THE WISDOM OF BEN SIRA

Volume 39

THE ANCHOR BIBLE is a fresh approach to the world's greatest classic. Its object is to make the Bible accessible to the modern reader; its method is to arrive at the meaning of biblical literature through exact translation and extended exposition, and to reconstruct the ancient setting of the biblical story, as well as the circumstances of its transcription and the characteristics of its transcribers.

THE ANCHOR BIBLE is a project of international and interfaith scope. Protestant, Catholic, and Jewish scholars from many countries contribute individual volumes. The project is not sponsored by any ecclesiastical organization and is not intended to reflect any particular theological doctrine. Prepared under our joint supervision, THE ANCHOR BIBLE is an effort to make available all the significant historical and linguistic knowledge which bears on the interpretation of the biblical record.

THE ANCHOR BIBLE is aimed at the general reader with no special formal training in biblical studies; yet, it is written with the most exacting standards of scholarship, reflecting the highest technical accomplishment.

This project marks the beginning of a new era of cooperation among scholars in biblical research, thus forming a common body of knowledge to be shared by all.

William Foxwell Albright
David Noel Freedman
GENERAL EDITORS

THE ANCHOR BIBLE

THE WISDOM OF BEN SIRA

A New Translation with Notes

By

†PATRICK W. SKEHAN

Introduction and Commentary

By

ALEXANDER A. DI LELLA, O.F.M.

Doubleday

NEW YORK

1987

NIHIL OBSTAT
Christopher Begg, S.T.D., *Censor Deputatus*

IMPRIMI POTEST
Alban A. Maguire, O.F.M., *Minister Provincial*

IMPRIMATUR
Rev. Msgr. Raymond J. Boland, *Vicar General*
Archdiocese of Washington
January 10, 1986

The *Nihil obstat* and *Imprimatur* are official declarations that a book or pamphlet is free of doctrinal or moral error. No implication is contained therein that those who have granted the *Nihil obstat* and *Imprimatur* agree with the content, opinions, or statements expressed.

Scripture quotations outside the Wisdom of Ben Sira are taken generally from the New American Bible, copyright © 1970 by the Confraternity of Christian Doctrine, Washington, D.C., and are used by permission of copyright owner. All rights reserved.

Part IX of the Introduction, "The Poetry of Ben Sira," was originally published in *Eretz-Israel* 16 (1982) 26*–33*, copyright © by the Israel Exploration Society, and is used by permission of copyright owner.

Material from *Women's Life in Greece and Rome* by M. R. Lefkowitz and M. B. Fant (Johns Hopkins University Press, 1977), used by permission of the copyright holder.

Library of Congress Cataloging-in-Publication Data

Bible. O.T. Apocrypha. Ecclesiasticus. English.
Skehan. 1987.
The Wisdom of Ben Sira.

(The Anchor Bible; vol. 39)
Bibliography: p. 93.
Includes indexes.
1. Bible. O.T. Apocrypha. Ecclesiasticus—
Criticism, interpretation, etc. I. Skehan, Patrick W.
(Patrick William), d. 1980. II. Di Lella, Alexander A.
III. Title. IV. Series: Bible. English. Anchor
Bible. 1964; v. 39.
BS192.2.A11964.G3 vol. 39 220.7'7 s [229'.4077] 86-8989
[BS1763]
ISBN 0-385-13517-3

THE APOCRYPHA

The term "Apocrypha" (or "deuterocanonical books" in Roman Catholic usage) is popularly understood to describe the fifteen books or parts of books from the pre-Christian period that the Roman Catholic, Orthodox, and Eastern churches accept, wholly or partially, as canonical Scripture but Protestants and Jews do not. The designation and the definition are inaccurate on many counts. An apocryphon is literally a "hidden writing," kept secret from all but the initiate, being too exalted for the general public; virtually none of these books makes such a claim. Roman Catholics do not accept all of them as canonical Scripture, for 1 and 2 Esdras and the Prayer of Manasseh are not included in the official Catholic canon drawn up at the Council of Trent (1545–63). Many Protestant churches have no official decision declaring these books to be noncanonical; in fact, up to the last century they were included in most English Protestant Bibles.

What is certain is that these books did not find their way into the final Jewish Palestinian canon of Scripture. Thus, despite their Jewish origins (though parts of 2 Esdras are Christian and Latin in origin), they were preserved for the most part in Greek by Christians as a heritage from the Alexandrian Jewish community and their basic text is found in the codices of the LXX. However, recent discoveries, especially that of the Dead Sea Scrolls, have brought to light the original Hebrew or Aramaic texts of some of these books. Leaving aside the question of canonicity, Christians and Jews now unite in recognizing the importance of these books for tracing the history of Judaism and Jewish thought in the centuries between the last of the Hebrew Scriptures and the advent of Christianity.

PREFACE

Shortly after I sent off the manuscript of *The Book of Daniel* (AB 23, 1978), a work I coauthored with Professor Louis F. Hartman, C.SS.R. (died August 22, 1970), Anchor Bible editor David Noel Freedman mailed back to me several pages of helpful observations, criticisms, and corrections. In the covering letter, dated January 23, 1977, Freedman first expressed his appreciation and gratitude for the work, and then, being the ever-conscientious editor who never misses an opportunity, invited me to contribute another volume to the Anchor Bible, The Wisdom of Ben Sira. My initial reaction was dismay. I had just begun to enjoy the relief that followed years of work on the Daniel volume. So I decided to reject the invitation. I then spoke with my friend and colleague, Professor Patrick W. Skehan, an acknowledged expert in the complicated text and ancient versions of Ben Sira, and told him I would like to suggest his name to Freedman for the project. Skehan said he enjoyed working on the text but would not feel comfortable writing the commentary. He then said to me, "Why not do the volume together? I'll do the translation and notes; you write the introduction and commentary." This was a harder offer to refuse; so I agreed. Freedman and Doubleday & Company did, too.

As of late August 1980 Professor Skehan had completed the translation and notes of the grandson's Foreword and of 1:1–38:23, 39:12–35, and 44:1–51:12 (including the litany of praise after 51:12 in MS B). Earlier that summer he had told me he was keeping the more difficult sections till later. Unfortunately, however, there was to be no later. On August 25, Skehan suffered a massive heart attack. When I visited him in the hospital, he insisted on telling me a story even though he was attached to monitors and an oxygen tank. He said, "You'll never guess what I was working on when I got my heart attack." I guessed it was work on Ben Sira. He said, "Right, but you'll have a good laugh when you hear which section it was. I was doing the poem that opens with the words: 'Make friends with the physician, for he is essential to you'" (38:1). The comedy and irony were even greater than Skehan realized. The section he had just finished before his final illness is entitled "Sickness and Death" (38:1–23). He died on September 9, a few days short of his seventy-first birthday. The text of 38:16 reads:

My son, shed tears for one who is dead
  with wailing and bitter lament;
As is only proper, prepare the body,
  absent not yourself from his burial.

I followed Ben Sira's injunctions.

I did the translation and notes of 38:24–34, 39:1–11, 40:1–43:33, and
51:13–30. In great measure I followed Skehan's procedure of adapting and
revising the NAB translation of Sirach, which years before had been done
mostly by him. I alone am responsible for the Introduction, general Bibliography, and commentary. Since I was away on sabbatical the academic year
before his death, Skehan read little of the materials I had written up to the
summer of 1980. Needless to say, the present volume would have been better
had Skehan lived for us to be in dialogue in all stages of production up to final
publication.

I have left Skehan's contribution just about as he wrote it, making minor
revisions only to eliminate inconsistencies and the like. Since death intervened
before he and I could discuss a few disputed matters, I decided to keep his
translation and notes virtually unchanged and to give my (alternate) views in
the commentary (see, for example, 10:19–11:6). I did this out of respect for
his outstanding ability and to preserve his views on the issues involved. In this
way the reader may benefit, I hope, from the occasional differences of opinion
Skehan and I express. On all other matters it may be assumed that he and I
are in basic agreement.

The chapter and verse numbers in the present translation of Ben Sira are
those found in J. Ziegler's definitive edition in the Göttingen Septuagint.
Since, however, in all the extant Greek MSS two sections of the text, 30:25–
33:13a and 33:13b–36:16a, are given in reverse order (see INTRODUCTION,
Part VIII, 3b), we have followed the chapter and verse numbers that Ziegler
in these places puts in parentheses in order to preserve the original order of
the material. Unfortunately, many translations of Sirach (e.g., NAB, RSV,
NEB) have chapter and verse numbers that correspond neither to the Greek
nor to the Latin numbering. Thus, for example, 42:1a–d of our translation is
listed as 41:23 in RSV and 41:23–24 in NAB and NEB; and 44:23fg, as 45:1ab
of RSV, NAB, and NEB. I appeal to all scholars and Bible translators to
adopt Ziegler's enumeration as described here, so that in future the references
to a specific passage in Ben Sira may be uniform. The New Revised Standard
Version (to be published probably in 1990) has already adopted Ziegler's
numbering system.

References to all other texts of the Hebrew Bible are given, as in NAB and
NJV, according to the chapter and verse numbering found in *BHK* and *BHS*,
the standard editions of the MT. Here, too, there is a discrepancy: the enumeration in many English Bibles differs from that found in MT. Thus, for

instance, Dan 3:31–33 of MT is listed as 4:1–3 in RSV, NEB, NIV, and TEV; and Dan 4:1–34, as 4:4–37. To avoid confusion, writers often refer to such passages in this way: Dan 3:31–33 (ET[=English Translation] 4:1–3), or Dan 4:1–3 (Heb 3:31–33), a cumbersome system, which could be avoided quite simply if translators and publishers of the English Bible used in future only the enumeration of the MT.

In order to conserve space, references to the various works cited in this volume are generally given in abbreviated form. For full bibliographical details the reader should first go to the Index of Authors, which provides (in addition to the usual information) an alphabetical listing of all authors found in the six sections of the Bibliography; an asterisk next to a number in that Index indicates the page of the Bibliography to be consulted.

I had the honor of writing a tribute to my esteemed colleague, Patrick W. Skehan, in *CBQ* 42 (1980): 435–37. I consider it a further privilege to dedicate my portion of the present work to his hallowed memory; and acting as his proxy and in my own name, I dedicate his portion of the volume to his sister, Margaret R. Skehan.

I received an award for Theological Scholarship and Research from the Association of Theological Schools in the United States and Canada to help defray costs of my 1979–80 sabbatical leave for work on Ben Sira. I am grateful to the A.T.S. for its generous grant. That sabbatical year I lived at St. George's Friary, the Newman Center of the University of Cincinnati. There my brother Franciscans, who welcomed me into their community, provided not only excellent company and stimulating conversation, but also a quiet and congenial atmosphere in which to study and write. I extend my thanks to them all for their fraternal hospitality and moral support. My gratitude goes also to General Editor David Noel Freedman for his many corrections, comments, and suggestions for improvement; to copy editor Elaine Chubb for her careful work; to Kathleen Weber for compiling the indexes; and to Administrative Editor Theresa M. D'Orsogna and her staff at Doubleday & Company for seeing the volume through to publication.

September 30, 1985   *Alexander A. Di Lella, O.F.M.*
Feast of St. Jerome   Department of Biblical Studies
                             The Catholic University of America
                             Washington, D.C. 20064

CONTENTS

PRINCIPAL ABBREVIATIONS

A	Codex Alexandrinus of the LXX
AB	Anchor Bible
AER	*American Ecclesiastical Review*
AJSL	*American Journal of Semitic Languages and Literature*
Akk	Akkadian
ALBO	Analecta lovaniensia biblica et orientalia
ALGHJ	Arbeiten zur Literatur und Geschichte des hellenistischen Judentums
AnBib	Analecta biblica
ANET	J. B. Pritchard, ed., *Ancient Near Eastern Texts* *
AnOr	Analecta orientalia
Anton	*Antonianum*
AOAT	Alter Orient und Altes Testament
APOT	R. H. Charles, ed., *Apocrypha and Pseudepigrapha of the Old Testament*
Ar	Arabic
Aram	Aramaic
ASTI	*Annual of the Swedish Theological Institute*
ATR	*Anglican Theological Review*
B	Codex Vaticanus of the LXX
BA	*Biblical Archaeologist*
BASOR	*Bulletin of the American Schools of Oriental Research*
BBB	Bonner biblische Beiträge
BeO	*Bibbia e oriente*
BETL	Bibliotheca ephemeridum theologicarum lovaniensium
BHK	R. Kittel, *Biblia hebraica*
BHS	*Biblia hebraica stuttgartensia*
Bib	*Biblica*
BibOr	Biblica et orientalia
BibS	Biblische Studien
BIOSCS	*Bulletin of the International Organization for Septuagint and Cognate Studies*

* For the full reference, see the general Bibliography.

BJRL	*Bulletin of the John Rylands Library*
BKAT	Biblischer Kommentar: Altes Testament
Box-Oesterley	G. H. Box and W. O. E. Oesterley, "Sirach," in *APOT**
BR	*Biblical Research*
BSOAS	*Bulletin of the School of Oriental (and African) Studies*
BTB	*Biblical Theology Bulletin*
BTFT	*Bijdragen: Tijdschrift voor Filosofie en Theologie*
BVC	*Bible et vie chrétienne*
BWANT	Beiträge zur Wissenschaft vom Alten und Neuen Testament
BZ	*Biblische Zeitschrift*
BZAW	Beihefte zur *ZAW*
C	Codex Ephraemi rescriptus of the LXX
CBQ	*Catholic Biblical Quarterly*
CBQMS	Catholic Biblical Quarterly Monograph Series
chap(s).	chapter(s)
ConB	Coniectanea biblica
Copt	Coptic
Cowley-Neubauer	A. E. Cowley and A. Neubauer, eds., *The Original Hebrew of a Portion of Ecclesiasticus**
CSCO	Corpus scriptorum christianorum orientalium
DBSup	*Dictionnaire de la Bible, Supplément*
DJD	Discoveries in the Judaean Desert of Jordan
Duesberg-Fransen	H. Duesberg and I. Fransen, *Ecclesiastico**
EBib	Études bibliques
EncJud	*Encyclopedia judaica* (1971)
ErIsr	Eretz-Israel
EstBib	*Estudios bíblicos*
EstEcl	*Estudios eclesiásticos*
Eth	Ethiopic
ETL	*Ephemerides theologicae lovanienses*
EvT	*Evangelische Theologie*
ExpTim	*Expository Times*
FBBS	Facet Books, Biblical Series
FRLANT	Forschungen zur Religion und Literatur des Alten und Neuen Testaments
G	Greek translation of Ben Sira
GI	Greek translation of the grandson

* For the full reference, see the general Bibliography.

GII	The expanded Greek translation of Ben Sira
Greg	*Gregorianum*
HALAT	W. Baumgartner et al., *Hebräisches und aramäisches Lexikon zum Alten Testament*
Hart	J. H. A. Hart, *Ecclesiasticus: The Greek Text of Codex 248**
HAT	Handbuch zum Alten Testament
Heb	Hebrew
Hen	*Henoch*
hend.	hendiadys
HKAT	Handkommentar zum Alten Testament
HPR	*Homiletic and Pastoral Review*
HR	*History of Religions*
HSM	Harvard Semitic Monographs
HTI	Hebrew original of Ben Sira
HTII	Expanded Hebrew text of one or more recensions
HTR	*Harvard Theological Review*
HTS	Harvard Theological Studies
HUCA	*Hebrew Union College Annual*
IB	*Interpreter's Bible*
IDB	G. A. Buttrick, ed., *Interpreter's Dictionary of the Bible* (Nashville: Abingdon, 1962)
IDBSup	*Interpreter's Dictionary of the Bible, Supplementary Volume* (1976)
IEJ	*Israel Exploration Journal*
Int	*Interpretation*
ITQ	*Irish Theological Quarterly*
JAOS	*Journal of the American Oriental Society*
JB	Jerusalem Bible
JBL	*Journal of Biblical Literature*
JCS	*Journal of Cuneiform Studies*
JE	*Jewish Encyclopedia* (1905)
JJS	*Journal of Jewish Studies*
JNES	*Journal of Near Eastern Studies*
JQR	*Jewish Quarterly Review*
JQRMS	Jewish Quarterly Review Monograph Series
JSJ	*Journal for the Study of Judaism*
JSOT	*Journal for the Study of the Old Testament*
JSOTSup	Journal for the Study of the Old Testament, Supplement Series

* For the full reference, see the general Bibliography.

JSS	*Journal of Semitic Studies*
JTC	*Journal for Theology and Church*
JTS	*Journal of Theological Studies*
K	*Kĕtîb*
KAT	Kommentar zum Alten Testament
KJV	King James Version
Knabenbauer	I. Knabenbauer, *Commentarius in Ecclesiasticum**
L	Lucianic Recension of the LXX (main group)=Codices 248–493–637
l	Lucianic Recension of the LXX (subgroup)=Codices 106–130–545–705
L'	*L+l*
l(1).	line(s)
Lat	Old Latin translation in the Vulgate MSS
LCL	Loeb Classical Library
LD	Lectio divina
Lévi	I. Lévi, *L'Ecclésiastique ou la Sagesse de Jésus, fils de Sira**
lit.	literally
LumVie	*Lumière et vie*
LXX	Septuagint
M	Masada Scroll of Ben Sira
Marcus	J. Marcus, *The Newly Discovered Original Hebrew of Ben Sira . . . The Fifth Manuscript**
mg	margin
MH	Mishnaic Hebrew
MS(S)	Manuscript(s)
MSU	Mitteilungen des Septuaginta-Unternehmens
MT	Masoretic Text: K. Elliger and W. Rudolph, eds., *Biblia hebraica stuttgartensia*
NAB	New American Bible
NCCHS	R. D. Fuller et al., eds., *New Catholic Commentary on Holy Scripture*
NCE	M. R. P. McGuire et al., eds., *New Catholic Encyclopedia* (1967)
NEB	New English Bible
NIV	New International Version
NJB	New Jerusalem Bible
NJV	New Jewish Version
NovT	*Novum Testamentum*
NovTSup	Novum Testamentum, Supplements

* For the full reference, see the general Bibliography.

NRT	*Nouvelle Revue Théologique*
NT	New Testament
NTS	*New Testament Studies*
O	Origen's Recension of the LXX=Codex 253 and Syh
OBO	Orbis biblicus et orientalis
OLZ	*Orientalische Literaturzeitung*
OT	Old Testament
OTL	Old Testament Library
OTS	*Oudtestamentische Studiën*
PEQ	*Palestine Exploration Quarterly*
Peters	N. Peters, *Das Buch Jesus Sirach oder Ecclesiasticus**
PG	J. Migne, ed., *Patrologia graeca*
Phibis	*Papyrus Insinger,* ed. F. W. F. von Bissing*
PL	J. Migne, ed., *Patrologia latina*
Prato	G. L. Prato, *Il problema della teodicea in Ben Sira**
PRS	*Perspectives in Religious Studies*
RB	*Revue biblique*
RBén	*Revue bénédictine*
REJ	*Revue des études juives*
RevQ	*Revue de Qumran*
RivB	*Rivista biblica*
RSR	*Recherches de science religieuse*
RSV	Revised Standard Version
RTL	*Revue théologique de Louvain*
RTP	*Revue de théologie et de philosophie*
Rüger	H. P. Rüger, *Text und Textform im hebräischem Sirach**
Ryssel	V. Ryssel, "Die Sprüche Jesus', des Sohnes Sirachs"*
S	Codex Sinaiticus of the LXX
Sam.	Samaritan Pentateuch
Sanders	J. T. Sanders, *Ben Sira and Demotic Wisdom**
SB	*Sources bibliques*
SBJ	La sainte bible de Jérusalem
SBFLA	*Studii biblici franciscani liber annuus*
SBLDS	Society of Biblical Literature Dissertation Series
SBLMS	Society of Biblical Literature Monograph Series
SBM	Stuttgarter biblische Monographien
SBS	Stuttgarter Bibelstudien
SBT	Studies in Biblical Theology
Schechter	S. Schechter, "Genizah Specimens . . . ,"*
Segal	M. H. Segal, *Sēper ben-Sîrā' haššālēm**

* For the full reference, see the general Bibliography.

Sem	*Semitica*
SJT	*Scottish Journal of Theology*
Smend	R. Smend, *Die Weisheit des Jesus Sirach erklärt* *
SNT	Studien zum Neuen Testament
Spicq	C. Spicq, "L'Ecclésiastique," in *La Sainte Bible* *
ST	*Studia theologica*
Strack	H. L. Strack, *Die Sprüche Jesus', des Sohnes Sirachs* *
SUNT	Studien zur Umwelt des Neuen Testaments
Syh	Syrohexaplar
Syr	Syriac Peshiṭta
Targ.	Targum
TBT	*The Bible Today*
TD	*Theology Digest*
TDNT	*Theological Dictionary of the New Testament*
TDOT	*Theological Dictionary of the Old Testament*
TEV	Today's English Version (1976)
Theognis	*Elegy and Iambus . . . ,* ed. J. M. Edmonds*
TGUOS	*Transactions of the Glasgow University Oriental Society*
TLZ	*Theologische Literaturzeitung*
TPQ	*Theologisch-Praktische Quartalschrift*
TQ	*Theologische Quartalschrift*
TRev	*Theologische Revue*
TRu	*Theologische Rundschau*
TSK	*Theologische Studien und Kritiken*
txt	text
TZ	*Theologische Zeitschrift*
UF	*Ugaritische Forschungen*
v(v)	verse(s)
V	Codex Venetus of the LXX
Vattioni	F. Vattioni, *Ecclesiastico: Testo ebraico con apparato critico e versioni greca, latina e siriaca* *
VD	*Verbum Domini*
VSpir	*Vie spirituelle*
VT	*Vetus Testamentum*
VTSup	Vetus Testamentum, Supplements
WMANT	Wissenschaftliche Monographien zum Alten und Neuen Testament
WUNT	Wissenschaftliche Untersuchungen zum Neuen Testament
WZKM	*Wiener Zeitschrift für die Kunde des Morgenlandes*
Yadin	Y. Yadin, *The Ben Sira Scroll from Masada* *

* For the full reference, see the general Bibliography.

ZAW	*Zeitschrift für die alttestamentliche Wissenschaft*
ZDMG	*Zeitschrift der deutschen morgenländischen Gesellschaft*
Ziegler	J. Ziegler, ed., *Sapientia Iesu Filii Sirach**
ZKT	*Zeitschrift für Katholische Theologie*
ZNW	*Zeitschrift für die neutestamentliche Wissenschaft*

* For the full reference, see the general Bibliography.

Introduction

I. TITLE AND CONTENTS OF THE BOOK

The book that is here called "The Wisdom of Ben Sira" (or "Sirach," for a short title) is known in English Bibles by several other titles. In the NAB it is entitled "The Book of Sirach," the "-ch" at the end of the word representing the transliteration of the letter *chi* with which the name is spelled in Greek. The JB and NJB have "Ecclesiasticus," a word taken over directly from the title of the book in many Latin Vulgate MSS. The NEB has "Ecclesiasticus or the Wisdom of Jesus son of Sirach," and the RSV has a similar title. The TEV has "Sirach: the Wisdom of Jesus, Son of Sirach (Ecclesiasticus)."

1. The Original Hebrew Title

Unfortunately, none of the extant Hebrew MSS contains the opening chapter of the book, so that the superscription or title of the book is not available. But the name of the author can be determined from another section near the end of the book. In 50:27, extant in Cairo Geniza MS B (as corrected; see NOTE), the author identifies himself as "Yeshua [or Jesus] ben [son of] Eleazar ben Sira." The name appears in the same form also after the last verse of the book (51:30), in the subscription of MS B (as corrected; see COMMENT).

The pertinent part of this subscription reads as follows: "The Wisdom of Yeshua [Jesus] son of Eleazar son of Sira," Heb *ḥokmat yēšûaʿ ben ʾelʿāzār ben sîrāʾ*. From this we may safely assume that the original Hebrew title of the book was exactly the same. This conclusion receives some support from the superscription and subscription found in most of the Greek MSS: "The Wisdom of Jesus son of Sira," Gr *Sophia Iēsou huiou S(e)irach*. This title is also reflected in the superscription of most Latin MSS, "The Book of Jesus son of Sirach." The superscription and subscription of the sixth-century British Library MS 12142, the oldest extant Syriac copy of the book, reads: "The Wisdom of the son of Sira," Syr *ḥekmĕtâ dĕbarsîrâ*.

Among the Jews the book received various titles. In the Talmud (Ḥagigah 13a, Niddah 16b, Berakot 11b) it is called "The Book of Ben Sira," Heb *seper ben sîrāʾ*. Saadia (d. 942) refers to it as "The Book of Instruction," Heb *seper mûsār,* while other rabbis speak of it as "The Instruction of Ben Sira," Heb *mûsar ben sîrā*. A certain Rabbi Joseph calls the book "The Proverbs of Ben Sira," Heb *mišlê ben sîrā*.[1]

We shall refer to the author of our book simply as Ben Sira, the name by which he is commonly known. His proper name, however, was Yeshua or Jesus, as the author's grandson states explicitly in the Foreword to his Greek translation of the book; Sira was the name of our author's grandfather, and Eleazar the name of his father. The use of the name of a grandfather or earlier male ancestor as a patronymic with *Ben* ("son of") prefixed was not unusual, particularly when the name of one's father was not sufficiently distinctive.[2]

2. Contents of the Book

The Wisdom of Ben Sira, in fifty-one substantial chapters, is one of the longest books of the Bible. In terms of form and content, it belongs to the Wisdom literature of Israel, together with Job, Proverbs, Qoheleth, the Wisdom of Solomon, and several so-called wisdom Psalms. The book contains a number of poems praising wisdom and its Author as well as a series of exhortations or bits of advice for the wise. It also provides a kind of handbook of moral behavior or code of ethics that a Jew of the early second century B.C. was expected to observe.

Except for chaps. 44–50, which in Cairo Hebrew MS B are appropriately entitled "Praise of the Ancestors of Old," the book manifests no particular order of subject matter or obvious coherence; hence only a descriptive list of topics, with some inevitable overlapping of classifications, can give an adequate impression of the contents of the book.

> I. Wisdom and the Wise (1:1–43:33): "The beginning of wisdom is the fear of the Lord" (1:14)—1:1–30; 4:11–19; 6:18–37; 16:24–17:23; 19:20–30; 24:1–31; 25:3–6, 10–11; 37:16–26.
>   A. Praise of Wisdom's Author: 39:12–35; 42:15–43:33.
>   B. Service of God and True Glory: 2:1–18; 7:29–31; 10:19–11:6; 17:24–18:14; 23:27; 32:14–33:15; 34:14–35:26.
>   C. Prayer for God's People: 36:1–22.
>   D. Autobiographical References: 24:30–34; 33:16–18; 34:12–13; most of 50:25–51:30.
>   E. The Wise: 3:29; 14:20–15:10; 20:1–31; 21:11–24; 38:24–39:11.
>   1. Wisdom applied to spiritual life
>   a. humility—3:17–24; 4:8; 7:16–17; 10:26–28.
>   b. charity—3:30–4:6, 8–10; 7:32–36; 12:1–7; 29:8–13.
>   c. virtues and vices of the tongue—5:9–6:1; 7:13; 19:5–

---

[1] Cf. Box-Oesterley, p. 271.
[2] Ibid., p. 292.

17; 20:5–8, 13, 16–20, 24–31; 22:6, 27–23:4, 7–15; 27:4–7; 28:12–26.

  d. pride, folly, sin in general—3:26–28; 10:6–18; 11:6; 16:5–23; 20:2–31; 21:1–22:2, 18; 25:2; 27:12–15, 28; 33:5; 35:22–24; 41:10.

  e. anger, malice, vengeance—1:22–24; 27:22–28:11.

  f. evil desire—6:2–4; 18:30–19:4; 23:5–6, 16–26.

  g. other virtues and vices—4:20–31; 5:1–8; 7:1–15; 8:1–19; 9:11–10:5, 29; 11:7–22; 15:11–20; 18:15–29; 25:1, 7–11; 27:8–21; 34:1–8.

 2. Wisdom applied to "practical" life

  a. parents—3:1–16; 7:27–28; 23:14; 41:17.

  b. children—7:23–25; 16:1–4; 22:3–4; 25:7; 30:1–13; 41:5–10.

  c. women (including wife and daughters)—7:19, 24–26; 9:1–9; 19:2–4; 22:3–5; 23:22–26; 25:1, 8, 13–26:18; 28:15; 33:20; 36:26–31; 40:19, 23; 42:6, 9–14.

  d. friends and associates—6:5–17; 7:18; 9:10; 11:29–34; 12:8–13:23; 22:19–26; 27:16–21; 33:6; 36:23–25; 37:1–15.

  e. wealth—10:30–31; 11:10–11, 14, 18–19, 23–28; 13:15–14:10; 25:2–3; 26:28–27:3; 31:1–11.

  f. poverty—10:30–11:6, 14; 13:18–14:2; 25:2–3.

  g. enjoying life—14:11–19.

  h. loans—29:1–7, 14–20.

  i. frugality—29:21–28.

  j. health and doctors—30:14–20; 38:1–15.

  k. death—38:16–23; 41:1–4.

  l. joy and pleasure—30:21–27; 40:1–27.

  m. manners and self-control at table—31:12–32:13; 37:27–31.

  n. household management—7:20–22; 33:19–33.

  o. travel—34:9–12.

  p. begging—40:28–30.

  q. good name—41:11–13.

  r. shame—41:14–42:1d.

  s. human respect—42:1e–8.

II. Praise of the Ancestors (44:1–50:21): "Now I will praise those godly people, our ancestors" (44:1).

III. Conclusion (50:22–51:30)

 A. Epilogue: 50:22–29.

    B. Song of Praise: 51:1–12.
    C. Alphabetic Canticle: 51:13–30.[3]

From this list one can see that Ben Sira included in his book almost every major topic with regard to religious and secular wisdom and personal behavior. To men and women of today some of his sayings may appear shockingly pragmatic or utilitarian rather than spiritually enlightened:

> Bilious distress, and loss of sleep,
>   and restless tossing for the glutton!
> Moderate eating ensures sound slumber
>   and a clear mind next day on rising.
> If perforce you have eaten too much,
>   once you have emptied your stomach, you will have relief
>   (31:20–21).

Maxims such as these were not uncommon in the Wisdom tradition of Israel. Thus, long before Ben Sira's day, Prov 5:7–14 appealed to what seems to be rank expediency for motivation in avoiding adultery:

> So now, O children, listen to me,
>   go not astray from the words of my mouth.
> Keep your way far from [the adulteress],
>   approach not the door of her house,
> Lest you give your honor to others,
>   and your years to a merciless one;
> Lest strangers have their fill of your wealth,
>   your hard-won earnings go to an alien's house;
> And you groan in the end,
>   when your flesh and your body are consumed;
> And you say, "Oh, why did I hate instruction,
>   and my heart spurn reproof!
> Why did I not listen to the voice of my teachers,
>   nor to my instructors incline my ear!
> I have all but come to utter ruin,
>   condemned by the public assembly!"

The mentality behind such aphorisms reflects a religious perspective quite different from our own. Some of the motivations suggested may appear inappropriate or even embarrassing to today's believer who takes God's word in the Bible seriously. Yet men and women with real flesh and blood, in all ages and cultures, do tend to be morally flabby or wicked. For this reason the Hebrew Wisdom writers bluntly state that improper or unseemly conduct is

---

[3] I gave a similar list of topics, but with verse numbers as in the NAB, in the article "Sirach, Book of," *NCE,* vol. 13, pp. 257–58.

to be avoided, not only because it is sinful, but also because it may undermine one's health or status or possessions.

At times Ben Sira also sounds like a male chauvinist, which he was, because male dominance was simply taken for granted in his society and culture:

> Worst of all wounds is that of the heart,
>> worst of all evils is that of a woman (25:13).
> No poison worse than that of a serpent,
>> no venom greater than that of a woman (25:15).
> There is scarce any evil like that in a woman;
>> may she fall to the lot of the sinner! (25:19)
> In a woman was sin's beginning;
>> on her account we all die (25:24).

Yet despite sentiments like these, Ben Sira has words of high praise for the good wife:

> Dismiss not a sensible wife;
>> a charming wife is more precious than corals (7:19).
> A wife is her husband's richest treasure,
>> a help like himself, a staunch support (36:29).

I call attention to these quotations not to disparage Ben Sira but rather to illustrate how fully he reflects the mentality of second-century B.C. Palestinian Judaism: its limitations and its grandeur, which are obvious to everyone who reads the book attentively.[4]

---

[4] For a full discussion of Ben Sira's attitude toward women, see Part X, 7.

II. BEN SIRA AND HIS TIMES

A summary statement about Ben Sira and his times is found in the Prologue to the Greek translation of the book made by the author's own grandson:

> . . . My grandfather Jesus, who had devoted himself for a long time to the study of the Law, the Prophets, and the other books of our ancestors, and developed a thorough familiarity with them, was prompted to write something himself in the nature of instruction and wisdom. This he did so that those who love wisdom might, by acquainting themselves with what he too had written, make even greater progress, living in conformity with the Divine Law.

Later in the Prologue the grandson states that he himself arrived in Egypt in the thirty-eighth year of the reign of King Euergetes, and that he had spent many sleepless hours of hard work in preparing his Greek translation for publication. The epithet "Euergetes" was attached to only two of the Lagid kings, Ptolemy III Euergetes I (246–221 B.C.) and Ptolemy VII Physkon Euergetes II (170–164 and 146–117). Since the former reigned only twenty-five years, he cannot be the Euergetes in question. Ptolemy VII, however, began to rule in 170, conjointly with his brother, Ptolemy VI Philometor (181–146), and he died fifty-three years later, in 117. Calculating from 170, the official accession year of Ptolemy VII, the thirty-eighth year would be 132 B.C.

This is the commonly admitted date when Ben Sira's grandson migrated to Egypt. He made the Greek translation of his grandfather's book in the following years, publishing the work, as some scholars hold, before 117 B.C.[1] Another theory as to the date of publication was proposed many years ago by U. Wilcken. He argued that the peculiar use of the preposition *epi* in Egyptian *koinē* Greek, the language the grandson used, before the name of a king (in this example, Euergetes) and the mention of an exact date (in this example, the thirty-eighth year) indicate that the king is no longer alive. Thus, according to this view, the grandson wrote the Prologue and published his translation after the death of Euergetes in 117 B.C.[2] Wilcken's argument, however, is

---

[1] Cf. Box-Oesterley, pp. 293 and 317.
[2] U. Wilcken, *Archiv für Papyrusforschung* 3 (1906): 321; 4 (1907): 205. This theory is accepted by Peters, pp. xxxii–xxxiii; M.-J. Lagrange, *Le Judaïsme avant Jésus-Christ*, p. 525, n. 2; and Duesberg-Fransen, p. 21.

flawed, as Smend (p. 3) correctly observed. Indeed, the facts that *epi* is used before the name of the reigning King Darius in Hag 1:1, 15; 2:10; and Zech 1:1, 7; and 7:1, and that an exact date is given in each of those texts, alone prove that Wilcken overstated his case. Smend (pp. 3–4) notes, however, that it is reasonable to argue for a date after 117 B.C. on the basis of the grandson's use of the Gr participle *synchonisas,* "while I was there at the same time [as Euergetes was king]," i.e., while I was there for the remainder of his reign. This view seems to be the most convincing. Thus the Prologue was written after the death of Euergetes II in 117 B.C.[3]

If the grandson was an adult on his arrival in Egypt in 132 B.C. (say, between twenty-five and forty years old), and if the average length of time between grandfather and grandson is taken into account (ca. forty to fifty years), then we may conclude that Ben Sira was practicing his profession as Wisdom teacher and was writing his reflections sometime in the first quarter of the second century B.C.

This date is confirmed by the book itself. In 50:1–21, Ben Sira has a long panegyric on a certain priest by the name of Simeon, son of Jochanan (Onias in some Gr MSS). It is commonly admitted that this person is Simeon II, who served as high priest from 219 to 196 B.C. From the vivid, colorful, and detailed descriptions of the high priestly vestments and liturgical actions, it seems certain that Ben Sira personally witnessed Simeon performing the elaborate rituals of the Daily Whole-Offering in the Jerusalem Temple. Ben Sira refers to Simeon in such a way as to imply that the high priest was already dead.

Moreover, Ben Sira does not mention or even allude to the troublous events that occurred in Palestine during the reign of the Seleucid Antiochus IV Epiphanes (175–164), who figures prominently as the archvillain in Daniel 7–12. The Seleucids long before Antiochus IV had pursued a policy of Hellenization that had been the dream of Alexander the Great (336–323). But to unify his realm Antiochus went much further than any of his predecessors by insisting on total Hellenization, even in religion. He succeeded in obtaining support also from some unscrupulous Jews. Notable among these was Jason, son of the high priest Simeon II on whom Ben Sira lavished great praise. Jason, unlike his father, was a scoundrel with vaulting ambition. He secured the high priesthood for himself by ousting from office his own brother Onias III, who legitimately held the office. Jason became high priest by offering to pay Antiochus IV a huge bribe of three hundred and sixty silver talents, and he also promised to take an active part in the royal policy of Hellenization, including the construction of a Greek gymnasium in Jerusalem (2 Macc 4:7–16).

[3] For other difficulties concerning the dates referred to in the Prologue, cf. A. H. Forster, "The Date of Ecclesiasticus," *ATR* 41 (1959): 1–9.

Three years later, however, Jason was expelled from office when Menelaus bought the high priesthood from Antiochus for a sum larger than the bribe of his predecessor (2 Macc 4:23–26). For orthodox Jews, though, the worst was yet to come. In 167 B.C. Antiochus determined to put an end once and for all to the practice of the Jewish religion in his domain. He abolished the celebration of Jewish sacrifices and festivals and prohibited circumcision and observance of the Sabbath and dietary laws. The ultimate villainy occurred in December 167 when he erected over the great altar of holocausts in the Jerusalem Temple a statue of the bearded Olympian Zeus. This disgraceful shrine—called "the appalling abomination" in Dan 8:13; 9:27; 11:31; and 12:11—remained in the temple for over three years.[4]

It is reasonable to assume that if Ben Sira had written his book during the disastrous years of Antiochus IV, he would have made some direct or indirect reference to the suffering the pious Jews endured. But he does not. Accordingly, it is safe to conclude that Ben Sira had died before 175 B.C., the year of Antiochus IV's accession to the throne, or at least had finished and published his book before that date.

Now that we have placed the literary activity of Ben Sira securely in the first quarter of the second century B.C.—the date of publication of his book being ca. 180—we turn to a consideration of the man himself. He was, first and foremost, a professional scribe (Heb *sôpēr*, Gr *grammateus*, cf. 38:24), which at this time meant wise man (Heb *ḥākām*). In fact, he has been called the last of the wise men of Israel and the first of the scribes.[5] As the grandson tells us in the Prologue, Ben Sira devoted himself to the diligent study of the Law, the Prophets, and the other Writings—all of which we now call Sacred Scripture. Accordingly, what we find in The Wisdom of Ben Sira is a composite work reflecting a lifetime of teaching and reflection. It seems that the lack of unity and coherence in the book (see Part I, "Title and Contents of the Book") may be due to the fact that individual sections or poems represent Ben Sira's final editing of class notes he had compiled over a period of years. This would account for the repetitions of the same theme or topic in several parts of the book, e.g., the discussion of children in 7:23–25; 16:1–4; 22:3–5; 25:7; 30:1–13; and 41:5–10.

Ben Sira doubtless was referring to himself when he wrote about the life of the scribe or sage in contrast to the life of manual laborers, whose talents and efforts are nevertheless essential for the good life:

> The scribe's profession increases wisdom;
>   whoever is free from toil can become wise.

[4] For a brief history of the reign of Antiochus IV, cf. L. F. Hartman and A. A. Di Lella, *The Book of Daniel*, AB 23, pp. 39–42.

[5] J. Hadot, *Penchant mauvais et volonté libre dans la sagesse de Ben Sira (L'Ecclésiastique)*, p. 76.

How can one become wise who guides the plow,
    who thrills in wielding the goad like a lance,
Who guides the ox and urges on the bullock,
    and whose concern is for cattle? (38:24–25)

Thus it seems that Ben Sira was a man of leisure whose exclusive concern was the pursuit of wisdom in the Israelite sense of that word.

In 38:34c–39:11, Ben Sira describes in detail the life and work of the Jewish scribe. Again, this section may be considered autobiographical:

How different the person who devotes himself to the fear of God
    and to the study of the Law of the Most High!
He studies the wisdom of all the ancients
    and occupies himself with the prophecies;
He treasures the discourses of the famous,
    and goes to the heart of involved sayings;
He studies the hidden meaning of proverbs,
    and is busied with the enigmas found in parables.

He is in attendance on the great,
    and has entrance to the ruler.
He travels among the peoples of foreign lands
    to test what is good and evil among people.
His care is to rise early
    to seek the Lord, his Maker,
    to petition the Most High,
To open his lips in prayer,
    to ask pardon for his sins.

Then, if it pleases the Lord Almighty
    he will be filled with the spirit of understanding;
He will pour forth his words of wisdom
    and in prayer give praise to the Lord.
He will direct his counsel and knowledge aright,
    as he meditates upon God's mysteries.
He will show the wisdom of what he has learned
    and glory in the Law of the Lord's covenant.

Many will praise his understanding;
    his fame can never be effaced;
Unfading will be his memory,
    through all generations his name will live.
The congregation will speak of his wisdom,
    and the assembly will declare his praises.

> While he lives he is one out of a thousand,
>> and when he dies he leaves a good name (38:34c–39:11).

One should not judge Ben Sira vain or immodest if he had himself in mind when writing this passage. For though he had a position of honor and respect as a scribe, he was aware of his responsibilities to the community:

> Now I am the last to keep vigil,
>> as one gleaning after the vintagers;
> Since by God's blessing I too have made progress
>> till like a vintager I have filled my winepress,
> Take notice that not for myself only have I toiled,
>> but for every seeker after guidance (33:16–18).

He realized that the talents he possessed were gifts from the Lord, which he used not for personal glory or gain (cf. 51:25) but for the common good, "for every seeker after guidance" (33:18b).[6]

Ben Sira lived in Jerusalem (according to 50:27 in the grandson's Greek version), where he had some sort of school or academy. He invited the unlearned to come to him so that they might no longer be deprived of wisdom (51:23–28). Presumably, his students were young men, for he often introduces a bit of advice or an admonition with the expression "My son" (Heb *běnî*)—2:1; 3:12; 4:1, etc. Like others in the Hellenistic period, Ben Sira traveled extensively in order to gain experience, often at great risk to his life (34:12–13; cf. 8:15–16). (Mugging with the intent to rob is not just a modern crime, as is obvious also from Jesus' Parable of the Good Samaritan in Luke 10:29–37.)

Indications of the kind of world in which Ben Sira lived and moved about in his travels are found in the book itself. It was a Hellenistic world—a world dominated by Greek ideas and ideals, customs and values, art and excellence; a world in which the Jews of Palestine were not politically free but subject to Egyptian or Syrian kings who fought many wars against each other to gain or maintain control of that strategically significant land. The prayer of Ben Sira in 36:1–22 sediments the deep feeling many pious Jews of that day must have felt toward the Gentile overlords in the Holy Land:

> Come to our aid, God of the universe,
>> and put all the nations in dread of you!
> Raise your hand against the foreign folk,
>> that they may see your mighty deeds (36:1–3).

---

[6] Though Ben Sira may have been a priestly scribe with special status, he was not an elitist. He considered it his responsibility to educate others in the wisdom of Israel, the key to which is fear of the Lord and personal piety. For more on these issues see H. Stadelmann, *Ben Sira als Schriftgelehrter: Eine Untersuchung zum Berufsbild des vor-Makkabäischen Sôfēr unter Berücksichtigung seines Verhältnisses zu Priester-, Propheten- und Weisheitslehretum* (WUNT 2/6, 1981).

Give new signs and work new wonders;
  show forth the splendor of your right hand and arm;
Rouse your anger, pour out wrath,
  humble the enemy, scatter the foe (36:6–9).

It took Alexander the Great little time in 332 to conquer Palestine, which had been under Persian domination from 539. He did not remain there long, however, but left the clean-up operations to his generals. After Alexander died in 323, the victim of a fever, the great empire he had acquired became a battleground once again. His successors, known as the Diadochoi, fought numerous battles to determine who would obtain which parts of the far-flung domain. With regard to our area of concern, only two of Alexander's generals are of importance, Ptolemy I Lagi and Seleucus I. Palestine became a bone of contention between the Hellenistic dynasties founded by these two men. In 301 B.C. Ptolemy I Lagi (323–285) of Egypt finally gained control of the area, and for a century afterward it remained under Egyptian sovereignty and influence.

During this period little is known of the fortunes of the Jews. But it seems that the Ptolemies adopted and possibly adapted the Persian administrative system under which the Jewish high priest was not only the spiritual leader of his people but also something of a secular prince, since it was his responsibility to collect the tribute owed to Egypt. Second-century B.C. documents clearly show that a priestly aristocracy had also been developing for some time. Apparently, as long as the imposed taxes were duly paid to the Egyptian crown, and law and order maintained, the Ptolemies kept their hands off internal affairs in Judea. Because, as it appears, the Jews remained submissive, they enjoyed relative peace and security.[7]

But the Ptolemies kept considerable military forces in Palestine because it was, after all, a borderland. Administration was in the hands of a governor with the rank of *stratēgos* (Greek for "general") who exercised supreme military and civil power. The *stratēgos,* usually a veteran soldier of the frequent wars in the area, was assisted by a finance officer in charge of collecting state revenues. Palestinian Jews shared in the economic prosperity of the Ptolemaic kingdom during the third century B.C. Greek methods of agriculture greatly increased crop yields, and trade with Egypt proved mutually advantageous. To satisfy the needs of the Greek population and of the military garrisons stationed in the principal towns and fortresses of Palestine, there were various imports, such as wine from the Aegean islands and other manufactured goods.[8]

Meanwhile, the Seleucid kings did not look kindly on Egyptian control of

---

[7] Cf. J. Bright, *A History of Israel,* 3d ed., p. 414.

[8] Cf. M. Stern, "Palestine under the Rule of the Hellenistic Kingdoms," in *A History of the Jewish People,* ed. by H. H. Ben-Sasson, pp. 186–90.

Palestine, but were in no position to change the situation despite several attempts to do so. Later in the third century, however, Syrian fortunes improved. The vigorous Antiochus III the Great (223–187) first concluded a series of successful campaigns to reassert Syrian sovereignty from Asia Minor (modern Turkey) to the frontier of India. Then he decided to set things right with Egypt, now ruled by Ptolemy IV Philopator (221–203). But Antiochus was decisively defeated in 217 at Raphia, at the southern border of Palestine, near the Mediterranean. After the young Ptolemy V Epiphanes (203–181) had ascended the throne, Antiochus again waged war on Egypt. This time he was successful in battle, smashing a large part of the Egyptian army in 198 at Panium (Caesarea Philippi of New Testament times), near the headwaters of the Jordan River, and driving what remained of the army from Asia. Palestine now became part of the Seleucid empire.[9]

According to Josephus (*Antiquities,* xii, 3, 3), the Jews in Palestine welcomed the change to Syrian rule, going so far as to provide supplies for Antiochus' army, including elephants (the tanks of antiquity). Under the leadership, presumably, of the high priest Simeon II, the Jews even joined the Syrian forces in besieging the garrison left by the Egyptian general Scopas in the citadel of Jerusalem. Antiochus rewarded the Jews for their cooperation and assistance. Timber for the repair of the Jerusalem Temple, which apparently had been damaged in the war, was exempt from any toll charges. (In 50:1–4, Ben Sira praises Simeon II for his work in renovating and fortifying the Temple precincts.) Temple personnel were exempt from the poll tax, crown tax, and salt tax. In order to accelerate economic recovery, the Jews as a group were excused from taxes for three years and from a third of their usual tribute. They were also allowed to live in accordance with their own laws—a right they had received earlier from the Persians and also, presumably, from the Egyptians.[10]

Antiochus III was ruined by his ambition. After bringing Seleucid power to its highest point, he foolishly decided to cross swords with Rome. He advanced into Greece, an adventure that prompted Rome to declare war in 192. The mighty Roman armies swiftly defeated Antiochus at Thermopylae, pursuing him into Asia. Then in 190 at the decisive battle of Magnesia, located between Sardis and Smyrna, the Roman general Lucius Cornelius Scipio overwhelmed Antiochus (cf. Dan 11:18), forcing him to submit to humiliating peace terms, which included payment of a huge indemnity. In 187, at Elymaïs in Elam, Antiochus III was assassinated while attempting to sack the treasury of Bel, one of his own gods, in order to meet his payments to Rome.

He was succeeded by his son, Seleucus IV Philopator (187–175), who

---

[9] Bright, *History,* p. 415.

[10] On administration and taxation in Palestine under the Ptolemies and Seleucids, cf. M. Hengel, *Judaism and Hellenism,* vol. 1, pp. 18–32; notes are located in vol. 2, pp. 13–25.

CHRONOLOGICAL TABLE

THE PTOLEMIES	THE JEWS	THE ZADOKITE HIGH PRIESTS	THE SELEUCIDS
Ptolemy I Lagi 323-285 Control of Palestine after Battle of Ipsos 301	Jews in Palestine under Ptolemies →	Onias I 323-300 (or 290) Simeon I the Just, son of Onias I (dates uncertain)	Seleucus I Nicanor 312/11-280 Antiochus I Soter 280-261
Ptolemy II Philadelphus 285-246 Ptolemy III Euergetes 246-221	Birth of Ben Sira ca. 250	Manasse, uncle of Simeon I (dates uncertain)	Antiochus II Theos 261-246 Seleucus II Callinicus 246-226 Seleucus III Ceraunus
Ptolemy IV Philopator 221-203	Jews in Palestine under Seleucids	Onias II, son of Simeon I d. 219 Simeon II, son of Onias II 219-196 (Sir 50:1-21)	226-223 Antiochus III the Great 223-187 Conquest of Palestine 200-198
Ptolemy V Epiphanes 203-181	← Wisdom of Ben Sira published ca. 180 Death of Ben Sira ca. 175 Desecration of Temple Dec. 167 ←	Onias III, son of Simeon II 196-174 Joshua (Jesus/Jason), brother of Onias III, 174-171	Seleucus IV Philopator 187-175 Antiochus IV Epiphanes 175-164
Ptolemy VI Philometor 181-146 (170-164: co-ruler Ptolemy VII)		Menahem (Menelaus), non-Zadokite usurper, 171-162 Jacim (Alcimus), illegitimate Zadokite, 162-159	Antiochus V 164-162 Demetrius I 162-150
Ptolemy VII Physkon Euergetes 146-117	Judas Maccabeus 166-160 Rededication of Temple Dec. 164 Greek Translation of Wisdom of Ben Sira in Egypt after 117	MACCABEAN HIGH PRIESTS Jonathan 152-143/2 Simon 142/41-134 John Hyrcanus I 134-104	Alexander Balas 150-145- Demetrius II 145-140 (Antiochus VI 145-142 Tryphon 142/41-138) Antiochus VII 138-129 Demetrius II (2d time) 129-126/5 Alexander Zebinas 128-122

turned out to be weak and ineffective as a ruler (cf. Dan 11:20). Although the new king confirmed the privileges his father had granted the Jews (cf. 2 Macc 3:2–3), he sent his foster brother and finance minister Heliodorus on a mission to Jerusalem to pillage the treasury of the Temple (cf. 2 Macc 3:4–40). Seleucus was assassinated in 175 and was succeeded by his younger brother Antiochus IV Epiphanes (175–164), of whom we spoke above.

These were the times in which Ben Sira lived. If, as we may assume, he was an old man when he published his book ca. 180, then he was born ca. 250 or earlier. Thus the Palestine he lived in was under Ptolemaic sovereignty for most of his life, from his birth to 198, and under Seleucid rule for the remainder, from 198 to his death sometime before 175.

In terms of Hellenization, however, it mattered little whether a Ptolemy or a Seleucid ruled over the Holy Land of Ben Sira's day. Monarchs of both dynasties vigorously promoted the policy of Hellenization instigated by Alexander the Great. In his travels, Ben Sira must have seen the baneful effects of Hellenization on the Jewish people. He must have met many Jews whose faith was shaken by the questions and doubts that Greek philosophy and religion had raised. These Jews had a gnawing, unexpressed fear that the religion of their Ancestors was inadequate to cope with the needs of social and political structures that had changed enormously.

To bolster the faith and confidence of his fellow Jews, Ben Sira published his book. His purpose was not to engage in a systematic polemic against Hellenism but rather to convince Jews and even well-disposed Gentiles that true wisdom is to be found primarily in Jerusalem and not in Athens, more in the inspired books of Israel than in the clever writings of Hellenistic humanism.[11] Yet Ben Sira himself often read non-Jewish literature and incorporated many of its insights in his own book (see Part VII). Being secure in his own Jewish faith, he had nothing to fear from Gentile writings. Ben Sira borrowed Gentile thoughts and expressions as long as these could be reconciled with the Judaism of his day.

[11] For further comments on Ben Sira's reaction to Hellenism, cf. A. A. Di Lella, "Conservative and Progressive Theology: Sirach and Wisdom," *CBQ* 28 (1966): 140–42; A. Moreno, "Jesús Ben Sira: Un judio en un tiempo de crisis," *Teología y Vida* 10 (1969): 24–42; A. Sisti, "Riflessi dell' epoca premaccabaica nell' Ecclesiastico," *RivB* 12 (1964): 215–56; and J. D. Martin, "Ben Sira—A Child of His Time," in *A Word in Season: Essays in Honour of William McKane*, ed. J. D. Martin and P. R. Davies (JSOTSup 42, 1986), pp. 141–61.

III. CANONICITY OF THE BOOK AND PLACE IN THE CANON

The Wisdom of Ben Sira is Vol. 39 of the Anchor Bible, and it appears first in the list of books designated "Apocrypha," which are placed, it should be observed, after the New Testament series. Jews and Protestants use the term "Apocrypha" to refer to the following religious writings, which, however, they do not accept as canonical: 1–2 Esdras (also known as 3–4 Esdras), Tobit, Judith, Additions to Esther, Wisdom of Solomon, Wisdom of Ben Sira, Baruch, Letter of Jeremiah (=Baruch 6 in the Vulgate and Roman Catholic editions), Song of the Three Jews (=Dan 3:24–90 in the Vulgate and Roman Catholic editions), Susanna (=Daniel 13 in the Vulgate and Roman Catholic editions), Bel and the Dragon (=Daniel 14 in the Vulgate and Roman Catholic editions), Prayer of Manasseh, and 1–2 Maccabees.

Roman Catholics, however, because they follow the ancient tradition of the Church that held these writings (with the exception of 1–2 Esdras and the Prayer of Manasseh) to be sacred and inspired by God, refer to them as deuterocanonical. In Roman Catholic editions of the Bible, The Wisdom of Ben Sira is located exactly where it should be, among the Wisdom books of the Old Testament in the following order: Job, Psalms, Proverbs, Qoheleth, Song of Songs, Wisdom of Solomon, and Wisdom of Ben Sira. This order of books is found also in the Latin Vulgate. The fourth-century Codex Vaticanus, one of the oldest copies of the LXX, has the same order of the Wisdom books with the exception of Job, which is placed after Song of Songs.[1]

The "Apocrypha," when included in Protestant editions of the complete Bible, are located either between the Old and New Testaments (as in the NEB) or at the end of the New Testament (as in the RSV).

Until some time in the 1960s the commonly accepted theory maintained that the so-called Alexandrian or Septuagint canon, which included all the deuterocanonical books, was the Sacred Scripture of Alexandrian Jews, whereas the shorter Palestinian or Hebrew canon, which contained only those books later declared to be canonical by the Pharisaic rabbis near the end of the first century A.D., was the Bible of Palestinian Jews, even in the Apostolic Age. It was the Alexandrian canon, according to this theory, that the Christian Church eventually accepted as its own official list of Old Testament

[1] H. B. Swete, *The Old Testament in Greek,* vol. 1, 4th ed., p. xvii.

books. The great biblical scholar St. Jerome (d. 420) made a distinction between "canonical books" and "ecclesiastical books," only, however, after he
had moved to the Holy Land and come under the influence of his Jewish
teachers.[2] The "ecclesiastical books," which came to be known as the deuterocanonical books, Jerome did not accept as Sacred Scripture.

The contemporary St. Augustine (d. 430) disagreed with Jerome's distinction, accepting the ancient tradition of the Church that all the books in the
LXX collection are equally authoritative. In the Reformation controversies of
the sixteenth century, however, Martin Luther broke with the tradition of the
Church and accepted Jerome's view of the so-called Palestinian canon as
alone being the list of Scriptures used by Jesus and the early Christians.
Luther was the first to separate the deuterocanonical writings from their
logical and time-honored locations in the canon (e.g., Tobit and Judith from
the historical books and The Wisdom of Solomon and The Wisdom of Ben
Sira from the Wisdom books). He called these books "Apocrypha" and
placed them in his German translation of 1534 in a separate section between
the Old and New Testaments. Most Protestant translations of the Bible, when
they include the "Apocrypha" at all, have followed Luther's lead in keeping
these writings segregated.

In several carefully researched publications beginning in 1958, A. C. Sundberg has successfully challenged the commonly accepted ideas with regard to
the history of the Christian Old Testament canon, and in particular the hypothesis of the Alexandrian or LXX canon.[3] He has shown that there never
was a Palestinian Hebrew canon in the days of Jesus, a canon that later in the
first century A.D. was authoritatively defined by the rabbis. Nor is it correct
to distinguish in the first century A.D. between a shorter Hebrew canon in
Palestine and a longer LXX canon in Alexandria. It is now certain that at the
turn of the era, and even before, many Greek-speaking Jews were living in the
Holy Land, and that they used the LXX as a collection of undifferentiated
religious writings long enough even to make a Palestinian revision thereof.
Thus there never was an actual Alexandrian (LXX) canon at all or a Palestinian (Hebrew) canon before ca. A.D. 90.

The Jews, including those who spoke and read Greek, did not have any
closed canon of sacred writings till the rabbis drew up their authoritative list
near the end of the first century A.D. Accordingly, the Church, which separated itself from Judaism before the First Jewish Revolt (A.D. 66–70), received from the Synagogue a group of undifferentiated writings that were

---

[2] A. C. Sundberg, "The Protestant Old Testament Canon: Should It Be Re-Examined?," *CBQ*
28 (1966): 199.
[3] A. C. Sundberg, "The Old Testament of the Early Church," *HTR* 51 (1958): 205–26; *The Old
Testament of the Early Church* (HTS 20); *CBQ* 28 (1966): 194–203; "The Bible Canon and the
Christian Doctrine of Inspiration," *Int* 29 (1975): 352–71. I am summarizing the results of
Sundberg's research in these paragraphs.

considered in some way sacred. Only after the destruction of Jerusalem in A.D. 70 did the Jews begin in earnest to define which of their religious scriptures should be received as divinely inspired and which should not. By ca. A.D. 90 the Pharisaic rabbis had defined and closed forever their official canon.

It should be recalled that the Church "received 'scriptures' from Judaism, but not a canon."[4] For the final determination of the Christian Old Testament canon was an activity of the Church that took place in the West at the Council of Hippo (393) and two Councils of Carthage (397 and 419).[5] That ancient Christian canon included, in addition to all the books of the Jewish or Hebrew canon, all the books Roman Catholics call deuterocanonical, but it did not include 1–2 Esdras and Prayer of Manasseh, which Protestants also list among the Apocrypha.[6]

Thus, Sundberg, who is himself a Protestant, concludes:

> Two different communities were involved in defining canons out of the common material of pre-70 Judaism. And since the church did define her OT canon for herself, what historical claim does the Jewish definition of canon about the end of the first century have for the church? Only that it was the assumed *a priori* claim of the Jewish canon, when it became known in the church following Origen, that pressured the church into defining its OT. But that assumed *a priori* claim of the Jewish canon did not succeed in restricting the OT of the church to the Jewish canon. This is true of the Eastern as well as the Western Church. If Protestant Christianity is to continue its custom of restricting its OT canon to the Jewish canon, then an entirely new rationale and doctrine of canon will have to be described. And any Protestant doctrine of canonization that takes seriously the question of Christian usage and historical and spiritual heritage will lead ultimately to the Christian OT as defined in the Western Church at the end of the fourth and beginning of the fifth centuries.[7]

From what has been said, there can be no doubt that The Wisdom of Ben Sira has been part of the Christian Old Testament from the time that the canon was officially and formally defined and closed by the Church in antiquity.

[4] Sundberg, *Int* 29 (1975): 356.
[5] Ibid., p. 357.
[6] The canonical list of Old Testament and New Testament books accepted by the Western Church was spelled out in Canon 47 of the Council of Carthage II (397) and is conveniently published by Denzinger-Bannwart-Umberg-Rahner (eds.), *Enchiridion symbolorum*, 29th ed. (Freiburg i.B.: Herder, 1953), no. 92, p. 46.
[7] Sundberg, *CBQ* 28 (1966): 201–2.

Now the question arises: What was the canonical status of our book among Jews before ca. A.D. 90, when the rabbis excluded it from the Jewish canon? It is clear, first of all, that for Greek-speaking Jews both in Palestine and in the Diaspora, The Wisdom of Ben Sira in pre-Christian times was considered one of their sacred writings, for it was included in the LXX. Second, the first-century B.C. Jewish community at Masada had a Hebrew copy of the book that had been written stichometrically, i.e., each verse receives a full line, the first colon or part of the verse appearing on the right-hand side of the column, and the second on the left-hand side.[8] This same writing practice was employed in two small first-century B.C. Hebrew fragments of the book discovered in Cave 2 at Qumran.[9] This procedure, usually reserved for books that were later received as canonical, is another indication of the special reverence the Essenes and others who were Palestinian Jews accorded to The Wisdom of Ben Sira. Third, the fact that from early in the first century B.C. the book underwent successive Hebrew and Greek recensions in Palestine clearly suggests that at least some Jews there accepted the work as sacred and inspired.[10]

Even the question of the status of the book among Pharisaic Jews in antiquity is complex. The reason is that rabbinical tradition itself is not consistent. Thus Rabbi Akiba (d. ca. A.D. 132) placed the book among the ḥîṣônîm, the "outside" or noncanonical books, the readers of which have no part in the world to come (J. Sanhedrin 28a).[11] Similarly, Tosephta (*Yadayim,* ii 13, ca. A.D. 250) says explicitly that "the books of Ben-Sira and all books written after the prophetic period do not defile the hands," i.e., they are not canonical.[12] Yet, curiously, the book remained popular among the Jews despite its official exclusion from the Jewish canon. Even the Talmud, the Midrashim, the Derek Ereẓ, and similar works show definite traces of its influence. Some eighty-two times The Wisdom of Ben Sira is quoted with approval in the Talmud and other rabbinical writings. Sometimes its sayings are even introduced by the formula "it is written," which is reserved only for quotations from the canonical Scriptures (Ḥagigah 12a; Niddah 16b; J. Berakot 11c).[13]

The evidence considered above seems to warrant the conclusion that the rabbis, the successors of the Pharisees, excluded The Wisdom of Ben Sira from the Jewish canon late in the first century A.D., but they nonetheless continued to quote the book, on occasion, paradoxically, even as Sacred Scripture.

---

[8] This arrangement is clearly discernible in cols. II–VII on the splendid plates 2–4, 6–8 published by Y. Yadin, *The Ben Sira Scroll from Masada.*

[9] The same arrangement of the text is found in Cairo Geniza MSS B, E, and F of the book.

[10] See Part VIII for a discussion of the various forms of the Heb text, the grandson's Gr version, and the second Gr recension.

[11] Cf. I. Lévi, "Sirach, The Wisdom of Jesus, the Son of," *JE,* vol. 11, p. 390.

[12] Cited in Box-Oesterley, p. 271.

[13] Cf. Cowley-Neubauer, pp. x, xix–xxx; Smend, xlvi–lvi; Lévi, *JE,* vol. 11, p. 390.

IV. LITERARY GENRES

Ben Sira was a lifelong and devoted student of the Scriptures—one of the principal reasons he became so popular in Jewish and Christian circles. In fact, his fame is due not so much to the originality of his thought as to the fidelity with which he reflected the sacred traditions of Israel's heritage and commented on them. He was not a creative thinker like the authors of Job and Qoheleth or a master stylist like the author of The Wisdom of Solomon. Nor was he an innovator in literary genres. In composing his book, he simply employed the forms of expression and literary styles he found ready-made in the Scriptures, especially the Wisdom literature, of which the Book of Proverbs was his overwhelming favorite.

The principal literary genres in The Wisdom of Ben Sira are the following: *māšāl,* hymn of praise, prayer of petition, autobiographical narrative, lists or onomastica, and didactic narrative.[1]

1. Māšāl

Though *māšāl* is not an English word but simply the transliteration of a Hebrew noun, it is used in biblical studies because there is no adequate equivalent for this literary genre, which appears very frequently in the Wisdom literature as well as the rest of the Bible. The noun *māšāl* (pl. *měšālîm*) derives from the Hebrew verb root *mšl,* which has two basic meanings: "to rule, have dominion over, reign," and "to be similar, to compare" (Akk *mašālu,* Ar *maṭal,* Aram *mětal*). In the OT, accordingly, *māšāl* may have one or more of the following meanings: "proverb, saying, aphorism, adage, maxim; comparison, similitude; ruling word, paradigm, model, exemplar; byword; word play; taunt song; allegory; didactic poem."[2]

A well-constructed proverb or maxim is brief, striking, loaded with meaning. "Prosperity makes friends; adversity tries them." "Wealth makes wit waver" (note the alliteration). "He is a fool who makes his physician his

---

[1] Cf. W. Baumgartner, "Die literarischen Gattungen in der Weisheit des Jesus Sirach," *ZAW* 34 (1914): 161–98.

[2] Cf. Duesberg-Fransen, pp. 65–68; G. von Rad, *Wisdom in Israel,* pp. 25–34; W. McKane, *Proverbs: A New Approach,* pp. 22–33; J. L. Crenshaw, "Wisdom," in *Old Testament Form Criticism,* ed. J. H. Hayes, pp. 229–39.

heir." The proverb sounds a responsive chord in the listener or reader. "The greatest wealth is contentment with a little." "A fool's tongue is long enough to cut his own throat." "Without wisdom wealth is worthless" (note the alliteration). The proverb stretches the mind, expands horizons, captivates the imagination. "If the wise erred not, it would go hard with fools." "Foolish tongues talk by the dozen." "He that is truly wise and great / Lives both too early and too late." The proverb rings true, especially on reflection, and commands respect. "He that is a wise man by day is no fool by night." "Every man is a fool sometimes, and none at all times." "An ounce of wit that's bought is worth a pound that's taught." The proverb is memorable, quotable, teachable. "A proverb has shortness, sense, and salt." "Better wit than wealth." "One man no man." "One of these days is none of these days." "The fool wanders; the wise man travels." The proverb heightens awareness, excites admiration, and prompts acceptance. "A wise man cares not for what he cannot have." "A fool may give a wise man counsel." "A wise man changes his mind, a fool never." The proverb is sometimes amusing, often satirical, always authoritative. "A wise man is never less alone than when he is alone." "What the fool does in the end the wise man does in the beginning." "He has great need of a fool that plays the fool himself." A good proverb exemplifies the classic definition: "A proverb is one man's wit and all men's wisdom" (attributed to Lord John Russell [1792–1878]). Or as Cervantes said, "A proverb is a short sentence based on long experience."

The proverb abounds among all peoples and nations and is often heard in daily speech. "A stitch in time saves nine." "A bird in the hand is worth two in the bush." "Easy come, easy go." "Birds of a feather flock together." "Business is business." "If you can't stand the heat, get out of the kitchen." "A fool and his money are soon parted." "Many hands make light work." A splendid collection of proverbs may be found in *The Oxford Dictionary of English Proverbs,* 3d ed. (Oxford: Clarendon, 1970).

Shakespeare turned out many sentences that have now become proverbial. "The devil can cite Scripture for his purpose" (*The Merchant of Venice,* I iii 99). "A young man married is a man that's marred" (*All's Well That Ends Well,* II iii 315). "What's in a name? that which we call a rose / By any other name would smell as sweet" (*Romeo and Juliet,* II ii 43–44). "My salad days, / When I was green in judgement" (*Antony and Cleopatra,* I v 73). "Pardon is still the nurse of second woe" (*Measure for Measure,* II i 270).

The *māšāl* can be found in all parts of the Bible. "Physician, heal yourself" (quoted by Jesus in Luke 4:23). "Like mother, like daughter" (Ezek 16:44). "Not as man sees does God see, because man sees the appearance but the LORD looks into the heart" (1 Sam 16:7). "In much wisdom there is much sorrow, and he who stores up knowledge stores up grief" (Qoh 1:18). "A live dog is better off than a dead lion" (Qoh 9:4). "Pride goes before disaster, and a haughty spirit before a fall" (Prov 16:18). "Better a dry crust with peace than a house full of feasting with strife" (Prov 17:1). "Face a bear robbed of her cubs, but never a fool in his folly!" (Prov 17:12). "Open reproof is better than love concealed" (Prov 27:5 NEB). "Better a thief than an inveterate liar" (Sir 20:24).

Proverbs or maxims or comparisons such as these, are, in general, sedimentations of commonly experienced phenomena, events, and intuitions that are expressed in elegant, picturesque, and memorable language, often with alliteration, assonance, and rhyme. As such, they presumably have their origin in the significant and often didactic lore of family, clan, tribe, and court. Literature of this type may be called pretheoretical or practical or recipe wisdom,[3] for it deals with the everyday arts and skills of living fully and well, and with basic attitudes toward God and the world that men and women are called to subdue (cf. Gen 1:28).[4]

R. B. Y. Scott has isolated and described seven different patterns of proverbs in the folk wisdom of many peoples. Scott, however, makes no references to The Wisdom of Ben Sira; hence, after his examples and references below[5] I have added instances of each pattern from Ben Sira.

a. Identity, equivalence, or invariable association. "A friend in need is a friend indeed." "What a man sows is what he will reap" (Gal 6:7). Cf. also Judg 8:21; Prov 14:4; 29:5. "A faithful friend is beyond price, no sum can balance his worth" (Sir 6:15). "Like an arrow lodged in a person's thigh is gossip in the breast of a fool" (Sir 19:12).

b. Nonidentity, contrast, or paradox. "All that glisters is not gold" (The Merchant of Venice, II vii 66). "A soft tongue can break a bone" (Prov 25:15). Cf. also Jer 23:28; Prov 27:7; Qoh 5:9; John 1:46. "Is a wolf ever allied with a lamb? So it is with the sinner and the just" (Sir 13:17). "A blow from a whip raises a welt, but a blow from the tongue smashes bones" (Sir 28:17).

c. Similarity, analogy, or type. "Time and tide wait for no man." "Like cool water to one faint from thirst is good news from a far country" (Prov 25:25). Cf. also Hos 4:9; Ezek 16:44; Ps 137:4; Prov 25:13, 19, 20. "Whoever touches pitch blackens his hand; whoever accompanies a scoundrel learns his ways" (Sir 13:1). "Like one slaying a son in his father's presence is whoever offers sacrifice from the holdings of the poor" (Sir 34:24).

d. What is contrary to right order and so is futile or absurd. "Don't count your chickens before they are hatched." "Can an Ethiopian change his skin, or a leopard his spots?" (Jer 13:23). Cf. also Prov 1:17; 17:16; 26:14; Amos 6:12. "If you satisfy your lustful appetites, they will make you the sport of your enemies" (Sir 18:31). "Tainted his gift who offers in sacrifice ill-gotten goods! Presents from the lawless do not win God's favor" (Sir 34:21–22).

---

[3] P. L. Berger and T. Luckmann (The Social Construction of Reality, p. 42) speak of "recipe knowledge," a phrase that suggested to me "recipe wisdom."

[4] Cf. A.-M. Dubarle, "Où en est l'étude de la littérature sapientielle?," ETL 44 (1968): 418–19.

[5] R. B. Y. Scott, Proverbs • Ecclesiastes, AB 18, pp. 5–8.

e. Classification and characterization of persons, actions, or situations. "A rolling stone gathers no moss." "The sluggard loses his hand in the dish; he will not even lift it to his mouth" (Prov 19:24). Cf. also Prov 13:1; 14:15; 19:13; 30:15–31. "Sand and salt and an iron lump are less of a burden than the stupid" (Sir 22:15). "A daughter is a treasure that keeps her father wakeful, and worry over her drives away sleep: Lest in her youth she remain unmarried, or when she is married, lest she be childless" (Sir 42:9).

f. Value, relative value or priority, proportion or degree. "Better late than never." "Better is the end of speech than its beginning" (Qoh 7:8). Cf. also Prov 19:22; 21:27; 22:1; Qoh 6:11; 1 Sam 15:22. "Better the worker who has goods in plenty than the boaster who is without sustenance" (Sir 10:27). "Better the one who hides his folly than the one who hides his wisdom" (Sir 20:31).

g. Consequence of human character and behavior. "Nothing venture, nothing win." "When they sow the wind, they shall reap the whirlwind" (Hos 8:7). Cf. also Jer 31:29; Ezek 18:2; Prov 15:13; 20:4; 26:27. "One person is silent and is thought wise; another, for being talkative, is disliked" (Sir 20:5). "A person may purchase much for little, but pay for it seven times over" (Sir 20:12).

Often in The Wisdom of Ben Sira a single *māšāl* introduces a series of other proverbs that develop a particular topic or theme from several points of view. The purpose is clearly didactic.

> Happy the husband of a good wife,
>   twice lengthened are his days;
> A worthy wife brings joy to her husband,
>   peaceful and full is his life.
> A good wife is a generous gift
>   bestowed upon him who fears the Lord;
> Be he rich or poor, his heart is content
>   and a smile is ever on his face (26:1–4).

Cf. also 15:11–20; 21:1–10; 23:16–21.

In like manner, a *māšāl* may serve as a topic sentence at the beginning of a longer admonition that contains several other proverbs.

> Go not after your lusts,
>   but keep your desires in check.
> If you satisfy your lustful appetites,
>   they will make you the sport of your enemies.
> Have no joy in the pleasures of a moment
>   which bring on poverty redoubled;
> Become not a glutton and a winebibber
>   with nothing in your purse.

Whoever does so grows no richer;
>   whoever wastes the little he has will be stripped bare.

Wine and women make the mind giddy,
>   and the companion of prostitutes becomes reckless.

Rottenness and worms will possess him,
>   for contumacious desire destroys its owner (18:30–19:3).

Cf. also 2:1–6; 16:1–4; 28:12–16.

Ben Sira frequently employs another type of *māšāl* he found in the earlier Wisdom books of the OT, the numerical proverb; cf. Job 5:19–22; 33:14–15; Ps 62:12; Prov 6:16–19; 30:15b–16, 18–19, 21–23, 29–31. A typical example is Prov 6:16–19:

There are six things the LORD hates,
>   yes, seven are an abomination to him;

Haughty eyes, a lying tongue,
>   and hands that shed innocent blood;

A heart that plots wicked schemes,
>   feet that run swiftly to evil,

The false witness who utters lies,
>   and he who sows discord among brothers.

This text illustrates the usual form: x/x-plus-one, with emphasis on the larger number to create suspense and stimulate interest.[6] The numerical proverb is found in Sir 23:16–18; 25:7–11; 26:5–6, 28; 50:25–26. It seems that proverbs of this kind served as mnemonic devices to aid in teaching and learning. The increasing numerical reference in these proverbs goes from one-two (e.g., Job 33:14–15) up to nine-ten (e.g., Sir 25:7–11).

The numerical proverb has much in common with the riddle. Take, for example, the following case:

These two things bring grief to my heart,
>   and the third rouses my anger:

A wealthy person reduced to want;
>   the intelligent held in contempt;

And the person who passes from justice to sin—
>   him the Lord makes ready for the sword (26:28).

---

[6] Cf. W. B. Stevenson, "A Mnemonic Use of Numbers in Proverbs and Ben Sira," *TGUOS* 9 (1938–39): 26–38; W. M. W. Roth, "The Numerical Sequence X/X+1 in the Old Testament," *VT* 12 (1962): 300–11; idem, *Numerical Sayings in the Old Testament;* G. von Rad, *Wisdom in Israel,* pp. 35–37; J. L. Crenshaw, "Wisdom," pp. 236–38. G. Sauer (*Die Sprüche Agurs,* pp. 70–112) has shown that a relationship exists between numerical proverbs in the OT and in the Ugaritic literature.

Implicit in the form of this *māšāl* are the following: (a) What are the three things that grieve me most? (b) I'll give you three guesses!⁷ Thus the numerical proverb served as a pedagogical technique.

Similar in form and function is another type of numerical proverb in which there appears a statement of things that total up to a single specified number given at the beginning of the text; cf. Prov 30:7–9, 24–28. In Ben Sira there are only two examples of this form:

> With three things I am delighted,
>   for they are pleasing to the Lord and to humans:
> Harmony among kindred, friendship among neighbors,
>   and the mutual love of husband and wife.
> Three kinds of people I hate;
>   their manner of life I loathe indeed:
> A proud pauper, a rich dissembler,
>   and an old person lecherous in his dotage (25:1–2).

The *māšāl* may also take the form of admonition (or exhortation), in either brief or extended compass, stated positively or negatively. Ben Sira and the other sages employed this type of proverb to urge on readers the proper patterns of behavior and right thinking. To achieve this purpose Ben Sira used motive clauses, questions, and other devices to provide incentives:

> The vengeful will suffer the Lord's vengeance,
>   for he remembers their sins in detail.
> Forgive your neighbor's injustice;
>   then when you pray, your own sins will be forgiven.
> Should a person nourish anger against another
>   and expect healing from the Lord?
> Should a person refuse mercy to another,
>   yet seek pardon for his own sins?
> If one who is but flesh cherishes wrath,
>   who will forgive his sins?
> Remember your last days, set enmity aside;
>   remember death and decay, and cease from sin!
> Think of the commandments, hate not your neighbor;
>   of the Most High's covenant, and overlook faults (28:1–7).

The sage also appeals to his own authority as grounds for compliance:

> I open my mouth and speak of her [wisdom]:
>   gain wisdom for yourselves, without money.

---

⁷ Cf. G. von Rad, *Wisdom in Israel,* p. 36.

> Submit your neck to her yoke,
> and let your mind weigh her message.
> She is close to those who seek her,
> and the one who is in earnest finds her.

> See for yourselves! I have labored only a little,
> but have found much (51:25–27).

Another of Ben Sira's favorites is the comparison or antithetic *māšāl*, which occurs frequently in the Book of Proverbs also (12:9; 15:16–17; 16:8, 16, 19; 17:1; 19:1; 21:9, 19; 25:24; 27:5, 10c; 28:6). The comparison or antithesis is one type of R. B. Y. Scott's sixth pattern of proverbs we described earlier. In addition to the texts cited there, the following examples may be listed: Sir 11:3; 19:24; 20:2, 18, 25; 30:14–17; 41:12; 42:14. The didactic intent of such proverbs is to put sin or folly or what is undesirable or inappropriate in the worst light so that the opposite may appear more appealing and worthwhile.

> Rather death than a wretched life,
> unending sleep than constant illness (30:17).

2. Hymn of Praise

There are two fundamental modes of calling on God: praise and petition. In fact, the Psalms, with few exceptions, may each be reduced to one or both of these modes.[8] Ben Sira utilizes both the hymn of praise and the prayer of petition. In his book, hymns in praise of God occur with some regularity: 1:1–10; 18:1–7; 39:12–35; 42:15–43:33; 50:22–24; 51:1–12. In the Cairo Geniza Hebrew text of MS B there is found after 51:12 another hymn of praise, 16 verses in length. Patterned on Psalm 136, it is, however, not attested in any of the ancient versions, for which reason many scholars question its authenticity (see COMMENT on 51:12 i–xvi).

In imitation of Proverbs 8, Ben Sira widens the scope of praise to include Wisdom, the first and most splendid of God's creatures. The hymn extolling Wisdom in Sir 24:1–33, near the middle of the book, is one of the high points of Ben Sira's poetic skill and religious sentiment. The hymn in 1:1–10 honors Wisdom and the Lord as Source of all Wisdom.

---

[8] Cf. C. Westermann, *Praise and Lament in the Psalms,* pp. 15–35, 152–53.

3. Prayer of Petition

Though not as common as the hymn of praise, the prayer of petition occurs in at least two places in our book: 22:27–23:6 and 36:1–22. It will be observed that these prayers have the same features as petitions in the Psalms.[9]

4. Autobiographical Narrative

The autobiographical narrative or confessional statement occurs in Wisdom literature when the sage appeals to his own experience or authority in order to make a point that is applicable to all his students or readers.[10] This literary genre had its origin in Egypt, as is clear from such works as the "Instruction for King Merikare" (*ANET,* pp. 414–18), written at the end of the twenty-second century B.C., and the "Instruction of King Amen-em-het" (*ANET,* pp. 418–19), extant copies of which date from 1500–1100 B.C. Examples from the OT are the following: Prov 4:3–9; 24:30–34; Ps 37:25, 35–36 (a wisdom psalm); Qoh 1:12–2:26; 3:10; 4:7–8; 5:17–19; 8:9–9:1, 11, 13–16; 10:5–7; Wisdom of Solomon 7–9.

Ben Sira employs the autobiographical genre to emphasize that his quest for wisdom was not for himself alone but for others also.

> Now I am the last to keep vigil,
> as one gleaning after the vintagers;
> Since by God's blessing I too have made progress
> till like a vintager I have filled my winepress,
> Take notice that not for myself only have I toiled,
> but for every seeker after guidance (33:16–18).

Ben Sira concludes his book with a long autobiographical poem; but even here the intent is primarily didactic, as is evident from the acrostic form of the poem. The first four bicola, beginning respectively with *aleph, beth, gimel, daleth* (=A, B, C, D of our alphabet) tell us that for Ben Sira the pursuit of wisdom began in youth and will continue till death:

> When I was young and innocent,
> I kept seeking wisdom.
> She came to me in her beauty,
> and until the end I will cultivate her.

---

[9] Cf. ibid., pp. 52–71.
[10] Cf. G. von Rad, *Wisdom in Israel,* pp. 37–38; J. L. Crenshaw, "Wisdom," pp. 256–58.

As the blossoms yielded to ripening grapes,
> the heart's joy,
So my feet kept to the level path,
> for from earliest youth I was familiar with her (51:13–15).

5. Lists or Onomastica

Lists or onomastica (pl. of *onomasticon*, Greek for "[book of] names") of geographical, mineralogical, cosmic, meteorological, and other natural phenomena became a literary genre in ancient Egypt and Mesopotamia and later were utilized in the Wisdom literature of Israel.[11] This genre is employed in Job 28; 36:27–37:13; 38:4–39:30; 40:15–41:26; Psalm 148; and the Hymn of the Three Jews (Dan 3:52–90, NAB); Wis 7:17–20, 22–23; 14:25–26.

Ben Sira makes good use of onomastica in his hymns in praise of God the Creator (39:16–35 and 42:15–43:33). In the latter poem, for example, he lists all the splendor and beauty of God's handiwork in the heights (sky, sun, moon, stars, rainbow, hail, lightning, thunder, winds, snow, frost, rain) and on the earth below (the sea and its stupendous and amazing creatures, islands in the midst of the sea, monsters of the deep). The purpose of this long list of natural phenomena is made clear at the end of the poem:

More than this we will not add;
> let the last word be "He is the all."
Let us praise him the more, since we cannot fathom him,
> for greater is he than all his works (43:27–28).
Beyond these, many things lie hid;
> only a few of his works have I seen.
It is the LORD who has made all things,
> and to those who fear him he gives wisdom (43:32–33).

6. Didactic Narrative

A striking example of didactic narrative is found in Prov 7:6–23: the portrayal of the lecherous woman with the restless feet, who roams the streets to seduce "a youth with no sense" (7:7). The woman's seductive actions and suggestive dialogue achieve their goal:

[The youth] follows her stupidly,
> like an ox that is led to slaughter;

---

[11] Cf. G. von Rad, "Job XXXVIII and Ancient Egyptian Wisdom," in *The Problem of the Hexateuch and Other Essays,* pp. 281–91; J. L. Crenshaw, "Wisdom," pp. 258–59.

Like a stag that minces toward the net,
 till an arrow pierces its liver;
Like a bird that rushes into a snare,
 unaware that its life is at stake (7:22–23).

The author's intention in depicting this vivid, almost lurid, scene is patently didactic:

So now, O children, listen to me,
 be attentive to the words of my mouth!
Let not your heart turn to her ways,
 go not astray in her paths;
For many are those she has struck down dead,
 numerous, those she has slain.

Her house is made up of ways to the nether world,
 leading down into the chambers of death (Prov 7:24–27).

Ben Sira provides a splendid example of didactic narrative in the long poem or hymn (44:1–50:24) entitled in Cairo MS B "Praise of the Ancestors of Old," and in most Greek MSS "Praise of the Ancestors." The didactic purpose of this composition is made clear in the opening and closing lines of the introductory section (41:1–15):

I will now praise those godly people,
 our ancestors, each in his own time— (44:1)
Their wealth remains in their families,
 their heritage with their descendants.
Through God's covenant with them their family endures,
 and their offspring for their sakes;
For all time their progeny will last,
 their glory will never be blotted out.
Their bodies are buried in peace,
 but their name lives on and on;
At gatherings their wisdom is retold,
 and the assembly declares their praises (44:11–15).

Beginning with Noah, Ben Sira writes a short theology of history (44:17–49:16) of the covenanted People of God, and he concludes with a lengthy panegyric (50:1–21) of the high priest Simeon II (219–196 B.C.).[12]

---

[12] Another example of didactic narrative is Wisdom of Solomon 10–19; cf. J. L. Crenshaw, "Wisdom," p. 262.

V. WISDOM TRADITIONS IN THE OLD TESTAMENT

In Jer 18:18, three classes of personnel are mentioned: the priest (Heb *kōhēn*) who gives instruction, teaching, and law (Heb *tôrâ*); the prophet (Heb *nābî*) who is witness to God's word and revelation (Heb *dābār*); and the wise man (Heb *ḥākām*) who imparts counsel (Heb *ʿēṣâ*). These three groups are also referred to in Ezek 7:26; but the prophet is said to experience vision (Heb *ḥāzôn*) instead of *dābār*, and *ʿēṣâ* is attributed to the elder (Heb *zāqēn*) rather than the *ḥākām*. Elsewhere in Isaiah and Jeremiah the *ḥākām* is associated with the rich and powerful as members of the upper class (Isa 5:21; 19:11–13; Jer 9:22; 51:57).

The words *ḥākām* (m.), *ḥăkāmâ* (f.), "wise person, sage" (m. pl. *ḥăkāmîm*, f. pl. *ḥăkāmôt*), and *ḥokmâ*, "wisdom, skill, cleverness," are also used in the OT to describe people who are trained in the various arts, crafts, and trades. Thus, in Exod 35:30–33, Moses says to the Israelites that Yahweh chose Bezalel and filled him with a divine spirit (Heb *rûaḥ ʾĕlōhîm*), with skill (Heb *ḥokmâ*), with understanding, with knowledge, and with all craftsmanship, to produce embroidery and articles of gold, silver, and bronze, to cut and set precious stones, to carve wood, and to have ability in every other craft. In Exod 28:3, those who are to fashion Aaron's elaborate vestments are called "experts, skilled laborers" (Heb *ḥakmê lēb*, lit., "wise of heart [=seat of intelligence]") whom God had endowed with an able mind (Heb *rûaḥ ḥokmâ*, lit., "spirit of wisdom"); cf. also Exod 36:1–2, 8. In Exod 35:25, every woman who spun the various yarns and fine linen thread for the construction of the meeting tent is referred to as an expert (Heb *ḥakmat lēb*, "wise of heart"). The skilled persons who worked on the sanctuary are called *ḥăkāmîm* in Exod 36:4.

Similarly, some form of the terms *ḥākām* and *ḥokmâ* is employed for silversmiths and goldsmiths (Jer 10:9), sailors (Ezek 27:8; Ps 107:27), professional wailing women (Jer 9:16), competent warriors (Isa 13:10), government advisers (Isa 29:14), experts in music, poetry, botany, and zoology (1 Kgs 5:10–13), an unprincipled but shrewd adviser (2 Sam 13:3), and even magicians, enchanters, and sorcerers (Dan 2:2, 12).[1]

---

[1] The Greek word *sophia* also originally meant cleverness or skill or ability in the trades, crafts, and arts (e.g., music, singing, poetry). Cf. Liddell-Scott-Jones-McKenzie, *Greek Lexicon*, pp. 1621–22, for references to the pertinent classical literature.

1. Recipe Wisdom

When we speak of the Wisdom traditions of the OT, however, we are not referring primarily to the occupations and activities mentioned above. We mean, rather, the type of material that has been put into writing in such books as Proverbs, Job, Qoheleth, Wisdom of Ben Sira, Wisdom of Solomon, and certain wisdom Psalms. The Wisdom traditions sedimented in these works have a long and complicated history.[2] Nevertheless, a study of these books will show that there are only two basic types of wisdom. The first may be called pretheoretical or practical or, as I prefer to call it, recipe wisdom,[3] because it deals with everyday attitudes, beliefs, customs, manners, and forms of behavior one should have toward God, one's fellows, and the world at large if one is to live fully and well as a faithful Israelite. Though found to some degree in all the Wisdom books of the OT, recipe wisdom is found in largest supply in Proverbs and The Wisdom of Ben Sira.

> Lying lips are an abomination to the LORD,
>> but those who are truthful are his delight (Prov 12:22).
>
> A mild answer calms wrath,
>> but a harsh word stirs up anger (Prov 15:1).
>
> He who mocks the poor blasphemes his Maker;
>> he who is glad at calamity will not go unpunished (Prov 17:5).
>
> Whoever hates correction walks the sinner's path,
>> but whoever fears the Lord repents in his heart (Sir 21:6).
>
> Whoever keeps the Law controls his impulses;
>> whoever is perfect in fear of the Lord has wisdom (Sir 21:11).
>
> When a sieve is shaken, the husks appear;
>> so do a person's faults when he speaks (Sir 27:4).
>
> To keep the Law is a great oblation,
>> and whoever observes the commandments sacrifices a
>>> peace offering (Sir 35:1–2).

The *Sitz im Leben,* or social context, of this kind of wisdom is presumably the significant lore of family, clan, tribe, and court that eventually became part of the literary and religious heritage of Israel.

---

[2] For attempts at tracing this history, cf. R. Gordis, *Koheleth—the Man and His World: A Study of Ecclesiastes,* 3d ed., pp. 8–38; R. B. Y. Scott, *The Way of Wisdom in the Old Testament,* pp. 1–47; G. von Rad, *Wisdom in Israel,* pp. 3–23.

[3] Cf. Part IV above, "Literary Genres." R. Gordis (*Koheleth,* p. 27) calls this type lower or practical wisdom.

2. Existential Wisdom

The second kind of wisdom may be called theoretical or, as I prefer to call it, existential wisdom,[4] because it attempts to provide meaning for one who is faced with such problems as natural disasters, untimely death, his lot after death, the basis of morality, the value of upright living, the dilemmas of the innocent sufferer, and the anomaly of the prosperous wicked. The *a priori* principle underlying this kind of wisdom is this: if one is to remain human, one simply cannot accept meaninglessness, ultimate absurdity, or hopelessness.[5]

The existential Wisdom writers do not attempt to make intelligible all the unpleasantries and absurdities of human life and experience, but merely try to show that these ineluctable realities may be faced squarely and honestly by the person who professes faith in a transcendent and loving God who has willed to become personally involved in human history. Absurdity becomes no less absurd, but it does become tolerable because the believer comes to accept mystery as an integral part of being human in a society in which other persons also have free will and often abuse it.

Existential wisdom, though present in all the Wisdom books to some extent, is found in largest measure in Job, Qoheleth, and The Wisdom of Solomon. It has as its *Sitz im Leben* a fairly widespread crisis in faith.[6]

What the books of Job, Qoheleth, and The Wisdom of Solomon have in common is the goal of supplying the believer with a theodicy, or a plausible legitimation of God's ways in view of the existence of moral and physical evil.[7] As P. L. Berger correctly notes, there is a fundamental attitude, in itself

[4] R. Gordis (*Koheleth,* p. 28) calls this type higher or speculative wisdom.

[5] Cf. P. L. Berger, *The Sacred Canopy: Elements of a Sociology of Religion,* p. 56.

[6] As a literature that attempts to legitimate and reinforce Israel's faith and practice, existential wisdom is perfectly in keeping with the other books of the Bible, in particular Proverbs and The Wisdom of Ben Sira. Hence I disagree with the following statement by R. Gordis (*Koheleth,* p. 28): ". . . The higher or speculative Wisdom books, particularly *Job, Ecclesiastes* and perhaps *Agur ben Yakeh* (Pr., ch. 30), are basically heterodox, skeptical works, at variance with the products of the practical Wisdom School."

[7] Cf. O. S. Rankin, *Israel's Wisdom Literature: Its Bearing on Theology and the History of Religion,* pp. 15–35. Berger (*The Sacred Canopy,* p. 53) writes: "Every nomos is established, over and over again, against the threat of its destruction by the anomic forces endemic to the human condition. In religious terms, the sacred order of the cosmos is reaffirmed, over and over again, in the face of chaos. It is evident that this fact poses a problem on the level of human activity in society, inasmuch as this activity must be so institutionalized as to continue despite the recurrent intrusion into individual and collective experience of the anomic (or, if one prefers, denomizing) phenomena of suffering, evil and, above all, death. However, a problem is also posed on the level of legitimation. The anomic phenomena must not only be lived through, they must also be explained—to wit, explained in terms of the nomos established in the society in question. An explanation of these phenomena in terms of religious legitimations, of whatever degree of theoretical sophistication, may be called a theodicy."

quite irrational, that underlies all theodicies. This attitude is the surrender of self to the meaningful cosmos, or nomos, or ordering of reality, that every group of its very nature provides for its members. In other words, every cosmos or nomos entails a transcendence of individuality and necessarily implies a theodicy. A religious nomos, as a meaningful construct of reality, comprehends the individual and every aspect of his or her biography, including painful and absurd experiences. "The nomos locates the individual's life in an all-embracing fabric of meanings that, by its very nature, transcends that life."[8] When the individual adequately internalizes these meanings, he understands himself "correctly," i.e., within the coordinates of reality as defined by his religious society. He can now suffer "correctly" and even have a "correct" or "happy" death.[9]

Thus the primary function of existential wisdom is the religious legitimation of anomic phenomena such as suffering, moral evil, and untimely death. As theodicy, such wisdom offers a person not happiness but meaning. One is reminded of the existential psychiatrist Viktor E. Frankl, who developed the theory and practice of logotherapy. He maintains that "the striving to find a meaning in one's life is the primary motivational force in man."[10]

The trouble with many theodicies, however, is that they are vulnerable to empirical disconfirmation.[11] According to the Deuteronomic doctrine of retribution, for example, God rewards the good that men and women do and punishes their evil, and only during the course of their earthly life; after death everybody goes to Sheol, the underworld, which is not a place of retribution because once there saint and sinner alike possess a colorless, dull, limp existence devoid of all vitality and strength (Job 3:17; Ps 88:5).[12] Job's anguish stems precisely from the fact that this doctrine did not apply in his own case. Without doubt, the author of Job perceived innumerable cases where upright people died without any apparent recompense for their virtue. It is noteworthy, however, that he did not reject the Deuteronomic doctrine, but rather, by means of the Yahweh speeches in chaps. 38–41, indicates that the suffering of the righteous becomes meaningful only in God's transcendent and mysterious order and plan, which are not subject to empirical verification. The solution presented in the Book of Job apparently proved meaningful to pious Israelites, who in faith accepted the empirically unverifiable religious nomos, or order of reality, assumed in the book.[13]

[8] Berger, *The Sacred Canopy*, p. 54.

[9] Ibid., pp. 54–55.

[10] *Man's Search for Meaning: An Introduction to Logotherapy*, p. 154.

[11] Berger, *The Sacred Canopy*, pp. 69–71.

[12] Cf. A. A. Di Lella, "The Problem of Retribution in the Wisdom Literature," in *Rediscovery of Scripture: Biblical Theology Today* (Report of the 46th Annual Meeting of the Franciscan Educational Conference), pp. 109–12.

[13] For a fuller account of the Book of Job, cf. A. A. Di Lella, "An Existential Interpretation of Job," *BTB* 15 (1985): 49–55.

Qoheleth has been called many names—skeptic, pessimist, and even saint.[14] I prefer to call him a realist. A. G. Wright has convincingly shown that the book speaks more clearly but says much less than was previously thought. The impossibility of understanding what God has done, which was always taken as *a* theme, is really *the* theme, which is built on the vanity motif prominent in the first part of the book (1:12–6:9).[15] Being a keen observer of the hard facts of life, Qoheleth rejected, among other things, the older retribution theology (8:10–15). In effect, he says one should not call into question God's justice simply because the righteous do not prosper or the wicked suffer. Qoheleth insists that divine justice is too mysterious to be put into the straitjacket of the Deuteronomic theory of retribution. "I recognized that man is unable to find out all God's work that is done under the sun, even though neither by day nor by night do his eyes find rest in sleep" (Qoh 8:17). Like the author of Job, Qoheleth legitimates God's ways by locating them in the transcendent order so that they become immune to empirical disconfirmation.

The Wisdom of Solomon contains the most meaningful and satisfying answer to the problem of retribution. "The souls of the just are in the hand of God, and no torment shall touch them" (3:1). They are not really dead (3:2), but "live forever" (5:15) "in peace" (3:3) and are "accounted among the sons of God" (i.e., the angels) and "the saints" (5:5). The wicked, however, "shall . . . become dishonored corpses and an unceasing mockery among the dead . . . ; [they] shall be in grief" (4:19).[16] Here for the first time in the Wisdom literature the afterlife becomes the locale of nomization, a locale that will produce no empirical counterevidence.

In addition to providing the religious legitimation of anomic phenomena such as suffering, moral evil, and untimely death, existential wisdom also has as one of its functions the validation and exaltation of Israel's unique heritage, especially the claim to be the Chosen People of God and partakers of God's own Wisdom. The three great poems in which Wisdom is personified— Job 28, Proverbs 8, and Wisdom of Ben Sira 24—are splendid illustrations of this point. A brief quotation from one of these poems will make clear this aspect of existential wisdom:

> Wisdom sings her own praises,
>   among her own people she proclaims her glory;

[14] W. Baumgartner, "The Wisdom Literature," in *The Old Testament and Modern Study*, ed. by H. H. Rowley (Oxford: Clarendon, 1951), p. 221, notes that Qoheleth has been described by Heine as "the quintessence of scepticism," but by F. Delitzsch as "the quintessence of piety."

[15] A. G. Wright, "The Riddle of the Sphinx: The Structure of the Book of Qoheleth," *CBQ* 30 (1968): 313–34. Cf. also O. Loretz, *Qohelet und der Alte Orient: Untersuchungen zu Stil und theologischer Thematik des Buches Qohelet* (Freiburg i.B.: Herder, 1964).

[16] Cf. A. A. Di Lella, "Conservative and Progressive Theology: Sirach and Wisdom," *CBQ* 28 (1966): 150–54.

In the assembly of the Most High she opens her mouth,
in the presence of his host she declares her worth:

"From the mouth of the Most High I came forth,
and mistlike covered the earth.
In the heights of heaven I dwelt,
my throne on a pillar of cloud.
The vault of heaven I compassed alone,
through the deep abyss I took my course.
Over waves of the sea, over all the land,
over every people and nation I held sway.
Among them all I sought a resting place:
in whose inheritance should I abide?

Then the Fashioner of all gave me his command,
and he who had made me chose the spot for my tent,
Saying, 'In Jacob make your dwelling,
in Israel your inheritance.'
Before the ages, from the first, he created me,
and through the ages I shall not cease to be.
In the holy Tent I ministered before him,
and then in Zion I took up my post.
In the city he loves as he does me, he gave me rest;
in Jerusalem is my domain.
I have struck root among the glorious people;
in the portion of the Lord is my inheritance" (Sir 24:1–12).

The faithful Israelite need not look to Athens for *sophia,* "wisdom," which every well-educated Greek treasured so highly. For wisdom in its richest and widest sense, including the perception of the primeval order willed by the Creator, is a special gift God has reserved for his own people who are willing to receive it and live according to its liberating demands.

3. Hermeneutical Implications of Existential Wisdom and Recipe Wisdom

If we take the hermeneutical problem to be the contrast between "What did Scripture mean when it was written?" (the goal of literal interpretation) and "What does Scripture mean to me today?" (the concern of the new hermeneutic),[17] then the approach that theoretical or existential wisdom is

---

[17] Cf. K. Stendhal, "Biblical Theology, Contemporary," *IDB,* vol. 1, pp. 418–32; and R. E. Brown, "Hermeneutics," *JBC,* pp. 614–15.

fundamentally a literature that gives meaning to anomic phenomena and legitimates Israel's heritage should help considerably.[18] Like their Israelite predecessors, contemporary men and women face disorder and chaos within and without. They need meaning and hope and security in religious beliefs just as desperately and poignantly as the faithful to whom the books of Job, Qoheleth, and The Wisdom of Solomon were originally addressed.[19] These books, as well as the parts of The Wisdom of Ben Sira that contain existential wisdom, all posit the need for faith in a transcendent and mysterious God who nonetheless loves men, women, and children and is concerned about them and the pains and absurdities of their life. The object of such faith is, of course, empirically unverifiable, but so is every other nomos or ordered structure of reality that attempts to make meaningful the anomalies of human existence.

> The Eternal is the judge of all alike;
>> the Lord alone is just.
> Whom has he made equal to describing his works,
>> and who can probe his mighty deeds?
> Who can measure his majestic power,
>> or exhaust the tale of his mercies?
> One cannot lessen, nor increase,
>> nor penetrate the wonders of the Lord.
> When a person ends he is only beginning,
>> and when he stops he is still bewildered.
> What is a human being, of what worth is he?
>> the good, the evil in him, what are these?
> The sum of a person's days is great
>> if it reaches a hundred years:
> Like a drop of the sea's water, like a grain of sand,
>> so are these few years among the days of eternity.
> That is why the Lord is patient with people
>> and showers his mercy upon them.
> He sees and understands that their death is grievous,
>> and so he forgives them all the more.
> A person may be merciful to his neighbor,

[18] Cf. B. L. Mack, "Wisdom Myth and Mytho-logy: An Essay in Understanding a Theological Tradition," *Int* 24 (1970): 46–60.

[19] Gordis (*Koheleth,* p. 16) writes: "Fundamentally . . . Torah and Prophecy remain concerned with the group, its present duties and its future destiny. . . . Wisdom . . . made the life of the individual its exclusive concern." The adjective "exclusive" is, at best, misleading. The interpretation I am suggesting here is this: true, both recipe wisdom and existential wisdom are directed toward the individual, but only as a member of the religious society known as Israel. Cf. P. L. Berger and T. Luckmann, *The Social Construction of Reality: A Treatise in the Sociology of Knowledge,* pp. 67–68.

but the Lord's mercy reaches all flesh,
Reproving, admonishing, teaching,
    as a shepherd guides his flock;
Merciful to those who accept his guidance,
    who are diligent in his precepts (Sir 18:1–14).

As regards pretheoretical or recipe wisdom, the hermeneutical implications are not as clear but are nonetheless present. If recipe wisdom is to be defined as the knowledge of how one is to live fully and well in one's vertical relationships with God and horizontal relationships with one's fellows, together with the knowledge of how to master the world, then I think Walther Zimmerli is right in emphasizing that such wisdom is to be located within the framework of the OT theology of creation.[20] *Hybris* is not what impels men and women to subdue the earth, but rather it is God's command and blessing: "Be fertile and multiply; fill the earth and subdue it. Have dominion over the fish of the sea, the birds of the air, and all the living things that move on earth" (Gen 1:28). A twofold attitude underlies recipe wisdom as a whole:

a. Human beings were formed as free agents in a good universe and are not the hapless victims of fate, heredity, or environment.

Say not, "It was God's doing that I fell away";
    for what he hates, he does not do.
Say not, "It was he who set me astray";
    for he has no need of the wicked.
Abominable wickedness the LORD hates;
    he does not let it befall those who fear him.
It was he, from the first, when he created humankind,
    who made them subject to their own free choice.
If you choose you can keep his commandment;
    fidelity is the doing of his will.
There are poured out before you fire and water;
    to whichever you choose you can stretch forth your hands.
Before each person are life and death;
    whichever he chooses shall be given him.
Copious is the wisdom of the LORD;
    he is mighty in act, and all-seeing.
The eyes of God behold his handiwork;
    he perceives a person's every deed.
No one did he command to sin,
    nor will he be lenient with liars (Sir 15:11–20).

[20] "The Place and Limit of the Wisdom in the Framework of the Old Testament Theology," *SJT* 17 (1964): 146–58. Zimmerli writes (p. 149): "Wisdom is *per definitionem tahbûlôth,* 'the art of steering', knowledge of how to do in life, and thus it has a fundamental alignment to man and his preparing to master human life."

b. As members of society, men and women have the God-given power and responsibility to live happily and to create their own destiny in community.[21]

> The Lord from the earth created humankind,
>   and makes each person return to earth again.
> Limited days of life he gives them,
>   with power over all things else on earth.
> He endows them with a strength that befits them;
>   in God's own image he made them.
> He puts the fear of humans in all flesh,
>   and allows them power over beasts and birds.
> Discretion, with tongues and eyes and ears,
>   and an understanding heart he gives them.
> With wisdom and knowledge he fills them;
>   good and evil he shows them.
> He puts into their hearts the fear of him,
>   showing them the grandeur of his works,
> That they may glory in his wondrous deeds
>   and praise his holy name.
> He has set before them knowledge,
>   a law pledging life as their inheritance;
> An everlasting covenant he has made with them,
>   his commandments he has revealed to them.
> His majestic glory their eyes beheld,
>   his glorious voice their ears heard.
> He says to them, "Avoid all evil";
>   to each of them he gives precepts about his neighbors
>   (Sir 17:1–14).

This twofold attitude is normative for the believer today, and it may be suggested that this attitude is the only basis on which the truth and authority of recipe wisdom as well as its conformity with the rest of the OT can be authenticated.[22]

---

[21] Cf. W. Brueggemann, "Scripture and an Ecumenical Life-Style: A Study in Wisdom Theology," *Int* 24 (1970): 3–19.

[22] Thus there is no need to posit a difference in authority between Law and Prophets on the one hand and wisdom on the other. Zimmerli, for example, writes ("The Place and Limit," pp. 152–53): ". . . the admonition of the teacher of wisdom is not to be confused with the commandment of the law-giver of the covenant. . . . Certainly we cannot say that counsel has no authority. It has the authority of insight. But that is quite different from the authority of the Lord, who decrees." For an excellent discussion of the truth and unity of the Bible, cf. N. Lohfink, "Über die Irrtumslosigkeit und die Einheit der Schrift," *Stimmen der Zeit* 174 (1963–64): 161–81; a summary of the article appeared in *TD* 13 (1965): 185–92.

VI. BEN SIRA AND THE OTHER BOOKS
OF THE OLD TESTAMENT

Ben Sira spent a lifetime immersed in the Scriptures of Israel. Before becoming a teacher and author himself, he had been a tireless student of the Torah (or Law), Prophets, and Writings that were already part of the nation's literary and religious heritage, as the grandson makes clear in the Prologue to his Greek translation of the book. As we saw in Part IV above, Ben Sira employed the literary genres he found in the earlier biblical books, especially the Wisdom literature, Proverbs, Job, and Qoheleth. As regards style, though, he wrote in the manner of the Pirqe 'Abot, a collection of maxims of the Jewish Fathers, the oldest generation of the rabbis. Thus Ben Sira may be considered the prototype of the rabbis. But unlike the rabbis, he wrote for the most part in the classical Hebrew of the late period, the kind of language he had often read in the biblical books he conscientiously and deliberately imitated.[1]

Ben Sira's procedure was to adapt the older Scriptures in order to popularize them and make them relevant to the new Hellenistic age in which he lived. Though he often quotes or refers to a sacred text, he does not hesitate to alter it or change the wording so that there is a new emphasis or a different meaning. Here are some examples:[2]

You shall love the LORD, your God, with all your heart, and with all your soul, and with all your strength (Deut 6:5).	With all your soul fear God, revere his priests. With all your strength, love your Maker, neglect not his ministers (Sir 7:29–30).
For me they listened and waited; they were silent for my counsel (Job 29:21).	The rich speaks and all are silent, his wisdom they extol to the clouds (Sir 13:23).
Joy and gladness shall be found in her, thanksgiving and the sound of song (Isa 51:3e–f).	Joy and gladness he will find; she will endow him with an everlasting name (Sir 15:6).

---

[1] Cf. Duesberg-Fransen, p. 68.

[2] Duesberg-Fransen, p. 69, list many of these examples as well as others which, however, are not as convincing as the ones offered here.

In the beginning, when God created the heavens and the earth . . . (Gen 1:1). God created man in his image; in the divine image he created him (Gen 1:27).

It was he, from the first, when he created humankind, who made them subject to their own free choice (Sir 15:14).

When you had found [Abraham's] heart faithful in your sight, you made the covenant with him to give to him and his posterity the land of the Canaanites, Hittites, Amorites, Perizzites, Jebusites, and Girgashites. These promises of yours you fulfilled, for you are just (Neh 9:8).

[Abraham] obeyed the Most High's command, and entered into a covenant with him; in his own flesh the ordinance was incised, and when tested, he was found steadfast (Sir 44:20).

In his exposition of wisdom motifs, Ben Sira cites or alludes to the Torah or Pentateuch (Genesis, Exodus, Leviticus, Numbers, Deuteronomy), Joshua, 1–2 Samuel, 1–2 Kings, 1–2 Chronicles, Nehemiah, Psalms, Job, Isaiah, Jeremiah, Ezekiel, Haggai, and Malachi. He mentions in passing the Judges (46:11–12), the Twelve Minor Prophets as a group (49:10), the Psalms as compositions of David (47:9), and Proverbs as the work of Solomon (47:14–17), but he does not refer at all to Ruth, Ezra, Tobit, Judith, Esther, Daniel, or Baruch. Thus Ben Sira occupies a position between the OT on the one hand and intertestamental literature on the other. This alone makes Ben Sira a figure of great importance in the history of Israel, for he opens the way for the later rabbis.[3]

Ben Sira often takes a single text from the Torah and expands it into a large didactic discourse which itself contains allusions to several other texts of the OT. A good illustration of this procedure is Sir 3:1–16, which is based on Exod 20:12 and Deut 5:16, both of which deal in almost the same words with the commandment to honor one's father and mother, that one may have a long life (cf. also Lev 19:3).

3:1 Children, pay heed to a father's right;
        do so that you may live.
  2 For the Lord sets a father in honor over his children;
        a mother's right he confirms over her sons.
  3 Whoever honors his father atones for sins;
  4   he stores up riches who honors his mother.
  5 Whoever honors his father will have joy in his children,
        and when he prays he is heard.

[3] Ibid.

6 Whoever honors his father will live a long life;
he obeys the Lord who honors his mother.

7 Whoever fears the Lord honors his father,
and serves his parents as masters.

8 In word and deed honor your father
that his blessing may come upon you.

9 For a father's blessing gives a family firm roots,
but a mother's curse uproots the growing plant.

10 Glory not in your father's disgrace;
his disgrace is no glory to you!

11 His father's glory is a person's own glory;
he multiplies sin who demeans his mother.

12 My son, be steadfast in honoring your father;
grieve him not as long as he lives.

13 Even if his mind fails him, be considerate of him;
revile him not in the fullness of your strength.

14 For kindness to a father will not be forgotten;
it will serve as a sin offering—it will take lasting root.

15 In time of trouble it will be recalled to your advantage;
like warmth upon frost it will melt away your sins.

16 A blasphemer is he who neglects his father;
he provokes God, who demeans his mother.

Ben Sira bases his observation in v 9 on Gen 27:27–29 (Isaac's blessing of Jacob); 48:15–20 (Israel's blessing of Ephraim and Manasseh); 49:8–12 (Jacob's blessing of Judah); and Judg 17:1–4 (the curse of Micah's mother later neutralized by the blessing she utters). In v 11a, Ben Sira rephrases an idea he found in Prov 17:6b: "The glory of children is their parentage." He makes the exhortation in v 11b by changing some of the terms of Prov 23:22b: "Despise not your mother when she is old." The comment in v 16 harks back to Exod 21:17 and Lev 20:9 (both of which texts speak of the death penalty for the person who curses his father or mother) and Proverbs:

He who mistreats his father, or drives away his mother,
is a worthless and disgraceful son (Prov 19:26).
There is a group of people that curses its father,
and blesses not its mother (Prov 30:11).
The eye that mocks a father,
or scorns an aged mother,
Will be plucked out by the ravens in the valley;
the young eagles will devour it (Prov 30:17).

There are many other examples of this procedure; see the commentary.

Being a wisdom teacher himself, Ben Sira chose to reflect and comment especially on the sacred literature most like his own, the Book of Proverbs. But he did not merely quote or paraphrase a maxim or other type of *māšāl* he found in Proverbs; rather, he explained it and developed its implications for his own day and his own society. Though he was content to be a glossator, his writing was by no means lacking in imagination and creativity. From his reading and study of Israel's holy books, particularly Proverbs, he compiled his own notes, comments, and reflections, which eventually he edited and published as a separate book.

Ben Sira's dependence on Proverbs can be detected in almost every portion of his book; see the commentary. Here it will suffice simply to give some examples from the first few poems of the book to show how Ben Sira takes a text of Proverbs and expands or summarizes or adapts it for his own didactic purposes.

The LORD begot me [Wisdom], the firstborn of his ways, the forerunner of his prodigies of long ago (Prov 8:22).

Before all things else wisdom was created; and prudent understanding, from eternity (Sir 1:4).

The fear of the LORD is the beginning of knowledge; wisdom and instruction fools despise (Prov 1:7).

The beginning of wisdom is the fear of the Lord; it is formed with the faithful in the womb (Sir 1:14).

With me [Wisdom] are riches and honor, enduring wealth and prosperity. My fruit is better than gold, yes, than pure gold, and my revenue than choice silver (Prov 8:18–19).

Fullness of wisdom is fear of the Lord; she inebriates them with her fruits. Her whole house she fills with choice foods, her granaries with her harvest (Sir 1:16–17).

The crucible for silver, and the furnace for gold, but the tester of hearts is the LORD (Prov 17:3).

For in fire gold is tested, and those God favors, in the crucible of humiliation (Sir 2:5).

Trust in the LORD with all your heart, on your own intelligence rely not; in all your ways be mindful of him, and he will make straight your paths (Prov 3:5–6).

Trust God and he will help you; make straight your ways and hope in him. You that fear the Lord, wait for his mercy, turn not away lest you fall. You that fear the Lord, trust him, and your reward will not be lost. You that fear the Lord, hope for good things, for lasting joy and mercy (Sir 2:6–9).

When he is dealing with the arrogant, he is stern, but to the humble he shows kindness (Prov 3:34).

Humble yourself the more, the greater you are, and you will find favor with God (Sir 3:18).

He who mocks the poor blasphemes his Maker; he who is glad at calamity will not go unpunished (Prov 17:5).
Refuse no one the good on which he has a claim when it is in your power to do it for him. Say not to your neighbor, "Go, and come again, tomorrow I will give," when you can give at once (Prov 3:27–28).

My son, do not mock the poor person's life, nor wear out the expectations of an embittered spirit. The hungry do not aggrieve, nor ignore one who is downtrodden. Do not inflame the bile of the oppressed; delay not giving to the needy. A beggar's plea do not reject; avert not your glance from the downtrodden. From one in need turn not your eyes, give him no reason to curse you; for if in the ache of his bitterness he curse you, his Maker will hear his prayer (Sir 4:1–6).

From these examples and the numerous others throughout the rest of the book, one can see readily that Ben Sira shares many of the concerns and themes of Proverbs. The two books are alike also in that both contain loosely connected groups of Wisdom sayings and exhortations. But unlike The Wisdom of Ben Sira, which had only a single author who edited and published all his materials himself, the Book of Proverbs in its present form represents an anthology of materials that in date of composition span several centuries. The final editor of Proverbs as a whole was also the author of chaps. 1–9, which serve as an introduction to the work; he published the book probably in the early fifth century B.C.[4]

Between Proverbs and Ben Sira there are, to be sure, differences in emphasis and in the problems addressed. For the political situation and the social framework reflected in the two books were not the same. But what is more important is that both books share in the same scholastic tradition of the sages and in the same religious heritage. Ben Sira, though, did not consider the authors of the several collections in Proverbs simply as colleagues in a long line of Wisdom writers but rather as inspired writers whose work was

---

[4] Cf. P. W. Skehan, *Studies in Israelite Poetry and Wisdom*, pp. 15–26.

already viewed as sacred and virtually canonical.[5] Accordingly, he commented on many passages from Proverbs in order to make them more understandable and more applicable to his own generation of believers.[6]

By doing this with Proverbs and the other books of the Old Testament, Ben Sira created a new synthesis that served the needs, interests, and preoccupations of the Jewish community of his own day. Precisely in this fact lie his originality, significance, and lasting contribution to the thought of Israel's sages.[7]

---

[5] The Jewish canon of Scripture was not officially defined, however, until the last decade of the first century A.D. See Part III, "Canonicity of the Book and Place in Canon."

[6] Duesberg-Fransen, p. 71.

[7] For a more detailed summary of Ben Sira's relation to Judaic tradition, cf. J. T. Sanders, *Ben Sira and Demotic Wisdom* (SBLMS 28, 1983): 3–26. Cf. also J. G. Snaith, "Biblical Quotations in the Hebrew of Ecclesiasticus," *JTS* n.s. 18 (1967): 1–12; and J. L. Koole, "Die Bibel des Ben-Sira," *OTS* 14 (1965): 374–96.

VII. BEN SIRA AND NON-JEWISH LITERATURE

Ben Sira vigorously opposed any compromise of Jewish values and traditions (cf. 2:12) and pronounced woe to those who forsook Israel's Law (41:8), with which wisdom itself, in his view, was to be identified (24:23). Yet he learned much from his travels abroad (34:9–13) and presumably from his contact with the Gentiles he met. In fact, what Ben Sira writes about the scribe, and hence about himself, leads us to believe that, in addition to the inspired writings of Israel, he indeed not only read foreign literature but actually pondered it deeply because it was his vocation to do so:

> He treasures the discourses of the famous,
>   and goes to the heart of involved sayings;
> He studies the hidden meaning of proverbs,
>   and is busied with the enigmas found in parables.
>
> He is in attendance on the great,
>   and has entrance to the ruler.
> He travels among the peoples of foreign lands
>   to test what is good and evil among people (39:2–4).

From this autobiographical account we may assume that Ben Sira gained wide experience of cultures other than his own and became acquainted first-hand with non-Jewish Wisdom literatures. It is not unreasonable to assume that he would employ in his own book some of what he learned from the Gentiles.

The Book of Proverbs itself, which was one of Ben Sira's principal sources (see Part VI above), provided a legitimate precedent for borrowing from Gentile Wisdom literature. R. B. Y. Scott calls Prov 22:17–24:22 "The Thirty Precepts of the Sages,"[1] a title suggested by 22:20: "Have I not written for you thirty precepts [so Scott; or more literally with NAB, the "Thirty," reading šělōšîm for MT K šilšôm, Q šālîšîm]." The expression the "Thirty" derives from the Egyptian *Instruction of Amen-em-ope* (*ANET*, pp. 421–24), which also contains exactly thirty precepts. The first ten exhortations (two are variants) of Prov 22:17–24:22 parallel nine of the thirty precepts of *Amen-em-ope*. There is a scholarly consensus that the exhortations of Prov 22:17–

---

[1] *Proverbs • Ecclesiastes,* AB 18, p. 133.

23:11 bear a significant resemblance to the Egyptian work,[2] and the dependency is of the former on the latter, not vice versa. *Amen-em-ope* may have been composed as early as the thirteenth century B.C. but was still being copied centuries later.[3]

There can be little doubt that portions of Ben Sira also derive from Gentile literature. But one must distinguish between *expressions* or *ideas* that Ben Sira borrows indirectly from pagan authors and pagan *works* that he read personally and then directly alludes to in his own book. An example of the former case is Sir 14:18, which shows a striking resemblance to *The Iliad*, vi 146–49 (see COMMENT on 14:18 for the passage from Homer). Even granting the dependence on Homer in this case, as do many commentators, one may not conclude that Ben Sira must have read *The Iliad*. It is equally probable that he read the passage in a chrestomathy or anthology containing Greek authors. More likely, however, the ideas and expressions in the passage became well known in Ben Sira's day, as, for example, the words from *Romeo and Juliet*, II ii 43–44, have become proverbial in our own language: "What's in a name? that which we call a rose / By any other name would smell as sweet." One may not assume that a person quoting these lines has read the whole play or even knows that Shakespeare is the author. Most people, even if they know that Karl Marx wrote, "Religion . . . is the opium of the people," have never read a page of his *Critique of Hegel's Philosophy of Right*, Introduction (1844). Likewise, one who calls a killjoy or miserly person a Scrooge need not have read Charles Dickens's *A Christmas Carol*. These examples suffice to make the point clear.

T. Middendorp provides a convenient overview of evidence adduced by scholars who have attempted to show parallels between The Wisdom of Ben Sira and various Greek authors.[4] He claims that approximately one hundred passages in Ben Sira have clear parallels in Greek literature.[5] The largest number of these parallels come from Theognis and smaller amounts from Euripides, Xenophon, Hesiod, Homer, Sophocles, and several other Greek authors. J. T. Sanders rightly criticizes Middendorp for exaggerating Ben Sira's dependence on Greek sources, and for proposing that Ben Sira deliberately chose those portions of Greek works that resemble Jewish proverbial literature in order to show his Jewish readers the value of Gentile wisdom, and to show his Hellenic readers "the great similarities between Hellenistic and Jewish thought."[6] Sanders, after examining all the parallels Middendorp

---

[2] For an analysis of the similarities between the two works, cf. W. McKane, *Proverbs*, pp. 374–85; Scott, *Proverbs • Ecclesiastes*, pp. 20–21, 135–43; and G. E. Bryce, *A Legacy of Wisdom: The Egyptian Contribution to the Wisdom of Israel*.

[3] Scott, *Proverbs • Ecclesiastes*, p. xxxv.

[4] T. Middendorp, *Die Stellung Jesu Ben Siras zwischen Judentum und Hellenismus*.

[5] Ibid., pp. 8–24.

[6] J. T. Sanders, *Ben Sira and Demotic Wisdom*, SBLMS 28, p. 29.

alleges, concludes that Ben Sira apparently did read and use in his work the elegiac poems of Theognis, at least Book 1. Perhaps the reason why Ben Sira borrowed from these poems is that they contain practical advice similar to what is found in Jewish Wisdom literature, and they employ the elegiac couplet that is similar to the *parallelismus membrorum*, the hallmark of Hebrew poetry.[7] But, as Sanders demonstrates satisfactorily, not all the parallels Middendorp suggests are close enough to convince readers that borrowing took place.[8] I agree with most of the Theognis–Ben Sira parallels that Sanders considers probable and with his analysis of the same.[9] Whenever a passage from Ben Sira seems to parallel material from Theognis I shall make reference, in the commentary, to Sanders's analysis.

Of the eight passages from Ben Sira that, according to Middendorp, parallel material from Homer, only one is in any way convincing: 14:18 resembles *The Iliad,* vi 146–49, as mentioned above. The other alleged correspondences between Ben Sira and Homer and the other Greek authors are far from certain or even likely.[10]

Sanders offers a satisfying explanation of Ben Sira's manner of borrowing from Greek sources.[11] Ben Sira used Hellenic material only when it suited his Jewish purpose, i.e., when he regarded it as true, in which case he claimed it for Judaism. "Thus, it is not that Ben Sira opposed Hellenic ideas *as such,* and he is even able, apparently, to read and use at least one Hellenic writer (Theognis); rather, he is entirely open to Hellenic thought *as long as it can be Judaized.* What he opposes is *the dismantling of Judaism. . . .*"[12] Accordingly, despite the probable use of Greek sources, what Ben Sira wrote was a completely Jewish work.

Apparently, Ben Sira was familiar with Egyptian Wisdom literature as well. The Egyptian work entitled "The Satire on the Trades" (*ANET,* pp. 432–34), also called "The Instruction [or Maxims] of Duauf," seems to be the source, directly or indirectly, of many ideas and expressions found in Sir 38:24–39:11 (see COMMENT). Sanders gives a fine overview of scholarly research and opinion regarding the other Egyptian influences on Ben Sira.[13] The most important source is *Papyrus Insinger,* which contains about three fourths of an Egyptian gnomic work, written in demotic and attributed to a certain Phibis, son of Tachos-pa-iana. This work is to be dated in or before the Ptolemaic period, so that we may safely assume that it could have been read by Ben Sira.[14] Sanders makes the interesting observation that "one finds

[7] Ibid., pp. 29–30.
[8] Ibid., pp. 33–38.
[9] Ibid., pp. 30–38.
[10] Ibid., pp. 39–45.
[11] Ibid., pp. 55–59.
[12] Ibid., p. 58.
[13] Ibid., pp. 61–91.
[14] Ibid., p. 70.

in *Phibis* exactly Ben Sira's characteristic ethics of caution based on shame and regard for one's name, a similarity which cannot be paralleled in any other known work which Ben Sira might conceivably have used."[15] Cf. Sir 6:13; 13:1–14:2; 29:20; 32:23; 41:11–13.[16] According to Sanders's calculations, over 15 percent of *Phibis* is reflected in Ben Sira; that's an astounding statistic. Aware of the dangers of "parallelomania" that have afflicted scholars over the years,[17] Sanders nonetheless makes a strong case that there are enough meaningful similarities between Ben Sira and *Phibis* to conclude that the Jewish sage borrowed from the Egyptian. But Sanders makes two key remarks that should be kept in mind. First, *Papyrus Insinger* "is perhaps not—and certainly not necessarily—the exact form of *Phibis* known to Ben Sira. . . . Ben Sira was under the influence not only of certain *sources* of *Papyrus Insinger* but indeed of an *edition* of the work of which *Papyrus Insinger* is the primary surviving exemplar."[18] Second, Ben Sira never quotes exactly from *Phibis* material; rather, "Ben Sira has derived *gnomic insight* from *Phibis*."[19] After other carefully nuanced analyses and generally convincing arguments, Sanders writes that *"Phibis* is much more like Ben Sira than such other literature, and that *Phibis* is *more* like Ben Sira, in both style and content, than is *any other collection of proverbs, Theognis included, save only the Book of Proverbs itself."*[20] Thus it is reasonable to conclude that Ben Sira liked much of what he read in *Phibis* and took over and adapted several of its proverbs, especially those dealing with the need to be cautious so as to secure for oneself a lasting good name.[21] In the commentary I shall make reference to Sanders in order to alert the reader to the principal *Phibis*–Ben Sira parallels.

The dependence of Ben Sira on several non-Jewish writings seems beyond question. As mentioned above, he probably even read, in whole or in part, the works of Theognis and Phibis, and incorporated into his own book some of their insights and ideas as well as others that were circulating at the time. But we must keep in mind that Ben Sira utilized certain Gentile expressions and aphorisms only because he considered these to be true and hence, in his mind, conformable to Jewish tradition and doctrine. In effect, what Ben Sira does with the non-Jewish material is to make it as Jewish as possible, and this procedure is far more important and significant for our understanding of his book than the fact that he has borrowed or adapted it in the first place. For

---

[15] Ibid., p. 97.

[16] For an excellent study of Ben Sira's concern for one's good name and the caution that he urges in his ethical teaching, cf. J. T. Sanders, "Ben Sira's Ethics of Caution," *HUCA* 50 (1979): 73–106.

[17] Cf. S. Sandmel, "Parallelomania," *JBL* 81 (1962): 1–13.

[18] Sanders, *Ben Sira and Demotic Wisdom,* pp. 98–99.

[19] Ibid., p. 102.

[20] Ibid., p. 105.

[21] Ibid.

this reason, I pay less heed, in the commentary, to the non-Jewish sources of Ben Sira, choosing instead to emphasize the biblical background of Ben Sira's thought and the literary skill with which he expresses himself.

An analogy may help to validate my choice. Sir Thomas North's translation (1595) of Plutarch's *Lives* is the source of three of Shakespeare's plays: *Julius Caesar, Coriolanus,* and *Antony and Cleopatra.* Though Shakespeare absorbed much of North's translation into his own plays, "turning noble prose into nobler verse,"[22] the magnificent poetry, the splendid imagery, and the masterful structure of these plays, which have captivated and entertained and enlightened audiences for centuries, can in no way be attributed to North or to Plutarch, but only to Shakespeare's unrivaled genius.

Similarly, when all is said and done, though Ben Sira utilized foreign authors, what he writes comes out as something completely his own, and accordingly must be described as something thoroughly Jewish and compatible with earlier biblical thought and sentiment. That is why his maxims, even when they may parallel material from Theognis or *Phibis,* have more the spirit and tenor of the Book of Proverbs than of either pagan source. Ben Sira adapted and adopted not only the earlier biblical literature, by far his major source (see Part VI), but also non-Jewish writings in order to create a Wisdom book that would inspire the Jews of his day to remain faithful to their heritage and to resist the blandishments of Hellenistic culture and religion. From his reading, Ben Sira knew how attractive pagan writings could be, and how they could lead Jews away from the practice of their faith. So he made use of these foreign sources, not because he was caught up in the spirit of compromise and syncretism that was rampant at the time, but because he felt he had to show others how the best of Gentile thought is no danger to the faith but could even be incorporated into an authentically Jewish work, the purpose of which was to encourage fidelity to their ancestral practices. Herein lie the religious genius and literary skill of Ben Sira.

[22] C. J. Sisson, ed., *William Shakespeare: The Complete Works* (New York: Harper & Brothers, 1954), p. 939.

VIII. THE ORIGINAL HEBREW TEXT
AND ANCIENT VERSIONS

That Ben Sira wrote his book originally in Hebrew is beyond question. In the Foreword to the Greek translation his grandson states explicitly that the book was originally written in that language. The original Hebrew text began to disappear, however, after the rabbis denied the book a place in the Hebrew canon; see Part III. For centuries the Hebrew text was known through only a few more or less exact quotations found in the Talmudic and rabbinical literature. The Greek and Syriac versions, from which all other translations (ancient and modern) have been made, became the principal sources of our knowledge of the book.

1. Discovery of the Hebrew Text

In 1896 S. Schechter, Reader in Talmudic Hebrew at Cambridge University, examined a leaf of an old manuscript, which had been brought from the East by Mrs. Lewis and Mrs. Gibson, and recognized it immediately to be a portion of The Wisdom of Ben Sira in the original Hebrew.[1] Between 1896 and 1900 many more fragments of Ben Sira in Hebrew were identified by scholars among the vast collection of materials recovered from the Cairo Synagogue Geniza (=storeroom for worn-out or discarded MSS). These were parts of four distinct manuscripts, generally called A, B, C, and D, and were dated from the tenth to the twelfth century. In 1931 J. Marcus discovered a new leaf of Hebrew Sirach among the fragments in the Adler Geniza collection housed at the Jewish Theological Seminary of America; this leaf was called MS E. In 1958 and 1960 J. Schirmann identified and published a few more leaves of MSS B and C. Qumran Cave 2 produced small fragments of Sirach (2Q18), which were published by M. Baillet in 1962. In 1965 J. A. Sanders published *The Psalm Scrolls of Qumran Cave 11* (11QPs[a]), in which is found an important portion of Sirach. In 1965 Y. Yadin published fragments of a Sirach scroll recovered from the ruins of Masada. Finally, in 1982, A. Scheiber found, among the Geniza materials of the Taylor-Schechter Ad-

---

[1] For details of this exciting discovery and first publication of the fragment, cf. S. Schechter, "A Fragment of the Original Text of Ecclesiasticus," *Expositor,* 5th Ser., 4 (1896): 1–15.

ditional Series collection at Cambridge University Library, a new leaf of Ben Sira and the corner fragment of a damaged leaf of MS C (first published in 1900). Scheiber states that the new leaf (containing 31:24–32:7 and 32:12–33:8) is from MS D. This identification, however, is wrong for two reasons: (1) the new leaf is written stichometrically (like MSS B and E and the Masada MS), whereas MS D is not so written; and (2) the handwriting is different from that of MS D. The leaf cannot be from MS E either, for MS E has some of the same bicola found in the new leaf, and the hands are not the same. Hence I conclude that what Scheiber has found is a portion of a sixth manuscript, hitherto unknown. I give the name MS F to this new leaf. Though Scheiber published the leaf in 1982, his article appeared in an obscure, not widely known Hungarian journal, *Magyar Könyvszemle*. As a result I became aware of this article only in late March 1987, when this volume was already in galleys. Hence I have been unable to utilize the peculiar readings of MS F in Skehan's translation and notes and in my commentary.

The suggested dates and contents of the various Hebrew fragments of Sirach are as follows:

A. THE 1896–1900 AND 1931 DISCOVERIES

A—six leaves, eleventh century, containing 3:6b–16:26.

B—nineteen leaves written stichometrically, twelfth century, containing 30:11–33:3; 35:11–38:27b; 39:15c–51:30 (with subscription).

C—four leaves, older than MSS A and B, a florilegium containing, in this order, 4:23, 30, 31; 5:4–7, 9–13; 6:18b, 19, 28, 35; 7:1, 2, 4, 6, 17, 20, 21, 23–25; 18:31b–19:3b; 20:5–7; 37:19, 22, 24, 26; 20:13; 25:8, 13, 17–24; 26:1–2a.

D—a single leaf, eleventh century, containing 36:29–38:1a.

E—a single leaf written stichometrically, undated by Marcus, containing 32:16–34:1.

B. SCHIRMANN'S LEAVES OF MSS B AND C

B—two leaves containing 10:19c–11:10; 15:1–16:7.

C—two leaves containing 3:14–18, 21–22; 41:16; 4:21; 20:22–23; 4:22–23b; 26:2b–3, 13, 15–17; 36:27–31.

C. THE QUMRAN CAVE 2 FRAGMENT

2Q18—two fragments, second half of first century B.C., containing only four complete words, at the ends of lines, and a few end letters of 6:20–31, written stichometrically, and three or four letters of 6:14–15 (or possibly 1:19–20).

D. THE QUMRAN CAVE 11 FRAGMENT

11QPs^a—part of a scroll, first half of first century A.D., containing 51:13–20, 30b (the last two words).

E. THE MASADA SCROLL

M—twenty-six leather fragments forming seven columns, written stichometrically like MSS B, E, and F, first half of first century B.C., containing portions of 39:27–44:17.

F. SCHEIBER'S FRAGMENT OF MS C AND LEAF OF MS F

C—the corner of a damaged leaf containing 25:8 and 25:20–21.
F—a single leaf written stichometrically, undated by Scheiber but probably eleventh century, containing 31:24–32:7 and 32:12–33:8[2]

About 68 percent of the book is now extant in Hebrew: about 2,200 cola of the 3,221 that are found in the complete book according to the Greek text of Codex Vaticanus.[3] Of these 2,200 cola, about 530 are extant in whole or in part (many of the Masada cola are, unfortunately, fragmentary) in two MSS at the same time, and 36 are found in three MSS (14 in B, C, and D: 36:29, 30, 31; 37:19, 22, 24; and 22 in B, E, and F: 32:16–22, 24; 33:1–2).

[2] For the publication of all six MSS, the Qumran fragments, and the Masada MS, see the Bibliography: A. Sources; 1. Geniza, Qumran, and Masada MSS of Ben Sira.
[3] The count from Codex Vaticanus (B) is given by H. B. Swete, *The Old Testament in Greek*, 3d ed., vol. 2, p. 754.

2. Authenticity of the Geniza MSS

Shortly after the initial excitement over the discovery of the original Hebrew text of Sirach, some scholars began to question the authenticity of the Geniza MSS. On the basis of his analysis of only Sir 12:10–11 and 51:13–30, G. Bickell (1899) argued that the Geniza text is in general a slavish translation of the Syriac.[4] In a 20-page pamphlet D. S. Margoliouth (1899) proposed a bizarre retroversion hypothesis: first Sirach was translated from Greek into Persian, and then a Persian Jew translated the Persian text into Hebrew. Margoliouth based his theory on the presence of a few Persian glosses in the margins of MS B.[5] Scholars were quick to reject Margoliouth's fanciful hypothesis.[6] E. Nestle (1902) attempted to prove that the Geniza fragments represent a text that is partly original and partly retranslated from Greek (MS C) and from Syriac (MS A).[7] Between 1896 and 1901 I. Lévi changed his opinion several times about the authenticity of the Geniza MSS. His final opinion is that the Cairo text is substantially authentic, but it contains some retroversions from the Syriac.[8] More recently, E. J. Goodspeed,[9] M. Hadas,[10] C. C. Torrey,[11] and H. L. Ginsberg[12] also questioned the authenticity of the Cairo MSS. The controversy has now abated, thanks in large measure to the discovery and study of the Masada scroll, which supports the authenticity of Cairo MS B and indirectly the other MSS as well. Y. Yadin writes: "The text of the scroll unquestionably confirms that *Btext* and the glosses of *Bmarg basically* represent the original Hebrew version! . . . In spite of many variants, the Scroll text is basically identical with that of the Genizah MSS."[13] The consensus today seems to be that the Cairo Geniza MSS are essentially authentic.[14]

[4] G. Bickell, "Der hebräische Sirachtext eine Rückübersetzung," *WZKM* 13 (1899): 251–56.

[5] D. S. Margoliouth, *The Origin of the "Original Hebrew" of Ecclesiasticus.*

[6] For details of the controversy and bibliography, cf. A. A. Di Lella, *The Hebrew Text of Sirach,* pp. 27–30.

[7] E. Nestle, "Sirach (Book of)," in *A Dictionary of the Bible,* 4 (ed. J. Hastings), pp. 547–49.

[8] I. Lévi, *The Hebrew Text of the Book of Ecclesiasticus* (Semitic Study Series 3); and "Sirach, The Wisdom of Jesus, the Son of," *Jewish Encyclopedia,* 11 (1905): 393–94.

[9] E. J. Goodspeed, *The Story of the Apocrypha,* p. 25.

[10] *The Apocrypha,* tr. E. J. Goodspeed, introduction M. Hadas, p. 222.

[11] C. C. Torrey, *The Apocryphal Literature,* p. 97; and "The Hebrew of the Geniza Sirach," in *Alexander Marx Jubilee Volume,* pp. 585–602.

[12] H. L. Ginsberg, "The Original Hebrew of Ben Sira 12:10–14," *JBL* 74 (1955): 93–95.

[13] Y. Yadin, *The Ben Sira Scroll from Masada,* pp. 7, 10.

[14] For detailed arguments against the opponents of authenticity as well as arguments for authenticity, cf. Di Lella, *The Hebrew Text,* pp. 23–105.

3. *The Confusing Textual Witnesses*

Perhaps the best overall approach to the complex textual problems that arise from a consideration of the extant Hebrew MSS, the two Greek forms, the Old Latin, and the Syriac, is that suggested by C. Kearns, whose analysis[15] I am generally adapting and expanding here and augmenting from the studies of J. Ziegler, whom Kearns also used, and others. Kearns speaks of the following: HTI, the Hebrew original of Ben Sira; HTII, the expanded Hebrew text of one or more recensions; GI, the grandson's Greek translation of HTI; GII, the expanded Greek translation based on HTII.

A. THE GREEK WITNESSES: GI AND GII

GI is contained, for the most part, in the uncials A, B, C, S, and their dependent cursives. J. Ziegler notes that GII is not preserved in any single MS, not even the celebrated Codex 248. The witnesses of GII, generally the *O* and *L'* MSS in Ziegler's critical edition (see below), actually transmit the text of GI, which was then expanded under the influence of one or more MSS. The translator of GII did not produce a new and independent translation; he had before him and used MSS of GI and translated from HTII only in those cases where he considered it to be necessary. Many of the peculiar readings of 248 and other GII MSS go back to an old Hebrew *Vorlage,* one of the recensions of HTII, which differed significantly from HTI. The additions found in the MSS do not offer the complete contents of GII but only a selection. All the daughter translations of Greek Sirach are important and useful, but only the Old Latin, the oldest of these translations, is fundamental (see below). The Greek text in the course of centuries of transmission has suffered a great deal and often is mutilated in the MSS; of all the books of the LXX, Sirach has the greatest number of emendations and conjectures. Accordingly, the textual critic has to take great pains to try to remedy these textual corruptions with more or less success.[16]

GII, derived ultimately from HTII, offers many additions. These may be: (a) an addition of a few words or even of a single word, which could give a new meaning to the phrase or colon in question (cf., e.g., 1:30e; 2:11a); (b) complete bicola or cola (cf. e.g., 1:5, 7, 10cd, 12cd, 18cd, 21; 2:5c, 9c). GII has about 300 cola not found in GI. In his splendid critical edition, Ziegler

[15] C. Kearns, "Ecclesiasticus, or the Wisdom of Jesus the Son of Sirach," in *NCCHS* (1969): 547–50.
[16] J. Ziegler, ed., *Sapientia Iesu Filii Sirach* (Septuaginta 12/2), pp. 74–75.

prints these extra cola right in the text itself, but in smaller letters, so that they are readily identifiable. In the present volume, the translation of GII is generally given at the end of a section of text. GII is found in two groups of MSS: (a) the Origenistic or hexaplaric, which Ziegler calls the O-group; and (b) the Lucianic, which Ziegler calls the L-group (the main group) and the l-group (the subgroup), L' being used when L and l witness to the same reading.[17]

The textual witnesses of O are cursive 253 and the Syrohexaplar (Syh) as well as uncial V and S^c (the seventh-century corrector of S) and sometimes the Armenian and Old Latin. The witnesses of L are 248-493-637 and sometimes the Armenian, Old Latin, and Syriac; of l, 106-130-545-705.[18]

B. THE OLD LATIN

The Old Latin, as already indicated, is an important witness to GII, either directly or indirectly. But Old Latin preserves the correct order of chapters after 30:24, whereas in all the extant Greek MSS two sections, 30:25–33:13a and 33:13b–36:16a, have exchanged places. These two sections are nearly equal. H. B. Swete writes:

> There can be little doubt that in the *exemplar* from which, so far as is certainly known, all our Greek MSS. of this book are ultimately derived the pairs of leaves on which these sections were severally written had been transposed, whereas the Latin translator, working from a MS. in which the transposition had not taken place, has preserved the true order.[19]

Old Latin's exemplar apparently contained many additions of the GII type. Smend (pp. ic–cxiii) lists 36 places in which Old Latin supports the addition of a bicolon or more in the GII witnesses, and gives the Old Latin of 75 more bicola that are found only in Old Latin. There is a dispute as to the form of Greek text that underlay the original Old Latin: (a) Smend (pp. xcviii, cxxiv) maintains that it was basically a MS of GI, which, however, had far more traces of GII than any of the surviving MSS. (b) D. De Bruyne disagrees, holding that Old Latin was translated directly from a GII MS but that many GI readings entered it later. In this opinion, Old Latin would be the only known direct witness of GII.[20]

The Old Latin, which was eventually incorporated into the Vulgate because

[17] Ibid., 58–64; and Kearns, "Ecclesiasticus," p. 548.

[18] Ziegler, *Sirach*, pp. 58–69; Kearns, "Ecclesiasticus," p. 548.

[19] H. B. Swete, *The Old Testament in Greek*, 3d ed., vol. 2, pp. vi–vii.

[20] D. De Bruyne, "Étude sur le texte latin de l'Ecclésiastique," *RBén* 40 (1928): 41–43, 46. Kearns ("Ecclesiasticus," p. 548) gives a good summary of this dispute.

St. Jerome did not make a fresh translation of the book, was made from a GII text tradition, probably in the second century. This early Latin version lacked the grandson's Prologue as well as the Praise of the Ancestors (chaps. 44–50); the latter was unknown to the Latin Fathers prior to Isidore of Seville (d. 636). This Latin text did contain, however, chap. 51 and also an intrusive chap. 52, the Prayer of Solomon (=2 Chr 6:13–22). In the fifth or sixth century, the Old Latin of Sirach began appearing in MSS of the Vulgate after it had first undergone many alterations by scribes and editors who also added the Prologue and chaps. 44–50. As a result of this complicated history, the Old Latin of Sirach has more doublets, variants, glosses, and interpolations than any other book of the Latin Bible. It is, nevertheless, of great importance for the textual criticism of the expanded text of Sirach.[21]

C. THE SYRIAC

The Syriac was translated directly from a Hebrew *Vorlage* which had fused the two Hebrew recensions that seem to underlie the extant Hebrew fragments (see below). In choosing between doublets in his *Vorlage,* the Syriac translator was often guided by the reading found in the Greek text he had with him, a text which was not identical with GII but which contained many of its readings. Syriac has 70 of the approximately 300 additional cola found in GII, as well as several shorter additions in common with GII. It also contains 74 cola and numerous shorter variants that are proper to itself. Many of these are probably of Christian origin, but quite a few others show the doctrinal trends of GII and Old Latin.[22] It is probable that Ben Sira was originally translated into Syriac by Ebionites no later than the early fourth century, and that it was revised in the late fourth century by orthodox Christians who gave it its present form.[23]

D. THE HEBREW MSS

The Geniza MSS seem to bear witness to the existence of more than one recension of the Hebrew text, viz., HTI and HTII. The existence of GII corroborates this conclusion, which is supported also by many of the Talmudic and rabbinical quotations of Sirach. HTII differs from HTI primarily

---

[21] Kearns, "Ecclesiasticus," p. 547.

[22] Ibid., p. 548.

[23] For a solid defense of this hypothesis, cf. M. M. Winter, "The Origins of Ben Sira in Syriac," *VT* 27 (1977): 237–53 and 494–507.

by additions. A. Fuchs has shown[24] that the Hebrew text in Geniza MSS A, B, and C contains (apart from the interpolated psalm after 51:12) 90 passages, each a bicolon or more in length, that have been added to HTI. Sixty-one of these are only alternative readings of HTI. Almost all the rest are editorial additions of doctrinal import, comparable to the additions we see in GII. The examples Kearns suggests are 11:15, 16; 15:14b, 15c; 16:15, 16; 31:6d; 51:1.[25]

Kearns' analysis of the confusing textual witnesses—GI and GII, HTI and HTII, Syriac, and Old Latin—is generally convincing. It seems to give, on the whole, the most reasonable and plausible account of the often elusive evidence. Retroversion, however, is one feature of the Cairo MSS that Kearns does not take seriously even though he mentions it in passing.[26] It is the contention of the authors of this volume that the Cairo Geniza MSS, though basically genuine, nevertheless contain some retroversions from the Syriac and from the Greek. The assumption is that these retroversions were made by a medieval Jewish scribe. I have argued for retroversion from Syriac in the following texts: 5:4–6; 10:31; 15:14, 15, 20; 16:3; and 32:16.[27] And I. Lévi has shown that the text of 51:13–30 in MS B (see COMMENT) was, for the most part, retroverted from Syriac.[28] Finally, J. Ziegler has demonstrated that parts of 11:2b; 20:13a; and 37:20b are retroversions from Greek.[29] H. P. Rüger, however, does not agree that the texts that Ziegler and I have proposed are examples of retroversion but argues that they are instead examples of the primary and secondary Hebrew text forms, similar to what Kearns calls HTI and HTII; these two text forms, Rüger says, explain all the doublets and other variants in the Cairo MSS.[30]

I believe, however, that the hypothesis that the Cairo MSS contain some retroversions made by one or more medieval Jews is compatible with, and even reinforces, the theory that these MSS (particularly MS B) witness to more than one recension of the Hebrew text, viz., HTI and HTII, the bases, respectively, of GI and GII (see above). The reason is that some of the passages that have been analyzed as medieval retroversions simply do not have the same kind of Hebrew as "the secondary Hebrew text-form" (Rüger) or HTII (Kearns), which dates back to the first century B.C. The diction and

[24] A. Fuchs, *Textkritische Untersuchungen zum hebräischen Ekklesiastikus* (BibS 12/5), pp. 112–15.

[25] Kearns, "Ecclesiasticus," p. 548.

[26] Ibid., p. 546.

[27] For a discussion of these retroversions, cf. Di Lella, *The Hebrew Text,* pp. 106–47.

[28] I. Lévi, *L'Ecclésiastique,* Part II, pp. xxi–xxvii. Lévi argues for other retroversions as well.

[29] For a discussion of these retroversions, cf. J. Ziegler, "Zwei Beiträge zu Sirach," *BZ* N.F. 8 (1964): 277–84; and "Ursprüngliche Lesarten im griechischen Sirach," in *Mélanges Eugène Tisserant,* 1, Studi e testi 231 (1964): 461–87.

[30] H. P. Rüger, *Text und Textform in hebräischen Sirach* (BZAW 112, 1970). Cf., esp., pp. 1–11.

grammar of these retroversions are often demonstrably Mishnaic[31] and hence quite different from what one would expect in HTII.

4. Textual Criticism of the Book

The textual witnesses to The Wisdom of Ben Sira are, as should be obvious from the above, enormously complicated, especially when the critic attempts to understand the relationships that exist between and among them. No other book of the Old Testament is as textually complex and difficult to work with.

These are some of the fundamental problems and factors that the textual critic of Sirach must face:

a. No extant witness in Hebrew gives us the complete text of the book.

b. Though the theory of more than one recension of the Hebrew text (HTI and HTII) seems most probable, it is not always easy to determine when an addition to the text should be analyzed as evidence of HTII or as a gloss or as a retroversion from Syriac (or Greek).

c. The Cairo Geniza MSS, especially MS B, have more than the usual share of scribal errors—dittography, haplography, misspellings, and misreadings of the exemplar being copied.[32]

d. Though GI remains the most reliable form of the book as a whole, it nevertheless contains many scribal errors and other corruptions as well as mistranslations due to the grandson's failure to understand the underlying Hebrew; see, for example, the NOTE on 42:18d.

e. On rare occasions, GII may be the only reliable witness to Ben Sira's thought; but it is not always obvious when this is the case. See, for example, NOTES and COMMENT on 11:15–16 and 33:26a.

f. At times, Syriac may provide the best text of an aphorism; see, for example, NOTES and COMMENT on 18:19, 21 and 25:1ab.

g. At other times, Syriac, because it is of Ebionite origin and was later reworked by orthodox Christians, deliberately omits, or changes the meaning of, a portion of the Hebrew text; thus, for example, in 35:1–10, Syriac avoids all mention of sacrifice.[33]

h. The Masada Scroll, the oldest and generally most reliable witness to the

---

[31] For clear illustrations of this point, see the discussion of 10:31 and 16:3 in Di Lella, *The Hebrew Text*, pp. 115–19, 134–42.

[32] For a reconstruction of the history of the Cairo Geniza Hebrew text of Sirach, cf. Di Lella, *The Hebrew Text*, pp. 150–51. For a splendid study of the doctrinal content and origin of the expanded text of Sirach, which is the basis of HTII and GII, cf. Kearns, "Ecclesiasticus," pp. 548–50.

[33] For a comparison and analysis of the Greek and Syriac texts of 35:1–10, cf. Winter, "The Origins of Ben Sira in Syriac," pp. 238–40.

original Hebrew text of Ben Sira, at times agrees with MS B^{txt}; at other times it agrees with B^{mg}; and at still other times it agrees with neither B^{txt} nor B^{mg}.[34]

i. The Old Latin, though an essential witness to the expanded GII text type, offers abundant difficulties of its own, viz., double and even triple renderings, additions, transpositions, Christian reworkings, and a few omissions as well.[35]

It should be obvious from a consideration of the above that there are no iron rules or golden rules for the textual criticism of The Wisdom of Ben Sira. The careful critic must take into account all these bewildering features and then make a judgment that seems most reasonable for the particular text under consideration. Even then, there will, of course, be legitimate differences of opinion on which form of the text best witnesses to Ben Sira's thought.

5. The Editions of Sirach

For information and data on the various editions of the Hebrew fragments, the Greek, Old Latin, Syrohexaplar, Syriac Peshitta, Arabic, Coptic, Ethiopic, and other versions, see the Bibliography: A. Sources.

Here I offer some comments on the availability, utility, and accuracy of the principal editions of Sirach.

A. THE HEBREW FRAGMENTS

The most widely available editions of the Geniza fragments identified up to 1900 are those of H. L. Strack, *Die Sprüche Jesus', des Sohnes Sirachs* (1903); I. Lévi, *The Hebrew Text of the Book of Ecclesiasticus* (1904; reprinted 1951); R. Smend, *Die Weisheit des Jesus Sirach, hebräisch und deutsch* (1906); and M. H. Segal, *Sēper ben-Sîrāʾ haššālēm*, 2d ed. (1958). Strack's edition is the most convenient to use because of the layout of the text when more than one MS is extant; but it contains a few errors in transcription. Lévi's edition is convenient for the same reason as Strack's, and it also contains a useful Hebrew-English and German glossary; but it contains too many errors to be of use for the serious textual critic. Smend's edition, which is more difficult to use, contains the most reliable transcription of the Cairo MSS.[36] Segal's edi-

---

[34] For details and lists of the agreements and disagreements of M, B^{txt}, and B^{mg}, cf. Yadin, *The Ben Sira Scroll from Masada*, pp. 8–10 and Tables 1–3 on pp. 7–9 and 11–13 of the Hebrew section.

[35] Cf. Ziegler, *Sirach*, pp. 23–29.

[36] I have been told that Smend is the one who smeared Vaseline on the Oxford fragments of Sirach in a (futile) attempt to read them more accurately. I examined these in the summer of 1963. They are difficult to read now even under ultraviolet light; hence the Vaseline damage seems to be permanent. Fortunately, however, the Oxford fragments were photographed before

tion, though readily available, is inconvenient to use and contains some errors.

In his edition Segal also includes MS E, which J. Marcus discovered and then published in 1931. For the most part, one must rely on the transcription of Marcus because the facsimiles he published are difficult or impossible to read, having been printed on cheap, dull paper instead of the usual glossy paper.

J. Schirmann's publication of the further leaves of MSS B and C in *Tarbiz* 27 (1957–58): 440–43 and 29 (1959–60): 125–34, are not as accurate as they could be. So from the original leaves of these MSS housed at the University Library, Cambridge, I made my own edition and published it, with facsimiles, in "The Recently Identified Leaves of Sirach in Hebrew," *Bib* 45 (1964): 153–67.

The small 2Q18 fragments of Sirach were competently published by M. Baillet, *Les "Petites Grottes" de Qumrân* (DJD 3, 1962). J. A. Sanders, *The Psalms Scroll of Qumrân Cave 11 (11QPsᵃ)* (DJD 4, 1965), gives an accurate transcription of the Sirach portion of the text; I disagree with him on the reading of only one word: I would read the third word of col. xxi, l. 17 *pr*š*[ty]*; Sanders reads *pt*ḥ*[ty]*.[37]

Y. Yadin, *The Ben Sira Scroll from Masada* (1965), offers a generally reliable edition and study of that most important text. One should, however, also consult J. Strugnell, "Notes and Queries on 'The Ben Sira Scroll from Masada,'" *ErIsr* 9 (1969): 109–19, for certain improvements on Yadin's readings.

F. Vattioni, *Ecclesiastico: Testo ebraico con apparato critico e versioni greca, latina e siriaca* (1968), prints all the Hebrew fragments except MS F (discovered in 1982); hence his edition is quite useful on that score alone. But, unfortunately, he reproduces I. Lévi's faulty edition of Cairo MSS A, B, C, and D; that lessens the value of the work. Vattioni's volume is arranged in polyglot form (another worthwhile feature): on the right-hand page, the Hebrew text, when extant, and its apparatus are given on the top, and the Syriac (a reduced facsimile of Lagarde's edition [see below]), is found underneath; on the left-hand page, the Greek (Ziegler's text but with no apparatus) is given on top, and the Old Latin (the Rome critical edition but with no apparatus) is found underneath.[38]

Smend applied the Vaseline, and were splendidly published in *Facsimiles of the Fragments Hitherto Recovered of the Book of Ecclesiasticus in Hebrew* (1901)—another important work that the scholar must consult when editions give different readings of the same text.

[37] Cf. A. A. Di Lella, review of Sanders's volume, *CBQ* 28 (1966): 92–95.

[38] For reviews of Vattioni's volume, cf. A. A. Di Lella, *CBQ* 31 (1969): 619–22; and P. W. Skehan, *Bib* 51 (1970): 580–82.

B. THE ANCIENT VERSIONS

For the Greek text of GI and GII, J. Ziegler's definitive Göttingen edition, *Sapientia Iesu Filii Sirach* (1965), now supersedes all other editions[39] and must be consulted for any serious study of the book. As mentioned in 3a above, Ziegler places GII right in the text itself, but in smaller print, and then gives the evidence for the particular GII reading in the apparatus. As in other volumes of the Göttingen Septuagint, Ziegler arranges, when possible, the 62 MSS collated into groups: *O L l a b c* 155' 157' 157" 315' 404' 534' 631' 744' —an invaluable service.

The Syrohexaplar is available in A. M. Ceriani's magnificent facsimile edition of Codex Ambrosianus, *Codex syro-hexaplaris Ambrosianus photolithographice editus* (1874).

A model critical edition of the Old Latin found in Vulgate MSS (see 3b above) was published by the Benedictines at the San Girolamo Abbey in Rome: *Biblia Sacra iuxta latinam vulgatam versionem, 12: Sapientia Salomonis, Liber Hiesu filii Sirach* (1964). In the apparatus for Sirach are found the readings of 27 MSS, 7 fragments, and 8 editions. This work now makes obsolete all the earlier editions of the Vulgate.

Until the Peshiṭta Institute critical edition of Sirach is published, one must consult A. M. Ceriani's sumptuous facsimile, *Translatio Syra Pescitto Veteris Testamenti ex codice Ambrosiano sec. fere VI photolithographice edita*, 2/4 (1878); P. A. de Lagarde, *Libri veteris testamenti apocryphi syriace* (1861), which for Sirach contains a diplomatic edition of the British Library Codex 12142 (sixth century); B. Walton, *Biblia sacra polyglotta*, 4 (1657), with variants found in vol. 6, pp. 46–47; and the Mosul Peshitta, *Biblia sacra juxta versionem simplicem quae dicitur Pschitta*, 2 (reprinted 1951).

[39] Cf. A. A. Di Lella, review of Ziegler's edition, *CBQ* 28 (1966): 538–40.

IX. THE POETRY OF BEN SIRA

That The Wisdom of Ben Sira is poetry and not prose is beyond question.* The book's 1,616 lines (the count in the Greek version)—mostly bicola with a rare tricolon—are discrete sense units akin to the poetic lines found in Job, Proverbs, Psalms, and parts of the prophetic and other literature of the OT. Moreover, the oldest copies of the book (the Masada scroll from the first century B.C.[1] and two first-century B.C. fragments from Qumran Cave 2[2]) were written stichometrically—a practice employed by the Qumran sect for such poetic compositions as Deuteronomy 32 (4QDeut)[3] and several Psalms, and by the later Masoretes for parts of Job, Psalms, and Proverbs.[4] Of the Geniza fragments of Ben Sira, MSS B, E, and F were also copied stichometrically.[5]

Soon after the discovery of the Geniza manuscripts at the end of the nineteenth century, the metrics and strophic structure of Ben Sira were studied by H. Grimme[6] and N. Schlögl.[7] Some years later, R. Smend, who rightly criticized the results of these two scholars, made his own attempt to analyze the prosody and strophes of Ben Sira but frankly admitted that the key to the riddle had not yet been discovered.[8] More recently, S. Mowinckel published his own study of Ben Sira's poetry.[9] The commentary of M. H. Segal[10] offers,

---

* Most of the content of this chapter appeared originally in the H. M. Orlinsky Volume, ed. B. A. Levine and A. Malamat, ErIsr 16 (Jerusalem 1982), pp. 26'–33'.

[1] Published by Y. Yadin, *The Ben Sira Scroll from Masada.* See esp. cols. ii–vii on the splendid plates ii–iv, vi–viii.

[2] Published by M. Baillet in *Les "Petites Grottes" de Qumrân* (DJD 3, 1962): pp. 75–77 and Plate xv.

[3] Cf. P. W. Skehan, *BASOR* 136 (1954): 12–14, and VTSup 4 (1956): 150.

[4] Cf. A. Fitzgerald, "Hebrew Poetry," in *The Jerome Biblical Commentary,* ed. R. E. Brown et al. (Englewood Cliffs, N.J.: Prentice–Hall, 1968): p. 239.

[5] For MS B, see *Facsimiles of the Fragments Hitherto Recovered of the Book of Ecclesiasticus in Hebrew* (1901), and A. A. Di Lella, "The Recently Identified Leaves of Sirach in Hebrew," *Bib* 45 (1964): 156–62 and plates i–iv. For MS E, see J. Marcus, "A Fifth Ms. of Ben Sira," *JQR* n.s. 21 (1930–31): 223–40.

[6] "Strophenartige Abschnitte im Ecclesiasticus," *OLZ* 2 (1899): 213–17; "Mètres et strophes dans les fragments du manuscrit parchemin du Siracide," *RB* 9 (1900): 400–13; "Mètres et strophes dans les fragments hébreux du manuscrit A de l'Ecclésiastique," *RB* 10 (1901): 55–65; 260–67; 423–35.

[7] *Ecclesiasticus (39,12–49,16) ope artis criticae et metricae in formam originalem redactus* (1901).

[8] *Die Weisheit des Jesus Sirach erklärt,* pp. xxxviii–xlvi.

[9] "Die Metrik bei Jesus Sirach," *ST* 9 (1955): 137–65.

[10] *Sēper ben-Sîrāʾ haššālēm* (2d ed., 1958).

however, the best analysis of the strophic structure. My colleague, the late
P. W. Skehan, who has done most of the translation and notes in the present
volume (see Preface), agrees in general with Segal but in several places suggests a different and better strophic division. I do not intend to enter into the
debate about the nature of Hebrew poetry (or, more precisely, verse) and
strophic structures. I simply accept the scholarly consensus about the commonly recognized conventions of Hebrew verse: (1) the basic sense unit is the
bicolon (or tricolon), in which there is a caesura between the two (or three)
cola; (2) the number of syllables may vary considerably from colon to colon
in the same bicolon (or tricolon), but each colon has usually two to four
accents; and (3) groups of bicola (or tricola) may form discrete stanzas within
a longer poem.[11]

Since commentators and other scholars have given little attention to the
poetic and rhetorical devices Ben Sira employed in composing his work, I
intend to examine here how Ben Sira used assonance, alliteration, rhyme,
chiasm, *inclusio,* and twenty-two- and twenty-three-line compositions to en-
hance the quality and force of his poetry. As regards metrics, it will be
observed that Ben Sira employed most frequently the $3+3$ accents in a
bicolon. There are, however, many cola in which there are two as well as four
accents. Occasionally he will also compose in the *qînâ* meter $(3+2)$; cf. 12:14
and 36:18–19 below. As regards the number of accents in a colon, I recognize
that there may be differences of opinion. I have provided a literal translation
to assist in the study of the texts below.

1. Assonance, Alliteration, and Rhyme

Assonance, alliteration, and rhyme, which make a bicolon more pleasing or
striking, are found often in the poetry of Ben Sira. I call attention here to the
more remarkable examples that I discovered as I was writing the commentary
of the book. Further examples are pointed out in the next section, Chiastic
Patterns.

5:6 A labial, *'ayin,* and liquid alliteration and *i* assonance: *kî raḥămîm
wěʾap ʿimmô / wěʾal rěšāʿîm yanniaḥ rogzô* $(3+3$ accents), "For mercy and
anger are with him, and upon the wicked alights his wrath." There is also
internal rhyme in *raḥămîm* and *rěšāʿîm* and end rhyme in *ʿimmô* and *rogzô.*

6:8 An *ē/î* and *ō* assonance and labial alliteration: *kî yēš ʾôhēb kěpî ʿēt /
wělōʾ* [MS A *wěʾal*] *yaʿămôd běyôm ṣārâ* $(3+3)$, "For there is a friend according to the occasion, but he will not be with you in time of distress."

[11] Cf., for example, the strophic analysis given by P. W. Skehan in "The Acrostic Poem in
Sirach 51:13–30," *HTR* 64 (1971): 387–400; and "Structures in Poems on Wisdom: Proverbs 8
and Sirach 24," *CBQ* 41 (1979): 374–79.

6:19ab A labial and *k/q* alliteration and *a* assonance: *kāḥôrēš wĕkazzôrēaʿ* [=Gr *speirōn;* MSS A and C *wĕkaqqôṣēr*] *qĕrab ʾēlêhā / wĕqawwēh lĕrōb tĕbûʾātāh* (4+3), "As one who plows and sows draw close to her [Wisdom], and await the abundance of her fruits."

7:4 A labial and *l* alliteration and *ē* assonance: *ʾal tĕbaqqēš mēʾēl mem-šālet / wĕkēn mimmelek môšāb kābôd* (3+3), "Seek not from God authority, nor from the king a seat of honor."

10:13ab A labial, *q,* and *z* alliteration: *kî miqwēh zādôn ḥēṭʾ / ûmĕqôrōh yabbîaʿ zimmâ* (3+3), "For sin is a reservoir of pride, and its source runs over with vice." The alliterated words *miqwēh* and *mĕqôrōh* and *zādôn* and *zimmâ* are also in synonymous parallelism.

10:22 An *r*, *g/k*, and sibilant alliteration: *gēr zār nokrî wārāš / tipʾartām yirʾat yhwh* [MS B] (4+3), "Tenant, wayfarer, alien, and pauper—their glory is the fear of Yahweh." For the parallel pair *zār* and *nokrî*, cf. Job 19:15; Prov 2:16; 5:20; 7:5; 20:16; 27:2, 13; Isa 28:21; Obad 11.

10:24 A sibilant, liquid, and labial alliteration and *ô* and *ē* assonance: *śar šôpēṭ ûmôšēl nikbādû* [MS B] / *[wĕʾê]n gādôl m[î]rēʾ ʾĕlōhîm* [MS A] (4+3), "Prince, judge, and ruler are in honor, but none is greater than he who fears God." It is to be noted that *śar* (sibilant+liquid) corresponds to the last syllable of *môšēl.*

10:27 An *ô* and *ē* assonance and labial alliteration: *ṭôb ʿōbēd wĕyôtēr hôn / mi[mmit]kabbēd [waḥă]s[ar] māzôn* [so Syr (cf. Gr); MS A *mattān*] (4+3), "Better the worker who has goods in plenty than the boaster who lacks sustenance." There is also internal rhyme in *ʿōbēd* and *mimmitkabbēd* and end rhyme in *hôn* and *māzôn.*

11:3 An *ō* assonance and labial and liquid alliteration: *ʾĕlîl* [MS A; MS B *qĕṭannâ*] *bāʿôp dĕbōrâ / wĕrōʾš tĕnûbôt piryāh* (3+3), "Least is the bee among flying things, but her fruit is supreme among produce." There is also end rhyme in *dĕbōrâ* and *piryāh,* in both of which words there is a labial and an *r*.

11:4cd A labial and *l* alliteration: *kî pĕlāʾôt maʿăśê yhwh / wĕneʿlām mēʾādām* [MS A; MS B *mēʾĕnôš*] *poʿŏlô* (3+3), "For wondrous are the works of Yahweh, and hidden from humans his deeds." There is an *a:b::b':a'* pattern in the words *maʿăśê:yhwh::mēʾādām:poʿŏlô.* In *wĕneʿlām* there occurs the combination *ʿayin-lamed*+labial, and in *poʿŏlô* the combination labial+*ʿayin-lamed.* Cf. discussion of 9:18 under Chiastic Patterns. In v 4d, note also that a labial ends the first word, begins and ends the second, and begins the third, thus creating a pleasing rhyme and rhythm.

12:13–14 An *n* alliteration and *e* and *o* assonance: *mî yāḥôn* [so Gr, Lat, Syr; MS A *yûḥan*] *ḥôbēr nāšûk / wĕkol haqqārēb ʾel ḥayyat šēn; kēn ḥôbēr ʾel ʾîš* [so Gr, Lat, Syr; MS A *ʾēšet*] *zādôn / ûmitgôlēl baʿăwônôtāyw* (3+3, 3+2), "Who pities a snake charmer who is bitten, or anyone who goes near a wild beast? So is he who associates with a proud person, and is involved in his sins." There is also a wordplay on the homonym *ḥôbēr*, which means "snake charmer" in v 13a (as also in Ps 58:6) and "he who associates" in v 14a.

13:1 A labial and liquid alliteration and *ô* assonance: *nôgēaʿ bĕzepet tidbaq yādô / wĕḥôbēr ʾel lēṣ yilmad darkô* (4+4), "Whoever touches pitch, it cleaves to his hand; and whoever associates with a scoundrel learns his ways." There is also end rhyme in *yādô* and *darkô*.

13:2ab A labial alliteration and *a* assonance: *kābēd mimmĕkā mah tiśśāʾ / wĕʾel ʿāšîr mimmĕkā mah titḥabbēr* (3+3), "Why pick up what is too heavy for you, and why associate with one who is wealthier than you?"

13:19 A liquid, *ʾaleph*, and labial alliteration and *î* assonance: *maʾăkal ʾărî pirʾê midbār / kēn marʿît ʿāšîr dallîm* (3+3), "Food for the lion are the wild asses of the desert; just so the feeding grounds for the rich are the poor."

13:24 An *o* and *î* assonance and labial, *nun,* and *ʿayin* alliteration: *ṭôb hāʾôšer ʾim ʾēn ʿāwôn / wĕraʿ hāʿŏnî ʿal pî zādôn* (3+3), "Wealth is good if there is no guilt; but poverty is evil by the standards of the proud." There is also end rhyme in *ʿāwôn* and *zādôn,* which are a parallel pair, as in 12:14.

14:17 An *ô* assonance and labial, liquid, and *k/g/q* alliteration: *kol habbāśār kabbeged yibleh / wĕḥôq ʿôlām gāwôaʿ yigwāʿû* (3+3), "All flesh wears out like a garment; the age-old law is: all must die."

15:1 A *y* and dental alliteration: *kî yĕrēʾ yhwh yaʿăśeh zōʾt / wĕtôpēś tôrâ yadrîkennâ* (3+3), "For whoever fears Yahweh will do this, and whoever is practiced in the Law will come to her [Wisdom]."

15:6 A labial and sibilant alliteration: *śāśôn wĕśimḥâ yimṣāʾ / wĕšēm ʿôlām tôrîšennû* (3+3), "Joy and gladness will he find, and she [Wisdom] will endow him with an everlasting name."

15:14 A labial and *y* alliteration: *ʾĕlōhîm mibbĕrēʾšît* [MSS A and Bᵐᵍ; MS Bᵗˣᵗ *hûʾ mērōʾš*] *bārāʾ ʾādām / wayyittĕnēhû yiṣrô* (4+2), "God from the beginning created humankind, and he made them subject to their free choice."

16:12 A *k,* liquid, and labial alliteration and *ô* assonance: *kĕrōb raḥămāyw kēn tôkaḥtô / ʾîš kĕmaʿălālāyw yišpōṭ* (3+3), "As great as his mercy, so is his punishment; he judges a person according to his deeds." There is internal rhyme in *raḥămāyw* and *kĕmaʿălālāyw.*

33:25ab A labial, sibilant, and liquid alliteration and *ô* assonance: *mispôʾ wĕšôṭ ûmaśśāʾ laḥămôr / leḥem* [so Gr; MS E omits by haplography] *ûmardût mĕlāʾkā lāʿă[bed]* (4+4), "Fodder and whip and burdens for the ass; bread and correction and work for the slave." The two cola are also in perfectly symmetrical parallelism.

36:18–19 A *k/q* alliteration and in v 19 an *a:b::b′:a′* chiastic pattern: *raḥēm ʿal qiryat qodšekā / yĕrûšālayim mĕkôn šibtêkā; mallēʾ ṣîyôn:ʾet hôdekā::ûmikkĕbôdĕkā:ʾet hêkālekā* (3+2, 3+2), "Take pity on your holy city—Jerusalem, the foundation of your throne; fill *Zion* with *your majesty,* and with *your glory, your temple.*" There is end rhyme -*kā* in these four cola, the final cola of a stanza in a prayer (36:1–22). There is also internal rhyme in *hôdekā* and *ûmikkĕbôdĕkā,* the *b* and *b'* elements of the pattern. For the synonymous parallelism of *hêkāl* and *ṣîyôn,* cf. Ps 65:2, 5. In Ps 79:1, *hêkāl* is in parallel with *yĕrûšālayim.*

2. Chiastic Patterns

In the cases of chiastic patterns given below, each of the two, three, or four elements after the double colon (::) is, in reverse order, either the same word or word root as its correspondent, or a word or phrase in synonymous, antithetic, or synthetic parallelism. Thus, in the first example (1:4), *protera pantōn* (the *a* expression) is in synonymous parallelism with *ex aiōnos* (the *a'* expression) as is *sophia* (the *b* word) with *synesis phronēseōs* (the *b'* phrase). Often the corresponding words are formulaic or fixed pairs found in other parts of the OT.

1:4 a:b::b':a' *protera pantōn (ektistai):sophia::kai synesis phronēseōs:ex aiōnos,* "Before all things wisdom was created, and prudent understanding from eternity." *Sophia* and *phronēsis* occur as a pair also in 19:22.

1:14-21 In these eight bicola (omit v 19a with several MSS) there are four stanzas. Each stanza, two bicola in length, begins with a noun in the nominative followed by the genitive *sophias.* These phrases are in an a:b::b':a' pattern: *archē sophias,* "the beginning of wisdom" (v 14a):*plēsmonē sophias,* "the fullness of wisdom" (v 16a)::*stephanos sophias,* "the crown of wisdom" (v 18a):*riza sophias,* "the root of wisdom" (v 20a).

2:5 a:b::b':a' *hoti en pyri:(dokimazetai) chrysos::kai anthrōpoi dektoi:en kaminō tapeinōseōs,* "For *in fire gold* is tested, and *people accepted (by God) in the crucible of humiliation.*"

3:3-4 a:b::b':a' *ho timōn patera:exilasetai hamartias::kai hōs ho apothē-saurizōn:ho doxazōn mētera autou,* "Whoever honors his father atones for sins, and as one who stores up treasure is whoever honors his mother." There is a double parallelism in the *a-a'* phrases.

3:30 a:b:c::c':b':a' *ʾēš lôḥeṭet:yĕkabbû:māyim::kēn ṣĕdāqâ:tĕkappēr:ḥaṭ-ṭāʾt* (3+3), "As water quenches flaming fire, so alms atones for sins." There is also a dental and labial alliteration. For *ʾēš,* "fire," as an image of evil and wickedness, cf. Isa 9:17; Prov 16:27.

4:12-14 a:b:c:b':a' *ʾôhăbêhā (ʾāhăbû ḥayyîm):ûmĕbaqqĕšêhā (yāpîqû rāṣôn mēyhwh):wĕtômĕkêhā (yimṣĕʾû kābôd* [with Gr, omit *mēyhwh,* dittography] *wĕyaḥănû bĕbirkat yhwh): (mĕšārĕtê qōdeš) mĕšārĕtêhā:wĕʾôhăbêhā* [so Gr; MS A corrupt] *(agapq kyrios)* (3+4, 3+3, 3+3), "Those who love her love life, and those who seek her win favor from Yahweh; and those who hold her fast find glory, and they shall dwell in the blessing of Yahweh. Those who serve her serve the Holy One, and those who love her the Lord loves." There is also internal rhyme, -*hā,* in the five words that form the pattern. The verbs *bqš* and *šrt* often have as direct object "God" or "Yahweh." For *bqš*, cf. Deut 4:28; Zeph 1:6; 2:3; Hos 3:5; 5:6; 1 Chr 16:10; 2 Chr 11:16; 20:4. For *šrt*, cf. Sir 7:30; Deut 10:8; 17:12; 21:5; Isa 61:6; Jer 33:21. The point of 4:12–14 is this: as those who seek Wisdom seek God, so those who serve Wisdom serve God. The verb *tmk* occurs in a similar context in Prov 3:18.

4:24 a:b:c::c':b':a' *kî bĕ'ômer:nôda'at:ḥokmâ::ûtĕbûnâ:bĕma'ănēh:lāšôn* (3+3), "For through speech becomes known wisdom, and understanding through the answer of the tongue." There is also a labial alliteration. For the parallel pair *ḥokmâ* and *tĕbûnâ*, which also rhyme, cf. Job 12:12; Prov 2:2; 3:13, 19; 5:1; 8:1; 24:3; Jer 10:12; 51:15.

5:5–6ab a:b:c::c:b:a *'el sĕlîḥâ ('al tibṭaḥ):(lĕhôsîp) 'āwôn 'al 'āwôn: (wĕ'āmartā raḥămāyw) rabbîm::lĕrôb:'āwônôtay:yislaḥ* (2+3, 3+3), "Of *forgiveness* be not overconfident, adding *sin upon sin*, and saying, 'Great is his mercy; *the multitude of my sins he will forgive.*'" There is also an *a* and *ô* assonance.

5:14 a:b::b':a ('al tiqqārē') ba'al štāyim:(ûbilĕšônĕkā 'al tĕraggēl [omit rēa'; cf. Gr] (kî 'al gannāb nibrĕ'â) bōšet::ḥerpâ ra'â [MS A rē'ēhû]: 'al [so Gr; MS A omits] ba'al štāyim (3+2, 3+4), "Be not called *double-tongued*, and with your tongue slander not, for *shame* was created for the thief, and *harsh disgrace* for the *double-tongued.*" For the parallel pair *bōšet* and *ḥerpâ*, cf. Isa 54:4.

6:5–6a a:b::b:a (ḥēk 'ārēb) yarbeh ('ôhēb):(wĕšiptê ḥēn šô'ălê) šālôm:: 'anšê šĕlômĕkā (yihyû) rabbîm / (ûba'al sôdĕkā 'eḥād mē'ālep (3+3, 4+4), "Pleasant speech *multiplies* friends, and gracious lips those that give *greeting* [i.e., *peace*]; let people at *peace with you* be *many*, but one in a thousand your confidant." There is also a sibilant, labial, and liquid alliteration, and *e* assonance, as well as internal rhyme (in *'ārēb* and *'ôhēb*, and *šĕlômĕkā* and *sôdĕkā*).

6:14 a:b::b:a' *'ôhēb 'ĕmûnâ ('ôhēl* [so Gr; MS A *'ôhēb*] *tĕqôp): ûmôṣĕ'ô::māṣā':hôn* (3+3), "*A faithful friend* is a sturdy shelter, *and whoever finds one finds wealth.*" There is also an *ō* assonance and labial alliteration.

6:22 a:b::b:a' *(kî) hammûsār (kišĕmô kēn):hî'* [MS A *hû'*, the confusion of *waw* and *yod*, as elsewhere]*::wĕlō' (lĕrabbîm) hî':nĕkôḥâ* (3+3), "For *discipline* like her name, so is *she*, and to many *she* is *not obvious.*" There is also a labial and a *k* alliteration. As in Prov 4:13, *mûsār* here has feminine agreement because it is a synonym for *ḥokmâ*. In this verse, Ben Sira plays on the word *mûsār*, using it as a noun, "discipline," and as the *hoph'al* participle of *sûr*, "withdrawn." It is this latter sense that the parallel *lō' nĕkôḥâ* is meant to suggest; cf. Prov 8:9.

6:37ab a:b::b':a' *wĕhitbônantā:bĕtôrat* [cf. Gr and 41:8b; 42:2a; 49:4c; MS A *bĕyir'at*] *'elyôn::ûbĕmiṣwātô:hĕgēh* [so Gr, Syr; MS A *wehĕgeh*] *tāmîd* (3+3), "Reflect on the Law of the Most High, and on his commandments meditate constantly." For the parallel pair *tôrâ* and *miṣwâ*, cf. Prov 3:1; 6:20, 23; 7:2.

6:37cd   a:b::b':a'   wĕhû yābîn:libbekā::waăšer iwwîtā:yĕḥakkĕmekā (3+2), "And he will inform your heart; and what you desire, he will make you wise." The *b* and *b'* expressions are in synthetic parallelism—the heart is the seat of desire. As regards the roots *bîn* and *ḥkm*, cf. discussion of 4:24 above. There is also a labial alliteration and end rhyme (in *libbekā* and *yĕḥakkĕmekā*).

7:10   a:b::b':a'   al titqaṣṣēr:bitĕpillâ::ûbiṣĕdāqâ:al tit^cabbar (2+2), "Be not impatient in prayer, and in almsgiving be not tardy." There is also a liquid, dental, and labial alliteration, and internal rhyme in *bitĕpillâ* and *ûbiṣĕdāqâ*. Here, as elsewhere in Ben Sira (cf., for example, 3:30 above), *ṣĕdāqâ* means "alms(giving)."

7:29   a:b::b':a'   (bĕkol libbĕkā) pĕḥad:ēl::wĕet kôhănāyw:haqdēš (3+2), "With your whole heart *fear God, and his priests revere.*" There is also a *k/q* alliteration.

7:30   a:b::b':a'   (bĕkol mĕôdĕkâ) ehab:^côšekā::wĕet mĕšārĕtāyw:lō ta-^căzōb (3+3), "With your whole strength *love your Maker, and his ministers you shall not neglect.*" There is also an *o* assonance.

7:33   a:b::b':a'   tēn mattān:lipnê kol ḥay::wĕgam mimmēt:al timna ^cḥāsed (3+3), "Give a gift to anyone alive, and from the dead withhold not a kindness." There is also a dental, *nun,* and labial alliteration.

8:2cd   a:b:c::c':b':a'   kî rabbîm:hiphîz:zāhāb::wĕhôn:yašgeh lēb:nĕdîbîm (3+3), "For gold has made many boastful, and wealth perverts the heart of princes." There is also a sibilant and labial alliteration and *î* assonance and internal rhyme (in *rabbîm* and *nĕdîbîm*).

8:8ab   a:b::b':a'   al tiṭṭôš:śîḥat ḥăkāmîm::ûbĕḥîdôtêhem:hitraṭṭēš (3+3), "Spurn not the discourse of the wise, and with their proverbs busy yourself." There is also a dental, sibilant, and *ḥ* alliteration.

9:10   a:b::b:a   (^cal tiṭṭôš ôhēb) yāšān:kî ḥādāš (lō yid[meh lô])::(yayin) ḥādāš (ôhēb) ḥādāš:wĕyāšān (^cahar tištennû) (3+3, 4+3), "Spurn not an *old* friend, for the *new one* cannot equal him; a *new* friend is (like) *new* wine, but when *old,* then you can drink it."

9:18   a:b::b':a'   nôrā bā^cîr [so Gr, Syr; MS A bĕ^cad]:îš lāšôn::wĕnôśē [so Syr; MS A ûmaśśā] ^cal pîhû:yĕšunnē (3+3), "Feared in the city is the person of tongue [=of railing speech; cf. 25:20b], and whoever speaks rashly is hated." There is also a sibilant, liquid, and *nun* alliteration. For the idiom *nś ^cal peh*, cf. Ps 50:16. Here, however, the context indicates that the expression means "to speak rashly" (cf. Gr *ho propetēs en logǭ autou,* "whoever is rash in his speech"), or "to speak wickedly." There is a wordplay and internal rhyme in *nôśē* and *yĕšunnē* (the *nun* and the *śin* are in an a:b::b:a pattern); cf. also *zār* and *rāz* in 8:18a.

10:3   a:b:c:d::d':c':b':a'   melek:pārûa^c:yašḥît:^cammô [so Gr, Lat, Syr; MS

A *ʿîr]::wĕʿîr:nôšebet:bĕšēkel:śārêhā (4+4), "A king undisciplined destroys his people, but a city becomes populous through the wisdom of its princes." There is also a labial, liquid, and sibilant alliteration. The *a-a'* and *d-d'* words are in synonymous parallelism, the *b-b'* and *c-c'* words are in antithetic parallelism.

10:29 a:b::b':a' maršîaʿ napšô:mî yaṣdîqennû::ûmî yĕkabbēd:maqleh napšô (3+3), "Whoever condemns himself, who will justify, and who will honor whoever dishonors himself?" There is also a labial and sibilant alliteration and *î* assonance.

11:4ab a:b::b':a' bĕʿôṭeh ʾēzôr:ʾal tĕhattēl::wĕʾal tĕqallēs:bimĕrîrî yôm [MS B] (3+3), "Whoever wears a loincloth mock not, nor scoff at the bitter person of the day." There is also a dental and liquid alliteration. For *mĕrîrî* as a masculine singular adjective, cf. Deut 32:24.

11:4cd a:b::b':a' For the text, see discussion of assonance and alliteration above.

11:25 a:b:c::c:b:a ṭôbat yôm:tĕšakkaḥ:hārāʿâ::wĕrāʿat yôm:tĕšakkaḥ:ṭôbâ (3+3), "The day's prosperity makes one forget adversity, and the day's adversity makes one forget prosperity." There is also end rhyme in *hārāʿâ* and *ṭôbâ*.

14:5a a:b::b':a' rāʿ:lĕnapšô::lĕmî:yêṭîb. "Whoever is evil [i.e., stingy] to himself, to whom will he do good?"

14:26 a:b::b':a' wĕyāśîm qinnô:bĕʿopyāh::ûbaʿănāpêhā:yitlônān (3+2), "And he places his nest in her [Wisdom's] foliage, and in her branches he lodges." There is also a *nun* and labial alliteration. For the parallel pair *ʿopyāh* and *ʿănāpêhā*, cf. Dan 4:9.

15:2 a:b::b':a' wĕqiddĕmathû:kĕʾēm::ûkĕʾēšet nĕʿûrîm:tĕqabbĕlennû (2+3), "And she [Wisdom] will meet him like a mother, and like a young bride she will receive him." There is also a *q/k* and labial alliteration and internal rhyme (in *wĕqiddĕmathû* and *tĕqabbĕlennû*).

15:3 a:b::b':a' wĕheʾĕkîlathû:leḥem śēkel::ûmê tĕbûnâ:tašqennû (3+3), "And she will feed him with the bread of learning, and the water of understanding she will give him to drink." The parallel pair *heʾĕkîl* and *hišqâ* is found also in Ps 80:6; Jer 9:14; 23:15; and Prov 25:21; *leḥem* and *mayim* in Gen 21:14; Exod 23:25; Isa 3:1; 21:14; Amos 8:11; Job 3:24; 22:7; Prov 9:17; 25:21; and Neh 9:15; and *śēkel* and *tĕbûnâ* in Neh 8:8. There is also internal rhyme in *wĕheʾĕkîlathû* and *tašqennû*.

15:7 a:b::b':a' lōʾ yadrîkûhā:mĕtê šāwʾ::wĕʾanšê zādôn:lōʾ yirʾûhā (2+3), "They shall not attain her [Wisdom], worthless people; and the haughty shall not see her." There is also a sibilant alliteration and internal rhyme (in *yadrîkûhā* and *yirʾûhā*).

15:9a, 10a a:b:c::c:a':b lōʾ nāʾâtâ:tĕhillâ:bĕpî rāšāʿ::bĕpî [MS B; MS A bĕpeh] ḥākām:tēʾāmēr:tĕhillâ (3+3), "Unseemly is praise in the mouth of the wicked. In the mouth of the wise is spoken praise." There is also an *ā/â* assonance. The antithetic parallel pair *rāšāʿ* and *ḥākām* occurs also in Prov 9:7b, 8b.

16:25 *a:b:c::b':a':c'* *ʾabbîʿâ:běmišqāl:rûḥî::ûběhaṣnēaʿ:ʾăhawweh:dēʿî* (3 + 3), "I will pour out with measure my spirit, and with modesty I will declare my knowledge." There is also a labial alliteration and end rhyme (in *rûḥî* and *dēʿî*). For the vocabulary and images, cf. Job 28:25; Prov 1:23; 18:4; Sir 18:29; 39:6, 8; Isa 29:10.

21:26 *a:b:c::c:b':a* *en stomati:mōrōn:hē kardia autōn::en de kardia̧: sophōn:stoma autōn.* "In the mouth of fools is their heart, but in the heart of the wise is their mouth." The antithetic parallel pair "fool(s)" and "wise" is common in the Wisdom literature.

23:4b–6 *a:b::b':a'* *meteōrismon ophthalmōn (mē dǫs moi):kai epithymian (apostrepson ap' emou)::koilias orexis kai synousiasmos (mē katalabetōsan me):kai psychę̄ anaidei (mē paradǫs me).* "A lifting up of the eyes [i.e., a proud look] give me not, and *concupiscence* ward off from me; let not *the desire of the belly and lust* [hendiadys, i.e., the lustful craving of the flesh] overtake me, and *to a shameless soul* give me not over." Proud eyes (the *a* phrase) express externally what the shameless soul/heart (the *a'* phrase) desires internally.

24:1 *a:b::b:a'* *(hē sophia) ainesei:(psychēn) autēs::(kai en mesǭ laou) autēs:kauchēsetai.* "Wisdom *praises her*self, and among *her* people *she is hon-ored."*

24:28 *a:b::b':a'* *ou (synetelesen):ho prōtos (gnōnai autēn)::(kai houtōs) ho eschatos:ouk (exichniasen autēn).* "Not fully did *the first human* know her [Wisdom]; so also *the last one* will *not* trace her out."

24:29 *a:b::b':a'* *apo gar thalassēs (eplēthynthē):dianoēma autēs::kai hē boulē autēs:apo abyssou megalēs.* "Deeper *than the sea* is her *understanding, and her counsel, than the great abyss."* For the parallel pair "sea" (Heb *yām*) and "abyss" (Heb *těhôm*), cf. Job 28:14 and 38:16; Isa 51:10 has the pair *yām* and *těhôm rabbâ* as here.

25:10b, 11a *a:b:c::c:b:a'* *all' ouk estin:hyper:ton phoboumenon ton ky-rion::phobos kyriou:hyper pan:hyperebalen.* "But he is not above whoever fears the Lord; fear of the Lord surpasses all else."

26:1a *a:b::b':a'* *ʾiššâ:ṭôbâ::ʾašrê:baʿlāh* *(ûmispar yāmāyw kiplāyim)* (3 + 3), "A good wife, happy her husband, and double is the number of his days." There is also an *a* assonance and sibilant and labial alliteration.

27:11–12 *a:b::b':a'* *(diēgēsis) eusebous (dia pantos sophia):ho de aphrōn (hōs selēnē alloioutai)::(eis meson) asynetōn (syntērēson kairon):(eis meson de) dianooumenōn (endelechize).* "The discourse *of the godly* is wisdom through-out, but *the fool* changes like the moon. In the midst *of fools* limit your time, but in the midst *of the thoughtful* abide continually." For the synonymous parallel pair "godly" (or "righteous") and "thoughtful" (or "wise"), cf. Prov 23:24; for the antithetic parallel pair "godly" and "fool," cf. Prov 10:21.

27:16–17 *a:b::b:a* *ho apokalyptōn mystēria (apōlesen pistin):(kai ou mē*

heurę̄) philon (pros tēn psychēn autou)::(sterxon) philon (kai pistōthēti met'
autou):ean de apokalypsę̄s ta mystēria autou (mē katadiōxę̄s opisō autou).
"Whoever reveals secrets destroys confidence; and he will never find an intimate *friend.* Cherish a *friend* and keep faith with him; but if *you reveal his
secrets,* follow him not."

31:27a,c a:b::b:a lĕmô [MS B lĕmî, confusion of *waw* and *yod*]
hayyayin:ḥayyîm le'ĕnôš::mah ḥayyîm:ḥăsar hayyāyin (4+3), "Indeed wine is
life to a person. What is life to the one who lacks wine?" There is also a *y* and
ḥ alliteration. The word *lĕmô* is a poetic form of the particle *lĕ-* (cf. Job 27:14;
29:21; 38:40; 40:4); here it is a particle of emphasis.

32:20 a:b::b':a' bĕderek môqĕšôt:'al tēlēk::wĕ'al tittāqēl:bĕnegep pa'a-
māyim (3+3), "On a way set with snares walk not, and stumble not on an
obstacle twice." There is also a labial and *k/g/q* alliteration.

32:21–22 a:b::b':a 'al tibṭaḥ:bĕderek mēḥetep::ûbĕ'ōrḥôtêkā:hizzāhēr
(3+2), "Trust not the road, for bandits, and on your paths be careful." There
is also a labial and dental alliteration. For *ḥetep* in the sense of "bandit,
robber," cf. Prov 23:28a and Sir 50:4a. For the synonymous parallel pair
derek and *'ōraḥ,* cf. Gen 49:17; Prov 3:6; 4:18–19; 9:15; 15:19; Pss 25:4; 139:3;
Joel 2:7.

33:10 a:b::b':a' [wĕkol 'îš:kĕ]lî ḥomer::ûmin 'āpār:nôṣar 'ādām (3+3),
"And every person is a vessel of clay, and from the ground was formed
humankind." There is also a liquid alliteration and *a* assonance. For *ḥōmer*
and *'āpār* in parallel, cf. Job 27:16 and 30:19. The principal reference is, of
course, to Gen 2:7.

33:19 a:b::b':a' šim'û 'ēlay:śārê 'am [omit *rab* of MS E; so Gr,
Syr]::ûmôšĕlê qāhāl:ha['ăzînû] (3+3), "Listen to me, leaders of the people;
and rulers of the assembly, give ear." There is also a liquid and sibilant
alliteration. This chiastic pattern is preserved also in Gr, Lat, and Syr. For
the synonymous parallel pair (which here also rhyme) *šim'û* and *ha'ăzînû,* cf.,
for example, Deut 32:1; Isa 1:2; 64:3; Ps 49:2.

35:1–2 a:b::b':a' ho syntērōn nomon:pleonazei prosphoran [so MSS V
307, some Lat MSS, and Syr; most Gr MSS *prosphoras*]::thysiazōn sōtēriou:ho
prosechōn entolais [other MSS *entolas*]. "Whoever keeps the Law makes a
great oblation; he sacrifices a peace offering who observes the commandments."

35:23bc a:b::b':a' 'ad yôrîš:šēbeṭ zādôn::ûmaṭṭēh rāšā':gādōa' yigdā'
(3+4), "Till he destroys [the meaning of *yôrîš* also in 20:22b (MS C) and
Exod 15:9] the scepter of the proud, and the staff of the wicked he breaks off
short." There is also a dental, sibilant, and *'ayin* alliteration and internal
rhyme (in *rāšā'* and *yigdā'*). For the image of cutting a staff in two, cf. Zech
11:10, 14. The phrase *šēbeṭ hāreša'* occurs in Ps 125:3a; *maṭṭēh rĕšā'îm* in Isa
14:5a; and *maṭṭēh reša'* in Ezek 7:11.

36:4 a:b:c::b:a':c ka'ăšer niqdaštā:lĕ'ênêhem:bānû::kēn lĕ'ênênû:hikkā-

bed:bām [so MS B^mg] (3+3), "As you sanctified yourself before their eyes in us, so before our eyes glorify yourself in them." There is also a labial, *k,* and *n* alliteration and *e* assonance, as well as internal rhyme (in *bānû* and *lĕ'ênênû*).

3. Inclusio

pasa and *sophia* (1:1a) and *pantōn* and *sophia* (1:4a), in the opening and closing bicola of the first stanza of a poem on wisdom (1:1–10).

pasa (1:1a) and *pasēs* (1:10a), and *met'* (*autou*) (1:1b) and *meta* (*pasēs*) (1:10a), in the opening and closing bicola of the poem.

phobos kyriou (1:11a) and *phobǭ kyriou* (1:30e), in the opening and closing bicola of a twenty-two-line poem on fear of the Lord.

proselthȩs and *en kardiǭ* (1:28b), in the first bicolon of a stanza (1:28–30ab), and *prosēlthes* (1:30e) and *hē kardia sou* (1:30f), in the closing bicolon of the following stanza (1:30cdef).

eleos in 2:7a and 2:9b, the opening and closing cola of a stanza.

mûsār in 6:18a, the opening colon of the first stanza of a poem, and in 6:22a, in the closing bicolon of the second stanza.

hokmâ (6:18b) and *yĕhakkĕmekā* (6:37d), in the opening and closing bicola of a twenty-two-line poem on striving for wisdom.

mû'āz (10:12a), the opening colon of a stanza, and *'azzût* (10:18b), the closing colon.

nikbād (10:19ab) and *niqleh* (10:19cd), in the two opening bicola of a poem, and *niqlû* (11:6a) and *nikbādîm* (11:6b), in the closing bicolon. These words form an *a:b::b:a* chiastic *inclusio.*

ra' 'ayin in 14:3b and 14:10a, in the opening and closing bicola of a stanza on the miser.

egō in 24:3a, 4a, the opening bicola of the first stanza of Wisdom's twenty-two-line speech, and in 24:16a, 17a, the opening bicola of the final stanza of her speech.

ho apokalyptōn mystēria (27:16a) and *ho apokalypsas mystēria* (27:21c), the opening and closing cola of a poem.

ekdikēsis in 27:28b and 28:1a, in the opening and closing bicola of a poem.

machē in 28:8a and 28:11b, the opening and closing cola of a poem on quarreling.

plēsion in 29:14a and 29:20a, in the opening and closing bicola of a poem on going surety for a neighbor.

mûsār in 32:14a and *paideian* (=*mûsār*) in 33:18b, the opening and closing cola of a section of the book.

'ĕlōhîm in 36:1 and 36:5b, the opening and closing cola of the first stanza of the prayer in 36:1–22.

zûlātekā in 36:5b, the closing colon of the first stanza, and *zûlātî* in 36:12b, the closing colon of the second stanza of the prayer.

'ĕlōhê hakkōl (36:1) and *kol* (36:22c) and *'el* (36:22d), in the opening and closing bicola of the prayer. These words form an *a:b::b:a* chiastic *inclusio*.

The composition of twenty-two bicola or lines (to equal the number of letters in the Hebrew alphabet) in 1:11–30, the opening poem of the book after the Introduction (1:1–10), forms an *inclusio* with the twenty-three-line alphabetic acrostic poem at the end of the book (see COMMENT on 51:13–30). This major *inclusio* indicates that the book was planned in the form in which we have it by a single compiler, namely, Ben Sira himself.

4. Twenty-two- and Twenty-three-Line Poems

Like the great Hebrew poets before him, Ben Sira often employed the technique of composing units of twenty-two, or by way of variation twenty-three, lines (for an explanation, see COMMENT on 51:13–30), to signal the opening or closing of a major part of his book, to show the unity of a section or portion of text, or simply to add elegance to his work. See, for example, 1:11–30 (the opening poem of the book); 5:1–6:4; 6:18–37 (the opening poem of Part III); 12:1–18; 13:24–14:19 (the closing poem of Part III); 21:1–21; 29:1–20; 29:21–30:13; 38:24–34; 49:1–16 (the closing unit on Israel's great ancestors); 51:13–30 (an alphabetic acrostic, the closing poem of the book). Ben Sira learned this technique of poetic composition from such biblical texts as Deut 32:1–14, 15–29, 30–43;[12] Proverbs 2; 6:20–7:6; 7:7–27; 31:10–31 (the final poem of the book); Psalms 9–10, 25, 33, 34, 37, 94, 111, 112, 119, 145; and Lamentations 1–5. Psalms 37 and 119 and each of the chapters of Lamentations 1–4 have twenty-two stanzas arranged as an alphabetic acrostic. Psalms 111 and 112 have twenty-two cola or half-lines in an alphabetic acrostic. Lamentations 5 and the other texts listed contain twenty-two or twenty-three bicola or lines, some of which are also alphabetic acrostics (e.g., Prov 31:10–31; Psalms 25, 34).

---

[12] Cf. P. W. Skehan, "The Structure of the Song of Moses in Deuteronomy (32:1–43)," in *Studies in Israelite Poetry and Wisdom* (CBQMS 1; Washington: Catholic Biblical Association, 1971): 67–77.

X. THE TEACHING OF BEN SIRA

When he wrote his book, Ben Sira had no intention of offering a systematic theology. Instead, he composed a series of reflections and aphorisms, based on the earlier biblical books, especially Proverbs, for all who seek after guidance (33:18). As mentioned in Part I above, there is no particular order or obvious coherence in the topics Ben Sira chose to discuss. As a result, one can come to appreciate the extent and depth of Ben Sira's teaching only after a careful reading and study of his book. What I give here is not meant to be exhaustive or strictly systematic, but rather selective; it is an attempt to show the dimensions and grandeur of the principal elements of Ben Sira's theology.[1] I shall also point out Ben Sira's limitations.

At the outset, it must be noted that Ben Sira's doctrine is above all traditional or conservative. His work reflects the teachings of Israel's Sacred Scriptures on such subjects as God; the election of Israel; retribution; anthropology; morality; repentance; faith; good works; almsgiving; kindness to the widow, orphan, and poor; fear of the Lord; and the like. His pervading theological outlook is Deuteronomic.

1. Wisdom, Fear of God, and the Law

There has been an ongoing dispute about the primary theme of The Wisdom of Ben Sira. J. Haspecker has made a good case that fear of God is the total theme (*Gesamtthema*) of the book.[2] But G. von Rad and J. Marböck disagree, insisting that wisdom is the fundamental theme.[3] I believe, however, that R. Smend suggests the best approach to this question when he writes (p. xxiii): "Subjectively, wisdom is fear of God; objectively, it is the law book of Moses (chap. 24)." Accordingly, I would argue that Ben Sira's primary theme is wisdom *as* fear of God, and that the fundamental thesis of the book

---

[1] Good surveys of Ben Sira's doctrine are found in Box-Oesterley (pp. 303–14); R. H. Pfeiffer, *A History of New Testament Times with an Introduction to the Apocrypha*, pp. 372–98; T. A. Burkill, "Ecclesiasticus," *IDB* (1962) 2.19–21; Duesberg-Fransen (pp. 53–64); and C. Kearns, "Ecclesiasticus, or The Wisdom of Jesus the Son of Sirach," in *NCCHS* (1969), pp. 543–46.

[2] J. Haspecker, *Gottesfurcht bei Jesus Sirach: Ihre religiöse Struktur und ihre literarische und doktrinäre Bedeutung* (AnBib 30, 1967), pp. 87–105.

[3] G. von Rad, *Wisdom in Israel*, p. 242; J. Marböck, *Weisheit im Wandel: Untersuchungen zur Weisheitstheologie bei Ben Sira* (BBB 37, 1971).

is the following: wisdom, which is identified with the Law, can be achieved only by one who fears God and keeps the commandments. Or, as Ben Sira himself writes:

> The whole of wisdom is fear of the Lord;
>   complete wisdom is the fulfillment of the Law (19:20).

The expression "fear of God," or its equivalent, occurs fifty-five to sixty times in our book. In the rest of the OT, only the Psalter, where the expression is found seventy-nine times, has a larger number of occurrences.[4] Obviously, fear of God is a paramount concern of Ben Sira. But so is wisdom, a noun that occurs about fifty-five times (in the grandson's Greek). The opening chapters (1:1–2:18) form the thematic introduction to the book. We find here a detailed treatise on wisdom as fear of God. The expression "fear of God" is found seventeen times in the two chapters. The word "wisdom," Gr *sophia*, however, occurs eleven times in the first chapter alone.

At the outset Ben Sira states his view on the source of wisdom:

> All wisdom is from the Lord,
>   and with him it remains forever (1:1).

He rephrases the same idea at the beginning of the second half of the book, when he has personified Wisdom say:

> From the mouth of the Most High I came forth,
>   and mistlike covered the earth.
> In the heights of heaven I dwelt,
>   my throne on a pillar of cloud (24:3–4).

Wisdom, in Ben Sira's view, existed before all other creatures:

> Before all things else wisdom was created;
>   and prudent understanding, from eternity (1:4).
> Before the ages, from the first, [God] created me [Wisdom],
>   and through the ages I shall not cease to be (24:9).

Ben Sira derived many of the ideas about wisdom in 24:1–22 from Prov 8:22–31. Wisdom is something that God alone possesses fully (1:8), for he "fashioned her . . . and . . . has poured her forth upon all his works" (1:9).

But God bestows the gift of wisdom only "upon his friends" (1:10b), i.e., on those who "keep the commandments" (1:26) of the Law and fear him (15:1; 43:33b). Ben Sira calls fear of the Lord "the beginning of wisdom" (1:14a, derived from Prov 9:10a), the "fullness of wisdom" (1:16a), "wisdom's garland" (1:18a), and "the root of wisdom" (1:20a). Thus fear of God

---

[4] Haspecker, *Gottesfurcht*, p. 82.

is the very essence of wisdom. It is also "glory and exultation, gladness and a festive crown. . . . [It] rejoices the heart, giving gladness and joy and length of days" (1:11–12). Fear of the Lord and wisdom make life meaningful and satisfying and full of days (1:20b; 34:14–20). Cf. Deut 6:24 and 30:15–20. Fear of the Lord is what "keeps sin far off . . . and turns back all [God's] wrath" (1:21). Thus Ben Sira can say:

> Nothing is better than the fear of the Lord,
>> nothing sweeter than obeying his commandments (23:27cd).
> Whoever finds wisdom is great indeed,
>> but not greater than the one who fears the Lord.
> Fear of the Lord surpasses all else,
>> its possessor is beyond compare (25:10–11).

Although wisdom holds sway over every land, people, and nation (24:6), she received the divine command to make her dwelling in Jacob, her inheritance in Israel (24:8). Wisdom "struck root among the glorious people" (24:12a). Thus true wisdom has her domain "in Jerusalem" (24:11b), and not in Athens or Alexandria. All of which is to say that Israelite wisdom is incomparably superior to Hellenistic wisdom and culture. In the splendid poem on wisdom in chap. 24, Ben Sira employs a colorful series of tree and vine images with which personified Wisdom compares herself (vv 13–17).[5] At the end of her speech, Wisdom invites the faithful who yearn for her to be filled with her fruits (v 19). Then, in v 23a, Ben Sira makes his most emphatic affirmation that wisdom is the Torah of Israel: "All this [what Wisdom says about herself] is true of the book of the Most High's covenant."

Though wisdom is a free gift of God, the faithful have to do their part in order to receive it. In addition to fearing the Lord and observing the Law, the faithful are to endure affliction as a test (2:1–10; 4:17–19). By remaining steadfast in time of trial, they are saved and not forsaken by the Lord (2:10–11). The faithful must also subject themselves to discipline if they hope to become wise:

> My son, from your youth embrace discipline;
>> thus you will gain wisdom with graying hair (6:18).

Ben Sira explains how one can come to wisdom:

> Put your feet into her net
>> and your neck into her noose.

---

[5] For a good study of the symbolism of these images, cf. A. Fournier-Bidoz, "L'Arbre et la demeure: Siracide xxiv 10–17," *VT* 34 (1984): 1–10. In addition to Sirach 24, Wisdom is personified also in 4:11–19; 6:18–31; 14:20–15:8; and 51:13–21. See also Job 28, Proverbs 8, and Wisdom 7:22–26; for a penetrating study of these texts, cf. R. E. Murphy, "Israel's Wisdom: A Biblical Model of Salvation," in *Voies de Salut: Studia Missionalia* 30 (1981): 29–39.

> Stoop your shoulders and carry her
> and be not irked at her bonds (6:24–25).

Though the effort to achieve wisdom is great, the rewards are many:

> Her net will become your throne of majesty;
> her noose, your apparel of spun gold.
> Her yoke will be your gold adornment;
> her bonds, your purple cord.
> You will wear her as your glorious apparel,
> bear her as your splendid crown (6:29–31).

Despite the manifold benefits wisdom confers (4:11–16), many do not strive for her because of the prerequisite discipline:

> For discipline is like her name:
> she is not obvious to many (6:22).

After attaining wisdom by loyalty to God and the Law, the believer must take care not to sin, for sin drives out wisdom:

> If he fails me [Wisdom], I will abandon him
> and deliver him over to robbers (4:19).

That is why sinners or fools—the terms are synonymous in Ben Sira's lexicon—can never find wisdom:

> Worthless people will not attain to her,
> the haughty will not behold her.
> Far from the impious is she,
> not to be spoken of by liars (15:7–8).

But the virtuous or wise person—these terms in Ben Sira are also synonymous—pursues wisdom "like a scout" (14:22a) and then "pitches his tent beside her and lives as her welcome neighbor" (14:25). The result is that:

> Motherlike she will meet him,
> like a young bride she will embrace him,
> Nourish him with the bread of learning,
> and give him the water of understanding to drink (15:2–3).

It is noteworthy that Ben Sira, despite his negative comments about women (see below, no. 7), personifies wisdom as a woman: Wisdom is teacher (4:11–19), mistress (6:18–31), welcome neighbor, mother, and wife (14:20–15:8), and lover to be wooed (51:13–21). Daring images for an inveterate misogynist.

In Ben Sira's theology, fear of the Lord is synonymous with love of the Lord (2:15–16). Those who fear and love the Lord: (a) "do not disobey his words" (2:15a); (b) "keep his ways" (2:15b); (c) "seek to please him" (2:16a); (d) "are filled with his law" (2:16b); and (e) "prepare their hearts and humble themselves before him" (2:17). These ideas are based, for the most part, on the great Deuteronomic equation: to fear God = to love him = to keep his commandments = to walk in his ways; cf. Deut 10:12–13 and 30:16. In Ben Sira's theology, the one who fears God must have a deep and abiding relationship of trust and love with God.[6]

From what has been said thus far, it should be clear that the term "wisdom" in Ben Sira, as also in the other Wisdom writings of the OT, has a much wider meaning than in classical or contemporary literature. In Ben Sira, "wisdom" never refers to pure learning or cleverness or intelligence, as it does, say, in many classical and modern authors.

Wisdom in our book may be considered as either speculative or practical. Speculative wisdom has the intellect as its focus, and one achieves it by study, travel, and reflection. It tries to solve problems that engage the mind. Hence, such wisdom is the goal of the scribe whom Ben Sira describes in 38:34cd–39:11. But even there a person becomes wise by first devoting "himself to the fear of God and to the study of the Law of the Most High" (38:34cd). Speculative wisdom also has its dangers (3:21–23); so Ben Sira warns:

Indeed, many are the speculations of human beings—
    evil and misleading fancies (3:24).

Practical wisdom, which has the will as its principal focus, includes what we would call today secular, ethical, and spiritual concerns and choices in daily life. For Ben Sira, however, practical wisdom is an essentially religious ability to distinguish and then choose between what is good and what is evil, between what is useful and what is harmful, and between what should be done and what should be avoided. When the faithful choose the first of these sets of alternatives, they are truly wise, for they have exercised their moral consciousness, which enables them to have a closer relationship to God than merely external observance of a ceremonial law.[7] Accordingly, Ben Sira teaches that believers must love and fear God, must walk in his ways and keep the commandments of the Law. By so doing, they are living out God's own wisdom, which is revealed in the Law, and as a result their practical wisdom approaches in some significant way the divine wisdom (cf. 24:28–29). One can now see more clearly why in 24:23a the Law and wisdom are identified (see above).

In sum, those who fear the Lord know they have a personal relationship with God by their faith, hope, and confidence in him, and by their obedience to him. They recognize the Lord as Master and Judge and as merciful and

---

[6] Haspecker, *Gottesfurcht*, p. 337.
[7] Cf. Box-Oesterley, p. 308.

compassionate Father who can also test them and make them acknowledge their sins.[8]

2. Doctrine of God

Ben Sira has much to say about God. He proclaims first of all that God is one and not many, and he prays that all nations may recognize him:

> Come to our aid, God of the universe,
>   and put all the nations in dread of you! . . .
> As you have used us to show them your holiness,
>   so now use them to show us your glory.
> Thus they will know, as we know,
>   that there is no God but you (36:1–2, 4–5).

God "is from eternity one and the same" (42:21b). "He is the all" (43:27b), an expression that must not be taken in any pantheistic sense, but rather in the sense in which the Old Latin renders the colon: "He is in all," i.e., God reveals himself in all his creatures; see COMMENT. Thus God is not only transcendent but also immanent in creation.

God is the Creator of all, including wisdom (24:8; cf. 42:15–43:33). He creates by simply uttering his all-powerful word (39:17–18; 42:15c); cf. Gen 1:3–24. He knows all things, including the deepest mysteries of the universe, and sees all things, even before they come to be (15:18–19; 23:19–20; 39:19–20a; 42:18–20). The marvelous order and dazzling beauty of the heavens as well as all the ordinary and awesome elements of nature are due to God's all-embracing wisdom and might (43:1–26).

> Yet even God's holy ones [=angels] must fail
>   in recounting all his wonders (42:17).

Each thing that God made exists in harmony and balance with the rest of creation and receives all that it needs (16:26–30). So Ben Sira exclaims:

> How beautiful are all his works,
>   delightful to gaze upon and a joy to behold! (42:22)

Though Ben Sira is particularistic and glories in the divine election of his people (17:17; 24:8–12), he nonetheless teaches that God is merciful not only to Israel but to every other nation as well:

> A person may be merciful to his neighbor,
>   but the Lord's mercy reaches all flesh,

---

[8] L. Derousseaux, *La Crainte de Dieu dans l'Ancien Testament,* p. 355.

Reproving, admonishing, teaching,
  as a shepherd guides his flock (18:13).

Cf. also 17:29. But God is also righteous; so he punishes the wickedness of Jews and Gentiles alike. The habitual, unrepentant sinner who quotes Heinrich Heine (1797–1856) on his deathbed, "God will pardon me; it is his trade," will receive no mercy. For as Ben Sira remarks:

Of forgiveness be not overconfident,
  adding sin upon sin,
And saying: "Great is his mercy;
  my many sins he will forgive";
For mercy and anger alike are with him—
  upon the wicked alights his wrath (5:5–6).

The same idea is expressed in 16:6–13, esp. v 12:

Great as his mercy is his punishment;
  he judges people, each according to his deeds.

Cf. also 11:26 and 35:15bc.

Ben Sira teaches that the true believer has a filial relationship with God and accordingly may address him confidently in these words:

Lord, my Father and the Master of my life (23:1a; cf. v 4a).
I extolled the LORD, "You are my Father!
  my mighty savior, only you!
Do not leave me in this time of crisis,
  on a day of ruin and desolation!" (51:10)

Because God is a loving Father, he listens especially to "the cry of the orphan" and to "the widow when she pours out her complaint" (35:17).

3. Sin and Free Will

Ben Sira's discussion of the origin of sin is a good indication of the complexity of the question that confronts biblical authors, philosophers, and theologians: How can one reconcile human freedom with God's freedom and foreknowledge? In other words, does God's foreknowledge of my choices predetermine those choices, thus depriving me of the freedom to choose between good and evil? Ben Sira has made significant advances over the earlier biblical books regarding this question, but he is far from offering a satisfactory solution. A text like Exod 11:10, for example, "The LORD made Pharaoh obstinate, and he would not let the Israelites leave his land," suggests that God was responsible for Pharaoh's sin. The same could be said of 2 Sam

24:1–10, which records David's sin in ordering the census of the people. Later biblical authors state that human beings have free choice to obey or disobey the Lord; cf., for example, Deut 11:26–28; 30:15–20.

But Ben Sira goes much further and explicitly denies that God is involved at all in human sin:

> Say not, "It was God's doing that I fell away";
>> for what he hates, he does not do.
> Say not, "It was he who set me astray";
>> for he has no need of the wicked.
> Abominable wickedness the LORD hates;
>> he does not let it befall those who fear him (15:11–13).
> No one did he command to sin,
>> nor will he be lenient with liars (15:20).

Ben Sira explains why human sin cannot be imputed to God:

> It was he, from the first, when he created humankind,
>> who made them subject to their own free choice.
> If you choose, you can keep his commandment;
>> fidelity is the doing of his will.
> There are poured out before you fire and water;
>> to whichever you choose you can stretch forth your hands.
> Before each person are life and death;
>> whatever he chooses shall be given him (15:14–17).

These verses are a clear statement of the doctrine of free will. Thus, human beings, because they possess the radical freedom of choice in moral matters, are responsible both for their virtuous deeds and for their sins.[9]

Yet despite this unambiguous affirmation, elsewhere Ben Sira *seems* to imply that God predestines some people for blessing and others for cursing:

> Yet in the fullness of his understanding the Lord makes people
>> unlike:
> in different paths he has them walk.
> Some he blesses and makes great,
>> some he sanctifies and draws to himself.
> Others he curses and brings low,
>> and expels them from their place.
> Like clay in the hands of a potter,
>> to be molded according to his pleasure,

---

[9] For further discussion of this important passage, cf. J. Hadot, *Penchant mauvais et volonté libre dans la sagesse de Ben Sira (L'Ecclésiastique)*, pp. 91–103; and G. Maier, *Mensch und freier Wille, Nach den jüdischen Religionsparteien zwischen Ben Sira und Paulus.*

> So are people in the hands of their Maker,
>> to be requited according as he judges them (33:11–13).

This text seems to say that God has decreed for each person either a blessed or a cursed destiny, independent of the person's free choice. But Ben Sira stops far short of attributing human sin to God and of saying that divine predestination destroys human freedom to choose between good and evil. In fact, the most likely meaning of 33:12cd, "Others he curses and brings low, and expels them from their place," is that God curses some people because they have chosen the path of wickedness; it is not that they are wicked because God has cursed them.

As regards the historical origin of sin, Ben Sira follows the traditional teaching:

> In a woman was sin's beginning;
>> on her account we all die (25:24).

This text derives from Gen 3:1–6 and 2:16–17 (cf. 1 Tim 2:14). All Eve's children have had a similar propensity to sin.

Though Ben Sira does not offer a systematic theology of sin and free will, we may conclude from the study of the texts above and others such as 4:26; 7:1–3, 8, 12–13; 8:5; 21:1–2; 23:18–20; and 27:8 that he firmly believed in the reality and prevalence of sin, on the one hand, and on the other, that human beings have the radical freedom of choice to be virtuous or wicked. Because of human freedom, there is hope even for the sinner: he can repent.

> Return to the Lord, and give up sin,
>> pray before him and make your offenses few.
> Turn again to the Most High and away from sin,
>> hate intensely what he loathes (17:25–26).
> How great the mercy of the Lord,
>> his forgiveness of those who return to him! (17:29)

Repentance is possible only because the sinner can freely choose to abandon sin and return to the Lord's way.

4. Teaching on Retribution

The traditional doctrine of retribution in Ben Sira's day was this: keeping the commandments and fearing the Lord brought prosperity, happiness, and longevity to nation and individual believer; failure to observe the Law brought adversity, distress, and early death.[10] Rewards and punishments in

---

[10] The material in this section is adapted from my article "Conservative and Progressive Theology: Sirach and Wisdom," *CBQ* 28 (1966): 143–46.

the afterlife were not even considered.[11] This doctrine has rightly been called the Deuteronomic theology of retribution[12] because it had been applied as an interpretive principle by the Deuteronomistic redactors of Israel's history, and is set forth in great detail in Deuteronomy 28. According to this theology, adversity could serve as a test of fidelity (cf. Judg 2:22–3:6). After death, all people—saints as well as sinners—went to Sheol, the netherworld; from there the dead, it was believed, would not rise again (Job 14:12). Sheol, therefore, could not be considered as a place of retribution. Moreover, its inhabitants shared alike a dark, listless, dismal survival separated from God.

In Ben Sira's view, reward (for virtue) and punishment (for sin) take place only in this life:

> Opt not for the success of pride;
> remember it will not reach death unpunished (9:12).

Since "death does not tarry" (14:12), Ben Sira writes:

> Give, take, and treat yourself well,
> for in the netherworld there are no joys to seek.
> All flesh grows old, like a garment;
> the age-old law is: all must die (14:16–17).

Thus human beings must seek their complete meaning and fulfillment only during the present life.

Since there is no coming back from Sheol, Ben Sira urges moderation in mourning for the dead, lest "heartache destroy one's health" (38:18b):

> Recall him not, there is no hope of his return;
> no good can it do, but it will do you harm (38:21).

Ben Sira leaves no doubt regarding the dull, gloomy, and pointless survival in Sheol:

> Who in the netherworld can glorify the Most High
> in place of the living who offer their praise?
> No more can the dead give praise than those who have never lived;
> they glorify the Lord who are alive and well (17:27–28).

For the Israelite, life without the worship and praise of God was totally meaningless.[13]

---

[11] For a good discussion of the traditional theology of virtue and sin, cf. G. von Rad, *Old Testament Theology*, 1.384–86.

[12] An excellent treatment of this theology is found in O. S. Rankin, *Israel's Wisdom Literature: Its Bearing on Theology and the History of Religion*, pp. 77–80.

[13] Von Rad (*Old Testament Theology*, vol. 1, pp. 369–70) writes: "Praise is man's most characteristic mode of existence: praising and not praising stand over against one another like life and death."

Ben Sira also speaks of suffering that may befall the faithful as a test of their loyalty and a means of purification:

> My son, when you come to serve the Lord,
>   prepare yourself for testing.
> Be sincere of heart and steadfast,
>   undisturbed in time of affliction (2:1–2).
> Accept whatever befalls you,
>   in periods of humiliation be patient;
> For in fire gold is tested,
>   and those God favors, in the crucible of humiliation (2:4–5).

In the long run, the faithful will never be disappointed; despite present adversity, they will be rewarded with the usual blessings: long life (1:12), good health (1:18), a good marriage (26:3), happiness (26:4), joy in their children (25:7c), and a good and lasting name (37:26; 39:11).

> Study the generations long past and understand:
>   has anyone hoped in the Lord and been disappointed?
> Has anyone persevered in his fear and been forsaken?
>   has anyone called upon him and been rebuffed? (2:10)

The obvious answer to these rhetorical questions is a resounding yes! And Ben Sira, as a keen observer of the disconcerting facts of life, knew it; he was painfully aware of the theological anomaly that the wicked often are prosperous and apparently happy right up to the time of their death. But, Ben Sira assures us, disaster awaits the sinner, though it may be delayed to the last hours of life:

> Say not, "I am self-sufficient.
>   What harm can come to me now?"
> It is easy for the Lord on the day of death
>   to repay a person according to his conduct.
> Brief affliction brings forgetfulness of past delights;
>   the last of a person tells his tale.
> Call no one happy before his death,
>   for by how he ends, a person is known (11:24, 26, 27–28).

After death, one of the ways a person lives on is in his children. A virtuous parent can approach death with serenity:

> At the father's death, he will not seem dead,
>   since he leaves after him one like himself,
> Whom he looks upon through life with joy,
>   and even in death, without regret (30:4–5).

But for a wicked parent death is grim, for he can expect only reviling from his children:

> Children curse their wicked father,
>   for they are in disgrace because of him.
> Woe to you, O wicked people,
>   who forsake the law of the Most High.
> If you have children, mischief will be theirs;
>   and if you become a father, it will only be for groaning.
> When you stumble, there is lasting joy;
>   and when you die, you become a curse (41:7–9).

The only other way a person survives death is in his good (or bad) name:

> The human body is a fleeting thing,
>   but a virtuous name will never be annihilated.
> Have respect for your name, for it will stand by you
>   more than thousands of precious treasures;
> The good things of life last a number of days,
>   but a good name, for days without number (41:11–13).

The possibility of rewards or punishments in some sort of afterlife receives no mention at all in the original Hebrew text of Ben Sira.[14] But the Greek translation does make definite allusions to retribution in the hereafter;[15] see, for example, 7:17b and 48:11b (cf. NOTE). This fact is not surprising, for Ben Sira's grandson made the translation of GI (see Part VIII) in Alexandria after the publication of the Book of Daniel, in which a blessed resurrection is assured to the faithful (Dan 12:1–2a), whereas apostate Jews "will become everlasting objects of contempt and abhorrence" (Dan 12:2b, AB).[16] GII has even more allusions to retribution in the world to come; see, for example, 2:9c; 16:22c (cf. NOTE on 16:22b); 19:19. The Syriac contains explicit references to "eternal life" (1:12b, 20; 3:1b, see COMMENT; 48:11b, cf. NOTE), which is the reward of the righteous who will wear an eternal crown and share the lot of the holy ones, i.e., the angels (1:24 in Syriac only); these statements, however, are all interpolations by Ebionite and orthodox Christian scribes (see Part VIII, 3c). The Old Latin, a Christian translation, adds its own glosses on a blessed (or damned) immortality. After 18:22b, for example, it adds: "for God's reward remains forever." Instead of "that end in the

---

[14] F. Saracino ("Risurrezione in Ben Sira?," *Hen* 4 [1982]: 185–203) thinks he has found evidence for a belief in resurrection in Sir 46:12 and 49:10 as well as in 48:11, 13. As should be obvious from the discussion thus far, I do not agree with his findings; see NOTES and COMMENT on these verses.

[15] Cf. M. Fang Che-Yong, *Quaestiones theologicae selectae libri Sira ex comparatione textus graeci et hebraici ortae,* pp. 37–54.

[16] Cf. L. F. Hartman and A. A. Di Lella, *The Book of Daniel* (AB 23, 1978), pp. 307–10.

depths of the netherworld" in 21:10b, it has: "and their end is hell and darkness and punishment." After 24:22b, it adds: "those who explain me [wisdom] shall possess eternal life." It adds a whole bicolon after 27:8: "And it [justice] will protect you forever, and on the day of reckoning you will find a strong foundation."

5. Prayer, Temple Worship, and Personal Morality

Our book contains many prayers of Ben Sira, the principal ones being the hymns of praise in 39:12–35 and 42:15–43:33; and the prayers of petition in 22:27–23:6 and 36:1–22. The splendid prayer in 51:1–12 combines both praise and petition. Prayer is the language of a dynamic faith in God; it is spoken correctly only by those who fear God because they have a personal relationship with him by their faith, hope, and confidence, and by their love for him.

Ben Sira also speaks highly of the priesthood and of temple worship:

> With all your soul fear God,
>   revere his priests.
> With all your strength love your Maker,
>   neglect not his ministers.
> Honor God and respect the priest;
>   give him his portion as you have been commanded:
> The flesh of sacrifices, contributions,
>   his portion of victims, a levy on holy offerings (7:29–31).

He waxes eloquent in his panegyric on Aaron (45:6–22), describing in minute detail his liturgical vestments and his priestly duties and rights. The glowing description of the High Priest Simeon II (50:1–21) officiating at the ceremonies for the Daily Whole-Offering suggests that Ben Sira attended the temple rituals regularly. He eulogizes David for his constant prayer (47:8a) and for making music an important part of the temple ritual (47:9–10).

But prayer and temple sacrifice and worship with beautiful liturgy are worthless if one's personal morality is not what it should be, especially in the area of social justice:

> Tainted his gift who offers in sacrifice ill-gotten goods!
>   Presents from the lawless do not win God's favor.
> The Most High approves not the gifts of the godless,
>   nor for their many sacrifices does he forgive their sins (34:21–23).

Israel's Law is essentially a moral law, for which there can be no substitute. Like the great prophets (Amos 5:21–25; Isa 1:10–20), who excoriated the practices of those who prayed earnestly and regularly and offered lavish sacrifices but at the same time shamelessly exploited the defenseless, Ben Sira

states categorically that sacrifice itself is an abomination when offered by one
who has violated the rights of the poor:

> Like one slaying a son in his father's presence
>> is whoever offers sacrifice from the holdings of the poor.
> The bread of charity is life itself for the needy;
>> whoever withholds it is a person of blood.
> He slays his neighbor who deprives him of his living;
>> he sheds blood who denies the worker his wages (34:24–27).

In contrast, observance of the moral law is the highest form of sacrifice and
worship of God.

> To keep the Law is a great oblation,
>> and whoever observes the commandments sacrifices a peace
>>> offering.
> In works of charity one offers fine flour,
>> and when he gives alms he presents his sacrifice of praise.
> To refrain from evil pleases the Lord,
>> and to avoid injustice is an atonement (35:1–5).

Although the offering of sacrifice is commanded in the Law, only "the just
person's sacrifice is welcomed" (35:9a). The Lord does not accept the sacrificial offerings or the contributions of those who are guilty of injustice:

> But offer no bribes; these he does not accept!
>> Trust not in sacrifice of the fruits of extortion,
> For he is the God of justice,
>> who knows no favorites (35:14–15).

In sum, Ben Sira teaches that observance of the Law covers both personal
morality, especially practical social action, and ceremonial ritual in the Temple. Though Ben Sira clearly distinguished these two aspects of obedience, he
was at pains to emphasize that social justice is the prerequisite for one who
wishes to please the Lord in the Temple cult. For Ben Sira, concern for social
justice is far more important and central to authentic religion than any prescribed ritual, no matter how colorful and emotionally satisfying it may be.[17]

6. Social Justice

As should be clear from the discussion above, true religion can never be a
matter of prayer and ceremonial ritual alone. Personal morality takes prece-
dence over all else, for without it religious practices, even the most sublime,

[17] Cf. J. G. Snaith, "Ben Sira's Supposed Love of Liturgy," *VT* 25 (1975): 167–74.

become sheer hypocrisy. The principal ethical concerns that Ben Sira speaks of are social justice and almsgiving. Of the former he writes:

> Give a hearing to the poor,
>   and return his greeting with deference.
> Deliver the oppressed from his oppressors;
>   let not right judgment be repugnant to you.
> To the fatherless be as a father,
>   help the widows in their husbands' stead;
> Then God will call you a son of his,
>   and he will be more tender to you than a mother (4:8–10).

Ben Sira derived his teaching on social justice from the biblical tradition[18] he knew so well; cf., for example, Exod 22:22; Deut 24:17–22; Lev 19:9–10; 23:22; Job 29:11–16; 31:13–22; Prov 14:13; 28:27; Amos 5:10–15; Isa 1:17; Tob 1:3, 8.

Since, as Jesus said, "The poor you will always have with you" (Matt 26:11; Mark 14:7; John 12:8), Ben Sira insists that they be treated kindly and generously. For "charity [or love] covers a multitude of sins" (1 Pet 4:8; cf. Prov 10:12b).

> As water quenches flaming fire,
>   so alms atones for sins.
> The kindness a person has done crosses his path as he goes;
>   when he falls, he finds a support (3:30–31).

In caring for the needy and the oppressed, you must never delay or behave in a condescending or patronizing way, for such conduct is insulting and may anger them, with the result that they may curse you to your own ruin:

> The hungry do not aggrieve,
>   nor ignore one who is downtrodden.
> Do not inflame the bile of the oppressed;
>   delay not giving to the needy.
> A beggar's plea do not reject;
>   avert not your glance from the downtrodden.
> From one in need turn not your eyes,
>   give him no reason to curse you;
> For if in the ache of his bitterness he curse you,
>   his Maker will hear his prayer (4:2–6).

Cf. also 7:10b; 29:8–13; and 35:3–4. At least from the time of the Book of Tobit, almsgiving was considered to be righteousness *par excellence;* cf. Tob

---

[18] For a splendid study of this tradition, cf. H. E. von Waldow, "Social Responsibility and Social Structure in Early Israel," *CBQ* 32 (1970): 182–204.

1:3; 2:10; 3:2; 14:9–11; Matt 6:1–2. The duty of helping the needy is a recurring biblical injunction; cf., for example, Deut 15:7–11; 24:13; Prov 14:21; 19:17; 22:9; 28:27; Tob 4:7–11; 12:8–9.

7. Attitude Toward Women

Much of what Ben Sira writes about women appears offensive to the contemporary Western reader. See the following texts (with COMMENT) that deal with woman as wife, mother, daughter, adulteress, or prostitute: 3:2–6; 7:19, 24–26; 9:1–9; 19:2–4; 22:3–5; 23:22–26; 25:1, 8, 13–26:18; 28:15; 33:20; 36:26–31; 40:19, 23; 42:6, 9–14. It should be observed, at the outset, that Ben Sira was a typical oriental male who wrote his book in a patriarchal society and culture in which a woman had few rights as a free and independent human being and was subject to either her father or her husband. In ancient Israel, woman was considered man's chattel, whom he could dispose of for his own advantage (Gen 12:12–20; 19:8; 20:1–18; Judg 19:24–30). In the conclusion of one form of the Ten Commandments, the wife is listed with a man's property (Exod 20:17). It was legal and moral for a man to sell his daughter as a slave, and she could not be freed (Exod 21:7), as could a male slave, at the end of six years (Exod 21:1–2). Such was the religiously legitimated social order in which Ben Sira lived. Accordingly, we can hardly expect that he would write things about women that would appeal to us who live in a Western (hence totally different) social order in which, for the most part, women are socially and politically equal with men, at least in law if not in fact.

In a lengthy monograph, W. C. Trenchard tries to prove that "Ben Sira wrote about women as he did, because he was motivated by a personal, negative bias against them."[19] What one senses throughout this study, however, is Trenchard's own negative bias against Ben Sira, which often affects his presentation and evaluation of the textual evidence.[20] This bias is a serious drawback in an otherwise significant contribution to scholarship. In the conclusion of the book, Trenchard writes: "[Ben Sira] makes remarks about women that are among the most obscene and negative in ancient literature."[21] Apparently, Trenchard overlooked much of that ancient literature. For if he had consulted the interesting anthology of M. R. Lefkowitz and M. B. Fant, *Women in Greece and Rome* (1977), now supplemented with new material

[19] W. C. Trenchard, *Ben Sira's View of Women: A Literary Analysis* (Brown Judaic Studies 8, 1982), p. 7.
[20] For critical reviews of the book, see A. A. Di Lella, *CBQ* 46 (1984): 332–34; and C. Meyers, *BSOAS* 47/2 (1984): 339–40.
[21] Trenchard, *Ben Sira's View of Women*, p. 172.

and retitled *Women's Life in Greece and Rome*,[22] he would have read really repulsive, hostile, and obscene remarks about women by ancient authors who make Ben Sira seem moderate by comparison. Three sample quotations from *Women's Life* will prove my point. (1) Semonides, *On Women,* sixth century B.C.: "Yes, this is the worst plague Zeus has made—women; if they seem to be some use to him who has them, it is to him especially that they prove a plague. The man who lives with a woman never goes through all his day in cheerfulness. . . . Just when a man most wishes to enjoy himself at home, . . . she finds a way of finding fault with him and lifts her crest for battle. . . . The very woman who seems most respectable is the one who turns out guilty of the worst atrocity" (p. 16). (2) Hipponax, sixth century B.C.: "The two best days in a woman's life are when someone marries her and when he carries her dead body to the grave" (p. 16). (3) Valerius Maximus, first century A.D.: "Egnatius Metellus [in Romulus' day] . . . took a cudgel and beat his wife to death because she had drunk some wine. Not only did no one charge him with a crime, but no one even blamed him. . . . [Gaius Sulpicius Gallus, consul in 166 B.C.] divorced his wife because he had caught her outdoors with her head uncovered: a stiff penalty, but not without a certain logic. 'The law,' he said, 'prescribes for you my eyes alone to which you may prove your beauty. . . . If you, with needless provocation, invite the look of anyone else, you must be suspected of wrongdoing.' Quintus Antistius Vetus felt no differently when he divorced his wife because he had seen her in public having a private conversation with a common freedwoman. For, moved not by an actual crime but, so to speak, by the birth and nourishment of one, he punished her before the sin could be committed, so that he might prevent the deed's being done at all, rather than punish it afterwards. . . . And so, long ago, when the misdeeds of women were thus forestalled, their minds stayed far from wrongdoing" (p. 176).

It is against the background of such sentiments that Ben Sira's negative comments about women are to be evaluated. True, his remarks are often misogynistic (e.g., 25:13–26) and at times downright gross (e.g., 42:14a); these are to be deplored. But in the patriarchal society in which he lived, such remarks would not have drawn any serious criticism, for women were viewed only in their sociologically validated and legitimated roles, i.e., in their relationship to men, and never as autonomous individuals or the equals of men. Moreover, Ben Sira wrote his book only for the instruction and enlightenment of young men in a male-centered and male-dominated society; hence his vocabulary and grammar are masculine-oriented. It was not his intention to instruct women. When we take these factors into account, we can understand why Ben Sira speaks about women in the way he does, even though today we may disagree with much of what he says and how he says it. Unfortunately

---

[22] Baltimore: Johns Hopkins University, 1982.

and unfairly, however, Trenchard gives the impression that Ben Sira would have written differently about women if only he were less biased toward them and had more pleasant experiences with them.[23] Such an attitude toward Ben Sira is not only wrong but wrongheaded.

For other studies of Ben Sira's comments about women, see J. W. Gaspar, *Social Ideas in the Wisdom Literature of the Old Testament;*[24] H. McKeating, "Jesus ben Sira's Attitude to Women";[25] K. E. Bailey, "Women in Ben Sirach and in the New Testament";[26] and M. Gilbert, "Ben Sira et la femme."[27]

[23] Trenchard dedicates his book "To Marilyn, whom Ben Sira should have known" (p. v).
[24] The Catholic University Studies in Sacred Theology 2/8, pp. 57–62.
[25] *ExpTim* 85 (1973–74): 85–87.
[26] In R. A. Coughenour (ed.), *For Me to Live: Essays in Honor of James Leon Kelso,* pp. 56–73.
[27] *RTL* 7 (1976): 426–42.

BIBLIOGRAPHY

A. SOURCES

1. *Geniza, Qumran, and Masada MSS of Ben Sira*

Adler, E. N. "Some Missing Chapters of Ben Sira [7,29–12,1]." *JQR* 12 (1899–1900): 466–80.

Baillet, M., J. T. Milik, and R. de Vaux. *Les "Petites Grottes" de Qumrân.* DJD 3. Oxford: Clarendon, 1962.

The Book of Ben Sira: Text, Concordance and an Analysis of the Vocabulary. Jerusalem: Academy of the Hebrew Language and Shrine of the Book, 1973 [in Hebrew].

Cowley, A. E., and A. Neubauer, eds. *The Original Hebrew of a Portion of Ecclesiasticus.* Oxford: Clarendon, 1897.

Di Lella, A. A. "The Recently Identified Leaves of Sirach in Hebrew." *Bib* 45 (1964): 153–67.

Facsimiles of the Fragments Hitherto Recovered of the Book of Ecclesiasticus in Hebrew. Oxford-Cambridge: Oxford and Cambridge University, 1901.

Gaster, M. "A New Fragment of Ben Sira [parts of chaps. 18, 19, and 20]." *JQR* 12 (1899–1900): 688–702.

Knabenbauer, I. *Textus Ecclesiastici Hebraeus.* Appendix to *Commentarius in Ecclesiasticum.* Cursus Scripturae Sacrae 6. Paris: Lethielleux, 1902.

Lévi, I. *L'Ecclésiastique ou la Sagesse de Jésus, fils de Sira.* 2 parts. Paris: E. Leroux, 1898, 1901.

———. "Fragments de deux nouveaux manuscrits hébreux de l'Ecclésiastique." *REJ* 40 (1900): 1–30.

———. *The Hebrew Text of the Book of Ecclesiasticus.* Semitic Study Series 3. Leiden: Brill, 1904.

———. "Un Nouveau Fragment de Ben Sira." *REJ* 92 (1932): 136–45.

Marcus, J. *The Newly Discovered Original Hebrew of Ben Sira (Ecclesiasticus xxxii, 16–xxxiv, 1): The Fifth Manuscript and a Prosodic Version of Ben Sira (Ecclesiasticus xxii, 22–xxiii, 9).* Philadelphia: Dropsie College, 1931. This is a corrected reprint of the article that appeared originally in *JQR* n.s. 21 (1930–31): 223–40.

Margoliouth, G. "The Original Hebrew of Ecclesiasticus XXXI.12–31, and XXXVI.22–XXXVII.26." *JQR* 12 (1899–1900): 1–33.

Peters, N. *Der jüngst wiederaufgefundene hebräische Text des Buches Ecclesiasticus untersucht, herausgegeben, übersetzt und mit kritischen Noten versehen.* Freiburg i.B.: Herder, 1902.

———. *Liber Jesu filii Sirach sive Ecclesiasticus hebraice.* Freiburg i.B.: Herder, 1905.

Sanders, J. A. *The Dead Sea Psalms Scroll.* Ithaca, N.Y.: Cornell University, 1967.

———. *The Psalms Scroll of Qumrân Cave 11 (11QPs^a).* DJD 4. Oxford: Clarendon, 1965.

Schechter, S. "A Fragment of the Original Text of Ecclesiasticus." *Expositor,* 5th Ser., 4 (1896): 1–15.

———. "A Further Fragment of Ben Sira [MS C: parts of chaps. 4, 5, 25, and 26]." *JQR* 12 (1899–1900): 456–65.

———. "Genizah Specimens: *Ecclesiasticus* [original text of 49:12–50:22]." *JQR* 10 (1897–98): 197–206.

———, and C. Taylor. *The Wisdom of Ben Sira: Portions of the Book Ecclesiasticus from Hebrew Manuscripts in the Cairo Genizah Collection Presented to the University of Cambridge by the Editors.* Cambridge: Cambridge University, 1899.

Scheiber, A. "A New Leaf of the Fourth [*sic;* read Sixth] Manuscript of the Ben Sira from the Geniza." *Magyar Könyvszemle* 98 (1982): 179–85, with 8 plates.

Schirmann, J. *"Dap ḥādāš mittôk sēper ben-Sîrā' hā-ʿibrî."* *Tarbiz* 27 (1957–58): 440–43.

———. *"Dappîm nôsĕpîm mittôk sēper 'ben-Sîrā'."* *Tarbiz* 29 (1959–60): 125–34.

Segal, M. H. *Sēper ben-Sîrā' haššālēm.* 2d ed. Jerusalem: Bialik Institute, 1958.

Smend, R. *Die Weisheit des Jesus Sirach, hebräisch und deutsch.* Berlin: Reimer, 1906.

Strack, H. L. *Die Sprüche Jesus', des Sohnes Sirachs.* Leipzig: Böhme, 1903.

Vattioni, F. *Ecclesiastico: Testo ebraico con apparato critico e versioni greca, latina e siriaca.* Pubblicazioni del Seminario di Semitistica, Testi 1. Naples: Istituto Orientale di Napoli, 1968.

Vigouroux, F. *L'Ecclésiastique. La Sainte Bible Polyglotte,* 5. Paris: A. Roger et F. Chernoviz, 1904.

Yadin, Y. *The Ben Sira Scroll from Masada.* Jerusalem: Israel Exploration Society, 1965.

2. *The Versions of Ben Sira*

Greek:

Hart, J. H. A. *Ecclesiasticus: The Greek Text of Codex 248.* Cambridge: Cambridge University, 1909.

Holmes, R., and J. Parsons. *Vetus testamentum graecum cum variis lectionibus,* 4. Oxford: Clarendon, 1827.

Rahlfs, A. *Septuaginta,* 2. 5th ed. Stuttgart: Württembergische Bibelanstalt, 1952.

Swete, H. B. *The Old Testament in Greek,* 2. 3d ed. Cambridge: Cambridge University, 1907.

Ziegler, J. *Sapientia Iesu Filii Sirach.* Septuaginta 12/2. Göttingen: Vandenhoeck & Ruprecht, 1965.

Old Latin:

Biblia Sacra iuxta latinam vulgatam versionem, 12: *Sapientia Salomonis, Liber Hiesu filii Sirach.* Rome: Typis Polyglottis Vaticanis, 1964.

Douais, C. *Une Ancienne Version latine de l'Ecclésiastique.* Paris: A. Picard, 1895.

Herkenne, H. *De veteris latinae Ecclesiastici capitibus I–XLIII.* Leipzig: Hinrichs, 1899.

Lagarde, P. de. *Die Weisheiten der Handschrift von Amiata.* Mittheilungen 1. Göttingen: Hoyer, 1884. Sirach, pp. 283–378.

Weber, R., ed. *Biblia sacra iuxta vulgatam versionem.* 2 vols. 2d ed. rev. Stuttgart: Württembergische Bibelanstalt, 1975. Sirach, 2.1029–95.

Syrohexaplar:

Ceriani, A. M. *Codex syro-hexaplaris Ambrosianus photolithographice editus.* Milan: Pogliani, 1874.

Syriac Peshitta:

Biblia sacra juxta versionem simplicem quae dicitur Pschitta, 2 (referred to as the Mosul edition). Beirut: Imprimerie Catholique, 1951. Sirach, pp. 204–55.

Ceriani, A. M., ed. *Translatio Syra Pescitto Veteris Testamenti ex codice Ambrosiano sec. fere VI photolithographice edita.* 2 vols. Milan: Pogliani, 1876–83.

Lagarde, P. A. de. *Libri veteris testamenti apocryphi syriace.* Leipzig-London: F. A. Brockhaus–Williams & Norgate, 1861.

Walton, B. *Biblia sacra polyglotta,* 4. London: Thomas Roycroft, 1657. Variants are contained in vol. 6, pp. 46–47.

Arabic:

Frank, R. M., ed. *The Wisdom of Ben Sirach (Sinai ar. 155. ix–x cent.).* CSCO 357. Louvain: CorpusSCO, 1974. This Arabic translation was made from the Greek.

Walton, B. *Biblia sacra polyglotta,* 4. London: Thomas Roycroft, 1657. This Arabic translation was made from the Peshitta.

Coptic:

Lagarde, P. de. *Aegyptiaca.* Göttingen: Hoyer, 1883. Sirach, pp. 107–206.

Ethiopic:

Dillmann, A. *Biblia veteris testamenti aethiopica,* 5: *Libri apocryphi.* Leipzig: Sumptibus F. C. G. Vogelii, 1894. Sirach, pp. 54–117.

For information concerning the other versions and editions thereof, see L. Bigot, "Ecclésiastique (Livre de l')," *Dictionnaire de théologie catholique,* 4, 2. Paris: Letouzey et Ané, 1911. Cols. 2031–33.

B. COMMENTARIES AND SPECIAL AND GENERAL STUDIES ON BEN SIRA

Abbott, T. K. "Margoliouth's Essay on the Place of Ecclesiasticus in Semitic Literature." *Hermathena: A Series of Papers on Literature, Science, and Philosophy* 16 (1890): 341–44.

Abrahams, I. "Schechter and Taylor's *Wisdom of Ben Sira.*" *JQR* 12 (1899–1900): 171–76.

A Lapide, C. *In Ecclesiasticum.* Commentaria in Scripturam Sacram 9–10. 9th ed. Paris: Vivès, 1868.

Alfrink, B. "Het gebed van Jesus Sirach (Eccl. 51, 1–17)." *Nederlandsche Katholieke Stemmen* 33 (1933): 137–44.

Alonso Schökel, L. "The Vision of Man in Sirach 16:24–17:14," in *Israelite Wisdom: Theological and Literary Essays in Honor of Samuel Terrien.* Ed. J. G. Gammie et al. Missoula: Scholars, 1978. Pp. 235–45.

————, et al. *Proverbios y Eclesiastico.* Los libros sagrados. Madrid: Cristiandad, 1968.

André, L. E. T. *Les Apocryphes de l'Ancien Testament.* Florence: O. Paggi, 1903.

Anonymous. "Ueber den liturgischen Gebrauch des Hohenliedes und des Ecclesiasticus im marianischen Cultus." *Der Katholik* N.F. 1 (1859): 111–21.

Anoz, J. "La muerte en el Ben Sira." *Mayéutica* 5 (1979): 7–13.

The Apocrypha according to the Authorized Version. London: Cresset, 1929.

Arduini, M. L. "Il tema 'vir' e 'mulier' nell' esegesi patristica e medievale di Eccli., XLII,14: A proposito di un' interpretazione di Ruperto di Deutz." *Aevum* 54 (1980): 315–30; 55 (1981): 246–61.

Arnald, R. *Critical Commentary upon the Apocryphal Books.* New ed., corrected by J. R. Pitman. London: R. Priestley, 1822.

————. *A Critical Commentary upon the Book of the Wisdom of Jesus the Son of Sirach.* London: W. Bowyer, 1748.

————. *Ecclesiasticus,* in *A Critical Commentary and Paraphrase on the Old and New Testament and the Apocrypha,* 3. London: R. Priestley, 1822. Pp. 936–1097.

Auvray, P. "Notes sur le Prologue de *l'Ecclésiastique,*" in *Mélanges bibliques rédigés en l'honneur de André Robert.* Paris: Bloud & Gay, 1957. Pp. 281–87.

Baars, W. "On a Latin Fragment of Sirach." *VT* 15 (1965): 280–81.

Bacher, W. "Four Quotations from the Hebrew Ben Sira." *JQR* 11 (1898–99): 344.

————. "The Hebrew Text of Ecclesiasticus." *JQR* 9 (1896–97): 543–62.

————. "An Hypothesis about the Hebrew Fragments of Sirach." *JQR* 12 (1899–1900): 92–108.

————. "Notes on the Cambridge Fragments of Ecclesiasticus." *JQR* 12 (1899–1900): 272–90.

————. "Notes sur les nouveaux fragments de Ben Sira. I." *REJ* 40 (1900): 253–55.

————. "Die persischen Randnotizen zum hebräischen Sirach." *ZAW* 20 (1900): 308–10.

Bailey, K. E. "Women in Ben Sirach and in the New Testament," in *For Me to Live: Essays in Honor of James Leon Kelso.* Ed. R. A. Coughenour. Cleveland: Dillon/ Liederbach, 1972. Pp. 56–73.

Bauckmann, E. G. "Die Proverbien und die Sprüche des Jesus Sirach: Eine Untersuchung zum Strukturwandel der israelitischen Weisheitslehre." *ZAW* 72 (1960): 33–63.

Bauer, J. " 'Kein Leben ohne Wein' (Jesus Sirach 31,27): Das Urteil der Hl. Schrift." *Bibel und Liturgie* 23 (1955–56): 55–59.

————. "Des Vaters Segen . . . , der Fluch der Mutter . . . [Sir 3:9]." *Bibel und Liturgie* 23 (1955–56): 295–96.

Bauer, J. B. "Der priesterliche Schöpfungshymnus in Gen. 1 [Sir 15:14]." *TZ* 20 (1964): 1–9.

———. "Sir. 15,14 et Gen. 1,1." *VD* 41 (1963): 243–44.

Baumgarten, J. M. "Some Notes on the Ben Sira Scroll from Masada." *JQR* 58 (1968): 323–27.

Baumgartner, W. "Jesus Sirach," in *Die Religion in Geschichte und Gegenwart*, 3. 2d ed. Tübingen: Mohr, 1929. Pp. 169–70.

———. "Die literarischen Gattungen in der Weisheit des Jesus Sirach." *ZAW* 34 (1914): 161–98.

Beavin, E. L. "Ecclesiasticus or the Wisdom of Jesus the Son of Sirach," in C. M. Laymon, ed., *The Interpreter's One-Volume Commentary on the Bible*. Nashville: Abingdon, 1971. Pp. 550–76.

Becker, J. *Gottesfurcht im Alten Testament*. AnBib 25. Rome: Biblical Institute, 1965.

Beentjes, P. C. " 'The Countries Marvelled at You': King Solomon in Ben Sira 47:12–22." *BTFT* 45 (1984): 6–14.

———. "De getallenspreuk en zijn reikwijdte: Een pleidooi voor de literaire eenheid van Jesus Sirach 26:28–27:10." *BTFT* 43 (1982): 383–89.

———. "Inverted Quotations in the Bible: A Neglected Stylistic Pattern [Sir 46:19]." *Bib* 63 (1982): 506–23.

———. "Jesus Sirach 7:1–17, Kanttekeningen bij de structuur en de tekst van een verwaarloosde passage." *BTFT* 41 (1980): 251–59.

———. "Jesus Sirach 38:1–15, Problemen rondom een symbool." *BTFT* 41 (1980): 260–65.

———. "The 'Praise of the Famous' and Its Prologue." *BTFT* 45 (1984): 374–83.

———. "Recent Publications on the Wisdom of Jesus ben Sira (Ecclesiasticus)." *BTFT* 43 (1982): 188–98.

———. "Sirach 22:27–23:6 in zijn context." *BTFT* 39 (1978): 144–51.

Bentzen, A. "Sirach, der Chronist, und Nehemiah." *ST* 3 (1949 [1951]): 158–61.

Ben Zeeb, I. L. *Ḥokmat Yĕhôšûaʿ ben-Sîrāʾ*. 3d ed. Vienna: Schmid, 1814.

Bickell, G. "Ein alphabetisches Lied Jesus Sirach's." *ZKT* 6 (1882): 319–33.

———. "Der hebräische Sirachtext eine Rückübersetzung." *WZKM* 13 (1899): 251–56.

Bigot, L. "Ecclésiastique (Livre de l')." *Dictionnaire de théologie catholique*, 4, 2. Paris: Letouzey et Ané, 1911. Cols. 2028–54.

Bissell, E. C. *The Apocrypha of the Old Testament. A Commentary on the Holy Scriptures*. Vol. 15 of the Old Testament. New York: C. Scribner's Sons, 1880. Pp. 274–409.

Blau, L. "Quelques notes sur Jésus ben Sirach et son ouvrage. I." *REJ* 35 (1897): 19–29.

Boer, P. A. H. de. "*bbrytm ʿmd zrʿm* Sirach xliv 12a." *VTSup* 16 (1967): 25–29.

Born, A. van den. *Wijsheid van Jesus Sirach (Ecclesiasticus) uit de grondtekst vertaald en uitgelegd*. Roermond: Romen & Zonen, 1968.

Box, G. H., and W. O. E. Oesterley. "Sirach," in *APOT* 1. Ed. R. H. Charles. Oxford: Clarendon, 1913. Pp. 268–517.

Bretschneider, C. G. *Liber Iesu Siracidae graece. Ad fidem codicum et versionum emendatus et perpetua annotatione illustratus.* Ratisbon: Apud Montgium et Weissium, 1806.

Brockington, L. H. *A Critical Introduction to the Apocrypha.* Studies in Theology 61. London: Athlone, 1961.

———. *Ideas of Mediation between God and Man in the Apocrypha.* London: Athlone, 1962.

Büchler, A. "Ben Sira's Conception of Sin and Atonement." *JQR* n.s. 13 (1922–23): 303–35; 461–502; 14 (1923–24): 53–83.

Burkill, T. A. "Ecclesiasticus." *IDB* 2. New York–Nashville: Abingdon, 1962. Pp. 13–21.

Burney, C. F. "Notes on Some Hebrew Passages: Ecclesiasticus iv 26b., v 10." *JTS* 21 (1919–20): 242–43.

Cadbury, H. J. "The Grandson of Ben Sira." *HTR* 48 (1955): 219–25.

Caquot, A. "Ben Sira et le Messianisme." *Sem* 16 (1966): 43–68.

Carmignac, J. "Les Rapports entre l'Ecclésiastique et Qumrân." *RevQ* 3 (1961): 209–18.

Caspari, W. "Der Schriftgelehrte besingt seine Stellung Sir 51,12–17 (29)." *ZNW* 28 (1929): 143–48.

———. "Über die Textpflege, nach den hebräischen Handschriften des Sira." *ZAW* 50 (1932): 160–68; 51 (1933): 140–50.

Celada, B. "El velo del templo [Sir 50]." *Cultura Biblica* 15 (1958): 109–12.

Chait, S. *Buddha and Sirach: A Comparative Study* (reprinted from the Hebrew Monthly *Hatoren* 10 [1923]: 1–16).

Chajes, H. P. "Notes critiques sur le texte hébreu de l'Ecclésiastique." *REJ* 40 (1900): 31–36.

Cheyne, T. K. "Ecclus. xi. 19." *JQR* 10 (1897–98): 13–17.

———. *Job and Solomon, or the Wisdom of the Old Testament.* London: K. Paul, Trench & Co., 1887.

———. "Note (on D. S. Margoliouth's 'The Language and Metre of Ecclesiasticus')." *Expositor,* 4th Ser., 1 (1890): 390–91.

———. "Note on Sirach L. 9." *JQR* 12 (1899–1900): 554.

Churton, W. R. *The Uncanonical and Apocryphal Scriptures.* London: J. Whitaker, 1884.

Conzelmann, H. "Die Mutter der Weisheit [Sir 24:3–7]," in *Festschrift R. Bultmann.* Tübingen: Mohr, 1964. Vol. 2, pp. 225–34.

Cook, S. A. "An Arabic Version of the Prologue to Ecclesiasticus," in *Proceedings of the Society of Biblical Archaeology* (May 14, 1902): 173–84.

Couroyer, B. "Un Égyptianisme dans Ben Sira iv,11." *RB* 82 (1975): 206–17.

Cowley, A. "Notes on the Cambridge Texts of Ben Sira." *JQR* 12 (1899–1900): 109–11.

———. "Review of *De Veteris Latinae Ecclesiastici capitibus i–xliii . . . , scripsit Dr. Theol. Henr. Herkenne.*" *JQR* 12 (1899–1900): 168–71.

Cox, D. *Proverbs, with an Introduction to Sapiential Books.* Old Testament Message 17. Wilmington, Del.: Michael Glazier, 1982.

———. "ṣĕdāqâ and mišpāṭ: The Concept of Righteousness in Later Wisdom." *SBFLA* 27 (1977): 33–50.

Crenshaw, J. L. *Old Testament Wisdom: An Introduction.* Atlanta: John Knox, 1981.

———. "The Problem of Theodicy in Sirach: On Human Bondage." *JBL* 94 (1975): 47–64.

———, ed. *Studies in Ancient Israelite Wisdom.* New York: Ktav, 1976.

———. "Wisdom," in *Old Testament Form Criticism,* ed. J. H. Hayes. San Antonio: Trinity University, 1974. Pp. 225–64.

———. "Wisdom in the OT." *IDBSup.* Nashville: Abingdon, 1976. Pp. 952–56.

Cronbach, A. "The Social Ideals of the Apocrypha and Pseudepigrapha." *HUCA* 18 (1943–44): 119–56.

Czajkowski, M. "Na tropach tradycji eschatologicznej i mesjańskiej u Ben-Syracha." *Ruch Biblijny i Liturgiczny* 16 (1963): 87–98.

Da S. Marco, E. "Ecclesiastico," in *La Sacra Bibbia, Il Vecchio Testamento,* 2. Turin: Marietti, 1960. Pp. 467–566.

Davidson, A. B. "Sirach's Judgment of Women." *ExpTim* 6 (1894–95): 402–4.

De Bruyne, D. "Étude sur le texte latin de l'Ecclésiastique." *RBén* 40 (1928): 5–48.

———. "Le Prologue, le titre et la finale de l'Ecclésiastique." *ZAW* 47 (1929): 257–63.

———. "Saint Augustin reviseur de la Bible." *Miscellanea Agostiniana* 2 (Rome 1931): 578–85.

De Fraine, J. "Het Loflied op de menselijke Waardigheid in Eccli 17,1–14." *BTFT* 11 (1950): 10–22 (French summary on pp. 22–23).

Delcor, M. "Le Texte hébreu du cantique de Siracide LI,13 et ss. et les anciennes versions." *Textus* 6 (1968): 27–47.

De Nicola, A. "Quasi cypressus in monte Sion (Eccli 24,17b)." *BeO* 17 (1975): 269–77.

Denton, R. C. *The Apocrypha: Bridge of the Testaments.* Greenwich, Conn.: Seabury, 1954.

De Pury, A. "Sagesse et révélation dans l'Ancien Testament." *RTP* 27 (1977): 1–50.

Derousseaux, L. *La Crainte de Dieu dans l'Ancien Testament.* LD 63. Paris: Cerf, 1970.

Desečar, A. J. "La necedad en Sirac 23,12–15." *SBFLA* 20 (1970): 264–72.

———. *La sabiduría y la necedad in Sirac 21–22.* [Pars dissertationis.] Rome: Edizioni Francescane, 1970.

———. " 'Sapiente' e 'stolto' in Eccli 27,11–13." *BeO* 16 (1974): 193–98.

Desečar, E. "De conceptu stultitae in libro graeco Jesu Sirach." Doctoral dissertation, Pontificium Athenaeum Antonianum. Jerusalem, Jordan, 1963.

Deutsch, C. "The Sirach 51 Acrostic: Confession and Exhortation." *ZAW* 94 (1982): 400–9.

Di Lella, A. A. "Authenticity of the Geniza Fragments of Sirach." *Bib* 44 (1963): 171–200.

———. "Conservative and Progressive Theology: Sirach and Wisdom." *CBQ* 28 (1966): 139–54.

———. "Ecclesiasticus." *NCE,* vol. 5. New York: McGraw-Hill, 1967. Pp. 33–34.

———. *The Hebrew Text of Sirach: A Text-Critical and Historical Study.* Studies in Classical Literature 1. The Hague: Mouton, 1966.

———. "The Poetry of Ben Sira," in H. M. Orlinsky Volume. Ed. B. A. Levine and A. Malamat. ErIsr 16 (1982): 26*–33*.

———. "The Problem of Retribution in the Wisdom Literature," in *Rediscovery of Scripture: Biblical Theology Today*. Report of the 46th Annual Meeting of the Franciscan Educational Conference. Burlington, Wis.: Franciscan Educational Conference, 1967. Pp. 109–27.

———. "Qumrân and the Geniza Fragments of Sirach." *CBQ* 24 (1962): 245–67.

———. "Sirach, Book of." *NCE*, vol. 13. New York: McGraw-Hill, 1967. Pp. 257–58.

———. "Sirach 10:19–11:6: Textual Criticism, Poetic Analysis, and Exegesis," in *The Word of the Lord Shall Go Forth: Essays in Honor of David Noel Freedman in Celebration of His Sixtieth Birthday*. Ed. C. L. Meyers and M. O'Connor. Winona Lake, Ind.: ASOR-Eisenbrauns, 1982. Pp. 157–64.

———. "Sirach 51:1–12: Poetic Structure and Analysis of Ben Sira's Psalm." *CBQ* 48 (1986): 395–407.

———. "The Wisdom of Ben Sira." *TBT* 101 (1979): 1954–61.

Driver, G. R. "Ben Sira, XXXIII, 4." *JJS* 5 (1954): 177.

———. "Ecclesiasticus: A New Fragment of the Hebrew Text." *ExpTim* 49 (1937–38): 37–39.

———. "Hebrew Notes on the Wisdom of Jesus Ben Sirach." *JBL* 53 (1934): 273–90.

Driver, S. R. "Note (on D. S. Margoliouth's 'The Language and Metre of Ecclesiasticus')." *Expositor*, 4th Ser., 1 (1890): 387–90.

Dubarle, A.-M. *Les Sages d'Israël*. Lectio divina 1. Paris: Cerf, 1946.

Duesberg, H. "La Dignité de l'homme: Siracide 16,24–17,14." *BVC* 82 (1968): 15–21.

———. "Ecclésiastique (Livre de l')." *Dictionnaire de Spiritualité*, 4. Paris: Beauchesne, 1958. Cols. 52–62.

———. "Il est le Tout: Siracide 43,27–33." *BVC* 54 (1963): 29–32.

———. "Le médecin, un sage (Ecclésiastique 38,1–15)." *BVC* 38 (1961): 43–48.

———. *Les Scribes inspirés: Introduction aux livres sapientiaux de la Bible*. 2 vols. Paris: Maredsous, 1966.

Duesberg, H., and P. Auvray. *Le livre de l'Ecclésiastique*. SBJ. 2d ed. Paris: Cerf, 1958.

Duesberg, H., and I. Fransen. *Ecclesiastico*. La Sacra Bibbia . . . di S. Garofalo: Antico Testamento. Ed. G. Rinaldi. Turin: Marietti, 1966.

Duhaime, J. L. "El elogio de los Padres de Ben Sira y el Cántico de Moisés (Sir 44–50 y Dt 32)." *EstBib* 35 (1976): 223–29.

Dukes, L. *Rabbinische Blumenlese, enthaltend: Eine Sammlung, Übersetzung und Erläuterung der hebräischen und chaldäischen Sprüche des Sirach, talmudischer Sprichwörter, Sentenzen und Maximen, nebst einem Anhange, Leichenreden und einem Glossen*. Leipzig: Hahn, 1884.

Eberharter, A. *Das Buch Jesus Sirach oder Ecclesiasticus*. Die Heilige Schrift des Alten Testamentes übersetzt und erklärt in Verbindung mit Fachgelehrten, 6,5. Bonn: P. Hanstein, 1925.

———. "Die 'Ekklesiastikuszitate' bei Klemens von Alexandrien. Gesammelt und mit LXX und Vulgata verglichen." *TQ* 93 (1911): 1–22.

———. "Die Ekklesiastikus-Zitate in den Pseudocyprianischen Schriften." *Bib* 7 (1926): 324–25.

———. "Zu Ekkli 16,14." *BZ* 6 (1908): 162–63.

————. "Exegetische Bemerkungen zu Ekkli. 16,1–5." *Der Katholik,* 4te Folge, 37 (1908): 386–89.

————. *Der Kanon des Alten Testaments zur Zeit des Ben Sira.* Alttestamentliche Abhandlungen 3, 3. Münster i.W.: Aschendorff, 1911.

————. "*KŠL* in Ps 105,3 and Ekkli 14,9." *BZ* 6 (1908): 155–61.

————. "The Text of Ecclesiasticus in the Quotations of Clement of Alexandria and Saint Cyrian." *Bib* 7 (1926): 79–83.

————. "Textkritische Bemerkungen zu Ekkli. Ekkli 6,19 IV; 8,10 I; 13,9 I." *BZ* 5 (1907): 22–26.

Ecclesiasticus: or, The Wisdom of Jesus, the Son of Sirach [Revised Version]. With Illustrations by V. Brunton and an Introduction by C. L. Hind. New York: Dodd, Mead, 1927.

Edersheim, A. *Ecclesiasticus,* in *Apocrypha,* 2, ed. by H. Wace. London: John Murray, 1888. Pp. 1–239.

Eissfeldt, O. *The Old Testament: An Introduction Including the Apocrypha and Pseud-epigrapha, and also the Works of Similar Type from Qumran.* Tr. P. R. Ackroyd. New York: Harper & Row, 1965.

Elmslie, W. A. L. *Studies in Life from Jewish Proverbs.* [Special reference to Proverbs and Sirach.] London: J. Clarke, 1917.

Eybers, I. H. "Some Light on the Canon of the Qumran Sect," in *New Light on Some Old Testament Problems.* Papers Read at 5th Meeting Held at the University of South Africa, Pretoria. Pretoria, South Africa: University of South Africa, 1962. Pp. 1–14.

Fang Che-yong, M. "Ben Sira de novissimis hominis." *VD* 41 (1963): 21–38.

————. "De discrepantiis inter textum graecum et hebraicum libri Ecclesiastici seu Ben Sira quarum origo sensus necnon momentum theologicum investigantur." Doctoral dissertation, the Pontifical Biblical Institute. Rome, 1963.

————. *Quaestiones theologicae selectae libri Sira ex comparatione textus graeci et hebraici ortae.* Rome: Biblical Institute, 1963 (published in 1964).

————. "Sir 7,36 (Vulg 7,40) iuxta hebraicam veritatem." *VD* 40 (1962): 18–26.

————. "Usus nominis divini in Sirach." *VD* 42 (1964): 153–68.

Ferrar, W. J. *The Uncanonical Jewish Books.* New York: Macmillan, 1918.

Fonck, L. " 'Quasi cedrus exaltata sum in Libano . . .' (Eccli. 24,17)." *VD* 1 (1921): 226–31.

Forster, A. H. "The Date of Ecclesiasticus." *ATR* 41 (1959): 1–9.

Fournier-Bidoz, A. "L'Arbre et la demeure: Siracide xxiv 10–17." *VT* 34 (1984): 1–10.

Fraenkel, S. "Zu Ben Sira." *ZAW* 21 (1901): 191–92.

————. "Zur Sprache des hebräischen Sirach." *Monatsschrift für Geschichte und Wissenschaft des Judenthums* 43 (1899): 481–84.

Fransen, I. "Les Oeuvres de Dieu (Sir 42,1–50,20)." *BVC* 81 (1968): 26–35.

Fritzsche, O. F. *Kurzgefasstes exegetisches Handbuch zu den Apokryphen,* 5. Leipzig: Hirzel, 1859.

Fruhstorfer, K. "Des Weisen curriculum vitae nach Sirach (39,1–15)." *TPQ* 94 (1941): 140–42.

Fuchs, A. *Textkritische Untersuchungen zum hebräischen Ekklesiastikus.* BibS 12, 5. Freiburg i.B.: Herder, 1907.

Fuss, W. "Tradition und Komposition im Buche Jesus Sirach." Doctoral dissertation, the University of Tübingen, 1963.

Gallus, T. " 'A muliere initium peccati et per illam omnes morimur' (Sir 25,24 [33])." *VD* 23 (1943): 272–77.

Garibay Kintana, A. M. *Proverbios de Solomon y Sabiduría de Jesús ben Sirak.* México: Editorial Porrúa, 1966.

Gaspar, J. W. *Social Ideas in the Wisdom Literature of the Old Testament.* Catholic University of America Studies in Sacred Theology, 2d Ser., 8. Washington: Catholic University of America, 1947.

Gasser, J. K. *Das althebräische Spruchbuch und die Sprüche Jesu Ben Sira in Bezug auf einige wesentliche Merkmale ihrer historischen Verschiedenheit untersucht.* Gütersloh: Bertelsmann, 1903.

———. *Die Bedeutung der Sprüche Jesu Ben Sira für die Datierung des althebräischen Spruchbuches untersucht.* Beiträge zur Förderung christlicher Theologie Jhrg. 8. Hft. 2, 3. Gütersloh: Bertelsmann, 1904.

Geiger, A. "Warum gehört das Buch Sirach zu den Apokryphen?" *ZDMG* 12 (1858): 536–43.

Gelin, A. "Ecclésiastique (Livre de l')." *Dictionnaire de théologie catholique, Tables générales.* Paris: Letouzey et Ané, 1956. Cols. 1087–91.

Germann, H. "Jesus ben Siras Dankgebet und die Hodajoth." *TZ* 19 (1963): 81–87.

Gigot, F. E. "Ecclesiasticus," in *The Catholic Encyclopedia,* 5. New York: Robert Appleton, 1909. Pp. 263–69.

Gilbert, M. "Ben Sira et la femme." *RTL* 7 (1976): 426–42.

———. "L'Éloge de la Sagesse (Siracide 24)." *RTL* 5 (1974): 326–48.

———. "La sequela della Sapienza: Lettura di Sir 6,23–31." *Parola, Spirito e Vita* 2 (1980): 53–70.

———. "Spirito, sapienza e legge secondo Ben Sira e il libro della Sapienza." *Parola, Spirito e Vita* 4 (1981): 65–73.

———, ed. *La Sagesse de l'Ancien Testament.* BETL 51. Gembloux/Louvain: Duculot/University, 1979.

Ginsberg, H. L. "The Original Hebrew of Ben Sira 12:10–14." *JBL* 74 (1955): 93–95.

Ginzberg, L. "Randglossen zum hebräischen Ben Sira." *Orientalische Studien, Theodor Nöldeke gewidmet,* 2. Ed. by C. Bezold. Giessen: Töpelmann, 1906. Pp. 609–25.

Girotti, G. "Ecclesiastico," in *La Sacra Bibbia commentata da M. M. Sales e G. Girotti, Il Vecchio Testamento, 6: I Sapienziali.* Turin: Lega Italiana Cattolica Editrice, 1938. Pp. 345–544.

Gonzalo Maeso, D. "Disquisiciones filológicas sobre el texto hebreo del Eclesiástico." *Miscelanea de estudios árabes y hebraicos* 8, 2 (1959): 3–26.

Goodspeed, E. J., tr. *The Apocrypha.* Introd. by M. Hadas. New York: Random House, 1959.

———, tr. *The Apocrypha,* in *The Complete Bible: An American Translation.* Chicago: University of Chicago, 1939. Pp. 91–136.

———. *The Story of the Apocrypha.* Chicago: University of Chicago, 1939.

Gray, G. B. "A Note on the Text and Interpretation of Ecclus. XLI. 19." *JQR* 9 (1896–97): 567–72.

Grimme, H. "Mètres et strophes dans les fragments du manuscrit parchemin du Siracide." *RB* 9 (1900): 400–13.

————. "Mètres et strophes dans les fragments hébreux du manuscrit A de l'Ecclésiastique." *RB* 10 (1901): 55–65; 260–67; 423–35.

————. "Strophenartige Abschnitte im Ecclesiasticus." *OLZ* 2 (1899): 213–17.

Grootaert, A. "L'Ecclésiastique est-il antérieur à l'Ecclésiaste?" *RB* n.s. 2 (1905): 67–73.

Habermann, A. M. "ʾĀlephbêtāʾ děben-Sîrāʾ nūshāh šělîšît (Hebrew University Hebrew MS 2203)." *Tarbiz* 27 (1957–58): 190–202.

Hadot, J. "L'Ecclésiastique ou le Siracide," in *La Bible, L'Ancien Testament*. Bibliothèque de la Pléiade, 2. Paris: Gallimard, 1959. Pp. 1708–1885.

————. *Penchant mauvais et volonté libre dans la sagesse de Ben Sira (L'Ecclésiastique)*. Brussels: Presses Universitaires, 1970.

Halévy, J. *Étude sur la partie du texte hébreu de l'Ecclésiastique récemment découvert.* Paris: Leroux, 1897.

Hall, B. G. "Ecclesiasticus iv. 26." *ExpTim* 37 (1925–26): 526.

Hamp, V. "Jesus Sirach (Ecclesiasticus)," in *Das Alte Testament nach den Grundtexten übersetzt und herausgegeben*. Würzburg: Echter-Verlag, 1955. Pp. 820–71.

————. *Sirach*. Die Heilige Schrift in Deutscher Übersetzung. Echter-Bibel: Das Alte Testament 13/2. Würzburg: Echter-Verlag, 1951.

————. "Zukunft und Jenseits im Buche Sirach," in *AT Studien, Festschrift Nötscher*. BBB 1. Bonn: Hanstein, 1950. Pp. 86–97.

Harrington, D. J. "The Wisdom of the Scribe according to Ben Sira," in *Ideal Figures in Ancient Judaism: Profiles and Paradigms*. Ed. J. J. Collins and G. W. E. Nickelsburg. Chico, Calif.: Scholars, 1980. Pp. 181–88.

Hart, J. H. A. "[Note on] Sir. xlviii 17a,b." *JTS* 4 (1902–3): 591–92.

————. "Primitive Exegesis as a Factor in the Corruption of Texts of Scripture Illustrated from the Versions of Ben Sira." *JQR* 15 (1902–3): 627–31.

Hartman, L. F. "Sirach in Hebrew and in Greek." *CBQ* 23 (1961): 443–51.

————, and A. van den Born. "Sirach, the Book of," in *Encyclopedic Dictionary of the Bible*. New York: McGraw-Hill, 1963. Cols. 2247–50.

Haspecker, J. *Gottesfurcht bei Jesus Sirach: Ihre religiöse Struktur und ihre literarische und doktrinäre Bedeutung*. AnBib 30. Rome: Biblical Institute, 1967.

Hatch, E. "On the Text of Ecclesiasticus," in *Essays on Biblical Greek*. Oxford: Clarendon, 1889. Pp. 246–82.

Hauer, C. H. "Water in the Mountains [Sir 48:17]." *PEQ* 101 (1969): 44–45.

Herford, R. T. *Talmud and Apocrypha*. London: Soncino, 1933.

Herkenne, H. *Die Textüberlieferung des Buches Sirach*. BibS 6, 1–2. Freiburg i.B.: Herder, 1901. Pp. 129–40.

Herz, N. "Dr. Ryssel on the Origin of the Doublets in the Hebrew 'Ben Sira.'" *ExpTim* 19 (1907–8): 189–90.

————. "The Hebrew Ecclesiasticus." *JQR* 10 (1897–98): 719–24.

Höffken, P. "Warum schwieg Jesus Sirach über Esra?" *ZAW* 87 (1975): 184–201.

Hogg, H. W. "Another Edition of the Hebrew Ecclesiasticus." *AJSL* 15 (1898–99): 42–48.

Holzmeister, U. "Pro morte defluente deprecatus (-a) sum [Eccli. 51,13 (9)]." *VD* 9 (1929): 30.

Hughes, H. M. *The Ethics of Jewish Apocryphal Literature.* London: Robert Culley, n.d. [1909].

――――. "The Social Teaching of the Hebrew Apocrypha," in *The Social Teaching of the Bible.* Ed. S. E. Keeble. New York: Eaton & Mains, 1909. Pp. 129–45.

Husslein, J. "Wisdom and the Toiler." *HPR* 22 (1922): 1299–1302.

Isaack, M. *Die Pädagogik des Jesus Sirach.* Sammlung pädagogischer Vorträge 12, 12. Bonn: F. Soennecken, 1900.

Iwry, S. "A New Designation for the Luminaries in Ben Sira [43:5] and in the Manual of Discipline (IQS)." *BASOR* 200 (1970): 41–47.

Jacob, E. "Wisdom and Religion in Sirach," in *Israelite Wisdom: Theological and Literary Essays in Honor of Samuel Terrien.* Ed. J. G. Gammie et al. Missoula: Scholars, 1978. Pp. 247–60.

Jacobs, J. "A Romance in Scholarship (the Discovery of Hebrew Sirach)." *Fortnightly Review* 72 (1899): 696–704.

Jansen, A. "Einige textkritische und exegetische Bemerkungen zum Buche Ekklesiastikus: Eccli 33,3; 50,1–5; 50,24a." *BZ* 4 (1906): 20–24.

Jenni, E. "Jesus Sirach," in *Die Religion in Geschichte und Gegenwart,* 3. 3d ed. Tübingen: Mohr, 1959. Pp. 653–55.

Johnson, N. B. *Prayer in the Apocrypha and Pseudepigrapha.* SBLMS 3. Philadelphia: Society of Biblical Literature, 1948.

Jongeling, B. "Un Passage difficile dans le Siracide de Masada (col. IV,22a=Sir. 42,11e)," in *Von Kanaan bis Kerala: Festschrift für Prof. Mag. Dr. Dr. J. P. M. van der Ploeg O.P. . . .* Ed. W. C. Delsman et al. AOAT 211. Kevelaer: Butzon & Bercker; Neukirchen-Vluyn: Neukirchener Verlag, 1982. Pp. 303–10.

Kahana, A. *Hassĕpārîm haḥîṣônîm: dibrê Šimʿôn ben-Sîrāʾ.* 2d ed. Tel Aviv: *Msdh,* 1955–56.

Kaiser, O. "Die Begründung der Sittlichkeit im Buche Jesus Sirach." *ZKT* 55 (1958): 51–63.

Kalt, E. *Das Buch Jesus Sirach übersetzt und erklärt.* Steyl: Missionsdruckerei, 1925.

Kaufmann, D. "Notes to Sirach XLIII. 20 and XL. 12." *JQR* 11 (1898–99): 159–62.

――――. "Sirach L. 5–8." *JQR* 10 (1897–98): 727–28.

――――. "Das Wort *tḥlyp* bei Jesus Sirach." *Monatsschrift für Geschichte und Wissenschaft des Judenthums* 41 (1897): 337–40.

Kearns, C. "Ecclesiasticus, or the Wisdom of Jesus the Son of Sirach," in *A New Catholic Commentary on Holy Scripture.* Ed. R. C. Fuller et al. London: Nelson, 1969. Pp. 541–62.

――――. "The Expanded Text of Ecclesiasticus: Its Teaching on the Future Life as a Clue to Its Origin." Doctoral dissertation, the Pontifical Biblical Commission. Rome, 1951.

Kearns, C. J. "La Vie intérieure à l'école de l'Ecclésiastique." *VSpir* 82 (1950): 137–46.

Kilpatrick, G. D. "*prosanoikodomēthēsetai* Ecclus. iii.14." *JTS* 44 (1943): 147–48.

Klawek, A. "Slowa Boze-pieśń ku czci Stworzyciela z księgi Ecclesiasticus 42,15–43,33." *Ruch Biblijny i Liturgiczny* 4 (1951): 329–32.

Knabenbauer, I. *Commentarius in Ecclesiasticum. Cursus Scripturae Sacrae, Commentariorum in Vet. Text. pars II, in libros didacticos VI.* Paris: Lethielleux, 1902.

Knabenbauer, J. "Einiges über die neuentdeckten hebräischen Stücke des Buches Sirach." *Stimmen aus Maria-Laach* 62 (1902): 526–39.

Köbert, R. "Ode Salomons 20,6 und Sir 33,31." *Bib* 58 (1977): 529–30.

König, E. *Die Originalität des neulich entdeckten hebräischen Sirachtextes.* Freiburg i.B.: Herder, 1899.

———. "Professor Margoliouth and the 'Original Hebrew' of Ecclesiasticus." *ExpTim* 10 (1898–99): 512–16; 564–66; 11 (1899–1900): 31–32.

Koole, J. L. "Die Bibel des Ben-Sira." *OTS* 14 (1965): 374–96.

Krauss, S. "Notes on Sirach: 1. The name Sirach; 2. The Author; 3. Sayings of Sirach in Rabbinic Literature; 4. The word *tḥlyp.*" *JQR* 11 (1898–99): 150–58.

Kroon, J. " 'Qui spernit modica, paulatim decidet' [Eccli. 19,1]." *VD* 5 (1925): 210–11.

Kuhn, G. "Beiträge zur Erklärung des Buches Jesus Sira." *ZAW* 47 (1929): 289–96; 48 (1930): 100–21.

Lamparter, H. *Die Apocryphen,* 1. *Das Buch Jesus Sirach.* Stuttgart: Calwer, 1972.

Lang, B. *Anweisungen gegen die Torheit: Sprichwörter Jesus Sirach.* Stuttgarter Kleiner Kommentar, AT 19. Stuttgart: KBW Verlag, 1973.

Lee, T. R. *Studies in the Form of Sirach 44–50.* SBLDS 75. Atlanta: Scholars, 1986.

Lefèvre, A. "Les Livres deutérocanoniques: L'Ecclésiastique (ou Siracide)," in *Introduction à la Bible,* 1. 2d ed. Ed. A. Robert and A. Feuillet. Tournai: Desclée, 1959. Pp. 771–76.

Le Frois, B. J. "Las lecciones Litúrgicas del Libro de Sirac." *Revista Biblica con Seccion Litúrgica* 19 (1957): 72–73.

———. "Our Lady and the Wisdom Passage from Sirach." *AER* 135 (1956): 1–8.

Lehmann, M. R. "Ben Sira and the Qumran Literature." *RevQ* 3 (1961): 103–16.

———. "11QPsᵃ and Ben Sira." *RevQ* 11 (1983): 239–51.

———. " 'Yom Kippur' in Qumran [and Ben Sira]." *RevQ* 3 (1961): 117–24.

Leloir, L. "Orientales de la Bible (Versions): II. Versions arméniennes." *DBSup* 6. Paris: Letouzey et Ané, 1960. Cols. 810–18.

Lesètre, H. *L'Ecclésiastique: Introduction critique, traduction française et commentaires.* La Sainte Bible avec commentaires. Ed. P. Brach and A. Bayle. 2d ed. Paris: Lethielleux, 1896.

Lévi, I. "Le Chapitre III de Ben Sira," in *Festschrift zu Ehren des Dr. A. Harkavy.* Ed. D. v. Günzburg and I. Markon. St. Petersburg, 1908. Pp. 1–5.

———. "Découverte d'un fragment d'une version hébraïque de l'Ecclésiastique de Jésus, fils de Sirach." *REJ* 32 (1896): 303–4.

———. *L'Ecclésiastique ou la Sagesse de Jésus, fils de Sira.* 2 parts. Paris: Leroux, 1898, 1901.

———. "Notes sur les ch. VII.29–XII.1 de Ben Sira édités par M. Elkan N. Adler." *JQR* 13 (1900–1): 1–17.

———. "Notes sur les nouveaux fragments de Ben Sira. II. III." *REJ* 40 (1900): 255–57.

———. "Les Nouveaux Fragments hébreux de l'Ecclésiastique de Jésus fils de Sira." *REJ* 39 (1899): 1–15; 177–90.

————. "Quelques notes sur Jésus ben Sirach et son ouvrage, II." *REJ* 35 (1897): 29–47.

————. "La Sagesse de Jésus, fils de Sirach: découverte d'un fragment de l'original hébreu." *REJ* 34 (1897): 1–50.

————. "Sirach, The Wisdom of Jesus, the Son of." *The Jewish Encyclopedia,* 11 (New York–London, 1905): 388–97.

Levison, J. "Is Eve to Blame? A Contextual Analysis of Sirach 25:24." *CBQ* 47 (1985): 617–23.

Liebermann, S. "Ben Sira à la lumière du Yerouchalmi." *REJ* 97 (1934): 50–57.

Lods, A. *Histoire de la littérature hébraïque et juive.* Paris: Payot, 1950.

Löhr, M. "Bildung aus dem Glauben: Beiträge zum Verständniss der Lehrreden des Buches Jesus Sirach." Doctoral dissertation, University of Bonn, 1975.

Luciani, F. "La giustizia de Enoch in Sir. 44,16b secondo la versione greca." *BeO* 23 (1981): 185–92.

Luzzi, G. "Ecclesiastico," in *Apocrifi dell' Antico Testamento.* La Bibbia tradotta dai testi originali e annotata da G. Luzzi. Florence: Società Fides et Amor, 1930. Pp. 345–504.

McHardy, W. D. "The Arabic Text of Ecclesiasticus in the Bodleian MS. Hunt[ington]. 260." *JTS* 46 (1945): 39–41.

————. "Ben-Ze'eb's Edition of the Peshitta Text of Ecclesiasticus." *ZAW* 61 (1945/1948): 193–94.

Mack, B. L. *Wisdom and the Hebrew Epic: Ben Sira's Hymn in Praise of the Fathers.* Chicago Studies in the History of Judaism. Chicago: University of Chicago, 1985.

McKeating, H. "Jesus ben Sira's Attitude to Women." *ExpTim* 85 (1973–74): 85–87.

McKenzie, J. L. "Reflections on Wisdom." *JBL* 86 (1967): 1–9.

MacKenzie, R. A. F. "Ben Sira as Historian," in *Trinification of the World: A Festschrift in Honor of F. E. Crowe.* . . . Ed. T. A. Dunne and J.-M. Laporte. Toronto: Regis College, 1978. Pp. 313–27.

————. *Sirach.* Old Testament Message 19. Wilmington, Del.: Michael Glazier, 1983.

McRae, C. A. "The Hebrew Text of Ben Sira [39,15–43,33]." Doctoral dissertation, University of Toronto, 1910.

Mader, J. "Zu Sir 51,13." *BZ* 11 (1913): 24–25.

Maertens, T. *L'Éloge des Pères (Ecclésiastique XLIV–L).* Collection Lumière et Vie 5. Bruges: l'Abbaye de Saint-André, 1956.

Maier, G. *Mensch und freier Wille, Nach den jüdischen Religionsparteien zwischen Ben Sira und Paulus.* WUNT 12. Tübingen: Mohr [Siebeck], 1971.

Malchow, B. V. "Social Justice in Wisdom Literature." *BTB* 12 (1982): 120–24.

Marbach, C. *Carmina Scripturarum, scil. antiphonas et responsaria ex sacro Scripturae fonte in libros liturgicos S. Ecclesiae Romanae derivata.* Hildesheim: G. Olm, 1963. Use of Sirach in liturgy, pp. 288–302.

Marböck, J. "Das Gebet um die Rettung Zions Sir 36,1–22 (G:33,1–13a; 36,16b–22) im Zusammenhang der Geschichtsschau Ben Siras," in *Memoria Jerusalem.* Ed. J. B. Bauer. Jerusalem/Graz: Akademische Druck- und Verlagsanstalt, 1977. Pp. 93–116.

————. "Gesetz und Weisheit: Zum Verständnis des Gesetzes bei Jesus Sira." *BZ* N.F. 20 (1976): 1–21.

————. "Henoch—Adam—der Thronwagen: Zu frühjüdischen pseudepigraphischen Traditionen bei Ben Sira." *BZ* N.F. 25 (1981): 103–11.

————. "Sir. 38,24–39,11: Der schriftgelehrte Weise. Ein Beitrag zu Gestalt und Werk Ben Siras," in *La Sagesse de l'Ancien Testament.* Ed. M. Gilbert. BETL 51. Gembloux/Louvain: Duculot/University, 1979. Pp. 293–316.

————. "Sirachliteratur seit 1966: Ein Überblick." *TRev* 71 (1975): 177–84.

————. *Weisheit im Wandel: Untersuchungen zur Weisheitstheologie bei Ben Sira.* BBB 37. Bonn: Hanstein, 1971.

Marcus, R. *Law in the Apocrypha.* Columbia University Oriental Studies 26. New York: Ams, 1960.

Margoliouth, D. S. "The Date of Ben-Sira," in *Occident and Orient . . . Gaster Anniversary Volume.* London: Taylor's Foreign Press, 1936. Pp. 403–8.

————. "The Destruction of the Original of Ecclesiasticus." *ExpTim* 16 (1904–5): 26–29.

————. "Ecclesiastes and Ecclesiasticus." *Expositor,* 7th Ser., 5 (1908): 118–26.

————. "Ecclesiasticus in Arabic Literature." *ExpTim* 18 (1906–7): 476–77.

————. "The Language and Metre of Ecclesiasticus." *Expositor,* 4th Ser., 1 (1890): 295–320; 381–87.

————. "Note on Ecclus. vii. 25." *ExpTim* 23 (1911–12): 234–35.

————. "Observations on the Fragment of the Original of Ecclesiasticus Edited by Mr. Schechter." *Expositor,* 5th Ser., 4 (1896): 140–51.

————. *The Origin of the "Original Hebrew" of Ecclesiasticus.* London: Parker, 1899.

————. "Three Notes on Ecclesiasticus." *ExpTim* 13 (1901–2): 331–32.

Margolis, M. L. "Ecclus. 7,6d." *ZAW* 25 (1905): 323.

————. "Ecclus. 6,4." *ZAW* 25 (1905): 320–22. [As regards this article, cf. I. Lévi, *ZAW* 26 (1906): 142; and Margolis's answer in *ZAW* 27 (1907): 276–77.]

————. "Ecclus. 3,27." *ZAW* 25 (1905): 199–200.

————. "Mr. Hart's 'Ecclesiasticus.'" *JQR* n.s. 1 (1910–11): 403–18.

————. "A Passage in Ecclesiasticus [34,16–17]." *ZAW* 21 (1901): 271–72.

Mari, F. "L'originale ebraico dell'Ecclesiastico recentemente scoperto." *Studi Religiosi* 3 (1903): 63–82; 170–82.

Marmorstein, A. "Jesus Sirach 51,12ff." *ZAW* 29 (1909): 287–93.

Martin, J. D. "Ben Sira—A Child of His Time," in *A Word in Season: Essays in Honour of William McKane,* ed. J. D. Martin and P. R. Davies. JSOTSup 42. Sheffield: JSOT, 1986. Pp. 141–61.

Martin Juárez, M. A. "Sabiduría y ley in Jesús Ben Sira." *Religión y Cultura* 25 (1979): 567–74.

Matthes, J. C. "Bemerkungen zu dem hebräischen Texte Jesus Sirachs und seiner neuesten Übersetzung." *ZAW* 29 (1909): 161–76.

————. "Das Buch Sirach und Kohelet in ihrem gegenseitigen Verhältniss. Die Prioritätsfrage." *Vierteljahrsschrift für Bibelkunde* 2 (1904–5): 258–63.

May, H. G., and B. M. Metzger, eds. *The New Oxford Annotated Bible with the Apocrypha: Revised Standard Version, Containing the Second Edition of the New Testament and an Expanded Edition of the Apocrypha.* New York: Oxford University, 1977.

Merguet, K. H. V. *Die Glaubens- und Sittenlehren des Buches Jesus Sirach.* 2 vols. Königsberg: Ostpreussische Druckerei, 1874, 1901.

Metzger, B. M. *An Introduction to the Apocrypha.* New York: Oxford University, 1957.

Michaelis, D. "Das Buch Jesus Sirach als Typischer Ausdruck für das Gottesverhältnis des nachalttestamentlichen Menschen." *TLZ* 83 (1958): 601–8.

Middendorp, T. *Die Stellung Jesus ben Siras zwischen Judentum und Hellenismus.* Leiden: Brill, 1973.

Milik, J. T. "Un Fragment mal placé dans l'édition du Siracide de Masada." *Bib* 47 (1966): 425–26.

Minisalle, A. *Siracide (Ecclesiastico): Versione-introduzione-note. Nuovissima Versione,* 23. Rome: Paoline, 1980.

Minocchi, S. "La Découverte du texte hébreu original de l'Ecclésiastique," in *Congrès scientifique des Catholiques, 1897. II: Sciences exégétiques.* Fribourg, Switzerland: Librairie de l'Oeuvre de St. Paul, 1898. Pp. 283–96.

Moffatt, J. "Literary Illustrations of the Book of Ecclesiasticus." *Expositor,* 7th Ser., 4 (1907): 279–88; 8th Ser., 1 (1911): 84–96.

Moreno, A. "Jesús Ben Sira: Un judio en un tiempo de crisis." *Teología y Vida* 10 (1969): 24–42.

Morenz, S. "Eine weitere Spur der Weisheit Ämenopes in der Bible (Sir 33,13 [Greek])." *Zeitschrift für Ägyptische Sprache* 84 (1959): 78–79.

Moulton, R. G. *Ecclesiasticus. The Modern Reader's Bible.* New York: Macmillan, 1896.

Mowinckel, S. "Die Metrik bei Jesus Sirach." *ST* 9 (1955): 137–65.

Müller, H.-P. *"ḥākam, ḥākām, ḥokmâ, ḥokmôt." TDOT* 4 (1980): 364–85.

Muraoka, T. "Sir. 51,13–30: An Erotic Hymn to Wisdom?" *JSJ* 10 (1979): 166–78.

Murphy, R. E. "Assumptions and Problems in Old Testament Wisdom Research." *CBQ* 29 (1967): 101–12.

———. "Hebrew Wisdom." *JAOS* 101 (1981): 21–34.

———. "Israel's Wisdom: A Biblical Model of Salvation," in *Voies de Salut. Studia Missionalia* 30 (1981): 1–43.

———. *Seven Books of Wisdom.* Milwaukee: Bruce, 1960.

———. "What and Where Is Wisdom?" *Currents in Theology and Mission* 4 (1977): 283–87.

———. "Wisdom and Creation." *JBL* 104 (1985): 3–11.

———. *Wisdom Literature and Psalms.* Interpreting Biblical Texts. Nashville: Abingdon, 1983.

Nebe, G. W. "Sirach 42,5c." *ZAW* 82 (1970): 283–86.

Nelis, J. T. "Sir 38,15," in *Von Kanaan bis Kerala: Festschrift für Prof. Mag. Dr. Dr. J. P. M. van der Ploeg O.P.* . . . Ed. W. C. Delsman et al. AOAT 211. Kevelaer: Butzon & Bercker; Neukirchen-Vluyn: Neukirchener Verlag, 1982. Pp. 173–84.

Nelson, M. D. "The Syriac Version of Ben Sira Compared to the Greek and Hebrew Materials." Doctoral dissertation, UCLA, 1981.

Nestle, E. "Ecclus. xii. 10,11." *ExpTim* 11 (1899–1900): 143.

———. "Jesus Sirach Neffe oder Enkel des Amos Sirach." *ZAW* 23 (1903): 128–30.

———. "Sirach (Book of)," in *A Dictionary of the Bible*, 4. Ed. by J. Hastings. New York: C. Scribner, 1902. Pp. 539–51.

———. "Zum Prolog des Ecclesiasticus." *ZAW* 17 (1897): 123–34.

Nic[c]acci, A. "Siracide 6,19 e Giovanni 4,34–38." *BeO* 23 (1981): 149–53.

Nickels, P. "Wisdom's Table—Daily Bread." *TBT* 19 (1981): 168–72.

Nickelsburg, G. W. E. *Jewish Literature between the Bible and the Mishnah: A Historical and Literary Introduction*. Philadelphia: Fortress, 1981.

———. *Resurrection, Immortality, and Eternal Life in Intertestamental Judaism*. Cambridge, Mass.: Harvard University, 1972.

Nöldeke, T. "Bemerkungen zum hebräischen Ben Sira." *ZAW* 20 (1900): 81–94.

———. "The Original Hebrew of a Portion of Ecclesiasticus." *Expositor*, 5th Ser., 5 (1897): 347–64.

Noorda, S. J. "Illness and Sin, Forgiving and Healing: The Connection of Medieval Treatment and Religious Beliefs in Ben Sira 38,1–15," in *Studies in Hellenistic Religions*. Ed. M. J. Vermaseren. Leiden: Brill, 1979. Pp. 215–24.

Oesterley, W. O. E. *The Books of the Apocrypha: Their Origin, Teaching and Contents*. London: B. Scott, 1915.

———. *An Introduction to the Books of the Apocrypha*. London: SPCK, 1935.

———. *The Wisdom of Ben-Sira (Ecclesiasticus)*. London: SPCK, 1916.

———. *The Wisdom of Jesus the Son of Sirach or Ecclesiasticus*. Cambridge: Cambridge University, 1912.

Ó Fearghail, F. "Sir 50,5–21: Yom Kippur or The Daily Whole-Offering?" *Bib* 59 (1978): 301–16.

Patterson, R. K., Jr. "A Study of the Hebrew Text of Sirach 39:27–41:24." Doctoral dissertation, Duke University, 1967.

Pautrel, R. "Ben Sira et le Stoïcisme." *RSR* 51 (1963): 535–49.

Pax, E. "Dialog und Selbstgespräch bei Sirach 27,3–10." *SBFLA* 20 (1970): 247–63.

Penar, T. *Northwest Semitic Philology and the Hebrew Fragments of Ben Sira*. BibOr 28. Rome: Biblical Institute, 1975.

Peters, N. *Das Buch Jesus Sirach oder Ecclesiasticus*. Exegetisches Handbuch zum Alten Testament 25. Münster i.W.: Aschendorff, 1913.

———. "Ekklesiastes und Ekklesiastikus." *BZ* 1 (1903): 47–54; 129–50.

———. *Die Sahidisch-koptische Uebersetzung des Buches Ecclesiasticus auf ihren wahren Werth für die Textkritik untersucht*. BibS 3, 3. Freiburg i.B.: Herder, 1898.

———. "Sirach," in *Lexikon für Theologie und Kirche*, 9. 2d ed. Freiburg i.B.: Herder, 1937. Pp. 594–95.

Pfeiffer, R. H. *A History of New Testament Times with an Introduction to the Apocrypha*. New York: Harper & Bros., 1949.

———. "The Literature and Religion of the Apocrypha." *IB* 1. New York: Abingdon-Cokesbury, 1952. Pp. 391–419.

Pietersma, A. "The 'Lost' Folio of the Chester Beatty *Ecclesiasticus*." *VT* 25 (1975): 497–99.

Pisani, V. "Acqua e fuoco [Sir 15,17–18]." *Acme* 1 (1948): 94.

Plath, S. *Furcht Gottes: Der Begriff jr' im Alten Testament*. Stuttgart: Calwer, 1963.

Poulssen, N. "Het wijsheidsideaal van Jezus Sirach: Een impressie." *Ons Geestelijk Leven* 54 (1977): 105–8.

Power, A. D. *Ecclesiasticus, or The Wisdom of Jesus, the Son of Sira.* London: Hodder and Stoughton, 1939.

———. *The Wisdom of Jesus the Son of Sirach Commonly Called Ecclesiasticus.* Chelsea [London]: Ashendene, 1932.

Prato, G. L. "La Lumière interprète de la sagesse dans la tradition textuelle de Ben Sira," in *La Sagesse de l'Ancien Testament.* Ed. M. Gilbert. BETL 51. Gembloux/Louvain: Duculot/University, 1979. Pp. 317–46.

———. *Il problema della teodicea in Ben Sira: Composizione dei contrari e richiamo alle origini.* AnBib 65. Rome: Biblical Institute, 1975.

Prelipceanu, V. "Actualitatea învăţătirilor moral-sociale dîn cartea lui Iisus fiul lui Sirah." *Studii Teologice* 7 (1955): 582–99.

Priest, J. "Ben Sira 45,25 in the Light of the Qumran Literature." *RevQ* 5 (1964–65): 111–18.

Procter, W. C. *The Value of the Apocrypha.* London: C. J. Thynne & Jarvis, 1926.

Purvis, J. D. "Ben Sira and the Foolish People of Shechem [Sir 50:25–26]." *JNES* 24 (1965): 88–94.

Rabinowitz, I. "The Qumran Hebrew Original of Ben Sira's Concluding Acrostic on Wisdom." *HUCA* 42 (1971): 173–84.

Rad, G. von. "Die Weisheit des Jesus Sirach." *EvT* 29 (1969): 113–33.

———. *Wisdom in Israel.* Tr. J. D. Martin. Nashville: Abingdon, 1972.

Rankin, O. S. *Israel's Wisdom Literature: Its Bearing on Theology and the History of Religion.* Edinburgh: T. & T. Clark, 1936.

Reiterer, F. V. *"Urtext" und Übersetzungen: Sprachstudie über Sir 44,16–45,26 als Beitrag zur Siraforschung.* Arbeiten zu Text und Sprache im Alten Testament, 12. St. Ottilien: EOS, 1980.

Rickenbacher, O. *Weisheitsperikopen bei Ben Sira.* OBO 1. Freiburg, Switzerland–Göttingen: Universitätsverlag–Vandenhoeck und Ruprecht, 1973.

Rinaldi, G. *"Ektisen . . . koinē* nell' Ecclesiastico (18.1)." *BeO* 25 (1983): 115–16.

———. "Onus meum leve: Osservazioni su Ecclesiastico 51 (v. 26, Volg. 34) e Matteo 11,25–30." *BeO* 9 (1967): 13–23.

Ring, E. *Det sedliga handlandets motiv enligt Siraks bok.* Stockholm: V. Petterson, 1923.

Rivkin, E. "Ben Sira and the Nonexistence of the Synagogue: A Study in Historical Method," in *In the Time of Harvest: Essays in Honor of Abba Hillel Silver.* New York: Macmillan, 1963. Pp. 320–54.

———. "Ben Sira—The Bridge between Aaronide and Pharisaic Revolutions." *ErIsr* 12 (1975): 95*–103*.

Rost, L. *Judaism outside the Hebrew Canon: An Introduction to the Documents.* Trans. D. E. Green. Nashville: Abingdon, 1976.

Roth, C. "Ecclesiasticus in the Synagogue Service." *JBL* 71 (1952): 171–78.

Roth, W. "The Lord's Glory Fills Creation: A Study of Sirach's Praise of God's Works (42:15–50:24)." *Explor* 6 (1981): 85–95.

———. "On the Gnomic-Discursive Wisdom of Jesus Ben Sirach." *Semeia* 17 (1980): 59–79.

———. "The Relation between the Fear of the Lord and Wisdom." *Beth Mikra* 25 (1980): 150–62 (Hebrew).

Rothstein, J. W. "Ein Spezimen criticum zu hebräischen Texte des Sirach-buches," in *Orientalische Studien, Theodor Nöldeke gewidmet*, 1. Ed. by C. Bezold. Giessen: Töpelmann, 1906. Pp. 583–608.

Rowley, H. H. *The Origin and Significance of the Apocrypha.* Rev. ed. London: SPCK, 1967.

Rudnitzky, N. *Die Apokryphen und Pseudepigraphen des Alten Testaments.* Pforzheim: A. Zutavern, 1926.

Rüger, H. P. *Text und Textform im hebräischen Sirach: Untersuchungen zur Textgeschichte und Textkritik der hebräischen Sirachfragmente aus der Kairoer Geniza.* BZAW 112. Berlin: De Gruyter, 1970.

Rydén, L. "LXX Sirach 37,2." *Eranos* 59 (1961): 40–44.

Ryssel, V. "Die neuen hebräischen Fragmente des Buches Jesus Sirach und ihre Herkunft." *Theologische Studien und Kritiken* 73 (1900): 363–403; 505–41; 74 (1901): 75–109; 269–94; 547–92; 75 (1902): 205–61; 347–420.

———. "Die Sprüche Jesus', des Sohnes Sirachs," in *Die Apokryphen und Pseudepigraphen des Alten Testaments*, 1. Ed. E. Kautzsch. Tübingen: Mohr, 1921. Pp. 230–475.

Sanders, J. T. *Ben Sira and Demotic Wisdom.* SBLMS 28. Chico, Calif.: Scholars, 1983.

———. "Ben Sira's Ethics of Caution." *HUCA* 50 (1979): 73–106.

———. "A Hellenistic Egyptian Parallel to Ben Sira." *JBL* 97 (1978): 257–58.

Sandmel, S., et al., eds. *Oxford Study Edition: The New English Bible with the Apocrypha.* New York: Oxford University, 1976.

Santoro, L. "L'inno al Creatore di Gesù Ben Sirac." *Città di Vita* 2 (1947): 253–61.

Saracino, F. "Risurrezione in Ben Sira?" *Hen* 4 (1982): 185–203.

Scazzocchio, L. "Ecclesiastico, Tobia, Sapienza di Salomone alla luce dei testi di Qumran." *Rivista degli Studi Orientali* 37 (1962): 199–209.

Schechter, S. "The British Museum Fragments of Ecclesiasticus." *JQR* 12 (1899–1900): 266–72.

———. "A Glimpse of the Social Life of the Jews in the Age of Jesus the Son of Sirach," in *Studies in Judaism, Second Series.* Philadelphia: Jewish Publication Society of America, 1908. Pp. 55–101.

———. "A Hoard of Hebrew Manuscripts I," in *Studies in Judaism, Second Series.* Philadelphia: Jewish Publication Society of America, 1908. Pp. 1–11.

———. "The Quotations from Ecclesiasticus in Rabbinic Literature." *JQR* 3 (1890–91): 682–706.

———. "Review of *The Origin of the 'Original Hebrew' of Ecclesiasticus.*" *The Critical Review* 9 (1899): 387–400.

Schiffer, S. "Le Paragraphe 40,13–17 de l'Ecclésiastique de Ben Sira," in *Oriental Studies Dedicated to Paul Haupt.* Baltimore: Johns Hopkins, 1926. Pp. 106–10.

Schildenberger, J. "Die Bedeutung von Sir 48,24f. für die Verfasserfrage von Is 40–66," in *AT Studien, Festschrift Nötscher.* BBB 1. Bonn: Hanstein, 1950. Pp. 188–204.

112 THE WISDOM OF BEN SIRA

Schilling, O. *Das Buch Jesus Sirach.* Herders Bibelkommentar. Die heilige Schrift 7/2. Freiburg i.B.: Herder, 1956.

Schlatter, A. *Das neu gefundene hebräische Stück des Sirach. —Der Glossator des griechischen Sirach und seine Stellung in der Geschichte der jüdischen Theologie.* Beiträge zur Förderung christlicher Theologie 1, 5–6. Gütersloh: Bertelsmann, 1897.

Schlögl, N. "Das Alphabet des Siraciden (Eccls. 51,13–29), eine textkritische Studie." *ZDMG* 53 (1899): 669–82.

———. *Ecclesiasticus (39,12–49,16) ope artis criticae et metricae in formam originalem redactus.* Vienna: Mayer, 1901.

Schmidt, N. *Ecclesiasticus.* The Temple Bible. London: Dent & Co., 1903.

Schmitt, E. *Leben in den Weisheitsbüchern Job, Sprüche und Jesus Sirach.* Freiburger Theologische Studien 66. Freiburg i.B.: Herder, 1954.

Schnabel, E. J. *Law and Wisdom from Ben Sira to Paul: A Traditional Historical Enquiry into the Relation of Law, Wisdom, and Ethics.* WUNT 2/16. Tübingen: Mohr, 1985.

Scott, R. B. Y. *The Way of Wisdom in the Old Testament.* New York: Macmillan, 1971.

———. "Wisdom; Wisdom Literature." *EncJud,* 16 (1971): 557–63.

Segal, M. H. *"Ben-Sîrā̓,"* in *Enṣîqlôpēdyāh miqrā̓ît,* 2. Jerusalem, Israel: Bialik Institute, 1954. Pp. 162–69.

———. "Ben Sira, Wisdom of." *EncJud,* 4 (1971): 550–53.

———. " ʻDappîm nôsēpîm mittôk sēper ben-Sîrā̓ ' (H. Šîrman, Tarbîṣ, kt, ʻm̓ 125–34)." *Tarbiz* 29 (1959–60): 313–23.

———. "The Evolution of the Hebrew Text of Ben Sira." *JQR* n.s. 25 (1934–35): 91–149.

———. *"ḥqr, nhqr bĕš[ēper] ben-Sîrā̓."* *Lĕšonénu* 21 (1957): 143.

———. *"Kĕtab-ha-yād ha-ḥămîšî šel ben-Sîrā̓ hā-ʻibrî."* *Tarbiz* 2 (1930–31): 295–307.

———. *"Sēper ben-Sîrā̓ bĕqûmrân."* *Tarbiz* 33 (1963–64): 243–46.

Seligmann, C. *Das Buch der Weisheit des Jesus Sirach (Josua ben Sira) in seinem Verhältniss zu den salomonischen Sprüchen und seiner historischen Bedeutung.* Breslau: Pruss & Jünger, 1883.

Selmer, C. "A Study of Ecclus. 12:10–19." *CBQ* 8 (1946): 306–14.

———. "Traces of the 'Sayings of the Seven Sages' in the Liber Ecclesiasticus." *CBQ* 5 (1943): 264–74.

Sheppard, G. T. "Wisdom and Torah: The Interpretation of Deuteronomy Underlying Sirach 24:23," in *Biblical and Near Eastern Studies.* Ed. G. A. Tuttle. Grand Rapids: Eerdmans, 1978. Pp. 166–76.

Siebeneck, R. T. "May Their Bones Return to Life! —Sirach's Praise of the Fathers." *CBQ* 21 (1959): 411–28.

Silverstone, H. S. *A Guide to the Prophets and the Apocrypha.* Baltimore: Kogan, 1942 [1945?].

Sisti, A. "Riflessi dell' epoca premaccabaica nell' Ecclesiastico." *RivB* 12 (1964): 215–56.

Skehan, P. W. "The Acrostic Poem in Sirach 51:13–30." *HTR* 64 (1971): 387–400.

———. "Didache 1,6 and Sirach 12,1." *Bib* 44 (1963): 533–36.

———. "The Divine Name at Qumran, in the Masada Scroll, and in the Septuagint." *BIOSCS* 13 (1980): 14–44.

———. "Ecclesiasticus." *IDBSup.* Nashville: Abingdon, 1976. Pp. 250–51.

———. "Sirach 30:12 and Related Texts." *CBQ* 36 (1974): 535–42.

———. "Staves, Nails and Scribal Slips (Ben Sira 44:2–5)." *BASOR* 200 (1970): 66–71.

———. "Structures in Poems on Wisdom: Proverbs 8 and Sirach 24." *CBQ* 41 (1979): 365–79.

———. *Studies in Israelite Poetry and Wisdom.* CBQMS 1. Washington: Catholic Biblical Association, 1971.

———. "They shall not be found in parables (Sir 38,33)." *CBQ* 23 (1961): 40.

———. "Tower of Death or Deadly Snare? (Sir 26,22)." *CBQ* 16 (1954): 154.

Smend, R. *Das hebräische Fragment der Weisheit des Jesus Sirach.* Abhandlungen der königlichen Gesellschaft der Wissenschaften zu Göttingen. Philologisch-Historische Klasse. N.F., 2, 2. Berlin: Weidmannsche, 1897.

———. "Nachträgliches zur Textüberlieferung des syrischen Sirach." *ZAW* 27 (1907): 271–75.

———. *Die Weisheit des Jesus Sirach erklärt.* Berlin: Reimer, 1906.

Smith, C. R. "The Social Teaching of the Apocryphal and Apocalyptic Books." *ExpTim* 37 (1925–26): 505–8.

Snaith, J. G. "Ben Sira's Supposed Love of Liturgy." *VT* 25 (1975): 167–74.

———. "Biblical Quotations in the Hebrew of Ecclesiasticus." *JTS* n.s. 18 (1967): 1–12.

———. *Ecclesiasticus or The Wisdom of Jesus, Son of Sirach.* Cambridge Bible Commentary, New English Bible. Cambridge: Cambridge University, 1974.

———. "The Importance of Ecclesiasticus (The Wisdom of Ben Sira)." *ExpTim* 75 (1963–64): 66–69.

Soggin, J. A. *Introduction to the Old Testament: From Its Origins to the Closing of the Alexandrian Canon.* Rev. ed. Tr. J. Bowden. OTL. Philadelphia: Westminster, 1980.

Sović, A. "Enkomij liječnicima u Svetom Pismu [Sir 38,1–15]." *Bogoslovsia Smotra* 26 (1938): 165–79 (Latin summary on p. 165).

Spadafora, F. "Ecclesiastico," in *Enciclopedia Cattolica,* 5. Vatican City: Ente per l'Enciclopedia Cattolica e per il Libro Cattolico, 1950. Pp. 40–45.

Spicq, C. "L'Ecclésiastique," in *La Sainte Bible,* 6. Ed. L. Pirot and A. Clamer. Paris: Letouzey et Ané, 1951. Pp. 529–841.

———. "Le Siracide et la structure littéraire du prologue de Saint Jean." *Mémorial Lagrange.* Paris: Gabalda, 1940. Pp. 183–95.

Squillaci, D. "La preghiera missionaria dall'Ecclesiastico (36,1–19)." *Palestra del Clero* 41 (1962): 260–63.

Stadelmann, H. *Ben Sira als Schriftgelehrter: Eine Untersuchung zum Berufsbild des vor-Makkabäischen Sōfēr unter Berücksichtigung seines Verhältnisses zu Priester-, Propheten- und Weisheitslehretum.* WUNT 2/6. Tübingen: Mohr, 1981.

Steinhardt, J. *Neun Holzschnitte zu ausgewählten Versen aus dem Buche Jeschu ben Elieser ben Sirach, mit einer Einleitung von Arnold Zweig.* Berlin: Soncino-Gesellschaft der Freunde des jüdischen Buches, 1929.

Stevenson, W. B. "A Mnemonic Use of Numbers in Proverbs and Ben Sira." *TGUOS* 9 (1938–39): 26–38.

Stöger, A. "Der Arzt nach Jesus Sirach (38,1–15)." *Arzt und Christ* 11 (1965): 3–11.

Storr, R. "Einige Bedenken gegen die Echtheit des hebräischen Jesus Sirach." *TQ* 106 (1925): 203–31.

Strauss, D. "Sprachliche Studien zu den hebräischen Sirachfragmenten." *Schweizerische Theologische Zeitschrift* 17 (1900): 65–80.

Strothmann, W. *Johannes von Mosul, Bar Sira, Syrische Texte: Übersetzung und vollständiges Wortverzeichnis.* Göttingen Orientforschungen 1, Syriaca 19. Wiesbaden: Harrassowitz, 1979.

Strugnell, J. "Notes and Queries on 'The Ben Sira Scroll from Masada,' " in W. F. Albright Volume. Ed. A. Malamat. ErIsr 9 (1969): 109–19.

Stummer, F. " 'Via peccantium complanata lapidibus' (Eccli 21,11)," in *Colligere Fragmenta.* Festschrift Alban Dold. Ed. B. Fischer and V. Fiala. Beuron in Hollenzollern: Beuroner Kunstverlag, 1952. Pp. 40–44.

Surburg, R. F. *Introduction to the Intertestamental Period.* St. Louis: Concordia Publishing House, 1975.

Swete, H. B. *An Introduction to the Old Testament in Greek.* 2d ed. Rev. R. R. Ottley. Cambridge: Cambridge University, 1902.

Swidler, L. *Women in Judaism: The Status of Women in Formative Judaism.* Metuchen, N.J.: Scarecrow, 1976.

Szczygiel, P. "Daniel i Judyta w ksiedze Siracha." *Przegląd Biblijny* 1 (1937): 117–47.

Taylor, A. F. *Meditations in Ecclesiasticus.* London: J. Clarke & Co., 1928.

———. "Meditations in the Apocrypha [Ecclus]." *ExpTim* 37 (1925–26): 40–42; 91–93.

Taylor, C. "The Alphabet of Ben Sira." *JQR* 17 (1904–5): 238–39.

———. "The Alphabet of Ben Sira." *Journal of Philology* 30 (1907): 95–132.

———. "Studies in Ben Sira." *JQR* 10 (1897–98): 470–88.

———. "The Wisdom of Ben Sira." *JQR* 15 (1902–3): 440–74; 604–26.

———. "The Wisdom of Ben Sira." *JTS* 1 (1899–1900): 571–83.

——— and J. H. A. Hart. "Two Notes on Enoch in Sir. xliv 16." *JTS* 4 (1902–3): 589–91.

Taylor, W. R. "The Originality of the Hebrew Text of Ben Sira in the Light of the Vocabulary and the Versions." Dissertation, University of Toronto, 1910.

Tedesche, S. S. *Prayers of the Apocrypha and Their Importance in the Study of Jewish Liturgy* (reprinted from Yearbook, vol. 26, Central Conference of American Rabbis, 1916).

Tennant, F. R. "The Teaching of Ecclesiasticus and Wisdom on the Introduction of Sin and Death." *JTS* 2 (1900–1): 207–23.

Thielmann, P. "Die europäischen Bestandteile des lateinischen Sirach." *Archiv für lateinische Lexikographie und Grammatik* 9 (1896): 247–84.

———. "Die lateinische Übersetzung des Buches Sirach." *Archiv für lateinische Lexikographie und Grammatik* 8 (1893): 501–61.

Thomas, D. W. "A Note on Ecclus 51:21a." *JTS* 20 (1969): 225–26.

———. "The LXX's Rendering of *snwt lb twb* in Ecclus. XXXIII 13." *VT* 10 (1960): 456.

Tobac, E. *Les cinq livres de Solomon.* Brussels: Vromant & Co., 1926. Pp. 173–214.

Torrey, C. C. *The Apocryphal Literature.* New Haven: Yale University, 1946.

——. "The Hebrew of the Geniza Sirach," in *Alexander Marx Jubilee Volume.* New York: Jewish Theological Seminary of America, 1950. Pp. 585–602.

Touzard, J. "Ecclésiastique," in *Dictionnaire de la Bible,* 2, 1. Paris: Letouzey et Ané, 1899. Cols. 1543–57.

——. "Nouveaux fragments hébreux de l'Ecclésiastique." *RB* 9 (1900): 45–62; 525–63.

——. "L'Original hébreu de l'Ecclésiastique." *RB* 6 (1897): 271–82; 547–73; 7 (1898): 33–58.

——. *Traduction française du texte hébreu de l'Ecclésiastique avec les variantes du grec et du latin.* Appendix to F. Vigouroux, *La Sainte Bible polyglotte, Ancien Testament,* 5. Paris: A. Roger et F. Chernoviz, 1904. Pp. 885–970.

Toy, C. H. "Ecclesiasticus," in *Encyclopaedia Biblica.* London: Macmillan, 1904. Pp. 1164–79.

——. "Remarks on the Hebrew Text of Ben-Sira." *JAOS* 23 (1902): 38–43.

——. "Sirach," in *Encyclopaedia Biblica.* London: Macmillan, 1904. Pp. 4645–51.

Trenchard, W. C. *Ben Sira's View of Women: A Literary Analysis.* Brown Judaic Studies 38. Chico, Calif.: Scholars, 1982.

Treves, M. "Studi su Gesù ben Sirach." *La Rassegna mensile di Israel* 22 (1956): 387–97; 464–73.

Trinquet, J. "Ecclésiastique (Livre de l')." *Catholicisme,* 3. Paris: Letouzey et Ané, 1952. Cols. 1244–49.

——. "Les Liens 'sadocites' de l'Écrit de Damas, des manuscrits de la Mer Morte et de l'Ecclésiastique." *VT* 1 (1951): 287–92.

Tromp, N. J. "Jesus Ben Sira en het offer: Proeve van een portret." *BTFT* 34 (1973): 250–66.

Tyler, T. "Ecclesiasticus: The Retranslation Hypothesis." *JQR* 12 (1899–1900): 555–62.

Vaccari, A. "Il concetto della Sapienza nell'Antico Testamento." *Greg* 1 (1920): 218–51.

——. "Eccli. 24,20s. de Beata Virgine." *VD* 3 (1923): 136–40.

——. "Ecclesiastici hebraice fragmentum nuper detectum." *VD* 11 (1931): 172–78.

——. *L'Ecclesiastico.* La Sacra Bibbia tradotta dai testi originali con note, a cura del Pontificio Istituto Biblico di Roma. Rome: Biblical Institute, 1961. Pp. 1179–1285.

——. "Ecclesiastico 37,10.11: critica ed esegesi." *EstEcl* 34 (1960): 705–13.

——. " 'Oratio Jesu, filii Sirach' (Eccli. 51,1–17)." *VD* 2 (1922): 71–72.

——. " 'Quasi plantatio rosae in Iericho' (Eccli. 24,18)." *VD* 3 (1923): 289–94.

Vargha, T. "De Psalmo hebraico Ecclesiastici c. 51." *Anton* 10 (1935): 3–10.

Vattioni, F. "Genesi 1,1 ed Eccli. 15,14." *Augustinianum* 4 (1964): 105–8.

——. "Nuovi fogli ebraici dell' Ecclesiastico." *RivB* 8 (1960): 169–79.

——. "San Girolamo e l'Ecclesiastico." *Vetera Christianorum* 4 (1967): 131–49.

Vawter, B. *The Book of Sirach with a Commentary.* Pamphlet Bible Series 40–41. 2 parts. New York: Paulist, 1962.

Vella, J. *Eclesiástico.* La Sagrada Escritura, Antiguo Testamento 5. Madrid: Editorial Católica, 1970. Pp. 1–218.

Vogt, E. "Novi textus hebraici libri Sira." *Bib* 41 (1960): 184–90.

———. "Novum folium hebr. Sir 15,1–16,7 MS B." *Bib* 40 (1959): 1060–62.

Volz, P. *Hiob und Weisheit (Das Buch Hiob, Sprüche und Jesus Sirach, Prediger).* Die Schriften des Alten Testaments 3, 2. 2d ed. Göttingen: Vandenhoeck & Ruprecht, 1921.

Wahl, O. *Der Sirach-Text der Sacra Parallela.* Würzburg: Echter-Verlag, 1974.

Walsh, M. E. *The Apocrypha.* Nashville: Southern Publishing Association, 1968.

Weber, T. H. "Sirach," in *The Jerome Biblical Commentary,* ed. R. E. Brown et al. Englewood Cliffs, N.J.: Prentice-Hall, 1968. Vol. 1. Pp. 541–55.

Wellhausen, J. "Reis im Buch Sirach [39,13]." *ZDMG* 64 (1910): 258.

Wicks, H. J. *The Doctrine of God in the Jewish Apocryphal and Apocalyptic Literature.* Introd. by R. H. Charles. New York: Ktav, 1971 [reprint of 1915 ed.].

Wieder, A. A. "Ben Sira and the Praises of Wine [Sir 31,27–28]." *JQR* 61 (1970–71): 155–66.

Wilmart, A. "Nouveaux feuillets Toulousains de l'Ecclésiastique." *RBén* 33 (1921): 110–23.

Wilson, R. D. "Ecclesiasticus." *The Presbyterian and Reformed Review* 11 (1900): 480–506.

Winter, M. M. "The Origins of Ben Sira in Syriac (Part I)." *VT* 27 (1977): 237–53; (Part II), pp. 494–507.

Winter, P. "Ben Sira (33[36],7–15) and the Teaching of 'Two Ways.' " *VT* 5 (1955): 315–18.

———. "Lukanische Miszellen: I. Lc 1,17 und Ben Sira 48,10c Heb." *ZNW* 49 (1958): 65–66.

The Wisdom of the Apocrypha. The Wisdom of the East Series. Introd. by C. E. Lawrence. London: J. Murray, 1910.

Wlosiński, M. "Implikacje teologiczne Syr 17,1–14." *Ruch Biblijny i Liturgiczny* 34 (1981): 163–73.

Wood, J. *Wisdom Literature. Studies in Theology.* London: G. Duckworth, 1967.

Zeitlin, S. "The Ben Sira Scroll from Masada." *JQR* 56 (1965–66): 185–90.

Zenner, J. K. "Ecclesiasticus 38,24–39,10." *ZKT* 21 (1897): 567–74.

———. "Zwei Weisheitslieder [Sir 24; Bar 3,9–4,4]." *ZKT* 21 (1897): 551–58.

Ziegler, J. "Hat Lukian den griechischen Sirach rezensiert?" *Bib* 40 (1959): 210–29.

———. "Die hexaplarische Bearbeitung des griechischen Sirach." *BZ* N.F. 4 (1960): 174–85.

———. *Die Münchener griechische Sirach-Handschrift 493: Ihre textgeschichtliche Bedeutung und erstmalige Edition durch den Augsburger Humanisten David Hoeschel (1604).* Sitzungsberichte der Bayerische Akademie der Wissenschaften, Philosophisch-Historische Klasse. Munich, 1962, Heft 4.

———. "Ursprüngliche Lesarten im griechischen Sirach," in *Mélanges Eugène Tisserant,* 1. Studi e testi 231. Vatican: Biblioteca Apostolica Vaticana, 1964. Pp. 461–87.

———. "Die Vokabel-Varianten der *O*-Rezension im griechischen Sirach," in *Hebrew and Semitic Studies Presented to Godfrey Rolles Driver.* Ed. D. Winton Thomas. Oxford: Clarendon, 1963. Pp. 172–90.

———. "Zum Wortschatz des griechischen Sirach." *ZAW* 77 (1958): 274–87.

———. "Zwei Beiträge zu Sirach." *BZ* N.F. 8 (1964): 277–84.

Zöckler, O. *Die Apokryphen des Alten Testaments.* Kurzgefasster Kommentar zu den heiligen Schriften Alten und Neuen Testamentes sowie zu den Apokryphen. Munich: Beck, 1891. Pp. 255–354.

Zorell, F. "Canticum Ecclesiastici. (Sir. 36)." *VD* 7 (1927): 169–71.

C. CONCORDANCES, DICTIONARIES, GRAMMARS, AND LEXICA

Barber, E. A., ed. *Greek-English Lexicon, A Supplement* to Liddell and Scott. Oxford: Clarendon, 1968.

Barth, J. *Die Nominalbildung in den semitischen Sprachen.* 2d ed. Leipzig: Hinrichs, 1894.

Barthélemy, D., and O. Rickenbacher. *Konkordanz zum hebräischen Sirach.* Göttingen: Vandenhoeck & Ruprecht, 1973.

Bauer, H., and P. Leander. *Historische Grammatik der hebräischen Sprache des Alten Testaments.* Halle an d.S.: Niemeyer, 1922.

Bauer, J. B., ed. *Bibeltheologisches Wörterbuch.* 2 vols. 3d ed. Graz: Styria, 1967.

Bauer, W., F. W. Gingrich, and F. W. Danker. *A Greek-English Lexicon of the New Testament and Other Early Christian Literature.* 2d ed. Chicago: University of Chicago, 1979.

Ben-Yehuda, E. *Millôn hallāšôn haʿibrît hayyĕšānāh wĕhaḥădāšāh: Thesaurus totius hebraitatis et veteris et recentioris.* 16 vols., repr. in 8 vols. New York: Yoselof, 1960.

Blass, F., and A. Debrunner. *A Greek Grammar of the New Testament and Other Early Christian Literature.* Tr. R. W. Funk. Chicago: University of Chicago, 1961.

Brockelmann, C. *Grundriss der vergleichenden Grammatik der semitischen Sprachen.* 2 vols. Berlin: Reuther und Reichard, 1908, 1913.

———. *Hebräisches Syntax.* Neukirchen: Erziehungsverein, 1956.

———. *Lexicon syriacum.* 2d ed. Halle an d.S.: Niemeyer, 1928.

Brønno, E. *Studien über hebräische Morphologie und Vokalismus auf Grundlage der Mercatischen Fragmente der zweiten Kolumne der Hexapla des Origenes.* Leipzig: Brockhaus, 1943.

Brown, F., S. R. Driver, and C. A. Briggs. *A Hebrew and English Lexicon of the Old Testament.* Corrected impression. Oxford: Clarendon, 1952.

Buttrick, G. A., ed. *The Interpreter's Dictionary of the Bible.* 4 vols. Nashville: Abingdon, 1962. *Supplementary Volume.* Ed. K. Crim. 1976.

Cazelles, H., and A. Feuillet, eds. *Supplément au Dictionnaire de la Bible.* Paris: Letouzey et Ané, 1928– .

Concordance to the Apocrypha/Deuterocanonical Books of the Revised Standard Version. Foreword by B. M. Metzger. Grand Rapids: Eerdmans, 1983.

Fischer, B. *Novae concordantiae bibliorum sacrorum iuxta Vulgatam versionem critice editam.* 5 vols. Stuttgart/Bad Cannstatt: Frommann-Holzboog, 1977.

Gesenius, W., and E. Kautzsch. *Hebrew Grammar.* Tr. by A. E. Cowley. 2d ed. Oxford: Clarendon, 1910.

Grossman, R., and M. H. Segal. *Compendious Hebrew-English Dictionary.* Tel-Aviv: Dvir, 1956.

Hartdegen, S. J. *Nelson's Complete New American Bible Concordance.* Nashville: Nelson, 1977.

Hartman, L. F., ed. *Encyclopedic Dictionary of the Bible.* New York: McGraw-Hill, 1963.

Hatch, E., and H. A. Redpath, *A Concordance to the Septuagint and the Other Greek Versions of the Old Testament (Including the Apocryphal Books).* 2 vols. Oxford: Clarendon, 1897.

Jastrow, M. *A Dictionary of the Targumim, The Talmud Babli and Yerushalmi, and the Midrashic Literature.* 2 vols. Repr. New York: Pardes, 1950.

Jenni, E., and C. Westermann, eds. *Theologisches Handwörterbuch zum Alten Testament.* 2 vols. Munich: Kaiser, 1971, 1976.

Joüon, P. *Grammaire de l'hébreu biblique.* 2d ed. Rome: Biblical Institute, 1947.

Koehler, L., and W. Baumgartner. *Lexicon in veteris testamenti libros,* with *Supplementum.* Leiden: Brill, 1958.

Kuhn, K. G., ed. *Konkordanz zu den Qumrantexten.* Göttingen: Vandenhoeck und Ruprecht, 1960.

Lampe, G. W. H., ed. *A Patristic Greek Lexicon.* Oxford: Clarendon, 1961.

Léon-Dufour, X. *Dictionary of Biblical Theology.* 2d ed. rev. and enlarged. Tr. P. J. Cahill and E. M. Stewart. New York: Seabury, 1973.

Levy, J., and H. L. Fleischer. *Neuhebräisches und chaldäisches Wörterbuch über die Talmudim und Midraschim.* 4 vols. Leipzig: Brockhaus, 1876–89.

Liddell, H. G., R. Scott, H. S. Jones, and R. McKenzie. *A Greek-English Lexicon.* A new ed., revised and augmented throughout. Oxford: Clarendon, 1953.

McKenzie, J. L. *Dictionary of the Bible.* Milwaukee: Bruce, 1965.

Mandelkern, S. *Veteris Testamenti concordantiae hebraicae atque chaldaicae.* 5th ed., with Addenda by F. Margolin and M. Gottstein. Jerusalem: Schocken, 1962.

Meyer, R. *Hebräische Grammatik.* 4 vols. Berlin: de Gruyter, 1966–72.

Moulton, W. F., and A. S. Geden. *A Concordance to the Greek Testament according to the Texts of Westcott and Hort, Tischendorf and the English Revisers.* 5th ed., rev. H. K. Moulton, with a supplement. Edinburgh: Clark, 1978.

Nöldeke, T. *Compendious Syriac Grammar.* Tr. from the 2d and improved German ed. by J. A. Crichton. London: Williams & Norgate, 1904.

―――. *Kurzgefasste syrische Grammatik.* 2d and improved ed. Leipzig: C. H. Tauchnitz, 1898.

Payne Smith, J. *A Compendious Syriac Dictionary.* Oxford: Clarendon, 1903.

Payne Smith, R., et al., eds. *Thesaurus syriacus.* 2 vols. Oxford: Clarendon, 1879, 1901.

Redpath, H. A. *Supplement* to *A Concordance to the Septuagint,* ed. by E. Hatch and H. A. Redpath. Oxford: Clarendon, 1906.

Reicke, B., and L. Rost, eds. *Biblisch-historisches Handwörterbuch.* 4 vols. Göttingen: Vandenhoeck & Ruprecht, 1962–79.

Rosenthal, F. *A Grammar of Biblical Aramaic.* Porta linguarum orientalium n.s. 5. Wiesbaden: Harrassowitz, 1961.

Schleusner, J. F. *Novus thesaurus philologico-criticus: sive, Lexicon in LXX. et reliquos interpretes graecos ac scriptores apocryphos Veteris Testamenti.* 3 vols. London: Duncan, 1829.

Segal, M. H. *A Grammar of Mishnaic Hebrew.* Oxford: Clarendon, 1958.

Smend, R. *Griechisch-syrisch-hebräischer Index zur Weisheit des Jesus Sirach.* Berlin: Reimer, 1907.

Smyth, H. W. *Greek Grammar.* Rev. G. M. Messing. Cambridge, Mass.: Harvard University, 1956.

Thackeray, H. St. J. *A Grammar of the Old Testament in Greek according to the Septuagint.* Cambridge: Cambridge University, 1909.

Vogt, E. *Lexicon linguae aramaicae Veteris Testamenti.* Rome: Biblical Institute, 1971.

Winter, M. M. *A Concordance to the Peshiṭta Version of Ben Sira.* Monographs of the Peshiṭta Institute, 2. Leiden: Brill, 1976.

Zorell, F. *Lexicon hebraicum Veteris Testamenti.* Ed. L. Semkowski. Completed by P. Boccaccio. Rome: Biblical Institute, 1984.

D. WISDOM ELSEWHERE IN THE OLD TESTAMENT AND ANCIENT NEAR EAST AND OTHER PROVERBIAL LITERATURE

Aletti, J. N. "Séduction et parole en Proverbes I–IX." *VT* 27 (1977): 129–44.

Bartlett, J. *Familiar Quotations: A Collection of Passages, Phrases and Proverbs Traced to Their Sources in Ancient and Modern Literature.* 15th ed. Rev. and enlarged by E. M. Beck et al. Boston: Little, Brown, 1980.

Beaucamp, E. *Man's Destiny in the Books of Wisdom.* Tr. J. Clarke. Staten Island, N.Y.: Alba House, 1970.

————. *Les sages d'Israël ou le fruit d'une fidélité.* Quebec: l'Université Laval, 1968.

Bergant, D. *What Are They Saying about Wisdom Literature?* New York: Paulist, 1984.

Bissing, F. W. F. von, ed. and tr. *Altägyptische Lebensweisheit.* Zurich: Artemis, 1955. *Phibis, Papyrus Insinger,* pp. 91–120.

Blank, S. H. "Wisdom." *IDB* 4. Nashville: Abingdon, 1962. Pp. 852–61.

Blenkinsopp, J. *Wisdom and Law in the Old Testament: The Ordering of Life in Israel and Early Judaism.* The Oxford Bible Series. Oxford: Oxford University, 1983.

Brown, J. P. "Proverb-Book, Gold Economy, Alphabet." *JBL* 100 (1981): 169–91.

Brueggemann, W. "Scripture and an Ecumenical Life-Style: A Study in Wisdom Theology." *Int* 24 (1970): 3–19.

Bryce, G. E. *A Legacy of Wisdom: The Egyptian Contribution to the Wisdom of Israel.* Lewisburg/London: Bucknell University/Associated University, 1979.

Cohen, J. M. and M. J., eds. *The Penguin Dictionary of Quotations.* Baltimore: Penguin Books, 1960.

Cox, D. "Fear or Conscience? *yirʾat yhwh* in Proverbs 1–9," in *Studia Hierosolymitana* 3. Ed. G. C. Bottini. Studium Biblicum Franciscanum, Collectio Major 30. Jerusalem: Franciscan Printing Press, 1982. Pp. 83–90.

Dictionary of Quotations. Collected and arranged and with comments by B. Evans. New York: Delacorte, 1968.

Di Lella, A. A. "An Existential Interpretation of Job." *BTB* 15 (1985): 49–55.

Drubbel, A. "Le Conflit entre la Sagesse profane et la Sagesse religieuse." *Bib* 17 (1936): 45–70; 407–28.

Dubarle, A.-M. "Où en est l'étude de la littérature sapientielle?" *ETL* 44 (1968): 407–19.

Eakin, F. E. "Wisdom, Creation and Covenant." *PRS* 4 (1977): 225–40.

Eichrodt, W. *Theology of the Old Testament.* OTL. 2 vols. Philadelphia: Westminster, 1961, 1967.

Fensham, F. C. "Widow, Orphan and the Poor in Ancient Near Eastern Legal and Wisdom Literature." *JNES* 21 (1962): 129–39.

Fontaine, C. "Proverb Performance in the Hebrew Bible." *JSOT* 32 (1985): 87–103.

Fox, M. V. "Aspects of the Religion of the Book of Proverbs." *HUCA* 39 (1968): 55–69.

Gammie, J. G., et al., eds. *Israelite Wisdom: Theological and Literary Essays in Honor of Samuel Terrien.* Missoula, Mont.: Scholars, 1978.

Gemser, B. "The Spiritual Structure of Biblical Aphoristic Wisdom," in *Studies in Ancient Israelite Wisdom.* Ed. J. L. Crenshaw. New York: Ktav, 1976. Pp. 208–19.

Goldstein, J. *Les Sentiers de la sagesse.* Paris: Source, 1967.

Gordis, R. *Koheleth—the Man and His World: A Study of Ecclesiastes.* 3d ed. New York: Schocken, 1968.

———. "The Social Background of Wisdom Literature." *HUCA* 18 (1943–44): 77–118.

Hermisson, H.-J. *Studien zur israelitischen Spruch-Weisheit.* WMANT 28. Neukirchen-Vlyun: Neukirchener Verlag, 1968.

Humbert, P. *Recherches sur les sources égyptiennes de la littérature sapientiale d'Israël.* Mémoires de l'Université de Neuchatel 7. Neuchatel: Secrétariat de l'Université, 1929.

Imschoot, P. van. "Sagesse et esprit dans l'Ancien Testament." *RB* 47 (1938): 23–49.

International Thesaurus of Quotations. Compiled by R. T. Tripp. New York: Thomas Y. Crowell, 1970.

Jansen, H. L. *Die spätjüdische Psalmendichtung, ihr Enstehungskreis und ihr "Sitz im Leben."* Oslo: J. Dybwad, 1937.

Khanjian, J. *Wisdom in Ugarit and in the Ancient Near East with Particular Emphasis on Old Testament Wisdom Literature.* Ann Arbor: University Microfilms International, 1978.

Lambert, W. G. *Babylonian Wisdom Literature.* Oxford: Clarendon, 1960.

Lang, B. *Frau Weisheit: Deutung einer biblischen Gestalt.* Düsseldorf: Patmos, 1975.

———. *Die weisheitliche Lehrrede.* SBS 54. Stuttgart: KBW Verlag, 1972.

Mack, B. L. *Logos und Sophia: Untersuchungen zur Weisheitstheologie im hellenistischen Judentum.* SUNT 10. Göttingen: Vandenhoeck und Ruprecht, 1973.

———. "Wisdom Myth and Mytho-logy: An Essay in Understanding a Theological Tradition." *Int* 24 (1970): 46–60.

McKane, W. *Proverbs: A New Approach.* OTL. Philadelphia: Westminster, 1970.

Marx, A. "An Aramaic Fragment of the Wisdom of Solomon." *JBL* 40 (1921): 57–69.

Morgan, D. F. *Wisdom in Old Testament Traditions.* Atlanta: John Knox, 1981.

Murphy, R. E. "The Faces of Wisdom in the Book of Proverbs," in *Mélanges bibliques et orientaux en l'honneur de M. Henri Cazelles.* Ed. A. Caquot and M. Delcor. AOAT 212. Kevelaer: Butzon & Bercker, 1981. Pp. 337–45.

———. *The Forms of the Old Testament Literature.* Vol. 13: *Wisdom Literature: Job, Proverbs, Ruth, Canticles, Ecclesiastes, Esther.* Ed. R. Knierim and G. M. Tucker. Grand Rapids: Eerdmans, 1981.

Noth, M., and D. W. Thomas, eds. *Wisdom in Israel and in the Ancient Near East.* VTSup 3. Leiden: Brill, 1955.

Oxford Dictionary of English Proverbs. 3d ed. rev. by F. P. Wilson with an Introduction by J. Wilson. Oxford: Clarendon, 1970.

Oxford Dictionary of Quotations. 3d ed., reprinted with corrections. New York: Oxford University, 1980.

Perdue, L. G. *Wisdom and Cult: A Critical Analysis of the Views of Cult in the Wisdom Literatures of Israel and the Ancient Near East.* SBLDS 30. Missoula, Mont.: Scholars, 1977.

Pinkuss, H. "Die syrische Uebersetzung der Proverbien." *ZAW* 14 (1894): 65–141; 161–222.

Rad, G. von. "Job XXXVIII and Ancient Egyptian Wisdom," in *The Problem of the Hexateuch and Other Essays.* Tr. E. W. Trueman Dicken. New York: McGraw-Hill, 1966. Pp. 281–91.

———. *Old Testament Theology.* 2 vols. New York: Harper & Row, 1962, 1965.

Richter, W. *Recht und Ethos: Versuch einer Ortung des weisheitlichen Mahnspruches.* SUNT 15. Munich: Kösel, 1966.

Roth, W. M. W. *Numerical Sayings in the Old Testament.* VTSup 13. Leiden: Brill, 1965.

———. "The Numerical Sequences X/X+1 in the Old Testament." *VT* 12 (1962): 300–11.

Rylaarsdam, J. C. *Revelation in Jewish Wisdom Literature.* Chicago: University of Chicago, 1946.

Sauer, G. *Die Sprüche Agurs.* BWANT 4/4. Stuttgart: Kohlhammer, 1963.

Schmid, H. H. *Wesen und Geschichte der Weisheit.* BZAW 101. Berlin: Töpelmann, 1966.

Scott, R. B. Y. "Folk Proverbs of the Ancient Near East," in *Studies in Ancient Israelite Wisdom.* Ed. J. L. Crenshaw. New York: Ktav, 1976. Pp. 417–26.

Sheppard, G. T. "The Epilogue to Qoheleth as Theological Commentary." *CBQ* 39 (1977): 182–89.

———. *Wisdom as a Hermeneutical Construct: A Study in the Sapientializing of the Old Testament.* BZAW 151. Berlin/New York: de Gruyter, 1980.

Theognis. *Elegy and Iambus . . . with the Anacreontea,* 1. LCL. Ed. and trans. J. M. Edmonds. Cambridge, Mass.: Harvard University, 1968.

Thompson, J. M. *The Form and Function of Proverbs in Ancient Israel.* The Hague: Mouton, 1974.

Towner, W. S. "The Renewed Authority of Old Testament Wisdom for Contemporary

Faith," in *Canon and Authority*. Ed. G. W. Coats and B. O. Long. Philadelphia: Fortress, 1977. Pp. 132–47.

Westermann, C. *Elements of Old Testament Theology*. Atlanta: John Knox, 1982.

Whybray, R. N. *The Intellectual Tradition in the Old Testament*. BZAW 135. Berlin: de Gruyter, 1974.

———. *Wisdom in Proverbs: The Concept of Wisdom in Proverbs 1–9*. SBT 45. Naperville, Ill.: Allenson, 1965.

Williams, J. G. "The Power of Form: A Study of Biblical Proverbs." *Semeia* 17 (1980): 35–58.

———. *Those Who Ponder Proverbs: Aphoristic Thinking and Biblical Literature*. Sheffield, England: Almond, 1981.

Williams, R. J. "Wisdom in the Ancient Near East." *IDBSup*. Nashville: Abingdon, 1976. Pp. 949–52.

Zimmerli, W. *Old Testament Theology in Outline*. Atlanta: John Knox, 1978.

———. "The Place and Limit of the Wisdom in the Framework of the Old Testament Theology." *SJT* 17 (1964): 146–58.

E. QUMRAN, TEXTUAL CRITICISM, AND OTHER PERTINENT WORKS

Albrektson, B. "Difficilior lectio probabilior: A Rule of Textual Criticism and Its Use in Old Testament Studies." *OTS* 21 (1981): 5–18.

Audet, J.-P. *La Didachè: Instructions des Apôtres*. EBib. Paris: Gabalda, 1958.

Bacher, W. "Qirqisāni, the Karaite, and His Work on Jewish Sects." *JQR* 7 (1894–95): 687–710.

Baillet, M. "Fragments du Document de Damas, Qumrân, Grotte 6." *RB* 63 (1956): 513–23.

———. "Le Travail d'édition des fragments manuscrits de Qumrân. Communication de M. Baillet." *RB* 63 (1956): 54–55.

Barthélemy, D. "Notes en marge de publications récentes sur les manuscrits de Qumrân." *RB* 59 (1952): 187–218.

———, and J. T. Milik. *Qumran Cave I*. DJD 1. Oxford: Clarendon, 1955.

Bentzen, A. *Introduction to the Old Testament*. 2 vols. 2d ed. Copenhagen: Gad, 1952.

Berger, P. L. *The Sacred Canopy: Elements of a Sociology of Religion*. Garden City, N.Y.: Doubleday/Anchor, 1969.

———, and T. Luckmann. *The Social Construction of Reality: A Treatise in the Sociology of Knowledge*. Garden City, N.Y.: Doubleday/Anchor, 1967.

Bidawid, R. S. *Les Lettres du Patriarche nestorien, Timothée I*. Studi e Testi 187. Vatican City: Biblioteca Apostolica Vaticana, 1956.

Bloch, J. "The Printed Texts of the Peshitta Old Testament." *AJSL* 37 (1920–21): 136–44.

Braun, O. "Ein Brief des Katholikos Timotheos I über biblische Studien des 9 Jahrhunderts." *Oriens Christianus* 1 (1901): 299–313.

———. "Der Katholikos Timotheos I und seine Briefe." *Oriens Christianus* 1 (1901): 138–52.

Brock, S. P., C. T. Fritsch, and S. Jellicoe. *A Classified Bibliography of the Septuagint*. ALGHJ 6. Leiden: Brill, 1973.

Brown, R. E. "The Messianism of Qumrân." *CBQ* 19 (1957): 53–82.

Burrows, M. *The Dead Sea Scrolls.* New York: Viking, 1955.

————. *"Waw* and *Yodh* in the Isaiah Dead Sea Scroll (DSIa)." *BASOR* 124 (1951): 18–20.

Charles, R. H. "Fragment of a Zadokite Work," in *APOT* 2. Ed. R. H. Charles. Oxford: Clarendon, 1913. Pp. 785–834.

Cowley, A. E., and R. H. Charles. "An Early Source of the Testaments of the Patriarchs." *JQR* 19 (1906–7): 566–83.

Cross, F. M. *The Ancient Library of Qumran and Modern Biblical Studies.* Rev. ed. Garden City, N.Y.: Doubleday/Anchor, 1961.

————. "The Development of the Jewish Scripts," in *The Bible and the Ancient Near East.* Essays in honor of William Foxwell Albright. Ed. by G. E. Wright. Garden City, N.Y.: Doubleday, 1961.

————, and S. Talmon, eds. *Qumran and the History of the Biblical Text.* Cambridge, Mass.: Harvard University, 1975.

Davies, P. R. *The Damascus Covenant: An Interpretation of the "Damascus Document."* JSOTSup 25. Sheffield, England: *JSOT,* 1983.

Devreesse, R. *Introduction à l'étude des manuscrits grecs.* Paris: Klinksieck, 1954.

Di Lella, A. A. "Daniel 4:7–14: Poetic Analysis and Biblical Background," in *Mélanges bibliques et orientaux en l'honneur de M. Henri Cazelles.* Ed. A. Caquot and M. Delcor. AOAT 212. Kevelaer: Butzon & Bercker, 1981. Pp. 247–58.

————. "Patrick William Skehan: A Tribute." *CBQ* 42 (1980): 435–37.

Driver, G. R. "New Hebrew Manuscripts." *JQR* n.s. 40 (1949–50): 359–72.

Eissfeldt, O. "Der gegenwärtige Stand der Erforschung der in Palästina neu gefundenen hebräischen Handschriften." *TLZ* 74 (1949): 595–600.

————. *The Old Testament: An Introduction.* Tr. P. R. Ackroyd. Oxford: Blackwell, 1965.

Elliger, K., and W. Rudolph, eds. *Biblia hebraica stuttgartensia.* Stuttgart: Deutsche Bibelgesellschaft, 1977.

Filson, F. V. "Some Recent Study of the Dead Sea Scrolls." *BA* 13 (1950): 96–99.

Fitzmyer, J. A. *The Dead Sea Scrolls: Major Publications and Tools.* Missoula, Mont.: Scholars, 1977.

Frankl, V. E. *Man's Search for Meaning: An Introduction to Logotherapy.* New York: Washington Square Press, 1963.

Gardthausen, V. E. *Griechische Palaeographie,* 2 Band: *Die Schrift, Unterschriften und Chronologie im Altertum und im byzantinischen Mittelalter.* 2d ed. Leipzig: Veit, 1913.

Gaster, T. H. *The Dead Sea Scriptures.* 3d ed. rev. and enlarged. Garden City, N.Y.: Doubleday, 1976.

Goshen-Gottstein, M. H. "The Textual Criticism of the Old Testament: Rise, Decline, Rebirth." *JBL* 102 (1983): 365–99.

Gottwald, N. K. *The Hebrew Bible—A Socio-Literary Introduction.* Philadelphia: Fortress, 1985.

Greenberg, M. "The Stabilization of the Text of the Hebrew Bible, Reviewed in the Light of the Biblical Materials from the Judean Desert." *JAOS* 76 (1956): 157–67.

————. "The Use of the Ancient Versions for Interpreting the Hebrew Text." VTSup 29 (1978): 130–48.

Grelot, P. "Notes sur le Testament araméen de Lévi." RB 63 (1956): 391–406.

Gribomont, J. "Latin Versions," IDBSup. Nashville: Abingdon, 1976. Pp. 527–32.

Harkavy, A. de. "Karaites," The Jewish Encyclopedia 7 (1904): 438–46.

Hartman, L. F., and A. A. Di Lella. The Book of Daniel. AB 23. Garden City, N.Y.: Doubleday, 1978.

Jellicoe, S. The Septuagint and Modern Study. Oxford: Clarendon, 1968.

Jonge, M. de. Testamenta XII patriarcharum. Leiden: Brill, 1964.

————, ed. Studies on the Testaments of the Twelve Patriarchs: Text and Interpretation. Studia in Veteris Testamenti Pseudepigrapha 3. Leiden: Brill, 1975.

Kaestli, J.-D., and O. Wermelinger, eds. Le Canon de l'Ancien Testament. Geneva: Labor et Fides, 1984.

Kahle, P. E. "The Age of the Scrolls." VT 1 (1951): 38–48.

————. The Cairo Geniza. 2d ed. Oxford: Blackwell, 1959.

Kenyon, F. Our Bible and the Ancient Manuscripts. Rev. by A. W. Adams. 5th ed. New York: Harper, 1958.

Kraft, R. A., ed. Septuagintal Lexicography. Missoula, Mont.: Scholars, 1975.

Lambert, G. "Les Manuscrits du désert de Juda: IV. Tient-on un nouveau chapitre de l'histoire de la grotte?" NRT 72 (1950): 199–202.

Lohfink, N. "Über die Irrtumslosigkeit und die Einheit der Schrift." Stimmen der Zeit 174 (1963–64): 161–81 (English summary in TD 13 [1965]: 185–92).

Mansoor, M. The Thanksgiving Hymns. Grand Rapids: Eerdmans, 1961.

Marchal, L. "Esséniens." DBSup 2. Paris: Letouzey et Ané, 1934. Cols. 1109–32.

Milik, J. T. Ten Years of Discovery in the Wilderness of Judaea. SBT 26. Tr. J. Strugnell. Naperville, Ill.: Allenson, 1959.

————. "Le Testament de Lévi en araméen." RB 62 (1955): 398–406.

Murphy, R. E. "Yēṣer in the Qumran Literature." Bib 39 (1958): 334–44.

Murphy-O'Connor, J. "The Essenes in Palestine." BA 40 (1977): 100–24.

Newman, A. A. "Saadia and His Relation to Palestine." JQR n.s. 33 (1942–43): 109–32.

Orlinsky, H. M. "The Septuagint as Holy Writ and the Philosophy of the Translators." HUCA 46 (1975): 89–114.

Pass, H. L., and J. Arendzen. "Fragment of an Aramaic Text of the Testament of Levi." JQR 12 (1899–1900): 651–61.

Paul, A. Écrits de Qumran et sectes juives aux premiers siècles de l'Islam. Recherches sur l'origine du qaraïsme. Paris: Letouzey et Ané, 1969.

Poznanski, S. "Philon dans l'ancienne littérature judéo-arabe." REJ 50 (1905): 10–31.

Pritchard, J. B. Ancient Near Eastern Texts Relating to the Old Testament. 3d ed. Princeton: Princeton University, 1969.

Rabin, C. "The Translation Process and the Character of the Septuagint." Textus 6 (1968): 1–26.

————. The Zadokite Documents: I. The Admonition. II. The Laws. 2d rev. ed. Oxford: Clarendon, 1958.

Ratzaby, Y. "Remarks concerning the Distinction between Waw and Yodh in the Habakkuk Scroll." JQR n.s. 41 (1950–51): 155–57.

Ridout, R., and C. Whitting. *English Proverbs Explained.* New York: Barnes and Noble, 1968.

Rowley, H. H. *The Zadokite Fragments and the Dead Sea Scrolls.* Oxford: Blackwell, 1952.

Schechter, S. *Fragments of a Zadokite Work.* Documents of Jewish Sectaries 1. Cambridge: Cambridge University, 1910. Reprinted with a Prolegomenon by J. A. Fitzmyer. New York: Ktav, 1970.

Siebeneck, R. T. "The Messianism of Aggeus and Proto-Zacharias." *CBQ* 19 (1957): 312–28.

Skehan, P. W. "The Biblical Scrolls from Qumran and the Text of the Old Testament." *BA* 28 (1965): 87–100.

————. "Communication: Professor Zeitlin and the Dead Sea Scrolls." *CBQ* 20 (1958): 228–29.

————. "Exodus in the Samaritan Recension from Qumran." *JBL* 74 (1955): 182–87.

————. "Gleanings from Psalm Texts from Qumran," in *Mélanges bibliques et orientaux en l'honneur de M. Henri Cazelles.* Ed. A. Caquot and M. Delcor. AOAT 212. Kevelaer: Butzon & Bercker, 1981. Pp. 439–52.

————. "The Period of the Biblical Texts from Khirbet Qumran." *CBQ* 19 (1957): 435–40.

————. "Qumran and Old Testament Criticism: The Structure of the Psalter at Qumran," in *Qumrân: sa piété, sa théologie et son milieu.* Ed. M. Delcor. BETL 46. Paris/Gembloux: Duculot, 1978. Pp. 163–82.

————. "Qumran and the Present State of Old Testament Text Studies: The Masoretic Text." *JBL* 78 (1959): 21–25.

————. "The Qumran Manuscripts and Textual Criticism." VTSup 4 (1957): 148–60.

Snijders, L. A. "The Meaning of *zar* in the Old Testament." *OTS* 10 (1954): 1–154.

Sundberg, A. C., Jr. "The Bible Canon and the Christian Doctrine of Inspiration." *Int* 29 (1975): 352–71.

————. "The Old Testament of the Early Church." *HTR* 51 (1958): 205–26.

————. *The Old Testament of the Early Church.* HTS 20. Cambridge, Mass.: Harvard University, 1964.

————. "The Protestant Old Testament Canon: Should It Be Re-examined?" *CBQ* 28 (1966): 194–203.

Talmon, S. "The Transmission of the Bible in Light of the Qumran Manuscripts." *Textus* 4 (1964): 93–132.

Teicher, J. L. "The Dead Sea Scrolls—Documents of the Jewish-Christian Sect of Ebionites." *JJS* 2 (1951): 67–99.

Tov, E. "The Criteria for Evaluating Textual Readings: The Limitations of Textual Rules." *HTR* 75 (1982): 429–48.

————. "A Modern Textual Outlook Based on the Qumran Scrolls." *HUCA* 53 (1982): 11–27.

————. "The Nature and Background of Harmonizations in Biblical Manuscripts." *JSOT* 31 (1985): 3–29.

————. "The Nature of the Hebrew Text Underlying the LXX: A Survey of the Problems." *JSOT* 7 (1978): 53–68.

————. *The Text-Critical Use of the Septuagint in Biblical Research.* Jerusalem Biblical Studies 3. Jerusalem: Simor, 1981.

————. "The Use of Concordances in the Reconstruction of the *Vorlage* of the LXX." *CBQ* 40 (1978): 29–36.

————, and R. A. Kraft. "Septuagint." *IDBSup.* Nashville: Abingdon, 1976. Pp. 807–15.

Ulrich, E. "Horizons of Old Testament Research at the Thirtieth Anniversary of Qumran Cave 4." *CBQ* 46 (1984): 613–36.

Van Puyvelde, C. "Manuscrits bibliques. I. Manuscrits hébreux. Les manuscrits de la geniza du Caire," *DBSup* 5. Paris: Letouzey et Ané, 1957. Cols. 798–800.

Vaux, R. de. "A propos des manuscrits de la Mer Morte." *RB* 57 (1950): 417–29.

————. "Exploration de la région de Qumrân." *RB* 60 (1953): 540–61.

Vermes, G. *The Dead Sea Scrolls: Qumran in Perspective.* Cleveland: Collins & World, 1978.

Vööbus, A. "Syriac Versions." *IDBSup.* Nashville: Abingdon, 1976. Pp. 848–54.

Waldow, H. E. von. "Social Responsibility and Social Structure in Early Israel." *CBQ* 32 (1970): 182–204.

Walters, P. (formerly Katz). *The Text of the Septuagint.* Ed. posthumously by D. W. Gooding. Cambridge: Cambridge University, 1973.

Westermann, C. *Praise and Lament in the Psalms.* Tr. K. R. Crim and R. N. Soulen. Atlanta: John Knox, 1981.

Wolff, H. W. *Anthropology of the Old Testament.* Tr. M. Kohl. Philadelphia: Fortress, 1974.

Zeitlin, S. *The Zadokite Fragments. Facsimile of the Manuscripts in the Cairo Genizah Collection in the Possession of the University Library, Cambridge, England.* JQRMS 1. Philadelphia: Dropsie College, 1952.

F. HISTORIES OF THE PERIOD

Abel, F.-M. *Histoire de la Palestine depuis la conquête d'Alexandre jusqu' à l'invasion arabe.* EBib. 2d ed. 2 vols. Paris: Gabalda, 1952.

Ackroyd, P. R., and C. F. Evans, eds. *The Cambridge History of the Bible.* Vol. 1: *From the Beginnings to Jerome.* New York: Cambridge University, 1970.

Baron, S. W. *A Social and Religious History of the Jews.* 8 vols. 2d ed. New York: Columbia University, 1952–60.

Ben-Sasson, H. H., ed. *A History of the Jewish People.* Cambridge, Mass.: Harvard University, 1976.

Bright, J. *A History of Israel.* 3d ed. Philadelphia: Westminster, 1981.

Hengel, M. *Judaism and Hellenism: Studies in Their Encounter in Palestine during the Early Hellenistic Period.* 2 vols. Tr. J. Bowden. Philadelphia: Fortress, 1974.

Josephus. *Jewish Antiquities* ix–xi and xii–xiv. LCL, *Josephus,* 6–7. Tr. R. Marcus. Cambridge, Mass.: Harvard University, 1958, 1961.

Lagrange, M.-J. *Le Judaïsme avant Jésus-Christ.* 2d ed. EBib. Paris: Gabalda, 1931.

Mann, J. *Texts and Studies in Jewish History and Literature.* Vol. 2: *Karaitica:* Philadelphia, 1935. Repr., New York: Ktav, 1972.

Moore, G. F. *Judaism in the First Centuries of the Christian Era.* 3 vols. Cambridge, Mass.: Harvard University, 1927–30.

Murphy-O'Connor, J. "The Essenes and Their History." *RB* 81 (1974): 215–44.

Nemoy, L. "Al-Qirqisānī's Account of the Jewish Sects and Christianity." *HUCA* 7 (1930): 317–97.

Rostovtzeff, M. I. *The Social and Economic History of the Hellenistic World.* 3 vols. 2d ed. Oxford: Clarendon, 1952.

Schlatter, A. *Geschichte Israels von Alexander dem Grossen bis Hadrian.* 3d ed. Stuttgart: Calwer, 1925.

Schürer, E. *Geschichte des jüdischen Volkes im Zeitalter Jesu Christi,* 3. 4th ed. Leipzig: Hinrichs, 1909.

———. *The History of the Jewish People in the Age of Jesus Christ (175* B.C.–A.D. *135).* Vol. 1. Rev. and ed. G. Vermes and F. Millar. Edinburgh: T. & T. Clark, 1973.

Tcherikover, V. *Hellenistic Civilization and the Jews.* Tr. S. Applebaum. Philadelphia: Jewish Publication Society of America, 1959.

Translation
Notes and Commentary

FOREWORD

[1]Many notable truths have been given us through the Law, the Prophets, and the later authors; and for these the instruction and wisdom of Israel merit praise. [2]Now, those who are familiar with these truths must not only themselves understand them; they must also, as lovers of wisdom, be able in speech and in writing to help those who are without them. [3]And so my grandfather Jesus, who had devoted himself for a long time to the study of the Law, the Prophets, and the other books of our ancestors, and developed a thorough familiarity with them, was prompted to write something himself in the nature of instruction and wisdom. [4]This he did so that those who love wisdom might, by acquainting themselves with what he too had written, make even greater progress, living in conformity with the Divine Law.

[5]You therefore are now invited to read it in a spirit of attentive goodwill, with indulgence for any apparent failure on our part, despite earnest efforts, in the interpretation of particular passages. [6]For what was said originally in Hebrew is not equally effective when translated into another language. [7]That is true not only of this book; the Law itself, the Prophets, and the rest of the books differ no little when they are read in the original.

[8]I arrived in Egypt in the thirty-eighth year of the reign of King Euergetes, and during my stay I came across the reproduction of[a] a good deal that is instructive. [9]I therefore considered myself in duty bound to devote some diligence and industry to the translation of this book. [10]Many sleepless hours of close application have I devoted in the interval to finishing the book for publication, for the benefit of those living abroad who wish to acquire wisdom and are disposed to live their lives according to the standards of the Law.

[a] A less well-attested reading would yield simply "I had access to."

Comment

The grandson's *prologos* (the Gr word from which the English word "prologue" is derived) resembles the classical historical prefaces written by Herodotus, Thucydides, and Polybius, and the prefaces of works on various subjects written by authors of the Hellenistic period, such as Dioscorides Pedanius (*De materia medica,* 1.1), Hippocrates (*De prisca medicina*), Aristeas (*Ep. ad Philocrates,* §1), and Josephus (*Against Apion,* 1.1 §§1–3; 2.1 §1). This prologue may be compared also to the prologue to Luke's Gospel, 1:1–4; cf. J. A. Fitzmyer, *The Gospel according to Luke* (I–XI) (AB 28A; Garden City, N.Y.: Doubleday, 1981), pp. 287–90. Ben Sira's grandson wrote the prologue in carefully crafted prose, employing the grammar and syntax of literary *koinē* Greek; he must have had a first-rate education in the rhetoric and literature of the period. Though the English translation given here has ten sentences, the grandson's Gr text has three fairly elegant periodic sentences; these three sentences correspond to the three paragraphs into which the English translation is divided. The quality of Greek in the prologue differs markedly from the kind of Greek the grandson uses in order to render accurately the Heb text of Ben Sira. The grandson usually translated quite literally, even on occasion utilizing Semitisms; thus he preserved as much as possible of the sense and flavor of the original Hebrew.

The Prologue, or Foreword, is found in all the great uncials and in most of the cursive MSS, including those of GII. It is also present in Lat and most of the daughter translations of G. But it is missing in Codex 248, one of the most famous of the GII MSS, and in a few other cursives, as well as the Ethiopic and Armenian, also daughter translations of G. Because Syr was translated from the Heb text, it, too, lacks the Prologue.

To facilitate reference I numbered each of the English sentences. The Prologue may be divided, in terms of its contents, into three paragraphs (see above): (1) the reasons why Ben Sira composed his book; (2) an invitation for the reader to study the book with indulgence for any failure of the grandson to render the Heb original effectively; and (3) the grandson's autobiographical note about his arrival in Egypt and his hours of tedious labor to produce the translation of his grandfather's book.

In no. 1, the "many notable truths," lit., "many and great things," are what God in his love and mercy has vouchsafed to Israel "through the Law, the Prophets, and the later authors," i.e., through the Sacred Scriptures, which are inspired by God. Here for the first time mention is made of the threefold division of the OT: the Law, Heb *tôrâ*, the Prophets, Heb *nĕbî'îm*, and "the later authors," or "the other books of our ancestors" (no. 3), or "the rest of the books" (no. 7). The third division, referred to in a somewhat general way by the grandson, came to be known later as the Writings, Heb *kĕtûbîm*. The Jews today still use these three divisions, calling the OT as a whole *Tanak*, an acronym formed from the initial Heb letter of the name for each division. This tripartite division is also found in Luke 24:44: ". . . the law of Moses and the prophets and the psalms . . ."—the only explicit mention in the NT. The grandson uses the expression "later authors" (lit., "the others who followed after them") to imply that these wrote after the prophets. The "instruction" (Gr *paideia*=Heb *mûsār*), or "discipline," is what enables one to possess "wisdom" (Gr *sophia*=Heb *hokmâ*), which in the thought of Ben Sira means fear of the Lord which equals keeping the Law; cf. COMMENT on 1:11–30; 6:32–37; 15:1; 19:20; 21:6; 23:27; 24:23–29. Because such "instruction" and "wisdom" (the two words occur together also in no. 3) have been given to the Jews through "the Law, the Prophets, and the later authors," Israel merits praise. Cf. Deut 4:6, 8. The grandson makes this remark for the benefit of his fellow Jews living in the Hellenized cities of Egypt. He says, in effect, that they can glory in their literary heritage as the Greeks do in theirs. Hence Jews need not feel culturally inferior to the Greeks.

In no. 2, the expression "those who are familiar with these truths" (Gr *tous anaginōskotas*, lit., "the readers") refers to the learned, the scribes, who can read the Scriptures in the original languages; cf. Ezra 7:11 and Neh 8:1, 4. Such persons must themselves first understand these truths, and then, "as lovers of wisdom" (lit., "lovers of learning"), help others "in speech and in writing"—cf. Neh 8:8–12. The expression "those who are without them" refers to the laity, or those who cannot read the original Scriptures without help. The scribes instructed the people primarily "in speech," or orally. The phrase "in writing" is noteworthy; it refers to such works as The Wisdom of Ben Sira and others of a similar nature, e.g., the Book of Tobit and perhaps even noncanonical works such as the Sayings of Ahiqar, a popular Wisdom book at the time. In no. 3, the grandson states that his grandfather Jesus was such a scribe, "who had devoted himself for a long time to the study [lit., reading] of" the Sacred Scriptures. Because Jesus Ben Sira had become thoroughly familiar with the Scriptures, he "was prompted to write something himself in the nature of *instruction and wisdom*" (the same phrase as in no. 1). He wrote in Hebrew for Palestinian Jews, "those who love *wisdom*" (lit., *learning*, cf. no. 2), so that they too "might . . . make even greater progress, living in conformity with the Divine Law" (no. 4)—the purpose of any reading and study of Scripture. Cf. 8:8–9; Prov 9:9–10.

In no. 5, the "you" are Jews in the Diaspora of Egypt where the grandson lived at the time he made his translation. He invites these Jews to read his grandfather's book in Greek, begging "indulgence for any apparent failure" on his part to render "particular passages" of the Heb original with true fidelity. In no. 6, the grandson articulates the anguish of translators throughout history: how to render one language into another in an idiomatic and accurate way and to capture at least some of the elegance of the original. Translation of poetry, which his grandfather's book is, is even more difficult. "A translation is no translation . . . unless it will give you the music of a poem along with the words of it" (John M. Synge, *The Aran Islands* [1907]). "It is impossible to translate poetry. Can you translate music?" (Voltaire, Letter to Mme. Deffaud, May 19, 1754). It is interesting that the grandson, who composed this Prologue sometime after 117 B.C., criticizes freely not only his own translation but also the LXX, most of which had already been translated (no. 7). Later the LXX acquired a quasi-canonical status, which would have precluded such frank criticism by a pious Jew.

The grandson migrated to Egypt, presumably from Palestine, "in the thirty-eighth year of the reign of King Euergetes" (no. 8), i.e., Ptolemy VII Physkon Euergetes II (170–164 and 146–117 B.C.); hence in 132 B.C. Cf. INTRODUCTION, Part II. U. Wilcken has argued on the basis of certain papyri (*Archiv für Papyrusforschung* 3 [1906] 321–22) that the peculiar use of the preposition *epi* in Egyptian *koinē* Greek before the name of a king (i.e., Euergetes) and the giving of the exact date (i.e., the thirty-eighth year) indicate that the king is no longer alive. Thus the grandson wrote this Prologue and published his translation after the death of Euergetes II in 117 B.C. But as Smend (p. 3) has remarked, this argument alone is hardly convincing. Indeed, one need only mention that *epi* is used before the name of the reigning King Darius in Hag 1:1, 15; 2:10; and Zech 1:1, 7; 7:1. However, Smend further notes (pp. 3–4) that an argument can be made for a date after 117 B.C. on the basis of the Gr participle *synchronisas* (here translated "during my stay"), lit., "while I was there at the same time (as he was king)," i.e., while I was there for the rest of his reign. Thus the Prologue was written after the death of Euergetes II in 117 B.C.

Some time between 132 and 117 B.C. the grandson "came across *the reproduction* [Gr *aphomoion;* cf. NOTE*ᵃ*] of a good deal that is instructive" (no. 8). The less well-attested reading, *aphormēn* (found in a few minuscule MSS), here translated "(I had) access to," is easier to interpret: the grandson learned a good deal from the Jewish community in Alexandria where he lived. Smend (p. 4) prefers this reading, as do Box-Oesterley (p. 317) and Duesberg-Fransen (p. 92). The weight of manuscript evidence, however, favors the reading *aphomoion,* "the reproduction," which probably refers to written copies (cf. Lat *libros relictos,* "books left behind") of the teachings of the scribes of the Jewish community in Egypt. These writings were instructive for the grandson who studied them and may have motivated him "to devote some diligence and industry to the translation of [his grandfather's] book" (no. 9). He devoted "many sleepless hours of close application . . . in the interval" to translating the book and readying it for publication (no. 10). The reference to "the interval" is to the years 132–117 (cf. no. 8 above). Thus the translation was made between 132–117, and the Prologue was written just before publication of the book in Greek sometime after 117 B.C. The grandson did his work "for the benefit of those living abroad [i.e., in the Dispersion or Diaspora] who wish *to acquire wisdom* [lit., *to love learning,* cf. nos. 2 and 4] and are disposed to live their lives according to the standards of the Law" (no. 10). The Law is mentioned in the opening and closing sentences of the Prologue, thus forming an *inclusio* (an inclusion). The Law was the cornerstone of Jewish religious life and worship and was a central concern not only of the grandson but also of Ben Sira himself, as the book makes abundantly clear.

PART I (1:1–4:10)

1. Introduction: The Origin of Wisdom
(1:1–10)

1 1 All wisdom is from the Lord,   G
      and with him it remains forever.
   2 The sand of the seashores, the drops of rain,
      the days of eternity: who can number these?
   3 Heaven's height, earth's breadth,
      the depths of the abyss: who can fathom these?
   4 Before all things else wisdom was created;
      and prudent understanding, from eternity.*

   6 To whom has wisdom's root been revealed?
      Who knows her subtleties?*
   8 There is but one, wise and truly awe-inspiring,
      seated upon his throne: the Lord.
   9 He it is who fashioned her, has seen her and taken note
                                                    of her;
      he has poured her forth upon all his works,
   10 Upon every living thing according to his bounty;
      he has lavished her upon his friends.*

---

* 5 The wellspring of wisdom is the word of God in the heights,   GII
   and its runlets are the ageless commandments.

* 7 An understanding of wisdom—to whom has this been   GII
                                             disclosed;
   her resourcefulness, who has known?

* 10cd Love of the Lord is ennobling wisdom;   GII
      to those to whom he appears he apportions it, that they
                                          may see him.

Notes

1 3. *depths of the abyss*, with Lat, Copt, Eth; "the great ocean," Syr. Most witnesses have "the abyss and wisdom." Cf. 24:5.
6. *her subtleties*, Heb *ma'ărûmêhā;* cf. 42:16; 51:19 in 11QPs^a.
7. A variant on 1:6; it supposes Heb *śēkel* rather than *šōreš* as the first word.
10. *lavished* supposes Heb *wayyaśpîqêhā;* in 15:18 and 39:33, *spq*=*śpq*. For *his friends* (cf. Judg 5:31; Ps 145:20) a few Gr MSS and Syr read "those who fear him." The latter reading would lead in to the next section (1:11–30); "friends" was seemingly in the Gr when 10cd was composed. Cf. 2:15–16.

Comment

The first major division of the book (chaps. 1–23) has a total of four parts, as does the second major division (chaps. 24–50). After the introduction to the book (1:1–10), there follows a lengthy poem in praise of wisdom (1:11–30). The second division will open in the same way (24:1–33).

The general theme of Part I (1:1–4:10) is wisdom as fear of the Lord in its various manifestations: trust and a lively hope in the Lord; patience in suffering and adversity; reverence and respect for parents; humility in one's attitudes and conduct toward others; docility, almsgiving, and concern for the disadvantaged.

The opening poem (1:1–10), which serves as Introduction to the book, has, in GI, two stanzas of equal length, 4+4 lines or bicola. GII and Lat give three extra bicola, vv 5, 7, and 10cd, which are clearly intrusive and secondary, for none of the three is present in Syr. V 5 is related to v 4 and anticipates 24:23–33; v 7 merely repeats the ideas of v 6. The gloss in v 10cd, which begins with the words "Love of the Lord" [Gr *agapēsis kyriou*], was occasioned by the final words of v 10b, "upon his friends" [Gr *tois agapōsin auton*, lit., "on those who love him"]. The use of Gr *pasa*, "all," in v 1a and *pasēs*, "all, every," in v 10a forms an *inclusio*, a commonly employed rhetorical device. Another *inclusio* can be seen in Gr *met' autou*, "with him," in v 1b, and *meta pasēs sarkos*, "with every living thing," in v 10a.

The theme of the poem, derived from Prov 8:22–31, can be stated simply:

all wisdom has its origin in God (v 1) and is given as a gift to those whom God chooses (vv 9–10). V 1 can be considered the topic sentence of the whole book. In vv 1, 4, and 8, God is declared to be the source and seat of wisdom from eternity; cf. Prov 2:6; 8:22–23, 30; Job 12:13; Wis 7:26–27; 9:4, 6; John 1:1–2; Jas 1:5, 17. For the expression "the sand of the seashores" (v 2a), cf. Gen 32:13; 1 Sam 13:5; Ps 78:27. The idea of numbering [Gr *exarithmēsei*] "the drops of rain" (v 2a) may be derived from the LXX of Job 36:27: "The drops of rain are numbered by [God]." "Days of eternity" (v 2b; also in 18:10), in Heb *yĕmê 'ōlām* (Isa 63:9), only the Lord can number; in v 9a, "[The Lord] . . . has . . . taken note of [Gr *exērithmēsen*, lit., numbered, or counted] her [wisdom]."

The words of v 3 are an echo of LXX Job 38:16, 18; cf. also Ps 102(103):11 (LXX); Hab 1:6; Dan 12:2 (LXX); Wis 9:16; Sir 16:18; 24:5–6. The verb and idea in v 3b, "Who can fathom [Gr *exichniasei*, lit., trace out] them," are taken up by Paul in Rom 11:33, "How untraceable [Gr *anexichniastoi*] are his ways!" Wisdom was created before all other creatures (v 4). In the thought of Ben Sira, wisdom is identified with the Law of Moses; cf. 1:26–27; 15:1; 21:11; 24:23; 34:8. The same idea was held by the rabbis. In the Midrash *Bereshith Rabba*, 8, a comment on Gen 1:26 states: "According to R. Simeon ben Laqish, the Torah was in existence 2,000 years before the creation of the world" (cited in Box-Oesterley, p. 318). Gr *synesis* (v 4b), "understanding," in Job 28:20 (LXX) equals Heb *bînâ*, a synonym for wisdom, Gr *sophia* (v 4a), Heb *ḥokmâ*. In v 4, there is a chiastic *a:b::b':a'* pattern—*before all things: wisdom::understanding:from eternity.*

In v 5 of GII, a gloss on v 4 (cf. above), the phrase "the wellspring of wisdom" is found also in Bar 3:12; cf. Jer 2:13. "The word of God," Gr *logos theou*, occurs in John 1:1–2. The phrase "ageless [Gr *aiōnioi*, lit., eternal] commandments," reflects the idea of R. Simeon ben Laqish quoted above. Hart (p. 285) observes that v 5 is a Pharisaic doublet of v 4.

In v 6b, "subtleties, secrets," Gr *panourgeumata*, occurs only one other time in the book, 42:18, for which the Heb is extant, *ma'ărummîm* (MS B and M); cf. also 51:19d (11QPs^a). The questions in v 6, resuming the questions of vv 2–3, emphasize the nature of wisdom as impenetrable to human beings. In answer to these questions, v 8 declares that the Lord alone possesses wisdom.

In v 7 (GII), a doublet of v 6 (cf. above), Gr *polypeiria*, "resourcefulness, great experience," occurs only one other time in the book, 25:6, and once more in the rest of the Gr OT, Wis 8:8. It is noteworthy that the Gr words *sophia, panourgeumata,* and *epistēmē* ("understanding") in cola 6a, b, and 7a, respectively, occur in exactly that order in Jdt 11:8, which is also the only other place in the Gr OT, except for Sir 1:6 and 42:18, where *panourgeumata* occurs.

The idea of v 8 is taken up again in 43:29. Pss 9:5; 47:9; and Isa 6:1 provide the image of the Lord "seated upon his throne." The purpose of v 8 is to answer the questions asked in vv 2, 3, and 6, and to state unambiguously that God is the transcendent and sovereign Lord of all creation, who alone possesses wisdom in and of himself and in a full and perfect way. Though the Lord is "truly awe-inspiring" [Gr *phoberos sphodra,* lit., greatly to be feared], he created wisdom in order to pour "her forth upon all his works, upon every living thing according to his bounty" (vv 9b, 10a). But "the beginning of wisdom is the fear of the Lord; it is formed with the faithful in the womb" (v 14; cf. comment below). Ben Sira insists here and elsewhere that wisdom is an attribute of God, a quality of the universe which he created, and his free gift to men and women (v 10). Though wisdom is sometimes personified in the OT (Prov 8:1–36; 9:1–6, 11; Sir 24:1–34), she is nonetheless a mere creature; and regardless of her grandeur and excellence she is never to be identified with God himself.

The thought and vocabulary of v 9a, "He it is who fashioned her, has seen her and taken note of [lit., numbered] her," Gr *autos ektisen autēn kai eiden kai exērithmēsen autēn,* are derived from LXX Job 28:26–27, *hote epoiēsen houtōs idōn erithmēse,* "When [God] made [the weight of the winds and the measures of the water], he saw and numbered them." The idea of v 9b is taken from Joel 3:1–2; cf. Acts 2:17–18.

In v 10a, "every living thing" [Gr *pasēs sarkos,* lit., all flesh] includes not only the Jews but also the Gentiles; cf. Prov 8:15–16. The phrase "according to his bounty," or gift, Gr *kata tēn dosin autou* is found also in 35:12a, for which MS B^txt has the corresponding Heb *kĕmattĕnātô.* The point of vv 9b and 10a is that God pours out wisdom on all creation but especially on human beings, including Gentiles, because he is generous in giving. The point of v 10b is that God "has lavished" [Gr *echorēgēsen,* lit., has equipped or furnished abundantly] wisdom "upon his friends" [Gr *agapōsin auton,* lit., those who love him], i.e., he has granted wisdom in greater measure to the faithful Jews who observe the Law; cf. 24:7–12; Deut 6:5; 10:12. The four cursive MSS of the *l*-group (a subgroup of the so-called Lucianic recension) and Syr read *phoboumenois,* "those who fear [him]," instead of *agapōsin;* Smend (p. 9) and Duesberg-Fransen (p. 94) prefer the former reading, but the latter is better (cf. NOTE).

The gloss in v 10 is found in some MSS of GII (but not in 248, the principal witness of the *L*-group) and in Lat (but as vv 14–15a).

For a detailed study of this Wisdom poem, cf. J. Marböck, *Weisheit im Wandel: Untersuchungen zur Weisheitstheologie bei Ben Sira,* pp. 17–34.

2. Fear of the Lord Is Wisdom for Humankind
(1:11–30)

1 ¹¹ Fear of the Lord is glory and exultation,   G
         gladness and a festive crown.
    ¹² Fear of the Lord rejoices the heart,
         giving gladness and joy and length of days.^a
    ¹³ He who fears the Lord will have a happy end;
         even on the day of his death he will be blessed.

    ¹⁴ The beginning of wisdom is the fear of the Lord;
         it is formed with the faithful in the womb.
    ¹⁵ With the godly she was created from of old;
         with their descendants her beneficence is constant.

    ¹⁶ Fullness of wisdom is fear of the Lord;
         she inebriates them with her fruits.
    ¹⁷ Her whole house she fills with choice foods,
         her granaries with her harvest.

    ¹⁸ Wisdom's garland is fear of the Lord,
         with blossoms of peace and perfect health.^b
    ^{19b}Knowledge and full understanding she showers down;
      c   she heightens the glory of those who possess her.

    ²⁰ The root of wisdom is fear of the Lord;
         her branches are length of days.

---

^a 12cd Fear of the Lord is the Lord's gift;   GII
         also for love he makes firm paths.

^b 18cd Both are gifts of God toward peace;   GII
         splendor opens out for those who love him.

21 The fear of the Lord keeps sin far off;   GII
    it stays with one and turns back all [God's] wrath.

22 No one can justify unjust anger;   G
    anger plunges a person to his downfall.
23 For a time the patient person stays calm,
    and then gladness comes back to him.
24 For a time he holds back his words,
    then the lips of many tell of his understanding.

25 Among wisdom's treasures is the model for knowledge;
    but to the sinner fear of the Lord is an abomination.
26 If you desire wisdom, keep the commandments,
    and the Lord will bestow her upon you.
27 Fear of the Lord is wisdom and discipline;
    trust and humility are his delight.

28 Be not faithless to the fear of the Lord,
    nor approach it with duplicity of heart.
29 Play not the hypocrite before others;
    over your lips keep watch.
30 Exalt not yourself lest you fall
    and bring upon you dishonor;

For then the Lord will reveal your secrets
    and in the midst of the assembly he will cast you
                            down,
Because you approached the fear of the Lord
    with your heart full of guile.

Notes

1   15. *godly* supposes the Heb phrase *'anšê ḥesed;* cf. 44:10–11. G's *themelion* read Heb *yĕsōd* for *ḥesed,* and its *enosseusen* supposes Heb *qnn* for *ạnh* or *tqn.* For the interplay of *ḥesed* and *'ĕmet* in vv 14–15, cf. Syr.

17. A revision in some Gr MSS reads: "Their whole house. . . ." "Her . . ." is the more common reading, supported by Lat and Syr.

18. Between v 18 and v 28, Syr has the equivalent of fourteen lines; it seems to have improvised to fill a gap.

18cd. *Both* are probably "fear of the Lord" and "love" from 12cd; i.e., 18cd builds on 12cd, while drawing on vv 12 and 18.

19a. G=9b repeated out of place.

19–20. 2Q18 has a small fragment with a few letters from the ends of these two verses; from the bottom of a column, it points to a format with columns eighteen lines in length, with a complete bicolon making up each line. By whatever coincidence, this is exactly the format observed throughout the pages of Cairo MS B. Cf. 6:20–31.

21. Though this verse is preserved only in GII, the structure of this part of Sirach requires at this point a line complementary to v 20; cf. vv 14–15, 16–17, 18–19, and now 20–21.

29. *before others*="in the sight of men," with hexaplaric MSS, Lat, Syr. G has "in the mouths of men": *stomasin* for *ommasin?*

30. G has "Because you did not approach . . ."; the negative was put in as a gloss when the line in its Gr form came to be misunderstood; cf. Lat and Syr.

Comment

Following the Introduction (1:1–10), this opening poem (1:11–30) contains twenty-two lines or bicola, the number of letters in the Hebrew alphabet; it forms an *inclusio* with 51:13–30, the closing poem, a twenty-three-line alphabetic acrostic. See INTRODUCTION, Part IX, 4. The present poem is divided into two parts, each with eleven lines. The second part begins in v 22a with Gr *ou,* Heb *lō',* the letter *lamed* being the start of the second half of the Heb alphabet. GII has intrusive material in vv 12cd and 18cd (cf. NOTE), which could scarcely have been part of the original poem. GII, however, also has v 21; though the v is missing in GI, it is necessary for the rhetorical structure of the poem (cf. NOTE). The poem has nine stanzas, five in the first half and four in the second, with the following arrangement: 3+2+2+2+2 and 3+3+3+2, for a total of twenty-two lines.

The purpose of the poem is to provide the identification of "wisdom," as Ben Sira understands the concept, with "the fear of the Lord." The two concepts are interwoven throughout the poem, especially in vv 25–27. Thus the poem is programmatic for an understanding of The Wisdom of Ben Sira.

The first half of the poem opens with a three-line stanza, vv 11–13, the topic of which is "fear of the Lord," an expression that occurs in each of the lines. Fear of the Lord is the source of the best things that life can offer. "Fear of the Lord" also recurs in vv 14a, 16a, 18a, and 20a, the first colon, respectively, of each of the following four stanzas. Moreover, at the beginning of these same four cola there occur four phrases arranged in a deliberate a:b::b':a' pattern—beginning of wisdom:fullness of wisdom::garland of wisdom:root of wisdom.

The second half of the poem, vv 22–30, contains moral advice and exhortation to practice certain virtues that are needed by the wise and to avoid the vices that are incompatible with "the fear of the Lord."

The poem begins (v 11a) and ends (v 30e) with "the fear of the Lord," thus forming a literary inclusio. It is probably not a coincidence that the expression "the fear of the Lord," or its equivalent, occurs a total of twelve times in the poem, twelve being a sacred and significant number in the Bible (twelve tribes of Israel, twelve months in a year).

Fear of the Lord is an essential component of faith; cf. Deut 4:9–10; 8:5–6; 10:12; 2 Chr 19:7; 26:5; Prov 1:7; 9:10; Job 28:28; Ps 111:10. It is not surprising, then, that fear of the Lord is a central theme in the teaching of Ben Sira; cf. INTRODUCTION, Part X, 1. "Fear of the Lord is glory and exultation, gladness and a festive crown" (v 11); it is the beginning (v 14a), fullness (v 16a), garland or crown (v 18a), and root (v 20a) of wisdom. "Fear of the Lord is wisdom and discipline" (v 27a). The one who fears the Lord will have a glad heart and length of days (v 12), and a happy and blessed end (v 13).

"Fear of the Lord is glory [Gr doxa] and exultation [Gr kauchēma], gladness [Gr euphrosynē] and a festive crown [Gr stephanos agalliamatos]" (v 11). Two of these Gr expressions are also found in a long poem of exhortation to strive for wisdom (6:18–37): doxa (MS A kābôd) and stephanos agalliamatos (MS A ʿăṭeret tipʾeret) (6:31). Euphrosynē connotes a good mental and moral state, a sense of serenity and happiness, resulting from an upright and virtuous life. The Gr word occurs also in vv 12b, 23b; 2:9b; 6:28b; 9:10d; 15:6a; 30:16b, 22a; 31:27d, 28a, 31b; 35:11b; 37:4a.

"Fear of the Lord rejoices the heart," Gr terpsei kardian (v 12a). The same Gr words are found in the LXX of Prov 27:9, "The heart rejoices [Gr terpetai kardia] in ointments and wines and perfumes." For "length of days" in v 12b Syr has "eternal life," a later concept introduced under Christian influence; it is at variance with the original thought of Ben Sira, who, in keeping with the older Deuteronomic theory of retribution only in this life, did not accept the doctrine of rewards and punishments in the afterlife; see INTRODUCTION, Part X, 4. Cf. A. A. Di Lella, "Conservative and Progressive Theology: Sirach and Wisdom," *CBQ* 28 (1966): 143–46. In vv 12b and 20b, the idea of "length of days," Gr *makroēmereusin,* as a reward for fidelity to the Lord is derived from Deut 6:2, which states that the Israelites are to fear Yahweh their God and to keep all his statutes and commandments all their lives so that their "days may be lengthened" [LXX uses the verb *makroēmereuein*]. Cf. v 20b; 3:6a; 30:22b; Exod 20:12; Deut 5:16; Ps 21:5; Prov 3:2, 16; 4:10; 10:27, 30.

The intrusive bicolon v 12cd, found only in the *O*-recension and four other cursives, explains that fear of the Lord is a gift [Gr *dosis*] from the Lord just as wisdom is said to be in v 10a. The mention of "love" in v 12d, Gr *agapēsis,* connects this gloss with the doublet in v 10, in colon c of which "love" also occurs.

In v 13b, Codex B and the *l*- and *b*-group of MSS read *heurēsei charin,* "he will find grace," in place of *eulogēthēsetai,* "he will be blessed." The former reading is apparently due to Christian influence (so Box-Oesterley, p. 319). Even though Ben Sira did not believe in the afterlife, he could rightly affirm in v 13 that the person who fears the Lord will be blessed even on the day of death because his earthly life had been blessed by the Lord (vv 11–12) and others after him will consider him to have been blessed. Cf. 1 Chr 29:28: "[David] died at a ripe old age, rich in years and wealth and glory."

Spicq (p. 565) writes that vv 11–13 emphasize two essential yet diverse aspects of Judaism: (1) the intimate connection of moral behavior and religion, i.e., virtue is the fruit of fear of the Lord; and (2) the utilitarian motivation of this moral behavior, i.e., virtue brings with it its own immediate recompense. Accordingly, it is to one's advantage to acquire wisdom. The wise work for their own good, while sinners are fools who do not understand even their own interests. Cf. 3:14–15, 25–28, 31; 16:14; 17:22–23.

The Gr word *archē,* Heb *rōʾš* or *tĕhillâ* (as in Prov 9:10), "the beginning," has three meanings: (1) point of departure or starting point, as in 15:14; (2) the most important part of the thing, as in 29:21 and 39:26; and (3) the best part or essence of a thing, as in 11:3. In v 14a, all three meanings are present; cf. Prov 1:7; 9:10; Ps 111:10. In v 14b, Ben Sira implies that wisdom is like an infused gift which together with the gift of life is given to the faithful in the womb (cf. Spicq, p. 566). Prov 8:31 is the background of the textually difficult v 15 (cf. NOTE and Smend, p. 11); cf. also 4:16; 24:9.

The idea of fullness in v 16a is taken up again in 2:16b; cf. Job 28:28. In v 16b, wisdom "inebriates" or intoxicates, Gr *methyskei,* the godly with her fruits; in 32:13b, God is said to intoxicate the faithful with his good things.

For the "fruits" of wisdom, cf. Prov 8:19; 11:30. In v 17, the concept of wisdom's house and food is derived from Prov 9:1–6.

The word "crown" or "garland," Gr *stephanos,* in v 18a occurs also in other wisdom texts; cf. 25:6 and Prov 17:6 (crown of old men); Prov 12:4 (crown of a husband); 16:31 (crown of glory). In v 18b and in the rest of the Bible, Gr *eirēnē,* Heb *šālôm,* means much more than our English word "peace." The word *šālôm* includes the ideas of well-being, prosperity, serenity, proper vertical and horizontal relationships, tranquillity, safety, contentment, and satisfaction. The connection between fear of the Lord and health may be seen also in 34:17–20 and Prov 3:7–8. The *O*-recension and Lat give the gloss in v 18cd (cf. NOTE) after 18b; but the *L*-recension gives v 18c before v 18a, and v 18d after v 18b.

The *O*-recension plus three other Gr MSS and some Lat MSS and Sahidic correctly omit v 19a, which merely repeats v 9b. The blessings of fidelity in vv 16b, 17, 18b, 19bc, 20b, and 21 are spelled out in even greater detail in Lev 26:3–13 and Deut 28:1–14. In v 20, as fear of the Lord is "the root," Gr *riza,* or inner essence of wisdom, so "her branches" produce the most precious fruit, viz., "length of days" (so Smend, p. 13). For this v, Syr has: "Her [wisdom's] roots are eternal life, and her flowers length of days." Cf. COMMENT on v 12b. The image of wisdom as a tree occurs also in 24:13–14, 16–17. Though absent in GI, v 21 is found in many Gr MSS: *O, L'*-672-694-743, and 768; it must be genuine, as was pointed out above. The mention of "all wrath" in v 21b leads in to the second half of the poem, which begins with a bicolon on human anger (v 22); cf. Peters, p. 16.

The evils and dangers of unjust anger (v 22) are often mentioned in the Wisdom literature; cf. 27:30; 28:3–11; Prov 10:18; 12:16; 14:29; 15:1, 18; 16:32; 20:3; 29:11. The one who is patient and remains calm is quickly restored to gladness (v 23); cf. vv 11, 12; Prov 19:2; 21:5; 25:15. Such a person also knows how to keep silent (v 24a); the result is that "many [Gr *polloi*] tell of his understanding [Gr *synesin autou*]" (v 24b); the same three Gr words occur in a similar context in 39:9. Silence was highly valued also in Egyptian wisdom; cf. H. Duesberg, *Les Scribes inspirés: Introduction aux livres sapientiaux de la Bible,* vol. 1, pp. 113–19.

"To the sinner fear of the Lord is an abomination" because he lacks wisdom and knowledge (v 25); cf. Prov 1:29–30. Gr *theosebeia* is the word in v 25b for "fear of the Lord." The word is very rare, occurring only once in The Wisdom of Ben Sira and three other times in the rest of the canonical Gr OT: in Gen 20:11, *theosebeia* translates Heb *yirʿat ʾĕlōhîm,* "fear of God"; in Job 28:28, *yirʿat ʾădōnay,* "fear of the Lord"; in Bar 5:4, no Hebrew is extant. In vv 25–27, Ben Sira refers to his great equation: fear of the Lord = wisdom = gift of the Lord = discipline = keeping the commandments. "Love of the Lord" (v 10c), which is another part of this great equation, is left out here, but is found in 2:15b. This equation in one form or another occurs elsewhere in the book. V 26 "offers a good example of the combination of grace and free-will" (so Box-Oesterley, p. 321). Cf. 1:9b, 10: Jas 1:5. In v 26b, the Gr verb *chorēgēsei*, "will bestow" (lit., will furnish abundantly) also occurs in v 10 (cf. COMMENT). In writing vv 25–27, Ben Sira must have been thinking of Prov 15:33, the MT of which is translated: "The fear of the LORD is training for wisdom, and humility [Heb *'ănāwâ*] goes before honors." In v 33a, the LXX has *phobos kyriou paideia kai sophia,* "fear of the Lord is discipline and wisdom," every word of which appears in a different order in the grandson's Greek of v 27a. In v 27b, Gr *pistis,* here translated "trust," also means faith, fidelity, firmness, unshakability, and constancy. The combination *pistis* and *prautēs,* "humility" (v 27b), occurs also in 45:4, for which the Heb (MS B) is extant: *'ĕmûnâ* and *'ănāwâ,* respectively. Cf. 3:17; 4:8; 10:28.

In v 27b, "trust" and "humility" will each be the subject of a separate poem in chap. 2 and in 3:17–24, respectively. The word *pistis,* "faith" (v 27b), leads in to the key idea of the next stanza, vv 28–30: "Be not faithless [Gr *apeithēsēs*] to the fear of the Lord" (v 28a). In 28b, "duplicity of heart," Gr *kardia dissē,* lit., double heart, is an idea taken from Ps 12:3: "Everyone speaks falsehood to his neighbor; with smooth lips they speak, and double heart" (Heb *lēb wālēb,* lit., heart and heart). In OT thought, the heart is the source of a person's interiority (intelligence and free will), and the tongue is the symbol of a person's external actions. Put differently, the heart is the root of choice, and the tongue is the expression of choice. Accordingly, heart and tongue are closely related, so that the expressions "evil heart" and "evil tongue" are similar in meaning. The same is true of "double heart" in v 28b, and "double tongue," Heb *ba'al štāyim,* Gr *diglōssos,* in 5:9(G), 14; 6:1; 28:13(G). For a good discussion of this point, cf. J. Hadot, *Penchant mauvais et volonté libre dans la sagesse de Ben Sira (L'Ecclésiastique),* pp. 177–92. Similar expressions are found in Jas 1:8, *anēr dipsychos,* "a double-minded man," and 4:8, *dipsychoi,* "double-minded ones."

The thought of v 29 flows quite naturally from v 28. One ought not to play the hypocrite but be single-hearted and sincere and speak the truth. Cf. 32:15. The maxim in v 30 is stated in various other ways in the Bible: cf. 10:15; Ezek 17:24; Dan 4:34; Job 22:29; Prov 11:2; 16:18; 18:12; 29:23; Matt 18:4; 23:12; Luke 1:52–53; 14:11; 18:14.

The poem ends with a stanza of two bicola (v 30c–f) in which Ben Sira speaks of the punishment in store for those who approach the fear of the Lord with a "heart full of guile." The "secrets" of v 30c are presumably the devious and evil machinations of the sinner's heart (v 30f). These secrets will be exposed and the sinner cast down "in the midst of the assembly," Gr *synagōgē,* publicly. The ideas here have as their source Prov 5:12–14:

> . . . Oh, why did I hate instruction,
>   and my heart spurn reproof!

> Why did I not listen to the voice of my teachers,
>   nor to my instructors incline my ear!
> I have all but come to utter ruin,
>   condemned by the public assembly!

With regard to the significance of the assembly in Ben Sira's day, cf. 4:7; 7:7; 23:24; 41:18; 42:11.

An *inclusio* can be seen in the verb "approach" in 28b, Gr *proselthēs,* and in 30e, *proselthes,* and also in the noun "heart" in v 28b and in v 30f. The Gr phrase *plērēs dolou,* "full of guile," occurs again in 19:26.

3. Trust in God
(2:1–18)

2 ¹ My son, when you come to serve the Lord,   G
    prepare yourself for testing.
² Be sincere of heart and steadfast,
    undisturbed in time of affliction.
³ Cling to him, forsake him not;
    thus will your future be great.

⁴ Accept whatever befalls you,
    in periods of humiliation be patient;
⁵ For in fire gold is tested,
    and those God favors, in the crucible of humiliation.ᵃ
⁶ Trust God and he will help you;
    make straight your ways and hope in him.

⁷ You that fear the Lord, wait for his mercy,
    turn not away lest you fall.
⁸ You that fear the Lord, trust him,
    and your reward will not be lost.
⁹ You that fear the Lord, hope for good things,
    for lasting joy and mercy.ᵇ

¹⁰ Study the generations long past and understand:
    has anyone hoped in the Lord and been disappointed?
Has anyone persevered in his fear and been forsaken?
    has anyone called upon him and been rebuffed?

ᵃ 5c In sickness and in poverty be confident in him.   G°

ᵇ 9c Because his reward is an everlasting gift, with joy.   GII

11 Compassionate and merciful is the Lord;
   he forgives sins, he saves in time of trouble.

12 Woe to craven hearts and drooping hands,
   to the sinner who treads a double path!
13 Woe to the faint of heart who trust not,
   who therefore will have no shelter!
14 Woe to you that have lost hope!
   what will you do at the Lord's visitation?

15 Those who fear the Lord do not disobey his words;
   those who love him keep his ways.
16 Those who fear the Lord seek to please him,
   those who love him are filled with his law.
17 Those who fear the Lord prepare their hearts
   and humble themselves before him.

18 Let us fall into the hands of the Lord
   and not into the hands of humans,
   For equal to his majesty is the mercy that he shows;
   his works are in keeping with his name.   s

Notes

2 1. *testing* supposes Gr *peirasmon* = Heb *nissāyôn;* cf. 4:17; 6:7.

5. *those God favors:* G points to Heb *'anšê rāṣôn* as the original; cf. Prov 3:12; 1QH 11:9 *bĕnê rĕṣônĕkā.*

5c. A variant on v 4b, in which place it is read by Syr; "sickness = Heb *ḥly;* "periods" in v 4b = Heb *ḥlp.*

9c. Expands 2:8–9.

18. *his works . . . his name,* thus Syr; the Heb line would have been incomplete without such a colon. Similar expressions appear in 6:17, 22.

Comment

In MS 248, this poem has the title "On Patience." It has six three-line stanzas and a concluding couplet. V 5c is a doublet of v 4b (cf. NOTE), and v 9c is a Christian gloss favoring the doctrine of the afterlife; see INTRODUCTION, Part X, 4.

In vv 1–6, Ben Sira warns his disciples about the adversity that the Lord allows as a test of whether or not fear of the Lord is genuine. The poem opens with the Gr word *teknon*, "my son." In the Wisdom literature, this is the usual form of address for one's disciples; cf., e.g., 3:12, 17; 4:1; 6:32; 10:28; 11:10; 14:11; 31:22; Prov 2:1; 3:1. Sometimes the plural form, "my children," is used: 3:1; 23:7; 39:13; 41:14; Prov 4:1. As v 1a, Syr reads: "My son, when you come *to the fear of God,*" a reading preferred by Smend (p. 18) and Duesberg-Fransen (p. 98); cf. 1:28, 30e. The idea of preparing oneself for testing even though one serves the Lord is part of the Deuteronomic theory of retribution that legitimated probationary suffering for the virtuous; cf. Judg 2:22–3:6. For a good discussion of the Deuteronomic theory, cf. O. S. Rankin, *Israel's Wisdom Literature: Its Bearing on Theology and the History of Religion,* pp. 77–80; for the application of this theory in The Wisdom of Ben Sira, cf. A. A. Di Lella, *CBQ* 28 (1966): 143–46.

In v 1, the idea of testing for the purpose of ascertaining how authentic a person's faith and practices may be is also found in 4:17b; 6:7a; 44:20d; cf. also Jas 1:2–4, 12; Matt 6:13; Luke 11:4. The rare Gr verb *kartereson,* "be steadfast or patient" (v 2a), also occurs in the LXX of Job 2:9; the only other occurrences in the canonical Gr OT are Sir 12:15b; Isa 42:14; and 2 Macc 7:17. In the NT, the verb occurs only once, Heb 11:27. In v 2b, the phrase "in time of affliction [or adversity, calamity]" simply means difficult or troublesome days; cf. G of 5:8b. A similar phrase occurs in v 11b. Despite the trials of adversity, the wise are called to "cling to [the Lord]" (v 3a), Gr. *kollētheti,* an idea taken from Deut 10:20, the LXX of which uses the same verb. For v 3b, Syr has: "so that you may be wise in your ways." Cf. Prov 19:20b.

For v 4b, Syr reads: "in disease and poverty be patient" (cf. NOTE on v 5c). The key to the first two stanzas of this poem (vv 1–6) is v 5, which is based on Prov 3:11–12. The phrase "those God favors" renders Gr *anthrōpoi dektoi,* lit., acceptable men. There is an *a:b::b':a'* chiastic arrangement in the principal words of this v: *in fire:gold::acceptable men:in the crucible.* For similar ideas, cf. Isa 48:10; Zech 13:9; Mal 3:3; Prov 17:3; 27:21; Ps 66:10; Wis 3:6;

Jas 1:12; 1 Pet 1:7. That God helps those who trust in him (Gr *pisteuson autǭ*) is clearly stated also in Pss 40:18; 46:2. Trust and hope (v 6) are two essential elements of biblical faith; cf. Pss 37:3; 71:5–6; Prov 3:5–6. An important variant in v 6b is found in the *O*-group of MSS and in Syr, which read: "hope in him, and he will make straight your ways."

In the next stanza (vv 7–9), each bicolon opens with the words "You that fear the Lord," followed by an imperative. In Jdt 8:17, Judith speaks to her fellow Israelites about "waiting for" (Gr *anamenein,* the same verb used in v 7a) salvation from God. In adversity, one must be patient and wait for God's mercy; if one becomes impatient and turns away, one falls or sins (v 7). The *mots crochets* or catchwords "trust" and "hope," in vv 8a and 9a, respectively, connect this stanza with the preceding (vv 4–6), in the last bicolon of which the same two verbs appear. For v 8b, Syr reads: "and he will not hold back your wages"; cf. Lev 19:13; Tob 4:14. In v 9b, the "lasting joy" is not the blessedness of the afterlife (cf. COMMENT on 1:12b) but rather the well-being of this life; the phrase is taken from Isa 35:10; 51:11; 61:7 (in Heb, *śimḥat ʿôlām*), where it has the same meaning. The word "mercy," Gr *eleos,* is found in the opening and closing cola (vv 7a and 9b) of the stanza, thus forming an *inclusio.* In place of "mercy" in v 9b, Syr has "salvation" (or "redemption").

The next stanza (vv 10–11) opens with a twofold imperative (v 10a); questions follow in each of the next three cola (v 10bcd); and the stanza concludes with a motive clause (v 11ab). In the opening colon, Ben Sira appeals to the testimony of past generations, and the rhetorical questions he asks all demand the answer "No." The experience of the Ancestors and of the upright men and women of Israel's history bears eloquent witness to the truth that trust in the Lord will never be in vain. In v 10b, the Gr verb *enepisteusen,* "has hoped in" (lit., has trusted in), and *enemeinen* in v 10c, "has persevered," are catchwords with *pisteusate* in v 8a, and *anameinate* in v 7a, thus connecting this stanza with the preceding; cf. COMMENT on vv 8a, 9a. The questions of v 10 are based upon Pss 22:5–6 and 37:25. In fact, the second verb of v 10b, *katēschynthē,* "has been disappointed" (lit., has been put to shame), is the same word used in the LXX of Ps 22:6. The motive clause in v 11 begins with Gr *dioti,* the equivalent of Heb *kî,* "for, because" (which does not appear in the above translation). The reason why the faithful will never be put to shame or be forsaken or rebuffed is that the Lord is "compassionate and merciful"; cf. v 18cd; Exod 34:6; Pss 86:5, 15; 103:8; 130:3–4; 145:8; Joel 2:13; Job 4:6–7. The Lord also forgives sins and saves his people in distress; cf. Pss 37:39–40; 103:3; 145:18–19.

The first word of vv 12, 13, and 14 is the Gr particle *ouai,* "woe." Thus these three verses clearly form a stanza. Instead of "craven [or fearful] hearts," Gr *kardiais deilais* (v 12a), Syh and a few other ancient versions read "double hearts," *kardiais dissais;* cf. v 12b. For the idea of fearful hearts, cf. Deut 20:8; Judg 7:3. The whole stanza is concerned with those Jews who have lost confidence and hope in the Lord and in the great promises made to Israel; cf. 1 Kgs 18:21; Isa 7:2, 9. Such Jews were tempted to compromise their faith by treading the "double path" (lit., two paths), i.e., the traditional path of the ancestral faith and the new path of Hellenistic culture and life-style. In 41:8, Ben Sira has harsher words for those who apostatize from the Lord. Cf. INTRODUCTION, Part II. With regard to the "two paths," cf. 1:28, which speaks of a "double heart." The Gr verb *pisteuei*, "trust," in v 13a, is a catchword connecting this stanza with the preceding stanzas; cf. vv 6a, 8a, 10b. The Lord holds each person accountable; loss of hope brings on judgment (v 14).

The next stanza has an obvious unity because of the repetition of "Those who fear the Lord" at the beginning of vv 15, 16, and 17; cf. vv 7–9. The point of this stanza is that true believers are obedient to the Lord's words and his law and do not seek or give in to the allurements of other ways. In v 15a, the Gr verb *apeithēsousin*, "disobey," also occurs in 1:28; cf. Pss 105:28; 107:11. Those who love the Lord "keep his ways" (v 15b) and do not tread "a double path" (v 12b); cf. Pss 18:22; 25:4. In vv 15 and 16, there is synonymous parallelism between "Those who fear the Lord" and "those who love him." Cf. COMMENT on 1:25–27. True religion means the recognition of who we are and who God is (v 17). The need for humility is often stressed by Ben Sira; cf. 3:18; 7:17; 18:21.

The final stanza of the poem is a couplet in praise of God's mercy (v 18). Sentiments similar to those of v 18ab are expressed in 2 Sam 24:14 and 1Chr 21:13; cf. Dan 13:23. The ideas of v 18cd are echoed also in 18:4–6; cf. Wis 11:23; 12:16. V 18d is not found in G; but Syr has the colon (cf. NOTE), which most likely was present in the lost original text, since it appears in MS A but in the wrong place (after 6:17b). For the notion of God's works, viz., of mercy (v 18c), being in keeping with his name (v 18d), cf. COMMENT on v 11. The name Ben Sira alludes to is *raḥûm*, Heb for "Merciful One," which he uses in 50:19b. Cf. Exod 34:6.

4. The Honor Due Father and Mother
(3:1–16)

3 ¹ Children, pay heed to a father's right;   G
    do so that you may live.
² For the Lord sets a father in honor over his children;
    a mother's right he confirms over her sons.
³ Whoever honors his father atones for sins;
⁴   he stores up riches who honors his mother.
⁵ Whoever honors his father will have joy in his children,
    and when he prays he is heard.
⁶ Whoever honors his father will live a long life;
    he obeys the Lord who honors his mother.

⁷ Whoever fears the Lord honors his father,   GII
    and serves his parents as masters.   G
⁸ In word and deed honor your father   A
    that his blessing may come upon you;   G
⁹ For a father's blessing gives a family firm roots,   A
    but a mother's curse uproots the growing plant.
¹⁰ Glory not in your father's disgrace;
    his disgrace is no glory to you!
¹¹ His father's glory is a person's own glory;
    he multiplies sin who demeans his mother.

¹² My son, be steadfast in honoring your father;
    grieve him not as long as he lives.
¹³ Even if his mind fails him, be considerate of him;
    revile him not in the fullness of your strength.
¹⁴ For kindness to a father will not be forgotten;
    it will serve as a sin offering—it will take lasting root.
¹⁵ In time of trouble it will be recalled to your advantage;
    like warmth upon frost it will melt away your sins.

¹⁶ A blasphemer is he who neglects his father;   C
he provokes God, who demeans his mother.

Notes

3   1. *right*=Lat *judicium*=hexaplaric *krima*=Heb *mišpāṭ;* G *emou* (*tou patros*);
Ziegler conj. *elegmon.*
live=Syr; G *sōthēte,* cf. LXX Ezek 33:12 *sōthēnai*=MT *liḥyōt*=live.
   6b. *obeys* with G=Heb *šmʿ;* Syr=Heb *šlm,* cf. 35:3, 13. *honors (his mother):* Heb
MS A begins here; G "gives rest [=comfort] to," cf. Gen 5:29.
   7a. =GII, Lat; required by 7b. 7b=G. 7ab lacking in MS A and Syr. Structure of
3:1–16 favors authenticity of GII+G in 7ab.
   8a. MS A, Syr *bĕnî,* "My son," overweights the colon; omit with G.
   8b. MS A, Syr "that all blessings may light upon you [or: come to you]" reworked
from Deut 28:2?
   11b. G="disgrace for her children is a mother in disrepute." MS A=*marbeh ḥeṭ'*
mĕqallēl 'immô; read *maqleh* (Smend), cf. G and Syr. For *mqll,* cf. 3:16; Exod 21:17.
   12a. G="My son, take care of your father when he is old."
   13b. *in the fullness of your strength*=G; MS A, Syr "all the days of his/your life"
from 12b.
   14a. *forgotten*=MS C, G, Syr; MS A="blotted out," cf. M 44:13b.
   14b. *tinnāṭaʿ* with MS A^{mg}, cf. v 9.
   16a. *who neglects*=*hāʿōzēb* with MS C, G; MS A *bōzeh*="who despises."
   16b. Reading *ûmakʿîs 'ēl maqleh 'immô;* MSS AC, Syr import new terms, cf. Qoh
12:1. G "accursed by God is he who provokes his mother"=Heb *ûmĕqullal 'ēl makʿîs*
'immô, transposing the participles.

Comment

This poem consists of three stanzas, each with five lines or bicola. It deals
with various responsibilities of children toward their parents. Fear of the
Lord has first place in the theology of Ben Sira (cf. 1:1–2:18 and INTRODUC-
TION, Part X, 1), but that is not enough. Believers (=those who love and fear
the Lord) must also love and honor their parents and care for them. Lat has
an interesting bicolon before v 1: "The children of wisdom are the congregation of the just; obedience and love are what they beget." Smend (p. 23)

observes that there must have been a Heb *Vorlage* for this Lat addition, but it is nonetheless secondary.

In v 1, "a father's right" (cf. NOTE) is to the obedience of his children so that they "may live" (cf. NOTE). In v 1b, Syr reads: "so that you may live *the life that is forever and ever.*" The italicized words are a Christian interpolation in favor of the doctrine of retribution in the afterlife; cf. COMMENT on 1:12 and INTRODUCTION, Part X, 4. In the Decalogue, the commandment to honor one's parents is the first one to which a promise is attached: "Honor your father and your mother, that you may have a long life in the land which the LORD, your God, is giving you" (Exod 20:12). V 2 is to be understood in light of this commandment. Reverence and respect for parents are a cornerstone of biblical ethics; cf. Exod 21:17; Lev 20:9; Deut 5:16; Tob 4:3–4; 14:12–13; Prov 1:8; 6:20; Matt 15:3–6; Mark 7:9–13; Eph 6:2–3. There is an *a:b::b′:a′* chiastic structure in vv 3–4: *whoever honors his father:atones for sins::he stores up riches:who honors his mother.* The Gr verb *apothēsaurizōn,* "he stores up riches," occurs only here in the entire Gr OT and only once in the NT, 1 Tim 6:19. We see in vv 3–4 "the beginnings of the development (especially in one direction) of the Jewish doctrines of atonement and mediation, which assumed great prominence in later times. . . . The observance of the Torah, or Law, became, as time went on, to an ever-increasing extent the main basis of practical religion among the Jews" (so Box-Oesterley, p. 324).

For maxims related to v 5a, cf. Prov 10:1; 15:20; 23:24–25; 29:3. The prayer of the one who honors his father "is heard" (v 5b) because the Lord hears "the prayer of the just" (Prov 15:29). In v 6a, Ben Sira restates Exod 20:12 and Deut 5:16. "Long life" is what the pious Jew looked for prior to the revelation of a blessed afterlife; cf. COMMENT on 1:12.

There is a striking synonymous parallelism between *obeying the Lord* (v 6b) and *fearing the Lord* (v 7a) by keeping the commandment to honor one's parents; cf. COMMENT on 1:25–27. One who fears and serves the Lord (cf. 2:1) must also serve "his parents as masters" (v 7b). The Gr word *despotēs,* "master," is one of the titles of God in the LXX; cf. 23:1; 34:29. In v 7b, the Gr verb *douleuein,* "to serve," seems to imply the service of a slave. The Law has been interpreted by some rabbis to mean that children were in the position of slaves to their father; cf. Exod 21:7; Neh 5:5. Some rabbis even taught on the basis of Gen 22:2–10, Judg 11:39, and 2 Kgs 23:10 that a father had the right of life and death over his children (Box-Oesterley, p. 324). Ben Sira, however, never says anything of this sort; in fact, the responsibilities to parents he speaks of here and in 7:27–28 are the services of love, honor, and care. Lip service alone will not do; children are to honor their parents also in deed (v 8a). Cf. Ps 78:36–37; Isa 29:13; Jer 12:2; Matt 14:8; 21:28–31; Mark 7:6.

The idea of a blessing for fidelity to the Law derives from Deut 28:2; cf. Prov 11:11. A father's blessing of his children (vv 8b–9a) was valued highly in the OT; cf. Gen 9:27; 27:27–38; 28:1, 6; 48:15–16; 49:25–26. Ben Sira borrowed the "root" metaphor (v 9a) from Prov 12:3. V 9b is in antithetic parallelism to v 9a, thus emphasizing the point being made; cf. Prov 20:20. A parent's word of blessing or of curse was considered irrevocable and efficacious; cf. Gen 9:25–27; 27:30–38; Judg 17:1–4. The Heb word *neṭaʿ*, "growing [or young] plant" (v 9b) occurs in this sense only here and in Job 14:9. On v 9, cf. J. Bauer, "Des Vaters Segen . . . , der Fluch der Mutter . . . [Sir 3:9]," *Bibel und Liturgie* 23 (1955–56): 295–96.

The truth of vv 10ab–11a is self-evident. It is senseless of children to glory or rejoice in the poverty, disgrace, or ill-fortune of their parents. Ben Sira may be alluding here to the sin of Ham, who saw his father drunk and naked and did nothing to cover the old man's disgrace but instead told his two brothers about it (Gen 9:21–22). Conversely, the glory of one's parents is also one's own glory. A similar idea is found in Sophocles' *Antigone*, 703–4 (ca. 441 B.C.): "For me, my father, no treasure is so precious as your welfare. What, indeed, is a nobler ornament for children than a prospering father's fair fame, or for father than son's?" In v 11b, Ben Sira paraphrases Prov 15:20b: "A foolish man despises his mother." Cf. Prov 23:22; 30:17. The thought of v 11b is repeated in v 16b.

The last stanza of the poem begins with Heb *bĕnî*, "my son" (v 12a), a sign that a new unit is beginning; cf. v 1. The stanza deals with the duty to honor one's parents especially when they are old, feeble, or senile. At the end of v 12b, MS A and Syr read "all the days of your life" instead of "as long as he lives," which is based on G. In v 13, a stark contrast is developed between the senile father who is in need of help and the son who in the vigor and strength of his mind and body is exhorted not to revile his aged father. In v 14a, "kindness" is Heb *ṣĕdāqâ*, lit., righteousness, Gr *eleēmosynē*, lit., almsgiving (or mercy). At least since the time of the author of the Book of Tobit (the third or second century B.C.) almsgiving was considered to be righteousness *par excellence;* cf. Tob 1:3; 2:10; 4:7–11; 14:9, 10, 11. In fact, vv 14–15 state in gnomic form what Tob 14:10–11 states in narrative form: "Because Ahiqar had given alms [*eleēmosynē*] to me, he escaped from the deadly trap Nadab had set for him. But Nadab himself fell into the deadly trap, and it destroyed him. So, my children, note well what almsgiving [*eleēmosynē*] does, and also what wickedness [Gr *adikia*, lit., unrighteousness] does—it kills!" In Matt 6:1–2, Gr *dikaiosynē*, lit., righteousness, and *eleēmosynē* are used synonymously. The thoughts of vv 14b–15ab are rephrased in vv 9a, 30–31. In v 14a, the reading of MS C, "(not) forgotten" (Heb root *škḥ*), supported by G and Syr, is probably to be preferred to that of MS A, "blotted out" (Heb *mḥh*) because of the parallelism between "not forgotten" and "recalled [or remembered]" (Heb *zkr*) in v 15a; however, in support of the reading of MS A, cf. Neh 13:14: "Remember [Heb *zkr*] me . . . and do not blot out [Heb *mḥh*] my good deeds." The reading of MS A (and Neh 13:14) suggests the image of God's book in which are indelibly recorded the good deeds of his people.

Matt 5:7 restates v 15: "Happy are they who show mercy [Gr *eleēmones*]; they in turn shall be shown mercy [Gr *eleēthēsontai*]." Cf. also Matt 25:34–40.

The poem concludes on a stern note: to neglect and demean one's parents is to blaspheme and provoke God. Cf. Exod 21:17; Lev 20:9; Deut 27:16; Prov 20:20; Matt 15:4; Mark 7:10. Ben Sira is affirming, in effect, that impiety to parents is impiety to God himself.

5. Humility
(3:17–24)

3   [17] My son, conduct your affairs with humility,   A
      and you will be loved more than a giver of gifts.   C
[18] Humble yourself the more, the greater you are,
      and you will find favor with God;
[20] *a*For great is the power of the Lord,   GI
      yet by the humble he is glorified.
[21] What is too sublime for you, seek not;   A
      into things beyond your strength, search not.
[22] What is committed to you, attend to;
      what is hidden is not your concern.
[23] With what is beyond you, meddle not;
      more than enough for you has been shown you.
[24] Indeed, many are the speculations of human beings—
      evil and misleading fancies.

---

a [19] Many are the lofty and the noble,   GII
      but it is to the humble he reveals his plan.

Notes

3   17a. *your affairs*=G *ta erga sou,* presumably Heb *běma'ăśêkā;* MS A, Syr "in your wealth (conduct yourself)"=Heb *bě'ošrěkā;* some conjecture *bě'ešqěkā,* "in your concerns," cf. vv 22, 23. MS C's *'et kol mal'ăkōtêkā* appears to be clumsy retroversion from G.

    17b. MS C, G=*'iš mattān;* cf. Prov 19:6; this is easiest *translated* by the ancient paraphrase of MS A (Syr), "giver of gifts."

18a. G=Heb kĕmô gādaltā, kēn hašpēl napšekā; cf. MS C and 7:11, 17 (also 2:17 G).

19–20. Where there was originally one bicolon, we have three alternatives for colon a and two for colon b. GI perhaps=Heb kî gĕdōlâ gĕbûrat Yhwh, waʿănāwîm yĕgaddĕlûhû; cf. for colon b (v 20b) Pss 34:3–4; 147:5–6; Sir 43:28, 30 (G also 31); 49:11. For colon a (v 19a), GII=Heb rabbîm rāmîm wĕnikbādîm; MS A, Syr (both of which read raḥămîm, "mercy," for ḥēn, "grace," to end 3:18b) have kî rabbîm raḥămê ʾĕlōhîm, "For abundant is God's mercy." For colon b (v 19b), GII, MS A, Syr all read, wĕlaʿănāwîm yĕgalleh sôdô. This last is dependent on Amos 3:7 and suggests a confusion between gdl and glh in the transmission of colon b (compare 43:28, MS B ngdlh, Bᵐᵍ nglh!). The GII, MS A, Syr form of colon b (v 19b), whether or not it is original (compare 4:18), is old enough to be a source for the oldest form of the sayings in Matt 11:25, 29; to the gospel passage, the GII form of colon a (v 19a) comes nearest, but the terms are not the same (cf. also Luke 10:21–22).

21. For this bicolon the paraphrases in medieval Jewish literature are many and various; see Segal, pp. 17–18. To judge from G, the earliest form will have been on the pattern Heb niplāʾ mimmekā ʾal tidrōš, wĕrām mimmekā ʾal taḥqōr, though the adjectives employed could have been different (qāšeh, ʿāmōq, rāḥōq, . . .). Possible parallels abound: Psalm 131; Deut 1:17; 2:10 LXX; Exod 18:26; Qoh 7:24.

22a. For MSS AC huršêtā, cf. CD xi, 20 lĕharšōt. The verb is an Aram borrowing into Heb, and vv 22–24 have an Aram tinge.

22b. "what is hidden"=Heb bĕnistārôt, cf. Deut 29:28.

23a. "meddle not"=Heb ʾal titʿaśśēq, cf. M 41:22; MS A's ʾl tmr is unintelligible.

23b. Heb horʾêtā, cf. Deut 4:35.

23–24. G expands slightly by paraphrase.

Comment

This poem consists of a single stanza of seven lines; cf. NOTE on vv 19–20. Ben Sira writes often of the need for the wise to practice humility: 1:27; 4:8; 7:16–17; 10:26–28; cf. 45:4. Similar exhortations to humility are found in the *Manual of Discipline* or *Rule of the Community* at Qumran; cf. 1QS ii 23–25; iii 8–9; iv 3; v 3, 24–25; ix 22–23.

The Heb word ʿānāwâ (Gr praütēs), translated here "humility," can also mean "modesty, meekness." In Prov 15:33, humility is spoken of in a context dealing with fear of the Lord and wisdom: "The fear of the LORD is training for wisdom, and humility goes before honors" (cf. Prov 11:2; 18:12). In Prov 22:4, humility and fear of the Lord are again linked together: "The reward of humility and fear of the LORD is riches, honor and life." The strongest statement on humility as a religious and moral virtue is found in Zeph 2:3: "Seek the LORD, all you humble of the earth, who have observed his law; seek righteousness, seek humility."

In v 17, Ben Sira seems to be advising humility in one's affairs for a somewhat utilitarian motive, viz., that one may "be loved more than a giver of gifts." But actually the sage is simply stating a commonly observed fact of life: everybody enjoys a humble or modest person but dislikes the arrogant. In v 17a, Smend (p. 72), Peters (p. 33), Box-Oesterley (p. 325), and Duesberg-Fransen (pp. 102–3) prefer the reading of MS A and Syr, "in your wealth" (cf. NOTE). The maxim in v 18a again sediments a conviction shared by most people everywhere: though all are to be humble, the rich and powerful have a more obvious need of humility and modesty than the poor and weak, who have little to boast about. The reward of humility is "favor with God" (v 18b); cf. Job 22:29; Prov 3:34; 29:23; Matt 23:12; Phil 2:3–9; Jas 4:10; 5:5; 1 Pet 5:5–6.

The humility Ben Sira urges in this poem is a combination of attitudes and virtues toward oneself and others, including an adequate self-image, patience, modesty, docility, meekness, awareness of one's limitations, respect for others, and above all, total dependence on God.

There is a problem with the text of vv 19–20; see the NOTE. "The power of the Lord" (v 20a, GI) is often the object of praise in the OT; cf. 1 Chr 29:11–12; 2 Chr 20:6–7; Pss 20:6; 21:14; 71:18; 74:13; 78:4; 89:14; Sir 15:18; 36:3; 43:29; 2 Macc 3:24. Though the Lord is great in power, it is not the powerful who give him glory but the humble (v 20b); cf. Luke 1:46, 48, 51–52, and the references given in the NOTE. See the NOTE for v 19, the alternate form of the bicolon in v 20.

The exhortation in v 21 has several possible parallels, as indicated in the NOTE. Ps 131:1, however, is the closest parallel to our text. In writing this verse, Ben Sira may also have had in mind Qoh 1:13: "I applied my mind to search and investigate in wisdom all things that are done under the sun. A thankless task God has appointed for human beings to be busied about." Spicq (p. 581) writes that the warning in v 21 was quite appropriate in an age when cosmogonic and theosophic speculations were found not only in the pagan Hellenistic world but also in Israel. More than half the present poem is devoted to the dangers of intellectual pride (vv 21–24) and to the failure to appreciate the grandeur of Israel's heritage.

In vv 21, 22b, 23a, 24, Ben Sira cautions his readers about the futility of Greek learning, its goals and techniques, and also reminds them of what the Lord has bestowed on them (vv 22a, 23b). The point of vv 22a and 23b is that the Law and the traditions of Israel are sufficient for the believer to live fully and well. What has not been handed down by the Ancestors should have no place in Israel. Thus, searching into the ultimate nature of the universe and of humankind—"what is too sublime for you" (v 21a), "things beyond your strength" (v 21b), "what is hidden" (v 22b; cf. NOTE), and "what is beyond you" (v 23a)—should not be a concern, even though the Greeks gloried in their intellectual curiosity and their achievements in science, technology, and philosophy. For Ben Sira the "speculations" of the Greeks (v 24a) are "evil and misleading fancies" (v 24b). Hence it is far better for the enlightened Jew to follow the certainties and true wisdom of the Law revealed to Moses than to strive after the often contradictory musings and uncertain opinions of the Greek thinkers.

6. Docility, Almsgiving, Social Conduct
(3:25–4:10)

3   ²⁵ Where the pupil of the eye is missing, there is no light,   A
       and where there is no knowledge, there is no wisdom.
  ²⁶ The stubborn will fare badly in the end,
       and he who loves danger will perish in it.   G
  ²⁷ The stubborn will have many a hurt;   A
       adding sin to sin is the madman's part.
  ²⁸ When the scoundrel is stricken, there is no cure;
       he is the offshoot of an evil plant.
  ²⁹ The mind of a sage appreciates proverbs;
       to the attentive ear, wisdom is a joy.

ALMSGIVING

  ³⁰ As water quenches flaming fire,
       so alms atones for sins.
  ³¹ The kindness a person has done crosses his path as he
                                         goes;
       when he falls, he finds a support.
4   ¹ My son, do not mock the poor person's life,
       or wear out the expectations of an embittered spirit.   G
  ² The hungry do not aggrieve,   A
       nor ignore one who is downtrodden.
  ³ Do not inflame the bile of the oppressed;
       delay not giving to the needy.
  ⁴ A beggar's plea do not reject;   G
       avert not your glance from the downtrodden.
  ⁵ From one in need turn not your eyes,
       give him no reason to curse you;   A

6 For if in the ache of his bitterness he curse you,
   his Maker will hear his prayer.

SOCIAL CONDUCT

7 Endear yourself to the assembly;
   before the city's ruler bow your head.
8 Give a hearing to the poor,
   and return his greeting with deference.
9 Deliver the oppressed from his oppressors;
   let not right judgment be repugnant to you.
10 To the fatherless be as a father,
   help the widows in their husbands' stead;
   Then God will call you a son of his,
   and he will be more tender to you than a mother.   G

Notes

3 25. Lacking in GI. For *there is no wisdom,* GII reads, "make no claims"; Syr=
"do not give persuasive advice." MS A, Syr have v 25 after vv 26–27.
   26b. MS A = "and he who loves what is good will be brought along by it."
   27b. *madman's part=mithôlēl;* MS A has *mithôlēl,* G "sinner," Syr "impudent."
   28a. Omit *ʿal tārûṣ lĕrappĕʾôt* and *kî* 1°: so G, Syr, and Lat.
   29a. To G's "proverbs," MS A, Syr add "of the wise."
   31a. *will cross his path=yiqrennû (bidĕrākāyw);* MS A has *yiqrāʾennû.* Cf. 12:17;
15:2. G reads "He who repays kindnesses [i.e., God] remembers for the future."
   4 1a. For MS A, Syr "mock," G reads "deprive"=paraphrase?
   1b. *expectations,* lit., "eyes," *ʿênê* with G. *embittered spirit=mar rûaḥ;* MS A has
nepeš ʿānî wĕmar nepeš: dwwḥ.
   2a. *aggrieve=*G, Syr; MS A *tāpûaḥ/tāpîaḥ=*"scorn."
   2b. G *parorgisēs* perhaps corrupt for *paraidēs;* cf. G in 3a and 2:10; 7:10; 8:8.
   3a. MS A adds *wĕqereb ʿānî ʾal takʾēb,* duplicating parts of vv 2b, 3a.
   4a. G, Syr show MS A's *wĕlōʾ tibzeh šĕʾēlôt dal* to be corrupt in orthography,
syntax, and word order.
   4b–5a. Lacking in MS A, Syr; in G they may be two separate attempts to repair the
inner-Greek corruption in 2b; see above.
   6b. *his Maker=yôṣĕrô=*G; MS A *ṣûrô* "his Rock"; Syr "his Creator."
   7b. *city=ʿîr,* as in Syr; MS A has *ʿôd.* G omits the word.

10b. For *the widows,* G paraphrases "their [the orphans'] mother."

10d. MS A has "and he will be kindly to you and will deliver you from the pit."

Comment

This section contains three poems that have little in common. It illustrates a tendency of Ben Sira to place together bodies of material that are unrelated; cf. INTRODUCTION, Part I, 2.

The first poem, entitled here "Docility," contrasts the stubborn with the wise. In v 25, Ben Sira says that as the eye that has been blinded can never see light, so the fool who refuses to acquire "knowledge" can never acquire wisdom. In the Hebrew mind, "knowledge" (Heb *da'at*) in v 25b is a matter not only of the intellect but also of the will that makes decisions affecting one's manner of life. Thus, if one knows a great deal but refuses to act in an upright manner, such a one can never be considered wise; cf. INTRODUCTION, Part X, 1.

In vv 26a and 27a, "the stubborn" renders Heb *lēb kābēd,* lit., a heavy heart, an expression used in Exod 7:14 to describe Pharaoh as "obdurate, stubborn"; cf. Exod 8:28. The "heavy" or "stubborn" heart (=mind and will in our Western categories; cf. v 29a) is the exact opposite of the "listening" or "obedient" heart, Heb *lēb šōmēa',* which Solomon, the person known proverbially for his wisdom, asked for in his prayer (1 Kgs 3:9). The grandson translated the expression by *kardia sklēra,* "hard heart," the same expression found in Syr (and Lat in v 26a; in v 27a, Lat has "evil" instead of "hard"); in English, an idiomatic rendering of the Heb phrase would be "hardhead." The stubborn "will fare badly" because they lack wisdom, the beginning of which is fear of the Lord (cf. 1:14 and COMMENT on 1:11–30). The "danger" (cf. NOTE) Ben Sira refers to in v 26b is not spelled out. Lat adds an extra bicolon after v 26, perhaps in an attempt to explain the danger: "The heart that walks the two paths shall not meet with success, and the depraved of heart shall stumble thereon." With regard to the "two paths" in the thought of Ben Sira, cf. COMMENT on 2:12–14.

V 27a is in parallelism with v 26a and has basically the same meaning (cf. above) but specifies further that the many hurts the stubborn will suffer are due to the corresponding number of sins committed. In the Deuteronomic theology of retribution that Ben Sira considered normative (cf. COMMENT on 1:12 and 2:1–6), sin was punished in this life. Hence, to add sin to sin "is the madman's part" (v 27b); cf. NOTE.

In v 28a (cf. NOTE), the stubborn person is now called a "scoundrel," Heb *lēṣ*, which also means "arrogant person, scorner." "There is no cure" for such people, for as offshoots "of an evil plant" (v 28b) they do not even admit their sin because of pride which has blinded them (cf. v 25). The older Wisdom literature has much to say about the *lēṣ;* here are some examples: "The *lēṣ* loves not to be reproved; to the wise he will not go" (Prov 15:12). "A wise son loves correction, but the *lēṣ* heeds no rebuke" (Prov 13:1). "When [God] is dealing with the *lēṣîm,* he is stern, but to the humble he shows kindness" (Prov 3:34). Cf. also Prov 9:7, 8; 14:8; 19:25, 29; 20:1; 21:11, 24; 22:10; 24:9. Ben Sira speaks again of the *lēṣ* in 8:11a and 13:1b.

In v 29a, Heb *lēb ḥākām,* here translated "the mind of a sage," can also be rendered "a wise heart," which contrasts sharply with the "heavy (or stubborn) heart" of vv 26a and 27a. For the expression *lēb ḥākām,* cf. Job 9:4; Prov 10:8; 16:21. The wise person "appreciates," Heb *yābîn* (lit., understands), "proverbs" because as sedimentations of Israel's wisdom they exhort the believer to live a righteous life. The sage also has an ear that gives attention to and rejoices (Heb *śmḥ*) in "wisdom" (v 29b), which in the thought of Ben Sira is equivalent to fear of the Lord; cf. COMMENT on 1:11–30. The first three words of v 29b in Heb are found, in different form and order, in Prov 2:2; cf. also Prov 15:31. The idea of wisdom bringing joy occurs also in Prov 23:15: "My son, if your heart be wise, my own heart also will rejoice [Heb *śmḥ*]."

The next poem deals with almsgiving, an important part of Jewish ethical teaching; cf. COMMENT on 3:14–15. The imagery in v 30 is striking; and the rhetorical *a:b:c::c':b':a'* arrangement of the words adds emphasis to the point being made: *flaming fire:quenches:water* (subject of the clause)::*alms:atones for:sins.* Heb *ṣĕdāqâ* and Gr *eleēmosynē* in v 30b are used in the sense of "alms, almsgiving" also in 7:10b, 12:3b, 16:14a, and 40:24b; in 29:8b, 12a, and 35:4 (and probably in 17:22a), where no Heb is extant, *eleēmosynē* has the same meaning. Cf. Prov 16:6; Deut 24:13; Tob 4:7–11; Dan 4:24. For the thought of v 31, cf. Tob 14:10–11. In v 31a, Heb *ṭôb,* "kindness," becomes in the grandson's Greek *charitas,* accusative pl. of the word *charis,* from which derives the word "charity." *Charis* also renders *ṭôbâ* (the f. form of *ṭôb*) in 8:19b and 20:13b.

In 4:1a, Gr has *aposterēsēs,* "deprive, cheat, defraud" (cf. NOTE), the verb St. Paul employs in 1 Cor 6:7–8. The Heb verb *l'g,* "mock, deride," is also found in Prov 17:5a (a passage Ben Sira doubtless had in mind when he wrote v 1a; cf. INTRODUCTION, Part VI): "He who mocks the poor blasphemes his Maker." Cf. also Prov 30:17 and Jer 20:7. The verb *d'b* in v 1b occurs elsewhere in the Heb OT only in Ps 88:10 and Jer 31:12, 25. The point of v 1a is that one should not make the poor feel inferior by mocking them; and of v 1b, that one should come to the rescue of the poor, the embittered spirits, as soon as possible and not let them wait for help, an injunction Ben Sira repeats in

29:8. In MS A, Heb *mar nepeš*, "embittered spirit" (cf. NOTE), is found as a plural in Prov 31:6b and Job 3:20b.

In v 2a, Heb *nepeš ḥăsêrâ*, lit., a needy person, is here translated "the hungry," following the legitimate interpretation of the Gr; cf. Ps 107:9. The Gr verb *lypēsęs*, the basis of the translation "aggrieve" (cf. NOTE), occurs also in the LXX of Job 31:39, the MT of which has *hippāḥtî*, from the root *nph*. The verb in MS A *tpwḥ*, vocalized *tāpûaḥ*, is from the root *pwḥ*. But it is probable that the medieval scribe misread a *yod* as a *waw*, so that in his *Vorlage* the verb was *tpyḥ*, vocalized *tappêaḥ*, also from the root *nph* found in the Job passage. For the confusion of *waw* for *yod* and vice versa in the Cairo MSS of Ben Sira, cf. A. A. Di Lella, *The Hebrew Text of Sirach*, pp. 97–101. Concern for the hungry was an essential part of Jewish ethics: cf. Tob 1:17; 4:16; and Mark 6:34–44 and parallels. As regards "one who is downtrodden" (v 2b), cf. Tob 4:7.

The imagery in v 3a would be forceful to the ancient Jew; the rare Heb verb *ḥmr*, used here in the *hiphʿil* or causative conjugation, means "to ferment, boil, or foam up." Hence, literally, v 3a can be translated: "Do not ferment the bowels [Heb *mēʿîm*] of the oppressed." Cf. Lam 1:20; 2:11. The word *mēʿîm*, "bowels, intestines, internal organs," was used figuratively in the OT to designate the seat of emotions; cf. Isa 16:11; 63:15; Jer 4:19; 31:20; Cant 5:4. G has changed the imagery: "Add not more trouble to a heart that is provoked to anger." The injunction in v 3b is an adaptation of Prov 3:28: "Say not to your neighbor, 'Go, and come again, tomorrow I will give,' when you can give at once." Seneca, the Roman philosopher, politician, and author of tragedies (d. A.D. 65), makes a similar point: *Qui tarde fecit, diu noluit*, "The one who does [a favor] late refuses to do it early" (*De beneficiis*, i 1).

The background of v 4 seems to be Ps 22:25: "For [Yahweh] has not spurned nor disdained the wretched in their misery, nor did he turn his face away from them, but when they cried out to him, he heard them." If so, Ben Sira in effect is urging his readers to imitate Yahweh in his love and care of the poor. Regarding v 4a, cf. Matt 5:42. Tob 4:7 has a virtually identical exhortation to v 4b: "Do not turn your face away from any of the poor," Gr *mē apostrepsęs to prosōpon sou apo pantos ptōchou*, every word of which, except for *pantos* ("any of"), is found in G. To the above words, Tob 4:7 adds: "And God's face will not be turned away from you." Cf. Deut 15:7–11; Prov 19:17.

V 5a is in synonymous parallelism with v 4b; v 5b depends on Prov 28:27b: "He who ignores [Heb *maʿlîm ʿênāyw*, lit., he who hides his eyes from] [the poor] gets many a curse." Regarding v 6, cf. 31:21 and Prov 14:31a: "He who oppresses the poor blasphemes his Maker." In v 6a, the Heb verb *ṣʿq*, here and in G translated "curse" (lit., cry out), and the Heb noun *ṣěʿāqâ* in v 6b, translated "prayer" (lit., cry, outcry), occur also in a similar context in Exod

22:22: "If ever you wrong [any widow or orphan] and they *cry out* to me, I will surely hear their *cry.*"

The next poem, dealing with "Social Conduct," continues some of the themes of the previous poems in this section. It contains precepts as to how one should behave toward others in the various classes of society.

In v 7a, Ben Sira presents a general exhortation. The phrase "endear yourself" (Heb *ha'ăhēb lěnapšô,* Gr *prosphilē poiei*) occurs also in 20:13 in G; see NOTE there on the corrected Heb text. "The assembly" (Heb *ʿēdâ,* Gr *synagōgē*) is the community of the Jews; cf. 7:7; 42:11. V 7a gives a general precept that one should endear oneself to the whole community; the rest of the poem specifies the various classes within it. Lat misses the point of v 7a by adding after "assembly" the word *pauperum,* "of the poor." In v 7b, instead of "ruler," *megistani,* many Gr MSS read "rulers," *megistasi;* Syr does the same. The reason for the plural may be that "there was no single ruler in Jerusalem, but a *Gerousia,* or assembly of great ones, which became known later on as the Sanhedrin" (so Box-Oesterley, p. 328). The singular in Heb and most Gr MSS, however, is to be preferred because "the ruler" (Heb *šilṭôn*) most likely means any individual member of the Jewish aristocracy before whom one is urged to be deferential; cf. INTRODUCTION, Part II.

Vv 8–10 contain injunctions regarding the vast majority of second-century B.C. Jews: the poor, the oppressed, the orphans, and the widows, all of whom are the religiously privileged and protected persons in the Bible. Cf. 35:15–22; Deut 24:17–22; Lev 19:9–10; 23:22; Job 29:11–16; 31:13–22; Amos 5:10–15; Isa 1:17; Tob 1:3, 8; Jas 1:27. In v 8a, the phrase "give a hearing," Heb *haṭ 'oznĕkā,* lit., incline your ear, is also found in Ps 17:6; cf. Jer 11:8. In v 8b, the Heb phrase *hăšîbēhû šālôm,* "return his greeting" (lit., return to him "peace"), was misunderstood by G, which has "answer him with *peaceable words* [*eirēnika*]." The word *šālôm,* "peace," has been the usual Jewish greeting from biblical times to the present.

Regarding v 9, cf. Ps 82:2–4. The perversion of justice was excoriated by the prophets; cf. Amos 1:6–7; 4:1; 5:7, 10–15, 21–24; Isa 1:15–17. In 34:21–27, Ben Sira takes up again the themes of injustice and oppression in greater detail. In v 10ab, the orphan and the widow are persons *par excellence* incapable of self-defense because they lack social and/or financial resources. For that reason they come under God's special protection; Ps 68:6: "The father of orphans and the defender of widows is God in his holy dwelling." Thus the faithful are in duty bound to assist the orphan and the widow, as is clear from the present text and Isa 1:17; Exod 22:21–23; and Deut 24:17, 19–21. By being a father to the orphan and a husband to the widow, a person will be called a child of God and will receive more love from God than his mother gave him (v 10cd). The imagery of God as mother in v 10d, translated from G, derives from Isa 49:15 and 66:13. For the thought and vocabulary of v 10d in MS A (see NOTE), cf. 51:2; Job 33:18, 24, 30; Ps 103:4; and Isa 38:17.

Smend (p. 38), Box-Oesterley (p. 328), and Duesberg-Fransen (p. 106) prefer the reading of MS A to that of G. Regarding the fatherhood of God in v 10c and elsewhere in the Bible, cf. 23:1, 4; 51:10; Deut 32:6; Isa 63:16; 64:7; Jer 3:19; 31:9; Hos 11:1, 3–4; Mal 1:6; 2:10; Prov 3:12; Wis 2:13, 16; 14:3; Matt 5:16; 6:1, 4, 6, 8–9, 14–15, 18, 26, 32; 7:11. Cf. M.-J. Lagrange, "La Paternité de Dieu dans l'ancien testament," *RB* n.s. 5 (1908): 481–99. In v 10cd, Ben Sira uses the biblical images of father and mother to describe God in his loving concern for the faithful. This metaphorical language, however, does not mean that God has gender (male or female), because he transcends sex and every other human category. God is far more than a father and a mother to creatures.

A final observation with regard to the ethical sensitivity toward the disadvantaged expressed in 3:30–4:10: the Greeks, despite their unquestioned accomplishments in philosophy, ethics, and law, had such a low regard for the poor that according to Plato (*The Laws,* ii) a certain Athenian actually proposed that each state enact a law banishing the poor; so Spicq, p. 588. It is to be further observed that Ben Sira, while urging benevolence and concern for the weak and powerless, does not condemn the rich simply because they are rich. Only those are warned who have the resources but neglect the poor.

PART II (4:11–6:17)

7. Wisdom's Rewards and Warnings
(4:11–19)

4   ¹¹ Wisdom teaches her children   A
        and admonishes all who can understand her.
      ¹² Those who love her love life;
        those who seek her out win the Lord's favor.
      ¹³ Those who hold her fast inherit glory;
        wherever they dwell, the Lord bestows his blessing.
      ¹⁴ Those who serve her serve the Holy One;
        those who love her, the Lord loves.   G

      ¹⁵ "Whoever obeys me will judge nations;   A
        whoever listens to me will dwell in my inmost
                             chambers.
      ¹⁶ If he remains faithful, he will have me as his heritage;   G
        his descendants too will possess me.

      ¹⁷ "Yet I will walk with him in disguise,   A
        and at first I will probe him with trials;
     Fear and dread I will bring upon him   G
        and test him with my discipline—
     Then when his heart is fully with me   A
      ¹⁸   I will set him again upon the straight path
        and reveal to him my secrets.
      ¹⁹ But if he fails me, I will abandon him
        and deliver him over to robbers."

Notes

4 11. *Wisdom*=Heb *ḥokmôt,* as in Prov 1:20; 9:1. *admonishes,* cf. Gen 43:3; Deut 8:19. *who can understand,* cf. Neh 8:2, 3.

12. Prov 8:17, 35; compare Sir 1:10; 2:15–16.

13a. Prov 3:35; 8:18, 21. Omit *myy* of MS A.

14b. MS A is jumbled here; Syr in a similar jumble reads Heb *'ohŏlô,* "his tent," for "those who love her." Cf. Wis 7:28.

15. The change to Wisdom as the speaker in MS A is very abrupt, but seems called for in vv 17–19; G has third person throughout. *nations*=G=Heb *'ummōt;* MS A, Syr *'ĕmet*="truly." Compare Prov 8:15–16 (the latter with variants *šōpĕṭê 'āreṣ/ṣedeq*); Wis 3:8.

16. Lacking in MS A; G, Syr have it.

17. There should be five cola here, the last one to be combined with v 18. G has the order *a, c, d, e, b;* Syr assimilates *b* and *d;* MS A lacks *c,* and reads a form of *d* after 19a. *probe*=*bḥr* as in Isa 48:10 and in Aram. *trials,* cf. 2:1–5; 6:18–23. *fear and dread,* cf. Exod 15:16.

18. *reveal to him my secrets,* cf. 3:19 (GII); 1:30; 39:6–8.

19. MS A has two corrupt forms for this, perhaps deriving from Heb *wĕ'im yāsûr ûnĕṭaštîhû, wĕhisgartîhû lĕšōdĕdîm;* G may have read at the end Heb *lîdê 'êdām/pîdām* or the like. *robbers,* cf. Obad 5; Jer 49:7–10.

Comment

Part II (4:11–6:17) falls into four sections on the general theme of Wisdom in everyday life: (1) Wisdom's rewards and warnings; (2) admonition against cowardice; (3) the dangers of presumption, duplicity in speech, and unruly passions; (4) true and false friendship.

The first poem (4:11–19) has three stanzas: four bicola in the first stanza; two bicola in the second stanza; and in the third stanza two bicola, a tricolon, and a bicolon, totalling four poetic lines that correspond to the four in the first stanza. In the first stanza (vv 11–14), Wisdom is referred to in the third person; in the second and third stanzas, Wisdom is the speaker (cf. NOTE on v 15).

In v 11a, "her children," Heb *bānêhā,* is a *mot crochet* (catchword) with *ben*, "son," in v 10c, thus connecting this section to the previous one. Throughout the poem, Wisdom is personified as a woman deeply concerned about her children. It is to be noted that the Heb verb *lmd*, "teach" (v 11a), is in parallelism with the verb *ʿwd*, "admonish, exhort solemnly" (v 11b). There is also a wordplay between *bānêhā* and *mĕbînîm*, "(all) who can understand (her)" (v 11b). Thus Ben Sira suggests that only those who understand Wisdom can be her children; cf. 15:2a. Cf. also Luke 7:35: "Wisdom is vindicated by all her children." Cf. B. Couroyer, "Un Égyptianisme dans Ben Sira iv,11," *RB* 82 (1975): 206–17.

In the next three verses there is an interesting flow of images that are rhetorically arranged in an *a:b:c:b':a* pattern: *those who love her* (v 12a):*those who seek her out* (v 12b):*those who hold her fast* (v 13a):*those who serve her* (v 14a): *those who love her* (v 14b). The verbs "seek" (Heb *bqš*) and "serve" (*šrt*) are often used in religious contexts with God or Yahweh as the direct object; for *bqš* cf., for example, Deut 4:28; Zeph 1:6; 2:3; Hos 3:5; 5:6; 1 Chr 16:10; 2 Chr 11:16; 20:4; for *šrt*, cf. 7:30; Deut 10:8; 17:12; 21:5; Isa 61:6; Jer 33:21. Accordingly, just as those who seek Wisdom seek God, so those who serve Wisdom also serve the Lord (v 14a).

The thought of v 12 is derived from Prov 3:16a, 18a; 8:17, 35; cf. also Wis 7:11–14; 8:16. In v 12b, the Heb word *rāṣôn* is used of God's "favor, good-will" also in Prov 12:2; 18:22; Pss 5:13; 30:6, 8; 51:20; 89:18; 106:4; Deut 33:16; Isa 60:10. The words "life" (Heb *ḥayyîm*) (v 12a) and "the Lord's favor" (v 12b) are in parallelism, thus suggesting that the attainment of a full life is due to the goodwill of the Lord. "Life" includes "glory, honor," Heb *kābôd* (v 13a), and the Lord's "blessing" (v 13b). In v 13a, the expression "those who hold her fast," Heb *tômĕkêhā*, is found in a similar context in Prov 3:18b. For the idea in v 13a, cf. also Prov 3:16b, 35a; 8:18a. In v 13b, the blessings of the Lord include those things that make for the good and long life (v 12a)—honor (v 13a), wealth (Prov 8:21), a worthy wife (Prov 18:22; cf. Prov 31:10–31).

A remarkable affirmation is made in v 14a: to serve Wisdom is to serve God himself. Here again Ben Sira implicitly equates Wisdom with fear of the Lord; cf. COMMENT on 1:11–30. The Heb verb *šrt*, "serve," is often used in cultic contexts; cf., for example, Deut 10:8; 17:12; 21:5; Jer 33:21. God is called "the Holy One," Heb *qôdeš* (lit., the Holiness), Gr *hagios,* because holiness is the divine attribute *par excellence;* cf. Isa 6:3. In Deutero-Isaiah, "the Holy One," Heb *qādôš,* is a favorite title of God; cf. Isa 41:14, 16, 20; 45:11; 47:4; 48:17; 49:7; 54:5; 55:5; cf. also Job 6:10; Isa 1:4; 5:19, 24; 10:20. In later Jewish literature, "the Holy One" is the term most frequently used when speaking of God; cf. 23:9 (G); 43:10 (G and Syr); 47:8 (G); 48:20 (G); Bar 4:22; 5:5. God loves those who love Wisdom (v 14b; see NOTE), because in the theology of Ben Sira Wisdom equals fear of the Lord; and God loves those who fear him by keeping the Law. Cf. Deut 7:12–13; 28:1–14; Prov 15:9; Ps 146:8.

The switch from Wisdom in the third person in the first stanza (vv 11–14) to Wisdom as speaker (in MS A and Syr but not in G) signals the beginning of the second stanza (vv 15–16), which specifies further the rewards of Wisdom. In v 15a, the consonants of 'mt in MS A, usually vocalized 'ĕmet ("truth," or "truly"), as Syr understood the word here, can also be vocalized 'ummōt, "nations" (cf. NOTE). The defective spelling of the word (but with a suffix) is found also in Gen 25:16, one of the three occurrences of the rare word in the MT, the others being Num 25:15 and Ps 117:1 (where the word is in parallelism with gôyīm, the common Heb word for "nations"). The idea of the just judging nations is found also in Wis 3:8, an idea taken up by St. Paul in 1 Cor 6:2; cf. Rev 3:21; 20:4. The LXX of Prov 29:9a expresses an idea similar to that in v 15a: "A wise man shall judge nations." Knabenbauer (p. 73), Smend (p. 40), Peters (p. 45), Box-Oesterley (p. 329), and Segal (p. 24 of Commentary) read 'mt as 'ĕmet. The image of Wisdom's "inmost chambers" (v 15b) derives from Prov 9:1: "Wisdom has built her house; she has set up her seven columns." Cf. 1:17. The wise must remain faithful to Wisdom in order to possess her as their heritage (v 16a). For the thought expressed in v 16b, cf. 1:15.

The final stanza of the poem (vv 17–19) has as its topic the concept of testing to determine whether or not the wise are faithful to Wisdom (v 16a). For the textual problems in v 17, see NOTE. The image of Wisdom walking with the wise (v 17a) occurs also in 6:24–25. Wisdom walks "in disguise" so that she may effectively probe the wise with trials (v 17b; see NOTE). The idea of God's "testing" a person's fidelity is found often in the OT: e.g., Gen 22:1; Exod 15:25; 16:4; 20:20; Deut 8:2, 16; 13:4; 2 Chr 32:31; Ps 26:2. It is curious that Wisdom speaks of bringing on the wise "fear and dread" (v 17c), which are precisely the unpleasant feelings that fell upon the Canaanites when they heard of the power of the Lord in redeeming his people (Exod 15:16). The grandson's use of the Gr basanizō (v 17d) is appropriate, for the verb means "to rub upon the touchstone; to test the genuineness of a thing." According to Ben Sira, "discipline" (Heb mûsār, Gr paideia) is a prominent part of the life of the wise; cf. 31:17a; 32:14a; 37:31a; 42:5b, 8a; 50:27a.

When Wisdom finds out that the heart of the wise "is fully" with her (v 17e), she again will set them on the right path (the Heb verb 'šr means literally "to lead on," as in Prov 23:19) and reveal to them her secrets (v 18). As regards Wisdom's "secrets" (Heb mistārîm, Gr krypta), cf. 39:3, 7b; 51:19f; Job 11:6; Dan 2:21–22. On vv 17–18, cf. Prov 3:11–12; Heb 12:5–13. If the wise "fail" (Heb yāsûr, lit., turn aside [from]) Wisdom, she "will abandon" them and "deliver [them] over to robbers" (v 19; cf. NOTE). The vivid imagery here may derive from Jer 49:7–10. The point Ben Sira makes is clear: if one refuses discipline and chastisement and the pain of trials (v 17a–d), one will never achieve genuine Wisdom (in the Heb sense of the word) but will be left devoid of any real sense of meaning in life (v 19).

8. Against Cowardice
(4:20–31)

4   20 My son, let your actions be timely; fear what is wrong,   A
        be not ashamed to be yourself.
  21 There is a sense of shame laden with guilt,
        and a shame that merits honor and respect.
  22 Show no favoritism to your own discredit;   C
        let no one intimidate you to your own downfall.   G
  23 Refrain not from speaking at the proper time,   C
        and hide not away your wisdom;   A
  24 It is through speech that wisdom becomes known,
        and understanding, through the tongue's rejoinder.

  25 Never gainsay the truth,   G
        and of your folly be ashamed.
  26 Be not ashamed to acknowledge your guilt,
        and struggle not against the rushing stream.   A
  27 Do not abase yourself before a fool,
        nor show favoritism before rulers.   G
  28 Even to the death fight for truth,   A
        and the LORD will battle for you.

  29 Be not haughty in your speech,
        nor lazy and slack in your deeds.
  30 Be not a lion at home,
        nor sly and suspicious with your servants.
  31 Let not your hand be open to receive
        and clenched when it is time to give.

Notes

4 20. MS A (*ʾēt*) *hāmôn* [Schechter *ûzĕman*]: omit with G, Syr; cf. Qoh 3:1.
22b. *let no one intimidate you* = Heb *wĕʾal tikkālēm* = G; read *lĕmikšôl lāk* with MS C.
25a. *truth* = G, Syr; MS A *hāʾēl.*
25b. G = Heb *wĕʾal ʾiwwaltĕkā hikkālēm;* MS A = *wĕʾel ʾĕlōhîm hikkānaʿ.*
26a. *to acknowledge your guilt* = G, Syr; MS A = "to draw back from guilt."
28. MS A introduces 8:14 before this verse and 5:14 after it. *fight* = G, Syr; the verb in MS A (*hēʿāṣēh,* written fully *hyʿṣh*) is an Aram loanword, and dubious. *truth* = G, Syr; MS A = *haṣṣedeq* = "righteousness."
30. *sly and suspicious* = MS A; "servants" = G, MS C *ʿăbuddātāk.*

Comment

This section contains sundry maxims about true and false shame (vv 20–28) and three unrelated sayings (vv 29–31). Shame is dealt with more extensively in 41:14–42:8 and more briefly in 20:22–23. There are three stanzas: 5+4+3 bicola.

The first stanza opens with *bĕnî,* "my son," thus signaling a fresh start. G and Syr omit the word, though Lat has it. Heb *ʿēt šĕmōr* means lit. "observe the appropriate time (or opportune moment)." Gr *kairos* has the same meaning as *ʿēt* in this and similar contexts, i.e., qualitative time and not quantitative or clock time. The "what is wrong" (Heb *raʿ,* lit., evil) in v 20a is not moral evil in general but probably a reference to the deadly compromise with Hellenism that many Jews were tempted to make; cf. INTRODUCTION, Part II. Thus, v 20b urges Jews not to be ashamed to be themselves. According to 1 Macc 1:11–15, a number of Jews in the reign of Antiochus IV Epiphanes (175–164 B.C.) gave up the practice of their faith for the allurements of the Greek way of life, even going so far as to cover over the mark of their circumcision so that they would suffer no ridicule when they engaged in sports naked, as was customary in the Greek gymnasium built in Jerusalem by "the ungodly pseudo-high-priest Jason," as 2 Macc 4:13 describes him. Though the Books of Maccabees refer to a period a few years later than our book, doubtless the temptation for Jews to accommodate to the Greek life-style was real also in Ben Sira's day.

Even the priests during Jason's high priesthood "despised what their ances-tors had regarded as honors, while they highly prized what the Greeks es-teemed as glory" (2 Macc 4:15). Accordingly, in the interpretation of this stanza I am suggesting, the point of v 21a is that to be ashamed to be a Jew is a "shame laden with guilt." On the contrary, when one is ashamed of one's sins and infidelities, such a shame "merits honor and respect" (v 21b). In 41:14–22, Ben Sira provides a detailed list of things that a faithful Jew should be ashamed of: immorality, falsehood, flattery, crime, disloyalty, breaking an oath, theft, lack of table manners, being tightfisted, fraud, lack of social graces, immoral thoughts and actions with a woman, unseemly language, betraying secrets.

In v 22a, the Heb expression *nś pānîm,* "show favoritism or partiality" (lit., lift up the face) occurs also in 35:16a and 42:1b and in this sense also in Deut 10:17; Lev 19:15; Job 13:8, 10; 34:19; Prov 18:5; Ps 82:2. V 22b, "let no one intimidate you [Heb *'al tikkālēm* (cf. NOTE), lit., do not be put to shame, dishonored, confounded] to your own downfall [Heb *lĕmikšôl,* lit., to (your own) stumbling]," probably is a warning not to abandon Judaism for a Helle-nistic way of life; cf. COMMENT on v 20 above. Parallelism would then war-rant the interpretation that v 22a also deals with an admonition about the blandishments of Hellenism.

The maxim in v 23 about the need to speak up "at the proper time" and to "hide not away your wisdom," shows us how deeply convinced Ben Sira was of his own Jewish faith, which he felt was far superior to anything the Greeks had to offer. The Jews had nothing to fear in their encounters with Greeks and should be courageous in speech about the glories of Israel. In v 23b, "wisdom" refers to the ancestral religion and way of life that the Jew prizes as his most precious possession. The reason why the Jew should speak up is given in v 24, which opens with the Heb particle *kî,* Gr *gar,* "for, because" (not given in the translation above): for only through speech can the wisdom of Israel become known, and understanding of Israel's heritage comes only through the tongue's reply. A rhetorically striking *a:b::b':a'* pattern brings this important stanza to a close: *through speech:wisdom::understanding: through the tongue's rejoinder.* Cf. Prov 16:1.

In v 25a, the verb *srb,* "gainsay, contradict," is an Aram loanword; Syr has *tesrōb.* The advice not to contradict the truth (cf. NOTE) or to lie, though part of any ethical system, has special significance for the Jew. In the Jerusalem Talmud, *Sanhedrin* i 18a, it is said that " *'Ĕmet* ['truth'] is the name of God" (quoted by Box-Oesterley, p. 330). Interestingly, instead of "truth," found in G and Syr, MS A reads "God." Cf. John 14:6, where Jesus says: "I am the way, and the truth, and the life." The injunction to be ashamed of one's folly (v 25b) comes from G; cf. NOTE. MS A has: "Humble yourself before God," and Syr, "Keep yourself away from your own folly."

In v 26a, the expression *"to acknowledge* your guilt" renders Heb *lāšûb mēʿāwôn,* lit., *to turn away* from guilt, or sin. The verb *šûb* in the OT often has this meaning; cf., for example, 1 Kgs 8:35; 13:33; Jer 15:7; 18:8; Ezek 3:19; 13:22. For repentance, i.e., turning away from evil, to be effective and sincere, one must confess one's sins (cf. Lev 5:5), make restitution when necessary (cf. Num 5:7–8), and humble oneself before the Lord (cf. 1 Kgs 21:29). It is all of this that Ben Sira counsels in v 26a. In v 26b, "struggle" translates Heb *ʿmd,* lit., stand. The interpretation of the colon is not clear, but it probably means "that one might as well try and stop the current of a river as seek to hide sins, i.e., from God" (so Box-Oesterley, p. 331). Apparently, v 26b was a proverb that urged against trying to do the impossible and thus was applicable to different situations. In the Syriac text of Aḥiqar we read: "My son, struggle not against a man in his day, and oppose not the current of a river."

W. M. W. Roth (*VT* 10 [1960]: 408) argues that "fool," Heb *nābāl,* in v 27a means an apostate from the Jewish faith. I would agree with that opinion in view of my interpretation of vv 20–24. See INTRODUCTION, Part X, 1. Regarding the translation "show favoritism" (v 27b), which comes from G, see COMMENT on v 22a above; cf. Jas 2:1–4. Compare v 27b with v 7b. In v 28a, Ben Sira advises Jews to fight (cf. NOTE) for truth even to the death. MS A reads *haṣṣedeq,* "righteousness, what is right, just," a reading also found in Lat; G and Syr read "truth," Heb *ʾĕmet.* If *ʾĕmet* is the correct reading, there is an *inclusio* between the opening and closing bicola of this stanza (vv 25 and 28). The "righteousness" or "truth" referred to is most likely the Jewish way of life; see COMMENT on vv 20–24. Cf. Ezek 14:14. The Jews who fight to the death for their faith need have no fear, for the Lord himself will battle for them (v 28b); cf. Exod 14:14; Prov 18:10; 2 Macc 14:15.

The next three verses (29–31) contain precepts for everyday life. Regarding v 29a, cf. Ps 12:4–5; for v 29b, cf. Prov 18:9. The exhortation in v 29 contrasts "speech" (Heb *lāšôn,* lit., tongue) and "deeds." One meaning of the verse may be "Don't talk big and then do little." Other possible interpretations are "Big talk is cheap; performance is what counts"; "Actions speak louder than words." Cf. 1 Cor 4:20. In v 30a, the reading "lion" (Heb *kĕʾaryēh,* lit., like a lion) is from MS C and is found also in G; MS A and Syr have "like a dog" (Heb *kĕkeleb*). Smend (p. 46) suggests that the original Heb reading may have been *kĕlābîʾ,* "like a lion." The Heb word *ʿabuddâ,* found in MS C (cf. NOTE), means household servants as a body; it occurs elsewhere in the OT only in Gen 26:14 and Job 1:3. The maxim in v 31 speaks for itself. The Heb verbs *ptḥ,* "open" (v 31a), and *qpṣ,* "clenched" (v 31b), are paired in a similar context also in Deut 15:7–8: "If one of your kinsmen . . . is in need . . . , you shall not harden your heart nor *close* your hand to him in his need. Instead, you shall *open* your hand to him and freely lend him enough to meet his need." Cf. Acts 20:35. This verse is freely cited in the *Didache*, iv 5, Epistle of Barnabas, xix 9, and Apostolic Constitutions, vii 12, 1: "Be not one that stretches out his hands to receive, but draws them in when it comes time to give."

9. Presumption, Duplicity in Speech, Unruly Passions (5:1–6:4)

AGAINST PRESUMPTION

5   1 Rely not on your wealth;   A
say not: "I have the power."
2 Count not on your mind and strength
in pursuing your own desires.
3 Say not, "Who can prevail against me?"
for the LORD will exact the punishment.

4 Say not: "I have sinned, yet what has befallen me?"
for the LORD bides his time.   C
5 Of forgiveness be not overconfident,   A
adding sin upon sin,
6 And saying: "Great is his mercy;
my many sins he will forgive";
For mercy and anger alike are with him—
upon the wicked alights his wrath.

7 Delay not your conversion to the LORD;
put it not off from day to day—
For suddenly his wrath flames forth:
at the time of vengeance you will be destroyed.
8 Rely not upon deceitful wealth;
it will be no help on the day of wrath.

AGAINST DUPLICITY IN SPEECH

9 Winnow not in every wind,
and start not off in every direction.   C

10 Be steadfast in your thoughts;   A
    consistent be your words.
11 Be swift to hear,
    but slow to answer.
12 If you have the knowledge, answer your neighbor;
    if not, put your hand over your mouth.

13 Honor and dishonor through talking!
    A person's tongue can be his downfall.
14 Be not called two-faced;
    use not your tongue for calumny.
 For the thief, shame was created;
    and harsh disgrace, for the two-faced.
15 Say nothing harmful, small or great,
6   1   be not a foe instead of a friend;
    A bad name, disgrace, and reproach will you acquire: G
    "This is what an evil, two-faced person is like!"   A

AGAINST UNRULY PASSIONS

2 Fall not into the grip of desire
    lest like fire it consume your strength;
3 Your leaves it will eat, your fruit destroy,
    and you will be left a dry tree,
4 For contumacious desire destroys its owner
    and makes him the sport of his enemies.

Notes

5   2a. *mind and*=G; MS A omits. MS A has another bicolon after v 2, a doublet.
3b. MS A alludes to Qoh 3:15, in what seems a reworked text.
4. MS A, Syr follow this verse with a form of 5:6ab, which MS A repeats in its proper place.
    7d. *the time of*=MS C, G; MS A="on the day of."
8. *wealth*=G; cf. v 1; MS A's *niksê*=Syr cannot be the authentic term.
9b. G follows this with a duplicate of 6:1c.
14d. MS A has "and disgrace; his neighbor"; G, Syr, "and harsh disgrace."

6 2b. Read *pen tĕbaʿēr kāʾēš ḥelekā;* MS A's *ʿālekā* is dittography from 6:3. G, Syr "consume like a bull" reflects the LXX understanding of Exod 22:4–5; for Ben Sira, passion is a fire, cf. 9:8; 23:16–17; and *bʿr* is "to burn with fire," cf. 8:10; 27:5; 40:30; 48:1. For the tree imagery with this, cf., e.g., Jer 11:16.

Comment

This section, the unity of which is suggested by the twenty-two-line structure (see COMMENT on 1:11–30 and 51:13–30), contains three poems: (1) against presumption (5:1–8); (2) against duplicity in speech (5:9–6:1); (3) against unruly passions (6:2–4). The first has $3+4+3$ lines. The opening and closing bicola (vv 1 and 8) have the word "wealth," thus forming an *inclusio* signaling the end of the poem.

Regarding the precept not to rely on wealth or to boast of power (v 1), cf. Ps 62:11–12. The Heb verb *šʿn,* "rely on" (lit., lean on), occurs also in v 2 (translated here "count on") and in 15:4: "[The one who fears the Lord] *will lean on* [Wisdom] and not fall." Cf. Luke 12:15–21; 1 Tim 6:17. In v 1b, the phrase "I have the power" is a translation of Heb *yš lʾl ydy.* A similar expression is found in 14:11 and in Gen 31:29; Deut 28:32; Neh 5:5; Prov 3:27; and Mic 2:1. The MT of Gen 31:29 vocalizes the words thus: *yeš-lĕʾēl yādî.* The meaning of the phrase has always been understood, but attempts to account for it grammatically have not been successful. W. G. E. Watson, "Reclustering Hebrew *lʾyd-,*" *Bib* 58 (1977): 213–15, argues that *lʾ* means "power" (etymology is *lāʾâ,* "to be strong, prevail," with cognates in Akkadian, Ugaritic, and Punic), and the expression should be divided thus: *lʾ lĕyād-,* "power in the hand of . . . ," which is a normal construction with *yēš,* "there is," or with *ʾēn,* "there is not." Thus the phrase in v 1b is translated lit. "There is power in my hand."

In v 2, Ben Sira urges against presumption based on one's intellectual ability or physical strength (cf. NOTE). In v 2b, the Heb phrase *hlk ʾaḥar,* translated here "in pursuing" (lit., in walking after), also occurs in Job 31:7b. The first colon of the doublet after v 2 in MS A, *(ʾal) tēlēk ʾaḥărê libbĕkā wĕʿênêkā,* "(do not) walk after your heart or your eyes," contains all the words of Job 31:7b, but in a different order and syntax: *wĕʾaḥar ʿênay hālak libbî,* "and my heart has walked after my eyes." The expression "(going astray) *after your heart(s) and your eyes*" is found also in Num 15:39. The second colon of the doublet, "by walking in evil desires," is an interpretation of v 2b.

The maxim in v 3a warns against presumption in speech. Instead of Heb *kōḥô,* "his strength," read *kōḥî,* "[Who can prevail against] my strength"; for the confusion of *waw* and *yod* in the Geniza MSS, cf. A. A. Di Lella, *The Hebrew Text of Sirach,* pp. 97–101. See Ps 13:5a for another example of the verb *ykl* with an object. The wording of MS A in v 3b is based on Qoh 3:15 (see NOTE). G has: "For the Lord will surely avenge you." Some Gr MSS and Lat omit "you"; other Gr MSS read "your pride." A dramatic illustration of the Lord avenging overweening pride is found in Dan 4:27–29.

The idea expressed in v 4 reflects Qoh 8:11–13. In v 4b, instead of "For the LORD *bides his time,"* one may translate "For the LORD *is slow to anger,"* Heb *'erek 'appayim,* lit., long of nostrils, the nose being in the Hebrew mind the place where anger manifests itself. The expression occurs also in Exod 34:6; Num 14:18; Neh 9:17; Pss 86:15; 103:8; 145:8; Nah 1:3. MS C reads "Yahweh," i.e., "LORD," MS A and Syr "God," most Gr MSS "Lord," the *O*-group of Gr MSS and Lat "the Most High"—a good example of the fluidity of the divine names in the book and its translations. The whole stanza (vv 4–6) concerns the arrogant sinner who presumes on God's mercy and forgiveness. MS A adds after v 4ab: "Do not say: 'Yahweh is merciful, and all my sins he will blot out' "; cf. Ps 51:3, 11; Isa 43:25; 44:22. This addition is a variant of v 6ab (cf. NOTE).

The Heb noun *sĕlîḥâ,* "forgiveness," occurs elsewhere in the singular only in Ps 130:4; the plural, used in the sense of "abundant forgiveness," is found in Neh 9:17 and Dan 9:9. In vv 5ab and 6ab, there is a striking *a:b:c::c:b':a* chiastic arrangement that adds emphasis to the point being made: *sĕlîḥâ/* forgiveness:*'āwôn 'al 'āwôn/*sin upon sin:*raḥămāyw rabbîm/*his mercy is great::*rôb/*greatness of, multitude of:*'ăwônôtay/*my sins:*yislāḥ/*he will forgive. V 6c is repeated in 16:11c in a context that develops the ideas contained in the present poem. The point of v 6 is that one must not remain in the state of sin by presuming on divine mercy, for the Lord of mercy who has compassion on those who repent is also a God of wrath who punishes those who continue to sin. The prophets often stress this twofold truth about God; cf., for example, Hos 2:4–25; 4:1–3; 6:1–3; Amos 5:15, 18–24; Isa 1:18–20.

The last stanza (vv 7–8) of the present poem urges that repentance be not postponed. In v 7a, MSS A and C read *lāšûb 'ēlāyw,* translated here "your conversion to the LORD" (lit., to turn back to him [the LORD]). Regarding the verb *šûb,* cf. COMMENT on 4:26. On v 7ab, cf. Prov 14:16. The Heb phrase *miyôm 'el yôm,* "from day to day," or "day after day," occurs, but in a different context, also in 1 Chr 16:23 and Ps 96:2. In v 7c, the concept of the Lord's wrath or indignation (Heb *za'am*) flaming forth (Heb *yṣ',* lit., coming forth) and destroying the wicked derives from texts such as Lev 10:2 ("Fire came forth [*yṣ'*] from Yahweh's presence and consumed [Nadab and Abihu]") and Num 16:35. The noun *za'am* is used of Yahweh's indignation in Isa 26:20; 30:27; Nah 1:6; Hab 3:12; Pss 38:4; 102:11; Dan 11:36. In Isa 26:21, Yahweh himself is said to go forth (Heb *yṣ'*) "from his place, to punish the wickedness of the earth's inhabitants." As regards the *suddenness* of Yahweh's wrath, cf. Mark 13:36. The phrase "the time of vengeance," the reading of MS C, which is followed by G and Syr, occurs also in 18:24b (G; the Heb text is not extant) but nowhere else in the OT. The phrase "the day of vengeance," the reading of MS A, occurs also in Isa 34:8; 61:2; 63:4; Prov 6:34. In v 7d, the *niphʿal* of the verb *sph*, "be destroyed, swept away," occurs in a similar context also in Gen 19:15, 17; Num 16:36; 1 Sam 12:25.

V 8 takes up by way of *inclusio* the thought of v 1 and develops it. In v 8a, Heb *nĕkāsîm*, "riches," the reading of MS A and Syr, is found also in Josh 22:8 and 2 Chr 1:11, 12, the LXX of which has in each of these places *chrēmata*, the word used in G here. Accordingly, *nĕkāsîm* appears to be the original reading; but cf. the NOTE for a different opinion. Regarding v 8b, cf. Prov 10:2; 11:4; Ezek 7:19; Matt 13:22; Mark 4:19; Luke 16:13. Instead of "wrath," the last word of v 8b, G reads "calamity, trouble," *epagōgēs*, the same word used in 2:2b. Cf. G. L. Prato, *Il problema della teodicea in Ben Sira*, pp. 367–69, for a discussion of vv 4–8, which he considers to be "a compendium of theodicy."

The next poem (5:9–6:1) contains precepts against duplicity in speech. It has two stanzas, 4+5 bicola. The two proverbs in v 9 seem to be exhortations to avoid fickleness and indecision. G adds a third colon, a duplicate of 6:1c, and thus appears to understand the proverbs in v 9ab as pertaining to sincerity and honesty in speech, about which the rest of the poem is concerned. V 10 may also be translated: "Be firm concerning what you know [Heb *daʿtekā*, lit., your knowledge, discernment, understanding]; let your word be one." The passive participle *sāmûk*, "firm, steadfast," occurs also in Isa 26:3 and Ps 112:8. The meaning of v 10 is that one's speech [Heb *dābār*, word] should coincide with what one knows to be true [*daʿat*]. The word *daʿat* signifies what is internal, i.e., in the mind; *dābār*, what is external, what emerges from and becomes independent of the speaker.

The thought of v 11 is taken up in Jas 1:19: "Let every one be quick to hear, slow to speak, slow to anger." Cf. Prov 18:13. A number of Gr MSS (*L*-743) add after v 11a: "and let your life be in truth." V 11b may also be translated: "and with patience, or deliberation [Heb *bĕʾōrek rûaḥ*, lit., with length of spirit], give answer." For the phrase *ʾōrek rûaḥ*, cf. Qoh 7:8, which contrasts "the patient spirit" (*ʾerek rûaḥ*) with "the lofty, or haughty, spirit" (*gĕbah rûaḥ*, lit., high, or lofty, of spirit). The equivalent of the Heb phrase *hāšēb pitgām*, "give answer," occurs in the Aram of Ezra 5:11 and Dan 3:16. Duesberg-Fransen (p. 113) cite a parallel to v 11 from the Egyptian Wisdom literature: "Be quiet . . . that is something more beautiful than the flower of Teftef; speak (only) if you know how to resolve (the difficulty)" (Ptah-hotep, *Lit.*, 24). Spicq (p. 595) calls attention to another parallel (*The History of Aḥiqar*, iii 5): "My son, make your path and your word straight; listen and do not hurry to give an answer."

The precept of v 11b receives further development in v 12. In v 12a, Ben Sira urges that one should have competence (Heb *'im yēš 'ittĕkā*, lit., if there is with you) in the matter under discussion for one to answer one's neighbor. Otherwise, one should keep silent, lit., your hand upon your mouth. The expression "(to put) the hand over the mouth" occurs also in Prov 30:32b and Mic 7:16 and signifies regret at having been foolish and proud. The same expression is found in Job 21:5b; 29:9b; 40:4b; and Wis 8:12c, and signifies the respect one has or should have for the speaker. Cf. B. Couroyer, "Mettre la main sur la bouche en Egypte et dans la Bible," *RB* 67 (1960): 197–209.

In v 13a MS A *bwṭ'* (MS C has *bwṭh*) should be read as a noun, "talking," as G translates, and not as a participle, "one who talks," as Syr translates. Smend (p. 51) suggests that the word be vocalized *bôṭ'* or *bêṭe'*; cf. 9:18a. The root *bṭ'/bṭh* in the MT occurs only in Lev 5:4 (*bis*); Prov 12:18; and Ps 106:33, and it means "to speak rashly, thoughtlessly." Here the word simply means "speech, talking," as the context makes clear. For the ideas in v 13, cf. Prov 12:18; 18:21; see also Matt 12:37 and especially Jas 3:2–10. The theme of the tongue and its uses and abuses, the topic of the present stanza (5:13–6:1), Ben Sira takes up again in 14:1; 19:6–17; 20:16–20; 22:27–23:1, 7–15; 25:8; 28:12–26.

In MS A, v 14a and most of v 14b are repeated after 4:28. The Heb expression *ba'al štāyim*, lit., master or owner of two (tongues), is idiomatically translated here "two-faced" (vv 14a and d). G has *psithyros*, "whisperer," in v 14a, a word he uses together with *diglōssos*, "double-tongued," in 28:13 (cf. also 21:28; Prov 16:28; 2 Cor 12:20); but in v 14d and 6:1c, G has *diglōssos*. V 14b may be translated, lit.: "and with your tongue do not slander [Heb *rgl*]" (MS A adds *rēa'*, "a neighbor," but the word is to be omitted since it is not present after 4:28 where the verse is also found). V 14b derives from Ps 15:3a. Instead of "slander," G reads "lie in wait" and Syr "stumble." By "the thief" in v 14c is meant one who has stolen, through slander, the good name of another (so Box-Oesterley, p. 333). Cf. Ps 140:2–4, 12; and Rom 1:29–30. In v 14d of MS A, instead of *rē'ēhû*, "his neighbor," after *ḥerpâ*, "disgrace, reproach," read *rā'â*, "evil, harsh, disagreeable," the reading of G and Syr. To stress the point being made in v 14, Ben Sira employs a rhetorical a:b::b':a chiastic pattern: *two-faced:shame::disgrace:two-faced*. This verse parallels *Phibis*, iii 2–8 (Sanders, pp. 82, 93).

In v 15, the Heb verb *šḥt*, here translated according to the context "say [something] harmful," means, lit., "to act corruptly" when it is used as an intransitive verb, as it is here and in 7:36b and 49:4b; see also Judg 2:19; 2 Chr 27:2; Isa 1:4; Ezek 16:47. G has *agnoeō* (the verb used in LXX Dan 9:15 to render Heb *pš'*, "to sin"), "to be in error, to make a mistake," a legitimate interpretation of *šḥt*, *pace* Smend (p. 52) and Box-Oesterley (p. 333); Syr has *srḥ*, "to commit sin, do iniquity." If one does not heed the advice of v 15, then one could indeed become "a foe instead of a friend" (6:1a). One would also acquire "a bad name, disgrace, and reproach [Heb *ḥerpâ*, the same word used in 5:14d]" (6:1b), all of which means a life without honor, a necessary constituent of a meaningful and worthwhile life; cf. Pss 31:10–14; 109:25; Ezek 5:15. In addition, one would get the reputation of being an "evil, two-faced [lit., two-tongued] person" (6:1c); this is the third mention of the "two-tongued" in this stanza (cf. 5:14a, d). The number three may be used to indicate the superlative degree or great emphasis; cf., for example, Isa 6:3; Jer 7:4.

The last poem in this section urges against unruly passions. The colorful and forceful language would make a profound impression on the young to whom the book of Ben Sira is primarily addressed. In 6:2a, the Heb expression *npl bĕyad*, lit., to fall into the hand of, is found also in Judg 15:18 and 2 Sam 24:14, both of which texts speak of coming under the control of one's enemies. The translation "desire, passion" is one of the several meanings of the Heb noun *nepeš*, which can also mean "the inner being of a person" (e.g., Ps 42:5, 7), "a living being (e.g., Gen 2:7), "life" (e.g., Exod 21:23), self and the personal pronoun "I/me" (e.g., Gen 49:6), "you" (e.g., Isa 43:14), "he" (e.g., Ps 25:13), "we" (e.g., Ps 124: 7), "they" (e.g., Isa 46:2), "the seat of the appetites" (e.g., Ps 107:9; Isa 58:10). As is obvious from 6:2b, the "desire" referred to here is impure and unholy; see NOTE for a discussion of the problems with the text of MS A, G, and Syr. The vivid metaphors in 6:3 are meant to emphasize the sad results of illicit passion; cf. Job 31:9–12. In a dramatic poem in Dan 4:7–14, Nebuchadnezzar is compared to a gigantic tree; because of his consummate arrogance, an angel gives the command to chop down the tree and lop off its branches and to strip off its leaves and scatter its fruit. Cf. A. A. Di Lella, "Daniel 4:7–14: Poetic Analysis and Biblical Background," AOAT 212 (1981): 247–58. Cf. Amos 2:9; Ps 37:35–36. In Isa 56:3, the eunuch describes himself as "a dry tree," Heb *'ēṣ yābēš*, the exact phrase Ben Sira uses in 6:3b. On the contrary, the righteous person is compared in Ps 1:3 to "a tree planted near running water, that yields its fruit in due season, and whose leaves never fade." Cf. Ps 128:1–4.

V 4 may also be translated: "For fierce [or strong, mighty] passion [i.e., uncontrolled desire] destroys its owners, and an enemy's joy overtakes them" (i.e., they become the joy of their enemies). In Isa 56:11, the blind leaders of the people are compared to "dogs *with a fierce appetite* [Heb *'azzê nepeš*, lit., fierce of appetite, desire], they know not when they have enough." In 6:4a, Ben Sira uses the same two words, *nepeš 'azzâ*, thus evoking a powerful image. The question of carnal lust (and of overindulgence in food and drink) is taken up again in 18:30–19:3.

10. True and False Friendship
(6:5–17)

6 5 Pleasant speech multiplies friends,   A
      and gracious lips prompt friendly greetings.
    6 Let your acquaintances be many,
      but one in a thousand your confidant.

    7 When you gain a friend, test him in the gaining,
      and be not too ready to trust him.
    8 For one sort of friend is a friend when it suits him,
      but he will not be with you in time of distress.
    9 Another is a friend who becomes an enemy,
      and tells of the quarrel to your shame.

    10 Another is a friend, a boon companion,
      who will not be with you when trouble comes.
    11 When things go well, he is your other self
      and lords it over your servants;   G
    12 But if disaster befalls you, he turns against you   A
      and hides when he sees you coming.

    13 Keep away from your enemies;
      be on your guard with your friends.
    14 A faithful friend is a sturdy shelter;
      whoever finds one finds a treasure.
    15 A faithful friend is beyond price,
      no sum can balance his worth.
    16 A faithful friend is a life-saving remedy,
      such as the one who fears God finds;
    17 Whoever fears the Lord makes firm his friendship,   G
      and his comrade will be like himself.   A

Notes

6   14a. *shelter*=G; MS A, Syr have "friend" a second time.
16a. *remedy*=G, Syr; MS A *ṣĕrōr,* dubious at best.

Comment

This poem on true and false friendship has four stanzas, 2+3+3+5 bicola. The first stanza (vv 5–6) introduces the general subject, and the other three provide specific injunctions and observations about friendship. Friendship is again discussed in 7:18; 11:29–12:18; 22:19–26; and 37:1–6. No other book of the Bible deals with friendship so extensively.

In v 5a, "pleasant speech" translates Heb *ḥêk (ʿārēb),* lit., (sweet) *palate* (or gums), used figuratively as the organ of speech; cf. Prov 5:3; 8:7, in both of which texts *ḥēk* (spelled without the *mater lectionis yod*) is parallel to *śĕpātayim,* "lips," the word Ben Sira employs in v 5b. The adjective *ʿārēb,* "sweet," is rare, occurring elsewhere only in Prov 20:17 and Cant 2:14. For the thought of v 5, cf. Prov 16:21. There is a recurring *e* sound in the first seven words of the verse and a *ś/š* sound in the fifth, seventh, and eighth words, thus creating a pleasant assonance and alliteration: *ḥêk ʿārēb yarbeh ʾôhēb/wĕśiptê ḥēn śôʾălê* [read as the final letter *yod* for *waw* of MS A] *šālôm.* Interestingly, Lat adds after v 5a: "and soothes enemies"; cf. Prov 15:1. A literal translation of v 5b: "and gracious lips (multiply) *those who ask for peace*" (i.e., those who give greetings); the phrase *śʾl šālôm* is the usual expression for greeting someone. Cf. Exod 18:7; Judg 18:15; 1 Sam 10:4; 17:22; 25:5; 30:21; 2 Sam 8:10; Jer 15:5; 1 Chr 18:10.

In v 6a, Heb *ʾanšê šĕlômĕkā,* "your acquaintances," means, lit., men of your peace. An *a:b::b:a* chiastic pattern links the two bicola of this stanza: *multiplies*/Heb *yarbeh* (v 5a):(those who ask for) *peace*/*šālôm* (v 5b)::(men of) *your peace*/*šĕlômĕkā* (v 6a):*many*/*rabbîm* (v 6a). The equivalent of the expression *ʾanšê šĕlômĕkā* occurs also in Ps 41:10; Jer 20:10; 38:22. In v 6b, Heb *baʿal sôdĕkā,* translated here "your confidant," means, lit., owner (or master) of your counsel (or your intimate circle, company); cf. Job 19:19:

mĕtê sôdî, "men of my intimate circle." The point of v 6 is clear: be friendly toward all, but reveal your inmost thoughts to a rare few. Similar ideas are expressed in 8:17–19.

The next stanza (vv 7–9) offers utilitarian and pragmatic advice about choosing freinds. In v 7, Ben Sira suggests that one should test new friends before trusting them. In 4:17, Lady Wisdom tests the wise to see if their hearts are fully with her.

In the words of v 8a, there is an *e/i* assonance: *kî yēš 'ôhēb kĕpî 'ēt.* The proverb stated in many words in v 8 is summed up neatly in our English proverbial expression "a fair-weather friend." A further reason for testing a friend is given in v 9: some friends turn into, or change into (the literal meaning of Heb *nehpāk*), enemies and proceed to embarrass you by telling everybody the reason why the friendship broke up. Cf. 27:16–21; Prov 17:9, 17; 18:24; 25:8–10.

The next stanza (vv 10–12) continues the theme of the fair-weather friend (v 8). A more literal translation of v 10: "Another friend is a table companion, but he will not be found on the day of trouble." This astute observation is the converse of the English proverb "A friend in need is a friend indeed." Cf. 13:21; Prov 14:20; 19:4, 6–7. In v 11, Ben Sira develops the idea of v 10a. In v 11b, MS A and Syr read: "When things go badly, he will depart from you." G, on which the translation here is based, is to be preferred, for it explains in a dramatic and ironic way how such a "friend" is "your other self." Ben Sira takes up a similar theme in 12:8–9. Regarding v 12, cf. the poignant plaint of Job (19:19–22) whose friends have turned against him because of his adversity. Cf. also Prov 18:24. With the thoughts expressed in this stanza compare Prov 17:17: "He who is a friend is always a friend, and a brother is born for the time of stress." Cf. also Sir 22:25.

The final stanza of this section begins with a pithy observation to avoid enemies and be on guard with friends (v 13), thus resuming ideas introduced in vv 7 and 10. In the four Heb words of v 13, Ben Sira demonstrates again that he is a hard-nosed and astute observer of the human scene; one ignores his advice at one's own peril or unhappiness. In v 14a, Heb *'ôhēb 'ĕmûnâ,* "a faithful friend," may also be translated "a reliable, or trustworthy, friend." It is such a person who is the subject of vv 14–16. In v 14, there is an *a:b::b:a'* pattern that makes the verse rhetorically forceful: *a faithful friend:whoever-finds-one::finds:a treasure.* The Heb word *hôn,* "treasure" (lit., wealth), occurs frequently in the Wisdom literature, esp. Proverbs (e.g., 1:13; 3:9; 6:31; 10:15; 18:11; 19:14; 24:4; 28:22; 29:3). The metaphor of v 14b receives further elaboration in v 15, where a faithful friend is depicted as "beyond price," an image taken up in v 15b, which may be translated more literally: "there is no weight for his worth." In antiquity, goods for trade as well as silver and gold used for money were weighed in the balance scale; thus the image is that no weight can be as heavy as a reliable friend. Cf. Gen 23:16; 24:22; Josh 7:21;

Judg 8:26; 1 Chr 22:3, 14; esp. Dan 5:27. In 7:18, Ben Sira writes: "Barter not a friend for money."

In vv 16–17, Ben Sira teaches that fear of God is the requirement for finding true friends and achieving the blessings of friendship. In v 16a, "life-saving remedy" (lit., medicine of life) is the reading of G and Syr. MS A reads *ṣĕrôr ḥayyîm,* "bundle of life, or of the living," a phrase also used in 1 Sam 25:29; Box-Oesterley (p. 335) prefer this reading. In Syriac patristic literature, Jesus Christ is often described as *sam ḥayyê,* "medicine of life." The clear implication of v 16b is that only those who fear God will find a faithful friend. MS A omits v 17a because of homoioarchton and adds after v 17b an extra colon: "and as his name, so are his deeds," which is in fact a repetition of 2:18d (cf. COMMENT above). The point of v 17 is that the pious Jew, "who fears the Lord," will have stable friendships with persons who are like himself in personality and particularly in observance of the Law. V 17b may be translated more literally: "for *like himself* so is *his neighbor.*" The italicized words render Heb *kāmôhû* and *rēʿēhû,* the same two expressions that occur in the well-known commandment (Lev 19:18, quoted by Jesus in Matt 19:19 and Luke 10:27) "You shall love *your neighbor as yourself,*" Heb *rēʿăkā kāmôkā.*

The material in this section has parallels in Theognis, 77–78, 81–82, 115–16, 299, 575, 643–44, 697–98, 929–30 (Sanders, pp. 30–31), and in *Phibis,* xi 23–xii 18 (Sanders, pp. 70–71).

PART III   (6:18–14:19)

11. Encouragement to Strive for Wisdom
(6:18–37)

6   18 My son, from your youth embrace discipline;   G
        thus you will gain wisdom with graying hair.
     19 As though plowing and sowing, draw close to her;   A
        then await her bountiful crops,
     For in cultivating her you will labor but little,
        and soon you will eat of her fruits.

     20 Jolting is she to the stupid—
        the fool cannot abide her;
     21 She will be like a burdensome stone to him
        and he will not delay in casting her aside,
     22 For discipline is like her name:
        she is not obvious to many.

     23 Listen, my son, and take my advice;   G
        refuse not my counsel.
     24 Put your feet into her net
        and your neck into her noose.
     25 Stoop your shoulders and carry her   A
        and be not irked at her bonds.

     26 With all your soul draw close to her;   G
        with all your strength keep her ways.
     27 Search her out, discover her; seek her and you will find   A
                                                          her.
     Then when you have her, do not let her go;
     28 Thus you will afterward find rest in her—
        she will be transformed into your delight.   C

29 Her net will become your throne of majesty;   A
    her noose, your apparel of spun gold.
30 Her yoke will be your gold adornment;
    her bonds, your purple cord.
31 You will wear her as your glorious apparel,
    bear her as your splendid crown.

32 If you wish, my son, you can become learned;
    if you apply yourself, you will be wise.
33 If you are willing to listen, you will gain;
    if you give ear, you will be instructed.

34 Frequent the company of the elders: G
    whoever is wise, stay close to him;
35 Be eager to hear every discourse,   A
    let no wise saying escape you.
36 If you see a prudent person, seek him out;
    let your feet wear away his doorstep!

37 Reflect on the law of the Most High,
    let his commandments be your constant meditation;
Then he will inform your mind,
    and the wisdom you desire he will grant you.

Notes

6   18a. *embrace*=G *epidexai* (Ziegler)=Lat (=Heb *qaḥ*); G MSS *epilexai.* Cf. 36:26.

19a. *(plowing) and sowing*=G=Heb *wĕkazzôrēaʿ;* MSS A, C *wĕkaqqôṣēr*="and reaping"; Syr "like the sower and like the reaper."

19c. *labor*=Heb *taʿămōl*=G, Syr, cf. 51:27 (again with *mĕʿaṭ*); MSS A, C *taʿăbōd.*

21. *burdensome*=Heb *maśśāʾ;* G reads "of testing"=Heb *massâ.*

22. Read *(kēn) hîʾ, mûsār* having feminine agreement (as a synonym for *ḥokmâ*) as in Prov 4:13; MS A=*hûʾ.* 2Q18, extant for most line ends of vv 20–31, reads *[nō]kaḥ* to end v 22; MS A *nĕkōḥâ.* V 22 is followed in MS A by 27:5–6; MS A omits vv 23, 24, 26, 34 from what follows.

24–25, 29–30. The imagery in v 24 is from hunters' nets and snares; in v 25 from the yoke and its leather straps. Each is taken up again, v 24 in v 29 and v 25 in v 30. Hence for G's *eis tas pedas autēs* in 24a read Heb *bĕrištāh*, as in Syr of 24a and MS A, Syr of 29a; the parallel in 24b should be *bĕḥablōtêhā* "into her noose [cords]," cf. MS A's *wḥblth*, 29b, and the discussion of 25b below. G, Syr in 24b and G in 29b introduce the yoke too soon, confusing with its straps (*mōsĕrōtêhā*, cf. MS A in 30b) the cords of the snare. In the books of the Hebrew canon, the snare is *ḥăbālîm* (Ps 18:6; Prov 5:22). The yoke itself (*'ullâ*) is not explicitly mentioned in the Hebrew till 30a, MS A, where G (*ep' autēs*=Heb *'ālêhā*) misreads it; it is implied in 25a, and the *desmoi* of G 25b, 30b is the standard LXX equivalent for *mōsĕrōt*, the straps of the yoke; cf. Isa 52:2; Jer 2:20; 5:5; 27:2; 30:8. In 25b, MS A's *bĕtaḥbûlōtêhā* is a further confusion from *bĕḥablōtêhā*, which would be the line-ending directly above (24b, missing in MS A) in a stichometrically written text; read instead *bĕmôsĕrōtêhā*=G.

29. The reading *bigdê kātem* is guaranteed by 2Q18; cf. then v 31; 45:8–11; 50:11; and Ps 45:10, 14.

33. *you will gain*=G *ekdexē*=Heb *tiqqaḥ;* MS A omits after *lišmōaʿ;* compare *lišmōaʿ* at the caesura in 35a; Syr="you will learn."

35a. *discourse*—G adds *theian*, "godly."

36. Read *mî (yābîn)*=Syr; MS A has *mâ*. Read *bĕsippô* with Syr (ignoring plural dots in Syr); cf. G; MS A has *sypy*.

37a. Read *bĕtôrat ('elyôn)* (Smend); cf. G *en tois prostagmasin Kyriou* and 41:4, 8 (M); 42:2 (M); 49:4. MS A, Syr=*bĕyirʾat*.

Comment

This poem, which encourages the Jew to strive for wisdom, has eight stanzas arranged in three groups: $3+3:3+3+3:2+3+2$ bicola for a total of 22, the number of letters in the Hebrew alphabet. It will be observed that each of these groups of stanzas has in its first colon (vv 18a, 23a, and 32a) the introductory word *bĕnî*, "my son," and has a thematic unity within the poem.

In MS A, v 18 is omitted completely; MS C has only the last two words of v 18b. The verse leaves no doubt as to how one can acquire wisdom: one must embrace discipline from youth in order to gain wisdom in old age. Cf. Lam 3:27 and Jer 2:20. In the Wisdom literature, the young were never thought to be as wise as the old; cf. 25:3–6. The Gr word *poliai*, "gray(ing) hair," occurs also in 25:4 (not extant in Heb). V 18 serves as topic sentence for the whole poem. The word "discipline" (Heb *mûsār*) occurs in v 18a, the opening colon of the first stanza, and in v 22a, in the closing bicolon of the second stanza, thus forming an *inclusio* that joins together the two stanzas of the group. The theme of these two stanzas is the need for discipline in the pursuit of wisdom.

In v 19, Ben Sira changes the image from youth and old age to plowing and sowing (cf. NOTE) and then awaiting the harvest; both images depict the process of growth and maturity. The metaphor of waiting for the harvest is taken up in Jas 5:7–8, which urges patience until the coming of the Lord. There is a *k/q* and *l/r* alliteration and *a* assonance in the Heb of v 19ab: *kāḥôrēš wĕkazzôrēaʿ qĕrab ʾēlêhā wĕqawwēh lĕrōb tĕbûʾātāh.* Biblical authors are fond of agricultural imagery: cf., for example, Isa 5:1–7; John 15:1–8; Matt 7:16–20; Mark 4:26–29; 1 Cor 3:6–9; 9:10–11; 2 Tim 2:3–6. The point of 19cd is that one must work for wisdom even though it is a gift of God (1:9–10; Wis 8:21–9:18), but the labor involved will be "little" in time and in effort, for "soon" (lit., tomorrow; cf. Isa 17:11) Wisdom bestows "her fruits."

In v 20, wisdom is compared to a path (cf. 4:17; Prov 2:9) which "to the stupid" is "jolting," Heb *ʿăqubbâ* (lit., steep, hilly), a word used only once in the MT (Isa 40:4). In v 20a, Heb *ʾĕwîl,* here translated "the stupid," also means "fool," in the sense not of intellectual but of moral deficiency. Cf. INTRODUCTION, Part X, 1. In the Book of Proverbs, the *ʾĕwîl* is said to despise wisdom and discipline, Heb *mûsār* (1:7; 15:5), and to be quarrelsome (20:3); it is useless to instruct him (27:22); cf. also Job 4:22; Isa 19:11; Jer 4:22. In v 20b, "the fool" translates Heb *ḥăsar lēb,* lit., "the one lacking in *heart*" (= the seat of intelligence and will); cf. COMMENT on 3:26. The expression *ḥăsar lēb* occurs also in Prov 6:32; 7:7; 9:4, 16; 10:13; 11:12; 15:21; 17:18; 24:30.

In v 21, wisdom is compared to "a burdensome stone" (lit., a stone that is a burden); cf. Matt 11:30. Instead of considering wisdom as something worth cultivating and cherishing, the foolish and careless person casts her aside as a troublesome weight, a burden, Heb *maśśāʾ,* a word occurring also in 51:26b. For the expression "a burdensome stone," cf. Zech 12:3. In v 22, Ben Sira plays on the word *mûsār,* "discipline," making it mean also "withdrawn" (*mûsār* being the *hophʿal* masculine singular participle of the verb *sûr,* which means "to turn aside, depart, withdraw"); cf. 51:23b. V 22 may be translated, lit.: "For *discipline,* as her name so is *she* [cf. NOTE], and to the many *she* is *not obvious.*" An *a:b::b:aʹ* pattern makes the wordplay on *mûsār* even more forceful: *discipline:she::she:not obvious.* The Heb word *nĕkôḥâ,* "obvious, plain," occurs in a speech by Lady Wisdom in Prov 8:9: "All [of my words] are *plain* to the person of intelligence."

The next three stanzas (vv 23–31) form a group the theme of which is the need for determination and zeal in the search for wisdom. In the first and third stanzas, the imagery is from hunting (vv 24 and 29) and the yoking of animals (vv 25 and 30); cf. NOTE. In v 23, Ben Sira appeals to his own authority in addressing his readers in the tone of a father: "Listen, *my* son, and take *my* advice; refuse not *my* counsel." In so doing, he was modeling himself on Prov 4:10: "Hear, my son, and receive my words." As a scribe, Ben Sira had the leisure to study and reflect on the Wisdom traditions of

Israel; and because in the process he became wise and experienced, he felt he had a right to teach with authority the youth of his day. The content of v 23 is based on Prov 19:20: "Listen to counsel and receive instruction, that you may eventually become wise." The hunting and yoking metaphors in vv 24 and 25 emphasize that wisdom involves self-discipline and constraint in what one does. In Matt 11:29–30, Jesus employs the images of burden (v 21a) and of yoke (vv 25 and 30) to describe Christian discipleship: "Take my yoke upon your shoulders and learn from me, . . . for my yoke is easy and my burden light."

The next stanza (vv 26–28) continues the imagery of hunting; in this case, however, the hunter is not Wisdom (as in vv 24 and 29) but the one who seeks Wisdom. In v 26, the expressions "with all your soul" (Syr reads "with all your heart") and "with all your strength" are from Deut 6:5: "You shall love the LORD, your God, with all your heart, and with all your soul, and with all your strength." As in hunting for prey, one should be diligent in searching for and discovering Wisdom; only in this way will one find her (v 27a). Then when one has taken hold of (or seized, Heb *ḥzq*) her, one must not let her go (v 27b); this colon derives from Prov 4:13a: "Take hold of [the same Heb verb] instruction; do not let her go [Heb *rph*, the same verb Ben Sira uses]." What one receives after taking hold of Wisdom is compared to the satisfaction one experiences at the end of a successful day's hunt (v 28); cf. 15:4–6.

Like the first stanza (vv 23–25), the third stanza (vv 29–31) of this group resumes the imagery of Wisdom as hunter. Being caught in Wisdom's net involves no loss of personal freedom. Rather, one becomes like a king (v 29a); cf. Prov 4:9; Ps 89:15; Wis 9:10–12. The constraints ("noose") Wisdom places on the wise make them appear as if clothed in gold (v 29b); cf. 21:19, 21. The metaphor of clothing as symbolic of moral virtues is often found in the Bible; cf. Job 19:9; 29:14; Ps 132:9; 1 Pet 5:5; Rev 7:9; 19:8. Wisdom's "yoke" (v 30a) does not hamper the wise but gives them a sure sense of direction in life. For that reason the yoke is dramatically compared to a "gold adornment," and Wisdom's "bonds" to a "purple cord" (v 30b). In the Bible, purple garments and gold were worn by kings, princes, high priests, and the wealthy; cf. Exod 39:1–31 (the high priest); Dan 5:7, 16, 29 (the nobility); Luke 16:19 (the rich). The expression "purple cord," Heb *pĕtîl tĕkēlet*, derives primarily from Num 15:38. The cord was used to fasten tassels on the corners of the garments, so that the sight of them may remind the Israelites "to keep all the commandments of the LORD, without going wantonly astray after the desires of [their] hearts and eyes" (Num 15:39). Thus Wisdom's "bonds" are the "purple cord" that reminds the faithful Jew to remain steadfast to the Law of Moses and not to stray after the allurements of Hellenistic learning and culture. As the high priest wore garments of "spun gold" (v 29b), ornaments of gold (v 30a), and vestments in which "purple cord" was used (v 30b; cf. Exod 28:28, 37; 39:21, 31), so the wise "will wear" Wisdom as their "glorious apparel" (v 31a; cf. 50:11), and bear her as their "splendid crown" (v 31b), Heb *ʿăṭeret tipʾeret,* Gr *stephanos agalliamatos* (cf. 1:11 with COMMENT; 15:6; Prov 4:9; 16:31). The wise, in other words, because of their fidelity to the Law will enjoy the splendor of royalty and the glory of the high priesthood.

The last group of stanzas (vv 32–37) in the poem has as its theme the exhortation to seek Wisdom by various means. The first stanza (vv 32–33), which states the theme in general terms, has a balanced rhetorical structure: each colon begins with a condition ("If you . . .") and ends with an affirmation ("You can/will . . ."); and there is synthetic parallelism between the conditional clauses of v 32a and b and between the main clauses of v 33a and b, and synonymous parallelism between the conditional clauses of v 33a and b (cf. NOTE) and between the main clauses of v 32a and b. In v 32, Ben Sira makes it clear that the desire for wisdom is a first step that must be followed by effective action: "if *you apply yourself,*" Heb *tāsîm libbĕkā,* lit., (if) you put your heart [=seat of intelligence and will] (to it). In other words, wishful thinking about wisdom without personal involvement and decision is worthless. V 33 spells out the means whereby one applies oneself: one must be willing to listen before one may hope to gain wisdom, for only by giving ear to the wise will one be instructed. Cf. Prov 8:32–33. In v 33b, Heb *tiwwāsēr,* "you will be instructed," is from the same root as the noun *mûsār,* "discipline, instruction," found in vv 18a and 22a; thus the first group of stanzas (vv 18–22) is connected to the last group (vv 32–37).

The next stanza (vv 34–36) specifies an important way to gain wisdom: seeking out the wise and their discourse. Regarding the significance of "the elders" (v 34a), cf. 8:9 and 32:3. The word "wise" in v 34b is in synonymous parallelism with "the elders," for wisdom was considered the prerogative of age; cf. v 18 with COMMENT and 25:4–6. The reason why one should "stay close" to "whoever is wise" (v 34b) is given in 13:16b: everyone associates with one's own kind. In v 35a, the Heb noun *śîḥâ,* "discourse," occurs also in 8:8a and 11:8b; in the MT, the word occurs only in Job 15:4, where it means "meditation," and in Ps 119:97, 99 where it means "(object of) musing, study." In Neo-Hebrew, it means "edifying discourse." In v 35b, "wise saying" translates Heb *mĕšal bînâ,* lit., a proverb/saying of intelligence; for a discussion of *māšāl,* cf. INTRODUCTION, Part IV, 1. The words *śîḥâ* and *mĕšal bînâ* are in synonymous parallelism. In v 36, the ideas of the stanza reach a climax: seek out a person who is prudent or wise (Heb *yābîn*); wear out his doorstep! Persistence, determination, and unflagging energy are required for one to acquire wisdom; there is no other way.

In the last stanza of the group (and of the poem) Ben Sira equates keeping the Law and achieving wisdom, as he does elsewhere; cf. 1:25–27 with COMMENT and 24:23 with COMMENT. God will grant the gift of wisdom only to those who observe the commandments. V 37ab may be translated, lit.: "Reflect on the law [cf. NOTE] of the Most High and on his commandments

meditate [read *ûbĕmiṣwôtāyw hĕgēh*] continually." A striking *a:b::b':a'* rhetorical pattern underscores the importance of Ben Sira's point: *reflect:law of the
Most High::his commandments:meditate.* V 37cd may be translated, lit.: "And
he himself will give understanding to your heart [=seat of intelligence and
will]; and what you desire, he will make you wise." Again an *a:b::b':a'* structure adds emphasis to the bicolon: *he will give understanding to:your
heart::what you desire* [an activity of the "heart"]:*he will make you wise.* Cf. 1
Kgs 3:11–12. It is to be noted that this long poem has *ḥokmâ* ("wisdom") in
the first bicolon (v 18) and the verb from the same root, *yĕḥakkĕmekā* ("he
will make you wise") in the last bicolon (v 37cd), thus forming an *inclusio.*

12. Conduct Toward God and Neighbor
(7:1–17)

7   1 Do no evil, neither let evil overtake you;   C
        2   avoid wickedness, and it will turn aside from you.   A
        3 Sow not in the furrows of injustice,   G
           lest you harvest it sevenfold.   A
        4 Seek not from God authority,
           nor from the king a place of honor.
        5 Parade not your justice before the Lord,
           and before the king flaunt not your wisdom.   G
        6 Seek not to become a judge
           if you have not strength to root out crime,
      Or you will be browbeaten by some prominent person   A
           and mar your integrity.
        7 Be guilty of no evil before the city court,   A
           nor disgrace yourself before the assembly.
        8 Do not plot to repeat a sin;
           not even for one will you go unpunished.
        9 Say not, "He will appreciate my many gifts;   G
           the Most High will accept my offerings."
      10 Be not brusque in your prayers;   A
           neither put off doing a kindness.
      11 Laugh not at an embittered person;
           there is One who exalts and humbles.
      12 Contrive no mischief against your brother,
           nor against your friend and companion.
      13 Take no pleasure in telling lie after lie;
           it never results in good.
      14 Do not hold forth in the assembly of the elders,   G
           nor repeat yourself when you pray.   A
      15 Hate not laborious work;   G
           work was assigned by God.

16 Do not esteem yourself better than your fellows;   s
    remember, his wrath will not delay.
17 More and more, humble your pride;   A
    what awaits humans is worms.

Notes

7   5a. *before the Lord*=G; MS A="before the king"; cf. v 5b.
6d. For G's *skandalon* read Heb *mûm,* cf. Syr and 33:23; 47:20; 1 Macc 9:10.
7a. *city court*=ʿ*ādat šaʿar;* MS A's ʿ*ādat šaʿărê* ʾ*ēl* includes dittography of the following *wĕ*ʾ*al.*
9. =G, Syr; it is lacking in MS A.
11b. MS A's "Remember (there is . . .)" omitted; cf. G, Syr, and 16b.
15. In MS A this verse stands between vv 9, 10; in Syr it is lacking.
15b. G+MS A suggest Heb read *wĕhî*ʾ *mē*ʾ*ēl neḥĕlāqâ,* referring to ʿ*ăbōdâ,* 15a, cf. 15:9; 41:4; for the construction *wĕhî*ʾ cf. 31:27d.
16. Understandable only as a sequel to v 15. G's 16a, with "among the multitude of sinners" for *better than your fellows,* is influenced by 16:6; Ps 1:1; it does not fit the present content. MS A is garbled here.
17. MS A follows this with the line "Do not hasten to say 'Disaster!' Rely on God and be content with his way"; this is a later comment on 17b, lacking in G and Syr, and dependent on Ps 37:5. (For *lprṣ* read *pāreṣ.*)

Comment

This section, being a collection of diverse ethical maxims, does not lend itself readily to strophic divisions. Smend (p. 62), however, and Box-Oesterley (pp. 338–39) divide the material into seven stanzas: 2+2+3+3+3+2+2 bicola. Having described the pursuit of wisdom in 6:18–37, Ben Sira now gives detailed precepts concerning the conduct of the wise. Since wisdom is defined as fear of the Lord (1:16) and keeping the commandments (1:26–27; 6:37), the wise must avoid sin in all its forms. Each saying, except v 17, begins with ʾ*al*+jussive: "Do not . . ."

V 1 is the topic sentence of this section: "Do no evil [Heb *raʿ*], neither let evil [*raʿ* here means *calamity*] overtake you." The avoidance of evil is essential if one is to acquire wisdom and live well and in peace. In v 2, Ben Sira shows his understanding of human behavior: "Avoid [lit., keep your distance from] wickedness [Heb ʿāwôn], and it will turn aside from you." The noun ʿāwôn means not only "wickedness, iniquity," a synonym for "evil" (v 1), but also "guilt, punishment of iniquity." Both meanings are present in this verse. In v 3, the image of sowing and reaping would strike a responsive chord in the minds and hearts of Ben Sira's readers and listeners. Agricultural metaphors are common in the Bible; cf. 6:19 with COMMENT and Isa 45:8; Hos 10:12; Job 4:8; Prov 22:8; Gal 6:8. The idea of "sevenfold" or "seven times" in v 3b is another frequent motif in Scripture; cf. 20:12b; 35:13b; Prov 6:31; Pss 79:12; 119:164; Gen 4:15, 24; Isa 30:26; Matt 18:22; Luke 17:4. The point of v 3 is that "injustice," like a seed sown in the ground, produces a harvest seven times larger than the normal yield—a profound insight into the social effects of injustice, Heb ʿāwel, Gr adikia.

In v 4, there is an m alliteration in four of the eight words of MS A: mēʾēl memšālet ("from God authority") mimmelek môšab ("from the king a place of [honor]"). In addition to these seven m's, there are four l's in the bicolon, which give it an added elegance. Authority and honors are to be avoided because "power tends to corrupt and absolute power corrupts absolutely" (Lord Acton, letter to Bishop Mandell Creighton, April 5, 1887); cf. Matt 20:20–28; Mark 10:35–45. In the courts of the Seleucids and Ptolemies of Ben Sira's day there were many functionaries who enjoyed political prestige and economic advantage, which doubtless led to abuses like those in the Maccabean period (cf. 2 Macc 3:4–13; 4:7–16). V 5a may also be translated: "Do not justify yourself before the Lord [cf. NOTE]." No one can claim innocence before God; cf. Job 9:2, 20; Ps 143:2; 1 Kgs 8:46; Luke 18:9–14; 1 Cor 4:4. Showing off before the king (or the powerful) (v 5b) has always been a risky enterprise; cf. Prov 25:6–7; Luke 14:7–11.

The exhortation in v 6 derives from Ben Sira's vast experience of social life and political realities. To be a good judge one must have unimpeachable integrity and dauntless courage; otherwise common criminals will go unpunished and the influential be set free even when guilty. V 6c may also be translated: "lest you be in fear in the presence of a prominent person."

Regarding v 7a, there are many possible evils one could commit in court: giving false witness, passing favorable judgment because of a bribe, showing partiality to the powerful or to the lowly, making an unjust accusation, not telling the whole truth. All these evils are explicitly condemned in the Bible; cf. Exod 20:16; 23:1–3, 6–8; Lev 19:15; Deut 1:17; 16:18–20; 19:16–21; Amos 5:15; Mic 7:3; Ps 82:2; Prov 18:5; 24:23; 28:21; 2 Chr 19:6–7; Dan 13:36–41, 52–62. By doing evil before the city court (v 7a), one would "disgrace [oneself] before the assembly" (v 7b). For the importance of the assembly in the eyes of the Jew, cf. Prov 5:14. M. Hengel (*Judaism and Hellenism,* vol. 1, pp. 133–34) is of the opinion that vv 4–7 are too concrete and specific to form a general Wisdom sentence and so may refer to the high priest Onias III, the successor of Simeon II. See INTRODUCTION, Part II. Unable to cope with party struggles and rich families, he erred in adopting a pro-Ptolemaic policy and in accepting a bribe from the Tobiad Hyrcanus in Transjordania. His opponents denounced him, with the result that he had to render an account of his conduct to Seleucus IV Philopator (187–175 B.C.) in Antioch and was detained there. While Onias was there, Seleucus was assassinated (2 Macc 4:1–7). If this view be correct, then vv 4–7 were written immediately before the accession of Antiochus IV Epiphanes, in September 175 B.C. (Onias was then deprived of the high priesthood when his brother Jason purchased the office from Antiochus.) Hengel is, I think, reading too much into these verses, which are quite in keeping with other types of Wisdom sayings by Ben Sira.

If v 8 continues the thought of v 7, it urges against conspiracy in juridical processes. If it is a miscellaneous maxim, which seems more likely, it reminds one that the repetition of the same sin because of a plot with others simply multiplies the punishment to come one's way eventually. Regarding the abominable futility of substituting sacrifices and offerings (v 9) for genuine service of the Lord and of one's neighbor, cf. 34:23–24; Prov 15:18; 21:27; Ps 50:7–15; Qoh 4:17; Jdt 16:15–16. The prophets in particular mince no words in excoriating the sinful and unrepentant Israelites for their foolish attempts at placating God by multiplying sacrifices and prayers: Isa 1:10–16; Amos 5:21–24; Mic 6:6–8; Jer 6:19–20; 7:2–7. Liturgy, sacrifices, and prayer are legitimate forms of worship and service of God only when they express publicly the inner conviction of a person willing to love God above all things (Deut 6:5) and neighbor as self (Lev 19:18); cf. 50:1, 5–21. See INTRODUCTION, Part X, 5.

V 10 may also be translated: "Be not impatient in prayer, and in alms(giving) be not tardy"—the a:b::b′:a′ rhetorical arrangement makes Ben Sira's point more forceful. Prayer to be worthwhile and pleasing to God must be patient and must be joined with almsgiving; cf. 3:30–4:10, with COMMENT, and Jas 1:6; Matt 21:21–22. In v 11a, Heb ʾal tibez, "do not despise," is understood by G in the sense of laughing to scorn, mocking. "An embittered person" (lit., a person in bitterness of spirit) may be an allusion to the misfortune that according to the Deuteronomic theory of retribution came upon a person as a result of sin or as a trial to test fidelity; cf. COMMENT on 2:1. Regarding v 11b, cf. 1 Sam 2:7; Luke 1:52. In v 11, Ben Sira warns against despising an embittered person for whatever reason he is suffering, because the Lord himself is the One who causes adversity and who brings prosperity. Cf. 11:4. Only the Lord knows why he "exalts" at one time and why he "humbles" at another; his manner of activity is beyond human scrutiny or understanding. A further dimension of Ben Sira's thought is suggested by the Lat proverb Hodie mihi, cras tibi, "Today me, tomorrow you!"

In v 12a, the Heb verb ḥrš, "to devise, contrive," also means "to plow," the sense in which G understands the word; cf. Prov 3:29; 6:14; 12:20; 14:22, in all of which texts the same verb is used. The noun *ḥāmās,* here translated "mischief," also means "violence, wrong." There is in the verse a descending order of intimacy: brother, friend, companion (or associate). Lying is also to be avoided especially since one lie often leads to another (v 13a). Ben Sira gives a pragmatic reason for the prohibition: "it never results in good" (v 13b), an observation confirmed by the experience of many. He brings up the subject of lying again in 20:24-26. Lying, esp. under oath, is vigorously condemned in the Bible; cf., for example, Exod 20:16; Hos 4:2; Jer 9:1-8; Isa 59:3; Mic 6:12; Lev 19:11-12; Col 3:9; Jas 3:14. Talkativeness (v 14a) is viewed with disdain by the Wisdom teachers (cf. Qoh 5:2), and it becomes even more despicable when indulged in the presence of "the elders" (cf. 32:9). In place of G's "elders," MS A and Syr read "princes." The injunction not to repeat oneself in prayer is similar to that found in Qoh 5:1 and Matt 6:7 ("In your prayer do not rattle on like the pagans"). The repetition of prayer formulas is hardly proscribed, as is obvious from Psalm 136, which Ben Sira certainly knew and in which the expression "for his mercy endures forever" occurs twenty-six times, and from Psalms 148 and 150, which repeat the verb "praise" (Heb *hallĕlû*) many times. Jesus himself, according to Matt 26:39-44, prayed three times, saying the same words; cf. Mark 14:35-39. The Apostle Paul also prayed three times to be relieved of "a thorn in the flesh" (2 Cor 12:7-8).

The precept in v 15 has a long biblical background, starting with Gen 2:15, where work on the land was commissioned by God himself to be a pleasant and satisfying enterprise. According to Gen 3:17-19, it was only after the sin of the first couple that farming would become a difficult task. But Ben Sira held manual labor in high esteem, for during this period there had occurred a transition from an agricultural to a commercial economy, with many people moving from rural areas to the city. The result was that many of the traditional moral values and personal virtues that originated in agricultural life were being called into question. Commerce introduced the people to new temptations; cf. 26:29-27:3.

For v 16a (cf. NOTE), G reads: "Number not yourself among the multitude of sinners." The reading of Syr, followed in the translation, is to be preferred in view of vv 15 and 17. The point of v 16 is that one should not allege social superiority as a pretext for avoiding manual labor (v 15); for if one esteems oneself above the common lot, God will not delay his wrath. Rather, one should continually flatten one's pride (v 17a; cf. 3:17-24 with COMMENT); the reason is, what awaits one is "worms" (v 17b; cf. Job 25:6). G reads "fire and worms" (cf. Isa 66:24; Jdt 16:17) because in the period between the composition of the book in ca. 180 B.C. and the translation by Ben Sira's grandson sometime after 117 B.C. (cf. INTRODUCTION, Part II) there developed the belief in rewards and punishments after death. In Ben Sira's time, this belief was not yet part of Israel's faith. See INTRODUCTION, Part X, 4.

For further study of this section, cf. P. C. Beentjes, "Jesus Sirach 7:1–17, Kanttekeningen bij de structuur en de tekst ven een verwaarloosde passage," *BTFT* 41 (1980): 251–59.

13. Maxims for Family Life, Religion, and Charity (7:18–36)

7 18 Barter not a friend for money,   A
      nor a true brother for the gold of Ophir.
   19 Dismiss not a sensible wife;
      a charming wife is more precious than corals.
   20 Mistreat not a servant who faithfully serves,   C
      nor a laborer who devotes himself to his task.
   21 Let a wise servant be dear to you as your own self;   A
      refuse him not his freedom.

   22 If you have livestock, look after them yourself;
      if they are dependable, keep them.
   23 If you have sons, chastise them;
      cure their stubbornness in their early youth.   G
   24 If you have daughters, keep them chaste,   A
      and be not indulgent to them.
   25 Giving your daughter in marriage is an end to anxiety;
      but give her to a sensible man.
   26 If you have a wife, let her not seem odious to you;
      but where there is ill feeling, trust her not.

   27 With your whole heart honor your father;   G
      your mother's birth pangs forget not.
   28 Remember, of these parents you were born;
      what can you give them for all they gave you?

   29 With all your soul fear God,   A
      revere his priests.
   30 With all your strength love your Maker,
      neglect not his ministers.
   31 Honor God and respect the priest;
      give him his portion as you have been commanded:

The flesh of sacrifices, contributions,
　　his portion of victims, a levy on holy offerings.

32 To the poor also extend your hand,
　　that your blessing may be complete;
33 Give your gift to anyone alive,
　　and withhold not your kindness from the dead;
34 Avoid not those who weep,
　　but mourn with those who mourn;
35 Neglect not to care for the sick—   G
　　for these things you will be loved.

36 In whatever you do, remember your last days,   A
　　and you will never sin.

Notes

7   18b. *true*=G *gnēsion;* MS A's *tālûy* is dubious at best.

21a. Read *ʾĕhôb (kĕnāpeš)* with MS C. MS B has this colon three times among its variant forms for 10:25. It reads *ḥābîb;* MS A has *ḥbb.* Cf. Rüger, pp. 45–46.

23b. *cure their stubbornness:* G supposes Heb *kōp rōʾšām,* literally "bow their heads," cf. 4:7; 30:12; 38:30; and Isa 58:5 (G's *trachēlon autōn* is its idiom for *rōʾšām:* cf. *CBQ* 36 [1974]: 536–37). MSS A, C, and Syr have, instead of this, "take for them wives (in their youth)," which fails to account for 30:12c in MS B, GII, and Syr. That colon, "bow his head in his youth," is a secondary duplication of a jumbled text (30:12a); it was adapted by a later glossator from this place in chap. 7 (*CBQ* 36 [1974]: 538–39). The same kind of glossing process has led to the introduction here, in MSS A, C, and Syr, of the recommendation of early marriage for sons. Rüger (p. 46) has not seen that 30:12c is secondary in that place, and makes the Heb-Syr reworking primary here in 7:23b.

27–28. Present in G and Syr, these verses are lacking in MS A; compare 3:1–16.

31c. *The flesh of sacrifices* supposes Heb *leḥem ʾiššîm;* MS A has been read *(leḥem) ʾšmym/ʾbrym.* G="firstfruits and guilt offering"=*ḥlb wʾšm;* for *ḥlb,* cf. Num 18:12, 29–32, MT and LXX. Compare 45:21–22.

32b. *complete:* cf. Deut 14:29.

35. Syr=G; MS A is garbled.

Comment

The maxims in this section may be divided into six groups or stanzas: 4+5+2+4+4+1 bicola. The section as a whole is concerned with personal responsibilities toward, or observations about, friends, brothers, wife, servants, cattle, children, parents, priests, the poor, the dead, the sorrowful, and the sick.

Since a "faithful friend" is "beyond price" (cf. 6:15 with COMMENT), one is urged not to endanger friendship for material gain (v 18a), a perennially valid precept. "A true brother" (cf. NOTE) is worth more than "gold of Ophir," a region on the coast of southern Arabia or eastern Africa, famous in antiquity for its gold; cf. 1 Kgs 9:28; 10:11; Isa 13:12; Job 22:24; 28:16; Ps 45:10. Hence, one should not manipulate a brother for personal advantage. A man should not "dismiss, or reject," a "sensible, or wise, wife" (v 19a; cf. 25:8) for another woman (cf. 9:3–9). In v 19b, "charming wife" translates Heb *ṭôbat ḥēn*, lit., "good in grace, well favored," an expression that occurs also in Nah 3:4. The parallelism suggests that "the wise wife" will also be "well favored, or charming." In v 19b, it is not certain whether the translation of Heb *pĕnînîm* should be "corals," "pearls," or "rubies"—cf. Job 28:18; Prov 31:10; Lam 4:7. Ben Sira has much to say about wives; cf. 9:1; 25:8; 26:1–4, 13–18; 36:27–31; and see INTRODUCTION, Part X, 7.

Servants, or slaves, could be either Jews or non-Jews (cf. Deut 15:12; 24:14); both deserve fair treatment free of personal abuse, especially when they serve "faithfully" (v 20a). Kindness to slaves was mandated in the Law; cf. Deut 15:12–18; 23:16. Ben Sira speaks of slaves also in 33:25–33. In v 20b, the "laborer" (Heb *śākîr*, lit., hireling, hired worker) who "gives himself" (the literal translation of the Heb phrase) also must be dealt with kindly, for the Law protects his rights, too; cf. Lev 19:13; 25:6, 53; Deut 24:14. V 21a (MS C) may also be translated: "Love a wise slave as yourself" (cf. Lev 19:18). The injunction in v 21b is a reference to the law that stipulated that after six years of service the Hebrew slave was to be set free; cf. Exod 21:2; Lev 25:39–43; Deut 15:12–15; Jer 34:8–20. See A. Phillips, *JSOT* 30 (1984): 51–66.

In v 22a, Heb *bĕhēmâ*, "livestock, cattle, beasts," may also mean "a riding animal," which Smend (p. 70), on the basis of Neh 2:12, 14, thinks is the sense here because of the adjective "dependable, reliable" in v 22b. Usually, however, *bĕhēmâ* means "livestock (in general)." Cf. Prov 27:23–27. It may strike a modern reader as odd that children (vv 23–25) and the wife (v 26) are mentioned in the same context as livestock; but in the world of Ben Sira, sons, daughters, and wife were considered as much a man's possessions as were his livestock. In v 23a, Heb *yassēr*, "chastise," may also mean "correct," or "discipline." Cf. 30:1–3, 13; Prov 13:24; 19:18; 23:13–14. A father is to cure the stubbornness (cf. NOTE) of his sons "in their early youth" (v 23b) while their characters are still being formed; otherwise, it will be too late. Cf. Deut 21:18–21. V 24a may be translated, lit.: "If you have daughters, watch [or guard] their *flesh*" (Heb *šĕʾēr*, also found with such a meaning in Ps 73:26 and Prov 5:11)—a rather blunt precept, which most fathers throughout history have sought to observe. V 24b may be translated, lit.: "and do not let your face shine on them" (cf. Qoh 7:3–4). Ben Sira takes up the theme of a father's concern for his virgin daughter again in 42:9–14. Although v 25a affirms that marrying off a daughter brings anxiety to an end, v 25b urges the father to give his daughter "to a sensible [or intelligent] man." A father arranged his daughter's marriage; she had no say in the matter.

V 26 may also be translated: "If you have a wife, abhor her not; but a hated [wife], trust her not." As regards the relatively rare Heb verb *tʿb*, "to abhor, regard as an abomination," cf. Deut 7:26; 23:8; Job 19:19; 30:10. The verb appears in parallelism with *śnʾ*, "to hate" (the passive participle of which occurs in v 26b) in Pss 5:6–7; 119:163; Amos 5:10. In the negative precept of v 26a, Ben Sira exhorts married men to respect their spouses, but he adds v 26b just in case the wife is not loved. Regarding "the unloved wife" (=Heb the hated wife), cf. Gen 29:31. Deut 21:15–17 protects the rights of the unloved wife and her children. The active participle of *śnʾ* means "enemy" in the OT; cf., e.g., 6:1, 4; 12:8; 25:1 (Heb not extant, but the same root appears in Syr); Exod 1:10; 23:5; Esth 9:1, 5, 10; Prov 26:24; 27:6.

Vv 27–28 were omitted in MS A probably because of homoioarchton: the scribe skipped from the first *bĕkol* (*libbĕkā*, "with [your] whole [heart]") (v 27a) to the second *bĕkol* (*napšĕkā* [so G; MS A has *libbĕkā*], "with [your] whole [soul]") (v 29a). The responsibility to honor one's parents (v 27) is part of the Decalogue: Exod 20:12 and Deut 5:16; cf. also Sir 3:1–16 with COMMENT; Tob 4:3; Matt 15:4–6; Mark 7:10–13; Luke 18:20; Eph 6:2. Regarding v 27b, cf. Tob 4:4. For v 28a, Syr and Lat read: "Remember that if it were not for them you would not be here." Adults are to honor and care for aging parents not only because the Law of God says so, but also because the law of gratitude demands as much (v 28b).

In G, the opening phrases of vv 27a ("With your whole heart"), 29a ("With all your soul"), and 30a ("With all your strength") (v 27 is missing in Heb, and in v 29a MS A reads "heart" instead of "soul") are taken from Deut 6:5: "You shall love Yahweh your God with your whole heart and with your whole soul and with your whole strength." Cf. Matt 22:37; Mark 12:30; Luke 10:27. In v 29, the faithful are enjoined not only to fear God (cf. 1:11–30 with

COMMENT) but also to "revere [lit., regard as holy] his priests"; cf. 45:6–22; 50:1–21. An *a:b::b':a'* pattern emphasizes the point: *fear:God::his priests:revere.* In v 30a, the phrase *bĕkol mĕʾôdĕkā,* "with all your strength," occurs only one other time in the rest of the OT (Deut 6:5); with the third person singular pronoun, the phrase occurs only in 2 Kgs 23:25, and with the third person plural pronoun, only in Tob 14:9. V 30 also is composed in an *a:b::b':a'* rhetorical pattern: *love:your Maker::his ministers:neglect not.* In v 31a, Ben Sira rephrases the precept given in v 29. The portion due the priests (v 31bcd) is specified in Num 18:9–20; Exod 29:27–28; Lev 2:1–10; 7:31–36; Deut 14:28–29; 18:1–8; cf. Tob 1:6–7.

The elite of Hellenistic Judea were the priests, of whose number the high priest was the acknowledged head of the Jewish people. In addition to being members of the Council of Elders or Gerousia, the priests were also the most important functionaries. The Judea of Ben Sira's day was ruled by priests who enjoyed many privileges even in the economic field, as is obvious from Sir 7:29–31. Cf. M. Stern, "The Social and Governmental Structure of Judea under the Ptolemies and Seleucids," in *A History of the Jewish People,* ed. H. H. Ben-Sasson, p. 194. See INTRODUCTION, Part II.

In Deut 14:28–29, the Levite along with the alien, orphan, and widow (the economically and socially disadvantaged of that society) are the recipients of the tithes the people are to bring so that God may bless them in all that they do. Ben Sira probably had this text in mind when composing these verses about responsibilities to the priests (vv 29–31) and to the poor and unfortunate (vv 32–35). Being openhanded with the poor (v 32a) makes one's "blessing . . . complete" (v 32b), for God has a special love for them and protects them. Cf. 3:30–4:10 with COMMENT and Matt 25:31–46. V 33, with an *a:b::b':a'* structure (*give a gift:to anyone alive::from the dead:withhold not kindness*) apparently extends the thought of v 32; the point is that one should help all the poor, those who are living and those who have died. By combining the living and the dead, Ben Sira creates a merism to include every poor person who is or who was. The meaning of v 33b, however, is not certain. The *ḥesed,* "kindness, mercy," Ben Sira urges may be "the bread of consolation" one should share with the family of the deceased (cf. Jer 16:7), or a food offering placed on his grave (cf. 30:18). Although both practices were prohibited in ancient times (Deut 26:14), later Jewish custom seems to have allowed them; cf. Ezek 24:17; Tob 4:17. The custom of holding a banquet after the burial of the dead was also common among Greeks and Romans (Tertullian, *Apology,* 39). This custom was taken up by the early Christians, as is attested by the discovery in the catacombs of St. Sebastian of a banquet room (*triclinium*) on the walls of which were graffiti signifying that pilgrims had satisfied a vow by celebrating a memorial banquet (*refrigerium*) in honor of Sts. Peter and Paul. There are also pictorial representations of such banquets in several tombs. By the end of the fourth century, however, this custom had become a scandal, and both Ambrose (*De Elia,* 17) and Augustine (Epistle 20, 10) took measures to suppress it. Cf. F. X. Murphy, *"Refrigerium,"* *NCE,* vol. 12, p. 197. It is also possible that in v 33b Ben Sira simply refers to the "kindness" of providing a decent burial for the poor; cf. Tob 1:16–19; 2:4, 8.

The precepts in v 34 are obligations one has toward the bereaved. Since death is an inexorable and inevitable fact of life, one should not try to hide from its unpleasantness by avoiding "those who weep" (v 34a). Rather one should share, and thus diminish, another's grief by "mourn[ing] with those who mourn" (v 34b). In Rom 12:15, St. Paul gives a similar injunction: "Weep with those who weep." Cf. Job 30:25; 1 Cor 12:26; 2 Cor 11:29. Ben Sira mentions duties toward the dead also in 22:11–12 and 38:16–23.

The care of the sick was another responsibility incumbent on the faithful Jew (v 35a); cf. Job 2:11–13; Matt 25:39, 44. In honoring this responsibility, not only does one achieve a sense of satisfaction in fulfilling God's law of love of neighbor (Lev 19:18), but also one is loved in return (v 35b).

In v 36, Ben Sira brings to a close this collection of ethical maxims by a general exhortation of overwhelming persuasiveness: "In whatever you do, remember *your last days* [Heb *'aḥărît,* lit., *the end*], and *you will* never *sin* [Heb *tiššāḥēt,* lit., *you will* (never) *be corrupt, or corrupted*]." The verb *šḥt* (found also in 5:15 and 49:4b) is used in the Flood Story to describe how corrupt the earth had become (Gen 6:11–12, the P tradition). Cf. M. Fang Che-yong, "Sir 7,36 (Vulg 7,40) iuxta hebraicam veritatem," *VD* 40 (1962): 18–26. In 28:6a (G; the verse is not extant in Heb), Ben Sira again uses the phrase "remember *the end,*" and in 28:6b the parallel is "[remember] death and decay."

14. Prudence in Dealing with Others
(8:1–19)

8   ¹ Contend not with the great,   G(A)
    lest you fall into his power.
  ² Quarrel not with the rich,   G
    lest he pay out the price of your downfall;
  For gold has unsettled many,   A
    and wealth perverts the character of princes.

  ³ Dispute not with a person of railing speech,
    heap no wood upon his fire.
  ⁴ Be not too familiar with the senseless,
    lest he show contempt for your forebears.

  ⁵ Revile not a repentant sinner;
    remember, we are all guilty.
  ⁶ Insult no one when he is old;
    some of us, too, will grow old.
  ⁷ Gloat not when a person dies;
    remember, we are all to be gathered in.

  ⁸ Spurn not the discourse of the wise,
    but busy yourself with their veiled maxims;
  In this way you will acquire the training
    to stand in the presence of princes.
  ⁹ Reject not the tradition of the elders
    which they have learned from their fathers;
  From it you will obtain the knowledge
    how to answer when the need arises.

  ¹⁰ Kindle not the coals of a sinner,   G
    lest you be consumed in his flaming fire.   A

11 Do not give ground before a scoundrel;
    it will set him in ambush against you.
12 Lend not to one more powerful than yourself;
    or when you lend, count it as lost.
13 Go not surety beyond your means;
    think any pledge a debt you must pay.

14 Contend not at law with a judge,
    for he will settle it according to his whim.
15 Travel not with the ruthless,
    lest he weigh you down with calamity;
For he will go his own way straight,
    and through his folly you will perish with him.
16 Show no defiance to the quick-tempered,
    nor ride with him through lonely country;
Bloodshed is nothing to him,
    and when there is no one to help you, he will destroy
          you.

17 Take no counsel with a simpleton,
    for he cannot keep a confidence.
18 Before a stranger, do nothing that should be kept secret,
    for you know not what it will engender later on.
19 Open your heart to no one;
    banish not your happiness.

Notes

8   1. MS A adds a variant form, and mixes the two; Syr has 1b, but takes MS A's variant for 1a.

2ab. Read *'al tārîb 'im 'îš 'āšîr/pen yišqal mišqālĕkā wĕ'ābadtā* with G (cf. Prov 28:11)+*'ābadtā* of MS A, the verb used by G, Syr to substitute for *hiphîz* in 2c.

2c. *rabbîm* could mean "great ones," but this is not Ben Sira's usage.

3b. *'ĕṣîm* is called for by G, Syr; MS A is damaged at the line's end. *his* here and in G merely applies the imagery.

4b. G *hoi progonoi sou* = *'ăbôtêkā;* read *la'ăbôtêkā,* cf. Cant 8:7. MS A's *lannĕdîbîm* is corrupt, from 2d.

6b. With G, Syr read *mimmennû mazqînîm*.

8c. For *mimmennû=In this way*, cf. 7:35.

10. MS A's *ʾl tṣlḥ bnḥlt* [*sic*, vs. Segal] *ršᶜ* is corrupted from *ʾl tṣyt bgḥlt ršᶜ*=G; Syr read *bgḥlt* but the expected equivalent *běgumrēʾ* (cf. 21:18) has undergone a reinterpretation to *gěmîrāʾ* and the extant Syr text is secondary.

14. *yišpôṭ*, MS A is lacking the end of the word. MS A at 4:27cd, and Syr here, give the variant "Do not sit with a wicked judge in a lawsuit, lest you give judgment with him according to his whim."

15b. *yakbîd* with G, Syr; MS A has *takbîd*.

15d. *with him* is interpretation, here and in G.

16b. G, Syr=*bammidbār;* MS A *badderek*.

Comment

This section gives advice on how one should behave with persons of diverse types—the rich and powerful, the loud-mouthed, the senseless, the repentant, the elderly, the dead, the wise, sinners, borrowers, judges, the ruthless, the quick-tempered, simpletons, strangers. The passage may be divided into seven stanzas: 3+2+3+4+4+5+3 bicola.

In v 1a, the variant in MS A, followed by Syr (cf. NOTE) reads: "Contend not with *one more mighty* [or severe, stubborn, hard] *than you.*" The Heb verb *rîb* means "to contend, strive," either physically (Deut 33:7) or verbally (hence, "to quarrel," as in v 2a and Gen 26:20) or juridically, i.e., in a lawsuit (Isa 3:13; 57:16). In v 1b, Ben Sira gives the commonly observed reason for the precept of v 1a: You don't stand a chance of winning. V 2ab is in synonymous parallelism with v 1; as is usually the case, the rich are also the great. V 2b makes reference to a bribe given to a judge in order to influence his verdict. The taking of a bribe was condemned by the OT: cf. Exod 23:8; Deut 16:19; 27:25; Amos 5:12; Sir 20:29. The motive clause in v 2cd, introduced by *kî* ("for, because") brings the stanza to an end. An *a:b:c::cʹ:bʹ:aʹ* rhetorical structure dramatizes the point *many* (direct object):*has unsettled:gold* (subject)::*wealth:perverts:princes.*

The next stanza concerns the loud-mouthed (v 3) and the senseless (v 4), often the same people, as is clear from the parallelism; cf. 20:5–8. In v 3a, "a person of railing speech" renders Heb *ʾîš lāšôn*, lit., a man of tongue, a colorful expression that occurs also in 9:18a; 25:20b uses the phrase "a woman of tongue." Cf. Jas 3:8. The imagery of words as pieces of wood placed on a fire (v 3b) is taken up again in 28:10. Here Ben Sira urges the wise person to avoid all disputes with the loud-mouthed, for they are given the excuse to speak even more when someone responds to their boisterousness. In the Psalms of Solomon xii 2, the tongue of a malicious person is compared to "fire in a threshing-floor that burns up the straw" (quoted in Box-Oesterley, p. 342). The sensible or wise are to avoid discussion or familiarity with the senseless or foolish; cf. 21:26; 22:13. The reason is that the wise by association with the foolish person will themselves be considered fools, and thus their forebears (see NOTE) will be disgraced for having engendered senseless children; cf. 3:11.

The next three verses form a stanza because vv 5b and 7b, the opening and closing bicola, begin with the imperative "remember" and the phrase "we are all. . . ." As regards the thought of v 5, cf. 27:30–28:7; Matt 7:4; and especially John 8:7. A similar idea is expressed in *Baba mezia* (Jerusalem Talmud), iv 10: "When a man repents say not to him, 'Remember your former sins'" (quoted in Box-Oesterley, p. 343). Regarding v 5b, cf. 1 Kgs 8:46; 2 Chr 6:36; Job 25:4; Qoh 7:20; Rom 5:12; Jas 3:2; 1 John 1:8. V 6 deals with another condition common to humankind: old age. In v 6a, the adjective *yāšîš*, "old," occurs elsewhere only in Job (12:12; 15:10; 29:8; 32:6). One reason why it is wrong to insult the aged is stated by Job 12:12: "With the old is wisdom, and with length of days understanding." Cf. v 9. Another reason is suggested by 3:13: senility. The sin of insulting the elderly will come back to haunt a person in his or her own old age (v 6b). The stanza ends with an exhortation (v 7) about a third condition that all men and women must face: death. No one should gloat or boast over a dead person, for sooner or later we must all die, or to use Ben Sira's colorful expression, "we are all to be gathered in," an expression he borrowed from Gen 25:8, 17; 49:29; Judg 2:10; 2 Kgs 22:20. In Gen 35:29 and 49:33, *wayyigwaʿ*, "and he died" (the participle of the same verb is used in v 7a), and *wayyēʾāsep*, "and he was gathered in," are used in parallelism, as in v 7.

The next stanza (vv 8–9), which contains an exhortation to learn from the wise and the elderly, begins with (v 8ab) a rhetorically balanced a:b::b':a' pattern: *spurn not:the discourse of the wise::with their veiled maxims:busy yourself.* As regards Heb *śîḥâ*, "discourse," cf. 6:35 with COMMENT. Heb *ḥîdôt*, "veiled maxims, riddles, enigmas," occurs elsewhere in the Wisdom literature only in 47:17a and Prov 1:6 (where it occurs in parallelism with *māšāl*, "proverb," *mĕlîṣâ*, "parable," and *dibrê ḥăkāmîm*, "words of the wise"). In 47:17a, *māšāl*, *ḥîdâ*, and *mĕlîṣâ* also are found in parallel. V 8cd is a motive clause, introduced by the usual *kî*, "for, because," which does not appear in translation here: for only by listening to the wise (= "in this way," cf. NOTE) can one "acquire the training *to stand in the presence of* princes" as servant or courtier. Cf. 38:3b; 47:1b; Job 1:6; 2:1; Prov 22:29. In v 9a, read *šĕmûʿâ*, "tradition" (lit., what has been heard) instead of MS A's *šĕmîʿâ* (confusion of *waw* and *yod;* cf. COMMENT on 4:2). The tradition of the elders (cf. v 6) must be respected because "they have heard" (Heb *šāmĕʿû* here translated "they have learned") it "from their fathers" (v 9b). Wisdom here is viewed as a tradition that was handed down from one generation to another. The *Pirqe Aboth,* i 1, states: "Moses received the Torah from Sinai, and he delivered it to Joshua, and Joshua to the elders [Josh 24:31; Judg 2:7], and the elders to the prophets, and the prophets delivered it to the men of the Great Synagogue" (quoted in Box-Oesterley, p. 343). Cf. Deut 4:9; 11:18–19; Ps 44:2; Job 8:8–10. V 9cd gives the motive clause, introduced as usual by *kî* (cf. vv 2c, 6b, 8a), which is not translated here. The Heb noun *śēkel,* "knowledge, prudence, good sense, insight, understanding," occurring more than a dozen times in the book, is an important word in the vocabulary of the Wisdom literature; cf. Prov 3:4; 12:8; 13:15; 16:22; 19:11; 23:9. The ability *to give an answer* (9d), Heb *lĕhāšîb pitgām* (lit., to return a word) is the mark of the wise; cf. 5:11; 11:8 (with *dābār,* the normal Heb noun for "word" instead of the Aramaism *pitgām*); Prov 22:21; 24:26 (see also Prov 15:28).

The next two verses (10–11) give advice about the "sinner" and the "scoundrel." The burning of coals is the classic image (v 10) of sinful passion and its destructive force; cf. 9:8d; Job 31:9–12; see also COMMENT on v 3 above. In v 11, the *lēṣ,* the Heb noun that means "scoundrel, scorner," is the concern of many Wisdom sayings; cf. 3:28; 13:1; 15:8; 31:26; 32:18; Ps 1:1; 1 Tim 1:13; and see the COMMENT on 3:28. In v 11a, the verb root *zwḥ,* here translated "Do (not) give ground," is an Aramaism; in Aram and Syr, it means "to move, stir, arouse oneself to action." The point of the verse is that the wise should not get excited or overreact to the statements of the scorner of religion or of morality, because by doing so they are playing into his hand (v 11b).

Caution with regard to loans is the subject of the next two verses (12–13); cf. also 29:1–7, where Ben Sira again takes up this important subject. The injunction of v 12a is sociologically validated by the experience of many recorded in v 12b. The reason why one should "count . . . as lost" the loan made to a person more powerful than oneself is that one has no way of effectively ensuring repayment; cf. vv 1–2 with COMMENT. Cf. also Prov 22:7. Though one should not be stingy in providing surety or collateral to a fellow Jew in need (cf. 29:14), one is urged to be realistic about the possible result of such an action (v 13a) because one may end up forfeiting the collateral in order to repay the debt (v 13b); cf. 29:14–20; Prov 6:1–5; 11:15; 17:18; 22:26–27.

The aphorism in v 14 is simply the sedimentation of a commonly observed situation. In v 14b, G makes the point even more striking: "for they [i.e., the judge's colleagues] will judge him according to his opinion [of the case]." Ben Sira alludes to his travel experience in v 15; cf. 34:9–13. In v 15a, the Heb word *'akzārî,* "ruthless, cruel, fierce," occurs as an adjective only in Isa 13:9; Jer 6:23; 50:42; Prov 12:10; 17:11; and as a noun only here and in 13:12a; 35:22d; 37:11f; Prov 5:9; 11:17; cf. Job 41:2. It is dangerous for people to go on a journey with a cruel person, for his conduct could bring them calamity (v 15ab). He will follow his own ruthless impulses (v 15c) and get into trouble; and through the folly of his unrestrained behavior they will perish along with him. Cf. 34:13. In v 16a, "the quick-tempered" translates Heb *ba'al 'ap*, lit., master, or lord, of anger; cf. Prov 22:24. "Show no defiance" is, lit., do not make bold (or strong) your brow (or forehead); cf. Ezek 3:7; Isa 48:4; Prov 7:13. The reason why one should not be defiant toward, or ride with, the quick-tempered through "lonely country" (lit., the desert; cf. NOTE) is given in v 16cd. Cain killed his brother Abel "in the field" (Gen 4:8), with nobody else around.

The last stanza (vv 17–19) speaks of the pitfalls of confiding in others. Taking counsel with, or confiding in, a simpleton or fool (v 17a), Heb *pôteh*, is to be avoided, "for he cannot keep [or conceal] a confidence [or a secret]" (v 17b). Cf. Prov 11:13, where the noun *sôd* ("confidence, secret, secret counsel") and the verb *ksh* ("to conceal") also occur; and Prov 20:19, where the noun *sôd* occurs along with the participle *pôteh*. Cf. also Prov 25:9b: "Another's secret [*sôd*] do not disclose." V 18a, which contains a wordplay on Heb *zār* ("stranger") by reversing the consonants to form the noun *rāz* ("secret"), may be translated, lit.: "Before a stranger make no secret." The word *rāz* is an Aramaism of Persian origin; it means "mystery, secret" in the Aram of Dan 2:18, 19, 27, 28, 29, 30, 47, and 4:6. It also occurs in the War Scroll from Qumran (1QM iii 9; xiv 9; xvi 11). Elsewhere in the OT the word occurs only in Sir 12:11c. In composing v 18b, Ben Sira may have had in mind the tragic experience of Samson, who revealed the secret of his strength to his girlfriend Delilah, who then told all to the Philistines (Judg 16:15–21). The final exhortation is the strongest and most inclusive; notice the ascending order: simpleton in v 17; stranger in v 18; "no one" (lit., no flesh) in v 19. Misery may be the outcome of revealing one's heart to another (v 19). As a parallel, Spicq (p. 614) quotes the pithy Latin proverb *Fide, sed cui vide*, "Confide, but choose your confidant carefully."

15. Advice Concerning Women and the Choice of Friends
(9:1–16)

9 1 Be not jealous of the wife of your bosom,   A
       lest you teach her to do evil against you.
     2 Give no woman power over you
       to trample upon your dignity.
     3 Do not go near a strange woman,
       lest you fall into her snares.
     4 Do not dally with a singing girl,   G
       lest you be captivated by her charms.
     5 Entertain no thoughts about a virgin,   A
       lest you be enmeshed in damages for her.
     6 Give not yourself to prostitutes,
       lest you surrender your inheritance.
     7 Gaze not about the lanes of the city   G
       and wander not through its squares;
     8 Avert your eyes from a comely woman;   A
       gaze not upon beauty that is not for you—
     Through woman's beauty many have perished,   G
       and love for it burns like fire.   S
     9 With a married woman recline not at table   G(A)
       nor drink intoxicants with her,
     Lest your heart incline toward her   A
       and you decline in blood to the grave.

     10 Discard not an old friend,
        for the new one cannot equal him;
     A new friend is like new wine
        which you drink with pleasure only when it has aged.
     11 Envy not the wicked;
        you know not when his day will come.

12 Opt not for the success of pride;
     remember it will not reach death unpunished.

13 Keep far from the person who has power to kill,
     and you will not be filled with the fear of death.
   But if you approach him, offend him not,
     lest he take away your life;
   Know that you are stepping among snares
     and walking over a net.

14 As best you can, take your neighbors' measure,
     and associate with the wise.
15 Exchange thoughts with the person who is
                         knowledgeable;
     let all your conversation be about the Law of the
                         the Most High.
16 Have just people for your table companions;
     in the fear of God be your glory.

Notes

9 1b. With G=*tĕlamměd ʿālêkā, you teach* (against yourself). For similar reflexive twists, even with second-person pronoun suffixes after second-person verb forms, cf. 7:7 (2×); 7:16. Syr understood *tilmad,* "(lest) she learn (against you)."

2a. *Give no[t]=ʾal tittēn* with G, Syr; MS A repeats *ʾal teqannēʾ* of 1a. This colon is less explicit than the reference to Solomon in 47:19, but carries the same implications.

2b. *trample upon your dignity:* the Heb borrows its imagery from Deut 33:29; Hab 3:19, and elsewhere, cf. J. L. Crenshaw, "*Wᵉdōrēk ʿal bāmŏtê ʾareṣ,*" *CBQ* 34 (1972): 39–53 (read rather *bomŏtê* for MT; here, K of Deut 32:13 and elsewhere, *bmwty=* approximately *bŏmôtê?*).

3–4. Since MS A inserts between these verses an additional bicolon, it becomes necessary to ascertain how much is authentic and where it fits. V 3 in MS A is close to G. For the verb in 3a, G reads *ʾal tiqqāreh/tiqqārēʾ/tiqqār,* "Do not meet (as if by chance) with (*ʾel*) a strange woman"; it supposes the situation of Prov 7:10–27, where the woman, dressed like a prostitute (v 10), indicates (v 19) that she is married. Syr in the context of Sirach simply makes her a prostitute. The verb in MS A is *(ʾal) tiqrab (ʾel),* "Do not approach (for intercourse)," an easy error for the form supposed by G. In Syr, the verb, *(lāʾ) teʿnē (ʿam),* "be not familiar with," is shown by its accompanying preposition to be a borrowing from what follows: the third colon in MS A has *ʿim zônâ ʾal tistayyād*. Thus the first of four cola in Syr, like the third of six in MS A, combines a subject from v 3 with a verb from v 4. For 3b, the basic witnesses (MS A, G, and Syr) all agree. MS A's fourth colon, *pen tillākēd blqwtyh*, has the verb of G's 4b (*mēpote*) *halǭs*, followed by a jumble of consonants patterned after the *bmṣwdtyh*, *into her snares*, that ends 3b. MS A's fifth colon has the correct noun for v 4, *(with) a singing girl*, though incorrectly plural as against G and Syr. With this, the proper verb would be *(ʾal) tistayyēd*, "Do not dally," already used by MS A (with medieval two *yod*'s for the doubled consonant, and Aramaizing *ā* in the last syllable, marked in the MS). Syr has this verb (*lāʾ tistawwad*, the direct counterpart of the form in MS A's third colon, and a doublet with the *lāʾ teʿnēʾ*, having the same sense, used by Syr in 3a). As for MS A, for the verb in this, its fifth, colon, it has *lʾ tdmwk*, "do not sleep (with)," the Jewish Aram imperfect in *u* of a familiar Aram stative verb that has ready equivalents but no cognate in Heb.

The knottiest problem in 4a is in the Gr, with its verb *(mē) endelechize*. In Sirach, *endelechōs* occurs twice (45:14; 51:11) for Heb *tāmîd*, "constantly, regularly, daily." Therefore, in three places where the cognate verb is used in the Gr (here in 9:4a, in 37:12, and in 41:6), Segal manufactures a *tatmîd/yatmîd* as the Heb counterpart. No one knows that such a *hiphʿîl* had been contrived anciently, though in 41:6 the remaining traces in the Masada MS verify the presence of at least the adverb (see the NOTE there). It is also curious that here MS A's incredible *tdmwk* has three of the same consonants. Yet whatever the Gr may have read in this place (or in 37:12, see the NOTE there), there is the strongest of evidence that *hstyd* as a verb stem based on the noun *sôd*, and meaning "make oneself the familiar companion/associate of (another)" was a real part of Ben Sira's personal vocabulary. The passages are 8:17; 9:14 (both in close context with the present place); and 42:12. In 8:17 and 9:14, G's *symboleuou* certainly corresponds to MS A's *tistayyēd/histayyēd;* in both places the Syr equivalent is with *qēṭar rāzāʾ*, an expression for "agree, conspire," and the like. In 6:6 are found the correspondences, MS A *baʿal sôdēkā*, G *symbouloi sou*, Syr *bēʿēl rāzāk*. Since in pre-Christian Qumran and in the Aram of Daniel, *sôd* and *rāz* respectively mean "mystery, secret," there is no mistaking the total ancient support for MS A's readings. Syr for 4b, "lest she destroy you by association with her," is a paraphrase that becomes slightly less obscure when one notices that in 9:15b *kol sôdēkā* of MS A is rendered in Gr by *pasa diēgēsis sou* and in Syr by *kolhēn šuʿyātāk*, "all your conversation," employing the same noun as does the "association with her" of 4b. 42:12 in MS B has *ʾl tstwyd*(!) with *ʾl tstyd* in the margin; G's *mē synedrue* and Syr *lāʾ tašpar šuʿyātāʾ* are paraphrases. The occurrence falls in a lacuna in the Masada MS. In the present translation of 9:4a, *ʾal tistayyēd* is taken to have been the original reading.

For 4b, the choice remains between MS A's fourth and sixth cola. Segal quotes from the Munich codex the former of these cited in b. Sanh. 100b as *pen tillākēd bimēṣûdôtêhā;* the verb can be retained (cf. G), but the prepositional phrase is from 3b (MS A, G, Syr). Rüger (p. 16) sees MS A's last colon of the six, *pen yiśrēpûkā bēpîpîyôtām*, as the later form of the colon, and follows Lévi and others in taking the Syr *tawbēdāk* as a corruption from *tawqēdāk*, "lest she set you on fire," echoing *śrp*. A double-edged sword (Heb *pîpîyôt*) is not a likely instrument for a singing girl either to make a catch or to ignite a flame with; Syr may have thought the *pîpîyôt* were something said or sung, given the etymology of "mouth" that underlies the double edge. The Gr with *epicheirēmasin* seems to credit the girl with efforts or enterprise, not specified. The present translation with *charms* reads *bîpēpîyôtehā,* based on the adjective *yĕpēpî,* derived from *yāpeh,* "beautiful," *yŏpî,* "beauty"; cf. Ps 45:3; Jer 46:20; and *HALAT;* the *tillākēd,* "be captivated," goes with this.

6b. *surrender=tāsēb;* MS A *tissōb.*

8c. *Through woman's beauty=bĕtô'ar 'iššâ=*G, Syr; MS A *bĕ'ad 'iššâ.*

9ab. Read *'im bĕ'ûlâ 'al tat 'aṣṣîl* [cf. 41:19], *we'al tisbā' 'immāh šēkār.*

10b. *equal him=*G, Syr; MS A illegible here.

10d. *with pleasure* is interpretation, here and in G.

11a, 12a. Cf. Prov 3:31.

15b. *about the Law of the Most High=bĕtôrat 'elyôn=*G; Syr similarly.

Comment

This section, dealing with conduct toward women (vv 1–9), friends (vv 10–12), and associates (vv 13–16), may be divided into four stanzas: $11+4+3+3$ bicola.

Ben Sira's advice about jealousy (v 1) is solid. Indeed, jealousy is one of the few vices from which one derives no (apparent) benefit, but only evil. "Ben Sira here gives a good reason for avoiding it—it may promote the realization of the thing feared" (so Box-Oesterley, p. 345). The graphic expression "the wife of your bosom" derives from Deut 13:7 and 28:54; cf. Mic 7:5. Regarding jealousy, cf. Num 5:14. V 2 is translated, lit.: "Give [cf. NOTE] not yourself to a woman to have her trample on your dignity [cf. NOTE]." Although Ben Sira, like other men in the society of that day, could be accused (from our perspective) of male chauvinism, he may not be indulging in it when he wrote v 2, because the verse may serve as an introduction to vv 3–4, which discuss women of questionable virtue. It is equally probable, however, that v 2 refers to the wife of v 1 and to the women of vv 3–4. In effect, Ben Sira says that while love should not be jealous (v 1), it should not be spineless either (v 2). On v 2, see *Phibis,* viii 4 (Sanders, p. 71). The Heb verb *qrb* (v 3a) means "to go near, approach," and "to come close (for sexual intercourse)," as in Gen 20:4; Lev 18:6, 14, 19; Deut 22:14; Isa 8:3; Ezek 18:6; both meanings are present in the verse. "A strange woman" (v 3a) is an expression derived from Prov 2:16; 5:3, 20; 7:5; 22:14; and 23:27, to designate "a prostitute or adulteress." As regards the "snares," or "nets," of the "strange woman," cf. Prov 7:22–23 and Qoh 7:26. As Duesberg-Fransen (p. 131) suggest, we should note the contrast between the nets of the strange woman and the net, noose, bonds, and yoke of wisdom; cf. 6:24–25, 29–30 with COMMENT. For the variant after v 3 in MS A, cf. NOTE. Regarding the fascination with singing girls (v 4), cf. 2 Sam 19:36. For the singing girl as prostitute, cf. Isa 23:15–16.

V 5a may also be translated: "Be not overly attentive to a virgin" (cf. Matt 5:28); cf. Job 31:1. If a man seduced a virgin, he was forced to pay her father a fine of fifty silver shekels (cf. v 5b) and then take her as his wife "because he has deflowered her" and could not subsequently divorce her (so Deut 22:29); cf. Exod 22:15–16. Wisdom writers repeatedly warn their students about consorting with whores (v 6a): Prov 5:3–14; 6:26; 7:10; 23:27; 29:3; cf. also Hos 4:12–14; Mic 1:7; Ezek 16:24–43. Prostitutes are to be avoided for a very practical reason, "lest you surrender your inheritance" (v 6b); cf. Prov 29:3; Luke 15:13, 30. The injunction of v 7 is again practical: if you wish to avoid contact with prostitutes or other loose women, you must not wander through the city streets looking for them; cf. Prov 7:7–12. In v 8, Ben Sira warns his students about the perils of lusting after a beautiful and shapely woman who is married or betrothed (= "beauty that is not for you" in v 8b). Self-control in these matters is the mark of the wise; cf. 18:30–31. Ben Sira's comment in v 8cd, however, is chauvinistic and unfair but not atypical in the social and religious milieu of that day. He blames a woman's beauty for the sinful lust (v 8d) a man experiences. It is as if one should view with suspicion delicious food and a good wine because some people are gluttons and drunkards. Cf. Job 31:9, 12 for the image of unholy passion being compared to fire (v 8d). In v 9, Ben Sira speaks of the possible pitfalls of sharing a dinner and drinking alcoholic beverages with a married woman. Terence (2d century B.C.) gives us the Latin proverb *Sine Cerere* [goddess of agriculture, hence of corn and grain] *et Libero* [god of wine] *friget Venus* [goddess of love], "Without Ceres and Liber, Venus grows cold." "Married women were often present with their husbands at banquets given to guests—such occasions are dangerous, says Ben-Sira" (so Box-Oesterley, p. 346). Cf. Amos 4:1. Compare the conduct of Jesus, who did not hesitate to speak alone with the Samaritan woman who had had five husbands and was living with a sixth man (John 4:7–26), and the narrow attitude of the disciples who "were surprised that Jesus was speaking with a woman" (John 4:27). Ben Sira employs a clever wordplay on the *hiph᷂il* (*taṭṭeh,* "incline," v 9c) and *qal* (*tiṭṭeh,* "decline," v 9d) of the verb *nṭh.* Cf. Prov 7:25–27 about the disastrous consequences of lusting after a married woman. The Law demanded the death penalty (v 9d) for those convicted of adultery: Lev 20:10; Deut 22:22; John 8:4–5. The reference in v 9d, however, may be to the vengeance of the husband who kills the adulterer (so Box-Oesterley, p. 347).

In v 10, there is a clever *a:b::b:a* chiastic pattern which adds elegance to Ben Sira's thought: *old (friend):new::new (friend):old.* For other maxims on friendship, cf. 6:5–17; 7:18; 37:1–6, as well as Theognis, 1151–52 (Sanders, p. 31). Regarding the imagery of v 10cd, cf. Luke 5:39. One should not envy the wicked in the sense of desiring to be like them; cf. Ps 37:1–2; Prov 3:31–32; 24:1–2. It is a temptation to envy sinners (vv 11a, 12a) because they seem to prosper and be successful, as Ps 73:2–16 describes so graphically. Yet the prosperity of the wicked ends suddenly (vv 11b, 12b), and they are hurled down to ruin, as Ps 73:18–19 goes on to say. In 16:6–13, Ben Sira gives examples of sinners who met with catastrophe because of their sin; cf. also 21:1–4, 8–10; and 40:10, 12–16.

In v 13, Ben Sira refers to the perils of court intrigues (cf., for example, 2 Macc 4:43–50). In Egypt, the Ptolemaic king, who was considered to be a god, had the absolute right of life or death over his subjects; military commanders had this right over their troops, and governors of subject provinces over the people. A similar situation prevailed with the Seleucid monarchs and their deputies. Hence the wisdom of Ben Sira's injunctions. For v 13a, cf. Prov 16:14; 20:2. For the fear or terror of death (v 13b), cf. Job 3:25; 15:21; Prov 3:25. You need to weigh your words and examine your actions in the presence of (v 13c) "the person who has power to kill" (v 13a), "lest he take away *your life* [Heb *nišmāteka*, lit., your breath, cf. Gen 2:7]" (v 13d). In v 13ef, the images, which are found also in Job 18:8–9, suggest that one should tread with extreme circumspection before the mighty who can kill at their whim (v 13a).

V 14a may also be translated: "As best you can, answer (or respond to, or advise) your neighbor," that is, teach and instruct him, but above all learn from the wise yourself; so Smend, p. 88. Association with the wise (v 14b) is often recommended in the Wisdom literature: 6:34; 8:8; Prov 13:14, 20; 15:31. In vv 15–16, Ben Sira again demonstrates that in his theology, pursuing Wisdom and striving to fulfill "the Law of the Most High" (v 15b) are the same thing; cf. 1:11–30 with COMMENT. Thus, for Ben Sira, only the righteous can be wise; and if one is wise, one is at the same time righteous, i.e., one fears the Lord by observing the Law. Accordingly, the wise should not associate with the unrighteous (=the foolish, the senseless); cf. 12:13–14; 13:17; 2 Cor 6:14–16. See INTRODUCTION, Part X, 1. Rather, the wise should have as "table companions" (v 16a) only "just people" (Heb *'anšê ṣedeq*, lit., people of righteousness), for the wise and the just both have as their glory "the fear of God" (v 16b); cf. Tob 2:2. The last word of v 16a, *laḥmeka*, rhymes with the last word of v 16b, *tip'arteka*.

16. About Rulers and the Sin of Pride
(9:17–10:18)

9   ¹⁷In skilled artisans their deftness is esteemed;   A
     but the ruler of his people is the skilled sage.
    ¹⁸Feared in the city is the person of railing speech
     and whoever talks rashly is hated.

10   ¹A wise magistrate lends stability to his people,   G
     and the government of a prudent person is well   A
                    ordered.
    ²As the people's judge, so are his ministers;
     as the head of a city, its inhabitants.
    ³A wanton king destroys his people,
     but a city grows through the sagacity of its princes.
    ⁴Sovereignty over the earth is in the hand of God,
     who raises up on it the person for the time;
    ⁵Sovereignty over everyone is in the hand of God,
     who imparts his majesty to the ruler.

    ⁶No matter what the wrong, do your neighbor no harm,
     and do not walk the path of arrogance.
    ⁷Odious to the Lord and to humans is arrogance,
     and both see oppression as a crime.
    ⁸Dominion is transferred from one people to another
     because of the violence of the arrogant.
    ⁹Why are dust and ashes proud?
     even during life the human body decays;
    ¹⁰A slight illness—the doctor jests;
     a king today—tomorrow he is dead.
    ¹¹When a person dies, he inherits corruption:
     worms and gnats and maggots.

    ¹²The beginning of pride is human effrontery
     in withdrawing one's heart from one's Maker;

13 For sin is the reservoir of pride,
    a source which runs over with vice;
    Because of it God sends unheard-of affliction
    and strikes humans with utter ruin.
14 The thrones of the arrogant God overturns
    and enthrones the humble in their stead;
15 The roots of the proud God plucks up,   G
    to plant the lowly in their place.
16 The last traces of the proud God sweeps away   A
    and digs out their roots from the subsoil.
17 He plucks them from the earth and roots them out,
    and effaces the memory of them from among men.
18 Insolence is not allotted to a human,
    nor impudent anger to one born of woman.

Notes

9   17a. *is esteemed*=*yĕḥāšēb;* MS A *yḥśk.*
17b. Read *ûmôšēl bĕ'ammô ḥăkam bînâ;* MS A *bîṭâ.*
18a. *in the city*=*bā'îr;* MS A *b'd.*
18b. *nōśē'* . . . *yĕśunnē'* (cf. Syr) is a wordplay like *zār* . . . *rāz* in 8:18a. The interpretation *speaks rashly* is G's.

10   1a. *lends stability to*=*yôsēd;* G's "instructs"=*yôsēr.* Cf. Wis 6:24b, "a prudent king [is] the stability of his people" (G *eustathia* would be Heb *yĕsôd*).
2–5. MS A has these vv in the order 3, 2, 5, 4.
3a. *his people*=G, Syr; MS A="the city."
10a. *jests;* MS A *yaṣhîb* unclear: "beams"(?), "blushes"(?).
12b. *one's heart*=G=*libbô;* MS A *mlbw.*
13c. Read *hiplî'*=G; MS A=*mālē' libbô.*
14b. *the humble*=G=*'ănāwîm;* MS A *'nyym.*
15. With G, Syr; MS A lacks this v. 15a *ethnōn* of G=*gôyīm;* read *gē'îm,* cf. Syr.
16a. Read *'iqĕbôt gē'îm ṭĕ'ṭē' ('ĕlōhîm);* MS A *'qbt gwym ṭmṭm.*
16b. Read *wayĕśārēšēm 'ad qarqa' 'āreṣ;* MS A *wšršm 'd 'rṣ q'q'.*
17a. *plucks them*=G=*nĕsāḥām;* MS A *wsḥm.*
17b. *from among men*=*mē'ādām,* cf. Syr; MS A *mē'āreṣ.*
18a. *not allotted*=*lō' neḥĕlaq,* cf. G, Syr; MS A *nā'weh.*

Comment

This section may be divided into three stanzas $(7+6+8$ bicola): one on rulers, and two on arrogance and pride, especially in rulers. G. L. Prato, *Il problema della teodicea in Ben Sira,* pp. 369–72, considers the section to be a tract on government.

The point of v 17, of which the text is uncertain (as the NOTES indicate), seems to be this: just as the "deftness" of "skilled artisans" is prized, so the wisdom of the sage is what makes him "ruler of his people." In contrast to "the skilled sage" is "the person of railing speech," Heb *ʾîš lāšôn,* lit., man of tongue (cf. 8:3a and 25:20b), who is "feared in the city" (v 18a). There is an *a:b::b':a'* pattern to the parallelism in v 18: *feared:man of tongue::whoever talks rashly:hated.* The verse parallels Theognis, 295–97 (Sanders, pp. 31–32). For the wordplay in the first and last words of v 18b, see NOTE. In vv 17 and 18, we can see a cross section of the populace in Ben Sira's day: skilled artisans (cf. 7:15 with COMMENT), the skilled sage as ruler (presumably the high priest; cf. 7:29–31 with COMMENT), and the babblers.

The value of good government leaders is the subject of 10:1–3. Prov 8:15–16 states that wisdom is what enables kings and princes to reign and lawgivers to establish justice. The purpose of government is to provide security, law, and order to a people and land. Only "a wise magistrate" can fulfill that purpose (v 1); cf. Prov 16:10–15; 19:12; 20:2, 8, 26; 25:4–5; 29:14; 31:8–9. The word "magistrate" translates Heb *šôpēṭ,* which also means "judge, ruler, governor." The word occurs again in v 2a, which may be translated: "As the people's governor, so are his ministers." V 2ab has echoes in proverbial literature. *Qualis pastor talis grex:* "As the pastor, so the flock." "Like mother, like daughter" (Ezek 16:44). Cf. Prov 14:35; 22:29; 29:12. In v 3ab, there is a clever *a:b:c:d::d':c':b':a'* chiastic pattern which emphasizes Ben Sira's point: *A king:undisciplined:destroys:his people::but-a-city:grows:through-the-wisdom:of-its-princes.* There is a wordplay on *yôšĕbāyw* ("its inhabitants") in v 2b and *nôšebet* (from the same *yšb* root = "becomes populous, grows") in v 3b. In contrast to "a wise magistrate" of v 1, and "the sagacity of [a city's] princes" in v 3b, "a wanton [or reckless, or unrestrained] king destroys his people" (v 3a). Regarding v 3a, cf. Prov 17:7; 28:15–16; 29:2, 4; 31:3–5; 2 Sam 13:23–29; 1 Kgs 16:9–10; 20:12, 16; Hos 7:5–7; 1 Macc 16:14–16. For v 3b, cf. Prov 14:28.

In vv 4 and 5, Ben Sira states a theological datum found in the OT and NT:

sovereignty over the earth and all humankind belongs to God alone, who delegates it to the ruler of his choice; cf. Dan 2:21; 4:14, 31–34; 5:26–28; 7:11–12, 14, 18, 22, 25–27; Ps 113:4–8; Wis 6:1–11; Luke 1:52. God raises up the ruler who is best suited "for the time" (v 4b); cf., for example, King Cyrus (Isa 44:28–45:3) and Jehu (2 Kgs 9:1–10). Both the Ptolemaic and Seleucid kings generally considered themselves to be gods. Such blasphemous arrogance is totally wrong, says Ben Sira, for the ruler who is raised up by God is a mere human being (v 4b). The "majesty," splendor, or dignity (Heb *hôd*) of the ruler is a gift from the King of kings (v 5). Ben Sira's allusions to the pagan kings are sufficiently veiled so as not to get him into trouble.

The precept in v 6a probably reflects Lev 19:16–18. Though v 6a seems to be out of place here (so Box-Oesterley, p. 349, and Duesberg-Fransen, p. 136), it may simply be a lead into v 6b. In other words, if one refuses to forgive the neighbor for a wrong and instead does him harm, such a one walks "the path of arrogance" (v 6b); cf. 28:1–7 and Theognis, 323–26 (Sanders, p. 32). The Heb of v 7a (and the translation) is rhetorically balanced in an *a:b::b':a'* fashion: *odious:to the Lord::and to humans:arrogance*. Both God and humans view "oppression" (Heb *ʿōšeq*, also = "extortion") as "a crime" (Heb *maʿal*, also = "treacherous act") (v 7b). The point of vv 6 and 7 seems to be that the ruler should do no harm, "no matter what the wrong" of the neighbor (v 6a); otherwise, he may engage in oppression (v 7b), one of the evil fruits of arrogance (vv 6b–7a). In this interpretation, the four cola of vv 6 and 7 are in an *a:b::b:a* parallelism: v 6a parallels v 7b, and v 6b parallels v 7a. Vv 6 and 7 thus serve as the lead into the important statement in v 8. V 8 probably refers to the battles of Raphia (217 B.C.) and Panium (198 B.C.). At Raphia, the Seleucid Antiochus III the Great (223–187) attempted to gain Palestine back from Egypt, now ruled by Ptolemy IV Philopator (221–203); he was defeated decisively. Several years after the accession of the young Ptolemy V Epiphanes (203–181), Antiochus attacked the Egyptian army at Panium, near the headwaters of the Jordan. This time he was successful; Palestine now became part of the Seleucid empire. Cf. Dan 11:10–19 with COMMENT in L. F. Hartman and A. A. Di Lella, *The Book of Daniel* (AB 23): 258, 290–93. Ben Sira lived through these violent times (cf. v 8b). Cf. INTRODUCTION, Part II.

Vv 9–11 probably refer to another event in Ben Sira's lifetime—the sudden death of Ptolemy IV in 203 B.C. after a life of debauchery. Smend (p. 93) writes that according to Dio Cassius and Trogus, Ptolemy died a horrible and painful death. In v 9a, the colorful phrase "dust and ashes" (Heb *ʿāpār wāʾēper*), which occurs again in 17:32 (G and Syr; Heb not extant) and 40:3, derives from Gen 18:27, a text in which Abraham uses the words to describe his lowly condition when he haggles with the Lord in an attempt to save Sodom. In Gen 2:7, God formed the man, *ʾādām*, out of the *ʿāpār min-hāʾădāmâ*, "dust [or soil, clay] from the ground." In v 9b, the Heb verb *rmm*, "to rot" (lit., to become wormy), is found only once in the MT, in Exod 16:20, where it is used to describe what happened to the manna that was kept overnight, contrary to Moses' instructions. The noun *giwyô,* "his [the human] body," means, lit., "his insides, intestines," as G understood the word. The first phrase of v 10a may be translated, lit.: "A whisper of disease." Cf. NOTE for the difficult *yaṣhîb.* The meaning of v 10, however, seems clear: what on one day is simply a report of the king's illness about which the physician is not worried (v 10a) terminates the next day in the death of the patient (v 10b). V 11 amplifies what Ben Sira states briefly in 7:17b where the noun *rimmâ,* "corruption, worms" (v 11a), also occurs. Though the language is elusive to protect himself from the pagan overlords, Ben Sira's graphic description of human frailty, impermanence, and corruptibility in vv 9–11 was probably meant as a stinging and grim diatribe against the Ptolemaic and Seleucid kings who claimed to be "gods on earth" and "masters of the world."

The final stanza (vv 12–18) of this section contains no precepts. Instead, Ben Sira writes an essay on the origin of pride, its roots and its fruits, and God's punishment of the proud. V 12 may be translated, lit.: "The beginning of pride—the human becomes shameless [Heb *mûʿāz,* cf. v. 18b], and from his Maker his heart [cf. NOTE] withdraws." In 1:14a, Ben Sira says: "The beginning of wisdom is the fear of the Lord." Thus wisdom and pride are opposites. The proud cannot be wise, nor are the wise proud. When a person's heart (=seat of intelligence and will) withdraws "from his Maker," he will not fear the Lord; rather, he "becomes shameless"—all of which is the "beginning (or origin, starting point) of pride." The thought is amplified in v 13ab, which may also be translated: "For sin [Heb *ḥēṭʾ*] is a reservoir of insolence [*zādôn* also means presumptuousness], and its source [*māqôr*= spring, fountain] overflows with vice [*zimmâ* also means wickedness, depravity]." The noun *zādôn* implies "aggressive wrongdoing—sinning with a high hand, contemptuous both of God and men" (so Box-Oesterley, p. 350). There is alliteration between the words *miqwēh* ("reservoir") and *ûmĕqôrōh* ("and its source"), and *zādôn* and *zimmâ.*

God's judgment of pride is given in vv 13cd–17. The Heb noun *negaʿ,* here translated "affliction" (v 13c), also means "plague, plague spot, mark," esp. of a disease, regarded as sent by God as a punishment; cf. Gen 12:17; Exod 11:1; 2 Sam 7:14; 1 Kgs 8:37, 38; Pss 38:12; 39:11; 89:33; 91:10. When God strikes the proud, they suffer "utter ruin" (v 13d). A similar conviction is found in Tob 4:13: "Do not be so proud-hearted toward your kinsmen, the sons and daughters of your people, as to refuse to take a wife for yourself from among them. For in such arrogance there is ruin and great disorder." The thought of v 14 echoes 1 Sam 2:7–8 and Ps 113:78; cf. also Job 5:11; Ps 147:6; Tob 4:19; Dan 4:14. Luke 1:52 rephrases v 14 but has basically the same ideas. V 15, present in G and Syr, was omitted in MS A because of homoioteleuton. "The root of wisdom is fear of the Lord" (1:20a), but "the roots of the proud [cf. NOTE] God plucks up, to plant the lowly in their place," because the lowly fear the Lord. Even "the last traces [Heb *ʿiqĕbôt*, lit., footprints] of the proud [so Syr] God sweeps away [cf. NOTE]" (v 16a). Not a single piece of the proud's roots will be left over in the "subsoil" (v 16b). Cf. Ps 44:3; Ezek 16:49–50. The worst of all punishments takes place when God *"effaces the memory of them* from among men" v 17b; cf. NOTE; cf. Deut 32:26 where the same verb (*šbt*) and direct object (*zikrām*) occur. Cf. also Pss 34:17; 109:15; Job 18:17. Since it was not yet part of Israel's faith to believe in rewards and punishments after death—the doctrine of retribution in the afterlife was revealed later in Dan 12:2 and Wis 3:1–5:23—children and a blessed memory were considered a vicarious immortality; cf. Prov 10:7. See INTRODUCTION, Part X, 4. Hence, for God to efface or destroy the memory of the proud would be their severest punishment.

The section ends with a global statement applicable to commoners as well as to kings (v 18): "Insolence [*zādôn,* also in v 13a] is not allotted to a human, nor *impudent anger* [*ʿazzût ʾap,* lit., fierceness of anger] to *one born of woman"* [*yĕlûd ʾiššâ*]. The opening colon of the stanza and the closing colon contain the Heb root *ʿzz* (*mûʿāz* in v 12a, and *ʿazzût* in v 18b), thus forming an *inclusio.* As regards the latter word, cf. 45:18d, where the expression *ʿĕzûz ʾappām* occurs. In Job 14:1, *yĕlûd ʾiššâ* is said to be "short-lived," hence, mortal.

Ben Sira excoriates pride in all its forms not only in the Egyptian and Syrian kings of his day (vv 6–11) but also in ordinary mortals, for pride "is the mother of all vice" (St. Augustine). Pride and its ugly effects are mentioned often in the Bible, beginning in Gen 3:4–6, which describes the first human sin as one of pride, of overstepping the bounds of creaturehood. See also Gen 11:1–9 (the story of the city and tower of Babel); Ezek 28:1–19 (the pride of the prince of Tyre and his punishment); and Dan 4:27–30, 37 (the arrogant claims made by Nebuchadnezzar and the dire consequences of his sin). Cf. Job 22:29; Prov 16:18; 29:1; Matt 23:12; Jas 4:6; and 1 Pet 5:5.

17. True Glory
(10:19–11:6)

10   ¹⁹ Whose offspring can be in honor? Human offspring.   G
         Which offspring are in honor? Those who fear God.
     Whose offspring can be in disgrace? Human offspring.   B
         Which offspring are in disgrace? Those who transgress
                           the Commandment.
²⁰ Among kindred their leader is in honor;   A
     such, in God's sight, is the one who fears him.^a
²² Be it sojourner, wayfarer, alien, or pauper,   B
     his glory is the fear of the LORD.
²³ It is not just to despise a person who is wise but poor,
     nor proper to honor any oppressor.
²⁴ The prince, the judge, the ruler are in honor;
     but none is greater than whoever fears God.   A
²⁵ When the free serve a prudent slave,   B
     the wise person does not complain.   G
²⁶ Prate not of wisdom in doing as you please,   A
     and boast not in your time of need.
²⁷ Better the worker who has goods in plenty
     than the boaster who is without sustenance.

²⁸ My son, with humility have self-esteem;
     prize yourself as you deserve.
²⁹ Who will acquit whoever condemns himself?
     Who will honor whoever discredits himself?
³⁰ The poor is honored for his wisdom
     as the rich is honored for his wealth;

---

^a ²¹ The beginning of acceptance is the fear of the Lord;   GII
     the beginning of rejection, effrontery and pride.

³¹ Honored in poverty, how much more so in wealth!   B
     dishonored in wealth, in poverty how much the more!

11   ¹ The poor person's wisdom lifts his head high   A
     and sets him among princes.
     ² Praise not a person for his looks;
     loathe not a person for his appearance.
     ³ Least is the bee among winged things,
     but she reaps the choicest of all harvests.
     ⁴ Mock not whoever wears a loincloth only,
     and jibe at no person's bitter day:
     For strange are the works of the LORD,
     hidden from humans his deeds.
     ⁵ The oppressed often rise to a throne,
     and some that none would consider wear a crown.
     ⁶ The exalted often fall into utter disgrace;
     the honored are given into enemy hands.

Notes

10   19. MS A lacks 19bc (omission by homoioarchton). The first extant leaf of MS B begins with 19cd, and extends to 11:10, see A. A. Di Lella in *Bib* 45 (1964): 156–59 plus plates I, II.

20b. *in God's sight*=G=*beʿênāyw*. MS A is defective, *bʿ*[; Smend supplied *bĕʿammô*. MS B (cf. Syr) has *mimmennû*.

21. This expansion of GII, unknown to Syr or Lat, imports the thought of 10:12, 13, 18 into the new section 10:19–24. It was written by someone who knew a text like MS A's for 10:12–18.

23. *just . . . proper*=G, interpreting the Heb infinitives (after *ʾên*).

25a. MS B has a variant (=7:21a) copied three times, besides the form vouched for by G; MS A is garbled.

28b. *prize yourself*=MS B *wĕtēn lāh* (i.e., *napšekā*) *ṭaʿam;* MS A *wytn.*

30b. *as the rich*=*wĕʿāšîr* (cf. MS B) for *wĕyeš* of MS A.

31ab. *in poverty* (2×)=*bĕʿonyô*=G, Syr; MSS A, B corrupt (*bĕʿênāyw*). For the wordy, late duplicate that appears in MSS A, B, see the discussion of A. A. Di Lella, *The Hebrew Text of Sirach*, pp. 115–19. Retroversion from the Syriac is the best explanation for it.

11   2b. Both MSS A and B+B^{mg} after *a person* add a qualifying gloss; A+B^{mg}= *mĕkôʿār*, "ugly"; B=*mʿzb.*

3. MS B duplicates the line. *qṭnh* is suspect of being secondary to *ʾlyl* (so MS A; MS B *ʾlwl*) for "insignificant, small"—*qṭn* is secondary in 51:27 (*HTR* 64 [1971]: 398), and in 30:12d (*CBQ* 36 [1974]: 539, 542). Was Prov 24:30 an influence on the transmission of Sir 11:3?

4ab. Smend, p. 102, makes the case against G's "Of enveloping garments do not boast; and on a day of glory be not lifted up." Not personal pride, but a negative judgment of others is the theme called for by the context, cf. v 5. The line present in both MSS A and B is the correct one, and B's added alternative is a corrupt variant. With B read *ʾēzôr, loincloth,* and point, with Smend, *bimĕrîrî yôm,* "at the bitter (individual) of the day"—cf. Deut 32:24. B's alternative, *kmryry ywm*=Job 3:5, is meaningless here.

5. The line present in both MSS A and B is the correct one; B again has a secondary variant.

6. Except for *wĕhošpĕlû yaḥad,* a gloss in both MSS A and B (lacking in G), the MS A form of this line is correct; for *bĕyād* with no qualifier, cf. 1 Sam 26:23, 2 Chr 25:20. G's *heterōn,* and *enemy* here, are interpretations.

Comment

In the translation above, this poem is divided into three stanzas: $9+4+7$ bicola. The poem, however, may also be divided into five symmetrical stanzas: 5 (vv 19–20, 22–23) +4 (vv 24–27) +2 (vv 28–29) +4 (10:30–11:2) +5 (11:3–6) bicola; it is this division that is discussed below.

G, which is followed in the translation here of v 19ab and in the interpretation of the Heb in v 19cd, has a question and an answer in each of the four cola. But v 19 may also be translated: "What can be an honorable seed? Human seed. (MS A) / The honorable seed is the one that fears God. (Syr) / What can be a dishonorable seed? Human seed. (MS B) / The dishonorable seed is the one that transgresses the Commandment" (MSS A and B). For a similar translation, cf. Box-Oesterley (pp. 350–51) and Duesberg-Fransen (p. 138). For a discussion of the textual problems of this verse, cf. A. A. Di Lella, *The Hebrew Text of Sirach,* pp. 60–63. V 19 is the topic sentence of the whole poem: human beings can be in honor only when they fear God; they are in dishonor when they transgress the Commandment, summarized in Deut 6:4–5; cf. Mark 12:28–30; Matt 22:36–38; Luke 10:26–28. There is a striking antithetic parallelism between vv 19b and 19d: *the honorable* (Heb *nikbād*) *seed* (v 19b) and *the dishonorable* (Heb *niqleh*) *seed* (v 19d); *the one that fears God* (v 19b) and *the one that transgresses the Commandment* (v 19d). The participles *nikbād* and *niqleh* occur together in Isa 3:5. Instead of "the Commandment," Heb *miṣwâ,* G, Lat, and Syr have "the commandments," a reading that perhaps depends on Qoh 12:13: "Fear God and keep his commandments." Cf. G. T. Sheppard, "The Epilogue to Qoheleth as Theological Commentary," *CBQ* 39 (1977): 184–85. Here again Ben Sira alludes to the great equation—to fear the Lord=to keep the Law. Cf. 1:25–27 with COMMENT and 32:23–24.

The translation above of v 20 brings out the comparison implied in the text. Heb *'aḥîm*, "kindred," also means "brothers, kin," members of the same religious or political community. As a religious or political leader is honored by his followers, so in God's eyes is the one who fears the Lord. The point of v 20 is that the honor which accrues to a person who fears the Lord is equal to the glory earthly leaders receive because of their office. V 20 is probably an allusion to the Joseph story (cf. Gen 42:1–47:12). In fact, Joseph, whom his brothers, in search for food in Egypt, do not recognize as yet, says of himself early in the story: "I *fear God*" (Gen 42:18), the words Ben Sira uses here. GII adds a bicolon (v 21; see NOTE) in which are found two technical theological terms: *proslēpsis* ("acceptance") and *ekbolē* ("rejection"), by God; *proslēpsis* and *apobolē* (a synonym for *ekbolē*) are used by St. Paul in Rom 11:15.

In v 22a, three of the four Heb words are monosyllabic; the fourth, bisyllabic. The noun *gēr* (translated "sojourner") occurs only here in the whole book, but very often in other books of the OT, where it means "temporary dweller, resident alien, newcomer (with no inherited rights)," as in Gen 23:4; Exod 12:19; Lev 24:16; Num 15:30. Used in the plural, *gērîm* usually refers to sojourners in Israel who had certain conceded rights; cf., for example, Exod 20:10; 23:12; Deut 5:14. They also had the obligations incumbent on Israel; cf. Exod 12:19, 48, 49; Lev 16:29; 17:8, 10, 12, 13, 15; 18:26. Oppression of the *gēr(îm)* was forbidden: Exod 22:20; 23:9; Lev 19:33; Deut 24:14, 17; Jer 7:6; 22:3. Kindness to the *gēr(îm)* was also enjoined by law: Lev 19:10, 34; 23:22; Deut 10:18, 19; 14:29; 24:19–21; 26:12–13. The word *zār* (translated "wayfarer") also means "stranger," and occurs several other times in the book: 8:18a; 14:4b; 37:5a; 40:29a; 45:13b. The feminine form, *zārâ*, occurs in 9:3a; cf. COMMENT above. The masculine plural, *zārîm*, is found in 45:18a. The word *nokrî* (translated "alien") also means "foreigner," and occurs only one other time in the book, 49:5b. The word *rāš* (translated "pauper") occurs only one other time in the book, 13:18b. It seems that Ben Sira refers to four distinct social groups, all of whom are disadvantaged. But the "glory" of these four groups is "the fear of the LORD" (v 22b); cf. Jer 9:22–23.

The wise poor person (Heb *dal maśkîl*, translated "a person who is wise but poor") should not be despised (v 23a), nor should "any oppressor" (*kol 'îš ḥāmās*, lit., any person of violence, or lawlessness) be honored (v 23b). The reason is that the wise, who keep the commandments and fear the Lord (1:25–27), should be in honor (v 19b) whereas the oppressor, who transgresses the Law, should be dishonored (v 19d). The verb root *kbd*, "to honor," occurs in the opening colon (v 19a) and closing colon (v 23b) of this stanza, thus forming an *inclusio*. In Gen 6:13 (the P tradition), *ḥāmās*, "violence, lawlessness," is the reason for the Flood. The *ʾîš ḥāmās*, "the violent, or lawless, person," occurs also in Pss 18:49; 140:12; Prov 3:31; 16:29. In the Psalms, "the poor" are the stalwart believers who put their hope and trust in the Lord; cf., for example, Pss 35:9–10; 40:18; 70:6; 72:12–14; 74:18–21; 86:1–7. The idea of the wise poor person being despised (v 23a) is found also in Qoh 9:15–16; cf. Jas 2:1–6.

The next stanza (vv 24–27) begins with three groups of people in the upper classes of society: "the prince" (Heb *śar*), "the judge" (*šōpēṭ*), and "the ruler" (*môšēl*)—all of whom "are in honor" (*nikbādû*) (v 24a). But Ben Sira insists that "none is greater than whoever fears God" (v 24b). It is to be noted that the *niphʿal* of the verb *kbd*, "to be honored, to be in honor," and the expression "the one who fears God" (*yěrēʾ ʾělōhîm*) occur in the opening bicolon both of the first (v 19ab) and of the second stanza (v 24). There is alliteration and assonance in the first three words of v 24a: *śar šōpēṭ ûmôšēl*—three sibilants (*ś, š, š*), two liquids (*r, l*), two labials (*p, m*), two *ô*'s, and two *ē*'s. Also *śar* corresponds to the last syllable of *ûmôšēl*, i.e., sibilant + liquid. The words *śar* and *šōpēṭ* occur together in the plural in Prov 8:16. As regards the thought of v 24b, cf. 40:25–27.

By combining the evidence of G and the fragmentary evidence of MSS A and B, we may now reconstruct the Hebrew of v 25b: *wěgeber maś[kîl]* (from MS B; cf. A. A. Di Lella, *Bib* 45 (1964): 156, l. 9) *[l]ōʾ yitʾônān* (from MS A). The phrase *ʿebed maśkîl*, "a prudent [or wise] slave," occurs also in Prov 17:2. As the *dal maśkîl*, the wise poor person, should not be despised (v 23a), so the *ʿebed maśkîl* will be served by "the free" or "nobles" (v 25a), and the *geber maśkîl*, "the wise person," will not complain (v 25b). What counts most of all is wisdom, and not social or economic status. Cf. Prov 19:10; 30:22; Qoh 10:6–7. The words *ḥôrîm*, "the free, nobles," and *śārîm*, "princes" (cf. v 24a) occur together in Isa 34:12. In v 26a, MS B reads *laʿăśôt* ("to do, make") instead of *laʿăbōd* of MS A ("to work, serve") *ḥepṣekā* ("your work"). The former reading is to be preferred on the basis of Isa 58:13, where a similar phrase occurs. V 26a may be translated, lit.: "Make not a display of wisdom in doing your own business, or *work*," as Gr *ergon* translates the last word. The point seems to be this: do not show off in doing the daily work required to sustain yourself; rather, do your job quietly and competently. The precept of v 26b then follows: "and boast not [i.e., do not make extravagant claims about what you might have done] in your time of need." The last word of v 26a, *ḥepṣekā*, rhymes with the last word of v 26b, *ṣorkekā*.

There is a remarkable antithesis presented in v 27: "the [energetic] worker" is contrasted with "the [idle] boaster," and "goods [*hôn*, lit., wealth] in plenty" with "without [(*ḥă)sa(r)*, lit., lacking in] *sustenance*" (read *māzôn*, as suggested by G and Syr, rather than *mattān* of MS A). The words *hôn* and *māzôn,* the last words of v 27a and v 27b, respectively, rhyme, as do the corresponding words in v 26 (cf. above)—a good way to end the stanza. In v 27a, each of the four words has an *ô* sound, creating assonance: *ṭôb ʿôbēd wĕyôtēr hôn.* For the thought and vocabulary of v 27, cf. Prov 12:9.

The next stanza (vv 28–29), the central stanza of the five in the poem, opens with *bĕnî,* "my son," and speaks of the value of accurate and humble self-esteem. V 28a may be translated, lit.: "My son, with humility honor yourself." On the importance and religious value of "humility" (Heb *ʿanāwâ*), cf. 3:17 with COMMENT. The noun *ʿanāwâ* occurs only four times in the MT: Zeph 2:3; Prov 15:33; 18:12; and 22:4. In the extant Heb text of Ben Sira, the word occurs a total of five times: 3:17a; 4:8b; 10:28a; 13:20a; and 45:4a; cf. 1:27. Regarding the thought of v 28a, cf. 7:17; 10:14; and 13:20. The point of the verse is that one achieves proper self-esteem only when one thinks of oneself with humility and not with pride. In v 29, Ben Sira deplores self-depreciation, which (contrary to popular opinion) is not what humility (v 28a) is all about. In the verse, there is a striking *a:b::b:a* chiastic pattern that underscores the thought: *"whoever-*condemns *himself":"who* will acquit"::*"who* will honor":*"whoever-*dishonors (discredits) *himself."* V 29b contains the two verb roots *kbd* ("to honor") and its antithesis *qlh* ("to dishonor"), which are also found in the opening couplet of the poem (v 19); v 29a likewise has two antithetic verbs, *ršʿ* ("to condemn") and *ṣdq* ("to acquit"). Self-depreciation is wrong also because it prompts others to condemn and dishonor the one who engages in the unwholesome practice.

The fourth stanza (10:30–11:2) of the poem speaks of the poor who are wise. The opening verse (10:30) again has the verb *kbd* in both cola, as do the opening verses of the first three stanzas (vv 19, 24, and 28). There is a remarkable balance in the strong sentiment expressed in v 30: the poor—honored for —wisdom; the rich (cf. NOTE)—honored for—wealth (cf. 13:21–23). Ben Sira clearly implies that the wise poor person is far better off than the rich who have wealth but no wisdom. V 31, which has the verbs *kbd* and *qlh* that occur also in v 19, restates and develops the thought of v 30: the wise poor, who are honored while they remain in poverty, will be even more honored when they become rich, whereas the rich, who are dishonored in wealth (presumably because they lack wisdom), will be even more dishonored when they become poor. In MS B and defective MS A, the reading *bʿynyw* (=*bĕʿênāyw,* "in his eyes"), is a mistake for *bʿwnyw* (=MT *bĕʿonyô,* "in his poverty"), occasioned by the confusion of the first *waw* for a *yod* (cf. COMMENT on 4:2); at this period it is not uncommon to use the *mater lectionis waw* where the MT would use a simple *o* vowel. In fact, even a short *ŏ* vowel of the MT can be written here with a *waw* as in *ʿwny* (=MT *ʿŏnî,* "poverty") in 13:24b. For the duplicate of v 31ab that is found in MSS A and B, see the reference to my book in the NOTE.

The subject of the wise poor person continues in 11:1. The Heb expression *nśʾ rōʾš*, "to lift up the head" (v 1a), occurs also in Gen 40:13 and 2 Kgs 25:27, in both of which texts it means, in effect, "to release from prison, to free." Thus Ben Sira implies that "the poor person's wisdom" frees him from the (apparent) confinement of his economic condition. Cf. Prov 15:33. The thought expressed in v 1b derives from 1 Sam 2:8c=Ps 113:8a (the same verb, *hiphʿil* of *yśb*, and noun *nĕdîbîm*, "princes," occur). The stanza concludes with the negative precept not to praise "a person for his [good] looks [or beauty]," or to loathe "a person for his [poor] appearance" (v 2). The reference again seems to be to the rich, who lack wisdom (cf. 10:30–31) but look good or beautiful because they can purchase expensive clothing, jewelry, and cosmetics (v 2a), and to the poor, who are wise (cf. 10:30–11:1) but lack a striking appearance because they cannot afford costly apparel or adornment (v 2b); cf. also vv 4–5. External appearances can be misleading, as Yahweh taught Samuel when the latter chose Eliab (1 Sam 16:6–7). Wisdom, which resides within a person, is all that really matters.

The fifth, and final, stanza of the poem (vv 3–6) begins with a metaphor. V 3 may be translated, lit., and with the same word order of the Heb: "Least among flying things is the bee [*dĕbōrâ*], but the best of produce is her fruit" [*piryāh*]. The final words of each colon—*dĕbōrâ* and *piryāh*—rhyme. There is also a striking antithetic parallelism between "least" (Heb *ʾĕlîl*, MS A, or *qĕṭannâ*, MS B; cf. NOTE) and "the best" (*rōʾš*, lit., the head). M. H. Segal (*Tarbiz* 29 [1959–60]: 316) thinks that *qĕṭannâ* is the better reading; I agree. An *ô* assonance in the middle four words of the verse—*bāʿôp* ("among flying things"), *dĕbôrâ*, *rōʾš*, and *tĕnûbôt* ("produce")—adds to the poetic skill Ben Sira displays here. V 4ab may be translated, lit., and with the same word order of the eight Heb words: "Whoever-wears a-loincloth *mock not,* and *scoff not* at-the-bitter-person of-the-day." The *a:b::b':a'* rhetorical pattern emphasizes Ben Sira's negative injunction. The noun *ʾēzôr*, "loincloth, waistcloth," occurs twice in Isa 11:5 as a metaphor for "righteousness" (Heb *ṣedeq*) and "fidelity" (*ʾĕmûnâ*). It is a relatively rare word (found also in 45:10c), occurring in 2 Kgs 1:8 (=part of apparel of Elijah); Jer 13:1, 2, 4, 6, 7 (2×), 10, 11 (=symbol of the closeness that Israel and Judah were intended to have with Yahweh); Job 12:18 (=a sign that a king is reduced to the condition of a slave whose garment is the waistcloth). For the expression "the bitter person of the day," cf. Amos 8:10. The point of v 4ab is that one should not judge a person by the quality and quantity of clothing (cf. v 2), as if sparse apparel ("loincloth") were a punishment resulting from the person's sin (cf. COMMENT on 2:1–6). The reason for not judging is given in v 4cd and amplified in vv 5–6; cf. Isa 55:8–9. Another *a:b::b':a'* structure can be seen in v 4cd: *the-works:of-the-Lord::from humans* [Heb *ʾādām*, MS A; MS B *ʾĕnôš*]:*his* [the Lord's]-*deeds.* There are four *m*'s and three other labials (two *p*'s and a *waw*) in the seven words of v 4cd. In the three words of v 4d, there is also a beautiful rhyme and rhythm: *wĕneʿlām mēʾādām poʿōlô;* notice also the *ʿayin-l*+*m* in *neʿlām* and the *p* (a labial like *m*)+*ʿayin-l* in *poʿōlô.*

V 5a may be translated, lit.: "Many oppressed [Heb *nidkāʾîm*] have sat on a throne." In Isa 57:15, Yahweh says: "On high I dwell, and in holiness, and with the *crushed* [*dakkāʾ*] and dejected in spirit, to revive the spirits of the dejected, to revive the hearts of the *crushed*" [*nidkāʾîm*]. V 5b is in parallelism with v 5a. For the sentiment expressed in vv 5 and 6, cf. 10:14; 1 Sam 2:7–8; Ps 113:7–8; and Luke 1:52. V 6 may be translated, lit.: *"Many exalted ones* [Heb *rabbîm niśśāʾîm*] *have been dishonored* [*qlh*] *completely, and the honored* [*kbd*] *are given into the hands of the little ones* [reading MS B: *bĕyad zĕʿîrîm;* cf. NOTE for a different opinion]." The thought and vocabulary probably derive from Isa 16:14: "The *glory* [*kābôd*] of Moab *shall be dishonored* [*qlh*] in all its *great* [*rab*] multitude; there shall be a remnant, a little, *a few* [*mizʿār*], not much." The word *zĕʿîrîm* was probably misread *zārîm,* "strangers," by G (*heterōn* = Lat *alterorum* = "others"); for in 14:4b, G uses *heteroi* to translate *zār.* Thus, in v 6, there is a sharp contrast between "many exalted ones" (*rabbîm niśśāʾîm*) and "the little ones" (*zĕʿîrîm*), and between "have been dishonored" (*niqlû*) and "the honored (*nikbādîm*). In fact, these words are in an *a:b::bʹ:aʹ* pattern to highlight the antithesis: *many exalted ones:have been dishonored::the honored:the little ones.* This verse, the last of the poem, contains the same two verbs (*niphʿal* of *kbd* and of *qlh*) found in the opening verse (10:19), forming an *inclusio* in an *a:b::b:a* chiastic pattern: *honored* (v 19ab):*dishonored* (v 19cd)::*dishonored* (v 6a):*honored* (v 6b). Also the last word of the poem, *zĕʿîrîm,* "the little ones," contains the same three consonants (but in a different order) as the first word in v 19, *zeraʿ,* "seed," thus forming a second *inclusio.*

For a fuller study of the strophic structure and text of this splendid poem, see A. A. Di Lella, "Sirach 10:19–11:6: Textual Criticism, Poetic Analysis, and Exegesis," in C. L. Meyers and M. O'Connor, eds., *The Word of the Lord Shall Go Forth: Essays in Honor of David Noel Freedman in Celebration of His Sixtieth Birthday,* pp. 157–64.

18. Providence and Trust in God
(11:7–28)

11   7 Before investigating, find no fault;   A
         examine first, then criticize.
       8 Before hearing, answer not,   B
         and interrupt no one in the middle of his speech.
       9 In what is not your quarrel do not become angry;   A
         in the strife of the arrogant take no part.

     10 My son, why increase your anxiety,
         since he who is avid for wealth will not be blameless?
       If you chase after it, you will never overtake it,   B
         nor will you be safe if you take to flight.
     11 One may toil and struggle and drive,   A
         and fall short all the same.
     12 Another goes his way a broken-down drifter
         lacking strength and abounding in weakness—
       Yet the eye of the LORD looks kindly on him;
         he shakes him free of the stinking mire,
     13 Lifts up his head and exalts him
         to the amazement of the many.

     14 Good and evil, life and death,
         poverty and riches, are from the LORD.ᵃ
     17 The Lord's gift remains with the just;   G
         his favor brings lasting success.   A

ᵃ 15 Wisdom and understanding and knowledge of the Law,   GII
         love and virtuous paths, are from the Lord.
     16 Error and darkness were formed with sinners from their
                                                                           birth,
         and evil grows old with those who exult in evil.

¹⁸ A person may become rich through a miser's life,
    and this is his allotted reward: G
¹⁹ When he says, "I have found rest,   A
    now I will feast on my possessions,"
He does not know how long it will be
    till he leaves them to others and dies.

²⁰ My son, hold fast to your duty, busy yourself with it,   G
    grow old while doing your task.
²¹ Marvel not how sinners live,
    but trust in the Lord and wait for his light,
For it is easy, as the Lord sees it,
    suddenly, in an instant, to make the poor man rich.

²² God's blessing is the lot of the just,   A
    and in due time his hope bears fruit.
²³ Say not, "What do I need?   G
    What further benefit can be mine?"
²⁴ Say not, "I am self-sufficient.
    What harm can come to me now?"
²⁶ It is easy for the Lord on the day of death
    to repay a person according to his conduct.

²⁵ The day's prosperity makes one forget adversity;   A
    the day's adversity makes one forget prosperity.
²⁷ Brief affliction brings forgetfulness of past delights;
    the last of a person tells his tale.
²⁸ Call no one happy before his death,
    for by how he ends, a person is known.

Notes

11   7. MS B follows 6d with what seem to be two forms of vv 7, 8; for v 7, MS B's second form is that of MS A and is the original, cf. G. Syr goes its own way with a caution about choosing a marriage partner.

8a. MS B had the original word order (cf. G); the doublet in MS B, with MS A, distorts this.

9a. Read *bĕʾên ʿeśqāk (ʾal tithār):* in G *chreia* = *ʿeseq* = *ʿēśeq,* cf. the next verse (for the sense, cf. the parallel 9b and Gen 26:20); *ʾal tithār* = G, Syr; compare Ps 37:1.

10cd. MS B has this bicolon in two forms; that which matches G is the original one (vocalize *tabrîaḥ* for *tbrḥ,* and read *timmālēṭ* for *tmlṭnw*). MS A and Syr share MS B's later and secondary form.

12b. *strength* with G, supposing *kôaḥ* for the *kōl* of MS A.

15, 16. These verses are present in MS A. They are absent from GI and do not appear in Lat till the Paris Bibles of the mid-thirteenth century. The form they take in GII seems to be reflected in Syr, which probably has them from that source, as does the later Lat. The GII form of text has its own interest: its treatment of v 15a borrows from GI of 33:3; also, *agapēsis,* whatever the underlying Heb term, becomes thematic in GII, cf. already 1:10, 12, 18 and (GI) 2:15. In v 16 *formed with (sinners) from their birth* = Gr *synektistai;* this understanding of the Heb (MS A *nwṣrh*) has led to an expansion of the thought in 16b. The text of MS A yields:

15 Wisdom and understanding and knowing how to speak are from the LORD;
     sin and virtuous paths are from the LORD.
16 Folly and darkness were made for sinners
     and evil abides with evildoers.

In this, "knowing how to speak" reflects 1 Sam 16:18, where it is a quality of David; it recurs in 33:3. "Sin" in v 15b is out of harmony with the rest of the verse (contrast v 16), and some such term as *ʾahăbâ* (= G) was probably the original. With v 16a compare 39:28–31. The uneven lengths of the Heb lines go to show that the two verses are an expansion of Ben Sira's text.

18b. The broken text of MS A here remains obscure.

20, 21. MS A is here legible only in part. *My son* in 20a follows MS A and Syr; so also *for his light* in 21b.

22–26. These verses are lacking in Syr, possibly because of homoioarchton between 21c and 26a. Segal has seen correctly that vv 25 and 26 have been transposed (before GI, the grandson's rendering); the unit in vv 22–24, 26 ends similarly to vv 20–21, and v 25 belongs with vv 27–28. MS A lacks v 26.

27b. In MS A, *wĕsôp ʾādām yaggîd ʿālāyw.* After 25b, MS A has a doublet for 27b that shares a faulty reading of Syr.

Comment

This section, which is not a single poem like the one in 10:19–11:6, may be divided into six minipoems: 3+6+5+3+4+3 bicola. The first (vv 7–9) gives six admonitions against hasty and rash judgments. The second (vv 10–13) is an essay (with no precepts) on the futility of undue anxiety. The third (vv 14, 17–19) is a discourse (again with no advice) on riches as a gift from the Lord. The fourth (vv 20–21) contains several injunctions urging fidelity and constancy in performing one's duty. The fifth (vv 22–24, 26) warns against presumption. The sixth (vv 25, 27–28) offers some observations about prosperity and adversity and concludes with a maxim not to evaluate a person's life until he or she dies.

As regards the thought of vv 7–8—wise advice in any age and culture—cf. 5:11–12. Failure to observe Ben Sira's admonitions would be not only unjust but also foolish and impolite; cf. Prov 18:13. A similar idea is found in *Pirqe Aboth*, v 10: "Seven things are in a clod, and seven in a wise man. [The wise man] . . . does not interrupt the words of his companion, and is not hasty to reply . . ." (cited by Box-Oesterley, p. 353). The one who keeps the maxim in v 9a will enjoy a more serene and pleasant life than the fool who ignores it. Apropos is the ditty of John Gay (1685–1732): "Those who in quarrels interpose, / Must often wipe a bloody nose" (*Fables*, xxxiv, "The Mastiff," l. 1). Moreover, the wise will take no part "in the strife of *the arrogant* [or proud]" (Heb *zēdîm*) (v 9b). As regards the *zēd(îm)*, cf. 10:13a with COMMENT and 12:5a; 32:18b; Prov 21:24; Pss 19:14; 86:14; 119:21, 51, 69, 78, 85, 122; Isa 13:11; Jer 43:2. The *zēdîm* are always spoken of as being opposed to Yahweh or to righteousness; hence, such people are to be avoided at all costs.

The next poem (vv 10–13) begins with "My son," an indication of a new subject matter. In v 10a, Heb *ʿiśqekā*, "your anxiety," is, lit., your business. V 10b may be translated, lit.: "he who hastens *to increase (it)* [Heb *lĕharbôt*] will not *be blameless,* or *exempt from punishment.*" The thought and vocabulary are derived from Prov 28:20, where three of the four same words occur: "he who hastens *to grow rich* [*lĕhaʿăšîr*] will not be blameless." Ben Sira has other warnings, too, on the possible evils of the business world and the pursuit of wealth; cf. 26:29–27:3 and 31:5–11. The meaning of v 10cd (cf. NOTE) is that one will never have enough wealth, no matter how energetically one chases after it (v 10c); nor will one be safe if one takes to flight with it (v 10d). For similar observations, cf. Prov 11:18, 28; 13:11; 15:27; 20:21; 21:6; 28:22; Qoh

5:9–11. The *Pirqe Aboth,* iv 14, has a similar precept: "Have little *business* ['ēseq, the equivalent of *'iśqĕkā* in v 10a] and be busied in Torah" (cited by Box-Oesterley, p. 354).

The accurate observations Ben Sira records in vv 11–13 receive emphatic confirmation in the experience of "many" (cf. v 13b). Some people are workaholics, totally involved in their jobs and almost oblivious of anything else; yet they still "fall short all the same" (v 11); cf. Qoh 4:8; 9:11. The colorful translation of v 12a captures the meaning of the text, which says, lit.: "Another goes his way beaten down and lost." Such a person lacks strength (cf. NOTE) and abounds "in weakness" (v 12b). Yet the Lord in his graciousness and kindness (v 12c) picks him up out of the gutter, to use our idiom, though Ben Sira's language is more forceful: "he shakes him free of the stinking mire" (v 12d); cf. 1 Sam 2:8. Not only that; the Lord also gives him a position of honor (v 13a), "to the amazement of *the many*" (v 13b), Heb *rabbîm,* i.e., the community, as in Isa 52:14 and 53:12. The main point of the poem is that success in life is not always the result of an individual's ambition and energy, for even those who seem to be going nowhere the Lord can raise on high. Cf. Pss 31:16; 127:1; Qoh 5:17–19.

The next poem (vv 14, 17–18) is summarized in the opening bicolon: the antinomies (or contraries) of life come from the Lord—good/evil, life/death, poverty/wealth. Cf. Isa 45:7; Job 1:21; 2:10. Regarding vv 15–16 in MS A and GII, see the extensive NOTE. Most scholars consider these verses as secondary; cf., for example, Smend (pp. 106–7), Peters (pp. 98–99), and Spicq (p. 626). Duesberg-Fransen, however (p. 142), take them as original but offer no reason why. In v 17, "the Lord's gift" and "his favor" are in parallelism; they abide "with the *just,* or *righteous*" [Heb *ṣaddîq,* as in the broken text of MS A] and bring "lasting success." Cf. Prov 13:22. Such is not the case with the sinner, the unrighteous, whose success is ephemeral; cf. Ps 49:17–21; Job 27:13–21; Prov 13:21. V 18a may be translated, lit.: "There is a man who becomes rich *by afflicting himself,*" Heb *mēhit'annôt,* which G aptly interprets "by his wariness and pinching." Of such a person Ben Sira ironically notes: "this is his allotted reward" (v 18b). In other words, the miser has wealth but none of the enjoyment that wealth can bring; in fact, he suffers from self-imposed want. Cf. 14:3–10, 14. Finally, when the miser thinks he has accumulated enough wealth to be at rest (v 19a), he says to himself: Now I will enjoy all my good things (v 19b). For how long, he knows not (v 19c); at death, he leaves them to others (v 19d). Cf. Ps 49:7–12; Qoh 2:18–22; 6:1–3; and the parable of the rich fool in Luke 12:16–21.

The next poem begins with *bĕnî,* "my son," which G and Lat omit. V 20 urges fidelity and devotion to duty. MS A, though fragmentary at this point, has the third word of v 20a, *ḥoqĕkā.* Instead of "your [prescribed] duty" (*ḥoqĕkā*), G and Lat read "your covenant, testament [with God]." For this use of *ḥōq,* cf. Exod 5:14. The principal duty prescribed for the Israelite was to fulfill the stipulations of the Covenant (hence, the interpretation of G, followed by Lat); all other responsibilities flowed therefrom. Cf. Neh 10:1–30. V 21a may be translated, lit.: "Marvel not at the works of the *sinner*" (several Gr MSS and Lat read *sinners*). The upright should not envy the prosperity and apparent success that sinners enjoy, but only for a brief time; cf. v 17; Prov 3:31–34; 13:9; 23:17–18; 24:1–2, 19–20; Ps 37:1–2. Rather, the upright should "trust [or believe] in the Lord and wait for *his light*" (the last expression is extant in MS A; G has *your labor,* though some Lat MSS have *his light*). The imperative to believe in (or trust in) the Lord is a fundamental obligation incumbent on the faithful; cf., for example, 2:6, 8, 10, 13; Gen 15:6; Exod 14:31; Num 14:11; Pss 78:22, 32; 106:12; 116:10; 119:66; Isa 7:9; 43:10; Hab 2:4; Rom 1:17; Gal 3:11; Heb 10:38. The "light" (Heb *'ôr*) of the Lord is a common image for salvation or deliverance (as in the present verse); cf. Isa 2:5; 10:17; 59:9–11; 60:19–20; Jer 13:16; Mic 7:8; Pss 27:1; 43:3; Tob 3:17; 5:10; 14:10; Rev 21:23; 22:5. V 21c is extant in MS A and may be translated, lit.: "for it is *easy* [*nākōaḥ*] in the eyes of Yahweh." The motivation in v 21d should not be considered less than noble (so Edersheim, referred to in Box-Oesterley, p. 355) but articulates the firm conviction that deliverance (v 21b), now expressed by the metaphor of the poor believer being made rich, can come "suddenly, in an instant." Cf. v 22b. V 21c is repeated in the first part of v 26a, the concluding bicolon also of the next poem.

In v 22a, the expression *"the lot* [Heb *gōrāl,* also=allotted portion] of the just [*ṣaddîq*]" finds an echo in Dan 12:13: "You [Daniel] will rise for *your allotted portion* [*gōrālĕkā*] at the end of the days." The just or righteous live not only by faith (see v 21b with COMMENT) but also by hope, a hope that "bears fruit" (v 22b); cf. 1:18; Prov 3:26; 10:22. In contrast to the fidelity of the righteous (v 22) is the presumption of sinner, who boasts that he has all he needs and is self-sufficient (vv 23–24a) and as a result can suffer no harm or evil (v 24b). Such an attitude is foolish, for as Ben Sira affirms, "It is easy for the Lord on the day of death to repay a person according to *his conduct* [lit., *his ways*]" (v 26). Ben Sira means retribution in the present life, not in the afterlife; cf. 7:17 with COMMENT. In the next poem (vv 25, 27–28), he explains how the Lord will punish the self-sufficient rich, who are unfaithful to the Law, on the day of their death. His theology of rewards and punishments taking place only here on earth demanded that he make the affirmation of v 26. See INTRODUCTION, Part X, 4.

In v 25, a carefully balanced *a:b:c::c:b:a* rhetorical chiasm gives emphasis to Ben Sira's explanation of how the Lord sets things right in the earthly life of both the righteous and sinners: *prosperity* (*ṭôb,* lit., good):*makes* (one) *forget:adversity* (*rā'â,* lit., evil)::*adversity:makes* (one) *forget:prosperity.* V 27a, in synonymous parallelism with v 25b, may be translated, lit.: "A time of *evil* [*rā'â*] makes (one) forget *delight* [*ta'ănûg*=daintiness (cf. Mic 1:16; 2:9); luxury (cf. Prov 19:10; Qoh 2:8); exquisite delight (of love) (cf. Cant 7:7)]." V

27b may be translated, lit.: "and the end [sôp] of a man will tell about him."
The noun sôp in the sense of "(death as) the end" occurs also in Qoh 7:2. The
point of v 27a is that regardless of the prosperity and wealth one may enjoy
now, a brief period of adversity and evil at the end of one's life will obliterate
"past delights." Hence, in v 27b Ben Sira suggests that only the final hours of
a person can tell us what kind of life he has lived: if he dies content and at
peace, his past poverty and affliction count as nothing; if he dies in disgrace
and anxiety, his past wealth and prosperity are meaningless. V 28 develops
the sentiment expressed in v 27b; cf. Qoh 12:14. In MS A, v 28 is given in two
different forms; the one followed in the translation here=G. The other form,
of which a few letters are illegible but easily reconstructed, "Before you examine a person do not call him blessed (or happy), for in his end a person is
blessed (or happy)"=Syr. In v 28b, G understood Heb bĕʾāḥărîtô—here
translated "by how he ends" (lit., in *his end*)—in the sense of "in *his posterity,*" and translated "in his children." In the MT and in Ben Sira, the noun
ʾaḥărît means "end" (cf., for example, 7:36a with COMMENT and 12:11d;
16:3c; Job 8:7; 42:12; Prov 5:11) and "posterity, descendants, children" (cf.,
for example, 16:3e [MS B]; Pss 37:37–38; 109:13; Dan 11:4). Solon (ca. 638–
ca. 559 B.C.) has a similar proverb: "Until he is dead, do not yet call a man
happy, but only lucky" (quoted by Herodotus, *Histories,* i 32). So too Aeschylus (525–456 B.C.): "Only when man's life comes to its end in prosperity can
one call that man happy" (*Agamemnon,* l. 928). And Sophocles (ca. 496–406
B.C.): "Let every man in mankind's frailty / Consider his last day; and let
none / Presume on his good fortune until he find / Life, at his death, a memory without pain" (*Oedipus Rex,* l. 1529).

19. Care in Choosing Friends
(11:29–12:18)

11   ²⁹ Bring not everyone into your house,   A
      for many are the wounds inflicted by the slanderer.
  ³⁰ Like a caged hunting falcon is the heart of the
                                           scoundrel;
      and like a spy he will pick out defects.
  ^{31a} The talebearer turns good into evil;
  ^{32a}   with a spark he sets many coals afire.
  ^{32b} The ne'er-do-well lies in wait for blood,
  ^{31b}   and plots against your choicest possessions.
  ³³ Look out for the wicked, since he breeds only evil,
      lest you incur a lasting stain.
  ³⁴ Lodge a stranger with you, and he will subvert your   G
                                             course,
      and make a stranger of you to your own household.

12   ¹ If you do good, know for whom you are doing it,
      and your kindness will have its effect.   A
  ² Do good to the just and reward will be yours,
      if not from him, from the LORD.
  ³ No good comes to him who gives comfort to the
                                    wicked,
      nor is it an act of mercy that he does.
  ⁴ Give to the good person, refuse the sinner;
  ⁵   refresh the downtrodden, give nothing to the proud:
      No arms for combat should you give him,
      lest he use them against yourself;
      With twofold evil you will meet
      for every good deed you do for him.
  ⁶ God himself hates sinners,
      and requites the wicked with vengeance.

8 In our prosperity we cannot know our friends;
　　in adversity an enemy will not remain concealed.
9 When a person is successful even his enemy is friendly;
　　in adversity even his friend disappears.
10 Never trust your enemy,
　　for his wickedness is like corrosion in bronze.
11 Even though he acts deferentially and peaceably toward
　　　　　　　　　　　　　　　　　　　　　　　　you,
　　take care to be on your guard against him.
　Treat him as one who would breach a confidence,
　　and be sure that in the end envy will still be there.
12 Let him not stand near you,
　　lest he oust you and take your place.
　Let him not sit at your right hand,
　　lest he then demand your seat,
　And in the end you appreciate my advice
　　when you groan over my neglected warning.

13 Who pities a snake charmer when he is bitten,
　　or anyone who goes near a wild beast?
14 So it is with the companion of the proud,
　　who is involved in his sins:
15 While you stand firm, he makes no move;
　　but if you slip, he cannot hold back.
16 With his lips an enemy temporizes,
　　but in his heart he schemes to plunge you into the
　　　　　　　　　　　　　　　　　　　　　　　abyss.
　Though your enemy has tears in his eyes,
　　given the chance, he will never have enough of your
　　　　　　　　　　　　　　　　　　　　　　　blood.
17 If evil comes upon you, you will find him at hand;
　　feigning to help, he will trip you up,
18 Then he will nod his head and shake his fist
　　and hiss repeatedly, and show his true face.

Notes

11 29–34. For these six bicola, MS A has eleven to correspond (one after 12:1). These include Jer 5:27, garbled doublets, and to go with v 30 an astonishing zoo: "like a wolf in ambush for prey," cf. 30b, and "the peddler waits in ambush like a bear, for the house of scoundrels." The oddly behaved bear (cf. Lam 3:10) may come from a retroverted Aram source (other than Syr) in which it was transmogrified from a wolf (for the reverse transformation in 1 Sam 17 and in the Syriac Psalms 152, 153, cf. *CBQ* 38 [1976]: 149–50, with discussion of the Aram forms). The wolf in its turn is an attempt to make something out of the caged bird in 30a, which the Gr calls a "hunting partridge"(!). MS A and Syr both have the caged bird (in Syr it is again a partridge), but in addition both proceed to turn the cage (Heb *kĕlûb*) into a dog (Heb *keleb*) that invades the house (cf. 29a) and snatches food or (Syr) throws the house into turmoil (cf. the Gr of 34a). Herkenne (pp. 127–29) already has in his Old Latin the partridge and an ensnared gazelle (cf. Sir 27:19–20), plus a line so obscure that he retroverts it into Gr and by rewriting a word gets dogs out of it, to match Syr. In the face of all this, the present translator should probably apologize for seeing in the partridge (Gr *perdix*) a *caged hunting falcon* (Gr *hierax*) compared to the *heart of the scoundrel: kĕnēṣ ṣayyād bikĕlûb lēb lēṣ.* That the alliteration with *lamed* is not too much is suggested by 13:1; for *hierax=nēṣ* cf. LXX Lev 11:16; Deut 14:15; Job 39:26; Job 39:13 Aquila.

29b. *wounds:* compare Prov 27:6; G has "ambushes."

30b. This colon reflects the language of Gen 42:9.

31–32. Read these four cola in the sequence (GI's) 31a (omit *enedreuei,* cf. 32b), 32a, 32b, 31b.

34a. *your course*=MS A *dĕrākĕkâ;* the Gr *en tarachais* reflects the sound rather than the sense of the Heb.

12 1a. For the garbled form of this in MS A (*'m ṭwb tdy' lmy ṭṭyb*) and the same garbling as already underlying a GII citation in *Didache,* 1,6 (*hidrōsatō=tdy'*) see *Bib* 44 (1963): 533–36.

5d. *will meet:* MS A and Syr add "in time of need," a gloss.

6. GII adds "and he keeps them for their day of vengeance," cf. 5:7 and Deut 32:35 LXX. "Day of vengeance" occurs three times in Isaiah.

7. G repeats v 4 here.

11cd. Between these cola MS A adds a gloss, "so that he may not be able to harm you"; G reads 11cd in terms of a corroded bronze mirror, cf. 10b.

12f. *over my neglected warning:* conj. *ûlĕtôkaḥtî;* cf. Prov 5:11–12; MS A *ûlĕ'anĕḥātî,* dubious.

14a. *proud [man]=['îš] zādôn:* MS A has *'ēšet,* "woman."

14b. After this colon, MS A introduces 23:16f, followed by a paraphrase of 12:15 preceding the normal text of that verse.

15. The verbs *ta'ămōd* and *timmôṭ* are misspelled in MS A.

Comment

This section, which advises care in choosing friends and associates, has an introductory poem (11:29–34) and a twenty-two-line poem in three stanzas, 7+8+7 bicola. For the confused state of MS A in the first poem (11:29–34), see the extensive NOTE.

The exhortation in v 29a makes good sense. Indeed, if the householder offers hospitality and friendship to anyone indiscriminately, he may well suffer unpleasant consequences, viz., "the wounds of the slanderers" (v 29b), concerning whom see Prov 11:13; 20:19; Jer 6:28; 9:3. For the reading of v 30a, cf. the clever emendation in the NOTE. In addition to the alliteration of the three *l*'s noted there, there are also three *ṣ*'s: *kĕnēṣ ṣayyad* ("like a hunting falcon") . . . *lēṣ* ("scoundrel"). The first word, *kĕnēṣ*, also rhymes with the last word, *lēṣ*. Thus the emendation not only makes good sense, but also embodies the type of poetic diction Ben Sira is capable of. The image in v 30a is powerful, suggesting that the scoundrel is on the watch for hapless prey. For similar imagery, cf. Jer 5:26–27. Ben Sira changes the metaphor in v 30b, comparing the scoundrel to a spy on the lookout for weak spots or "defects," Heb *'erwâ*, lit., "nakedness," language borrowed from Gen 42:9, 12.

In v 31a, Heb *[nir]gān* (the reconstruction of MS A is virtually certain), here translated "talebearer," may also mean "backbiter, slanderer." The word in this sense is found only in Prov 16:28; 18:8; and 26:20, 22—all of which deplore the evils of the backbiter. Ben Sira probably borrowed the imagery of v 32a to complete the bicolon 31a–32a (cf. NOTE) from Prov 26:20: "For lack of wood, the fire dies out; and where there is no talebearer [backbiter], strife subsides." In the bicolon 32b–31b, "the ne'er-do-well" translates Heb *'îš bĕlîya'al*, lit., man of worthlessness, a good-for-nothing, a base fellow. The word *bĕlîya'al* (used only here in the book) occurs also in Prov 6:12; 16:27; 19:28; Job 34:18. Here "the ne'er-do-well," in parallelism with the backbiter of v 31a–32a, is compared to the murderer who "lies in wait for [Heb *'rb*] blood" (v 32b). The verb *'rb* occurs also in Prov 1:11 in a similar context. In v 31b, *mahămaddekā*, "your choicest possessions," refers to the injured person's good name and reputation, which the backbiter (v 31a), who is also a good-for-nothing (v 32b), turns from "good" to "evil" (v 31a) and so in effect acts like a killer lying "in wait for blood" (v 32b).

In the nine short Heb words of v 33, there are six liquids (three *r*'s and three *l*'s) and six *m*'s, which give the bicolon a pleasant sound. "The wicked," or evil, man (Heb *raʿ*) is to be avoided because "he breeds (only) evil," Heb *raʿ;* cf. Isa 59:4. The Heb word *mûm* in the expression "a lasting *stain*" (v 33b) occurs also in 33:33lb; 44:19b; and 47:20a. The Gr word *mōmos*, which translates *mûm*, occurs likewise in 18:15a and 20:24a, where the Heb text is not extant. The "lasting stain" one may incur by association with the wicked is a bad name. The word *mûm* is used also in the sense of a physical defect or blemish which excludes a man from priestly service (Lev 21:17–18, 21, 23), or which disfigures a man (2 Sam 14:25) or a woman (Cant 4:7), or which makes an animal unsuitable for sacrifice (Lev 22:20–21, 25; Num 19:2; Deut 15:21; 17:1. In v 34, the "stranger" who "will subvert your course" may be the pagan or the Hellenized Jew who has given up his faith. Either of these characters could "estrange you from your own" (the lit. translation of G, v 34b), i.e., alienate you from your own people and your glorious Jewish heritage. Spicq (p. 629) interprets the verse in a similar way.

The opening stanza (12:1–6) of the twenty-two-line poem contains advice and exhortations that are typical of the mentality of Ben Sira and of the later rabbis. The maxims are at variance, however, with the teaching of the NT. V 1a is the topic sentence of the stanza. V 1b may be translated, lit.: "And there will be hope for your goodness (or kindness)," i.e., hope for a return of the benevolence you have given. V 2 explains v 1b: when you do good to the *just* (Heb *ṣaddîq,* also = "righteous") you will receive your reward, or recompense, "if not from him, from *the Lord*" (so the *O*-group of Gr MSS, followed by Lat; all other Gr MSS have "the Most High"); Syr has "from *his Lord.*" Cf. 35:13. The words of Jesus in Matt 5:43–47 flatly contradict the observations and precepts of Ben Sira in vv 3–6a; cf. also Rom 12:21. The meaning of v 3 is that benevolence to the wicked is not even accounted "an act of mercy" (Heb *ṣĕdāqâ,* also = "alms(giving)," as in 3:14a, 30b; 7:10b; 16:14a). A similar thought is found in the Midrash, *Qoh. rabba* v (Tanch. *ḥqt* §1), where a proverb is attributed to Ben Sira, "Do not good to the evil, and evil shall not befall you," and then adds, "and if you do good to the evil, you have done evil" (cited in Box-Oesterley, p. 359). A parallel is seen in Theognis, 105, 108 (Sanders, p. 32). Compare the sentiments expressed here with Prov 25:21–22: "If your enemy be hungry, give him food to eat, if he be thirsty, give him to drink; For live coals you will heap on his head, and the LORD will vindicate you." Cf. Rom 12:20.

The order found in G is followed in vv 4–6; and v 7, found only in G, repeats v 4, except that v 4 has *tō eusebei,* "to the godly person," whereas v 7 reads *tō agathō,* "to the good person" (=Heb). After v 3, MS A has the following order: vv 5de, 5bc, 6ab, 4, 5a. Compare Ben Sira's advice in vv 4 and 5a with the command of Jesus in Luke 6:27–28: "To you who hear me, I say: Love your enemies, do good to those who hate you; bless those who curse you and pray for those who maltreat you." The exhortation in 5bc is pragmatic, appealing to common sense and legitimate self-interest. In v 5b, the rare word *lāḥem,* "combat, war," occurs elsewhere only in Judg 5:8. V 5de amplifies the thought of v 3 (see above). Compare the statement of Ben Sira in v 6a with the conduct of Jesus in Luke 15:1–2: "The tax collectors and sinners were all gathering around to hear [Jesus], at which the Pharisees and the scribes murmured, 'This man welcomes sinners and eats with them.' " Cf. Luke 19:5–7. The punishment God metes out to the wicked (v 6b) who do not repent is spelled out fully in Deut 28:15–68.

The next stanza (vv 8–12) offers practical notes and maxims about friends and enemies. V 8, which serves as the topic sentence of the stanza, is a commonsense observation: in prosperity it is impossible to know one's friend, and in adversity one's enemy will always be there. V 9 explains the reason why: in prosperity an enemy becomes a companion, or an acquaintance (Heb *rēaʿ*), whereas in adversity a *rēaʿ* disappears. Prov 19:4 contains a similar observation: "Wealth adds many friends [Heb *rēʿîm*], but the friend [*rēaʿ*] of the poor man deserts him." Cf. Prov 14:20 and 19:7 and Sir 6:10–12; 13:21–23. Cicero quotes (*De Amicitia,* 64) the elegant Latin proverb of Quintus Ennius (239–169 B.C.): *Amicus certus in re incerta cernitur,* "A sure [or certain] friend can be discerned in an unsure [or uncertain] matter." Richard Barnfield (1574–1627) expresses a similar sentiment: "Every man will be thy friend / Whilst thou hast wherewith to spend; / But if store of crowns be scant, / No man will supply thy want. / He that is thy friend indeed, / He will help thee in thy need" (*Poems: In Divers Humours* [1598]). Ben Sira seems to distinguish between "(real) friend" (Heb *ʾōhēb,* also = lover) in v 8a and *rēaʿ,* "(mere) acquaintance," in v 9. The precept in v 10a is practical and is not meant to suggest a high religious ideal, as Jesus does in Luke 6:27. V 10b offers the explanation by comparing the enemy's wickedness with bronze, which corrodes in many different ways. The image of the rusting of metals is taken up again in 29:10b and in Matt 6:19 and Jas 5:3. The five bicola of vv 11 and 12 provide examples of an enemy's potential wickedness.

The point of 11ab is that one should be on guard especially when an enemy begins to act "deferentially" and "peaceably" [or humbly (the literal meaning of *bĕnaḥat)]*. V 11c shows one way in which a person can observe the maxim not to trust an enemy (v 10a). In v 11d, Ben Sira explains that envy is the usual result when an enemy sees another's prosperity. Compare this comment with the observation of Aeschylus (525–456 B.C.): "It is in the character of very few men to honor without envy a friend who has prospered" (*Agamemnon,* 1. 832). V 12b and v 12d, in synonymous parallelism, give two illustrations of what the envy of an enemy can produce if Ben Sira's warnings in v 12a and v 12c are not kept in mind. The stanza concludes (v 12ef) with an exhortation for one not to be slow to appreciate the sage advice Ben Sira offers, lest one "groan over [his] neglected warning" (see NOTE). Here again

Ben Sira appeals to his wide experience and his authority as a Wisdom teacher, implying that it would be foolish not to heed his advice. Apropos of v 12ef is the famous maxim of Benjamin Franklin (1706–90): "Experience keeps a dear school, but fools will learn in no other" (*Poor Richard's Almanac* [1743]).

The final stanza (vv 13–18) of this poem offers sage comments about the behavior of the proud who pretend to be friends. In v 13, the strong images— borrowed from Pss 22:14, 22; 57:5; and 58:5–7—are meant to dramatize the importance of Ben Sira's advice. In v 13a, Heb *ḥôbēr,* here translated "a snake charmer," means, lit., "a charmer." In Ps 58:6, the word is used specifically of the snake charmer. Cf. Jer 8:17; Qoh 10:11. The same word is used in v 14a but with its more usual meaning of "companion, associate." The point of v 14 is that the one who is foolish enough to be "the associate" (*ḥôbēr*) of the proud (cf. NOTE) so as to become involved with their sins deserves no more pity than "a snake charmer" (*ḥôbēr*) who gets bitten (v 13a), or the person who recklessly approaches "a wild beast" (lit., beast of tooth; cf. Ps 57:5) (v 13b). Cf. 3:26 with COMMENT. "The proud" (v 14a), feigning friendship, "makes no move" as long as you stand firm (v 15a) and show no weakness, economic or social. But should you fall, the proud reveals how false his friendship has been (v 15b). Cf. Prov 6:12–14. In v 16a, the false friend is now called *ṣār,* "adversary, enemy," who "with his lips . . . temporizes" (cf. Prov 26:24a), "but in his heart" he plots your downfall (cf. Prov. 26:24b). Hence the comment in v 16cd, the background of which is the sneaky and treacherous behavior of Ishmael, son of Nethaniah. With tears in his eyes, he asked the eighty men from Shechem, Shiloh, and Samaria who were bringing offerings for the house of Yahweh to come to Gedaliah, whom unbeknownst to them Ishmael and his men had murdered two days before in Mizpah. When the eighty were inside the city, Ishmael and his men killed seventy of them; so Jer 41:4–7. In effect, Ben Sira urges extreme caution when your enemy weeps, for his are crocodile tears. A similar proverb was written by John Gay (1685–1732): "An open foe may prove a curse, / But a pretended friend is worse" (*Fables,* xvii, "The Shepherd's Dog and the Wolf," l. 33).

Vv 17–18 explain further why the false friend should be avoided at all costs. If misfortune befalls you, he will be there (v 17a). He will pretend to be "like a man who gives support" (the literal translation of *kĕʾīš sômēk* in v 17b), but in reality "he will search for your heel" (v 17b), i.e., he will make sure your downfall is complete. In v 18, the enemy now makes obscene gestures of utter contempt: he will shake [or wag] his head (*rōʾš yānîaʿ;* the same expression is used in 13:7e and in Pss 22:8; 109:25; Lam 2:15) and wave his hand (cf. Lam 2:15; Ezek 25:6; Nah 3:19) and "hiss repeatedly" (cf. Lam 2:15) and finally "show his true face" (lit., change his face, i.e., from that of a "friend" to that of the real enemy he is). Cf. Matt 27:39. On vv 10–18, cf. C. Selmer, "A Study of Ecclus. 12:10–19," *CBQ* 8 (1946): 306–14.

20. The Rich and the Poor
(13:1–14:2)

13   1   Whoever touches pitch blackens his hand;   A
     whoever accompanies a scoundrel learns his ways.
   2   Why take up a burden too heavy for you;
     why go with someone wealthier than yourself?
   How can the earthen pot go with the metal cauldron?
     when they knock together the pot will be smashed.
   3   The rich does wrong and boasts of it,
     the poor is wronged and begs forgiveness.
   4   As long as the rich can use you he will enslave you,
     but when you are exhausted he will have nothing to
                                         do with you.
   5a While you own anything, he will be part of your   G
                                         household,
   6b   and with smiles he will win your confidence;
    c He will make you gracious promises and ask what you
                                         need,
   7a   and embarrass you with gifts of delicacies.
   6a As soon as he needs you, he will trick you;
   7b   twice or three times he will intimidate you,
   5b   then reduce you to penury without a qualm.
   7d Afterward he will gloat over you, pretend to be angry
                                         with you,
    e   shake his head at your downfall
    c   and finally laugh you to scorn.
   8   Guard against being easily upset,   A
     and do not come to grief with the uninformed.

   9   When approached by a person of influence, keep your
                                         distance;
     then he will urge you all the more.

10 Be not too forward with him lest you be rebuffed,
    but be not too standoffish lest you be taken for an
                    enemy.
11 Do not suppose you can be free with him,
    trust not his fulsome conversations;
    For by prolonged talk he will test you,
    and though smiling he will probe you.
12 Mercilessly he will store up your words as a threat   GII
                 against your life,
    and he will be unsparing of oppression or chains.
13 Be on your guard and take care   A
    never to accompany men of violence.[a]

15 Every living thing loves its own kind,
    every person a human being like himself.
16 Every living being keeps close to its own kind;
    with his own kind every person associates.
17 Is a wolf ever allied with a lamb?
    So it is with the sinner and the just.
18 Can there be peace between the hyena and the dog?   G
    Or between the rich and the poor can there be
                  peace?
19 Lions' prey are the wild asses of the desert;   A
    just so the poor are feeding grounds for the rich.
20 The proud abhors lowliness;
    so does the rich abhor the poor.
21 When the rich stumbles he is supported by a friend;
    when the poor trips he is repulsed by a friend.
22 Many are the supporters for the rich when he speaks;
    though what he says is repugnant, it wins approval.
    When the poor speaks they say, "Come, come, speak
                  up!"
    but though he is talking sense, they will not give him
                  a chance.

---

[a] 14 If you hear these things in your sleep, wake up!   GII
    With your whole life, love the Lord
    and call on him for your salvation.

23 The rich speaks and all are silent,
    his wisdom they extol to the clouds.
    The poor speaks and they say, "Who is that?"
    If he stumbles they knock him down.

24 Wealth is good where there is no guilt;
    but poverty is evil by the standards of the proud.
25 The heart of a person changes his looks,
    either for good or for evil.
26 The sign of a good heart is a radiant look;
    withdrawn and perplexed is the toiling schemer.

14 1 Happy the person whose mouth causes him no grief,
    whose heart brings him no remorse.
  2 Happy the person whose conscience does not reproach
                                 him,
    who has not lost hope.

Notes

13 2d. *will be smashed.* MS A and Syr add the intrusive colon "or why should the rich man associate with the poor man?"

5a–7c. The various sources here show textual confusion, already present in the Gr; Syr and MS A are weaker witnesses here.

8b. *come to grief* supposes *(ʿal) tiddam* for the *(ʾl) tdmh* of MS A; cf. Jer 25:37; 49:26; 50:30; and especially 51:6. For similar thought patterns, cf. Hos 4:6; Prov 5:23.

12a. *Mercilessly he will store up your words* is the reading of Origen's recension (253+Syr); Lat is similar. *As a threat against your life* makes conjectural use of the *ʿl npš rbym* of MS A and Syr, plus the *animus illius* of Lat (*inmitis animus illius conservabit verba tua*); their widely different applications suppose the presence of *nepeš* in the basic text.

17. MS A has an extra colon, "and so for the rich man keeping close to the (poor) man," where "poor" (=*rāš*) is a conjecture for *ʾīš* of the MS, which makes no sense.

18. MS A is garbled.

20a. *The proud*=G=*gēʾeh* here, though often G's *hyperēphanos*=*lēṣ;* MS A has *gʾwh,* "pride." Syr omits the verse.

21b. *repulsed by a friend:* G = "repulsed by (his) friends"; MS A = "pushed off from friend to friend."

22c. *speaks*=*mĕdabber*=Syr; MS A has *nāmôṭ* (cf. v 21b).

14   1b. Read *wĕlōʾ hēbîʾ ʿālāyw dāwôn libbô;* MS A *wlʾ ʾbh ʿlyw dyn lbw.*
   2a. *reproach him = ḥissĕdattû;* MS A *ḥsrtw.*

Comment

This section contains various observations and maxims concerning the rich and poor and their association with each other. It may be divided into four stanzas: the first with seven bicola, two tricola, and a bicolon (ten poetic lines); the second six bicola; the third eleven bicola; and the fourth five bicola. Thus the first two stanzas (10+6) have the same number of lines as the last two (11+5).

The first stanza (vv 1–8) opens with a general remark (v 1a) applicable to the many situations described later in the section. V 1a has become a popular proverb, being quoted twice in Shakespeare (1564–1616): "They that touch pitch will be defiled" (*Much Ado About Nothing,* III iii 61); "This pitch, as ancient writers do report, doth defile; so doth the company thou keepest" (*King Henry IV,* Part I, II iv 460). V 1b makes an application of the proverb, as does Shakespeare in the second quotation. The *lēṣ,* "scoundrel, scorner," is to be kept at a distance lest one learn "his ways." Regarding the *lēṣ,* cf. 3:28a; 8:11a; 15:8a; 32:18b. In v 1b, each of the five words has a liquid (*l* or *r*) in it: *wĕḥôbēr ʾel lēṣ yilmad darkô.* A parallel to v 1 is found in Theognis, 35–36 (Sanders, p. 32). In v 2ab, there is an *m* alliteration in the comparative particle *mimmĕkā* and the interrogative *mah,* found in each colon. The colorful images in the two bicola of v 2 emphasize the incompatibility of rich and not so rich. Ben Sira's comment in v 3 sediments what many people have observed or experienced. Cf. Prov 18:23. Rich and poor do not receive equal treatment either before the law or from society at large.

In vv 4–7 (cf. NOTE), Ben Sira gives examples of how the rich abuse and manipulate the poor for selfish gain. In v 4a, the Heb expression *yaʿăbōd bĕkā,* "he will enslave you," occurs also in Jer 30:8. Though Ben Sira makes the remarks in vv 4–7c (note the order of the cola in the translation above) about individual rich people who use the poor for their own purposes, what he says is applicable in modern times also to rich nations which have pursued a policy of colonialism and subjugated poor peoples for economic, military, or geopolitical advantage, only to abandon them later. The bicolon in v 5a–6b, from G, may be translated, lit.: "If you have anything, he will live with you, and he will smile at you and give you hope." In other words, the rich will move in on you, ingratiate themselves with you, and give you hope of a better tomorrow. Vv 6c–7a describe further the scheming of the rich: they pretend interest by making you promises (lit., he will speak fine things to you) and even inquire about your needs; they embarrass you with their expensive meals. But as soon as the rich need you for their own purposes, they trick you, intimidate you, and "reduce you to penury without a qualm" (lit., empty you out and not be sorry for it) (vv 6a, 7b, 5b). V 7dec may be translated, lit., from G: "Afterward when he sees you he will forsake [or abandon] you, and shake his head at you [cf. 12:18] and finally laugh you to scorn." The point is clear: after the rich have obtained through trickery what they want from you, they abandon you and ridicule you. V 8a may also be translated: "Be on your guard; do not *act too boldly*" (the Heb verb *rhb* in Isa 3:5 has such a meaning). For the verb in v 8b, cf. NOTE. If the alternate translation of v 8a is correct, then the colon urges against any bold conduct that would put one in the position of the persons Ben Sira speaks of in the previous seven verses. Failure to heed what is said brings one "to grief with *the uninformed*" (Heb *ḥăsêrê maddaʿ*, lit., those lacking in intelligence, or knowledge).

The next stanza (vv 9–13) issues appropriate warnings about contacts with the nobility. *Pirqe Aboth,* ii 3, expresses similar sentiments: "Be cautious with (those in) authority, for they let not a man approach them but for their own purposes; and they appear like friends when it is to their advantage, and stand not by a man in the hour of his need" (quoted in Box-Oesterley, p. 363). In v 9a, "a person of influence" translates Heb *nādîb,* lit., a noble, as in 1 Sam 2:8; Job 21:28; 34:18; Prov 8:16; Pss 47:10; 83:12; 113:8. The first two consonants of the verb *qārēb* (lit., when a noble *approaches*), the first word of the colon, are found in reversed order in the adjective at the end of v 9a, *rāḥôq,* "[keep] *distant.*" The reason for the advice is given in v 9b, which may be literally translated "and so much the more will he let you draw near." Cf. Prov 25:6–7 and Luke 14:7–11. V 10 may be translated, lit.: *"Do* not *draw* [too] *close* [*qrb*], lest you *be put at a distance* [*rḥq*], and *do* not *stay at* [too long] *a distance* [*rḥq*], lest you be hated." The point is to avoid either extreme—getting too close or remaining too distant. Proper distance is the ideal; cf. 32:9b. Dom Calmet attributes to Alexander the Great (ruled 336–323 B.C.) the remark that one should approach nobility as one approaches a fire—close enough to feel the heat, but far enough away not to be burned (quoted by Spicq, p. 635). In v 11, Ben Sira urges caution especially when the noble engages an inferior in extended and seemingly amiable conversation, the purpose of which in reality is to "test" and to "probe" the person (v 11cd). In making the observation in v 12, Ben Sira may have had in mind undue familiarity of Jews with their pagan overlords who could and did oppress them; cf. Ps 120:6–7. One should avoid at all costs the company of "men of violence" (v 13); cf. 10:23b with COMMENT; 15:12b; Prov 1:10–15; 3:31; 16:29. The "men of violence" may also refer to the pagan nobility in the Holy Land; cf. 10:6–18 with COMMENT and INTRODUCTION, Part II. A parallel to vv 10–13 is found in *Phibis,* x 12–xi 23 (Sanders, pp. 92–93). GII and Lat add v 14, a tricolon that urges attention and watchfulness regarding what has been said in the stanza, and advises further that one "love the Lord" and "call on him for . . . salvation"—good advice that will help one avoid the temptations and dangers described in the stanza.

The next stanza (vv 15–23) describes how like associates with like, and how the rich and poor are treated so differently. The maxim in v 15a has many echoes, as, for example, in the proverb "Like loves like," which is the rough English equivalent of the Lat *Similis simili gaudet,* "Like rejoices in like." V 15b is in parallelism with v 15a. V 16a and b give variations on the same proverb. Cicero has a similar saying: *Pares autem vetere proverbio cum paribus facillime congregantur,* "Indeed equals, according to the old proverb, most easily assemble with equals." In v 17a, the question—"Is *a wolf* [Heb *zěʾēb*] ever allied with *a lamb* [*kebeś*]?"—has as background Isa 11:6, in which the same two Heb words appear; cf. Matt 7:15; 10:16. The reason for stating the five proverbs in 15ab, 16ab, and 17a is to emphasize the point in v 17b: the sinner (Heb *rāšāʿ,* lit., "the evil, or wicked, person") and the righteous (*ṣaddîq*) have no likeness to each other and nothing in common; cf. Prov 29:27 where the same Heb nouns occur in a similar context. The imagery in v 18a would suggest a great deal to Palestinians, for dogs were used to protect the troops in the field (cf. Isa 56:10) and flocks (cf. Job 30:1) from the strong and rapacious hyenas which were numerous at that time (cf. Jer 12:9). The hyena and the dog were natural enemies. In like manner the rich and poor cannot live in "peace" (v 18b), for the rich (like hyenas) prey upon the helpless poor; cf. v 19. The powerful images of v 19a and b are made even more emphatic by the liquid alliteration (three *l*'s and five *r*'s) in seven of the eight words: *maʾăkal* (food for) *ʾărî* (the lion) [are] *pirʾê* (wild asses of) *midbār* (the desert), *kēn* (in like manner) *marʿît* (the pasture for) *ʿāšîr* (the rich man) [are] *dallîm* (the poor). There are also six labials (four *m*'s and a *p* and *b*). It is to be noted that "the rich" and "the poor" in vv 18b and 19b are in synonymous parallelism with the wicked and the righteous, respectively, in v 17b; cf. Jas 2:6. In Job 24:4–5, the poor are compared, as in v 19, to the "wild asses of the desert." For the lion as a figure for the wicked and the rich, cf. Pss 35:17; 58:7.

In v 20, "the proud" (cf. NOTE) is in parallel with "the rich," and "lowliness [or humility]" with "the poor." Rich and poor can never get along together, for "the poor is *an abomination to* [*tôʿăbat*] the rich" (the literal translation of v 20b), just as in Prov 29:27, "the one whose path is upright is *an abomination* to the wicked." The observation Ben Sira makes in v 21 receives empirical validation in the experience of many: when the rich are in trouble they find many to help them; when the poor need help, they are avoided even by their "friends." The poor have only God to turn to; cf. Ps 13:4–5. In vv 22–23, Ben Sira gives other illustrations of the vast differences that exist between the lives and behavior of the rich and of the poor. Many rally around the rich when he speaks, and approve of what he says though it be "repugnant" (Heb *měkôʿārîm,* also = "dark, ugly, repulsive, unseemly"; cf. NOTE on 11:2b). But when the poor speaks modestly and humbly, people act condescendingly toward him and do not "give him a chance" (lit., *there is no place for him*) though he "is talking sense" (v 22cd). A similar sentiment is expressed in Qoh 9:16: "The wisdom of the poor man is despised and his words go unheeded." "The rich speaks" and commands respectful silence from the listeners (cf. Job 29:9), who extol his wisdom "to the clouds" (v 23ab); cf. Job 20:6. "The poor speaks," and people ask the snide question, "Who is that?" (Heb *mî zeh,* Gr *tis houtos*) (v 23c). The same Gr pronoun is used in a sarcastic manner by the people of Nazareth when they refer to Jesus in Matt 13:55. Then if the poor person "stumbles they knock him down" (v 23d), doubtless with unholy glee. Aḥiqar (55) has observations similar to Ben Sira's in vv 21–23: "He whose hand is full is called wise and honorable; but he whose hand is empty is called wicked, poor, needy, and indigent, and no one honors him" (cited in Duesberg-Fransen, pp. 151, 153).

The final stanza (13:24–14:2) of this section offers various maxims about wealth and poverty and a good conscience. In v 24, there is an *o* assonance and an *n* and an *ʿayin* alliteration as well as rhyme at the end of the two cola: *ṭôb* (good) [is] *hāʿôšer* (wealth) *ʾim ʾên* (if there is no) *ʿāwôn* (guilt), *wěraʿ* (but evil) [is] *hāʿŏnî* (poverty) *ʿal pî zādôn* (by the standards of pride). Ben Sira may be speaking ironically in v 24a, since it would be rare to find wealth without guilt; cf. 11:10ab with COMMENT and Prov 28:20; Matt 19:23–24. It is possible, however, for the rich to be blameless; cf. 31:8a. The point of v 24b is that poverty which is not due to a person's sin or laziness is not evil even though the proud consider it so. But poverty is deplorable when it results from laziness (Prov 6:6–11; 10:4; 20:4, 13; 24:30–34) or from idle talk (Prov 14:23) or from idle pursuits (Prov 28:19; cf. 12:11) or from pleasure-seeking (Prov 21:17; 23:20–21; Sir 18:30–19:4).

In v 25, Ben Sira makes the perceptive observation that a person's interior disposition (= "the heart of a person" in Heb thought categories) manifests itself outwardly (= "changes his looks," lit., changes his face); cf. Prov 15:13; Ps 104:15; Qoh 8:1; Matt 6:16–18. V 26 gives illustrations of the two dispositions mentioned in v 25b: "a radiant look" (lit., a shining face) indicates "a good heart," a "perplexed" look indicates a "toiling schemer." The Heb text of v 26b is problematic. Syr has: "and a multitude of discourses are the thoughts of sinners." Gr reads: "and the finding [the meaning] of parables is a wearisome toil of the mind." The two beatitudes in 14:1–2 refer to persons with a clear conscience. Since in the Heb mentality "the mouth" is the external instrument of "the heart" (the internal source of ideas, accountability, and sentiments), 14:1 can speak of the former causing "no grief" and the latter bringing "no remorse." As regards the mouth, cf. 25:8c; Jas 3:2–10. For the combination of mouth (or tongue) and heart in contexts related to the present text, cf. Pss 17:3; 39:4; 141:3–4. V 2a may be translated, lit.: "Happy the person *whose soul* [*napšô*=his inner being, self (cf. 6:2 with COMMENT)] does not *reproach him"* (cf. NOTE); this colon is in parallel with v 1b. The implication of v 2b is that the person whose conscience reproaches him or her is a person who has no *hope* (Heb *tôḥelet*) of a blessed future; cf. Ps 39:8; Prov 10:28–30; 11:7. The point of 14:1–2 is that true happiness and fulfillment do not come from the accumulation of wealth; rather, inner serenity results from a clear conscience. Indeed, one can experience a deep and abiding sense of satisfaction and peace only when one has honored the commitments and responsibilities of one's life; cf. Pss 1:1–3; 34:9–23.

21. The Use of Wealth
(14:3–19)

14   3 Wealth ill becomes the mean person;   A
         and to the miser, of what use is gold?
    4 What he denies himself, he collects for someone else,
         and in his possessions a stranger will revel.
    5 To whom will he be generous who is stingy with himself
         and does not enjoy what is his own?
    6 There is no one worse off than he who is stingy with
                                 himself;
         he punishes his own avarice.
    7 If ever he is generous, it is by mistake,   G
         and in the end he displays his greed.
    8 An evil person is the miser:
         he refuses his neighbor and neglects himself.
    9 The greedy sees his share as insufficient,
         but his stinginess withers his appetite.
  10 Though the miser's eye is rapacious for food,   A
         there is none of it on his table.

  11 My son, use freely whatever you have,
         and enjoy it as best you can;
  12 Remember that death does not tarry,
         nor have you been told the grave's appointed time.
  13 Before you die, be good to your friend,
         and give him a share in what you possess.
  14 Deprive not yourself of present good things,   G
         let no choice portion escape you.
  15 Will you not leave your riches to others,   A
         and your earnings to be divided by lot?
  16 Give, take, and treat yourself well,
         for in the netherworld there are no joys to seek.

¹⁷ All flesh grows old, like a garment;
  the age-old law is: all must die.
¹⁸ As with the leaves that grow on a vigorous tree:
  one falls off and another sprouts—
  So with the generations of flesh and blood:
  one dies and another flourishes.
¹⁹ All of a person's works will perish in decay;
  his handiwork will follow after him.

Notes

14   3b. *of what use* = *lāmmâ zeh* = G; Syr and MS A repeat the *ill becomes* of 3a (*lŏʾ nāʾweh*).

5b. *enjoy* = G, Syr; MS A *yqrh,* dubious.

7–8. These are lacking in MS A; v 8 is lacking also in Syr. 7a: *by mistake* = Syr; G has "through forgetting."

9b. *his stinginess* supposes *ʿayin rāʿâ* for G's *adikia ponēra* = *ʿāwōn raʿ;* cf. 7:2, where G's *adikou* (neuter) = *ʿāwôn.* V 9 in MS A cannot be supposed to have been the original (so Segal).

10b. Read *mĕʾûmâ* for MS A's *mhwmh.* MS A has two forms of v 10, one matching GI, the other related to Syr.

12ab. MS A expands by introducing here the language of 16b.

14b. For the formulation, compare Wis 2:7. Syr and MS A are of no help here.

16b. Syr and MS A follow this with two cola in the spirit of Qoh 9:10; 11:9.

Comment

This poem on the proper uses of wealth may be divided into two stanzas: 8 + 10 bicola. The strophic structure is reasonably certain because the first stanza has "the miser" in the opening bicolon (v 3) and in the closing (v 10), thus forming an *inclusio;* and the second stanza begins with *bĕnî,* "my son" (v 11a), which is one of the usual ways to indicate the start of a new section. Each stanza also has a certain unity of subject matter. If we combine the last five bicola of the preceding section (13:24–14:2) with the present poem (note that 13:24 and 14:3 both begin with the word "wealth") we have a twenty-three-line poem used by Ben Sira to bring Part III of the book to a close just as he used a twenty-two-line poem to open this part (6:18–37).

The first stanza (vv 3–10) deals with the miser and the miserable life he leads despite his wealth; cf. COMMENT on 14:1–2. V 3, which serves as topic sentence of the stanza, may be translated, lit.: "To *the small heart* [=*the mean person*] ill-becoming is wealth, and to *the man evil of eye* [=*the miser*] of what use [cf. NOTE] is gold?" The colorful phrase "the small heart," Heb *lēb qāṭān,* is the reverse image of our English expression "big-hearted" (= generous). The phrase *"the evil of eye"* (=greedy person or miser), Heb *raʿ ʿayin,* occurs in Prov 23:6; and in Prov 28:22 is found the expression *ʾîš raʿ ʿayin,* "the man evil of eye," which Ben Sira uses here. "The small heart" (v 3a) is in parallel with "the man evil of eye" (v 3b). Vv 4–6 explain why wealth is unbecoming to "the mean person," and why gold is useless to "the miser." The miser, by depriving himself of the benefits of his wealth, amasses a fortune for a stranger who "will revel" in it (v 4); cf. Qoh 6:2–3. The point of v 5a is made more emphatic by an elegant *a:b::b':a'* rhetorical pattern: *he-who-is-evil (raʿ):to-himself (lĕnapšô)::to-whom (lĕmî):will-he-be-good (yêṭîb).* The miser "is *evil* to himself" by depriving himself of his own *goods* (v 5b). V 6 may be translated, lit.: "He who is evil to himself, there is none more evil than he, and with him [is] the recompense of his evil." Cf. 11:18–19 with COMMENT and Qoh 5:9–12.

If the miser ever is "generous," it is "by mistake" (so Syr; Gr has "in forgetfulness, or inadvertently"); eventually, however, "he displays his greed" (v 7). The miser is evil because his wealth benefits neither others nor himself (v 8); cf. 4:4–5; Qoh 4–8; Tob 4:7–11. Like spoiled and unruly children, the greedy think their "share" is "insufficient" (v 9a). But, ironically, their "stinginess withers [their] appetite" (v 9b), i.e., they are so tight-fisted that they suppress their desire for the satisfaction of their legitimate needs in order to prevent any diminution of their wealth. Though the miser is greedy for food not his own (v 10a; cf. 31:12–13), his own table is bare (v 10b). Such is the miserable existence of the miser, whom Ben Sira cordially excoriates. Apropos of v 10b is the proverb attributed to John Davies of Hereford (ca. 1565–1618): "A man shall as soon break his neck as his fast / In a miser's house" (*The Scourge of Folly,* written in 1611).

For the opening colon (v 11a) of the next stanza, in which Ben Sira speaks of the good uses of wealth, MS A has two forms: "My son, if you have anything, serve yourself," which is the reading of Syr; and "If you have anything, do good to yourself," which is the reading of G. For the Heb idiom *lᵉ lĕyādĕkā* (here translated "as best you can"), cf. COMMENT on 5:1b. The reason why one should enjoy the blessings of prosperity is that death will eventually be one's lot (v 12). For the thought of vv 11–12, cf. Qoh 5:17–19; Ps 49:18–20. In v 12, Ben Sira emphasizes that while death is certain, "the grave's appointed time" for any individual (lit., the decree of Sheol) remains uncertain; only God knows when one will die. Thus one is urged not only to do good to oneself (v 11) and so avoid the miseries of the miser, but also to do good to one's friend before one dies (v 13a). One is to be generous in sharing one's possessions. For the thought, cf. Prov 3:27–28. V 14 (cf. NOTE) rephrases the thought of v 11: enjoy God's gift of the good life; cf. 11:14; Qoh 7:14; 9:7–10. If you do not, you will "leave your riches to others," and your earnings to *those who cast the lot* (v 15); cf. 11:19; Ps 49:11. Box-Oesterley (p. 358) explain that in Palestine brothers divided their inheritance by lot as late as the second century B.C. Cf. Joel 4:2–3.

V 16a takes up again the idea of vv 11 and 14, and vv 16b–19 develop further the thought of v 12. In Ben Sira's view, there are "no joys to seek" in Sheol, the netherworld (v 16b), because rewards for a life of virtue (and punishment for a life of sin) take place not in the afterlife but only in the present life; cf. COMMENT on 7:17 and 11:26, and Qoh 9:9–10. See INTRODUCTION, Part X, 4. The aphorism in v 17 is made more memorable by the *b* and *k* alliteration in the first colon and the *ô* assonance in the second: *kol habbāśār* (all flesh) *kabbeged* (like a garment) *yibleh* (wears out), *wĕḥôq ʿôlām* (and the age-old decree) [is:] *gāwôaʿ yigwāʿû* (all shall surely die). The expression *kabbeged yibleh* is found also in Isa 50:9; 51:6; and Ps 102:27; cf. Job 13:28. In the last century, R. C. Trench wrote this amusing comment: "The Italians have a proverb . . . of the tardiness of the despatch of all business in Spain . . . : 'May my death come to me from Spain' (*Mi venga la morte da Spagna*), for so it will come late or not at all" (*On the Lessons in Proverbs*, iii 53, 1853).

The imagery in vv 18–19 depicts graphically the precariousness of human existence; cf. also 30:17; 41:1–4; Pss 39:5–7, 12; 62:10; Qoh 6:12. In Isa 40:6–8, human life is compared to grass that withers and the flower of the field that wilts; for similar metaphors cf. Job 8:11–13; 14:1–2; Ps 37:2; Jas 1:10; 1 Pet 1:24. In Isa 34:4, the figure of the leaf that wilts on the vine is used to underscore the transitoriness of the heavens and their host. Here Ben Sira uses the image of one leaf falling and another sprouting "on a vigorous tree" to portray the death of one generation and the growth of another (v 18); cf. Qoh 1:4; Isa 64:5; Ps 1:3. Homer employs a similar image: "People come and go as leaves year by year upon the trees. Those of autumn the wind sheds upon the ground, but when spring returns the forest buds forth with fresh ones. Even so is it with the generations of humankind, the new spring up as the old are passing away" (*The Iliad*, vi 146–49); cf. also *The Iliad*, xxi 463–64. For the thought of v 18, cf. Qoh 2:18–22. In v 18c, the expression "flesh and blood" (Heb *bāśār wĕdām*, Gr *sarx kai haima*), which occurs also in 17:3lb (not extant in Heb) is not found in the MT or in the nonbiblical Qumran fragments published prior to 1960. Interestingly, the expression *sarx kai haima* occurs in Matt 16:17; 1 Cor 15:50; and Gal 1:16; and *haima kai sarx* in Eph 6:12 and Heb 2:14. The Heb phrase *bāśār wĕdām* is found frequently in the rabbinical literature (cf. M. Jastrow, *A Dictionary of the Targumim, the Talmud Babli and Yerushalmi, and the Midrashic Literature*, vol. I, p. 199). The Heb verb *rqb*, "to decay, rot," in v 19a is found only twice in the MT: in Isa 40:20 (to describe a timber "that *will* not *rot*") and in Prov 10:7 (to state that "the name of the wicked *will rot*"). In v 19, Ben Sira insists that human works are as transitory as men and women themselves, because there is no retribution in the afterlife; cf. COMMENT on 7:17 and 11:26. Later, when the doctrine of a blessed immortality for the righteous and of punishment for the wicked was revealed, human works were viewed in a different light; cf. Rev 14:13.

PART IV (14:20–23:27)

22. The Search for Wisdom and Her Blessings (14:20–15:10)

14 ²⁰ Happy the person who meditates on Wisdom,   A
        and fixes his gaze on understanding;
    ²¹ Who ponders her ways in his heart
        and pays attention to her paths,
    ²² Pursuing her like a scout
        and watching her entryways;
    ²³ Who peeps through her window
        and listens at her doors;
    ²⁴ Who encamps near her house
        and fastens his tent pegs next to her walls;
    ²⁵ Who pitches his tent beside her
        and lives as her welcome neighbor;
    ²⁶ Who builds his nest in her leafage
        and lodges in her branches;
    ²⁷ Who takes refuge from the heat in her shade
        and dwells in her home.

15 ¹ He who fears the LORD will do this;
        he who is practiced in the Law will come to Wisdom.
    ² Motherlike she will meet him,
        like a young bride she will embrace him,
    ³ Nourish him with the bread of learning,
        and give him the water of understanding to drink.
    ⁴ He will lean upon her and make no misstep,
        he will trust in her and not be put to shame.
    ⁵ She will exalt him above his fellows;
        in the assembly she will make him eloquent.

6 Joy and gladness he will find;
   she will endow him with an everlasting name.
7 Worthless people will not attain to her,
   the haughty will not behold her.
8 Far from the impious is she,
   not to be spoken of by liars.
9 Unseemly is praise on a sinner's lips,
   for it is not allotted to him by God;
10 But praise is offered by the tongue of the wise,
   and its rightful master teaches it.

Notes

14 21b. *her paths* = *nĕtîbôtêhā;* MS A has *tbwntyh;* G and Syr diverge.
22b. *her entryways:* MS A adds "all," not vouched for by G, Lat, or Syr.
27a. Isa 4:6; the allusion explains G's choice of *doxē* "glory," in 27b.
27b. *her home:* more likely *ûbĕmiškĕnôtêhā* (cf. Pss 84:2; 87:2) than MS A's improbable *wbmʿnwtyh* (cf. Job 37:8).

Comment

This discrete poem, which is neatly divided into two stanzas (8 + 10 bicola), describes the blessedness of the person who seeks Wisdom and her ways and her paths. In the first stanza (vv 20–27), a variety of images portray the person on the quest for Wisdom.

In v 20a, the verb *hgh,* "to meditate," occurs also in 6:37b and 50:28a; cf. Ps 119:15, 23, 148. That person is declared "happy" who "meditates on *Wisdom"* (Heb *hokmâ*) and its parallel, "understanding" (*tĕbûnâ*) (v 20b). The same two Heb nouns are found in a similar passage in Prov 3:13: *"Happy* the person who finds *wisdom,* the one who gains *understanding."* The two nouns appear in parallel also in Exod 36:1. Cf. 14:1–2; 31:8a; 50:28a; and Ps 1:1 for other beatitudes. In v 21, Wisdom's "ways," *dĕrākêhā,* and "her paths," *nĕtîbôtêhā* (cf. NOTE) occur together also in Prov 3:17: "[Wisdom's] *ways* are pleasant *ways,* and all *her paths* are peace." On the thought of v 21, cf. Prov 8:32b: *"Happy* [are] those who keep *my* [i.e., Wisdom's] *ways."* In vv 22–23, the pursuit of Wisdom is compared to the clandestine activity of "a scout," or "a spy." Cf. 2 Sam 10:3. For Wisdom's "entryways" (v 22b) cf. Prov 8:34: "Happy the person watching daily at my gates, waiting at my doorposts." In vv 22–25, Ben Sira employs metaphors in which Wisdom is assumed to dwell in a house; cf. Prov 8:34 and 9:1. The searcher of Wisdom is to peer through the windows of her house (v 23a), as the lover gazes through the window of his beloved's house (Cant 2:9), and is to listen "at her doors" (v 23b) so that he may learn all he can about her. All this is in sharp contrast to the conduct of the fool described in 21:22–24.

The word "tent" (vv 24–25) in the OT usually refers to one's place of residence (as, for example, in Pss 52:7 and 69:26); but the word may also be used metaphorically to denote one's existence or moral life (as in Job 8:22; 22:23; 29:4). In vv 24 and 25, Ben Sira seems to be using the tent imagery in both senses. By encamping next to the walls of Wisdom's house (v 24) and living as her "welcome neighbor" (v 25), the pursuer of Wisdom can come to learn her secrets and her instruction; cf. 4:11–19; 6:18–22. The metaphor changes in vv 26 and 27: Wisdom is now depicted as a tree with foliage and branches; and the person in search of Wisdom is compared to a bird building its nest in her branches; cf. Ps 104:12. For the images in v 27, cf. Isa 4:6 and 25:4. Wisdom alone, says Ben Sira, can provide security and protection from "the heat" of life's pains and misfortunes; cf. Prov 1:33; Qoh 7:12.

The second stanza (15:1–10) details the blessings Wisdom bestows on those who energetically pursue her. In v 1a, there is a *y* alliteration in the middle three words: *kî* (For) *yĕrê°* (he who fears) *Yahweh* (usually abbreviated in MS A, *yy*) *ya'ăśeh* (will do) *zō°t* (this). A *dental* (*t* and *d*) alliteration occurs in the words of v 1b: *wĕtôpēś* (and he who *grasps,* or *is practiced in*) *tôrâ* (the Law) *yadrîkennâ* (will come to her, i.e., Wisdom). The stanza opens with *kî*, "for, because," thus indicating a motive clause. V 1 repeats again Ben Sira's teaching that Wisdom becomes available only to those who fear the Lord by keeping the Law. Cf. COMMENT on 1:11–30 and 6:32–37. In contrast to those who fear the Lord are the "worthless" and "haughty" who will never achieve Wisdom or "behold her" (v 7). In Jer 2:8, the expression *tôpēś tôrâ* (v 1b) refers to the priests who were supposed to shepherd the people. Here the expression refers to the scribe, whether he be priest or not; cf. 38:24–39:11. Eventually, a special office developed; it is to these scribes that the NT refers (cf. Matt 22:35; Luke 5:17; 7:30; 10:25; 11:45–53; 14:3; Acts 5:34; 1 Tim 1:7). The scribes devoted themselves to the study and teaching of Scripture, especially the Law.

In v 2, an *a:b::b':a'* rhetorical pattern lends emphasis to Ben Sira's point: *And-she-will-meet-him:like-a-mother::and-like-a-wife-of youth:she-will-receive-him.* For the mother imagery (v 2a), cf. Isa 49:15 and 66:13. The phrase "young bride" (v 2b) appears also in Prov 5:18; cf. also Prov 7:4; Cant 4:9, 12;

5:1–2; Jer 3:4. The point of v 2 is that Wisdom will show a motherly concern for those who seek her by fearing the Lord and observing the Law, and she will also receive them as enthusiastically and passionately as a young bride. Another perfectly balanced *a:b::b':a'* pattern (v 3) continues the thought of v 2: *And-she-will-feed-him:with-the-bread-of learning::and-with-the-waters-of understanding:she-will-give-him-to-drink.* For the expression "bread of learning," cf. Prov 9:5a. In v 3, Ben Sira speaks of Wisdom giving food and drink to those who seek her; in Isa 55:1, Yahweh gives the same things. Box-Oesterley (p. 369) mention that in the later Jewish literature the "water" and "bread" of the Torah are often referred to, e.g., in the Babylonian Talmud, *Shabbath,* 120a, the Midrash *Bereshit Rabba,* lxx, and the Midrash *Shir Rabba,* i 4. Cf. also the words of Jesus in John 4:10–15.

Because the wise "lean upon" (Heb *šʿn*) or depend on Wisdom, they "make no misstep" (v 4a); trusting in her, they are not "put to shame" (v 4b). In Ps 18:19, it is Yahweh who is "the support" (*mišʿān*) of the afflicted person; and in Pss 22:6 and 25:2, it is in Yahweh that the faithful trusted and were thus not put to shame. V 5b may be translated, lit.: "and in the midst of the assembly [*qāhāl*] she will open his mouth." The idea of Wisdom exalting the wise above their fellows (v 5a) is echoed later in *Pirqe Aboth,* vi 1: "And [the Torah] magnifies him and exalts him over all things" (cited in Box-Oesterley, p. 370). As regards v 5b, cf. 21:17. Though the wise are to open their mouths to speak and teach in the assembly, the fool is to remain silent (cf. Prov 24:7). The artisan—important as he is for the people—does not enjoy a place of honor in the assembly (38:33). There is a sibilant alliteration in v 6: *śāśôn* (joy) *wĕśimḥâ* (and gladness) *yimṣāʾ* (he will find) *wĕšēm ʿôlām* (and an everlasting name) *tôrîšennû* (she will endow him with). For v 6a, cf. Isa 51:3. In Isa 56:5, it is Yahweh who gives the faithful eunuchs "an eternal, imperishable name."

Wisdom can never be attained by the wicked, those who disregard and disobey the commandments. In v 7a, the phrase "worthless people" (*mĕtê šāwʾ,* lit., men of emptiness, vanity, worthlessness), which occurs also in Job 11:11 and Ps 26:4, is in synonymous parallelism with "the haughty" (*ʾanšê zādôn*) (v 7b), an expression similar to one found in Jer 43:2. An *a:b::b':a'* structure to the words in v 7 dramatizes Ben Sira's observation: *they-shall-attain-her not:worthless men::and haughty men:shall-see-her not.* Cf. v 1b. Like the "worthless" and the "haughty," the "impious" (*lēṣîm,* lit., scorners, mockers, as in 3:28a; 8:11a; 11:30a; 13:1b; 31:26b; 32:18b) will never come near Wisdom, nor will "liars" (*ʾanšê kāzāb,* lit., men of deceit) speak words of Wisdom (v 8). For the thought of v 8, cf. Prov 14:6 and Wis 1:4–5. In vv 9a and 10a, there is a clever *a:b::b:a* chiastic pattern that sharply contrasts the wicked and the wise: (unseemly is) *praise [tĕhillâ]:in-the-mouth-of the wicked [bĕpî rāšāʿ]::in-the-mouth-of the wise [bĕpî* (so MS B) *ḥākām]:praise [tĕhillâ]* (is spoken). In Ps 148:3–4, 7–10, the sun and moon and stars, the highest heavens and the waters above the heavens, the sea monsters and all depths, fire and hail, snow and mist and storm winds, mountains and hills, fruit trees and cedars, wild beasts and tame animals, creeping things and winged fowl, are all urged to praise Yahweh, for "he gave them a duty which shall not pass away" (Ps 148:6), i.e., all these creatures fulfill the purposes for which they were created. But praise has not been allotted by God to the wicked (v 9) because, as Ps 50:17 explains, they "hate discipline and cast [God's] words behind [them]," i.e., they do not fulfill the purposes for which they have been created. Cf. also Prov 17:7. Only the wise can utter the praises of an all-wise and all-holy God (v 10), for they fear God and keep the Law he established for them; cf. v 1 and Ps 33:1–5. The wise alone are the masters of praise and can teach it (v 10b); this colon may be a reference to the *hymns of praise* (Heb *hôdāyôt*) that the wise know how to compose and to teach others.

23. Free Will and Responsibility
(15:11–16:23)

15   ¹¹ Say not, "It was God's doing that I fell away";   A
     for what he hates, he does not do.
  ¹² Say not, "It was he who set me astray";
     for he has no need of the wicked.
  ¹³ Abominable wickedness the Lord hates;
     he does not let it befall those who fear him.
  ¹⁴ It was he, from the first, when he created humankind,   B
     who made them subject to their own free choice.
  ¹⁵ If you choose, you can keep his commandment;
     fidelity is the doing of his will.
  ¹⁶ There are poured out before you fire and water;   A
     to whichever you choose you can stretch forth your
                      hands.
  ¹⁷ Before each person are life and death;
     whichever he chooses shall be given him.
  ¹⁸ Copious is the wisdom of the Lord;
     he is mighty in act, and all-seeing.
  ¹⁹ The eyes of God behold his handiwork;
     he perceives a person's every deed.
  ²⁰ No one did he command to sin,
     nor will he be lenient with liars.

16   ¹ Do not yearn for worthless children,
     or rejoice in wicked offspring.
  ² Many though they be, rejoice not in them
     if they have not the fear of the Lord.
  ³ Count not on their length of life,
     have no hope in their future,
   For one can be better than a thousand;
     rather die childless than have impious children!

⁴ Through one wise person a city can be peopled;   B
    through a clan of rebels it becomes desolate.

⁵ Many such things my eye has seen,   A
    even more than these has my ear heard.
⁶ Against a sinful band fire is enkindled;
    upon a godless people wrath flames forth.
⁷ He forgave not the princes of old
    who were rebellious in their might;
⁸ He spared not the neighbors of Lot,
    abominable in their pride;
⁹ Nor did he spare the doomed people
    who were dispossessed because of their sin;
¹⁰ Nor the six hundred thousand foot soldiers
    who went to their graves for the arrogance of their
         hearts.
¹¹ And had there been but one stiff-necked person,
    it were a wonder had he gone unpunished;
For mercy and anger alike are with him
    who remits and forgives, but also pours out wrath.
¹² Great as his mercy is his punishment;
    he judges people, each according to his deeds.
¹³ A criminal does not escape with his plunder;
    a just person's hope God does not leave unfulfilled.
¹⁴ Whoever does good has his reward,
    which each receives according to his deeds.
¹⁵ [The LORD hardened the heart of Pharaoh so that he
         did not recognize him
    whose acts were manifest under the heavens;
¹⁶ His mercy was seen by all his creatures,
    and his light and his darkness he apportioned to
         humankind.]

¹⁷ Say not, "I am hidden from God;
    in heaven who has me in mind?
Among so many people I pass unnoticed;
    what am I in the universe of spirits?
¹⁸ Behold, the heavens, the heaven of heavens,
    the earth and the abyss tremble at his visitation;

19 The very roots of the mountains, the earth's
foundations,
at his mere glance, quiver and quake.
20 Of me, therefore, he will take no thought;
with my ways who will concern himself?
21 If I sin, no eye will see me;
if all in secret I am disloyal, who is to know?
22 Who tells him of just deeds;
or what expectation is there, since the end is far off?" G
23 Such are the thoughts of the senseless, A
which only the foolish knave will think.

Notes

15:11–16:7. MS B, of which a leaf first published in 1958 begins with 15:1 and continues through 16:7, runs textually very close to MS A in the first 10 verses (above) of chap. 15. From 15:11 on, MS B is filled with doublets and glosses, though some of its readings are still superior to those of MS A. See Di Lella, "The Recently Identified Leaves of Sirach in Hebrew," pp. 160–63, with tabs. III, IV; and Rüger, pp. 75–86 with a further summation on pp. 86–93.

15 11. MS B has an expanded double rendering of this verse, with variants.

12b. *he has no need* = *'ên lô ṣōrek;* MSS A, B^mg *'ên ṣōrek;* MS B *'ên lî ḥēpeṣ.*

13a. *Abominable wickedness* = *rāʿâ wĕtôʿēbâ* of MSS A, B^mg; the text of MS B, plus G's "every abomination," should not be taken to indicate the hendiadys was not original (otherwise, Rüger).

14b. MSS B, A both include here an extra colon, "and he puts him into the hand of his kidnappers," which is based on a verbal resemblance of the actual 15:14b to Syr of 4:19b; the expansion (see Di Lella, *The Hebrew Text of Sirach,* pp. 121–25) makes flagrant nonsense in this place.

15b. *fidelity* = *'ĕmûnâ;* MSS A, B^mg have the secondary variant *tĕbûnâ.* MSS A, B add: "and if you believe (*taʾămîn*) in him you too will live," based on Hab 2:4. In Syr this colon is present to the exclusion of 15b; Di Lella, *Hebrew Text,* pp. 127–29, sees the Heb of it as one more retroversion from Syr. It anticipates v 17 and could easily have been prompted by John 11:25.

16b. *you can stretch forth* = MS B *tšlḥ* = GI; MS A, GII, Lat, Syr read the imperative.

18a. *Copius* = *sāpĕqâ;* in earlier Heb *śpq,* see 1 Kgs 20:10. MS B has a doublet that looks suspiciously like retroversion from the Gr (otherwise, Rüger).

19a. The Gr has been accommodated to Ps 32(33):18.

20b. Read *wĕlōʾ yaḥmōl ʿal ʾanšê kāzāb;* MS A has *wĕlōʾ heḥĕlîm ʾanšê kāzāb,* with its verb not supported by either G or Syr. Compare Di Lella, *Hebrew Text,* pp. 129–34. MSS A, B, and Syr all add further verbiage in efforts to repair the text.

16 1a. The "many" of G and Syr anticipates v 2; the *tw'r* of MS A is based on dittography.

3b. The expansion after this colon by a later hand in Codex Sinaiticus and a few other Gr sources appears to be a purely Gr addition. It reads: "For you will groan in untimely mourning, and will know of their sudden end." Cf. Wis 14:15; Sir LXX 11:27.

4a. MS A and Syr expand this colon slightly. MS B has two forms of it: a longer paraphrase and the form translated above, which is also that of the Gr; MSS A, B, and G agree on 4b, which MS B gives twice.

5b. Read *'ṣmwt m'lh.* G rightly also gives the comparative degree, *ischyrotera,* which Syr (with *men*) confirms. Neither *k'lh* (MS A) nor *b'lh* (MS B) can express this in the language of Ben Sira (vs. Rüger, etc.).

6a. *fire is enkindled=ywqdt 'š* of MSS A, Bᵐᵍ; MS B's *ršph lhbh* is suspect: the frequent parallel *'eš // lěhābâ* is varied here to *'eš // ḥēmâ.* Otherwise, Rüger, who compares 43:21.

7a. The *'šr* of MSS A, B is not vouched for by G, Syr. The allusion to Gen 6:1–4 seen by the Gr (*archaiōn gigantōn*) is certainly present; but the choice (MSS A, B) of *něsîkê qedem, princes of old,* by Ben Sira, instead of the familiar *něpîlîm,* is conscious avoidance of the mythological overtones to the Genesis narrative so familiar from the Enoch literature and (later) Jubilees.

8b. *abominable=*G*=hammětô'ăbîm;* MS A's *hmt'brym,* which could be translated "overweening," does not reflect Ben Sira's use of the verb in question.

9b. After this colon, the late hand in Codex Sinaiticus inserts the gloss "All these things he did to the hard-hearted nations, and toward the multitude of his holy ones he did not relent." Two Gr minuscules have the same gloss after v 10b.

10b. After this colon, GII has the insert "Striking, sparing, smiting, healing, the Lord persisted in mercy and chastisement." For the thought and patterning of this gloss, cf. 18:13.

11d. *but also pours out wrath=*G*=wěšōpēk ḥēmâ;* for this, MS A substitutes a variant on 5:6d.

13b. *a just person's hope=tiqwat ṣaddîq=*G; MS A has *t'wt ṣdyq l'wlm.*

14a. Perhaps *lěkōl ṣědāqâ yeš śākār;* the text of MS A is overburdened.

14b. *receives=yimṣā'=*G; MS A has *yṣ' lpnyw;* Syr*=ymṣ' lpnyw.*

15–16. These two verses are present in MS A (in 15b read *wěhoškô* for *wšbḥw* of the MS), in GII, and in Syr; they are not vouched for by GI or Lat, and represent a late expansion of the text. The *wšbḥw,* "and his praise," of MS A, using an Aram/late Heb stem that Ben Sira does not employ, shows concern to avoid a dualistic view of creation such as obtained currency at Qumran, with "children of light" opposed to "children of darkness."

17d. *spirits:* MS A and Syr add "of all humankind," a gloss based on Num 27:16. Saadia quotes the line without the gloss, which is lacking also in GII.

18b. *tremble at his visitation=běpoqdô yirgāzû=*G, Lat; MS A varies (*bpqdw wkrgšw*) and includes also a seeming allusion to Isa 63:19–64:2. After this colon, GII adds the line "The whole world past and present is in his willing [it]."

22b. To this colon GII adds "and a scrutiny for all [will come] in the end/at death," which seems to depend on Wis 1:9; 3:17–19; and related passages.

Comment

This unit on free will, impious children, punishment of the wicked, and accountability for sin may be divided into four stanzas: $10 + 5 + 11 + 8$ bicola. As is obvious, the stanzas are only loosely related.

The first stanza (15:11–20), one of the key passages of the book, contains Ben Sira's theology of free will and sin. V 11a may be translated, lit.: "Say not, 'From God is my sin.' " The Heb noun *peša'* means "sin, transgression" against other human beings (cf. Gen 31:36; 50:17) or against God (cf. Amos 5:12; Mic 1:5, 13; Isa 58:1; 59:12; Ezek 18:22, 28). The point of v 11a is that personal sin does not have its origin in God. V 11b explains why one may not blame God for one's sins: "for what [God] hates, he does not do." Cf. Wis 11:24 and Jas 1:13. In some of the earlier books of the OT there are statements that seem to imply that God was the cause of sin; cf., for example, Exod 11:10; 2 Sam 24:1; Jer 6:21; Ezek 3:20. Here Ben Sira explicitly denies that God has any part in human sin. V 12a may also be translated: "Say not, 'It is he who made me stumble.' " The point of the colon is that God is not the occasion of sin either, "for he has no need of the wicked [*'anšê ḥāmās*, lit., men of violence, lawlessness; cf. COMMENT on 10:23b]." Cf. Job 22:2–3. In v 13a, *rā'â wĕtô'ēbâ*, lit., "wickedness (or evil) and abomination," is an hendiadys (cf. NOTE); hence the translation "abominable wickedness." V 13a is in synonymous parallelism with v 11b—the Lord hates sin and wickedness. Those who fear the Lord will not commit "abdominable wickedness"; hence Ben Sira may affirm that God "does not let it befall those who fear him" (v 13b). Cf. Prov 12:21.

The next four bicola (vv 14–17) are crucial for an understanding of Ben Sira's doctrine of free will. In v 14a, instead of *hû' mērō'š*, "It was he, from the first," of MS B, MS A and MS B^mg read *'ĕlōhîm mibbĕrē'šît*, "God from the beginning [created humankind]," two words taken from Gen 1:1: "In the beginning God created the heavens and the earth." V 14b may be translated, lit.: "And he placed them in the hand of their free will [*yēṣer*]." Cf. F. Vattioni, "Genesi 1,1 ed Eccli. 15,14," *Augustinianum* 4 (1964): 105–8; and J. B. Bauer, "Sir. 15,14 et Gen. 1,1," *VD* 41 (1963): 243–44. In the MT, the noun *yēṣer* means "vessel (formed by the potter)," as in Isa 29:16, or "form of man (made of clay)," as in Ps 103:14, or "that which is formed in the mind, imagination, purpose," as in Gen 6:5; 8:21; Deut 31:21; 1 Chr 28:9; 29:18; Isa

26:3. Here the word means "free choice, free will," as is obvious from the next three verses. In 27:6b, *yēṣer* means "(human) nature." In v 14, Ben Sira teaches that human beings from the time of their creation have enjoyed freedom of choice. He explains this teaching in vv 15–17. Keeping "his commandment," i.e., the Law (cf. Prov 19:16; Qoh 8:5)—G and Syr have "the commandments"—is a matter of personal decision and not of fate or predestination (v 15a): "If *you* choose." In v 15b, MSS A and B^mg read *tĕbûnâ,* "understanding," instead of "fidelity." The expression "to do *God's will*" (so MS B; MSS A and B^mg have "his will") is in parallelism with keeping "his commandment." Hence, to be faithful one must keep the Law and so do God's will. Faith in the biblical sense of the word implies not only an act of the intellect, which accepts God's word as true and normative, but also the activity of the will that puts belief into action. On the need for faith in OT theology, cf. also COMMENT on 11:21b. Ben Sira employs the verb "to choose," Heb *ḥpṣ,* three times in as many verses, thus emphasizing that human beings enjoy personal freedom in deciding whether or not to observe the Law (v 15) and in choosing life or death (v 17). Though in Deut 4:24 Yahweh is described as "a consuming fire, a jealous God," "fire and water" in v 16a are not symbols of "good and evil" as are "light and darkness" (John 1:5; 3:19; 8:12; 12:46; 1 John 2:8). "Fire and water" correspond to "life and death" (v 17a) merely as opposing elements; cf. 3:30a. By using these images, Ben Sira insists on the radical freedom human beings have of choosing one extreme or the other and, by implication, anything in between. The doctrine of free will is nothing new; Ben Sira found the elements of it in Deut 11:26–28 and 30:15–20, esp. v 19: "I [Moses] have set before you life and death, the blessing and the curse. Choose life, then, that you and your descendants may live." Cf. also Jer 21:8. For a fuller discussion of vv 14–17, cf. J. Hadot, *Penchant mauvais et volonté libre dans la sagesse de Ben Sira (L'Ecclésiastique),* pp. 91–103; and G. L. Prato, *Il problema della teodicea in Ben Sira,* pp. 237–46. Cf. also V. Pisani, "Acqua e fuoco," *Acme* 1 (1948): 94.

In vv 18–19, Ben Sira extols the wisdom, power, and omniscience of the Lord. In the context of the present stanza, vv 18–19 imply that God knows not only every person's deeds but also all his or her choices for good or for evil; cf. 42:17–21. For the teaching that God sees all things (vv 18b and 19b), cf. Prov 15:3; Job 34:21–22; Pss 33:13–15; 90:8; 139:1–4; Heb 4:13. The omnipotence of God is also a given in the Bible; cf., for example, Pss 46:2–10; 66:3–7. In v 20a, the concluding verse of the stanza, Ben Sira resumes, by way of *inclusio,* the thought of v 11, the opening verse. God not only is not responsible for human wickedness (vv 11–12), but also commands no one to sin. Accordingly, one should not say about one's personal evil: "God made me do it." However, should one make such an affirmation, one would be a liar; hence the strong statement in v 20b. On the *'anšê kāzāb,* lit., "men of deceit," cf. 15:8b. On free will in Ben Sira, see INTRODUCTION, Part X, 3.

The next stanza (16:1–4) tells why children, a blessing from God when they are pious, are undesirable when they are wicked, i.e., when they abuse their freedom (15:14–17). This theme is commonly found in the Wisdom literature; cf. 40:15–16; 41:5–13; Job 8:14–19; 27:14–15. Cf. A. Eberharter, "Exegetische Bemerkungen zu Ekkli. 16,1–5," *Der Katholik*, 4te Folge, 37 (1908): 386–89. Children were considered a sure sign of prosperity and well-being; cf. Gen 12:2; 15:5; 22:17; 24:60; Deut 28:4; Prov 17:16; Qoh 6:3; Pss 127:3–5; 128:3–4. But it is pointless, says Ben Sira, to "yearn for worthless children, or rejoice in wicked offspring" (v 1); cf. Wis 3:11–12. V 2a may be translated, lit.: "And even if they are faithful, rejoice not in them." The point is that a large number of children and of grandchildren is no cause for joy unless "they have . . . the fear of the LORD" (v 2b). The reason why one should not rely on "their length of life" (lit., their life) or "hope in their future" (v 3ab) is that the wicked will come to an untimely end; cf. Ps 55:24; Deut 28:15–19. The translation of v 3c is based on an emended Heb text; MSS A and B read: "For one who does the will [of God, so MS B] is better than a thousand." V 3d in MSS A and B also has a retroversion from Syr. For detailed discussion of the cumbersome verse in MSS A and B, cf. A. A. Di Lella, *The Hebrew Text of Sirach*, pp. 134–42. The point of v 3c is clear: one child who does the will of God (as the gloss has it in MSS A and B) and obeys the Law is better than a thousand wicked children. V 3d makes the point even more forceful: it is better to "die childless than have impious children!" (lit., a posterity of insolence)—a bold statement, since to be childless was considered a reproach (cf. Luke 1:25). V 4b alludes to the story of Sodom in Gen 18:16–32. MS A and a secondary form of MS B have as v 4a: "Through *one childless person who fears Yahweh* a city can be peopled"—a clear reference to Abraham, who was childless by his wife, Sarah, when he bargained with God in an attempt to save Sodom from destruction; the conception and birth of Isaac are recorded later, in Gen 21:2. The text of MS B translated here—"one wise person"—may be an allusion to the fact that Abraham, though he had only one son by Sarah, became the father of a numerous posterity.

The next stanza (vv 5–14) describes how God punishes without fail the wicked for their sins. In v 5a, Ben Sira appeals to his personal experience—apparently he had seen how evil men and women were afflicted because of their crimes. In v 5b, he tells how he had heard even more than he had seen—a reference not only to stories about contemporary sinners, but especially to stories of notorious sinners in the OT, as is clear from the rest of the stanza. The "sinful band" in v 6a are probably Korah, Dathan, and Abiram together with the two hundred and fifty Israelites who followed them; Num 16:1–35 tells the story how these rebels were destroyed by fire and earthquake. Cf. 45:18–19. V 6b is an allusion to Num 11:1–3. The expression "godless [or impious, or apostate] people [or nation]," Heb *gôy ḥānēp*, occurs also in Isa 10:6. In v 7, Ben Sira alludes not only to the giants of Gen 6:1–4 (cf. NOTE and Wis 14:6) but also to such "princes of old" as the king of Babylon in Isa 14:4–21 and Nebuchadnezzar in Dan 4:7–30 (a Daniel story Ben Sira probably knew; cf. L. F. Hartman and A. A. Di Lella, *The Book of Daniel*, AB 23, pp. 173–74).

In v 8, Ben Sira refers to the people of Sodom, "the neighbors of Lot." The reason why the Lord did not spare Sodom is that there were not even ten righteous persons to be found in the city (cf. Gen 18:32). It is to be noted that the crime of the Sodomites is one of "pride," Heb *ga'ǎwâ* (v 8b), as in Ezek 16:49–50. In Gen 19:4–5, "the neighbors of Lot" committed a different kind of sin. The devastation of Sodom is described in Gen 19:24–25. In v 9, "the doomed people who were dispossessed because of their sin" are the Canaanites, who were notorious for their licentious fertility cults and other religious abominations; cf. Exod 23:33; 34:11–16; Deut 7:1–2; Num 33:51–56; Wis 12:3–7. With regard to "the six hundred thousand foot soldiers," cf. 46:8b; Exod 12:37; Num 11:21, all of which refer to the number of people Moses led in the desert after the Exodus. Because they angered the Lord by murmuring against him, they were all slain despite the attempts of faithful Moses, Aaron, Joshua, and Caleb to intercede for them; cf. 46:1, 7–8; Num 14:1–12, 23–24, 38; 26:65; Deut 1:35–38. Interestingly, Ben Sira calls the sin of the disgruntled people "the arrogance [or insolence] of their hearts," Heb *zědôn libbām;* cf. COMMENT on 10:13a. In v 11a, "stiff-necked" is a reference to Exod 32:9 and 33:3, 5, in which Yahweh himself uses that expression to describe the sinful Israelites. The point of v 11ab is that it would have been virtually impossible for even a single member of the Chosen People to "go unpunished" if he or she were insolent or proud.

The pithy aphorism in v 11c, found also in 5:6c, is made more elegant by the alliteration of the six labials (four *m*'s, a *w*, and a *p*): *kî* (For) *raḥămîm* (mercy) *wĕ'ap* (and anger) *'immô* (are with him). This lapidary statement about God conveys a key teaching of the Bible. V 11d simply rephrases v 11c in a pedestrian way. For the expression "pour out wrath" (cf. NOTE), cf. Ps 79:6; Isa 42:25; Jer 10:25; Ezek 14:19. The rhetorically balanced proverb in v 12a is made more memorable by a *k* and an *r* alliteration and an *o* assonance: *kěrôb* (As great as) *raḥămāyw* (his mercy is) *kēn* (so is) *tôkaḥtô* (his punishment). This colon restates v 11c. In v 12b, Ben Sira speaks again of the Jewish doctrine of the efficacy of works—people are judged by God according to their deeds. Cf. 3:14–16, 30–31; 11:26; 15:19; 17:22–23; 29:11–12. Vv 13–14 develop the idea in v 12b. For the emendation "(a just person's) *hope*" (cf. NOTE) in v 13b, cf. 44:10. The point of v 13 is that the criminal and the righteous both receive what they deserve. The stanza comes to a close on a happy note: the one who does *good* (lit., *righteousness*) shall receive (cf. NOTE) the reward according to his deeds (v 14). For the added two bicola (vv 15–16) that are here placed in brackets because they do not seem original, cf. NOTE. Peters (p. 137) considers these two verses original. The hardening of

Pharaoh's heart (v 15a) is mentioned in Exod 7:3; 9:12; 10:27; 11:10; 14:4, 8, 17. As regards v 15b, cf. Exod 7:3. For the thought of v 16a, cf. Exod 9:16 and Rom 9:17.

The final stanza (vv 17–23) deals with a recurring question: In such a vast and marvelous and mysterious universe, why would God take thought of insignificant me? In stark contrast to the thought of v 17, compare Ps 139:7–18. The questions in v 17 are often found in the hearts or on the lips of people in distress, perhaps with a greater poignancy nowadays because of our knowledge of the incredible expanse and complexity of the known universe with its numberless heavenly bodies. Vv 18 and 19 seem to be a parenthesis because the questions of v 17 continue in vv 20–22. In v 18, "the heaven of heavens" is God's abode; "the heavens," the place of the sun, moon, and stars; "the earth," the habitation of human beings, plants, and animals; and "the abyss" (Heb *tĕhôm*, as in Gen 7:11), the subterranean waters. These were the four parts of the universe, according to the ancient Near Eastern mind. For the expression "the heaven of heavens," cf. Deut 10:14; 1 Kgs 8:27; in 2 Cor 12:2, Paul uses the expression "the third heaven." The idea of the earth trembling (v 18b) and the activity of the "roots of the mountains" in v 19 derive from Judg 5:4–5; Mic 1:3–4; Jonah 2:7; Pss 18:8–16; 97:5; 104:32; 114:4–7. The upheavals of nature described in vv 18–19 are the usual accompaniments of a theophany in the OT; cf., for example, Exod 19:16, 18; Nah 1:3–6. The "visitation" of God (v 18b) often signifies punishment; cf. Isa 10:3, 12; Jer 9:24.

The skeptical questions of v 17 resume in vv 20–22. V 20 serves as introduction to vv 21–22. The point of v 20 seems to be that the skeptic feels the individual to be inconsequential in view of the rest of creation. The questions in v 21 receive fuller expression in 23:18; cf. also Ps 10:4, 11, 13. In v 21, the skeptic says, in effect: Since no one sees me when I sin, who can know when I am unfaithful in secret, or who would care? In v 22, the skeptic is consistent because he disallows that "just [or righteous] deeds" make any difference either. In v 22b, "the end" translates Gr *diathēkē* = Heb *ḥôq*, which in 14:12 is equivalent to Heb *māwet*, "death." The gloss in GII (see NOTE) explains v 22b in terms of death. The "expectation," or "hope" (v 22b), is that of reward for practicing virtue. V 22b seems to say that the hope of retribution for virtue is not sufficient to motivate one, for one never knows when retribution will take place or how one will be by the time of death, which is "far off." Cf. 11:28 with COMMENT. The questions of vv 17 and 20–23 Ben Sira describes as "the thoughts of the senseless [lit., those who are lacking in heart; cf. 6:20b], which only the foolish knave [lit., foolish man] will think" (v 24). Cf. Pss 14:1; 53:2.

24. Divine Wisdom and Mercy as Seen in the Creation of Humankind (16:24–18:14)

16   24 Hearken to me, my son, take my advice,   G
         apply your mind to my words;
      25 I will pour out by measure the spirit that I have,   A
         and impart knowledge in a careful way.
      26 When God created the first of his works   G
         and, as he made them, assigned their tasks,
      27 He ordered for all time what they were to do
         and their domains from generation to generation.
       They were not to hunger, nor grow weary,
         nor ever desist from their rounds.
      28 Not one should ever crowd its neighbor,
         nor should they ever disobey his word.
      29 Then the Lord looked upon the earth
         and filled it with his good things.
      30 Its surface he covered with all manner of life
         which must return into it again.

17   1 The Lord from the earth created humankind,
         and makes each person return to earth again.
       2 Limited days of life he gives them,
         with power over all things else on earth.
       3 He endows them with a strength that befits them;
         in God's own image he made them.
       4 He puts the fear of humans in all flesh,
         and allows them power over beasts and birds.*

---

*5 They received the use of the Lord's five faculties;   GII
    of mind, the sixth, he granted them a share,
    as also of speech, the seventh, the interpreter of his
                                                    actions.

6 Discretion, with tongues and eyes and ears,
  and an understanding heart he gives them.
7 With wisdom and knowledge he fills them;
  good and evil he shows them.
8 He puts into their hearts the fear of him,
  showing them the grandeur of his works,
9 That they may glory in his wondrous deeds
10 and praise his holy name.
11 He has set before them knowledge,
  a law pledging life as their inheritance;
12 An everlasting covenant he has made with them,
  his commandments he has revealed to them.
13 His majestic glory their eyes beheld,
  his glorious voice their ears heard.
14 He says to them, "Avoid all evil";
  to each of them he gives precepts about his neighbors.
15 Their ways are ever known to him,
  they cannot be hidden from his eyes.*b*
17 Over every nation he places a ruler,
  but the Lord's own portion is Israel*c*
19 All their actions are clear as the sun to him,
  his eyes are ever upon their ways.
20 Their wickedness cannot be hidden from him;
  all of their sins are before the Lord.*d*
22 A person's goodness God cherishes like a signet ring,
  a person's virtue, like the apple of his eye.
23 Later he will rise up and repay them,
  and requite each one of them as they deserve.

---

b 16 Their ways are directed toward evils from their youth,   GII
  and they are unable to make their hearts fleshly rather
                                       than stony.

c 18 Israel, as his firstborn, he cares for with chastisement;
  the light of his love he shares with him without neglect.

d 21 But the Lord, being good and knowing how they are
                                       formed,
  neither neglected them nor left off sparing them.

THE WISDOM OF BEN SIRA

²⁴ But to the penitent he provides a way back;
  he encourages those who are losing hope!

²⁵ Return to the Lord, and give up sin,
  pray before him and make your offenses few.
²⁶ Turn again to the Most High and away from sin,
  hate intensely what he loathes;
²⁷ Who in the netherworld can glorify the Most High
  in place of the living who offer their praise?
²⁸ No more can the dead give praise than those who have
  never lived;
  they glorify the Lord who are alive and well.
²⁹ How great the mercy of the Lord,
  his forgiveness of those who return to him!
³⁰ The like cannot be found in humans,
  for not immortal is any human being.
³¹ Is anything brighter than the sun? Yet it can be eclipsed.
  How obscure then the thoughts of flesh and blood!
³² God holds accountable the hosts of highest heaven,
  while all humans are dust and ashes.

18 ¹ The Eternal is the judge of all alike;
  ² the Lord alone is just.^a
  ⁴ Whom has he made equal to describing his works,
  and who can probe his mighty deeds?
  ⁵ Who can measure his majestic power,
  or exhaust the tale of his mercies?
  ⁶ One cannot lessen, nor increase,
  nor penetrate the wonders of the Lord.
  ⁷ When a person ends he is only beginning,
  and when he stops he is still bewildered.
  ⁸ What is a human being, of what worth is he?
  the good, the evil in him, what are these?

---

^a 2b and there is no other than he;
³ He controls the world within the span of his hand,
  and everything obeys his will;
  For he in his might is the King of all,
  separating what is holy among them from what is profane.

GII

9 The sum of a person's days is great
   if it reaches a hundred years:
10 Like a drop of the sea's water, like a grain of sand,
   so are these few years among the days of eternity.
11 That is why the Lord is patient with human beings
   and showers his mercy upon them.
12 He sees and understands that their death is grievous,
   and so he forgives them all the more.
13 A person may be merciful to his neighbor,
   but the Lord's mercy reaches all flesh,
Reproving, admonishing, teaching,
   as a shepherd guides his flock;
14 Merciful to those who accept his guidance,
   who are diligent in his precepts.

Notes

16   26a. *God:* with MS A and Syr; G has "the Lord." *created* = MS A = *ktisei,* Ziegler; the correction is modern: MSS *krisei.*

   26b. *tasks* = *ḥuqqōtām* = Syr; G has "their allotments" = *ḥelqêhem.*

17   5. This purely Gr gloss seems to have been prompted by the five items enumerated in v 6 and by the subsequent text of vv 7–10. It has nothing to commend it.

   8a. *the fear (of him)* = *phobon:* so Ziegler, with a few witnesses; most MSS of G have *ophthalmon,* "eye," so that the colon reads: "He looks with favor on their hearts," lit., "He puts his eye on . . . ," cf. Gen 44:21.

   8b–10. At least two separate attempts to repair a damaged text have been made in the Gr here. As 8c GII adds, "and he gave it them throughout the ages to glory in his wondrous deeds"; the placing of this, as also of vv 10, 9 (usually in that order) in the text is unstable from one witness to the next, and the verb form in v 10 clashes with its general context. It has here been assumed that vv 8b, 9, which in GI repeat an identical phrase, should contain once *the grandeur of his works,* and as an alternative in the other place, to "glory in his wondrous deeds" of 8c, which alone appears of that line in Syr and in some Gr witnesses. Then either *showing them* in 8b or "that they may recount" of GI in 9a overweights the text. Here the last named has been dropped in the reconstruction. Syr lacks vv 7, 8a, and the verb from 8c; its equivalent for v 9 is "That they may be recounting in the world his fear," which is followed by v 10.

   11b. This is followed in GII by the line "That they may know that they who are now alive are mortal."

   16. This gloss of GII is built up out of Gen 8:21 and Ezek 11:19; 36:26.

17a. Before this verse, GII inserts "For in the dividing up of the nations of all the world," an allusion to Deut 32:8–9, on which Ben Sira's v 17 depends.

18. This expansion by GII is a blending of Prov 3:12; Exod 4:22; and Deut 31:6–8; compare the note on v 21 below.

21. Cf. LXX Ps 102(103):14 and Deut 31:6, 8, out of which this gloss was built up.

22. After this verse, GII adds "apportioning repentance to his sons and daughters"; compare v 24 and the gloss, v 18.

26a. GII follows this colon with "For he it is who leads out of darkness into the light of life," based on the narrative of Genesis 1; cf. Luke 1:79; 1 Pet 2:9.

30a. *The like:* reading *tauta* for G's *panta;* so Syr.

18 1a. *the judge:* reading *ekrinen* for G's *ektisen;* so Syr. Contrast 16:26a.

2b–3. GII's gloss here is again a pastiche of biblical expressions, from 1 Sam 2:2; Isa 40:12; Lev 10:10; or Ezek 42:20, and elsewhere.

4a. *Whom* = *tini,* with GII, Lat, Syr; GI's *outheni* = "No one."

9. Gr has only one colon for this verse; Syr joins it (awkwardly) with v 10, but does not have enough for a second colon. GII adds "but the death (*koimēsis*) of each one is beyond the calculations of all."

Comment

This lengthy section may be divided into four smaller poems: $8 + 19 + 8 + 13$ bicola. It deals with God as Creator and with human beings as creatures whose dignity derives from being fashioned in the image of God (17:3b). It also details the relationships and bonds that exist between the Chosen People and their Lord, who called them to be his "own portion" (17:17b).

The first poem (16:24–30) extols God's wisdom as seen in the order, beauty, and providence of created reality. Vv 24–25, which are introductory, set the scene for the new section—Ben Sira's personal reflection on the marvels of creation. In v 24a, "my son" is not found in MS A or Syr. Ben Sira begins by urging his students to "hearken," "to listen" (Heb *šmʿ,* Gr *akouein*), to him, to take his "advice," and to apply their "mind" (Heb *lēb,* "heart" = seat of intelligence and will) to his "words" (v 24). To become wise, one must listen to the wise (cf. also 23:7a) and learn from their experience and skill. Cf. Prov 1:8; 4:10, 20. An *a:b::b':a'* rhetorical pattern adds elegance to v 25: *I will pour out:by measure* (my spirit)::*in a careful way:I will impart* (my knowledge). Also the final words of v 25a and b rhyme: *rûḥî* (*my* spirit) and *dēʿî* (*my* knowledge). In v 25a, Ben Sira boldly employs words placed in the mouth of personified Wisdom in Prov 1:23: *"I will pour out* [Heb *ʾabbîʿâ,* same verb as here] to you my spirit [*rûḥî*]." The verb *nbʿ,* "to pour out," also occurs in 50:27c. For the images in v 25, cf. also Job 28:25; Prov 18:4; Sir 18:29; 39:6, 8; Isa 29:10.

The rest of the poem (vv 26–30) extols God's wisdom in ordering his creation so marvelously. From the first moment of creation God "assigned" to all "his works" their [appointed] tasks" (v 26; cf. NOTE); cf. Gen 1:1, 20, 25. "He ordered . . . what they were to do," lit., "He set in order his works" (v 27a). Gr *kosmeō*, "to order, arrange," is the verb from which derives the noun *kosmos*, which originally meant "order, set form," and later came to mean "the universe" because of its perfect "arrangement." Cf. Ps 104:24. The author of The Wisdom of Solomon (11:20) expresses a similar idea: "You [the Lord] have disposed all things by measure and number and weight." It is God who has arranged the "domains [of the heavenly bodies] from generation to generation" (v 27b); cf. 17:32; Gen 1:16, 18; Pss 103:22; 136:8–9. In the OT theology of creation, Yahweh is sovereign Lord of nature, and the elements of nature are mere creatures and not personalized forces to be feared or placated or worshipped. Everything in nature was created to exist in harmony and equilibrium with the rest of creation and to do precisely what the Lord had intended (v 27cd; cf. 43:10; Isa 40:26). All parts of nature function in their assigned places (v 28); that is to say, the heavenly bodies, because they have been set in order (v 27a), follow their prescribed courses without question and never interfere with each other. Cf. Pss 104:19; 148:5–6. After creating the heavens and their host, God turned his attention to, or "looked upon," "the earth and filled it with his good things" (v 29); cf. Gen 1:20–31; Ps 104:24, 28. The expression "all manner of life" in v 30a is similar to the LXX of Gen 1:21, 24. The point of the colon is that all life on earth is due to God's creative activity; cf. Ps 104:24–30. All life, however, must ultimately return into earth again (v 30b); cf. 40:11; Gen 3:19; Job 34:15; Ps 104:29; Qoh 3:20; 12:7.

The next poem, the longest of the section (17:1–4, 6–15, 17–20, 22–24), speaks of the creation of human beings, of the many gifts God has endowed them with, and of God's knowledge of all human acts and his recompense of human virtue and sin. Gen 2:7 and 3:19 are the texts on which v 1 is based; cf. also Ps 146:4. The creation of humankind from the earth explains human frailty, inconstancy, and incompatibility with divine commands and the penchant to transgress them (so Duesberg-Fransen, p. 165); cf. 8:5; 17:30–32. Though God allots human beings only a limited number of days (v 2a; cf. 18:9–10; Ps 90:10; Job 14:1–2; Isa 65:20), he has granted them authority "over all things else on earth" (v 2b; cf. Gen 1:28; 9:2; Ps 8:6–9; Wis 9:2–3). He has also endowed human beings "with a strength that befits them," Gr *kath' heautous* (v 3a). Ziegler, following Grotius and Rahlfs, emends the text to read *heauton*, "(like) his own." Smend (p. 155), Box-Oesterley (p. 375), and Duesberg-Fransen (p. 164) agree with the emendation, which in our judgment is uncalled for, since the reading of all the Gr MSS makes good sense. The point of 3a is that God has given human beings all the strength they need in order to fulfill the purposes of their creation, viz., to subdue the earth and to "have dominion over the fish of the sea, the birds of the air, and all the living things that move on the earth" (Gen 1:28). God made human beings "in [his] own image" (v 3b; cf. Gen 1:26–27)—the charter statement of human dignity and equality of all men, women, and children in the sight of God. The affirmation in v 4a is based on Gen 1:28 and esp. 9:2; v 4b, like v 2b, derives from Gen 1:28; Ps 8:6–9; Wis 9:2–3. As regards the inner Gr gloss in v 5, cf. NOTE. Smend (p. 156) quotes Grotius to the effect that this addition was inserted by a Stoic reader of the book, for Stoics used to speak of three other senses in addition to the usual five (sight, touch, smell, hearing, taste); the third extra sense, however, is omitted in the gloss.

God's splendid gifts to humankind are enumerated in vv 6–10. Sensory and psychological, intellectual and moral endowments (vv 6–8) the Creator has granted human beings so "that they may glory in his wondrous deeds and praise his holy name" (vv 9–10). In v 6a, Gr *diaboulion*, "discretion," is the same word the grandson employed to translate Heb *yeṣer* in 15:14b, in which text the word means "free will" (cf. COMMENT on 15:14). The arrangement of the various human endowments in v 6 is interesting: the first (discretion) and last (understanding heart) are intellectual-moral; the middle three (tongue, eyes, ears) are sensory-physical. Regarding the "understanding heart" (lit., a heart to understand), cf. 1 Kgs 3:9. Wisdom and knowledge are not human accomplishments but are gifts with which God fills people (v 7a). V 7b is a clear allusion to Gen 2:17 and 3:5, 22. Even the fear of the Lord is a divine gift, one of the purposes of which is to show human beings "the grandeur of his works" (v 8); cf. 18:4. To glory in God's "wondrous deeds" and to "praise his holy name" (vv 9–10) are an essential part of Israelite life and religious observance, i.e., of the fear of the Lord. G. von Rad (*Old Testament Theology*, vol. 1, pp. 369–70) writes: "Praise is man's most characteristic mode of existence: praising and not praising stand over against one another like life and death." Cf. vv 27–28; 15:9–10; 51:17, 22, 29.

In v 11, the "knowledge," which God "set before" (read Gr *proetheken* instead of *prosetheken* of all the MSS and versions) the Chosen People, is explained as "a law pledging life" (lit., the law of life); that is to say, the Law is Israel's true knowledge and wisdom, which no other society can match. Cf. 1:11–30 with COMMENT. "The law of life," a phrase that occurs also in 45:5d, is described in Deut 30:11–20; cf. Bar 4:1–4. The "everlasting covenant" (v 12a), which is called "the law that endures forever" in Bar 4:1b, is the covenant made on Sinai when God revealed "his commandments" (v 12b) to Moses; cf. Exod 19:2–20:17 and Deut 5:1–22. What the Israelites saw of God's "majestic glory" and heard of "his glorious voice" (v 13) is described in Exod 19:16–19 and 24:15–17; cf. 45:5; Isa 30:30. In v 14a, the injunction to "avoid all evil" is a summary of all the negative commandments, "Thou shalt not . . ."—especially the prohibitions against idolatry, false worship, and work on the sabbath, about which the first part of the Ten Commandments (Exod 20:1–11; Deut 5:6–15) is concerned. The "precepts about [our] neighbors" (v 14b) refer to the second part of the Decalogue (Exod 20:12–17; Deut 5:16–21). Thus v 14 alludes to the great commandments of the Law—to love God above all things (Deut 6:5) and to love our neighbor as ourself (Lev 19:18); cf. Matt 22:34–40; Mark 12:28–34; Luke 10:25–28; 1 John 4:21; Rom 13:8–10. Cf. J. De Fraine, "Het Loflied op de menselijke Waardigheid in Eccli 17,1–4," *BTFT* 11 (1950): 10–22; and H. Duesberg, "La Dignité de l'homme: Siracide 16,24–17,14," *BVC* 82 (1968): 15–21.

Some authors consider vv 15–24 as a separate poem—so Box-Oesterley (pp. 376–77); Spicq (pp. 653–54); Ziegler (pp. 203–4); and Duesberg-Fransen (pp. 166–67). These verses describe God's clear knowledge of human acts and thoughts and the divine retribution to be accorded to all men and women as they deserve. The Lord knows human "ways" because "they cannot be hidden from his eyes" (v 15); cf. Ps 90:8. In the Law revealed on Sinai, Yahweh traced out the "way" the Israelites should walk; cf. Deut 5:32–33; 8:6; 10:12; 11:22; 19:9; 26:17; 30:16. But as the gloss in GII (cf. NOTE) explains, the ways of human beings are "directed toward evils" rather than toward God. In v 17, Ben Sira refers either to the fact that Gentile nations have merely secular rulers whereas Israel has God himself as sovereign, or more probably to the belief that each of the pagan nations has an angel to act as God's intermediary in its behalf (cf. Deut 32:8; Dan 10:13–21), whereas Israel has no intermediary but has immediate access to God because Israel is "the Lord's own portion" (cf. Deut 32:9). The OT affirms that Israel was Yahweh's own "peculiar people," Heb ʿam sĕgullâ; cf. Exod 19:5; Deut 7:6; 14:2; 26:18; Ps 135:4; Mal 3:17. For the gloss (v 18) in GII, cf. NOTE. Whatever people do is "clear as the sun" to God (v 19a), who knows "their ways" (v 19b); cf. 16:17, 20–23; 23:19; Ps 94:11. Their "wickedness" and "sins" are also "before the Lord" (v 20); cf. Qoh 12:14; Ps 33:15; Isa 65:6; Jer 51:5; Dan 7:10. Cf. NOTE for the gloss (v 21) in GII.

A person's "goodness," Gr eleēmosynē (lit., almsgiving; cf. COMMENT on 3:14–15), on the other hand, "God cherishes like a signet ring," i.e., like something very precious (v 22a; cf. 49:11; Jer 22:24; Hag 2:23), and his "virtue [Gr charis], like the apple of his eye" (v 22b; cf. Deut 32:10; Ps 17:8; Prov 7:2; Zech 2:12). In 40:17, charis and eleēmosynē, rendering Heb ḥesed and ṣĕdāqâ, respectively, also refer to human virtue. The "signet ring" or "seal" (Gr sphragis, Heb ḥōtām) was hung by a cord about the neck (Gen 38:18) or worn on a finger of the hand (Jer 22:24); both customs are alluded to in Cant 8:6. The ḥōtām was used to attest a royal letter (1 Kgs 21:8) or to seal a precious article (Tob 7:14; 9:5). For the idea that God "cherishes" (Gr syntērēsei, lit., keeps, preserves) human "goodness" and "virtue," cf. Tob 12:12 and Acts 10:4. See NOTE regarding the extra colon found in GII. V 23 resumes the thought of v 20: God "will rise up" in judgment and repay sinners (v 23a). V 23b may be translated, lit.: "and their retribution he will render on their own head," a sentiment Ben Sira borrowed from Joel 4:4, 7, on the LXX of which the grandson modeled his Gr translation. Cf. also Ps 7:17; Jer 23:19; Ezek 22:31. In v 24, "the penitent" are those who "turn away" from their sinful ways and "turn back" (Heb šûb) to the Lord; cf. COMMENT on 4:26a and 5:7a. The "way back" (v 24a) is to divine grace and favor. Repentance is a central message of the prophets (cf., for example, Isa 31:6; 44:22; Jer 3:12, 14, 22; 18:11; 25:5; 35:15; Ezek 14:6; 18:30; 33:11; Hos 14:2) and of Jesus (cf. Luke 5:32; 15:7; Rev 2:5, 16, 21, 22; 3:3, 19). For the belief expressed in v 24a, cf. Ezek 33:11: "As I live, says the Lord Yahweh, I swear I take no pleasure in the death of the sinner, but rather in the sinner's turning away from his way, that he may live. Turn, turn from your evil ways! Why should you die, O house of Israel?" For the idea in v 24b, cf. Ezek 37:11-14. V 24 serves as a transition to the next poem.

Ben Sira opens the poem in vv 25-32 with a prophetic call to repentance. Vv 25-26 contain the various acts sinners must do and attitudes they must cultivate if conversion is to be sincere. "Return to the Lord" (v 25a; cf. 5:7; Mal 3:7) is the global invitation to repent. But one cannot return to the Lord unless one gives up sin and prays (cf. 39:5) and does one's best to minimize one's "offenses" (v 25b), which, owing to human weakness, are inevitable. To "turn to the Most High" means to "turn away from sin" (v 26a) and to "hate intensely what he loathes" (lit., the abomination; v 26b; cf. 15:13a). In 2 Chr 33:12-19, Manasseh is reported to have undergone a conversion by doing the things Ben Sira describes here. Cf. NOTE for the gloss that GII has between the two cola of v 26; regarding the idea that God "leads out of darkness into the light of life," cf. also Tob 14:10. In vv 27a and 28a, Ben Sira expresses the belief, which was normative up to his time, that "the netherworld," or Sheol (Gr Hades), was not a place of retribution after death; rather in Sheol, the dead—saints and sinners alike—shared a dark, listless, dismal existence separated from God; cf. Ps 88:4-7. Cf. COMMENT on 7:17 and 11:26 and INTRODUCTION, Part X, 4; see also A. A. Di Lella, CBQ 28 (1966): 143-46. Only the living can "offer their praise" to God (vv 27b and 28b); cf. Pss 6:6; 30:10, 88:11-13; 115:17-18; Isa 38:18-19. Thus, in vv 27-28, Ben Sira suggests good reasons why sinners should repent, viz., to stay alive so that they may glorify the Lord. V 28a compares the dead to "those who have never lived"—another strong denial of life after death. Syr omits the verse, probably because of this denial, which was contrary to the Christian belief in rewards and punishments after death; on the Christian origin of the Syriac Peshiṭta translation of Ben Sira, cf. INTRODUCTION, Part VIII, 3c.

In v 29, Ben Sira continues the theme of repentance by extolling the greatness of the Lord's "mercy" and "his forgiveness." Cf. Pss 86:5, 15; 103:8; 111:4; 117:2; 145:7-9; Joel 2:13; Jonah 4:2. God knows how weak and fragile human beings are, how they tend to be wayward and unfaithful; hence he is merciful to those who, having sinned, "return to him" (v 29b); cf. 8:5; Gen 6:5, 8:21; Ps 103:11–13; Jas 3:2. The point of v 30a seems to be that human beings are not as understanding, compassionate, and merciful as the Lord, for they are mortal (v 30b); cf. v 1; Ps 103:15–18. For v 30b, Syr reads: "nor is his [God's] thought like the thought of human beings"—cf. Isa 55:8–9; Jdt 8:16. In v 31, Ben Sira employs an analogy of peculiar logic to make his point: just as the sun, which is brightest of all, can be eclipsed, so "obscure" (lit., evil) are "the thoughts of flesh and blood." In more logical terms, the verse says: If the sun, most brilliant of the stars, can at times fail to give light, how much more can a human fail, who is but "flesh and blood." For similar metaphors, cf. Job 15:14–16; 25:4–6. V 32 continues the imagery of v 31a. "The hosts of highest heaven" (v 32a) are the sun, moon, and stars (cf. 24:2; 42:16–17; Deut 4:19; 17:3; Isa 34:4; Matt 24:29). God holds them "accountable" because the pagans and even unfaithful Israelites worshipped them as gods; cf. Isa 24:21 and Jer 8:2. In using the expression "the hosts of highest heaven," Ben Sira probably had in mind also the angels; cf. Job 38:7; Dan 12:3. The point of v 32, therefore, is that if the heavenly bodies and angels come under God's judgment, how much more do human beings, who are but "dust and ashes," a phrase used also in 10:9a and 40:3b (cf. COMMENT on 10:9a); cf. Job 4:17–21; 15:15–16; 25:4–6. God, however, does not judge human beings harshly but mercifully—a theme taken up in the next poem.

The last poem (18:1, 2a, 4–14) of this section is a hymn extolling the Lord as righteous and merciful judge. In contrast to human beings, who are "dust and ashes" (17:32b), the Lord is "the Eternal" (lit., the One who lives forever) and "the judge [cf. NOTE] of all alike" (v 1). Regarding the divine title "the One who lives forever," cf. Dan 4:31; 6:27; 12:17. For the sentiment of v 2a, cf. Ps 51:6. Cf. NOTE for an explanation of the gloss (vv 2b–3) in GII. In vv 4–7, Ben Sira states that it is impossible for men and women to appreciate the splendor and majesty of God as manifested in creation. The rhetorical questions in vv 4 and 5 make it clear that no one is capable of celebrating the Lord's works and majestic power in the measure they deserve. Cf. 1:3, 6; 42:17; Ps 145:3; Job 9:10. For the thought of v 6, cf. also 42:21. The point of v 7, which employs hyperbole to dramatize the conviction expressed in v 6, is that when a person "ends" contemplating "the wonders of the Lord" (v 6b; cf. Ps 77:12–13; 78:12) in order to "penetrate" them, he is "only beginning," and "when he stops" altogether, "he is still bewildered" by the impossibility of the task. The question in v 8a is an echo of Ps 8:5 that is found also in Ps 144:3 and Job 7:17. In view of God's utter transcendence and of human insignificance in the presence of divine majesty, "the good" and "the evil" in men and women are hardly worthy of consideration (v 8b); cf. Job 35:5–8. Vv 9 and 10 continue the idea of human smallness before God. Even if a person should live to be a hundred (v 9; cf. Ps 90:10), "these few years" are "like a drop of the sea's water [cf. Isa 40:15], like a grain of sand . . . among the days of eternity" (v 10). For a parallel to v 9, see *Phibis,* xvii 21 (Sanders, p. 71). Cf. 1:2; 17:2; Ps 90:3–6. For the addition after v 9 in GII, cf. NOTE.

Because human beings are so puny and short-lived, the Lord of the universe "is patient" with them "and showers his mercy upon them" (v 11). Being all-knowing and all-seeing, God "understands that their death [lit., overthrow] is grievous [lit., evil]"; hence "he forgives them all the more" (v 12). Cf. Ps 36:6–10. Vv 11 and 12 depict the tender love and mercy of God for men and women who are painfully conscious of their impermanence and mortality; cf. Matt 11:28. A person tends to "be merciful to his neighbor," but the Lord, who makes no distinctions, has mercy on "all flesh" (v 13ab). The Lord will be the "shepherd" of all his people, guiding (lit., bringing back) his flock by "reproving, admonishing, [and] teaching" them (v 13cd). Cf. 2 Macc 6:12–16; Wis 12:19–22. The beautiful image of the Lord as Shepherd derives from Isa 40:11; Ezek 34:11–16; Pss 23; 80:2. Jesus appropriates to himself the title of "Good Shepherd" in John 10:11–18; cf. 1 Pet 2:25; Heb 13:20; Rev 7:17. The Lord is especially "merciful to those who accept his guidance" (lit., instruction; cf. 1:27; 4:17; 6:18, 8:8) and "who are diligent in his precepts" (v 14; cf. Ps 119:20, 30, 43, 52, 62, 75, 102, 106, 108, 120, 164, 175). Such are the wise who fear the Lord by keeping his commands; cf. 1:11–30; 6:32–37; 15:1; 21:6; Prov 10:8. Thus this lengthy section opens with an exhortation to the wise (16:24) and closes with a remark about the mercy accorded to the wise (18:14). For further study of this passage, cf. L. Alonso Schökel, "The Vision of Man in Sirach 16:24–17:14," in J. G. Gammie et al., eds., *Israelite Wisdom: Theological and Literary Essays in Honor of Samuel Terrien,* pp. 235–45.

25. Prudential Warnings
(18:15–19:17)

18   15 My son, to your charity add no reproach,   G
         nor spoil any gift by harsh words.
     16 Like dew that abates a burning wind,
         so does a word transform a gift.
     17 Sometimes the word means more than the gift;
         both are offered by a kindly person.
     18 Only a fool upbraids before giving;
         a grudging gift wears out the expectant eyes.

     19 Be informed before speaking;
         before sickness prepare the cure.
     20 Before you are judged, examine yourself,
         and at the time of scrutiny you will meet with
                                           forgiveness.
     21 Before you fall, humble yourself;
         when you have sinned, show repentance.
         Delay not to forsake sins,   s
         neglect it not till you are in distress.
         Do not set a time for abandoning sin;
         remember that death will not delay.

     22 Let nothing prevent the prompt payment of your vows, G
         wait not to fulfill them when you are dying.
     23 Before making a vow have the means to fulfill it;
         be not one who puts the Lord to the test.
     24 Think of wrath and the day of death,
         the time of punishment when he will hide his face.
     25 Remember the time of hunger in the time of plenty,
         poverty and want in the day of wealth.
     26 Between morning and evening the weather changes;
         before the Lord all things are fleeting.

27 The wise is circumspect in all things;
    when sin is rife he keeps himself from wrongdoing.
28 Any learned person should make wisdom known;   S
    he who attains to her should declare her praise:
29 Those trained in her words must show their wisdom,
    pouring out proverbs in a careful way.

30 Go not after your lusts,   G
    but keep your desires in check.
31 If you satisfy your lustful appetites,
    they will make you the sport of your enemies.
32 Have no joy in the pleasures of a moment   C
    which bring on poverty redoubled;
33 Become not a glutton and a winebibber
    with nothing in your purse.

19 1 Whoever does so grows no richer;
    whoever wastes the little he has will be stripped bare.
2 Wine and women make the mind giddy,
    and the companion of prostitutes becomes reckless.   G
4 He who lightly trusts in them has no sense,
    and he who strays after them sins against his own life.
3 Rottenness and worms will possess him,
    for contumacious desire destroys its owner.   C

5 He who gloats over evil will meet with evil;   S
6   he who repeats an evil report has no sense.
7 Never repeat gossip,
    and you will not be reviled.
8 Tell nothing accusing to friend or foe;   G
    unless withholding it would be sinful, reveal it not,
9 For he who hears it will hold it against you,
    and in time become your enemy.
10 Let anything you hear die within you;
    be assured it will not make you burst.
11 When a fool hears something, he is in labor,
    like a woman giving birth to a child.
12 Like an arrow lodged in a person's thigh
    is gossip in the breast of a fool.

13 Admonish your friend—he may not have done it;
   and if he did, that he may not do it again.
14 Admonish your neighbor—he may not have said it;
   and if he did, that he may not say it again.
15 Admonish your friend—often it may be slander;
   every story you must not believe.
16 Then too, a person can slip and not mean it;
   who has not sinned with his tongue?
17 Admonish your friend before you break with him;
   give due place to the Law of the Most High.

Notes

18   28–29. For the language here, following Syr, compare the related passage 16:24–25.

29b. GII adds here the gloss "Better is confidence in the one Lord than clinging with dead heart to a dead idol."

33. GII follows this verse with "for you will be plotting against your own life"; cf. 19:4b.

19   4, 3. V 3 is missing from Syr, which has v 4a (but *in them* is not present in either G or Syr). For 4b, Syr has "The one who condemns himself, who will acquit?" which is 10:29a transposed here. The excerpt in MS C breaks off after 19:1, 2a, 3b (with 2b, 3a lacking). Two MSS of GII substitute "the one who is incontinent" for v 4's *he who strays,* and it is this limited clue that suggests relating v 4 to the context of vv 1–3 rather than to vv 5–12, with which it seems to have no connection. *(strays) after them* (the *prostitutes* of 2b) interprets 4b of GI in that sense; Lat is not helpful.

5. *will meet with evil=yērōaʿ;* Syr read this as from *rʿ* II, hence, "it will be the breaking of him"; G *katagnōsthēsetai* supposes *ydʿ.*

5, 6. Between these two lines, GII has two other lines apparently contrived to furnish, as 5b and 6a, parallels for each. They read: "But he who resists pleasures crowns his life" (compare perhaps 6:31); and: "he who controls his tongue will live without strife." In v 6, for *repeats=šōnēh=*Syr, GI read *śōnēʾ=*"hates," which obscures the sense.

8b. Both Syr and Lat read this line without the negative present in G, yielding "if you have a fault." G, *ei mē estin soi hamartia, unless* (withholding it) *would be sinful* (for you), seems to be based on the circumstances of Lev 5:1, according to which it would be sinful for a properly adjured witness to withhold damaging testimony. The other versions have oversimplified the special case by supposing a personal fault in the speaker rather than information detrimental to a third party. Cf. Segal.

17b. *give due place to the Law:* an allusion to Lev 19:17.

Comment

This section contains a series of minipoems filled with exhortations and wise observations about various activities in the life of the Israelite. There is little connection between the poems.

The first poem (vv 15–18), one of the shortest of the group, with only four bicola, deals with the art of gift-giving. The inspiration of this poem comes from the subject matter of the previous poem (18:1–14) on God's benevolence and mercy, which serve as a model for the courtesy and kindness men and women should show one another. In the maxim of v 15, Ben Sira manifests again his truly human sensitivity and refinement. Readers can easily identify with the wisdom of his words; for indeed many a gift has been spoiled "by harsh words" (v 15b). A kind word, however, can "transform a gift" (v 16b) like the "dew that abates a burning wind" (v 16a); cf. 43:22; Hos 13:15; Jonah 4:8. How one gives means more than what one gives (v 17a); both the courteous word and the gift "are offered by a kindly [or a charitable, gracious] person" (v 17b). Thus, if one is to be truly charitable, one must offer kind words as well as goods. The fool, however, "upbraids before giving" (v 18a), and the ungracious and "grudging" manner in which he gives his gift ruins the excitement and expectation of the recipient (v 18b); cf. 20:14–15. It is noteworthy that Ben Sira implies that graciousness is part of wisdom, and discourtesy a manifestation of folly. In Jas 1:5, God is said to give "generously and ungrudgingly to all"—it is this attitude in the art of giving that Ben Sira proposes.

The next poem (vv 19–21) gives a series of practical injunctions that are related to the thoughts about God's abundant forgiveness in 18:1–14. One should not speak unless one is adequately informed (v 19a). V 19b states that one should be prepared for sickness before it strikes. For v 19, Syr reads: "Before you fight, seek for yourself a helper, and before you become ill, seek for yourself a physician"—a reading preferred by Box-Oesterley (p. 380) and Duesberg-Fransen (p. 170). Cf. 48:12–15. The two aphorisms about the need for being prepared in v 19 seem to serve as introduction to vv 20–21. Thus the point of this poem is that just as one should be properly informed before speaking so as to avoid embarrassment (v 19a) and be prepared for illness so as to avoid it altogether or shorten it as much as possible (v 19b), so one should be ready for God's judgment by examining oneself (v 20a) and thereby "meet with [God's] forgiveness" (v 20b). V 21 develops this thought further.

In v 21a, "before you fall" is from Syr; G has "before you get sick." One prepares oneself for the inevitable "falls" all human beings are prone to by humbling oneself (v 21a); on the need for humility, cf. 1:27; 3:17–24; 4:8; 7:16–17; 10:26–28. Then when one sins, one should "show repentance" (v 21b), i.e., one should *turn away* from sin and *turn back* to God by seeking his forgiveness; cf. COMMENT on 4:26. Syr alone has v 21c–f, but then omits v 22. In v 21c–f, Ben Sira gives four more maxims urging that repentance be not neglected. V 21f is a repetition of 14:12a, but here the reminder about death is motivation for repenting of sin without delay, for sin brings on the sinner an untimely death; cf. Deut 28:15–20. Repentance is a key doctrine of Jewish and Christian faith. In the Babylonian Talmud, *Sanhedrin* 43b, for example, we read: "He who sincerely repents is doing as much as he who builds temple and altar, and brings all sacrifices" (cited in Box-Oesterley, p. 380). Cf. COMMENT on 17:24.

The next poem (vv 22–26) opens with two bicola about the need to be circumspect in making vows. If one makes a vow, one should fulfill it in due time (v 22a) and not wait till the time of death (v 22b); cf. Qoh 5:3; Num 30:3; Deut 23:22–24; Ps 50:14. One should not vow rashly (v 23a), for to make a vow and not keep it is to put "the Lord to the test" (v 23b); cf. Deut 6:16; Prov 20:25; Qoh 5:4–5; Mal 1:14. The rest of the poem is a reminder that the Lord holds men and women accountable for their religious and moral life. "Wrath" is the divine response to human infidelity, which then occasions an untimely death for the sinner (v 24a; cf. COMMENT on v 21f). "The day of death" (v 24a) is "the time of punishment" (v 24b); cf. 11:27–28, with COMMENT. When the Lord hides, or turns away, "his face," he repudiates and punishes the sinner; cf. Deut 31:17–21; 32:20–25; Ps 10:1. To "think of wrath" and "the time of punishment" can, therefore, be salvific, for it may motivate one who is tempted to compromise to remain faithful instead. V 25 continues the same idea: in time of plenty and of wealth one should remember that sin can result in "hunger" and "poverty"—two of the divine punishments the sinner was repeatedly told to expect; cf., for example, Deut 8:10–20; 28:31–34. The image about the changeability of the weather (v 26a) underscores how "before the Lord all things are fleeting" (v 26b), so that one should not become proud or think one is self-sufficient when one has been blessed with wealth and plenty (v 25); cf. Job 4:17–21; Ps 90:4–6; Luke 12:16–21.

The next poem, only three bicola (vv 27–29) in length, describes the attitude and conduct of the wise with regard to the questions discussed in the three previous poems (vv 15–18; 19–21; and 22–26). The wise are, of course, those who heed the exhortations Ben Sira writes in this section. Being "circumspect" or discreet (Gr *eulabēthēsetai;* the noun from this verb occurs in the LXX of Prov 28:14) "in all things," the wise always walk the way of the Lord and keep themselves "from wrongdoing" regardless of the outside pressure to give in to sin (v 27). To be wise means to keep the Law by fearing the Lord; cf. COMMENT on 1:11–30 and INTRODUCTION, Part X, 1. It is the responsibility of the wise to "make wisdom known" and to "declare her praise" (v 28) so that others may be encouraged to pursue her. Since the wise are "trained in her words" (cf. Prov 1:23; 13:13) they "must show their wisdom" by "pouring out proverbs in a careful way" (v 29), as Ben Sira is doing in this passage; cf. 20:30–31; Prov 18:4. In 39:6; 47:8; and 51:17, it is God himself who is praised as Source of wisdom. See NOTE for the gloss that GII adds after v 29b.

In the next poem (18:30–19:3), Ben Sira warns against sensual desires that are inordinate, hence unlawful. Syr opens the poem with "My son." Most Gr and Lat MSS have before v 30 the title "(On) self-control of the soul." V 30 serves as topic sentence of the poem. The following verses specify which "lusts" and "desires" in particular need to be held "in check" (v 30); cf. 2 Tim 2:22; Jas 1:14. Giving in to "lustful appetites" makes one "the sport of [one's] enemies" (v 31). A similar thought is expressed in 6:4; cf. also 42:11a–d. The reason why one should beware of "the pleasures of a moment" (v 32a) is that the sinful satisfaction of carnal desires brings financial ruin (cf. 9:6; Prov 5:10) and poor health together with untimely death (cf. Prov 2:16–19; 5:3–6, 11–12; 7:27), the "poverty redoubled" of v 32b. For the prohibition against gluttony and drunkenness (v 33a), cf. Deut 21:20 and Prov 23:20. The idea of drinking (and eating) "with nothing in your purse" (v 33b) brings to mind the lines of Henry Sambrooke Leigh (1837–83): "The rapturous, wild, and ineffable pleasure / Of drinking at somebody else's expense" ("Stanzas to an Intoxicated Fly"). For the addition after v 33b in GII, cf. NOTE. These two forms of overindulgence lead to poverty (19:1); cf. Prov 21:17 and 23:21. For the idea that wine as well as whores can be a source of evil (v 2), cf. 31:25–30; Hos 4:10–11; Prov 20:1; 31:3–5. See also *Phibis*, v 22 (Sanders, pp. 71–72). For the sense and arrangement of vv 4 and 3, in that order, see NOTE. It is the fool, the person with "no sense," who "lightly trusts in" prostitutes (v 4a), for such a person sins "against his own life" (v 4b), a thought already mentioned in 18:31–32. "Rottenness and worms will possess him," i.e., he will die an early death; cf. Gal 6:8. Cf. 10:11 for what happens to all people when they die. V 3b repeats 6:4a verbatim. Petrarch (1304–74) has a variant of the thought in v 3b: "A short cut to riches is to subtract from our desires" (*Epistolae de rebus familiaribus*, vii 10).

In the next poem (vv 5–12), Ben Sira warns against the evils of gossip. Not only is repeating gossip a wicked thing and a sign of folly (v 6), but to gloat over or rejoice in evil will result in evil for the perpetrator (v 5). For the two extra cola that GII has between vv 5 and 6, see NOTE. As a keen observer of the human scene, Ben Sira implies here that sins of the tongue as well as carnal desires are among the principal vices men and women are prone to; cf. 22:27–23:27 and 28:13–26. Gossipmongers, though they have a ready audience, are trusted by no one and reviled by all, for one never can be sure when one will become the subject of gossip from such persons—the point of v 7; cf. Prov 17:9; 25:9–10. Gossip is vicious because, as Alexander Pope (1688–1744) remarked: "At every word a reputation dies" (*The Rape of the Lock,* iii, 16). Gossip is tempting because it "is vice enjoyed vicariously" (Elbert Hubbard [1856–1915], *Philistine,* xix). What is said in v 7 is an echo of the famous saying of Hesiod (eighth century B.C.): "If you say a bad thing, you may soon hear a worse thing said about you" (*Works and Days,* 721). V 8a repeats the idea of v 7a. The point of v 8b is that one should not speak of another's faults unless by keeping silence one should become an accomplice in another's sin by withholding testimony after one has sworn to tell the truth (cf. NOTE). The person who hears the gossip "will hold it against you, and in time become your enemy" (v 9) for, as the Spanish proverb puts it, "Whoever gossips to you will gossip about you." The advice in v 10a to let any gossip "you hear die within you" is sound. The thought of v 10b derives from Job 32:18–19. When the fool hears gossip, "he is in labor, like a woman giving birth" (v 11); he simply cannot refrain from gossiping. Another colorful image (v 12a) suggests how powerful is the fool's urge to get out gossip once it lodges in his "breast" (lit., belly).

The last poem (vv 13–17) in this section is concerned with the fraternal correction one owes one's friend after hearing gossip about him. The imperative "admonish" (Gr *elegxon*) occurs from time to time in the five bicola. Vv 13–14 states delicately the situation one is often confronted with when one hears unsavory stories about friends. The gossip you heard may have no truth in it, but still it is wise to tell or "admonish" your friend about it, lest his reputation be hurt even more (vv 13a, 14a). And if he did (v 13b) or said (v 14b) what the gossip alleges of him, you should admonish him, "that he may not do it again" (v 13b) or "say it again" (v 14b). Often the malicious gossip you hear is nothing but slander (v 15a), which "you must not believe" (v 15b). "What some invent the rest enlarge" (Jonathan Swift [1667–1745], *Journal of a Modern Lady*). Cf. Deut 13:13–15; 17:4; 19:18. The charitable and courteous admonition one owes a friend in the circumstances described in vv 13–15 should be given in a spirit of mercy and kindness because the friend may have slipped and not meant it (v 16a). One should also be keenly aware of one's own weakness, and should be especially careful not to sin "with [one's] tongue" (v 16b); cf. 20:18a; 21:7(G); 25:8c; 28:26. Cf. John 8:7; Matt 7:1–5. You should admonish your friend "before you *break with* him" (v 17a; Gr *apeilēsai,* lit., threaten, but in the LXX of Gen 27:42 this verb renders Heb *mitnaḥēm,* which means "ease oneself [by taking vengeance]"; it is this Heb that probably lay at the basis of G; hence the translation here). But

above all, "give due place to the Law of the Most High" (v 17b), a reference
to Lev 19:17–18: "Though you may have to reprove your fellow man, do not
incur sin because of him. Take no revenge and cherish no grudge against your
fellow countrymen. You shall love your neighbor as yourself."

26. Wisdom and Folly in Word and in Deed
(19:18–20:32)

19 ^a

20 The whole of wisdom is fear of the Lord;   G
    complete wisdom is the fulfillment of the Law.^b
22 The knowledge of wickedness is not wisdom,
    nor is there prudence in the counsel of sinners.
23 There is a resourcefulness that is detestable,
    while the fool may be free from sin.   S
24 Better those with little understanding who fear God,   G
    than those of abounding intelligence who violate
                the Law.
25 There is a shrewdness, keen but dishonest,
    which turns to duplicity to win a judgment.
26 There is the wicked who is bowed in grief,
    but is full of guile within;
27 He bows his head and feigns not to hear,
    but when not observed, he will take advantage of
                you:

---

^a 18 Fear of the Lord is the source of a welcome;   GII
    and wisdom from him obtains love.
19 Knowledge of the Lord's commandments is life-giving
                instruction;
    those who do what pleases him will harvest the fruit of
             the tree of immortality.

^b 20c and awareness of his universal sovereignty.
21 The slave who says to his master, "What pleases you I will
                not do,"
    even if afterward he does it, provokes the one who has
             him in his care.

28 Even if lack of strength keeps him from sinning,
    when he finds the opportunity he will do harm.
29 One can tell a person by his appearance;
    the prudent is known as such when first met.
30 A person's attire, his hearty laughter, and his gait
    proclaim him for what he is.

20   1 An admonition can be untimely,
    and a person may be wise to hold his peace.
2 An admonition is too good to be resented,
3   for one who admits his fault will be kept from
                    disgrace.
4 Like a eunuch lusting for intimacy with a maiden
    is he who does right under compulsion.
5 One person is silent and is thought wise;   C
    another, for being talkative, is disliked.
6 One person is silent because he has nothing to say;
    another is silent, biding his time.
7 The wise is silent till the right time comes,
    but a boasting fool ignores the proper time.   G
8 He who talks too much is detested;
    he who pretends to authority is hated.

9 Some misfortunes bring success,
    some things gained are a person's loss.
10 Some gifts do no one any good,
    and some must be paid back double.
11 Humiliation can follow fame,
    while from obscurity a person can lift up his head.
12 A person may purchase much for little,
    but pay for it seven times over.
13 A wise speaker makes himself accepted,
    but fools' blandishments are poured out in vain.
14 A gift from a rogue will do you no good,
    for in his eyes his one gift is equal to seven.
15 He gives little and criticizes often,
    and like a crier he shouts aloud.
  He lends today, he asks it back tomorrow;
    hateful indeed is such a person.
16 The fool says, "I have no friends,
    nor thanks for my generosity";

Those who eat his bread, with mocking tongue
17   again and again laugh him to scorn.

18 Lost footing is not as bad as a slip of the tongue;
    that is why the downfall of the wicked comes so
                                                quickly.
19 A delicacy served up insipid is the tale untimely told;   s
    the heedless are always ready to offer it.   G
20 A proverb when spoken by a fool is unwelcome,
    for he does not utter it at the proper time.

21 A person through want may be unable to sin;
    when he comes to his rest he need not have regrets.
22 One may destroy oneself through shame,   C
    and bring on one's own ruin by foolish posturing.
23 One may give false hopes to a friend out of shame,
    and have him for an enemy needlessly.

24 A lie is a foul blot in a person,   G
    yet it is constantly on the lips of the heedless.
25 Better a thief than an inveterate liar,
    yet both will suffer disgrace;
26 A liar's way leads to dishonor,
    his shame remains ever with him.

27 A wise speaker advances himself;
    a prudent person pleases the great.
28 He who works his land has a heaping yield;
    he who pleases the great can make amends for guilt.
29 Favors and gifts blind the eyes;
    like a muzzle over the mouth they silence reproof.
30 Hidden wisdom and unseen treasure—
    of what value is either?
31 Better the one who hides his folly
    than the one who hides his wisdom.[a]

---

[a] 32 It is better to await the inevitable while serving the Lord   GII
    than to be the ungoverned helmsman for the careening of
                                                one's life.

Notes

19   18–22. GII here clusters several glosses around the beginning of a new section of Ben Sira's text (vv 20, 22).

23b. *free from sin* = Syr; G = "lacking in wisdom."

25c. GII adds the gloss "and there is the wise who judges justly."

20   3. *disgrace* = *ḥesed* II, cf. 41:22 (M); G's *elattōseōs* supposes *ḥōser*.

4. This verse appears again in GI and Syr with some variation as 30:20, where it is attested in two separate forms in MS B. In the present context, a case could be made for reading it before 19:28.

5b. *for being talkative* = *bĕrōb* *(śîaḥ)* = Syr; MS C has *bĕrîb* *(śîaḥ)*; G = *mĕrōb*.

7b. *a boasting fool* = GI. MS C has no equivalent for *boasting;* its form of this line is reflected in GII as an addition to 18:27. From GI, Syr, and Lat, it is not clear what qualification is to be added to *fool* here, though each supposes an added term.

8b. GII adds "How good it is to show repentance when rebuked; for thus you will flee deliberate sin." This seems a paraphrase of v 3 as it has been understood above.

13. MS C has a secondary form of this verse after its citation of 37:26. For discussion, cf. Rüger, pp. 2–3; he argues against *en oligois*, which Ziegler has taken from GII. V 13a seems to have been influenced (also in MS C) by an expanded form of 27a.

14a. After this line, GII adds "and likewise that [gift] from a miser out of some need of his."

17. After this line, GII has "For he did not hold in esteem his having what he had, and not having it is all the same to him."

19. *A delicacy served up insipid:* the image in Syr is quite specific, in the much expanded rendering "Just like the fatty tail (of a sheep), which cannot be eaten without salt, is the word untimely spoken." The special portion reserved by Samuel for Saul at a feast (1 Sam 9:24) included the fatty tail for which Near Eastern sheep were noted; that text has been obscured in the extant Heb because of a seeming conflict with the laws of sacrifice in Exod 29:22; Lev 3:9; 7:3; 8:25; 9:19. See Peters (1913); Segal. Syr does not have 19b, which in G is identical with 24b. The Gr of 19a has "[Like] an unpleasant man [is] an untimely tale."

27. A heading, "Proverbial Sayings," precedes this verse in G (later recensions omit it); it appears also (garbled) in Syr. It is an inappropriately placed gloss.

29a. *blind the eyes:* GI adds "of the wise"; Lat and Bohairic add "of judges"; Syr has neither of these glosses.

30–31. These verses recur in 41:14–15 already in G, where the two halves of 41:16 are separated by them. M (in chap. 41) has the Heb form of the two verses without the confusion that attends the Gr (and Lat) texts; so does Cairo MS B.

32. This verse is present in a single Gr manuscript (248). The image in 32b is that of a charioteer rather than a navigator; the vehicle is hurtling aimlessly.

Comment

This section on the nature of true wisdom and folly contains several loosely connected poems. The expression "the Law" in vv 17b and 20b serves as a *mot crochet* that links this section to the previous one (18:15–19:17).

GII inserts two bicola (vv 18–19) before, and adds three cola (vv 20c–21) after, the opening bicolon (v 20) of this new section; cf. NOTE. "The fruit of the tree of immortality" (v 19b) is a clear reference to a blessed afterlife (cf. Rev 22:19)—a doctrine foreign to the thought of Ben Sira. Cf. COMMENT on 7:17; 11:26; and INTRODUCTION, Part X, 4. In v 20, Ben Sira again equates "wisdom" with "fear of the Lord" and "fulfillment of the Law." Cf. COMMENT on 1:11–30; 6:32–37; 15:1; 21:6. V 21 in GII is a Christian interpolation based on Matt 21:30. The Greeks, who gloried in their knowledge of philosophy, science, and technology, considered themselves wise. But Ben Sira asserts: Not all knowledge is wisdom (v 22a), nor is "the counsel of sinners" (cf. Wis 1:3–5) prudence (v 22b); cf. Ps 1:1. For a certain type of "resourcefulness" (Gr *panourgia*) is "detestable" (lit., an abomination). *Panourgia* (v 23a) means, lit., "ability to do all things," hence, "craftiness, *savoir faire.*" For the Jew, such an attitude is indeed an "abomination," for it leads to arrogance and an attitude of total self-sufficiency, which are contrary to authentic religion. Cf. 21:12b; 23:1. There is, however, a "resourcefulness" that is quite legitimate; cf., for example, Prov 1:4a, where *panourgia* is used by the LXX to translate Heb *'ormâ,* "prudence, skill," a noun in parallel with *da'at,* "knowledge," and *mĕzimmâ,* "purpose, discretion." In contrast to the sinner who is clever and resourceful (v 23a) there is "the fool" who is "free from sin" (v 23b). The point of v 23 is that it is better to be considered "a fool" in the eyes of others but "free from sin" in the eyes of God than to be a clever person who is an abomination. V 24 restates the thought of v 23: it is better to be less intelligent and to "fear God" than to be very intelligent and to "violate the Law." This short poem is important for an understanding of Ben Sira's view that wisdom is essentially a practical matter of fearing the Lord (vv 20a and 24a) and keeping the Law (v 20b), and not a speculative matter of intelligence or schooling alone (vv 22–24). See INTRODUCTION, Part X, 1.

The next poem (vv 25–30) is connected to the previous one by the *mot crochet panourgia* (v 25a), now translated "shrewdness" (cf. above). It deals with the attitudes and conduct of the wicked who are crafty. Then as now, people often consider a person to be shrewd, if through dishonesty and "duplicity" he or she knows how "to win a judgment" (v 25b), but God considers such injustice an abomination (cf. Exod 23:6–8; Ps 18:27–28 = 2 Sam 22:27–28). For the gloss after v 25b, cf. NOTE. Even when the wicked are "bowed in grief," one should be on guard, for they are hypocrites, "full of guile within" (v 26); cf. 12:11ab; Ps 42:10; Mal 3:14. "To show an unfelt sorrow is an office / Which the false man does easy" (Shakespeare, *Macbeth* [1605–6], II iii 142). "With devotion's visage / And pious action we do sugar o'er / The devil himself" (Shakespeare, *Hamlet* [1600], III i 47). With head bowed, the wicked schemer pretends "not to hear" what is going on about him, "but when not observed, he will take advantage of you" (v 27). Hence the wily hypocrite cannot be trusted even when he seems humbled. "Spread yourself upon his bosom publicly, whose heart you would eat in private" (Ben Jonson, *Every Man Out of His Humour* [1599], iii 1). If the cunning hypocrite keeps from sinning for "lack of strength" (v 28a), when the occasion presents itself "he will do harm" (v 28b). In v 29a, Ben Sira affirms that a person can be known by his appearance. (Apparently he did not subscribe to the old adage "You can't tell a book by its cover.") After stating that "the prudent is known as such when first met" (v 29b), Ben Sira lists three things that "proclaim [a person] for what he is" (v 30b): his "attire, his hearty laughter [lit., laughter of the teeth], and his gait" (v 30a). Evidently Ben Sira believes these three things will enable one to judge whether others are hypocrites (vv 26–28) or "prudent" persons (v 29b). Cf. 13:25–26; 21:20; 2 Macc 6:18–28; 15:12–13.

The next poem (20:1–8) gives wise comments and observations on the value of silence and of appropriate speech. Though admonitions may be called for in certain circumstances (cf., for example, the cases discussed in 19:13–17), there are other occasions when "an admonition can be untimely" (lit., not in season) (v 1a). Under such circumstances, the wise will keep silent (v 1b). "We need a reason to speak, but none to keep silent" (Pierre Nicole [1625–95), *De la paix avec les hommes,* ii 1). "A sage thing is timely silence, and better than any speech (Plutarch, "The Education of Children," *Moralia* [ca. A.D. 100]). V 2 may also be translated: "It is much better to admonish than to be angry [GII adds: secretly]." The reason is that the one admonished may admit "his fault" and thus "be kept from disgrace" (v 3; see NOTE here and on v 8b); cf. 19:13–14. The point of v 4 is that just as a eunuch cannot deflower a virgin, so a sinner cannot be compelled to do what is upright. The aphorism in v 5a has many echoes. "Let a fool hold his tongue and he will pass for a sage" (Publilius Syrus, *Moral Sayings* [first century B.C.], 914), which is a variant of Prov 17:28: "Even a fool, if he keeps silent, is considered wise." "Silence is the wit of fools" (Jean de La Bruyère [1645–96], *Les Caractères*). "Silence is golden." "Blessed is the man who, having nothing to say, abstains from giving us wordy evidence of the fact" (George Eliot [Mary Ann Evans, 1819–80], *The Impressions of Theophrastus Such,* iv). Nobody likes a babbler (vv 5b and 8a); cf. 22:6a. "They always talk, who never think" (Matthew Prior, "Upon This Passage in Scaligerana" [1697]). V 6a is a variation of the idea expressed in v 5a: having nothing to say, a person remains silent (6a) and is thus thought to be wise (v 5a). V 6b and v 7a are in synonymous parallelism: the wise remain silent "till the right time comes." Cf. Prov 15:23; 25:11; 26:7. "Let your speech be better than silence, or be silent" (Dionysius the Elder [fourth century B.C.]). But the "boasting fool [hendiadys; lit., the braggart and the fool; cf. NOTE] ignores the proper time" (v 7b). Cf. 20:20; Qoh 3:7. V 8b adds another dimension to the thought expressed in vv 5b and 8a: the babbler is despised also because he "pretends to authority," presumably the authority of the wise who have the right to speak; cf. Ps 12:4–5.

The next poem (vv 9–17) contains perceptive remarks about the appearances of things. The observation in v 9 rings true in the experience of many: what at first seemed to be a "misfortune" later brought "success," and what seemed to be a "gain" turned out to be a person's "loss." The end result of a situation determines whether it is a success/gain or loss/misfortune. The following verses give illustrations. Even a gift may prove to be expensive because the giver expects double in return (v 10). "That is the bitterness of a gift, that it deprives us of our liberty" (Thomas Fuller, *Gnomologia* [1732], 4359). "You pay a great deal too dear for what's given freely" (Shakespeare, *The Winter's Tale* [1610–11], I i 18). The thought of v 11 has several biblical counterparts: 1 Sam 2:4–9; Pss 75:8; 113:7–9; Luke 1:51–53. V 12 is a timely comment about the price one may ultimately pay for what one thinks was at first a bargain. In v 12b, the "seven times," according to the biblical symbolism of the number being employed, means many times; cf. 7:3; Gen 4:15, 24. The acceptance that the wise speaker wins for himself (v 13a; cf. NOTE) is the antithesis of the abhorrence one feels for the fool "who talks too much" (v 8a). Even the "blandishments" or pleasantries (Gr *charites,* lit., "kindnesses") of the fool are utterly wasted (v 13b). The "wise speaker" is again discussed in v 27.

When a "fool" (Gr *aphrōn,* here translated "rogue") gives you a gift, he does you no good, for he thinks his one gift is worth seven (v 14). The number "seven" in v 14b comes from Lat and Syr (cf. v 12b); G has "many." Cf. v 10. The fool thinks that the "little" he gives entitles him to criticize much (Gr *polla;* v 15a). Moreover, his criticisms are not quiet and private but loud and public (v 15b). Because he is an impatient lender who expects quick repayment (v 15c), he is "hateful" (v 15d; GII and Syr add "to God and to men"— cf. 10:7a). The reason why the fool has no friends or thanks for his generosity (v 16ab) is that he always seeks to be repaid for any gift he gives; cf. v 10. Even those who share his table mock him for his foolish attitudes about generosity (vv 16c–17); compare the sentiment expressed in Ps 41:10. Cf. NOTE for the two extra cola GII adds after v 17.

The next three verses (18–20) form a minipoem about inappropriate speech. The maxim in v 18a is an echo of the proverb attributed to Zeno of Citium, the Stoic (335–263 B.C.): "Better to slip with the foot than with the tongue" (cited by Diogenes Laërtius, *Lives and Opinions of Eminent Philosophers*, vii 26 [third century of our era]). As quick as a slip of the tongue is "the downfall of the wicked" (v 18b). For the literal translation of v 19a and its background, cf. NOTE. The colorful image used to deride "the tale untimely told" (v 19a) would be especially meaningful to Near Eastern people who prized as a delicacy the fatty tail of a sheep. Cf. Job 6:6. It is only "the heedless," "the uneducated, ignorant" (Gr *apaideutoi*) who tell such tales (v 19b). Even a proverb from the mouth of a fool loses its worth because it is out of place (v 20); cf. 15:9; Prov 26:7, 9.

The next poem (vv 21–23) contains maxims about poverty and shame. Poverty may help one avoid the occasions of sin (v 21a) so that at the end of the day one "need not have regrets" (v 21b). Cf. 19:28. For the thought of vv 22–23, cf. 4:21; 41:14–42:8. V 22b may be translated, lit.: "and destroy oneself by folly of face." Ben Sira may be referring to the activity of those Jews who in order to gain social acceptance and economic advantage compromised their religious faith by becoming Hellenized (= "foolish posturing"); cf. COMMENT on 4:20–22 and INTRODUCTION, Part II. Cf. also Luke 9:24–26. In v 23, the reason why one may turn a friend into "an enemy needlessly" is that one either gives promises that one cannot fulfill or raises "false hopes" "out of shame."

The next poem, which like the previous two is only three verses in length (24–26), deals with the evils of lying, a subject Ben Sira discusses also in 7:13 and 25:2; cf. Prov 6:16–19; Ps 5:7. Though "a lie is a foul blot in a person, it is continually in the mouth of the heedless [or uneducated, ignorant]" (v 24) (Gr *en stomati apaideutōn endelechisthēsetai,* the same words found in v 19b). Even a thief is preferable to "an inveterate liar," though to be sure, "both will suffer disgrace" (v 25). In 5:14, the thief and the two-faced (or double-tongued; see COMMENT) are also said to be the objects of disgrace. Dishonor and shame are ever present to the liar (v 26). "In plain truth, lying is an accursed vice. We are not men, nor have other tie upon one another, but by our word" (Montaigne, "Of Liars," *Essays* [1580–88]).

The next poem (vv 27–31; cf. NOTE on v 27) contains various maxims about the wise and the prudent, and the dangers of gifts and the uselessness of hidden wisdom. In v 27a, "a wise speaker" (Gr *ho sophos en logois*) is the same expression as in v 13a (cf. NOTE). The "prudent person" (v 27b), in synonymous parallelism with "a wise speaker," "pleases the great"—a reference to Jewish sages at the court of the Gentile rulers of Palestine (so Smend, pp. 187–88). The idea expressed in v 27b occurs also in the romance of the successful or wise courtier. Several examples of this literary genre are found in the OT: Joseph at the court of Pharaoh (Genesis 37–41); Mordecai in the Book of Esther; Aḥiqar at the court of Esarhaddon (Tob 1:22); and Daniel at the courts of Nebuchadnezzar (Daniel 1–4), of Belshazzar (Daniel 5), and of Darius the Mede (Daniel 6). Cf. L. F. Hartman and A. A. Di Lella, *The Book of Daniel,* AB 23, pp. 55–61. In v 28, Ben Sira compares the diligent farmer who "has a heaping yield" with the wise "who pleases the great" at court and can thus "make amends for guilt," i.e., the displeasure of the foreign rulers because of some Jewish practice or custom incompatible with the Hellenization policy of the crown. Cf. Dan 1:5–20; 3:4–23, 27[94]–30[97]; 6:5–29; Prov 14:35; 16:13–14; 22:11. In v 29a, after "eyes" G adds "of the wise," a gloss (see NOTE) based on Deut 16:19. For the thought of v 29a, cf. Exod 23:8; Deut 16:19. The taking of bribes was severely condemned in the OT; cf. Prov 15:27; 17:23. It is the responsibility of the wise to reprove the unlearned and the young. Gifts tend to "silence reproof" (v 29b); hence it is risky for the wise to accept them. Vv 30–31 (cf. NOTE) speak of the futility of "hidden wisdom." These verses are related to v 29b in that the wise who remain silent hide their wisdom; cf. Matt 25:14–30. As regards the extra bicolon found in Codex 248, cf. NOTE.

27. Sin and Folly of Various Kinds
(21:1–22:18)

21 1 My son, if you have sinned, do so no more,
    and for your past sins pray to be forgiven.
2 Flee from sin as from a serpent
    that will bite you if you go near it;
  Its teeth are lion's teeth,
    destructive of human souls.
3 Every offense is a two-edged sword;
    when it cuts, there can be no healing.
4 Panic and pride wither wealth away;
    it is thus the household of the proud is uprooted.
5 Prayer from the lips of the poor is heard at once,
    and justice is quickly granted him.
6 Whoever hates correction walks the sinner's path,
    but whoever fears the Lord repents in his heart.
7 Widely known is the ready speaker,
    but the wise knows when he is at fault.
8 Whoever builds his house with another's money
    is collecting stones for his funeral mound.
9 A band of criminals is like a bundle of tow;
    it will end in a blazing fire.
10 The path of sinners is smooth stones
    that end in the depths of the netherworld.

11 Whoever keeps the Law controls his impulses;
    whoever is perfect in fear of the Lord has wisdom.
12 He can never be taught who is not shrewd,
    but one form of shrewdness is thoroughly bitter.

13 The knowledge of the wise wells up in abundance,
    and his counsel is a life-giving spring;

14 A fool's mind is like a broken cistern:
   no knowledge at all can it hold.

15 When the intelligent hears words of wisdom
   he approves them and adds to them;
   The wanton hears them with distaste,
   and casts them behind his back.

16 A fool's chatter is like a load on a journey,
   but there is charm to be found on the lips of the
                                              wise.
17 The views of the prudent are sought in an assembly,
   and his words are taken to heart.

18 Like a house in ruins is wisdom to a fool;
   to the stupid, knowledge is incomprehensible
                                          chatter.
19 Like fetters on the legs is learning to a fool,
   like a manacle on his right hand.
21 Like a chain of gold is learning to the wise,
   like an armlet on his right arm.

22a The fool steps boldly into a house,
23b   while the well-bred person remains outside;
23a A boor peeps through the doorway of a house,
22b   but a tactful person keeps his glance cast down.   S
24 It is rude for one to listen at a door;   G
   a cultured person would be overwhelmed by the
                                        disgrace of it.

20 A fool raises his voice in laughter,
   but the prudent at the most smiles gently.
25 The lips of the arrogant talk of what is not their   GII
                                              concern,
   but the words of the prudent are carefully weighed.   G
26 Fools' thoughts are in their mouths,
   the words of the wise are in their hearts.

27 When the godless curses his adversary,
   he really curses himself.

28 A slanderer besmirches himself,
and is hated by his neighbors.

22   1 The sluggard is like a filthy stone
so vile that everyone hisses at it.
2 The sluggard is like a lump of dung;
anyone who picks it up scours his hand.

3 An unruly son is his father's shame;
if it be a daughter, she was born for his disrepute.
4 A sensible girl will be a treasure to her husband;
a shameless one is her father's grief.
5 A hussy shames her father and her husband;
by both she is despised.

6 Like a song in time of mourning is inopportune talk,
but lashes and discipline are at all times wisdom.[a]
9 Teaching a fool is like gluing a broken pot,
or like disturbing someone in the depths of sleep;
10 He talks with a slumberer who talks with a fool,
for when it is over, he will say, "What was that?"

11 Weep over the dead, for his light has gone out;
weep over the fool, for sense has left him.
Weep the more gently over the dead, for he is at rest;
but worse than death is the life of a fool.
12 Seven days of mourning for the dead,
but for the fool, a whole lifetime.

13 Speak but seldom with the stupid,
be not the companion of a brute;
Stay clear of him lest you have trouble
and be spattered when he shakes himself;

---

[a] 7 Children whose upbringing leads to a wholesome life   GII
veil over the ignoble origins of their own parents.
8 Children whose pride is in scornful misconduct
besmirch the nobility of their own family.

> Turn away from him and you will find rest
> and not be wearied by his lack of sense.

14 What is heavier than lead—
>   what but "Fool" is the name for it?

15 Sand and salt and an iron lump
>   are less of a burden than the stupid.

16 Masonry bonded with wooden beams
>   is not loosened by an earthquake;
> Neither is a resolve constructed with careful
>   deliberation
> shaken in a moment of fear.

17 A resolve that is based on prudent understanding
>   is like the carved embellishment on a smooth wall.

18 Small stones lying on an open height
>   will not remain when the wind blows;
> Neither can a timid resolve based on foolish plans
> withstand fear of any kind.

Notes

21   4b. *uprooted* = Lat and Syr; thus (*ekrizōthēsetai*) Smend and Ziegler restore GI, which in the manuscripts has the same verb as in 4a (*erēmōthēsetai*).

7. *ready speaker* = "one wise (= skilled) with his tongue"; the description is ironic. *when he is at fault:* either the *ready speaker* or, more likely, the *wise* himself.

13–14. These verses echo the language of Jer 2:13; for *cistern* the Lat (*vas confractum*, "a broken jar") obscures this, and the Gr is at best ambiguous, cf. Prov 5:15 LXX.

13a. *wells up:* with Syr, which read *mabbûaʿ*, "well, source" where G read *mabbûl*, "flood."

18. *house in ruins:* Syr reads "prison," which may be the original; for *incomprehensible chatter*, Syr has "like fiery coals." The Gr speaks of the wisdom *of* the fool, the knowledge *of* the stupid; Syr and the context call for how wisdom appears *to* the fool, how knowledge is seen by him. Since the terms used for comparison by G and Syr do not provide us with a parallel pair, the precise imagery of the lost Heb verse seems beyond recovery.

19, 21. These verses are a matching pair, like 13–14; 15ab, cd; 16–17. V 20, here transposed before v 25, does not belong between them, though both G and Syr have it in that place.

21a. *chain of gold:* G does not specify the nature of the ornament; Syr has "armlet," transposed from 21b. The *chain* (Gen 41:42) and the *armlet* (2 Sam 1:10) were princely insignia.

22b, 23b. G and Syr both transpose these lines: the parallels with 22a, 23a require the order given here. 22b, *tactful* supposes G's *polypeiros* = *ʾîš mĕzimmôt* of the citation in *Pirqēʾ dĕrabbēnû haqqādôš* 14; cf. Smend (1906), Vattioni.

20b. *at the most* is interpretive expansion in G.

25a. *arrogant* = *zēdîm,* cf. Syr, "the wicked man"; G supposes *zārîm. what is not their concern* is an attempt by GII to restore a damaged text: GI "these things" is meaningless; Syr may reflect a text meaning "(according to) his whim."

22   3b. *disrepute* supposes *ḥesed* in the pejorative sense, as in Syr; so in 41:22 (MS B^ms, M). G and Syr read *ḥeser/ḥōser,* "poverty."

4a. *be a treasure to* supposes *tanḥîl;* G read *tinḥal,* and Syr lacks the verse.

7-8. These verses, secondary in G, are an expansion lacking the concrete imagery Ben Sira employs consistently in the context into which they have been placed.

11ab. The syntax followed is that of GII (*synesis*) and Lat; in GI (*synesin*) the dead and the fool have left behind them, respectively, the light and good sense.

12b. *for the fool:* G and Lat have "for the wicked fool," or "for the fool and the wicked." This probably represents a duplication of the term for *worse* in 11d.

13b. *of a brute:* after this, GII adds "for he will treat you with total and callous disregard."

17b. *carved:* supposes *glymmatos* (with Smend, Ziegler) = Syr for the *psammōtos* of the manuscripts.

Comment

This section on the various kinds of sin and folly opens with two poems (21:1–21), each containing eleven bicola, for a total of twenty-two lines—a characteristic feature of Ben Sira's poetry. The rest of the material is divided into shorter units mostly of two or three bicola; a ten-bicolon poem (22:13–18) concludes the section.

The opening poem (21:1–10) begins with "my son," which usually is found at the start of a new unit. The first four bicola (vv 1–3) speak about sin in general; vv 4, 6–9 give examples of different types of sin; and the poem ends with a general comment on the outcome of the sinner (v 10). It may be significant that the middle bicolon of the poem (v 5) affirms that the prayer of the poor is efficacious and justice is granted him. The poem opens with an exhortation to stop sinning and to pray for past sins (v 1). The translation "(pray) to be forgiven" is interpretive, as is the Lat *(deprecare) ut tibi remit-tatur.* Cf. 17:25. V 2a alludes to the serpent who tempted the woman in the Garden of Eden (Gen 3:1–5). As regards v 2b, Prov 23:32 compares overin-dulgence in wine to the bite of a serpent. For the lion imagery of v 2c, cf. 27:10 and Joel 1:6. The statements in 1 Pet 5:8—"Stay sober and alert. Your opponent the devil is prowling like a roaring lion looking for someone to devour"—are an allusion to v 2. The lethal capability of "a two-edged sword" (v 3) was proverbial; cf. Judg 3:16; Prov 5:4; Ps 149:6–7; Heb 4:12; Rev 1:16; 2:12. In vv 2–3, Ben Sira employs the powerful images of serpent, lion, and two-edged sword to evoke in his readers a horror of sin. In v 4a, the Gr noun *kataplēgmos* is a hapax legomenon in the LXX. As Smend (p. 189) points out, the word may have a transitive or an intransitive meaning; hence, either "intimidation, striking panic (in others)," or "panic (in oneself)." In the former sense, the wicked instill fear in those with whom they deal; in the latter sense, the wicked themselves are in "panic" over what to do with their wealth or how to protect it. In either sense, *kataplēgmos,* like pride, is inap-propriate and only hastens the loss of one's wealth. The thought of v 4b is derived from Prov 15:25. In composing v 4, Ben Sira may have also had in mind the sad case of Rehoboam in 1 Kgs 12:12–19 (=2 Chr 10:12–19). In contrast to the proud and wealthy who will suffer adversity are the poor whose prayer "is heard at once" (lit., comes to his [God's] ears) (v 5a), and for whom justice "is quickly granted" (v 5b); cf. Ps 17:1–2.

In v 6a, Ben Sira again speaks of those who walk the sinner's path and thus hate "correction"; cf. v 10 and 32:17. On the need for "correction, discipline" (Heb *mûsār*), cf. COMMENT on 6:18–22. The antithesis of the arrogant sinner is the person "who fears the Lord" and accordingly "repents in his heart" (v 6b); for a discussion of the concept of repentance in the OT, cf. COMMENT on 4:26a; 17:24; and 18:21. V 7a may be translated, lit.: "Widely known is he that is mighty in tongue" (cf. NOTE); the description is ironic, as is clear from the contrast with "the wise" (v 7b) who has the humility to recognize and confess "when he is at fault." "To build one's house" (v 8a) is a metaphor that means "to become wealthy"; cf. Ps 49:17. The colon refers to the amass-ing of wealth by oppressing the defenseless poor; cf. 40:13–14. By so doing, the unjust rich are building their "funeral mound" (v 8b), i.e., they shall die prematurely as punishment for their exploitation of the disadvantaged; cf. COMMENT on 7:17. The reading "funeral mound" *(chōma)* is from GII (the *L'*-group of MSS) and Syr; GI reads: *ch(e)imona,* "winter." An early death also awaits "criminals" (Gr *anomoi,* lit., the lawless, the ungodly), who are compared to "a bundle of tow" that will "end in a blazing fire" (v 9). Cf. Isa 1:31; Judg 16:9; Mal 3:19. The images of "tow" and "blazing fire" are meant to suggest the impermanence of the wicked in the present life, and not their punishment by fire in the afterlife; cf. COMMENT on 7:17 and 11:26 and INTRODUCTION, Part X, 4. In v 10, Ben Sira rephrases the belief in the early death that awaits the sinner. "The netherworld," or Sheol in Heb (Hades in Gr), was not a place of retribution, but merely the place where all the dead—saints and sinners alike—were believed to be gathered; cf. COMMENT on 14:16; 17:28; and 22:11, as well as Qoh 9:9–10. On v 10, cf. F. Stummer, "'Via peccantium complanata lapidibus' (Eccli 21,11)," in *Colligere Fragmenta—A. Dold,* pp. 40–44.

In v 11, Ben Sira restates his doctrine that wisdom=keeping the Law= fear of the Lord; cf. COMMENT on 1:11–30. The "impulses" in v 11a are presumably temptations to violate the Law. Instead of "impulses" (Gr *ennoēmatos*), Syr reads *yaṣreh,* "his *yēṣer*" (cf. COMMENT on 15:14), a reading preferred by Box-Oesterley (p. 388). One must be "shrewd" (Gr *panourgos*) in order to be taught (v 12a), but "one form of shrewdness" (*panourgia*) is undesirable, "thoroughly bitter" (v 12b), i.e., a cause of grief or pain to others. Cf. COMMENT on 19:23, where *panourgia* is also used in a pejorative sense.

On the next couplet (vv 13–14), see NOTES. The image Ben Sira employs here is taken up in *Pirqe Aboth,* vi 1, where it is said that the one who concerns himself with the Law is like "a spring that ceases not, and like a river that continues to flow on." In the same Jewish tractate, ii 10, Rabbi Eleazar ben Arak is called a "welling spring" because he studied the Law with untiring devotion (Box-Oesterley, p. 389). In stark contrast to the wise, the fool has a mind "like a broken cistern" (cf. Jer 2:13); it can hold no knowledge (v 14).

In the next couplet (v 15), Ben Sira again contrasts the conduct of the wise (=virtuous) and the fool (=sinner). The "intelligent" not only welcome and appreciate "words of wisdom," but they also add their own perceptive comments for the benefit of others. But the fool (the reading of Syr), who is here called "the wanton," has no taste for wisdom and rejects it. For the image of the wanton casting words of wisdom "behind his back," cf. 1 Kgs 14:9, in which Jeroboam, unlike faithful David, who followed the Lord with his whole heart (1 Kgs 14:8), angered the Lord and "cast [him] behind [his] back." Ezekiel (23:35) uses the same image to describe the infidelity of Jerusalem; cf. also Neh 9:26.

The next couplet (vv 16–17) depicts another contrast between the foolish and the wise. The fool's "chatter" (lit., discourse, explanation) is "like a load on a journey," i.e., burdensome and disagreeable (v 16a). But the conversation of the wise is charming (16b); cf. Ps 45:3; Prov 22:11; Qoh 10:12. Moreover, "the views [Gr *stoma,* lit., mouth] of the prudent are sought in an assembly" (v 17a), the religious place of honor; cf. Luke 4:14–15. For the thought of v 17, cf. 15:5; Job 29:7–23; Wis 8:10.

For the textual problems of v 18 and for the arrangement of vv 19, 21, cf. NOTES. To a fool, wisdom is as unappealing as "a house in ruins," or, if Syr is to be preferred, "a prison" (v 18a). To the stupid, "knowledge is incomprehensible chatter" (or, talk without sense; Syr has "like fiery coals"). The undisciplined and pitiable fool considers wisdom to be a wasteland, and knowledge incomprehensible speech; cf. v 15. To emphasize the point, Ben Sira employs the powerful images of fetters and manacle (v 19)—the fool considers learning a hampering of his person. Contrast this passage with the advice and images given in 6:23–31. The wise person, however, cherishes and displays learning "like a chain of gold" and "like an armlet on his right arm" (v 21); cf. NOTE. Learning is something to be prized and to be proud of.

As regards the order of the cola in vv 22–23, cf. NOTE. In vv 22–26, Ben Sira compares the social conduct of the foolish and the wise. In his typical impetuous and indiscreet way, the fool "steps boldly into a house" (v 22a); courtesy and consideration of others are virtues he fails to practice. But "the well-bred [lit., the educated] person remains [lit., stands] outside" (v 23b), presumably until he is invited inside after the usual amenities are extended at the door. The "boor [lit., fool] peeps through the doorway of a house" (v 23a), being nosy and totally insensitive to the right of privacy of people in their own homes. The "tactful person" (cf. NOTE), because he respects the rights of others, "keeps his glance cast down" (v 22b). The fool is also "rude" because he listens "at a door" (v 24a), again oblivious of the rights of others. The "cultured person," being "the mirror of all courtesy" (as "bounteous" Buckingham is described by Shakespeare in *Henry VIII* [1613], II i 53), is "overwhelmed [or grieved] by the disgrace [or dishonor]" of eavesdropping (v 24b).

The fool raises his voice when he converses with others, and his laughter is boisterous (v 20a) and annoying—further evidence of his lack of restraint. But the "prudent [Gr *panourgos,* as in v 12a] smiles . . . gently" (cf. NOTE). In v 25a, the fool is now described as "arrogant" (cf. NOTE); he is a person who talks "of what is not [his] concern" (cf. NOTE), a person who cannot mind his own business. The "words of the prudent" (Gr *phronimoi,* wise), however, "are carefully weighed [lit., are weighed in the balance]," for such people are ever conscious of right order in their relationships with others (v 25b). For the image of "weighing in the balance," cf. 16:25 and esp. 28:25a; cf. also Prov 16:23. A clever *a:b:c::c:b':a* rhetorical arrangement makes the point of v 26 even more forceful; it may be translated, lit.: "In the *mouth:of fools:*(is) their *heart* (=seat of intelligence)::in the *heart:of the wise:*(is) their *mouth.*" The fool talks without thinking; the sage thinks before talking. "They never taste who always drink, / They always talk, who never think" (Matthew Prior [1664–1721], *Upon This Passage in Scaligerana*). "Speech is a mirror of the soul: as a man speaks, so is he" (Publilius Syrus [first century B.C.], *Moral Sayings,* 1073).

The next couplet (vv 27–28) deals with cursing and slander. In v 27a, "his adversary" translates Gr *ton satanan,* presumably based on Heb *haśśāṭān,* which originally meant "adversary" and not "Satan" (as a proper noun); cf.

Num 22:22, 32; 1 Sam 29:4; 2 Sam 19:23; 1 Kgs 5:18; 11:25. The meaning of v 27 probably is that the "godless" in cursing his adversary (who is presumably a Jew) "really curses himself" because his curse recoils on his own head; cf. Gen 12:3: "I will bless those who bless you and curse those who curse you." Cf. also Gen 27:29 and Num 24:9. The "slanderer" attempts to dirty his victim but instead "besmirches himself" (v 28a) and at the same time "is hated by his neighbors" (v 28b); cf. 5:14–6:1; 28:13; Jas 3:6. "Slander, like coal, will either dirty your hand or burn it" (Russian proverb). "He that flings dirt at another dirtieth himself most" (Thomas Fuller, *Gnomologia* [1732], 2107).

The sluggard is the subject of the next couplet (22:1–2). He is compared to "a filthy stone" (v 1a), i.e., a stone (presumably smooth) that was used by the ancients (and by some desert Bedouin today) for wiping oneself after a bowel movement. Cf. Job 2:8. For v 1b, Syr has a more graphic reading: "and everyone flees from its stench." Hissing (in the G of v 1b) was a sign of derision and contempt; cf. Jer 19:8; 49:17; 50:13; Lam 2:15, 16; Ezek 27:36; Zeph 2:15. The sluggard is also likened to "a lump of dung" (v 2a), an even stronger metaphor that Ben Sira employs to evoke a feeling of disgust. The point of v 2b is that the sluggard, like dung, is so foul that anyone who comes in contact with (Lat reads *touches*) him "shakes out [the literal meaning of Gr *ektinaxei*] his hand." Cf. Isa 33:15. Sloth is excoriated by the sages; cf. Prov 6:9–11; 10:4–5; 15:19; 20:4; 24:30–34; 26:13–16.

Ben Sira now turns his attention to wicked children. V 3a may be translated, lit.: "A father's shame is in having begotten an untrained [or uneducated] son." For the thought expressed here, cf. Prov 17:21 and Sir 16:1–5. The sentiment in v 3b is misogynistic, reflecting an ancient Near Eastern and Jewish bias against women in general. The Jew of that time considered it a misfortune to beget daughters; cf. *Menachoth,* 43b, where it is urged that a man bless God daily for not having made him a woman or a slave. In the daily morning prayer of the Jewish liturgy is the following: "Blessed are you, O Lord our God, King of the Universe, who have not made me a woman." If a daughter be "sensible," or prudent, however, she was said to be "a treasure to [cf. NOTE] her husband" (v 4a); but even here the woman's value derived from the benefit she brought to her husband and not from what she was in herself. Cf. 26:1–4, 13–18; Prov 12:4; 18:22; 31:10–12, 23–28. A "shameless" daughter is a "grief" to her father (v 4b) not primarily because her conduct is deplorable but because it implies that he failed in his duty to discipline her properly from her youth; cf. 42:9–14. Again in v 5, the "hussy" is despised by both her father and her husband principally because she brings them shame, and not because her bold behavior damages her own reputation. Regarding Ben Sira's attitude toward women, see INTRODUCTION, Part X, 7.

The "inopportune talk" (v 6a) probably refers to merely using words to correct a child when stronger measures are required, viz., "lashes and discipline," which "are at all times wisdom" (v 6b); cf. Prov 22:15; 29:15. For the added vv 7–8 in GII, cf. NOTE. The imagery of v 9 is colorful and dramatic: just as it is futile to glue a "broken pot" because it becomes virtually useless, or to expect a person awakened out of a deep sleep to be alert right away, so it is a waste of time to teach a fool. Cf. Prov 1:7; 27:22. V 10a varies the image of v 9b but makes the same point; v 10b emphasizes how ineffective it is to speak with a fool. The fool simply cannot understand sensible talk any more than a sleeper can hear what you say. "Talk sense to a fool / and he calls you foolish" (Euripides, *The Bacchae* [c. 405 B.C.]).

In the next three bicola, Ben Sira continues to deplore the life of the fool. Weeping for the dead person is appropriate, "for his light has gone out" (Gr *exelipen;* v 11a), i.e., his life has ended, and there is nothing to expect beyond the grave; cf. COMMENT on 7:17; 11:26; 14:16; and 17:28. Cf. also Prov 20:20, 27. The fool should also be mourned, "for sense [or understanding; cf. NOTE] has left him" (*exelipen;* v 11b); in other words, the fool is already dead because he lacks intelligence, which is essential for a life that claims to be human. The dead, who are "at rest" (i.e., free of the toils and pains of life), are to be mourned less (v 11c) than the fool those life is "worse than death" (v 11d), because he lacks wisdom, which alone makes life meaningful and worthwhile. In other words, the fool was never really alive in the first place. "Seven days of mourning for the dead" (v 12a) is the customary period even for orthodox Jews today; it is called "shibah" (from the Heb word *šib'â*, "seven"). Cf. Gen 50:10; Jdt 16:24. The fool (cf. NOTE), however, should be mourned "a whole lifetime" (v 12b), lit., "all the days of his life." Vv 11–12 contain Ben Sira's severest indictment of the fool. These verses also speak of the two great tragedies that occur in life—death and folly.

The final poem (vv 13–18), which serves as conclusion to this section, again deals with the fool, whom the wise are urged to avoid. Even speaking with "the stupid [or foolish]" is to be kept to a bare minimum (v 13a), lest one "be . . . the companion of a brute" (lit., an unintelligent being; v 13b). Instead of "brute," Syr reads "pig," a reading preferred by Smend (p. 199), Box-Oesterley (p. 391), and Duesberg-Fransen (p. 188). For the extra colon after v 13b in GII, cf. NOTE. The wise are to "stay clear" of the fool lest they "have trouble [v 13c] and be spattered when he shakes himself" (v 13d)—a colorful reference to the outpouring of a fool's nonsense, which is compared to the filth that the pig shakes from itself after having wallowed in the mire (so Box-Oesterley, p. 391). The pig was considered in the OT to be an unclean animal, which the Israelites were forbidden to eat; cf. Lev 11:7–8. Only by keeping one's distance from the fool can one "find rest" (v 13e) and "not be wearied" by "his lack of sense" (or folly, or madness; v 13f). In v 14, the fool is said to be "heavier than lead"—a graphic image suggesting that the fool is intolerable, a dreadful bore; cf. 21:16. In v 15, the "stupid [or senseless]" is depicted as more of a burden than "sand and salt and an iron lump"—three elements traditionally viewed as heavy and troublesome to carry; cf. Prov 27:3; Job 6:3; Deut 28:48; Jer 28:13–14. In Syriac Aḥiqar 45–46, lead, salt, and iron are also used as images for heavy burdens difficult to bear.

In striking contrast to the fool is the "resolve" (Gr *kardia,* lit., heart [=mind]) of the wise who make up their minds after "careful deliberation" (v 16c). Hence, their "resolve," which is not "shaken in a moment of fear" (v 16d), is compared to a skillfully planned and constructed building, the masonry of which cannot be "loosened by an earthquake" (v 16b). The bonding of masonry "with wooden beams" (v 16a), a common practice in antiquity, assured solid construction; cf. 1 Kgs 7:12. The "resolve" of the wise is also compared to "the carved [cf. NOTE] embellishment on a smooth wall" (v 17), such as was carved in the walls of Solomon's temple (1 Kgs 6:29). The poem ends with a derogatory comment on the "timid resolve based on foolish plans" (v 18c), which cannot "withstand fear of any kind" (v 18d). Ben Sira uses construction imagery again when he compares such a resolve to "small stones . . . on an open height" (v 18a), which "will not remain when the wind blows" (v 18b). The reference in v 18a is to the small stones placed on top of the walls around vineyards and gardens in Palestine. These were put there so that when jackals or foxes jumped onto the wall to enter the area, the stones would rattle and thus alert the watcher. Since these stones were in an exposed position on the wall, they were easily blown down by gusty winds. So Ryssel (pp. 343–44).

28. The Preservation of Friendship
(22:19–26)

22 19 One who jabs the eye brings tears: G
       he who pierces the heart bares its feelings.
   20 He who throws stones at birds frightens them off,
       and he who insults a friend breaks up the friendship.
   21 Should you draw a sword against a friend,
       despair not, it can be undone.
   22 Should you speak sharply to a friend,
       fear not, you can be reconciled.
      But a contemptuous insult, a confidence broken,
       or a treacherous attack will drive any friend away.
   24 Before flames burst forth comes billowing smoke;   S
       so does abuse come before bloodshed.

   23 Make fast friends with a person while he is poor;   G
       thus you will enjoy his prosperity with him.
      In time of trouble remain true to him,
       so as to share his inheritance with him when it comes.
   25 From a friend in need of support   S
       do not hide in shame;
   26 If harm comes to him on your account   G
       all will stand aloof from you who hear of it.

Notes

22 22cd. With these two cola should be considered the intrusive line in Heb MS B following 31:2, which reads: "A trusty friend, insult will drive away, / but one who keeps secrets concealed is an intimate friend." Where MS B has it, the only function of the line is as a gloss on the expression "drive away sleep" in 31:2. For the rest, it is

closer (with Strack) to reflecting the content of 22:22 than that of 27:16, where some attempt to put it. Its vocabulary rings true, but the line is loosely constructed (with "insult" and "one who keeps secrets concealed" as parallel subjects), and is scarcely authentic in that form. Most likely the line originated as a gloss on 22:22 that said: "A trusty friend wards off (*yānîd*) insult, / and one . . ." (as above).

24. Both GI and Syr carry this verse after 23d, *share his inheritance with him.* There it so breaks the continuity between vv 23 and 25–26 that it must have been transposed from elsewhere; the present placement is an attempt to reduce the lack of sequence. In the Gr, the *smoke* comes from an oven; Syr suggests the language of Joel 3:3; Cant 3:6.

23d. After *inheritance with him* (and before v 24), GII adds the two cola "For there should never be any despising of a person's appearance, / nor is the senseless rich to be marveled at."

25–26. Both G and Syr appear to have had difficulties with these verses; in G, the verbs are largely first-person forms, very likely influenced by v 27, which, however, begins a new section of Ben Sira's discourse.

Comment

The relatively brief poem in this section contains two stanzas: 6+4 bicola. The first stanza (vv 19–22, 24) offers observations on the ways friendship can be destroyed and advice on how to avoid hurting a friend. The second stanza (vv 23, 25–26) speaks of the duties one has toward a friend.

The eye and the heart are two of the body's most delicate and sensitive organs. The heart is the seat not only of intelligence, but also of a person's higher emotions. The eye is the organ that expresses externally the sentiments found inside the heart. Thus tears flowing from the eyes can indicate the joy or sorrow that fills the heart. In v 19a, Ben Sira refers to the *physical* jabbing of the eye, which immediately fills with tears. He uses this image to suggest that the *metaphorical* piercing of the heart just as surely "bares its feelings" (v 19b). By speaking of these two sensitive organs, v 19 aptly introduces this poem on friendship and the sensitivity one should cultivate in relationships with friends. An insult can end a friendship just as throwing a stone frightens off birds (v 20). Cf. 20:15. The point of vv 21–22 is that a legitimate quarrel or even a serious disagreement with a friend (drawing "a sword against a friend" [v 21a] and speaking "sharply to a friend" [v 22a]) can be resolved amicably (vv 21b, 22b). But "a contemptuous insult, a confidence broken, or a treacherous attack" will put an end to any friendship (v 22cd; cf. NOTE); there is no hope of reconciliation, for the guilty party has no genuine sensitivity toward his erstwhile friend. Cf. 27:16–21; 42:1; Prov 11:13; 20:19; 25:9. The maxim in v 24a (cf. NOTE on the placement of the verse) is a variant of the modern proverb "Where there's smoke, there's fire." Ben Sira uses his maxim to illustrate the equally inevitable truth that "abuse [comes] before bloodshed" (v 24b); cf. 27:15.

Ben Sira also urges compassion and fidelity in friendship. If you are a steadfast friend to a person "while he is poor" (v 23a), you will still be a friend if his economic situation improves, in which case you too can enjoy some of his prosperity (v 23b). Remaining true to your friend "in time of trouble" (v 23c) also has its rewards—you can share in "his inheritance with him" (v 23d). When a friend needs help (v 25a; cf. NOTE on vv 25–26), don't be ashamed to assist him (v 25b). Otherwise, if he suffers harm because of you (v 26a), all "who hear of it" "will stand aloof from you" (lit., will watch out for you; v 26b). Compare this stanza with 6:10–12, 13–17, and with 19:13–17. The advice Ben Sira gives on friendship is quite pragmatic and self-serving. The attitudes he describes cannot be considered disinterested. The teaching of Jesus on friendship and on the duties of Christian love (Gr *agapē*) is totally different; cf. Luke 6:27–38.

29. Warning Against Destructive Sins
(22:27–23:27)

22   ²⁷ Who will set a guard over my mouth,   G
      and upon my lips an all-purpose seal,
    That I may not fail through my lips,
      that my tongue may not destroy me?
23   ^{1a} Lord, my Father and the Master of my life,
    ^{1c}   permit me not to fall because of them!

    ² Who will apply the lash to my thoughts,
      to my mind the rod of discipline,
    That my failings may not be spared,
      nor the sins of my heart overlooked;
    ³ Lest my failings increase,
      and my sins be multiplied;
    Lest I succumb to my foes,
      and my enemy rejoice over me?
    ^{4a} Lord, my Father and God of my life,
    ^{1b}   abandon me not into their control:
    ^{4b} A brazen look allow me not;
    ⁵   ward off passion from my heart,
    ⁶ Let not the lustful cravings of the flesh take hold of
                                    me,
      nor shameless appetites rule over me.   S

    ⁷ Give heed, my children, to the instruction I pronounce,   G
      for he who keeps to it will not be ensnared.
    ⁸ Through his lips is the sinner caught;
      by them are the railer and the arrogant tripped up.
    ⁹ Let not your mouth form the habit of swearing,
      nor become too familiar with the holy Name.
    ¹⁰ Just as a slave that is constantly under scrutiny
      will not be without welts,

So one who swears continually by the holy Name
will not remain free from sin.

11 A person who often swears heaps up offenses;
the scourge will never be far from his house.
If he swears in error, he incurs guilt;
if he neglects his obligation, his sin is doubly great.
If he swears without reason, he cannot be found just,
and all his house will suffer affliction.

12 There are words which merit death;
may they never be heard among Jacob's heirs.
For all such words are foreign to the devout,
who do not wallow in sin.

13 Let not your mouth become used to coarse talk,
for in it lies sinful matter.

14 Keep your father and mother in mind
when you sit among the mighty,
Lest in their presence you commit a blunder
and disgrace your upbringing,
By wishing you had never been born
or cursing the day of your birth.

15 A person who has the habit of abusive language
will never mature in character as long as he lives.

16 Two types of people multiply sins,
a third stirs up wrath:
Burning passion is a blazing fire,
not to be quenched till it burns itself out;
The man who is lewd with his own kindred
never stops till the fire breaks forth;

17 The rake to whom all bread is sweet
is never through until he dies.

18 The man who dishonors his marriage bed
says to himself, "Who can see me?
Darkness surrounds me, walls hide me;
no one sees me; who is to stop me from sinning?"   S
Of the Most High he is not mindful,   G
19   fearing only the eyes of humans;

He does not understand that the eyes of the Lord,
    ten thousand times brighter than the sun,
Observe every step a person takes
    and peer into hidden corners.
20 The One who knows all things before they exist
    still knows them all after they cease to be.
21 Such a man will be denounced in the streets of the city;   s
    when he least expects it, he will be apprehended.   G

22 So also with the woman who is unfaithful to her
                                            husband
    and offers as heir her son by a stranger.
23 First, she has disobeyed the law of the Most High;
    second, she has wronged her husband;
Third, in her wanton adultery
    she has raised up children by another man.
24 Such a woman will be dragged before the assembly,
    and her punishment will extend to her children;
25 Her children will not take root;
    her branches will not bring forth fruit.
26 She will leave an accursed memory;
    her disgrace will never be blotted out.

27 Thus all who dwell on the earth shall know,   s
    and all who remain in the world shall understand,
That nothing is better than the fear of the Lord,   G
    nothing sweeter than obeying his commandments.*

---

*28 It is a great glory to follow after God,   GII
    and for you to be received by him is length of days.

Notes

23 1. *of my life:* after this, G gives the colon (1b) that has been read here after 4a, where it is found in Lat and Syr.

2. Syr, with *lash* and *rod,* retains a concrete parallelism that has been weakened by the terms used in G.

3d. *rejoice over me:* after this colon, GII adds "for these things, the hope of your mercy is remote," a gloss on 2cd, 3ab.

1b. See the note on v 1 above. It appears likely that Syr first used for **bᵉṣtm,* the obvious Heb source for G's *en boulē autōn,* an equivalent *bᵉṭthwn* (cf. Dan 2:14, also Egyptian Aram and Job 22:18 in 11QtgJob). The noun does not survive in Syriac literature, and has been corrupted into *bĕṭaʿyûtĕhon* in Syr as we have it.

5. For this line, GII (with Clement of Alexandria) has "Remove always from your servant vain hopes / and improper desires turn aside from me / and sustain always him who wishes to serve you."

11a. *heaps up offenses:* supposes that the Heb underlying G will have read *marbēh šĕbûʿâ marbēh pešaʿ,* and that the translation was free.

16b. *stirs up wrath:* Prov. 15:1, cf. Ps 78:21; so Syr.

18e, 19a. These two cola are lacking in Syr; G construes 18e with what precedes, obtaining "no one sees me; why should I be afraid? The Most High will not be mindful of my sins."

Comment

This section, which concludes Part IV of the book (14:20–23:27), opens with a prayer consisting of two stanzas (3+7 bicola) structured in parallel. The first stanza (22:27–23:1) becomes the theme of 23:7–15 while the second (23:2–6) is thematically pursued in 23:16–26. The entire section (as well as the first four parts of the book) is summed up in the concluding phrases, "the fear of the Lord" (23:27c) and "obeying his commandments" (23:27d), which are prepared for by the phrases "the lash to my thoughts" (23:2a) and "the rod of discipline" (23:2b). Cf. P. C. Beentjes, "Sirach 22:27–23:6 in zijn context," *BTFT* 39 (1978): 144–51. Other prayers are found in 36:1–13a, 16b–22, and 51:1–12.

The opening stanza of this prayer asks God to protect Ben Sira, and the person who recites the prayer, from sins of the tongue. For the thought and wording of 22:27a, cf. Ps 141:3a. Cf. also 28:24–26. "An all-purpose seal" (22:27b) is, lit., "a seal of shrewdness." The dangers of the lips and tongue (22:27cd) are detailed also in Prov 13:3; 18:7, 21; cf. also Prov 21:23; Ps 39:2; Jas 3:5–12. Invoking God as "Lord, my Father, and the Master of my life" (23:1a) manifests the filial confidence with which the faithful are to pray and their willingness to obey the commandments (cf. 4:7–10). In other books of the OT, God is called Father of the Israelite people (1 Chr 29:10; Isa 63:16; Mal 2:10). In our book, the pious Jew can call God "my Father" (cf. 23:1a, 4a in Syr and 51:1a, 10a). Since God alone is the source of the moral life (cf. Ps 36:10; Jer 2:13; 17:13), only he can help one avoid sins of the tongue (23:1b). Cf. NOTE on 23:1 for the arrangement of the text.

The second stanza (vv 2–6) of this prayer asks God for help in avoiding sins of lust and illegitimate passion. As regards "lash" and "rod" in v 2ab, cf. NOTE. "The rod of discipline" (v 2b) is an expression that derives from Prov 22:15b. Ben Sira insists, as do other Wisdom writers, that only through lashes and discipline (cf. 22:6) can one avoid the "failings" and "the sins of [one's] heart" (v 2cd) and stop multiplying one's faults and moral compromises (v 3ab). Sin brings adversity in the present life (cf. COMMENT on 14:16); hence the sentiment expressed in v 3cd (cf. 12:16–18). For the thought of the enemy rejoicing over one's downfall (v 3cd), cf. Pss 13:5; 38:17. For the extra colon found in GII after v 3d, cf. NOTE. V 4a is a variant on the titles found in v 1a. As regards the placement of v 1b, cf. NOTE. In v 1b, Ben Sira prays to be delivered from the control (cf. NOTE) of his "thoughts" and "mind" (lit., heart) mentioned in v 2ab, since it is here that sin has its origin. He also prays to be freed from the tyranny of impure desires. There is an *a:b::b':a'* structure in vv 4b, 5, 6ab: *a brazen look* (lit., a lifting up of the eyes, which expresses externally what the heart desires; cf. COMMENT on 22:19):*passion::lustful cravings of the flesh:shameless appetite* (which exists inside the heart). For the variant of v 5 in GII, cf. NOTE. The "brazen look [or eye]" (v 4b) does not refer to pride in this instance, as the expression usually does (cf., for example, Isa 2:11; 5:15; Ps 131:1; Prov 21:4), but, as the structure mentioned above demonstrates, it refers to the depraved eye that fuels the fires of lust in the heart. Cf. 26:9; Gen 39:7; Prov 6:25; Matt 5:28. "The brazen eye," as used here, suggests the gleam of unholy passion.

The next two stanzas (vv 7–11 and 12–15) take up the theme introduced in the first part of Ben Sira's prayer (22:27–23:1a,c). Before v 7, many Gr MSS have the title "Instruction concerning the mouth," which is hardly accurate in this place, for the title conflicts with the structural and thematic elements of 22:27–23:27, as Beentjes points out (*BTFT* 39 [1978]: 144–51). This title is taken from the first two words of v 7a (*paideian stomatos*). In v 7a, "the instruction I pronounce" is, lit., "the instruction of *my* mouth," the reading of only one Gr MS (with some versions dependent on G) and Syr; all the other Gr MSS and Lat read "the instruction of *the* mouth [or about the mouth]." This stanza and the next deal with the sins the mouth is capable of; cf. Jas 3:1–12. The one who heeds the present instruction "will not be ensnared" (v 7b) by what one says, for as Ben Sira states in v 8, "the sinner [is] caught" and "the railer and the arrogant tripped up" by their "lips." Cf. 20:18; Prov 6:2; 11:6.

"The habit of swearing" (v 9a), especially when one calls upon "the holy Name [of God]" in oaths (v 9b) when there is no sufficient reason, is to be avoided; cf. Matt 5:34–37; 23:18–22; Jas 5:12. V 9b may be translated, lit.: "Do not make a habit of naming the Holy One." "The Holy One " is one of the titles of God in the OT; cf. Isa 1:4; 5:19, 24; 10:20; 41:14, 16, 20; 45:11; 47:4; 48:17; 49:7; 54:5; 55:5; Job 6:10; Sir 4:14; 43:10; 47:8; 48:20; Bar 4:22; 5:5. In v 10a, the phrase "that is . . . under scrutiny" may also be translated "that is being questioned." The Gr verb here, *exetazō,* means "to examine well or closely" or "to scrutinize," and also "to question, examine by torture"; cf. Acts 22:24. It is the latter meaning that is intended here, as is obvious from v 10b. The person "who swears continually" (v 10c) is presumably one who has no serious reason to do so (cf. v 11e). He is guilty of sin (v 10d), because he profanes "the holy Name" by using it to lie under oath; cf. Exod 20:7; Lev 19:12; Deut 5:11. V 11ef is a variation of v 11ab. The "scourge" (v 11b; cf. Ps 39:11) and "affliction" (v 11f; cf. Ps 91:10) that come on the "house" (v 11b,f) of the person who swears "often" (v 11a), i.e., "without reason" (v 11e), are punishment for his "offenses" (v 11a) and lack of justice (v 11e). In the Deuteronomic theory of retribution in this life, sin brought with it affliction and even disaster; cf. COMMENT on 7:17. "If a person swears in error" (the reading of Syr; Gr reads, lit., "if a person offends"), "he incurs guilt" (v 11c), as Lev 5:4 states. If a person "neglects" to do what he has sworn, "his sin is doubly great" (v 11d): the first sin is swearing rashly; the second is failure to fulfill the oath. Cf. Wis 14:28–31; Prov 19:5, 9, 29; 21:28; 25:18.

The next stanza (vv 12–15), also devoted to abuses of the tongue, advises against blasphemy, "coarse talk," and "abusive language." In v 12, the expression "words which merit death" is a reference to blasphemy, the punishment for which was the death penalty; cf. Lev 24:11–16; 1 Kgs 21:10, 13; Matt 26:65–66; John 10:33. Ben Sira had such a horror of the crime of blasphemy that he uses a euphemism to describe it and prays that it may "never be heard among Jacob's heirs" (v 12b). The "devout" (v 12c), i.e., those who fear the Lord and so "do not wallow in sin" (v 12d), never are tempted to utter such heinous words. Moreover, "coarse talk" is to be avoided because it, too, is sinful (v 13). What Ben Sira refers to is indecent and lewd conversations or remarks; cf. Gal 5:19. You should be mindful of your parents (v 14a) by being careful to avoid improper speech particularly when you sit "among the mighty" (v 14b) in whose presence you may "commit a blunder and disgrace your upbringing" (v 14cd). Social disasters of this sort make one wish one "had never been born" (v 14e; cf. 3:11, 16; Jer 20:17–18) and curse "the day of [one's] birth" (v 14f; cf. Job 3:3–10; Jer 20:14). Ben Sira concludes this two-stanza section on improper speech (vv 7–15) by the general observation that the person accustomed to "abusive language" (v 15a) "will never mature in character" (lit., will never become educated, v 15b). Such a person is indeed a boor and a fool, completely lacking in wisdom. Cf. A. J. Desečear, "La necedad en Sirac 23,12–15," *SBFLA* 20 (1970): 264–72.

The next three stanzas (vv 16–26: 4+7+6 bicola) resume the theme of illegitimate passion introduced in the second part of Ben Sira's prayer (vv 2–6). The first stanza (vv 16–17) describes and denounces lewd desires, incest, and adultery. In this stanza, Ben Sira employs a literary convention called the numerical proverb. Other examples of this proverb are found in 25:1–2, 7–11; 26:5–6, 28; 50:25–26; Prov 6:16–19; 30:15b–16, 18–19, 21–23, 29–31; Job 5:19–22; 13:20–22; 33:14–15; Ps 62:12 (cf. INTRODUCTION, Part IV, 1). Three types of lecherous persons "multiply sins" (v 16a) and thereby "[stir] up wrath" (v 16b; cf. NOTE): (1) the one whose "burning passion" is not "quenched till it burns itself out" (v 16cd), i.e., the person of unrestrained sexual desires (cf. v 6); (2) the person who commits incest (v 16ef), the various forms of which are described and condemned in Lev 18:6–18 and 20:11–12, 14, 17, 19–21; and (3) the adulterer ever on the quest for new liaisons ("to whom all bread is sweet," v 17a; cf. Prov 9:13–18), who never stops looking "until he dies" (v 17b). In v 16f, the clause "till the fire breaks forth," is a reference to the divine punishment that will come upon the person guilty of incest.

In the next stanza (vv 18–21), Ben Sira offers accurate observations about the psychology of the adulterer and the rationalizations he alleges in order to dull his conscience. For the thought of v 18b, cf. Job 24:15. As regards the expressions in v 18cd, cf. Isa 29:15 and Ezek 8:12. The adulterer is "not mindful" "of the Most High" (v 18e; cf. NOTE). Thus he violates the Deuteronomic injunction *to remember* the Lord and all the great wonders Israel experienced in her history because of divine election and mercy; cf. Deut 5:15; 7:18; 8:2, 18; 9:7, 27; 15:15; 16:3, 12; 24:9, 18, 22; 25:17; 32:7. Deuteronomy also commands the Israelite *not to forget* the Lord or the Covenant or the marvelous deeds he performed on behalf of his Chosen People; cf. Deut 4:9, 23, 31; 6:12; 8:11, 14, 19; 9:7; 25:19; 26:13; 31:21. On the Deuteronomic theology of remembering, cf. A. A. Di Lella, "The Deuteronomic Background of the Farewell Discourse in Tob 14:3–11," *CBQ* 41 (1979): 384–85.

The adulterer fears "only the eyes of humans" (v 19a), i.e., he is careful not to be caught in the act of adultery because of the public disgrace he would have to suffer (cf. v 21). Because of his unbridled lust, the adulterer does not want to "understand," or to "know, perceive" (Gr *egnō*), that the "eyes of the Lord" are "ten thousand times brighter than the sun" (v 19c) and can see everything human beings do (v 19d) or think, no matter how hidden or unobserved they feel their activity may be (v 19e). Cf. 17:19–20; Prov 15:3, 11; Ps 33:13–15. Divine omniscience is total—God knows not only all things that exist but even those things that are yet to be (v 20a) and things that later "cease to be" (v 20b). Cf. 42:18; Ps 139:1–16. Despite all precautions taken to remain undetected in his sin, the adulterer is often caught and "denounced in the streets of the city," i.e., publicly (v 21a). The adulterer is "apprehended" "when he least expects it" (v 21b), i.e., when he thinks his sin has been adequately concealed. V 21b may also be translated: "and where he does not suspect he will be taken"—the reference would then be to the public place of punishment. Apparently, in Ben Sira's day death by stoning, the penalty the Law decreed for adulterers (cf. Lev 20:10; Deut 22:22–24; Ezek 16:36–40; John 8:4–5), was not enforced since it is not alluded to in v 21 or in vv 22–26. Under Talmudic law the adulterer was scourged. Perhaps the same penalty is referred to in the alternative translation of v 21b given above; cf. Prov 5:11– 14; 6:32–33. Cf. *JE,* vol. 1, p. 217a.

The next stanza (vv 22–26) describes the evils the adulteress commits and the punishment she will receive. In v 22a, the "so also" may refer to the adulteress being brought to the public place (of scourging) alluded to in the alternative translation of v 21b. "The woman who *is unfaithful to"* is, lit., "the woman who *leaves"* (her husband); Syr has ". . . who *sins,* or *trespasses, against."* V 22b assumes that the adulteress will have a child by the man, "a stranger," with whom she sins; so also in vv 23d, 24b, 25. In v 23, Ben Sira lists three reasons why the adulteress will be punished, the number three perhaps being used here to balance the numerical proverb given in v 16ab ("two types of people . . . a third"). The first, and of course principal, reason is that she broke "the law of the Most High" (v 23a; cf. v 18e), a clear reference to Exod 20:14 and Deut 5:18: "You shall not commit adultery." Second, she commits an injustice against her husband (v 23b). Third, she may have children "by another man" (v 23d). It is to be noted that Ben Sira does not speak at all about the injustice the adulterer commits against his wife, or about the possibility that the adulterer may also have children by another woman. Like the adulterer in the alternative translation of v 21b, the adulteress will also "be dragged before the assembly" (v 24a) for public punishment (perhaps scourging; see COMMENT on v 21b). Under Talmudic law, the husband of the adulteress was forbidden to condone her crime (*Sotah,* vi 1), but was compelled to divorce her; she also lost all her property rights under her marriage contract. Cf. *JE,* vol 1, p. 217a.

As regards the punishment that "will extend to her children" (v 24b and v 25), cf. Wis 3:16–19. For the imagery of her children "not [taking] root," and her branches "not [bringing] forth fruit" (v 25), cf. Isa 37:31; Mal 3:19; Wis 4:3–6; and Hos 2:6. The children born of adulterous unions were not considered as belonging to the congregation of Israel (cf. *Qiddushin,* 78b); so Box-

Oesterley, p. 396. Instead of a blessed memory (cf. 45:1; 46:11), the adulteress leaves "an accursed memory" (v 26a); cf. Pss 9:6; 34:17; 109:15; Jer 29:22. The "disgrace" of her adultery "will never be blotted out" (v 26b); cf. Ps 109:14. Compare the punishments described here with the blessings and honor the faithful scribe receives in 39:9–11, and with the hallowed memory the godly ancestors enjoy in 44:10–15.

This section comes to a close with v 27, which neatly sums up the first four parts of the book (1:1–23:27) as well as the present poem (22:27–23:27). Cf. 50:28–29. In v 27ab, the reading of Syr is to be preferred to the Gr, which has only one colon: "And those who remain shall know." There is a rhythmic balance and synonymous parallelism between "all who dwell on the earth" (v 27a) and "all who remain in the world" (v 27b), and between "shall know" (v 27a) and "shall understand" (v 27b), and also between "nothing better than" (v 27c) and "nothing sweeter than" (v 27d), and between "the fear of the Lord" (v 27c) and "obeying his commandments" (v 27d). The point of this elegant conclusion is that those who have paid heed to the contents of this section and of the rest of the first four parts of the book will "know" and "understand" that "the fear of the Lord," which equals "obeying his commandments" (cf. COMMENT on 1:11–30; 6:32–37; 15:1; 19:20; 21:6), is the best and sweetest (i.e., most satisfying) course of action one can pursue. There is no other way, Ben Sira says in effect, to live fully and well and to achieve happiness in one's sojourn here on earth. See INTRODUCTION, Part X, 1.

The gloss in GII expands the thought but disturbs the balance of v 27cd by adding a third element (v 28a): "great glory" it is "to follow after *God*" (two Gr MSS and many Lat MSS have "the Lord"). The "length of days" (v 28b) is probably an allusion to eternal life, which GII has several references to (cf. INTRODUCTION, Part X, 4). The gloss, which also was meant to serve as a conclusion to the first four parts of the book, seems to be a deliberate application of the language of Ps 73:24 in the LXX to the thought of v 27.

PART V (24:1–33:18)

30. Praise of Wisdom
(24:1–33)

24 1 Wisdom sings her own praises,
　　among her own people she proclaims her glory;
2 In the assembly of the Most High she opens her
　　　　　　　　　　mouth,
　　in the presence of his host she declares her worth:

G

3 "From the mouth of the Most High I came forth,
　　and mistlike covered the earth.
4 In the heights of heaven I dwelt,
　　my throne on a pillar of cloud.
5 The vault of heaven I compassed alone,
　　through the deep abyss I took my course.
6 Over waves of the sea, over all the land,
　　over every people and nation I held sway.
7 Among them all I sought a resting place:
　　in whose inheritance should I abide?

8 "Then the Fashioner of all gave me his command,
　　and he who had made me chose the spot for my
　　　　　　　　　　tent,
Saying, 'In Jacob make your dwelling,
　　in Israel your inheritance.'
9 Before the ages, from the first, he created me,
　　and through the ages I shall not cease to be.
10 In the holy Tent I ministered before him,
　　and then in Zion I took up my post.
11 In the city he loves as he does me, he gave me rest;
　　in Jerusalem is my domain.

12 I have struck root among the glorious people;
  in the portion of the Lord is my inheritance.

13 "Like a cedar on Lebanon I am raised aloft,
  like a cypress on Mount Hermon.
14 Like a palm tree in Engeddi I stand out,
  like a rose garden in Jericho;
  Like a fair olive tree in the foothills,
   like a plane tree I am lofty beside the water.
15 Like cinnamon, or fragrant cane, or precious myrrh,
  I give forth perfume;
  Like galbanum and onycha and mastic,
   like the odor of incense in the holy Tent.

16 "I spread out my branches like a terebinth,
  my branches so bright and so graceful.
17 I bud forth delights like the vine,
  my blossoms yield to fruits fair and rich.[a]
19 Come to me, you that yearn for me,
  and be filled with my fruits;
20 You will remember me as sweeter than honey,
  better to have than the honeycomb.
21 He who eats of me will hunger still,
  he who drinks of me will thirst for more;
22 He who obeys me will not be put to shame,
  those who work with me will never fail."

---

[a] 18 I am the mother of fair love, of reverence,   GII, Lat
  of knowledge, and of holy hope;
  To all my children I give   GII
   to be everlasting: to those named by Him.

23 All this is true of the book of the Most High's
            covenant,
    "the Law which Moses enjoined on us
      as a heritage for the community of Jacob."[b]

25 It is brimful, like the Pishon, with wisdom—
      like the Tigris at the time of the new crops.

26 It runs over, like the Euphrates, with understanding;
      like the Jordan at harvesttime.

27 It floods, like the Nile, with knowledge;
      like the Gihon at vintage time.

28 The first human never knew wisdom fully,
      nor will the last succeed in fathoming her.

29 Deeper than the sea are her thoughts;
      her counsels, than the great abyss.

30 Now I, like a rivulet from her stream,
      channeling the waters forth into a garden,

31 Said to myself, "I will water my plants,
      my flower bed I will drench";
    And suddenly this rivulet of mine became a river,
      then this stream of mine, a sea.

32 Again will I send my teachings forth shining like the
            dawn,
      to spread their brightness afar off;

33 Again will I pour out instruction like prophecy,
      and bequeath it to generations yet to come.

---

[b]24 Do not grow weary of striving with the Lord's help,   GII
    but cling to him that he may reinforce you.
The Lord Almighty alone is God,
    and apart from him there is no savior.

Notes

24 1–33. For a reconstructed Heb of this poem, concerned to illustrate its strophic divisions, cf. *CBQ* 41 (1979): 374–79.

12b. *my inheritance:* with Ziegler; the Gr MSS have, "in the portion of the Lord, his inheritance," but compare v 7b.

14d. *beside the water:* restored with GII and Syr; GI omits.

15. The division in the Gr (and in Heb) between 15a and 15b comes after *cane.*

18a,b. These two cola of GII are followed in the Lat by "In me is every gift of life and truth [or: of the way and of truth]; / in me is all hope of life and of virtue." At least in its final form this would seem to have been shaped in Lat for alliterative effects.

18c,d. Not present in the Lat. The Gr is obscure, and the translation follows a conjecture of de Groot (*aei genesthai* for *aeigeneis/-ēs* of the MSS), cited by Ziegler.

24. *Lord Almighty* is the conventional equivalent for the Gr *Kyrios pantokratōr;* the underlying Heb would be *Yhwh ṣĕbā'ôt,* not used in the extant Heb of Ben Sira. The Gr title occurs in GI only in 42:17 (a text misread by G) and in 50:14, 17 by way of expansion on the Heb.

27a. The Gr of this colon is based on a false reading in (or of) the Heb, combining the verb used in 32b with *'ôr,* "light"; *the Nile* is, in Heb, *yĕ'ôr.* Syr reflects the correct text.

33. The Gr text that follows this, as v 34, has its proper place as 33:18. In chap. 24 (where it is not present in the Syr), it is a harmonizing expansion by a copyist; cf. *CBQ* 41 (1979): 376. Though it is plausible enough in this place to have won acceptance from modern scholars (e.g., Segal) there is perhaps an additional reason at work, besides the "harmonizing" one, for the presence of this bicolon after 24:33. Toward the end of Sirach, GII repeats the last colon from the end of chap. 43 (*and to those who fear him he gives wisdom*) at the end of chap. 50, and follows it with a doxology. This cannot be separated from the circumstances that chaps. 44–50 were lacking completely in the basic African (Old Lat) rendering of Sirach and (with chap. 51 as well) in two early forms of the Armenian; nor from the colophons for the end of the book quoted by Ziegler from two Gr MSS, one Lat MS (Q, dated c. A.D. 900), and the Armenian, as appearing at the end of chap. 43. A similarly truncated edition of the book passing over 25:1–33:18 altogether could have achieved its object with some finesse by appending the bicolon 33:18 to the end of chap. 24; this would have had to occur before the transposition within the Gr tradition that affects chaps. 30–36 in our extant codices. Collation of one such truncated copy against a text of the full book could then have brought the traveling bicolon into the Gr tradition of chap. 24 on which our codices depend.

Comment

Part V (24:1–33:18) begins the second major division of the book (chaps. 24–50), which has a total of four parts, as does the first division. As an introduction to this division, there is a long poem in praise of wisdom (24:1–33), as was the case also at the opening of the first division (1:11–30).

This splendid poem, which in most of the Gr MSS has the title "Praise of Wisdom," has seven stanzas (2+5+6+5+6+6+5 poetic lines): all bicola (but note that v 23a is prose). After a brief introduction (vv 1–2), Wisdom delivers in the first person a twenty-two-line speech (vv 3–17, 19–22), which has four stanzas (5+6+5+6 lines). Next comes a six-line stanza (vv 23, 25–29) equating Wisdom with the Law. The final stanza, 5 lines (vv 30–33), contains Ben Sira's description of his own functioning as a Wisdom teacher. In this composition, Ben Sira shows his awareness of the five-line stanzas with which the author of Proverbs 8 developed his theme. Ben Sira's poem has thirty–five lines, exactly the number in Proverbs 8 (seven stanzas, each of five lines). In shortening Wisdom's speech in his own poem, Ben Sira adopts for it the conventional length based on alphabetic acrostic considerations (cf. Proverbs 2; 31:10–31; and Lamentations). He composed two other poems in lengths of twenty-two lines each: 1:11–30; 6:18–37; cf. 51:13–30. Finally, this chapter is not a single draft composition like Proverbs 8 but rather the putting together of three related themes. The longest theme is developed in Wisdom's speech; the second theme (vv 23, 25–29) and the third (vv 30–33) each receive a single stanza. The lengths of these latter stanzas (6+5) were determined by the earlier pattern of 5s and 6s employed in Wisdom's speech. So P. W. Skehan, "Structures in Poems on Wisdom: Proverbs 8 and Sirach 24," *CBQ* 41 (1979): 375. In this chapter, the most famous part of the whole book, Ben Sira is at his best in displaying his poetic skills.

In the introductory couplet, the theme of the poem is stated: "Wisdom sings her own praises" and "proclaims her glory" "among her own people" (v 1), i.e., among the Israelites, as "the People of God," the reading of Syr, clearly suggests; cf. v 8cd. Smend (p. 216), however, thinks that the expression refers to the heavenly companions that Wisdom has. In v 2, "the assembly of the Most High" and "his host" are indeed the angelic attendants at God's throne, where Wisdom personified is also said to reside; cf. Ps 82:1; Isa 34:4. The phrase "she opens her mouth," derives from Prov 8:6–8; cf. also Prov 31:8–9, 26. Thus, in vv 1–2, Wisdom addresses herself to God's people on earth and to her companions in heaven. Wisdom alone is capable of speaking of her excellence because she came forth "from the mouth of the Most High" (v 3a).

In the first stanza (vv 3–7) of her twenty-two-line speech, Wisdom speaks of her origin from God and of her activity in heaven and on earth. It is to be noted that Gr *egō*, "I," is the first word of vv 3a and 4a, the opening bicola of Wisdom's address, and also the first word of vv 16a and 17a, the opening bicola of the final stanza of her speech. This feature is reminiscent of the two stanzas in Prov 8:12–16 and 17–21 that were introduced by Heb *ʾănî*, "I." So Skehan, *CBQ* 41, p. 377. The personification of Wisdom is an idea Ben Sira borrowed likewise from Proverbs (1:20–33; 8:4–36; 9:1–6, 11). Folly is also personified in Proverbs (9:13–18). Though Wisdom is personified and has her origin from God (v 3a), she remains nonetheless a creature (cf. v 8ab). Wisdom is said to come forth from God's mouth (v 3a) and accordingly is considered to be a spirit—an idea derived from Prov 8:23a, which speaks of Wisdom as "poured forth." Because she is a spirit, Wisdom is compared to a mist covering the earth (v 3b); cf. Gen 1:2, where the spirit (or wind) of God hovers over the primeval waters of chaos prior to the creative word that comes forth from God's mouth (Gen 1:3; Jdt 16:14). Thus Wisdom is poured out on the whole earth and is manifested in creation, which in turn proclaims the glory and handiwork of God (cf. Ps 19:2–5). In vv 23, 25–27, the Law or Torah (Heb *tôrâ*), which in the thought of Ben Sira is identified with Wisdom (cf. COMMENT on 1:11–30 and 6:32–37), is compared to a river at high water, which "runs over" and "floods, like the Nile." So the Law, too, is viewed as a spirit. In v 33a, Ben Sira says of himself, "I pour out instruction"—the imagery used of Wisdom in Prov 8:23a.

"In the heights" and "I dwelt" of v 4a are echoes of Prov 8:2, 12. The "pillar of cloud" (v 4b) in Exod 13:21–22; 14:19–20; 33:9–11; and 40:38 was the means by which the Lord manifested his presence to the Israelites during the period of the Exodus. By using these images in v 4, Ben Sira states that Wisdom dwells with God. According to Philo Judaeus (a Hellenizing Jewish philosopher of Alexandria, ca. 15 B.C.–ca. A.D. 45), the "pillar of cloud" was Wisdom (*Quis Rer. Div. Heres.*, 42). Cf. v 10 and Exod 33:9–10. In Wis 10:17, Wisdom is said to have conducted the Israelites "by a wondrous road" and become "a shelter for them by day and a starry flame by night" (cf. Exod 13:21). She is the one who "took them across the Red Sea and brought them through the deep waters" (Wis 10:18). Cf. Exod 14:15–29. In Wis 9:4, Solomon prays for Wisdom, "the attendant of [God's] throne" (cf. Wis 9:10 and John 1:1).

"The vault of heaven" imagery (v 5a; cf. 43:12a and Job 22:14) derives from Prov 8:27–28, and "the deep abyss" (v 5b; cf. 1:3) from Prov 8:24. The idea that Wisdom "held sway" (v 6b) over the sea (cf. Prov 8:29), the land (Prov 8:28), and every people and nation (v 6ab) reflects the theme of Prov

8:15–16; cf. v 11b, which states that Wisdom's special "domain" is Jerusalem. In vv 5–6, Ben Sira declares that Wisdom has been present and active throughout history, as she was present in the days of creation (Gen 1:1–31); cf. Prov 8:27–30. Finally, Wisdom sought for herself an earthly "resting place" (v 7a) "among them all," i.e., among "every people and nation" (v 6b), asking herself where she should abide (v 7b). In the Midrash *Pesiqta*, 186a, it is said that the Law was originally offered to all, but that Israel alone of the nations accepted it; so Box-Oesterley, p. 397. Cf. Bar 3:37. Like the dove, which sought "a resting place" (Gr *anapausin*, the same word found in the LXX of Gen 8:9, the MT of which has *mānôaḥ*) after Noah sent it forth from the Ark, so, too, did Wisdom seek such a place (v 7a). The stanza opens with "I" (Gr *egō*, Heb *'ănî*) and closes with a first-person-singular verb, "should I abide." Cf. H. Conzelmann, "Die Mutter der Weisheit [Sir 24:3–7]," *Fest-schrift R. Bultmann* 2, pp. 225–34.

The second stanza (vv 8–12) of Wisdom's speech begins with "then" (Gr *tote*, Heb *'āz*) followed by a perfect-tense verb in Heb (aorist in Gr). In Ps 89:20, a new stanza begins in exactly the same way. So Skehan, *CBQ* 41, p. 377. This stanza describes how Wisdom, after searching for a place to reside on earth, was commanded by the Creator to make her dwelling in Israel (v 8). In v 8a, the expression "Fashioner of all," an allusion to Prov 8:27–29, also occurs in the litany of praise (v iv) that follows 51:12 in MS B of the Cairo text: *yôṣēr hakkōl*, a phrase found also in Jer 10:16 and 51:19. V 8b implies that God himself had to choose "the spot for [Wisdom's] tent" because she was unsuccessful in her search (v 7). In v 8cd, there is perfect balance and synonymous parallelism between "in Jacob" and "in Israel," and between "make your dwelling" (Gr *kataskēnōson;* cf. John 1:14) and "(make) your inheritance" (cf. v 7b). V 9a alludes to Prov 8:22–23; cf. 1:1, 4, 9, 15. Wisdom is everlasting, "shall not cease to be" (v 9b). In v 10a, Wisdom is said to minister before the Creator "in the holy Tent"—an allusion to Wisdom (= the Law) stipulating the religious and liturgical rules to be followed in the worship of the Lord. The "Tent" is the Tabernacle or Dwelling that Yahweh commanded Moses to build; cf. Exod 25:8–9; 26:1–37. V 10b refers to Wisdom ministering to the Lord when the Jerusalem (=Zion) Temple took the place of the Tent. V 11 is in parallel with v 8: the Creator gave Wisdom rest (cf. vv 7a and 8b) "in the city he loves [cf. Ps 50:2] as he does me [= Wisdom]," i.e., "in Jerusalem" (v 11b). As regards Wisdom's "domain" (v 11b), cf. the verb phrase "I held sway" (v 6b): both words derive from the same Heb root *mšl* (cf. 10:4a in Heb and G). "The glorious people" (v 12a) is an obvious reference to Jacob-Israel (v 8cd). Wisdom's "inheritance" (v 12b; cf. NOTE) is "in the portion of the Lord," i.e., in Israel; cf. 17:17b; Deut 32:9; Zech 2:16. It is to be noted that the word "inheritance" occurs in the last colon (v 7b) of the first stanza of Wisdom's speech and in the last colon (v 12b) of the second stanza; cf. also v 8d.

The five bicola or lines of the third stanza of Wisdom's speech (vv 13–15) are linked together in a formal unity by the word "like" (Gr hōs, Heb kĕ-), which begins each line (vv 13a, 14a,c, 15a,c), and by "and like" (the "and" does not appear in the translation here), which opens the second colon of each line (vv 13b, 14b, 15b,d), with a variation in word order only in v 14d (where the "like" appears as the third word in G so as to ward off monotony; so Skehan, CBQ 41, p. 378). In Proverbs 8, the only plant imagery is found in v 19. In this stanza, Wisdom proclaims her excellence and desirability by a series of images, some of which may strike a modern Western reader as bombastic. The trees and plants (some of the finest among the flora of Palestine) and other exotic elements (some of which are used in the liturgy) are meant to evoke in the reader or listener a feeling of pleasure and a desire for Wisdom. The "cedar of Lebanon" (v 13a) is the most majestic and celebrated tree in Syria-Palestine and was used as a metaphor for strength and beauty; cf. Ps 92:13; Num 24:6; Cant 5:15. Cf. L. Fonck, " 'Quasi cedrus exaltata sum in Libano . . .' (Eccli. 24,17)," VD 1 (1921): 226–31. The "cypress" (v 13b) was noted for its great height; cf. 50:10. "Mount Hermon" (v 13b) is located in the northeastern border of Palestine, over against Lebanon. Adjoining the tableland of Bashan, it stands at the southern end and is the culminating point of the range of the Anti-Lebanon Mountains. Mount Hermon towered high above the ancient city of Dan and the sources of the Jordan; cf. Ps 133:3; Cant 4:8. "Engeddi" (v 14a), a town located on the western shore of the Dead Sea, in the wilderness of Judaea, was widely known for its date palms (cf. Josephus, Antiquities, xiv 4, 1), which grew splendid featherlike leaves and produced delicious clusters of dates. The town was also known as Hazazon-tamar, i.e., Hazazon of the palms; cf. 2 Chr 20:2. "Jericho" (v 14b), the famous city of Benjamin in the Jordan plain west of the river, was a fertile garden spot, well watered and luxuriant. It was also called "the city of palm trees" (2 Chr 28:15). Apparently the rose gardens in Jericho were spectacular, as v 14b implies; cf. 39:13. Cf. A. Vaccari, " 'Quasi plantatio rosae in Iericho' (Eccli. 24,18)," VD 3 (1923): 289–94.

The "olive tree" (v 14c) is the principal fruit-bearing tree of the Holy Land (and of the other Mediterranean countries). It is described here as "fair" or "beautiful in appearance" as it grows in abundance "in the foothills," the area known as the Shephelah (cf. Josh 10:40; 12:8). The "plane tree" (v 14d), mentioned only two other times in the OT (Gen 30:37 and Ezek 31:8), is found chiefly in the north of Palestine and in small numbers. For the phrase "beside the water," cf. NOTE and 39:13; Ps 1:3; Jer 17:8. In v 15 (cf. NOTE), Ben Sira changes the imagery to the perfumes and incense used in the service of the Meeting Tent in the desert. "Cinnamon" (cf. Prov 7:17; Cant 4:14), "fragrant cane," and "precious myrrh" (v 15a) were combined with cassia (the bark of a tree, used as a spice) and blended with olive oil to produce a sacred perfume ointment to be used in the anointing of the Tent, the ark of the commandments, and many other sacred appurtenances, as well as Aaron and his sons (Exod 30:23–30). "Galbanum" (v 15c) is a bitter, aromatic gum or resin extracted from a plant; "mastic" is the aromatic gum of the mastic tree. "Onycha" is "generally believed to be the operculum of some species of marine mollusc. The operculum is a horny or calcareous plate attached to the foot of certain Gasteropodous molluscs, the function of which is to close the aperture of the shell when the animal has withdrawn into the interior" (*Encyclopedia Biblica,* vol. 3, p. 3511). Galbanum, onycha, and mastic were blended with pure frankincense to produce the incense used in the liturgical service of the Tent (Exod 30:34–35). In v 15d, Wisdom compares herself to "the odor of incense in the holy Tent," i.e., something sacred, acceptable, and pleasing to the Lord; something which was forbidden to be used for non-liturgical purposes (cf. Exod 30:38) and which was to be offered only by authorized personnel (cf. Num 16:6–7, 17–35; 2 Chr 26:16–19). The pleasant smell of incense was proverbial; cf. Prov 27:9; Cant 3:6. V 15 adds a new dimension to Wisdom—Wisdom serves a liturgical and priestly function; it is an intermediary between God and human beings; cf. 2 Cor 2:15.

Like the opening stanza of Wisdom's speech, the final stanza (vv 16–17, 19–22) has "I" as the first word of the first two bicola; cf. COMMENT on v 3. The imagery returns to flora, as in vv 13–14. The "terebinth" (v 16a), a deciduous tree with pinnate leaves and red berries, was noted for its far-reaching and lovely branches. In Judg 6:11, the angel of Yahweh who spoke with Gideon sat under the terebinth in Ophrah. In Israel's past, the terebinth, probably because it was such a prominent and lofty tree, had been associated with cultic prostitution at idol shrines; cf. Isa 1:29; 57:5; Hos 4:13. Like the vine (v 17a) which produces the grape for wine that "cheers gods and men" (Judg 9:13), Wisdom buds forth "delights" (lit., grace). When her blossoms fall off, Wisdom produces "fruits fair and rich" (v 17b), lit., fruits of honor and wealth—the classical fruits of Wisdom. Cf. 4:21b; Prov 3:16; 8:18–19, 21. As regards v 18, found in GII, cf. NOTES. For a good study of the symbolism of the tree and vine images, cf. A. Fournier–Bidoz, "L'Arbre et la demeure: Siracide xxiv 10–17," *VT* 34 (1984): 1–10.

In v 19, Wisdom now offers the customary invitation to her disciples, whom she calls "you that yearn for me." One must accept her invitation in order to "be filled with [her] fruits," which are "fair and rich," as v 17b puts it. Cf. 6:18–38; Prov 8:4–10, 32–36; 9:4–6, 11; Matt 11:28–30. Wisdom describes herself as "sweeter than honey" (v 20a) and "better . . . than the honeycomb" (v 20b); cf. Ps 19:11, where the "ordinances of Yahweh" are said to be "sweeter than syrup or honey from the comb." Cf. also Ps 119:103; Prov 16:24; 24:13–14. The point of v 21 is that the one who eats and drinks of Wisdom's delights (cf. vv 17, 19–20) "will hunger" and "thirst for more." Compare the words of Jesus in John 4:14; 6:35. The one who "obeys" Wisdom (cf. Prov 8:32a) "will not be put to shame" (v 22a; cf. Ps 22:6), whereas the fool, i.e., the person who does not keep the Law, will experience shame and disgrace (cf. 5:14; 6:1; 20:26). Moreover, "those who work with [Wisdom]," i.e., those whose obedience to her is put into practice, *"will never fail"* (Gr *hamartēsousin,* Heb *yeḥṭāʾû* in Skehan's retroversion). Skehan writes (*CBQ* 41, p. 378): "Perhaps the most interesting lexical link between [Proverbs 8 and Sirach 24] occurs with *ḥōṭěʾî* in Prov 8:36 and *lōʾ yeḥṭāʾû* in Sir 24:22. 'He who misses me [that is, Wisdom]' is the sense in Proverbs, and 'will not fail' is the meaning in Sirach—the only two cases in biblical literature in which *ḥṭʾ* has its basic physical sense of falling short, missing the mark, and does not rather convey the derived sense of 'sin.' " It is also to be observed that the Heb verb *ḥṭʾ* (Gr *hamartanein*) occurs in the last line of the poem in Proverbs 8 (v 36a) and in the last lines of Wisdom's speech in our poem (v 22b).

The next stanza (vv 23, 25–29), in which Ben Sira is again the speaker, identifies Wisdom with the Law (Torah). Skehan remarks (*CBQ* 41, p. 379): "[V] 23a can only be described as a descent into prose; I know of no one who tries to make of it a full line." V 23a is, however, one of Ben Sira's most emphatic statements that Wisdom is the Torah of Israel. Cf. COMMENT on 1:11–30; 6:32–37; 15:1; 19:20; 21:6; 23:27. "The book of the . . . covenant" (v 23a) is an expression taken from Exod 24:7. V 23bc is a direct quotation of Deut 33:4, the LXX of which G quotes word for word. The Torah given to Moses to enjoin on the people is Jacob's "heritage" (v 23bc). For further study of v 23, cf. G. T. Sheppard, "Wisdom and Torah: The Interpretation of Deuteronomy Underlying Sirach 24:23," in G. A. Tuttle, ed., *Biblical and Near Eastern Studies,* pp. 166–76. For v 24 in GII, cf. NOTE. The Torah, like Wisdom in v 3, is viewed as a spirit. Hence Ben Sira can speak of the Torah being "brimful, like the Pishon [the first river that branched from the river in Eden; Gen 2:11], with wisdom" (v 25a), or "like the Tigris at the time of the new crops" (v 25b), i.e., in spring, when many rivers are at their high-water mark. The Torah is not only full with Wisdom (v 25a), but it also "runs over, like the Euphrates [a river which flows some 2,235 miles from east-central Turkey, through northeastern Syria and central Iraq, to the Tigris, with which it forms the Shatt-al-Arab] with understanding" (v 26a), or "like the Jordan [Palestine's own best-known river] at harvesttime" (v 26b); cf. 1 Chr 12:15. Instead of "at harvesttime," Syr reads "in the days of Nisan," the first month of the religious year, i.e., March–April, when the harvest was brought in. The flooding, in September, of the *Nile* (cf. NOTE) (at 4,145 miles in length the longest river in Africa, and in the Near East) was proverbial (cf. Amos 8:8; 9:5); so, too, the Torah "floods . . . with knowledge" (v 27a). The Gihon (v 27b) was the second river that branched from the river in Eden; cf. Gen 2:13. In the LXX of Jer 2:18, the Gihon is identified with the Nile. The omission of *kai,* "and," before "like" in v 27b in GI seems to reflect the same identification. But the *kai* is well attested in GII and many other Gr MSS, as well as Syh and Syr. Most likely, the original Heb text had "and" before "like," thus giving perfect balance to vv 25–27, one river in each of the six cola. The "vintage time" was September–October. It should be observed that the names of the first and sixth rivers in vv 25–27 derive from Gen 2:11, 13, which together with the rest of Genesis 1–11 contain the prehistory of Israel, whereas the other rivers named are connected with the real history of Israel— the Tigris and Euphrates with Assyria and later Babylon, which were Israel's enemies, and where Israel went into exile after the destruction of Jerusalem in 587 B.C.; the Jordan, which was the principal river of Palestine; and the Nile in the land of Egypt, where the children of Abraham were oppressed by the Pharaohs.

"The first human" (v 28a), i.e., Adam (another reference to Genesis 2) "never knew wisdom fully" because the Torah, which *is* wisdom, was not yet revealed; Moses was the one to whom the Torah was given. Israel's wisdom, her Torah, is so inexhaustible and profound that not even "the last [human]" on earth could "succeed in fathoming her" (v 28b). The reference to "the first human" and "the last human" implies a merism: i.e., wisdom is beyond all human beings and their attempts to attain her. In the Bible, water was often employed as an image of divine bounty and goodness; cf., for example, Isa 12:3; Jer 2:13; 17:13; Ps 36:9–10; John 4:14; 7:37. In v 29, Wisdom is compared to water that is "deeper than the sea . . . than the great abyss," the abyss being another reference to prehistory in Genesis (1:2). There is in v 29 a well-balanced *a:b::b':a'* chiastic structure that emphasizes the point and also brings the stanza to a close: (deeper) *than the sea:her thoughts::her counsels:than the great abyss.*

The final stanza of this superb poem, which now has as speaker Ben Sira himself, opens with "and I" (Gr *kagō,* Heb *waʾănî*), translated here "now I." The same pronoun opens the first (v 3) and the last stanzas (v 16) of Wisdom's speech; cf. COMMENT on vv 3–4. Because he is a Wisdom teacher, Ben Sira boldly compares himself to "a rivulet from her stream" (v 30a), thus continuing the imagery of vv 25–27. Wisdom's "stream" (lit., river) is so abundant that it can be channeled into many rivulets (like Ben Sira and other sages). Since Ben Sira is "a rivulet . . . channeling the waters forth into a *garden"* (v 30b; cf. 40:27a; Isa 58:11), he says to himself, "I will water my plants, my flower bed I will drench" (v 31ab); i.e., he is of a mind at first to use the waters of Wisdom for his personal benefit. But suddenly his "rivulet . . . became a river" (v 31c), his "stream [lit., river] . . . a sea" (v 31d), apparently even bolder metaphors because Wisdom herself is compared to a river in v 30a (cf. vv 25–27) and to the sea in v 29a. Cf. Ezek 47:1–12; Joel 4:18. But Ben Sira's "teachings" (v 32a) are not really his own, nor are they to be viewed as a personal achievement (like Aristotle's); but rather his wisdom is simply the Torah, which he learned from his glorious tradition, and of which he was the first to benefit. Accordingly, he can send forth the teachings of the Torah "shining like the dawn" (v 32a), "to spread their brightness afar off," i.e., even to the Diaspora, so that they are not confined merely to the Jewish inhabitants of the Holy Land. The image of the Law as light is found also in Ps 119:105; Isa 2:5; Wis 18:4. Finally, Ben Sira says he will "pour out [cf. COMMENT on v 3] instruction like prophecy" (v 33a), i.e., he is aware of his own inspiration from God, as the prophets of old were of theirs (cf. Jer 1:7, 9); and like them, he utters his wisdom for the benefit of others. He bequeaths his instruction "to generations yet to come" (v 33b), so that not only his contemporaries will profit from his teachings but also all future believers all over the world (cf. v 32b).

For a more detailed study of this chapter, see the excellent article by M. Gilbert, "L'Éloge de la Sagesse (Siracide 24)," *RTL* 5 (1974): 326–48.

31. Gifts That Bring Happiness
(25:1–12)

25   1 With three things I am delighted,   S
　　　for they are pleasing to the Lord and to humans:
　　Harmony among kindred, friendship among neighbors,   G
　　　and the mutual love of husband and wife.
　2 Three kinds of people I hate;
　　　their manner of life I loathe indeed:
　　A proud pauper, a rich dissembler,
　　　and an old person lecherous in his dotage.

　3 What you have not gathered in your youth,
　　　how will you acquire in your old age?
　4 How becoming to the gray-haired is judgment,
　　　and a knowledge of counsel to those on in years!
　5 How becoming to the aged is wisdom,
　　　understanding and prudence to the venerable!
　6 The crown of the elderly is wide experience;
　　　their glory, the fear of the Lord.

　7 There are nine who come to my mind as blessed,
　　　a tenth, whom my tongue proclaims:
　　Happy is whoever finds joy in his children,
　　　and whoever lives to see his enemies' downfall.
　8 Happy is whoever dwells with a sensible wife,
　　　and whoever is not plowing with an ox and a donkey   S
　　　　　　　　　　　　　　　　　　　　combined.
　　Happy is whoever sins not with his tongue,   G
　　　and whoever serves not his inferior.
　9 Happy is whoever finds a friend,
　　　and whoever speaks to attentive ears.
　10 Whoever finds wisdom is great indeed,
　　　but not greater than the one who fears the Lord.

¹¹ Fear of the Lord surpasses all else,
   its possessor is beyond compare.ᵃ

ᵃ ¹² Fear of the Lord is the beginning of loving him,   GII
   and fidelity is the beginning of clinging to him.

Notes

25 1ab. Ziegler restores the corrupt Gr text for these two cola, on the basis of the Syr and following the analogy of similar numerical proverbs; see his introduction, pp. 76–78.

7cd–10. The pattern of this numerical proverb calls for ten separate types named for approval. In the Gr, there are only nine, in the Syr, eleven; of these, eight are in more or less agreement.

8b. Lacking in G, this colon is taken from Syr. Two words only of it survive in a damaged leaf of Heb MS C; they are ḥwrš kšwr, "one plowing as (with) a bull. . . ." But the Syr has bĕtawrâ wĕbaḥĕmârâ ʾakḥĕdâ, with an ox and a donkey combined, the normal allusion to Deut 22:10. The allusion in the context of Sirach is certainly to an incompatible marriage; here it is being understood of one man married to two incompatible women (compare 37:11a). That the incompatible pair should be husband and wife is an application that has been made (viz., to Dinah and Shechem, Genesis 34; see Segal); since the terms more precisely mean "with a bull and a jackass combined," such an application multiplies incongruities to the straining point.

9a. *a friend:* so Lat and Syr; G has "knowledge"; compare 10a.

12. Note here a recurrent theme of GII, last seen in 19:18–19 and 24:18, 24.

Comment

This section, comprised of three loosely connected poems (4+4+7 bicola), contains numerical proverbs in the first (vv 1–2) and third (vv 7–11) units. Cf. COMMENT on 23:16–17 and INTRODUCTION, Part IV, 1.

The first poem (vv 1–2), with two numerical proverbs, introduces in v 1d the theme of this section and the next (25:13–26:18[27]), viz., the blessings of a good marriage and the kinds of husbands and wives that are found in such marriages. On v 1ab, cf. NOTE. "Harmony among kindred" (v 1c) is a cherished grace in any society, but particularly in a society with close family bonds as in ancient Israel; cf. 7:12; Psalm 133. "Friendship among neighbors" (v 1c) was also important, because the Israelites viewed other individuals of their group as kinsmen; cf. Tob 4:13. But the third, and hence finest, thing is "the mutual love of husband and wife," lit., a husband and a wife who are suited to each other (v 1d); cf. 40:23b. Curiously, GI has the word order "a wife and a husband." GII, Lat, and Syr have husband before wife. As could be expected from a writer of that day and culture, Ben Sira devotes only two bicola (v 2) to evil men and husbands. The rest of this section (vv 3–11) speaks of the blessings that the good husband experiences. In the next section (25:13–26:18[27]), however, Ben Sira has far more to say about the evil woman or wife (25:13–26; 26:5–12, 22–27) than about the good one (26:1–4, 13–18). See INTRODUCTION, Part X, 7. Ben Sira hates "a proud pauper" (v 2c) because pride is a vice that is despicable in anyone (cf. 10:7–18, with COMMENT), but especially in the poor, who have little to boast of in the first place. Lying is also loathsome (cf. 20:24–26, with COMMENT), but particularly in the rich (v 2c), who have all their needs satisfied and thus have little temptation to lie or use fraud. V 2d may be translated, lit.: "and an old man who is an adulterer lacking in sense." The old man is supposed to be, in view of his age and experience, a model of virtue and wisdom (cf. vv 4–6). When he commits adultery, however, he is despicable because he violates his station in life by proving to be "lacking in sense" as well as in virtue. It is bad enough when a young man gives in to youthful lust; but when an old man succumbs to illicit passion, it is utterly degenerate, as in the case of the two lecherous elders of the people who conspired to commit adultery with beautiful Susanna. She repelled their sinful advances even though they attempted to blackmail her (Dan 13:5–27).

The next stanza (vv 3–6) continues the theme of old age, opening with a strong reminder that what one has not gathered in youth it is too late to acquire in old age (v 3); cf. 6:18–37. Vv 4–6 may be autobiographical, for Ben Sira was well "on in years" (v 4b) when he published his book; cf. INTRODUCTION, Part II. These verses describe the wisdom and virtue that should be the possessions of the aged who throughout their lives have feared the Lord (v 6b), as Ben Sira apparently did. "Judgment" (v 4a) and "a knowledge of counsel" (v 4b), "wisdom" (v 5a), "understanding and prudence" (v 5b), and "wide experience" (v 6a; cf. 21:22b) are becoming to old age and are "the crown of the elderly" (v 6a; cf. 1:18a). But above all else is "the fear of the Lord," which is the "glory" of the aged (v 6b; cf. 1:11). Compare v 2d.

The final stanza (vv 7–11) contains Ben Sira's ten beatitudes; cf. Matt 5:3–11; Luke 6:20–22. Cf. NOTE on vv 7cd–10. The stanza is a typical example of an "x and x + 1" numerical proverb; cf. INTRODUCTION, Part IV, 1. Children were considered a blessing from the Lord (cf. Ps 127:3–5; Sir 40:19a); but not all children gave "joy" (v 7c) to their parents; cf. 16:1–4. The sentiment about living long enough to see the downfall of one's enemies (v 7d) is hardly Christian; compare Matt 5:43–47. That sentiment, however, was not uncommon in the OT; cf., for example, Pss 18:38–39, 40–43, 48–49; 54:7; 112:8. Dwelling "with a sensible wife" (v 8a) was another divine blessing the Jewish male hoped for; cf. v 1d and 26:1–4. On the face of it, v 8b calls happy the man who does not plow with an ox and an ass yoked together—something explicitly forbidden in the Law (Deut 22:10); cf. 2 Cor 6:14. But as the context clearly indicates, a statement about an undesirable marriage is being made; cf. NOTE. Cf. also vv 13–26; 26:7–9. Ben Sira gives another beatitude about the person who controls his tongue (v 8c) in 14:1a; cf. Jas 3:2. Serving an inferior (v 8d) was considered a social disgrace; compare Luke 22:27 and John 13:13–16. Friendship (v 9a; cf. NOTE) was another great blessing, about which Ben Sira had much to say; cf. 6:5–17 and 37:1–6. The wise are indeed happy if there are "attentive ears" (v 9b) to speak to; cf. 3:29b, which in G reads: "An attentive ear is the desire of the wise." The ninth beatitude calls great the one who "finds wisdom" (v 10a), and the tenth extols as even greater the one "who fears the Lord" (v 10b). Since in the thought of Ben Sira wisdom is identified with fear of the Lord (cf. COMMENT on 1:11–30; 6:32–37; 24:23–29), the ninth and tenth beatitudes—the two most significant in the series—call happy the person who does the same thing, i.e., "finds wisdom" and "fears the Lord." To emphasize the supreme value and importance of fear of the Lord, Ben Sira adds an extra line (v 11) to the ten beatitudes; cf. 1:11–21, 25–27. See INTRODUCTION, Part X, 1. GII goes one better by adding another line (v 12); cf. NOTE and 1:10cd.

32. Wicked and Virtuous Women
(25:13–26:18[27])

25   13 Worst of all wounds is that of the heart,   G
          worst of all evils is that of a woman.
    14 Worst of all afflictions is that from one's foes,
          worst of all vengeance is that of one's enemies:
    15 No poison worse than that of a serpent,
          no venom greater than that of a woman.
    16 With a dragon or a lion I would rather dwell
          than live with an evil woman.
    17 Wickedness changes a woman's looks,
          and makes her sullen as a female bear.
    18 When her husband sits among his neighbors,
          a bitter sigh escapes him unawares.

    19 There is scarce any evil like that in a woman;
          may she fall to the lot of the sinner!
    20 Like a sandy hill to aged feet
          is a railing wife to a quiet man.
    21 Stumble not through a woman's beauty,
          nor be greedy for her wealth: S
    22 Harsh is the slavery, great the shame,
          when a wife supports her husband.   G

    23 Depressed mind, saddened face,
          broken heart—these from an evil wife.
    Feeble hands and quaking knees—
          from a wife who brings no happiness to her husband.
    24 In a woman was sin's beginning:
          on her account we all die.
    25 Allow water no outlet,
          and be not indulgent to an erring wife;

26 If she walks not by your side,
 cut her away from your flesh with a bill of divorce.

26 1 Happy the husband of a good wife,
 twice lengthened are his days;
2 A worthy wife brings joy to her husband,
 peaceful and full is his life.
3 A good wife is a generous gift
 bestowed upon him who fears the Lord;
4 Be he rich or poor, his heart is content
 and a smile is ever on his face.

5 There are three things at which my heart quakes,
 a fourth before which I quail:
Though false charges in public, trial before all the
         people,
 and lying testimony are each harder to bear than
         death,
6 A wife jealous of another wife is heartache and
        mourning
 and a scourging tongue like the other three.

7 A bad wife is a chafing yoke;
 whoever marries her has a scorpion in his grasp.
8 A drunken wife arouses great anger,
 for she does not hide her shame.
9 By her eyelids and her haughty stare
 an unchaste wife can be recognized.

10 Keep strict watch over an unruly wife,
 lest, finding an opportunity, she make use of it;
11 Follow close if her eyes are bold,
 and be not surprised if she betrays you:
12 As a thirsty traveler with eager mouth
 drinks from any water that he finds,
So she sits down before every tent peg
 and opens her quiver for every arrow.

13 A gracious wife delights her husband,
 her thoughtfulness puts flesh on his bones;
14 A gift from the Lord is her governed speech,
 and her disciplined virtue is of surpassing worth.

15 Choicest of blessings is a modest wife,
    priceless her chaste person.
16 Like the sun rising in the Lord's heavens,
    the beauty of a virtuous wife is the radiance of her
                                            home.
17 Like the light which shines above the holy lampstand
    are her beauty of face and graceful figure.
18 Golden columns on silver bases
    are her shapely limbs and steady feet.*

---

*19 My son, keep intact the prime of your life   GII
    by not surrendering your strength to strangers;
20 Single out from all the land a goodly field
    and there with confidence sow the seed of your
                                            increase—
21 So shall you have your offspring around you
    growing up confident in their breeding.

22 Though a woman for hire be thought of as a trifle,
    a married woman is a deadly snare for those who
                                        embrace her.
23 An impious woman will be given as spouse to the lawless
                                                    man,
    but a devout wife is given to whoever fears the Lord.
24 The shameless hussy wears out reproach,
    but an exemplary daughter will be modest even before
                                            her husband.
25 The unruly wife will be thought of as a bitch,
    but the one with a sense of shame fears the Lord.
26 The woman who respects her husband will be seen by
                                        everyone as wise,
    but the one who proudly scorns her spouse all will know
                                            to be impious.
    Happy the husband of a good wife;
        each year of his life counts for two.
27 But a loud-mouthed, scolding wife can be recognized
    as a battle trumpet signaling attack.
    Any human being who matches that challenge
        will spend his life amid the turbulence of war.

Notes

25   15. *poison . . . venom:* the Heb will have been *rōʾš* and *ḥēmâ*, cf. Deut 32:33.
The Gr has misunderstood the terms.

16a. *dragon . . . lion:* these creatures come from Ps 91:13.

17a. *Wickedness changes a woman's looks:* "The wickedness of a woman turns her
husband's face green," says Syr. It is sure from G, Syr, and MS C that "her husband"
belongs in 18a; the earlier shift of reference is unwarranted. Cf. v 23.

18. *sits*=Syr, MS C (*yšb*); the Gr seems to have read *šwb. unawares*=GII (cod.
248), Syr, and MS C; so Ziegler, repairing the corrupt *akousas,* "having heard," of GI.
The *bitter* in G may be an expansion.

22a. *great*=G; Syr has *bĩštāʾ*="dire."

26b. *with a bill of divorce:* based on GII (248), with Syr. GI does not have this
explanation.

26   3b. *him who fears:* with Syr and MS C; G makes this plural.

10a. *unruly wife:* the context and Syr require this. G has fused the language of 10a
here and of the similar colon 42:11a, as the Masada text of the later passage helps to
prove. The "daughter" of G, instead of *wife,* comes from 42:11, where in turn the
adiatreptǭ, unruly, has been added by way of expansion. The Heb here in 10a will have
had *ʿazzat pānîm* (so Segal), which is to be understood of a wife rather than of an
unmarried person.

12c. *sits:* a euphemism for "lies"; in the basic Heb, this will have been *tšb* for *tškb.*

19–27. This series of expansions on 25:13–26:18 has been transmitted in both GII
and Syr. The presumption is that the verses were composed in Heb, though they are
not extant in that language.

22. Cf. Prov 6:26. *deadly snare:* both GII and Syr have "tower of death"; but in
view of the dependence on Proverbs, the presumption is very strong that the Heb read
mĕṣûdat māwet, and that not a tower but a snare was meant; cf. also Qoh 7:26; 9:12;
Sir 9:3; and *CBQ* 16 (1954): 154.

22–26cd. This series of antitheses is built up out of the language and thought
patterns of 25:13–26:18, with the doublet of Prov 6:26 (v 22) to open the series, and a
doublet of Sir 26:1 (v 26cd) to conclude it. V 23 is an elaboration of 25:19; 26:3.

26d. *for two.* After this, Syr has the line "Complaint by a wife should be made in
meekness, / and show itself in a slight flush"; this is accepted by Peters (instead of
26cd=26:1, see above) and by Segal. It breaks, however, the pattern otherwise visible
both in G and in Syr whereby in vv 22–27 seven successive sayings begin with the
same word for "woman/wife." That pattern suggests that vv 22–26 were compiled out
of familiar materials (see above) to provide a setting for the longer v 27, which (whatever else one thinks of it) is not found elsewhere.

27c. *that challenge:* both GII and Syr are vague, saying only "these"; but the
reference should be to the trumpet blasts of 27b.

Comment

This section on wicked and virtuous women resumes the theme introduced in 25:1d. As was noted in the COMMENT on 25:2, Ben Sira (like other authors of that society and age) writes a great deal more about the evil woman or wife (25:13–26; 26:5–12, 22–27) than about the good one (26:1–4, 13–18). The unflattering observations made here should not be explained away or exaggerated; they are simply accurate reflections of the kind of training for life the young Jewish male received in the early second century B.C. See INTRODUCTION, Part X, 7.

In the opening stanza (vv 13–18, six bicola), the first verse sets the somber tone for the comments Ben Sira makes about the evils women are capable of. Heartache indeed hurts more than any other pain (v 13a), and what a wicked woman can do to one's heart is the "worst of all evils" (v 13b). Vv 14–15 refer to the evils of polygamy, which was still practiced in Ben Sira's day (so Smend, p. 229, and Box-Oesterley, p. 401); cf. 25:8b; 26:6a; 37:11a. If a man's wives did not get along with each other, they became "foes" to each other as well as to their husband, and all suffered the "worst of all afflictions" (v 14a). V 14b is in parallel with v 14a; the "vengeance" (v 14b) refers to what the rival wives, who have become "enemies," try to wreak on one another. The "venom" (v 15b; cf. NOTE) of the feuding wives is said to be even greater than the dangerous "poison" of a serpent (v 15a). As regards the problems, envy, and jealousy that arose in polygamous marriages, cf. Gen 29:31–30:24.

Ben Sira states he "would rather dwell" "with a dragon or a lion" (v 16a; cf. NOTE) than "with an evil woman" (v 16b)—a somewhat daring, if not preposterous, hyperbole. Prov 21:19 and 25:24 make the point more subtly; cf. Prov 27:15. For the reading of Syr in v 17a, cf. NOTE. The Heb text of MS C is also extant for v 17a; it reads: "The wickedness of a woman makes black the appearance of (her) husband." The point of v 17a in G, which is closest to the original wording of Ben Sira, is that a woman's wickedness manifests itself in her appearance. V 17b may be translated, lit.: "and it [wickedness] darkens her face *like a bear*" (=MS C and most Gr MSS; Codex B of G has *like sackcloth;* Syr, *like the color of sackcloth;* Lat, *like a bear and like sackcloth*). The bear was known for its ferocity; cf. 47:3 (where bears are mentioned in parallel with lions); 1 Sam 17:34, 36–37; 2 Sam 17:8; Hos 13:8. In English and in French, the bear is a symbol of an ill-mannered person. When the wicked woman's husband "sits [cf. NOTE] among his neighbors" (v 18a), they receive an inkling of the grief he experiences in his marriage by the "bitter sigh [which] escapes him unawares" (v 18b; cf. NOTE). Contrast such a husband with the husband of the good wife described with lyrical enthusiasm in Prov 31:23, 28.

In the next stanza (vv 19–22), Ben Sira continues the dismal litany of woes that an evil woman brings upon her husband. The harsh statement in v 19a should be taken as an example of Semitic hyperbole, for Ben Sira must have known from the history of his own people that men caused more evil than women; cf., for instance, the history of the monarchy in Israel and in Judah as well as the prophetic denunciation of kings and princes, nobles and priests. An evil woman is such a misfortune that Ben Sira expresses the wish that she become the wife of a sinner (v 19b), and not of a righteous man; cf. 7:25; Qoh 7:26. The point of the vivid comparison in v 20 is that just as it is difficult, or even impossible, for the aged to climb a hill where the footing is poor because of sand, so it is troublesome, if not intolerable, for "a quiet man" to live with "a railing wife" (cf. 8:3). The advice in v 21 is sound: a man should not marry a woman simply for her beauty or her wealth. Smend writes (p. 231): "The rich woman is bait and trap together." Cf. 31:6. An interesting variation on the ideas expressed in vv 20b–21 is the saying of Thomas Fuller: "Choose a wife rather by your ear than your eye" (*Gnomologia* [1732], 1107). In comparing a wife who "supports her husband" (because he married her for the money she brings in) to "harsh slavery," Ben Sira alludes to the oppressive service the wealthy Egyptians imposed on the Israelites; cf. Exod 1:14; 6:9; Deut 26:6.

The next stanza (vv 23–26) describes the distress an evil wife brings on her husband and gives some advice on what he should do with her. Just as a woman's wickedness manifests itself exteriorly in her "looks" (v 17a), so a husband's grief, his "depressed mind" (v 23a) and "broken heart" (v 23b), at being married to "an evil wife" (v 23b) shows itself in his "saddened face" (v 23a) and "feeble hands [cf. Jer 47:3] and quaking knees [cf. Ps 109:24]" (v 23c); cf. Isa 35:3; Job 4:3–4; Heb 12:12. It is to be noted that "an evil wife" is defined in the parallel v 23d as "a wife who brings no happiness to her husband." Contrast what is said here with Prov 31:10–12. In v 24a, Ben Sira alludes to Gen 3:6—chronologically the woman in the Garden of Eden was the first to sin; her husband ate the forbidden fruit afterward. A similar idea is expressed in 2 Cor 11:3 and 1 Tim 2:14. With regard to the statement that "on her account we all die" (v 24b), it is to be observed that later Jewish theology generally taught that Adam was the real cause for the entrance of sin and death into the world (so Box-Oesterley, p. 402). St. Paul says the same thing in Rom 5:12, 14–19; 1 Cor 15:22. Cf. Wis 2:23–24. Cf. F. R. Tennant, "The Teaching of Ecclesiasticus and Wisdom on the Introduction of Sin and Death," *JTS* 2 (1900–1): 207–23; T. Gallus, "'A muliere initium peccati et per illam omnes morimur' (Sir 25,24 [33])," *VD* 23 (1943): 272–77;

H. Cazelles, *VT* 9 (1959): 212–15, a review of A.-M. Dubarle, *Le Péché originel dans l'Écriture* (Paris, 1956). J. Levison ("Is Eve to Blame? A Contextual Analysis of Sirach 25:24," *CBQ* 47 [1985]: 617–23) argues on the basis of the context and of a fragmentary poem from 4Q that v 24 "refers not to Eve but to the evil wife. Therefore it must be translated: 'From the [evil] wife is the beginning of sin, / and because of her we [husbands] all die' " (p. 622). I find Levison's argument unconvincing. As one dams up water to prevent a flood (v 25a), so a husband should not give free rein "to an erring wife" (v 25b). Cf. 1 Cor 14:34 and 1 Tim 2:11–12. If the erring wife does not become properly submissive (v 26a), the husband is advised to divorce her (v 26b). Cf. 24:1–4; Matt 5:31; 19:3–9. Gen 2:24 speaks of a husband and wife becoming "one flesh." Hence Ben Sira uses the strong language, "cut her away from your flesh," when he refers to divorce (v 26b); cf. NOTE.

Finally, in the next stanza (26:1–4), Ben Sira speaks, however briefly, of the good wife. But even here the woman is not extolled for what she is in and of herself, but only for what she is and does for her husband. Cf. 36:26–31. In v 1a, there is an elegant *a:b::b':a'* rhetorical arrangement to the four words also extant in Heb MS C: *a wife:good::happy:her-husband*. Cf. Prov 12:4. A good wife even gives length of days to her husband's life (v 1b); modern psychology and medicine have proved the validity of this ancient observation. For the thought of v 2, cf. Prov 31:10–12. V 13a is a rephrasing of v 2a. A long life (v 1b) that is "peaceful and full" (v 2b) was the desire and prayer of the pious Jew; cf. Prov 3:2, 16–17; Pss 37:11; 119:165; 122:6–9; 128:1–6. V 3 is important for a proper perspective on Ben Sira's ideas about the good wife: she is "a generous gift [presumably from God] bestowed on him who fears [cf. NOTE] the Lord." Accordingly, the key to finding a good wife and enjoying a happy marriage is fear of the Lord. Cf. Prov 18:22; 19:14. Wealth, though it helps, is not necessary in marriage (v 4a); what is essential is a cheerful (lit., good) heart on the inside and "a smile" on the outside (v 4b), and these come only when the husband, who is himself God-fearing (v 3b), has "a good wife" (v 3a). Cf. 36:29.

The next stanza (vv 5–6) is a numerical proverb; cf. COMMENT on 23:16–17. The first three things (v 5cd), which Ben Sira describes as each being "harder to bear than death" (v 5d), are (1) public judicial proceedings in which (2) "false charges" are made and (3) "lying testimony" is given. Cf. 1 Kgs 21:8–13. The first and third things are sins of the tongue, concerning which cf. 28:18–21. The fourth thing is "a wife jealous of another wife [or woman]"—she is "heartache and mourning" (v 6a). Here Ben Sira again alludes to the difficulties and tensions of polygamy; cf. COMMENT on 25:14–15 and 37:11. "A scourging tongue" (v 6b; cf. Job 5:21) is "like the other three" (lit., like all [the rest]), i.e., like the first three things of v 5cd; cf. 28:17.

The theme of the bad wife continues in the next stanza (vv 7–9). She is "a chafing yoke" (v 7a), a constant irritation; and her husband can be said to have "a scorpion in his grasp" (v 7b)—a vivid image because the scorpion's sting was thought to be deadly (cf. Deut 8:15; Luke 10:19; Rev 9:3, 5). If the husband were to correct or reform such a wife, he would be sure to feel her sting, which indeed could be described, with the words used earlier in a similar context, as "harder to bear than death" (v 5d). Another evil is "a drunken wife," whose inhibitions are taken away by alcohol; she boldly commits adultery (i.e., "she does not hide her shame"), thereby arousing in her husband "great anger" (v 8). Others can recognize "an unchaste wife" (lit., the whoredom of a woman/wife) by her looks (cf. 25:17a), i.e., "by her eyelids and her haughty stare" (v 9); cf. v 11; 23:4b; Prov 6:25. For the ancient Near Eastern customs and methods of making up the eyelids and eyebrows, cf. 2 Kgs 9:30; Jer 4:30; Ezek 23:40.

The "unruly wife" (v 10a; cf. NOTE) is the theme also of the next stanza (vv 10–12). The husband is urged to "keep strict watch" (v 10a) over such a woman, "lest, finding an opportunity, she make use of it" (v 10b), for she is ever on the quest for new lovers (cf. v 12). The "unruly wife" occurs also in v 25. Special surveillance is necessary "if her eyes are bold" (v 11a; cf. v 9a), for she is seeking ways to betray her husband (v 11b). The graphic and blunt comparison in v 12 is meant to dramatize how eager the unruly wife is to commit adultery with any man she meets. For "drinking water" as a metaphor for adultery, cf. Prov 9:17 and also Sir 23:16–17. As regards the verb "sits" (v 12c), cf. NOTE. The "tent peg" and "arrow" in v 12cd are euphemisms for the penis, as "quiver" (v 12d) is for the vagina.

In stark contrast to the unruly wife of the preceding stanza (vv 10–12) is the "gracious wife" of the present stanza (vv 13–18). She not only "delights her husband" (v 13a) but also fattens him up (the Gr is, lit., "her thoughtfulness will fatten his bones"); cf. Prov 15:30 for the phrase "fatten the bones." In those days, being fat was considered a desirable condition to be in and a sign of God's blessing; cf., for example, Deut 31:20 and Neh 9:25. "Her governed speech" (v 14a) renders Gr *gynē sigēra*, lit., "a silent wife" (Lat has "a sensible and silent wife"); cf. 36:28. "Her disciplined virtue" (v 14b) is, lit., "a well-instructed (or disciplined) soul (or mind)." Discipline (Heb *mûsār*) is essential not only to the wise man but also to the good wife; cf. COMMENT on 6:18–22. "A modest wife" is "choicest of blessings" (v 15a), lit., grace upon grace. After "modest," Gr Codex 248 adds, "and faithful." Lat reads "a holy and modest wife." In v 15b, "(her chaste) *person*" renders Gr *(egkratous) psychēs*, lit., (her chaste) *soul, person;* G, and the English translation here, use a euphemism for the euphemism of the original Heb extant in MS C, which reads *(ṣĕrûrat) peh,* "(restricted, shut up of) *mouth,*" a euphemism for the vagina (cf. v 12d). For *ṣĕrûrat,* cf. 2 Sam 20:3. A "modest" and "chaste" wife is "priceless" (v 15b); cf. 6:15; 7:19; Prov 31:10–11. On the beauty of the sun and "the Lord's heavens" (lit., the Lord's heights), with which the "virtuous wife" (v 16) is compared, cf. 43:1–5, 9. The good wife also has the "face and graceful figure" that are as beautiful as "the light which shines above the holy lampstand" (v 17; cf. 1 Macc 1:22; 4:49–50); i.e., she has the dignity and splendor one finds in the sacred liturgy of the Temple—the highest praise Ben Sira can think of, for to him the liturgical service was of supreme value (cf. 50:1–21). The same imagery continues in v 18; "her shapely limbs and steady *feet*" (lit., *heels* in S* and three minuscule MSS; Lat reads "soles [of the feet]"; most other Gr MSS read *sternois*, "breast, chest [as seat of affection], heart") are like the columns of the Temple, which presumably were covered with gold; cf. 1 Macc 1:22. The daring metaphors of vv 17 and 18 are to be taken into account when one evaluates Ben Sira's attitude toward women.

As regards vv 19–27, cf. NOTE. The view is taken here that these verses are an integral part of the original book; so also Peters, p. 218. The next stanza (vv 19–21) begins with "My son," a usual way to indicate a new start. The stanza is an exhortation to the young men of that day not to ruin their health by pursuing erotic adventures with loose women, but rather to find a good wife and beget children they can take pride in. The advice in v 19 is commonplace in the Wisdom literature; cf. 9:6; Prov 5:7–14; 7:24–27; and esp. 31:3 for the idea of giving one's "strength" (i.e., one's seed; cf. v 20b) to "strange" (i.e., immoral) women. In v 20, the young man is urged to find a good wife ("a goodly field") from among the Jews ("from all the land") and beget a family ("sow the seed"); cf. Tob 4:12–13. The children born in such a marriage will "[grow] up confident in their breeding" (v 21b), i.e., they are certain that their father is the husband of their devout mother (the "goodly field" of v 20a). Compare the situation described here with the deplorable case of the wife who wantonly commits adultery (23:22–26).

The final stanza (vv 22–29) of this section contrasts the impious wife and the devout wife and admonishes the young man that he must fear the Lord if he wishes to find a good wife. In v 22a, the Gr word *sialō*, here translated "(as a) trifle," means, lit., "spittle," a term that graphically depicts the scorn with which the men of that day looked upon the prostitute, even though many were willing to pay for her sexual favors. "A married woman," however, is more of a danger; in fact, Ben Sira calls her "a deadly snare [cf. NOTE] for those who embrace her" (v 22b). "The lawless man," i.e., one who does not fear the Lord (cf. COMMENT on 1:11–30; 6:32–37), will have "as spouse" (lit., as [his] portion) "an impious woman" (v 23a), i.e., a woman as bad as he is. Cf. 25:19. But the man who "fears the Lord" (i.e., who keeps the Law) will be given "a devout wife," i.e., a woman as pious as he is (v 23b). Cf. 11:17; 26:3. "The shameless hussy" (v 24a), a parallel to the "impious woman" (v 23a), "wears out [lit., rubs down, rubs away, exhausts] reproach [or shame]"; i.e., any shame she might have had has long since disappeared. The "exemplary daughter," lit., the "daughter with a sense of shame," however, "will be modest even before her husband" (v 24b); cf. v 15. "The unruly wife" (v 25a), also mentioned in v 10a (cf. COMMENT), is another way to describe the "impious woman" (v 23a) and the "shameless hussy" (v 24a). Such a woman will be considered "a bitch," a term of opprobrium that was much stronger for the ancient Jew than it is for us today; cf. Deut 23:19. The wife "with a sense of shame fears the Lord" (v 25b); cf. v 23. The good wife will respect her husband and will thus be considered "by everyone as wise" (v 26a). It is significant that Ben Sira applies the same standard for women as he does for men: to be wise (v 26a)=to fear the Lord (v 25b); cf. COMMENT on 2:15–17; 15:1; 19:20. The bad wife "proudly scorns her spouse" and will thus be seen by all "to be impious" (v 26b), i.e., lacking in wisdom. V 26c repeats verbatim v 1a, and v 26d is a variant form of v 1b; cf. COMMENT above. See NOTE on v 26d. The unflattering metaphors in v 27 are meant to suggest how dreadful it is for a man to be married to a "loud-mouthed, scolding wife." For this military imagery, cf. Josh 6:4–20; Job 39:24–25; Amos 2:2; Zeph 1:16; Zech 9:14.

33. Hazards to Integrity and to Friendship (26:28–27:21)

26   28 These two things bring grief to my heart,
     and the third rouses my anger:
  A wealthy person reduced to want;
     the intelligent held in contempt;
  And the person who passes from righteousness to sin—
     him the Lord makes ready for the sword.

  29 A merchant can hardly remain without fault,
     or a shopkeeper free from sin;
27   1 For the sake of profit many sin,
     and the struggle for wealth blinds the eyes.
  2 Like a peg driven between fitted stones,
     between buying and selling sin is wedged in.
  3 Unless one holds fast to the fear of the Lord,
     with sudden swiftness one's house will be thrown
                   down.

  4 When a sieve is shaken, the husks appear;
     so do a person's faults when he speaks.
  5 As the test of the potter's work is in the furnace,
     so in his conversation is the test of a person.
  6 The fruit of a tree shows the care it has had;
     so too does a person's speech show the bent of his
                   mind.
  7 Praise no one before he speaks,
     for it is then that people are tested.

  8 If you strive after righteousness you will attain it,
     and put it on like a splendid robe.
  9 Birds nest with their own kind,
     and fidelity comes to those who live by it.

10 As a lion crouches in wait for prey,
   so does sin for evildoers.
11 Ever wise are the discourses of the just,
   but the fool is inconstant as the moon.
12 Limit the time you spend among fools,
   but frequent the company of the thoughtful.
13 The conversation of the wicked is offensive;
   their laughter is wanton guilt.
14 Their oath-filled talk makes the hair stand on end,
   their brawls make one stop one's ears.
15 Wrangling among the haughty ends in bloodshed,
   their cursing is painful to hear.

16 Whoever betrays a secret destroys confidence;
   he will never find an intimate friend.
17 Cherish your friend, keep faith with him,
   but if you betray his secret, follow him not;
18 For as one might kill another,
   you have killed your neighbor's friendship.
19 Like a bird released from the hand,
   you have let your friend go and you cannot recapture
                                                    him.
20 Follow him not, for he is far away;
   he has escaped like a gazelle from the snare.
21 A wound can be bound up, and railing speech forgiven,
   but whoever betrays secrets does hopeless damage.

Notes

27 16. See the NOTE to 22:22cd.
18. *another:* reading *nekron* with Ziegler, based on limited Gr and Lat evidence (most MSS *echthron*); in Syr, too, the received *měnâteh* seems a corruption for *mîteh/mayîteh*, which then matches Ziegler's reading.

Comment

This section on hazards to integrity and friendship opens with a numerical proverb (26:28, three bicola); cf. COMMENT on 23:16–17. The reading "wealthy person" (26:28c) is from Syr, which has, lit., "a free person, noble, well-born." Gr has "man of war, warrior," an inferior reading. In view of the antitheses in 26:28de, the antithesis in 26:28c should be between "wealthy person" and "want," and not between "warrior" and "want." As Smend (p. 240) suggests, G mistranslated either Heb *ʾîš ḥayil* (lit., person of strength or wealth) or *gibbôr ḥayil* (lit., mighty man of valor or wealth; cf. Ruth 2:1). The second thing that grieves Ben Sira and rouses his anger (26:28ab) is: "the intelligent [Gr *andres synetoi*] held in contempt" (26:28d). It is precisely such a dismal plight that Job found himself in; cf. esp. Job 29:2–30:10. Cf. also Qoh 9:11, 13–16. The third thing is the one who turns from righteousness (Gr *dikaiosynē*) to sin (26:28e). Such a person "the Lord makes ready for the sword" (26:28f); cf. Ezek 18:24.

In the next poem (26:29–27:3), Ben Sira speaks of the moral dangers involved in commerce. The proverbs in 26:29–27:2 sediment feelings shared by many in every age and place; cf. Amos 8:4–6; Lev 19:35–36; Prov 11:1; 20:10. "The usual trade and commerce is cheating all round by consent" (Thomas Fuller, *Gnomologia* [1732], 4814). "Honour sinks where commerce long prevails" (Oliver Goldsmith, *The Traveller* [1764], l. 91). "It is difficult but not impossible to conduct strictly honest business. What is true is that honesty is incompatible with the amassing of a large fortune" (Mohandas K. Gandhi, *Non-Violence in Peace and War* [1948], vol. 2, p. 127). The literal translation of 27:1b is: "and whoever seeks to enrich himself *turns away his eye(s).*" The italicized expression derives from the LXX of Prov 28:27b. In this minipoem, Ben Sira may have had in mind the unfortunate social situation of his day which required even Jewish merchants to deal with the pagans, and which tempted them to engage in unethical practices. Cf. 31:5–11; Jas 4:13; Rev 18:11–19. The colorful metaphor of 27:2a would be meaningful to the people of that day: as a tent peg was driven in "between fitted stones" to ensure that it not be shaken loose, so firmly is sin "wedged in" "between buying and selling" (27:2b). Having made these observations about the ethical perils one encounters in business (26:29–27:2), Ben Sira now issues a stern warning in 27:3: if one does not hold "fast to the fear of the Lord," no matter how much money one has acquired, "one's house will be thrown down." Cf. 13:16; Prov 3:33; 12:7; 14:11; 15:25.

The next poem (vv 4–7) deals with the criteria for appraising a person's value. The Gr word *logismos* is used in vv 4b, 6b, and 7a; it can mean "reckoning, computation; consideration, reasoning, reflection." In v 5b, *dialogismos* is used; it can mean "settling of accounts; calculation, reasoning; discourse, conversation." In the LXX, *logismos* renders Heb *maḥăšebet/ maḥăšābâ* ("thought; device; plan; purpose") or *ḥešbôn* ("account, reckoning"), or *ḥiššābôn* ("device, invention")—nouns derived from the verb root *ḥšb*, "to think, account; devise, plan, mean; esteem, regard." The underlying Heb original probably had *ḥešbôn* in each case, for in vv 5b and 6b (where MS A is extant) that is the noun which is used. The translation of vv 4–7 here interprets *(dia)logismos/ḥešbôn* in the sense of "speech, conversation." In v 4a, "the husks" is, lit., "dunghill, dung, refuse" (Gr *kopria*). The wheat that "has been threshed for the first time is placed in [the sieve] and sifted; the refuse, i.e., the dung of the oxen which has been trodden into the straw, remains behind, while the grain passes through the sieve" (so Box-Oesterley, pp. 405–6, and Smend, p. 243). The point of the comparison in v 4 is that a person's faults (lit., "filth") remain behind "when he speaks," i.e., his filth becomes obvious to all who hear him. The imagery and comparison in v 5 are less startling, at least to a modern reader, and more to the point: as a potter tests his vessels "in the furnace," so others test a person "in his conversation." Cf. 13:11. V 6 uses an agricultural metaphor that would have had immediate significance for the people of that day: as the fruit shows how well a tree has been cultivated and tended, so speech shows the thoughts of a person's mind (lit., heart), i.e., whether or not he has a disciplined, trained, and upright mind. Cf. Matt 7:16–19; 12:33–37. Ben Sira concludes this poem with a general aphorism (v 7) that summarizes vv 4–6: one should not praise another before testing him by his speech. Cf. 20:5–8 with COMMENT.

The next poem (vv 8–15) may also be split into two units, viz., vv 8–10 and 11–15; so, for example, Box-Oesterley (p. 406), Spicq (pp. 702–3), and Duesberg-Fransen (pp. 212–15). The first unit (vv 8–10) contains general observations on righteousness and sin. For one to attain righteousness (or justice) it is necessary to "strive after" or "pursue" it (v 8a); wishful thinking will hardly do. Cf. Zeph 2:3. By seeking righteousness, one will "put it on like a splendid robe" (v 8b), lit., a robe of glory; cf. 6:31; Isa 61:10; Job 29:14; Rev 1:13. The image here calls to mind the splendid robes of the high priest described in 45:7–13. Cf. also Wis 18:24. In v 9, Ben Sira gives a variant form of our English proverb "Birds of a feather flock together" (so, as far back as George Wither, *Abuses* [1613], 72), an aphorism made more memorable by the alliteration between "feather" and "flock," and by the rhyme between "feather" and "together." Cf. INTRODUCTION, Part IV, 1. See also 13:15 for a similar saying. As like associates with like (v 9a), so "fidelity [Gr *alētheia,* also means truth; Heb *'ĕmet*] comes to those who live by it" (v 9b; lit. practice, or work at, it). V 10 is a counterpart to v 9; the "lion" (v 10a) appears also in 21:2c; cf. Ps 17:12. In vv 9–10, "fidelity" and "sin" are personified. Cf. E. Pax, "Dialog und Selbstgespräch bei Sirach 27,3–10," *SBFLA* 20 (1970): 247–63; and P. C. Beentjes, "De Getallenspreuk en zijn reikwijdte: Een pleidooi voor de literaire eenheid van Jesus Sirach 26:28–27:10," *BTFT* 43 (1982): 383–89.

The second unit (vv 11–15) takes up the theme of speech introduced in vv 4–7. Since a person can be tested by his conversation (vv 5–7), the speech of the upright (or just) is "ever wise" (v 11a; lit., always wisdom). But "the fool is inconstant [lit., changes] as the moon" (v 11b)—a phenomenon obvious to all; cf. 5:10; 43:8. In vv 11–12, there is an *a:b::b:a* chiastic arrangement in the order of the cola: the upright (or just) are mentioned in v 11a; the fool in v 11b; the fool in 12a; and the "thoughtful" (=upright) in v 12b. Duesberg-Fransen (p. 215) are of the opinion that v 12 interrupts the flow of thought between vv 11 and 13, and suggest that it be placed after v 15. But in view of the chiastic arrangement I just noted, the order as we have it in G is in no need of correction. Since time among fools is a total waste, one is urged to keep to a minimum "the time [one spends] among fools" (v 12a) when one cannot avoid them altogether. Cf. 22:13–15. As regards "the company of the thoughtful" (v 12b), however, one should delight in their presence, for with them there is no such thing as a waste of time. "The conversation of the wicked [the reading of Lat *peccantium,* lit., sinners; G and Syr, fools] is offensive" (v 13a; lit., an offense, Gr *prosochthisma,* which in the LXX of 2 Kgs 23:13, 24 and Ezek 5:11; 7:20 renders Heb *šiqqûṣ,* "abomination"). For the thought of v 13b, cf. 21:15cd; Prov 10:23a. As regards the "oath-filled talk" (v 14a) one hears from the mouth of the fool, cf. 23:11. For the expression "makes the hair stand on end" (v 14a), cf. Job 4:15. V 14b implies that when fools gather together, their "oath-filled talk" (v 14a) invariably leads them into a brawl that is so vile that one stops one's ears. In v 15, the fools are now called "the haughty" (cf. 10:7, 12; 16:8), whose "wrangling . . . ends in bloodshed" (cf. 22:24). "Their cursing [Gr *dialoidorēsis,* also means reviling; cf. *loidoria,* "railing speech," in v 21a] is painful to hear" (lit., wretched hearing).

The final poem (vv 16–21) of this section deplores a common vice, viz., revealing a confidence. In the opening colon (v 16a) and the closing (v 21b), there occurs the phrase "whoever betrays a secret [or secrets]" thus forming an *inclusio,* which gives the poem a definite unity. As regards the thought of v 16, cf. 22:22cd and its NOTE; Prov 20:19; 25:8–10. Without respecting another's confidence, one can never "find an intimate friend" (v 16b). The rest of the poem is devoted to the need for friends to observe mutual trust and confidence, which are essential components of friendship. In v 17a, "cherish" and "keep faith" are parallels which emphasize the truth that genuine love for a friend involves fidelity; cf. 29:3. If, however, one breaks faith by betraying a friend's secret, one should no longer follow him (v 17b), for the friendship has been destroyed, as v 18 (cf. NOTE) states in strong language. The image of the "bird released from the hand" (v 19a) suggests how irretrievable is the friendship one has lost by betrayal of a friend's secrets (v 19b). V 20 restates the same idea, using instead the metaphor of a gazelle that has escaped from a trap. The imagery of a bird (v 19) and gazelle (v 20) is found also in Prov 6:5. "A wound can be bound up" (i.e., can be healed), and "railing speech [Gr *loidoria*] forgiven" (v 21a), since *loidoria* is far less damaging than Gr *oneidos*, "(contemptuous) insult," in 22:22c; cf. COMMENT on that verse. But the one who "betrays secrets does hopeless damage" (v 21b; lit., has no hope). In addition to the *inclusio* mentioned in the COMMENT on v 16, there is a theological relationship between the words *pistin*, "confidence, faith" (v 16a) and *(aph)ēlpisen*, "he has (no) hope" (v 21b), for faith (*pistis*) and hope (*elpis*) are essential virtues one must have if one is to be an authentic believer; cf., for example, Pss 16:9–10; 22:5–6, 9; 78:7–8; Rom 4:18.

34. Malice, Anger, Vengeance, and the Evil Tongue
(27:22–28:26)

27 22 Whoever has shifty eyes plots mischief;   G
   whoever knows him will give him a wide berth.
  23 In your presence he uses honeyed talk,
   and admires your every word,
  But later he changes his tune
   and twists your words to your ruin.
  24 There is nothing that I hate so much,
   and the Lord hates him as well.
  25 As a stone falls back on the head of the one who
           throws it up,
   so a blow struck in treachery injures more than one.
  26 As the one who digs a pit falls into it,
   and whoever lays a snare is caught by it,
  27 Whoever does harm will be involved in it
   without knowing whence it came upon him.

  28 Mockery and abuse will befall the proud,
   and vengeance lies in wait for them like a lion.
  29 Traps and snares seize those who delight in them,   S
   and pain will consume them before they die;   G
  30 Wrath and anger are loathsome things,
   which the sinful person has for his own.
28   1 The vengeful will suffer the Lord's vengeance,
   for he remembers their sins in detail.

  2 Forgive your neighbor's injustice;
   then, when you pray, your own sins will be forgiven.
  3 Should a person nourish anger against another
   and expect healing from the Lord?
  4 Should a person refuse mercy to another,
   yet seek pardon for his own sins?

5 If one who is but flesh cherishes wrath,
    who will forgive his sins?
6 Remember your last days, set enmity aside;
    remember death and decay, and cease from sin!   s
7 Think of the commandments, hate not your neighbor;   G
    of the Most High's covenant, and overlook faults.

8 Avoid strife and your sins will be fewer,
    for the quarrelsome kindles disputes,
9 Commits the sin of disrupting friendship,
    and sows discord among those at peace.
10 The more wood, the greater the fire,
    the more underlying it, the fiercer the fight;
    The greater a person's strength, the sterner his anger,
    the greater his power, the greater his wrath.
11 Resin and pitch make fires flare up,   s
    and insistent quarrels provoke bloodshed.   G

12 If you blow upon a spark, it quickens into flame,
    if you spit on it, it dies out;
    yet both you do with your mouth!
13 Cursed be the gossiper and the double-tongued,
    for they destroy the peace of many!
14 A meddlesome tongue subverts many,
    and makes them refugees among the peoples;
    It destroys walled cities
    and overthrows powerful dynasties.
15 A meddlesome tongue can drive virtuous women from
                    their homes
    and rob them of the fruit of their toil;
16 Whoever heeds it will have no rest,
    nor can he dwell in peace.

17 A blow from a whip raises a welt,
    but a blow from the tongue smashes bones;
18 Many have fallen by the edge of the sword,
    but not as many as by the tongue.
19 Happy is whoever is sheltered from it,
    and has not endured its wrath;

Who has not borne its yoke,
    nor been fettered with its chains;
20 For its yoke is a yoke of iron
    and its chains are chains of bronze!
21 Dire is the death it inflicts,
    beside which even the netherworld is a gain.
22 It will not take hold among the just;
    they will not be burned in its flame,
23 But those who forsake the Lord will fall victims to it,
    as it burns unquenchably among them!
    It will hurl itself against them like a lion;
    like a panther, it will tear them to pieces.
24a As you hedge round your vineyard with thorns,
25b   set barred doors over your mouth;
24b As you seal up your silver and gold,
25a   so balance and weigh your words.
26 Take care not to slip by your tongue
    and fall victim to your foe waiting in ambush.

Notes

27 22b. In most Gr MSS this colon reads: "and no one can ward him off"; Ziegler repairs the text with materials from GII.

29. *Traps and snares:* so Syr; compare the structure of 28a, 30a. G recasts and expands this colon.

28 1b. *remembers . . . in detail:* supposes the minority Gr reading *diatērōn diatērēsei,* supported by Lat, accepted by Ziegler.

6b. *and cease from sin!:* so Syr, where G "and abide by the commandments" breaks down the interlinear parallelism of vv 6, 7. Segal reconstructs the two cola of v 6 with an end rhyme (*waḥădal liśnōʾ . . . ûmĕnaʿ mēḥăṭōʾ*) that appears altogether plausible.

11a. *Resin and pitch:* so Syr; as in 27:29, see above. G has obscured the concrete imagery—this time by duplicating a phrase from 11b.

13. *Cursed:* the form is that indicated by Syr and Lat; the Gr MSS have it garbled.

24–25. In most Gr MSS these four cola appear as 24a, 25b, 24b, 25a; Ziegler has reestablished the normal sequence with Syr, Lat, and some Gr evidence.

Comment

This section contains a series of poems on various subjects: malice (27:22–27), anger and vengeance (27:28–28:1), forgiveness (28:2–7), quarreling (28:8–11), and evils of the tongue (two poems: 28:12–16 and 28:17–26).

In the first poem (27:22–27), Ben Sira deplores the evils of malice coupled with insincerity and treachery. "Whoever has shifty eyes" (27:22a) is, lit., "Whoever winks with his eye(s)," Gr *dianeuōn ophthalmǭ* (*-mois*), an expression similar to the LXX of Prov 6:13, *enneuei ophthalmǭ*, "he winks with his eye," and Prov 10:10, *enneuōn ophthalmois*, "whoever winks with his eyes." Winking was considered a sign of duplicity (cf. Prov 16:30 and Ps 35:19), for such a person *"plots mischief."* For the italicized expression, in Heb *ḥrš rāʿ(â)*, cf. 11:33; Prov 3:29; 6:14. The reason why those who know such a person "give him a wide berth" (27:22b; cf. NOTE) is that they are never certain what his external actions may mean, as 27:23 makes clear. "He uses honeyed talk" (lit., he *sweetens* his mouth, the same verb found in G of 12:16a; cf. 6:5a and Prov 16:21), "and admires your every word" (27:23ab), i.e., he gives all the appearances of being friendly and appreciative of what you say. "Later," i.e., when you are no longer present, "he changes his tune" (27:23c), lit., he will twist his mouth, Gr *diastrepsei to stoma autou.* He "twists your words to your ruin" (27:23d), lit., "he makes a stumbling block with your words," thus combining hypocrisy and treachery. For the stumbling block, cf. 7:6d in G. For a parallel to 27:22–23, see Theognis, 93–96 (Sanders, pp. 33–34). In 27:24, Ben Sira expresses his strong feeling toward such a person: many things are detestable, but nothing is as hateful as the hypocritical double-dealer, whom the Lord himself hates as well. In 27:24b, Syr reads: "God also hates him and curses him." Without the extra phrase in Syr, the colon may be too weak and short (so Smend, p. 248). Cf. Prov 6:16–19; 8:13.

The last part (27:25–27) of this poem tells of how the evil that the schemer plans comes right back to him. The first image employed (27:25a) is a variant of the one in Prov 26:27b, which reads: "A stone comes back upon him who rolls it" (cf. Qoh 10:9). The translation of 27:25b is an interpretation of G, which reads, lit.: "and a deceitful blow opens wounds," a reading that makes little sense. Syr has "and he who strikes in secret will be given over to destruction." In view of the parallelism in 27:25a, 26ab, and 27a, the original text of 27:25b must have contained something similar to the translation given here. Cf. Pss 7:17; 9:17. For the imagery of "pit" and "snare" in 27:26, cf. Ps

9:16; Prov 26:27a; Qoh 10:8. The final bicolon (27:27) restates in general terms, and without specific imagery, the principle that "whoever does harm" (lit., evil things) will himself experience the evil he plans for others, "without knowing whence it came upon him."

The next poem (27:28–28:1) continues the same line of thought. "Mockery and abuse will befall the proud" (27:28a) according to the principle articulated in 27:27a, because mockery and abuse are what they pour out on others. The same is true of "vengeance" (27:28b); cf. 28:1. Perhaps, in composing this poem, Ben Sira had in mind proud Haman's vicious plot to kill Mordecai and all the other Jews because Mordecai refused to "kneel and bow down to" Haman (Esth 3:2, 5). The "traps and snares" (27:29a; cf. NOTE) may be an allusion to the gibbet Haman had erected with the intention of hanging Mordecai on it (Esth 5:14). Because Haman in his anger at Mordecai had conspired to kill all the Jews, "mockery and abuse" (27:28a) and "pain" (27:29b) befell him when King Ahasuerus ordered him to clothe Mordecai, his enemy, with the royal robe and place him on the royal horse to ride in the public square of the city (Esth 6:6–12). Haman became angry when Mordecai refused to pay him homage (Esth 3:5; 5:9); Ben Sira says: "Wrath and anger are loathsome things, which the sinful person [i.e., Haman] has for his own" (27:30). Because Haman sought to have his revenge by hanging Mordecai, he suffered "the Lord's vengeance" (28:1a) when he himself was hanged on the gibbet he had erected for the execution of Mordecai (Esth 7:9–10; 9:1–16, 24–25). For the idea of the Lord's vengeance, cf. Deut 32:35–36; Rom 12:19. The word "vengeance" (Gr *ekdikēsis*) occurs in the opening (27:28b) and the closing bicolon (28:1a) of the poem, thus forming an *inclusio*. Regarding the Lord's remembering "sins in detail" (28:1b; cf. NOTE), cf. Ps 130:3; Job 14:16–17.

The following poem (28:2–7) addresses the duty to forgive others and not to hold grudges. The "injustice" (28:2a) is Gr *adikēma*, lit., injury, hurt, wrong done. It is interesting to see how, in 28:2, Ben Sira connects one's forgiveness of others with the Lord's forgiveness of oneself. Cf. 8:5. Although the sentiments expressed in 28:2–5 sound Christian (cf. Matt 6:12, 14–15; 18:32–35; Mark 11:25; Luke 11:4; Jas 2:13), there are other Jewish writings that contain similar ideas: "Love one another from the heart; and if a person sin against you, speak peaceably to him, and in your soul hold not guile; and if he repent and confess, forgive him. But if he deny it, do not get into a passion with him, lest catching the poison from you, he take to swearing, and so you sin doubly. . . . But if he be shameless, and persist in his wrongdoing, even so forgive him from the heart, and leave to God the avenging" (*Test. XII Patr.*, Gad vi 3–7). "God forgives whoever forgives his neighbor" (*Rosh Ha-shanah*, 17a). "In the measure with which a person has had mercy on his neighbor, in that same measure the Lord will have mercy on him. . . . Therefore, have compassion in your hearts, for as a person acts toward his neighbor, so does the Lord act toward him" (*Test. XII Patr.*, Zebulon v 3). The texts just cited from *Test. XII Patr.* may, however, be interpolations in the Christian copies of that document. Not only must a person forgive his neighbor if he wishes to be forgiven by the Lord (28:2), but he must not "nourish anger" against his fellows if he expects "healing from the Lord" (28:3). The healing here is to be understood in general—healing from sin (i.e., forgiveness, as in 28:2, 5) and healing from sickness and pain (cf. Jer 17:14). Cf. Isa 6:10; Matt 13:15; Jas 5:15–16. The point of 28:3 is that one who holds a grudge against another (presumably with the notion of getting even with him by inflicting pain on him) cannot expect the Lord to heal him from his own hurts (especially injured feelings) and sins (especially of anger); cf. 28:5. For the notion of God as healer, cf. Gen 20:17; Exod 15:26; Hos 6:1; 7:1; 14:5. The one who refuses mercy to his neighbor should not expect the Lord to pardon his own sins (28:4). Cf. Matt 12:7. "So long as we are merciful, God is merciful to us; but if we are not merciful to others, God is not merciful to us" (*Megillah* 28a, cited in Box-Oesterley, p. 408). "The quality of mercy is not strained, / It droppeth as the gentle rain from heaven / Upon the place beneath: it is twice blessed; / It blesseth him that gives and him that takes" (Shakespeare, *The Merchant of Venice* [1596–97], IV i 184–87). For the expression, "one who is but flesh" (28:5a), cf. 17:31. V 5 restates the thought of 28:3. The poem concludes with two bicola that begin with Gr *mnēsthēti* (28:6a and 7a), "remember" (in v 7a, the translation "think of" is only for variation in English). The reason why one should remember one's "last days" (Gr *ta eschata,* lit., the last things) is that the Lord will set all things right before one's death; cf. 11:26–28. Remembering is considered a salutary activity for the believer; cf. 7:16, 36; 8:5, 7; 9:12; 14:12; 18:24–25; 38:20; 41:3. One should "set enmity aside" and "cease from sin" (cf. NOTE); otherwise "death and decay" (28:6) may come prematurely. One should remember "the commandments," especially the commandment "You shall love your neighbor as yourself" (Lev 19:18), which Ben Sira states negatively: "Hate not your neighbor" (cf. Lev 19:17) and "overlook faults" (28:7). Cf. Matt 19:19; 22:39–40; Luke 10:26–27.

The next poem (28:8–11), the subject of which is quarreling, has in its opening (28:8ab) and closing bicola (28:11b) the Gr word *machē*, "strife, dispute, quarrel," thus forming an *inclusio* that gives the poem a tight unity. Avoiding strife diminishes the number of one's sins (28:8a). The "quarrelsome" (Gr *thymōdēs,* lit., passionate, hot-tempered) "kindles disputes" (lit., strife, *machē*). Cf. Prov 15:18; 26:17, 21; 29:22, in the LXX of which *thymōdēs* is also found. V 9a may be translated, lit.: "And a sinful person disrupts (or troubles) friends." The expression "sinful person" is in synonymous parallelism with the "quarrelsome" or hot-tempered of 28:8b. Such a person "sows [lit., casts] discord [Gr *diabolē,* lit., slander, calumny; Lat and Syr, enmity] among those at peace" (28:9b). Perhaps the original Heb noun

was *šiṭnâ,* "opposition, hostility," as in Gen 26:21, where the Syr uses
bĕʿeldĕbābûtâ, "enmity," as here (so Smend, p. 251). Instead of promoting
peace as one should (cf. Ps 34:15), the hot-tempered person spreads hostility
(28:9b). For the image of wood in 28:10a, cf. Prov 26:20–21 and Jas 3:5. The
more there is to a dispute (*machē*), "the fiercer" will it be (28:10b), just as the
greater the wood, the larger the fire (28:10a). There is synonymous parallelism between 28:10c and d: the greater a person's "strength" (28:10c) and
"wealth" (28:10d, Gr *ploutos,* "riches," here translated *power*), the greater his
"anger" (28:10c, Gr *thymos*) and his "wrath" (28:10d, Gr *orgē*). As "resin
and pitch [cf. NOTE] make fires flare up" (28:11a; for the imagery, cf. Isa
34:9–10), so "insistent [lit., hasty] quarrels provoke bloodshed" (28:11b). As
regards the thoughts contained in this poem, compare Matt 5:21–26.

The last two poems of this section deal with evils of the tongue. The first
(28:12–16) deplores "the double-tongued" and "the third tongue" (Gr *glossa
tritē,* here translated *meddlesome tongue*). Regarding the vivid images and the
point of 28:12, compare 5:13; Prov 15:1; and Jas 3:9–10. Ben Sira calls down
a curse (cf. NOTE) on "the gossiper [lit., whisperer] and the double-tongued"
(28:13a), "for," as the Gr has it, lit., "they destroy many who were at peace"
(28:13b); cf. 28:9. Cf. 5:14–6:1 with COMMENT for more material on "the
double-tongued." The "third tongue" (28:14a) is an expression that appears
also in the rabbinical literature; it means "the tongue of the slanderer." So
Box-Oesterley (p. 409), who write: "cp. e.g. *Arakin* 15*b:* 'The third tongue
kills three,' viz. the slanderer, the slandered, and he who believes the slander;
on the last of these see *v.* 16." Such a tongue is called "third" because it butts
in between two others as a third and sows discord (cf. Knabenbauer, p. 301).
In 28:14–15, Ben Sira is probably speaking in general about the great evils the
"third tongue" can cause, although he may also have had in mind such
historical episodes as the slanderous letter the Samaritans wrote to King
Artaxerxes because the Jews refused to allow them to assist in rebuilding the
Temple (Ezra 4:1–16). The "third tongue" can also "drive virtuous women
from their homes" (28:15a, lit., drive out virtuous [or worthy, brave] women),
because their husbands will divorce them on the basis of false allegations
reported to them; cf. 25:26. For the expression "virtuous woman" (Gr *gynē
andreia*), cf. 26:2. In 28:15b, "the fruit of their toil" is an interpretive translation of G, which simply says, lit., "their labors." What is meant is the "fruit,"
i.e., the acceptance, praise, and gratitude, which the virtuous woman has a
right to enjoy because she has been a good wife and mother; cf. Prov 31:10–
31. Whoever heeds slander "will have no rest" or "peace" (28:16, lit., quiet),
because the listener is also a victim of the sin; cf. the quotation from *Arakin*
15b, above, regarding 28:14. The point of this verse is especially true of the
husband whose wife has been slandered.

The final poem (28:17–26) of this section also excoriates the mischief the
wicked tongue can cause. The thought of 28:17b derives from Prov 25:15b:

"A soft tongue will break a bone." Cf. also Prov 15:4. The Japanese have a proverb similar to 28:18: "The tongue is more to be feared than the sword." Contrast, however, the children's jingle "Sticks and stones may break my bones, but words can never hurt me." As regards 28:19a, cf. Ps 31:21. For the wrath that the tongue can arouse (28:19b), cf. 28:8–11. It is interesting that Ben Sira uses the images of "yoke" and "chains" (28:19cd–20ab) also with regard to personified Wisdom in 6:24–25, 29–30. The "yoke of iron" (28:20a) is an allusion to Jer 28:13–14, where it signifies the oppressive service the people will endure under Nebuchadnezzar, king of Babylon. The person who is victimized by another's tongue may accurately be described as bearing "a yoke of iron" and "chains of bronze" (28:20). Indeed, calumny is an intolerable burden to bear. "The death [the wicked tongue] inflicts" is "dire" (28:21a, lit., an evil death); cf. COMMENT on 28:14a. "The netherworld" (28:21b), i.e., physical death, is preferable to the living death (28:21a) the "third tongue" can cause; cf. 26:5cd. In 28:22, Ben Sira engages in a bit of wishful thinking, for the "just" (or upright) are also "burned in [the wicked tongue's] flame"; cf. 28:14. For the image of the tongue as a flame (28:22b–23ab), cf. Jas 3:5–6. But the unrighteous, "who forsake the Lord," are natural victims for the tongue's flame, which "burns unquenchably among them" (28:23ab), for their evil deeds provide adequate fuel for the fire of calumny. The imagery now changes from flame to "lion" and "panther" (28:23cd), wild animals whose ferocity is proverbial. The tongue, "like a panther," can indeed "tear [someone] to pieces" (28:23d), or completely mutilate, the literal meaning of the Gr verb *lymaneitai*. Regarding the order of the cola in 28:24–25, cf. NOTE.

By way of conclusion to these two poems on the potential evils of the tongue, Ben Sira issues some good advice on how to avoid sin through speech. The image of the vineyard in 28:24a would be especially meaningful to a Palestinian. As a person places a hedge of thorns around the vineyard to keep wild animals from overrunning and destroying it, so he should "set barred doors [hendiadys, lit., door and bar (pl. in one form of GII and Lat)] over [his] mouth" (28:24a, 25b). Cf. 22:27; Pss 39:2; 141:3. For the custom of binding up or sealing silver and gold (28:24b), cf. 2 Kgs 5:23 and Tob 9:5. Though Ben Sira uses a mixed metaphor in 28:24b, 25a, he nonetheless makes a valid point: just as a person uses great care in sealing up silver and gold, so he should be equally careful in balancing and weighing his words (lit., [one should] make a balance and a weight for [one's] words; cf. 16:25; 21:25b). One is to "take care not to slip by [one's] tongue" (28:26a); cf. 25:8c and also 14:1a. "Better to trip with the feet than with the tongue" (Zeno of Citium [c. 300 B.C.], quoted in Diogenes Laërtius [third century of our era], *Lives and Opinions of Eminent Philosophers*). Cf. Jas 3:2. If one does slip with the tongue, one "fall[s] victim to [one's] foe waiting in ambush" (28:26b, lit., fall[s] before him who lies in wait), i.e., an enemy will rejoice over the slip of the tongue and use it against one. Lat adds: ". . . and your case will become incurable, leading to death."

35. Loans, Alms, and Surety
(29:1–20)

29   ¹ He does a kindness who lends to his neighbor,   G
     and he fulfills the precepts who holds out a helping
                                         hand.

² Lend to your neighbor in his hour of need,
     pay back your neighbor when a loan falls due;
³ Keep your promise, be honest with him,
     and you will always come by what you need.
⁴ Many a person who asks for a loan   S
     adds to the burdens of those who help him;   G
⁵ Till he gets it, he kisses the lender's hand
     and speaks softly of his creditor's wealth;
But when payment is due, he puts it off,
     makes excuses, and asks for time.
⁶ If the lender is able to recover barely half,
     he considers it a find;
If not, he is cheated of his wealth
     and acquires an enemy at no extra charge;
With curses and revilement the borrower pays him back,
     with abuse instead of honor.
⁷ Many refuse to lend, not out of meanness,
     but from fear of being cheated to no purpose.

⁸ With the poor, however, be generous;
     keep him not waiting for your alms:
⁹ Because of the precept, help the needy;
     do not send them away empty-handed in their want.
¹⁰ Spend your money for kindred or friend,
     and leave it not under a stone to rot;
¹¹ Dispose of your treasure as the Most High commands,
     for that will profit you more than the gold.

12 Store up almsgiving in your cash box,
   and it will save you from every evil;
13 Better than a stout shield or a sturdy spear
   it will fight for you against the foe.

14 A good person goes surety for his neighbor,
   and only the shameless would play him false;
15 Forget not the kindness of your backer,
   for he offers his very life for you.
16 The wicked turns the favor of a pledge into disaster,
17   and the ungrateful schemer abandons his protector:
18 Going surety has ruined many prosperous people
   and tossed them about like the surging sea,
   Has exiled the prominent
   and sent them wandering through foreign lands.
19 The sinner through surety comes to grief,
   and whoever undertakes too much falls into lawsuits.
20 Go surety for your neighbor according to your means,
   but take care lest you fall thereby.

Notes

29 4a. *who asks for a loan:* with Syr; the Gr here introduces the language of 6b.
10b. *to rot:* the Gr supposes the corrosion of copper coins.

Comment

This section contains three poems on related themes: making loans (vv 1–7), giving alms (vv 8–13), and going surety (vv 14–20). Each of these themes is concerned with the person in need of assistance, to whom one should be generous. The section contains exactly twenty-three bicola; cf. COMMENT on 1:11–30 and 51:13–30.

The expression "to do a kindness" (v 1a) is Gr *poiein eleos*, Heb *'āśâ ḥesed,* as in 46:7a and 49:3b (MS B). To lend to one's neighbor "in his hour of need" (vv 1a, 2a) was considered an act of piety (cf. Pss 37:26; 112:5) and the fulfillment of the commandments (v 1b); cf. Exod 22:24–26; Lev 25:35–37; Deut 15:7–11; 23:20–21; 24:10–13; Ezek 18:8, 17; Prov 19:17. Ben Sira says nothing about interest on the loan, for interest-taking was explicitly forbidden; cf. Exod 22:24; Lev 25:36–37. Deut 23:20–21 disallowed interest on a loan made to a fellow Israelite but permitted it on a loan made to a Gentile. One also is obliged to pay back a loan when it is due (vv 2b, 3a); cf. Ps 37:21. Compare Luke 6:34–35. By repaying a loan on time (v 2b), i.e., by keeping one's "promise" (lit., word) and being "honest" (v 3a, lit., keeping faith), one will have no trouble obtaining a future loan, the point of v 3b. Hence prompt repayment of a loan is not only a religious obligation, but also a sound practice in terms of one's self-interest. For the text of v 4a, cf. NOTE. The rest of the poem (vv 4–7) offers sage comments and keen observations about abuses in borrowing and about the failure to repay a loan graciously and promptly. V 4 sets the tone for the remarks to follow: the prospective borrower often causes grief to those who help him. To obtain the loan he hypocritically "kisses the lender's hand" (v 5a) and "speaks softly [i.e., with hushed awe] of his creditor's wealth" (v 5b), thus suggesting, none too subtly, that the money requested would be a trifling sum in view of such wealth. When it is time for repayment, however, "he puts it off, makes excuses, and asks for time" (v 5cd). In v 6, Ben Sira reflects the unpleasant experience many have had throughout the ages. Getting back the loan or even part of it is a "find" (v 6ab). Often it is never recovered (v 6c), with the result that the lender "acquires an enemy *at no extra charge*" (v 6d, Gr *dōrean,* lit., freely, as a free gift: note the irony). Or if the borrower does repay, he does so "with curses and revilement" (v 6e), "with abuse instead of honor" (v 6f), i.e., obnoxiously instead of gratefully. It is no wonder, then, that "many refuse to lend, not out of meanness [Gr *ponēria,* lit., wickedness; cf. COMMENT on vv 1–2a regarding the duty to lend to one's neighbor], but from fear of being cheated to no purpose" (v 7; *dōrean* here has the derived meaning of "undeservedly"—cf. v 6d). The point of vv 4–7 was neatly and concisely summarized in the famous advice Polonius imparted to his son, Laertes: "Neither a borrower nor a lender be; / For loan oft loses both itself and friend" (Shakespeare, *Hamlet* [1600], I iii 75–76).

The following poem (vv 8–13) opens with a big "but, however" (Gr *plēn*), to emphasize that the case of the poor is totally different from that of the unprincipled borrower. Though one may have reasons for refusing a loan (v 7), one may not refuse alms (Gr *eleēmosynē*) to the poor or keep them waiting for alms (v 8). Cf. 3:14–15 and 3:30–4:6 with COMMENT; Prov 14:21, 31; 19:17; 21:13, 26; 22:9; 25:21–22. One must "help the needy" "because of the precept" (v 9a), which is contained in Deut 15:7–11. For v 9b, Syr reads: "and if there is a loss, do not bring it to mind," i.e., pay no attention to it. In v

10, "spend" is, lit., "lose" (Gr *apoleson*); and v 10b may be translated, lit.: "and let it not rust under a stone to be lost" (cf. NOTE). For the idea of rusting, cf. 12:10b. The point of v 10 is that one should be generous toward "kindred or friend" in distress and not allow money to rust away in its hiding place, "under a stone." Cf. Isa 45:3 and Matt 25:18. For the thought of wealth rotting and money rusting away, cf. Matt 6:19 and Jas 5:2–3. One is to dispose of wealth in accord with the commandments of the Most High (v 11a); cf. COMMENT on v 9a, above. Such generosity is more profitable "than the gold" (v 11b) one loses for the sake of others (cf. v 10a). V 12 continues the same notion: *locking up* (the literal meaning of G) alms*giving* in one's treasuries (note the paradox) "will save [one] from every evil." Cf. Matt 6:20; 19:21; Luke 12:33; 16:9. For the efficacy of almsgiving, cf. COMMENT on 3:14–15, 30–31; 12:2; and Tob 1:3; 2:10; 4:7–11; 14:9, 10–11. The images of v 13 dramatize the value of almsgiving.

In the final poem (vv 14–20) of this section, Ben Sira offers advice and observations about the pitfalls involved in going surety. Cf. also 8:13 with COMMENT. The Book of Proverbs (6:1–5; 11:15; 17:18; 20:16; 22:26–27; 27:13) uniformly advises against providing surety (or collateral) for another. Ben Sira, however, considers going surety for one's neighbor to be an act of virtue (v 14a), but he also urges restraint lest one be ruined (vv 18–20). It is only "the shameless" who would take advantage of one who provides surety (v 14b). Yet despite this risk, one should provide collateral when another is in need (v 14a). If you have received the benefit of collateral, you should not forget "the kindness of your backer" (v 15a) because he risks his life for you (v 15b)—an exaggeration to dramatize the point. Cf. Prov 22:26–27. The "wicked" (v 16, lit., sinner, Gr *hamartōlos*), however, who is called in the parallel "the ungrateful schemer" (v 17), takes advantage of his benefactor, "his protector" (v 17), by failing to honor the obligations of his debt that were backed by another's collateral. Because of such irresponsibility, "many prosperous people" (v 18a) have suffered financial ruin, with the result that they were forced to leave their homeland in order to make a living in "foreign lands" (v 18bcd, lit., strange nations). In v 19a, Ben Sira speaks of "the sinner" (*hamartōlos,* as in v 16) coming "to grief" because he tried to take advantage of others "through surety"; e.g., he would keep garments taken as collateral if the one who borrowed money failed to repay it. Such a practice was explicitly forbidden in the Law (cf. Exod 22:25 and Deut 24:12–13); and Amos 2:8 mentions it as a crime committed by the wealthy. The expression "whoever undertakes too much" (v 19b) is in parallel with "the sinner" (v 19a), and probably refers to the person who readily accepts the pledge of debtors in the hope that they cannot repay the loan, which would then give him the right to keep the pledge. But by undertaking too much, such a person "falls into lawsuits" (v 19b), perhaps because his victims hale him into the religious courts for his violation of the law stated in Exod 22:24–26 and Deut

24:10–13; cf. also Lev 25:39–43. In v 20a, "go surety" is from Syr; Gr has "assist, help." The final exhortation of the poem is to go surety for the neighbor "according to [one's] means" (lit., power), but at the same time one should be careful not to suffer harm thereby (v 20); cf. also 8:13. The Gr word *plēsion*, "neighbor," occurs in vv 14a and 20a, in the opening and closing of the poem, thus forming an *inclusio*.

36. Frugality and the Training of Children (29:21–30:13)

29 21 Life's prime needs are water, bread, and clothing;   G
        a house, too, for decent privacy.
22 Better a poor person's fare under the shelter of one's
                           own roof
        than sumptuous banquets among strangers.
23 Be it little or much, be content with what you have,
        so as not to hear reproach as a parasite.
24 A miserable life it is to go from house to house,
        for as a guest you dare not open your mouth.
25 The visitor has no thanks for filling the cups;
        besides, you will hear these bitter words:
26 "Come here, stranger, set the table;
        give me to eat the food you have in hand!
27 Away, stranger, for one more worthy;
        for my relative's visit I need the room!"
28 Painful things to a sensitive person
        are rebuke as a parasite and insults from his
                           creditors.

30 1 Whoever loves his son chastises him often,
        that he may be a joy to him when he grows up.
2 Whoever disciplines his son will benefit from him,
        and boast of him among his intimates.
3 Whoever educates his son makes his enemy jealous,
        and shows delight in him among his friends.
4 At the father's death, he will not seem dead,
        since he leaves after him one like himself,
5 Whom he looks upon through life with joy,
        and even in death, without regret:
6 The avenger he leaves against his foes,
        and the one to repay his friends with kindness.

7 Whoever spoils his son will have wounds to bandage,
    and will quake inwardly at every outcry.

8 A colt untamed turns out stubborn;
    a son left to himself grows up unruly.

9 Pamper your child and he will be a terror for you,
    indulge him and he will bring you grief.

10 Share not in his frivolity lest you share in his sorrow,
    when finally your teeth are gritted in remorse.

11 Give him not his own way in his youth,   B
    and close not your eyes to his follies.

12 In his lack of discipline, belabor his ribs,   GI
    and smite his flanks while he is still a boy,   B
    Lest he become stubborn, disobey you,   GI
    and your last breath be brought on by him.   B

13 Discipline your son, make heavy his yoke,
    lest through his impudence you be thrown down   G
                                 headlong.

Notes

29   23b. Ziegler's reading here follows Bretschneider in reconstructing the Gr (*paroikias ou mē*) on the basis of the Lat, against the Gr codices.

28. *as a parasite:* the reading *paroikias* (cf. 23b) is from Smend, accepted by Ziegler; it is attested (*hospitalitatis*) by two Lat codices only: the Amiatinus (A), where it occupies the place of *creditors* (most Lat codices, *foenoratoris*), and the now destroyed Codex Z, from Metz, in which it was the reading of the first hand, later "corrected."

30   11. A portion of MS B is extant from this point to 33:3, by which time it overlaps with MS E (from 32:16).

11–12cd. For these three bicola, GI was able to translate only the first colon in each case, evidently because the grandson's Heb prototype was stichometric by the full line (like the Masada MS and 2Q18—see the NOTES above at 1:19–20 and 6:22), and the left-hand (second) colon of each line was damaged in that source. Thus 30:11b is missing from GI; present in GII, Lat, Syr, and MS B, it is certainly authentic. In v 12, GII has introduced (12a in Ziegler) a borrowing from 7:23b; see the NOTE in that place. This was because by the time of GII the Heb text of the original first colon in v 12 had become hopelessly garbled (*kĕpeten* . . . in MS B). After substituting the colon from chap. 7, GII became confused by the similarity of the Heb second colon in 30:12 to GI's translation of the *first* colon in the verse (*thlason* . . . , now 12b in Ziegler) and left that to fill out his bicolon—so that the Gr tradition now shows no real equivalent at all for the second colon. Here the first colon is rendered from GI (which reconstructs to *kptyw ṣl'tyw rṣṣ*); on the basis of two forms of it in MS B, plus Syr, the second colon is being read as *wpg' mtnyw 'wdnnw n'r*. V 12c occupies the same relative position in all witnesses; the *yšqh* of MS B's running text should be read *yaqšeh* = G's *sklēryntheis* (with Smend, cf. Exod 13:15). For 12d, GI is lacking, Syr is defective, GII is weak, and MS B is the best source: perhaps read *wěnôlad lěkā*, note the ease with which the *lěkā* (G *soi*) could be lost by haplograpy. Cf. *CBQ* 36 (1974): 535–42.

13b. With G and Syr; the verb in MS B (*ytl'/ytʾl bk*) is unintelligible.

Comment

This section, which has exactly twenty-two poetic lines, contains proverbs and observations about two unrelated subjects: the satisfactions of the simple life (29:21–28) and the necessity of strict training of sons (two poems: 30:1–6 and 7–13).

Ben Sira states that the basic necessities of life are: "water, bread, and clothing" and "a house . . . for decent privacy" (29:21, lit., to cover shame). He expresses a similar notion but adds a few more items in 39:26. The point of this poem is that the wise are content with what they have (cf. 29:23a) and would never trade their independence by living beyond their means (cf. 29:24–28): sound advice in any age. In 29:22a, "(a poor person's) fare" is, lit., life; as regards the thought of the verse, cf. 40:29. Being satisfied with what one has (29:23a) is not only a mark of wisdom but also an indication that one is truly rich; cf. 1 Tim 6:8; Heb 13:5. On the contrary, if a person is not content with the "little or much" he has, he is not only foolish but poor, for he risks the charge of "parasite" ("freeloader" in American slang) when he enjoys more sumptuous food and drink in the houses of others (29:23b; cf. NOTE). It is also "a miserable life" to depend on others for food and lodging, "for as a guest you dare not open your mouth" (29:24)—a painful fact of life many have experienced when, either by choice or by necessity, they have lived with, and depended on, others. A literal translation of 29:25a is "You will entertain and give drinks without thanks," i.e., as a person who depends on the largess of others, you will be pressed into service as a house servant who receives no gratitude for his labors. Moreover, you will receive commands that will be "bitter words" (29:25b), especially because of the manner in which the householder speaks to you: "Come here, stranger, set the table" (29:26a)—words that hardly promote cordiality or a feeling of being welcome. You cannot even enjoy the meals because the householder begrudges you your food (29:26b). Then, if he expects a visit from a relative ("brother" in the Semitic sense of the word), he asks you to leave "for one more worthy" (29:27). In other words, he tolerates you only because no one else in his family has claimed his hospitality. "Painful things to a sensitive person [lit., one who has understanding; Syr, a wise person] are rebuke as a parasite [cf. NOTE] and insults from his creditors" (29:28). By this comment, Ben Sira connects this poem to the preceding one on going surety (29:14–20); cf. esp. 29:16–17.

In the next poem (30:1–6), the first of two on the proper training of sons, Ben Sira extols the value of strict discipline if one hopes to rear a good son. In many Gr and Lat MSS this section is entitled "On Children." The father who "loves his son chastises him often" (30:1a; lit., will continue the whips with him). The physical punishment of children was taken for granted in Israelite society; cf. 22:6b; Prov 13:24; 19:18; 22:15; 23:13–14; 29:15. If a father disciplines his son in youth, he will have joy in him as an adult (30:1b); cf. Prov 22:6. "Train up a fig-tree in the way it should go, and when you are old sit under the shade of it" (Charles Dickens, *Dombey and Son* [1848], p. 19). A father "will benefit" from the son he has disciplined (30:2a) and "boast of him" to his friends (30:2b); cf. Prov 29:17. Sound discipline includes the education or training of a son (30:3a). Why a person's enemies become jealous (30:3a) is that his son is so well behaved and wise. Such a person delights in his son "among his friends" (30:3b), because the son gives the father reason to be proud. " . . . Men pray to see dutiful children grow up around them in their homes—that such may requite their father's foe with evil, and honor, as their father does, his friend. But he who begets unprofitable children—what shall we say that he has sown, but troubles for himself, and much triumph for his foes" (Sophocles, *Antigone* [442–441 B.C.], 640–45). In death, a father "will not seem dead, since he leaves after him one like himself" (30:4). In Tob 9:6, Gabael says to Tobiah: "O noble and good child, son of a noble and good, upright and charitable man. . . . Blessed be God, because I have seen the very image of my cousin Tobit!" Since there was no belief in a blessed immortality at that time, children gave parents a sense of continuance; hence it was important to train children to be upright, wise, and pious. See INTRODUCTION, Part X, 4. In life, a father can look upon his disciplined son "with joy" (30:5a; cf. 25:7c); and when such a man dies, he has no regrets (30:5b) since his son, who is "like himself" (30:4b), carries on his good name. Cf. Prov 27:11. The son becomes the father's "avenger . . . against his foes" (30:6a), i.e., those who threaten his family because he has died; cf. Ps 127:5. The dutiful and well-trained son also repays his father's friends "with kindness" (30:6b), thus adding to the blessedness of his father's name.

The second poem (30:7–13) on child-rearing spells out many of the sad results that occur when a father fails to discipline his son. The spoiled or pampered son will incur wounds from his recklessness and folly; the father who was negligent in his duty to train such a son must then bandage the wounds (30:7a). "Every outcry" the father hears will make him "quake inwardly" (30:7b), for his son has either been injured in one of his senseless escapades or caused injury to another. The image of the untamed colt in 30:8a emphasizes the need to check a son "left to himself" lest he become "unruly" or "headstrong" (Gr *proalēs*, lit., springing forward; abrupt); cf. Prov 29:15. Syriac Aḥiqar offers advice similar to the comments of Ben Sira: "My son, withhold not your son from stripes, for the beating of a child is like manure to the garden, or like rope to an ass [the gloss adds: or any other beast], or like tether on the foot of an ass. My son, subdue your son while he is yet a child, before he grows stronger than you and rebels against you, and you become ashamed of all his corrupt doing" (3,32). There is intralinear parallelism between the two cola of 30:9: to pamper a child is to indulge him with the result that "he will be a terror for you . . . and . . . bring you grief." The parent foolish enough to share in his child's "frivolity" will "share in his sorrow" and grit his teeth "in remorse" (30:10); cf. Jer 31:29; Ezek 18:2; Matt 8:12; 13:42; 22:13; 24:51; 25:30; Luke 13:28.

As regards the text of 30:11–12, cf. NOTE. Giving a son "his own way in his youth" (30:11a) is a sure way for a father to spoil him. A son's "follies" (30:11b) indicate a "lack of discipline" (30:12a), in which case a father should "belabor" or "beat" his son's "ribs" (30:12a) and "smite his flanks" (30:12b). Otherwise, the boy will become "stubborn" and "disobey" his father (30:12c) and bring on his "last breath" (30:12d). The Law provided severe penalties for a stubborn, unruly, and disobedient son; cf. Deut 21:18–21; Ps 78:8. Ben Sira concludes this section by urging a father to discipline his son by making "heavy his yoke" (30:13a; the phrase derives from 1 Kgs 12:10–11); cf. 7:23. A father should do this not only because he loves his son (30:1a), but also because it is in his self-interest to do so (30:13b; cf. NOTE).

37. Health, Cheerfulness, and Riches
(30:14–31:11)

30 14 Better the poor in vigorous health   B
      than the rich with bodily ills.
 15 I had rather sturdy health than gold,
      and a blithe spirit than coral.
 16 No riches surpass a healthy body;
      no happiness matches that of a joyful heart!
 17 Rather death than a wretched life,
      unending sleep than constant illness.
 18 Dainties set before one who cannot eat
      are like food offerings placed before a tomb.   G
 19 Of what use is an offering to an idol
      that can neither eat nor smell?
    So it is with the one being punished by the Lord,
 20   who groans at the good things his eyes behold!

 21 Do not give in to grief
      or afflict yourself with brooding;
 22 Gladness of heart is the very life of a person,
      and cheerfulness prolongs his days.
 23 Distract yourself, renew your courage,   B
      drive resentment far away from you;
    For grief has brought death to many,
      nor is there aught to be gained from resentment.
 24 Envy and anger shorten one's life;
      anxiety brings on premature old age.
(27) One who is bright and cheery at table   G
      benefits from his food.

31 1 Wakefulness over riches wastes away the flesh;
 2   more than a serious illness, it washes out sleep.

3 The rich labors to pile up wealth,   B
   and if he rests, it is to enjoy pleasure;
4 The poor toils for a meager subsistence,
   and if ever he rests, he finds himself in want.
5 The lover of gold will not be free from sin;
   whoever pursues profit is led astray by it.
6 Many have they been who were entrapped by gold,
   who put their confidence in corals;
7 This is a stumbling block for fools—
   by it any simpleton will be ensnared.

8 Happy the rich found without fault,
   who turns not aside after wealth!
9 Who is he, that we may praise him?
   He, of all his kindred, has done wonders,
10 For he has been tested by gold and come off safe,   G
   and this remains his glory:
   He could have gone wrong but did not,   B
   could have done evil but would not,
11 So that his possessions are secure,
   and the assembly recounts his praises.

Notes

30   17. In MS B, 17c,b are the original line; its 17a,d and Syr 17b are a debased text.

18b. *before a tomb:* so G, Syr; MS B, "before an idol." Despite the ingenuity that relates *gillûl* of MS B to *gōlēl,* the rolling stone closing the entrance to a tomb, the evidence of G and Syr deserves to be respected in its own right; who knows how MS B came by *gillûl?*

19–20. Here there are five cola in GI (GII adds 20:4b as a borrowed sixth), seven in the Syriac, and nine in MS B. Certainly out of place is the addition from 20:4b, though it is present in GII, Syr, and MS B. The first four cola of GI contain the basic text and are translated above. They are followed in GI by the line "like a eunuch embracing a maiden and groaning"; though this appears also in Lat, Syr, and (with a doublet) in MS B, it is best seen as an inept application of 20:4a to the present context, to which GI links it by repetition of *who groans* (as: *kai stenazōn,* "and groaning") from v 20b. Both Syr and MS B (in its doublet) link this expansion with the language of Sir 5:3b by adding, "but the LORD will require it at his hand." Sir 5:3b is also the source of *being punished* in GI's v 19c. In the latter colon, *ekdiōkomenos* was read by Syh as *ekdikoumenos* (*mttbᶜ*), as Ziegler notes, following Smend and Hart. For comparison, Ziegler refers to 39:30; this passage is also a reflection of 5:3.

21, 22. The text of MS B is again corrupt, and would need to be rewritten in the light of GI, Syr; but in 21b read *bĕᶜeṣeb*, with or without a suffix, for G's *en boulē̦ sou* (see Segal). In 22b, MS B has been contaminated from Prov 19:11 under the influence of v 23 (Segal).

23c. *grief=dāwôn*=G, *lypē;* MS B *dîn,* false copy of an older *dāwôn.*

24a. *and anger*=G, Syr; MS B *wĕdîn,* compare 23c above.

(27). Though there are only twenty-four verses counted in the preceding Gr of this chapter, Ziegler numbers this last one 30:27 in deference to the Lat, which has chap. 30 in proper sequence, and has been made to count twenty-seven verses. This is the first verse of the several chapters that have undergone a major transposition in the Gr, in which it comes to be numbered 33:13b, with the following chapters 31 and 32 becoming 34 and 35. Further confusion occurs with chap. 33 (36), in which the other half of the transposition begins: see INTRODUCTION, Part VIII, 3.

27a. *bright and cheery* (of heart): this is G's double translation of *ṭôb (lēb)* in a colon that appears corrupt in MS B.

31 1–2. These verses are a nearly hopeless jumble. Before GI and Syr, 42:9b, "and anxiety for it drives away sleep," had already been imported here to become 31:1b. V 31:2a in G, "The anxiety of wakefulness drives away slumber," is a tautology created (before G) to provide a new parallel to the *sickness* colon, now 2b in the Greek. In Syr, the "wakefulness" of the tautology became "sustenance" (*māzōnāᵓ*), which the medieval Heb offers as *miḥyâ* (cf. Judg 6:4) and carries back also into 31:1 to provide a noun instead of the vague pronoun attached to "anxiety" there. MS B then imports a line that plays on 22:22 (see NOTE in that place) for no other purpose than to illustrate another verb for "drive away" than the two incredible ones (*tpryᶜ* and *tpryg*) it already had in the three cola preceding. Here the first colon of G has been kept as 31:1, and its fourth colon as 31:2 (note the parallel verb forms *ektēkei, eknipsei/eknēpsei*). The corresponding Heb is in its 31:1a, 2b (also flawed: *šeqer* for *šeqed; tapríaᶜ?*). Where MS B got its comparative particle to go with *sickness* (*mēḥŏlî*) one might wonder; but the point of the colon would seem to be a comparison between the sick man of vv 16–18 and the plight of the miser (31:1–7), and that is supposed in the translation given here. *washes out* (=*eknipsei,* with a few MSS and Grotius cited by Ziegler; the received *eknēpsei* is hopeless) is dubious—but some verb of similar form and meaning is required.

3a. Read *ᶜāmēl ᶜāšîr liqbōṣ lô hôn,* cf. Syr; for 3b, cf. 41:1d (M).

4. In MS B's double recording, 4ab is the better line; read *miḥyâ,* cf. the Gr, for *bêtô/kōḥô* (for the latter, cf. again 41:1d, M).

5. MS B has the verbs in this line transposed, cf. G, Syr.

6. Read *hazzāhāb* and *wĕhabbôṭĕḥîm.* Note that the Gr understood the latter word (which it saw followed by *ᶜal pĕnêhem*) as from *bṭḥ* II (cf. *HALAT,* 116), "to fall flat," in the light of Jer 12:5, and recognized that root though LXX Jer did not (vs. Segal). After this verse, Syr adds: "But they [i.e, their possessions, in the underlying Heb *pĕnînîm*] were unable to deliver them from disaster, or to save them on the day of

wrath." This is a gloss that cuts v 7 away from its context. Of this Syr, the Heb of MS B is a manifest retroversion, reading *wĕlā' 'eškaḥw*, "but they were unable," as *wĕlō' māṣĕ'û*, "but they did not find (a way)," and changing the subjects of both that verb and the two following infinitives (vs. Segal).

7. Where MS B reads *lā'ĕwîl, for fools*, G's *enthousiazousin autǭ* (so Ziegler, on limited direct evidence) probably represents *lĕ'ōwê lô;* the Lat, with *vae* (='ôy) *illis* shows another misreading of *l'wyl*.

8. For *'îš* of MS B, read *'āšîr, the rich*, cf. G, Syr, Lat. The Lat liturgical reading *beatus vir* reflects rather the text of Pss 1:1; 112:1; and the like, than any Heb reading for this passage in Sir.

10ab. Here MS B and its margin have a spate of jumbled phrases.

11b. *his praises:* G reads: "his pious deeds" = *ḥăsādāyw*.

Comment

This section contains four loosely connected poems: the blessing of good health (30:14–20); the benefits of cheerfulness (30:21–[27]); the anxieties of the rich (31:1–7); and the blessedness of the blameless rich (31:8–11).

The proverb in 30:14 receives hearty endorsement from perceptive people everywhere: "vigorous health" with poverty is preferable to wealth without health. "The first wealth is health" (Ralph Waldo Emerson, "Power," *The Conduct of Life* [1860]). "Sturdy health" is preferable to "gold" (30:15a, Heb *pāz*, "refined, pure gold"), and "a blithe spirit" (Heb *rûaḥ ṭôbâ*, lit., "a good spirit") than "coral" (30:15b). For the images, cf. Prov 3:14–15; 8:10–11; 31:10. "Look to your health; and if you have it, praise God, and value it next to a good conscience; for health is the second blessing that we mortals are capable of; a blessing that money cannot buy" (Izaak Walton, *The Compleat Angler* [1653], i 21). Before 30:16, some Gr MSS (B*, S, 248, and other cursives) have the title "On Foods" (Codex A, "On Health"). V 16 may be translated, lit.: "There is no wealth above the wealth of a sound body, and no good above a good heart" (=disposition). The sentiment in 30:17 (cf. NOTE) has been expressed by many sufferers; cf., for example, Tob 3:6, 10, 13, where Tobit in Nineveh and Sarah in Ecbatana both pray for death in order to be relieved of their miseries. Cf. also Job 3:11, 13, 17; Qoh 4:1–2. For the expression "constant illness" (30:17b), cf. Deut 28:59. V 17 is close to the thought of Theognis, 181–82 (Sanders, p. 34). Good food "set before one who cannot eat" (30:18a) is as useless as "food offerings placed before a tomb" (30:18b; cf. NOTE), a custom perhaps alluded to in Tob 4:17; cf. COMMENT on 7:33. This thought is amplified in 30:19–20 (cf. NOTE), with a change of imagery: the person who has before him good things he cannot eat because he is ill (his illness is here considered divine punishment; cf. John 9:2) feels like an idol "that can neither eat nor smell." Cf. Qoh 6:2. For the pagan custom of offering food and drink to idols, cf. Isa 57:6; Dan 14:1–22 (the story of Bel). The biblical authors ridiculed both idols and their devotees; cf. Deut 4:28; Ps 115:4–7; Isa 44:9–11.

As regards the text of 30:21–22, cf. NOTE. The sound advice given in 30:21 reminds us of the words of Jesus in Matt 6:34. Cf. Qoh 11:10. Modern psychology and medicine have proved the validity of the comments made in 30:22–24, (27). For the thought of 30:22, cf. Prov 17:22a; Qoh 11:9. Resentment and grief (cf. NOTE) can be fatal (30:23). "Nothing on earth consumes a man more quickly than the passion of resentment" (Friedrich Nietzsche, *Ecce Homo* [1888]). "Sorrow breaks seasons and reposing hours, / Makes the night morning and the noon-tide night" (Shakespeare, *Richard III* [1592–93], I iv 76–77). Envy, anger (cf. NOTE), and anxiety also "shorten one's life (30:24). "As iron is eaten away by rust, so the envious are consumed by their own passion" (Antisthenes [5th–4th century B.C.], quoted in Diogenes Laërtius, *Lives and Opinions of Eminent Philosophers* [third century of our era]). "The envious die not once, but as oft as the envied win applause" (Baltasar Gracián, *The Art of Wordly Wisdom* [1647], 162). "To be angry is to revenge the fault of others upon ourselves" (Alexander Pope, *Thoughts on Various Subjects* [1727]). "Anger would inflict punishment on another; meanwhile, it tortures itself" (Publilius Syrus, *Moral Sayings* [1st cent. B.C.], 1009). "Care is no cure, but rather corrosive, / For things that are not to be remedied" (Shakespeare, *Henry VI*, Part I [1591–92], III iii 3–4). Cf. Wis 17:12. As regards the numbering of 30:(27), cf. NOTE. Ben Sira concludes this poem with a clinically accurate observation: being "bright and cheery" (cf. NOTE) enables one to derive the most benefit from the food one eats. Cf. Prov 15:15.

The text of 31:1–2 is in a confused state; cf. NOTE for an attempt to make sense out of this jumble. The sinner, the fool (cf. 31:7), in the present case the rich, are said to suffer from insomnia because of their bad consciences (31:1–2); cf. 40:5–8; Qoh 5:11; Wis 17:11–15. Concern for an unmarried daughter also causes sleeplessness (42:9ab). In Ben Sira's perspective, the sinful rich (31:5–7) labor for only one reason, "to pile up wealth" (31:3a), and when they relax, "it is to enjoy pleasure" (31:3b)—ideas that are embodied in Jesus' parable of the rich fool in Luke 12:16–20; so Peters (p. 252). For the text of 31:3ab, cf. NOTE. Poverty, which makes life miserable and subsistence precarious (31:4a; cf. NOTE), is, however, not something desirable, for the poor can rest and relax only at the risk of experiencing "want" (31:4b). The poor and their plight are mentioned here only to provide a sharp contrast with the rich and their surfeit of the "good things" of life. The Jewish ideal was a virtuous life together with sufficient wealth to ensure the necessities of life and to enjoy some degree of prosperity (cf. 31:8–11). Those who are avid for wealth, however, "will not be free from sin," and those who seek "profit" are "led astray by it" (31:5; cf. NOTE); cf. 14:3; Prov 28:20b; Qoh 5:9; 1 Tim 6:9–10. The avaricious are trapped by the very "gold" they yearn for, because they "put their confidence in corals" (31:6; cf. NOTE), i.e., in their assets and other wealth yet to be hoped for. Thus greed becomes "a stumbling block for fools," a trap for the "simpleton" (31:7; cf. NOTE); cf. Prov 11:4. "Riches serve a wise man but command a fool" (English proverb). "There are men who gain from their wealth only the fear of losing it" (Antoine Rivaroli, *L'Esprit de Rivarol* [1808]).

In the next poem (31:8–11), Ben Sira lauds the rich who are wise, i.e., who are "without fault," who "turn not aside" or "stray not" "after wealth" (Heb *māmôn,* whence derives our English word "mammon"). Ben Sira is the first to use the Heb word *māmôn;* the word (*mamōna* in Gr) occurs also in Matt 6:24 and Luke 16:9, 11, 13. The question "Who is he . . . ?" (31:9a) clearly implies that a rich person who is also righteous was as rare in Ben Sira's day as he was in Jesus' day; cf. Matt 19:23–24; Mark 10:23–25; Luke 16:13. Indeed, the rich without fault, "of all [their] kindred," are said to do "wonders" (31:9b), another indication of the rarity of such people. What makes the virtuous rich praiseworthy is that they have been "tested" by gold and "come off safe" (31:10ab; cf. NOTE); they "could have done evil but would not" (31:10d). "There is a time when a man distinguishes between the idea of felicity from the idea of wealth; it is the beginning of wisdom" (Ralph Waldo Emerson, *Journals* [1830]). Cf. Matt 16:26. Because virtue, according to the Deuteronomic theory of retribution Ben Sira believed in, is rewarded only in this life, the "possessions" of the pious rich are "secure" (31:11a; cf. COMMENT on 2:1–6), and "the assembly recounts [their] praises" (31:11b; cf. NOTE), as it does the praises of the Ancestors in 44:15. The rabbis had a saying, "The salt of mammon is almsgiving" (so Box-Oesterley, p. 419).

38. Food, Wine, and Banquets
(31:12–32:13)

31 12 Are you seated at a banquet table?   G
    Bring to it no greedy gullet!
Say not, "What a spread this is!"
  13 Remember, gluttony is a bad thing.
God hates the eye's greed;   B
    was ever any creature greedier?
That is why it shifts with everything it sees,
    and sends tears streaming down the face.
15 Recognize that your neighbor feels as you do,
    and keep in mind your own dislikes;
14 Toward what he is looking at, do not put out a hand;
    nor reach when he does, for the same dish.
16 Eat, like anyone else, what lies before you   G
    and be not rapacious, lest you become loathed.   B
17 Be the first to stop, as befits good manners;
    gorge not yourself, lest you be despised.
18 If there are many with you at table,
    be not the first to reach out your hand.
19 Does not a little suffice for a well-bred person?
    When he lies down, it is without wheezing.
20c Bilious distress, and loss of sleep,   G
  d and restless tossing for the glutton!
  a Moderate eating ensures sound slumber
  b and a clear mind next day on rising.
21 If perforce you have eaten too much,   B
    once you have emptied your stomach, you will have
                    relief.

22 Listen to me, my son, and scorn me not;
    later you will find my advice good.

In whatever you do, be moderate,
and no addiction will afflict you.

23 On a person generous with food, blessings are invoked,
and this testimony to his goodness is lasting;

24 Whoever is miserly with food is denounced in public,
and this testimony to his stinginess is lasting.

25 Let not wine-drinking be the proof of your strength,
for wine has been the ruin of many.

26 As the forge probes the work of the swordsmith,
so does wine the hearts of the insolent.

27 Wine is very life to humans,
if taken in due measure.
Does one really live who lacks the wine
which was created from the first for his joy?

28 Joy of heart, good cheer, and delight
is wine enough, drunk at the proper time.

29 Headache, wormwood, and disgrace
is wine drunk amid anger and strife.

30 More and more wine is a snare for the fool;
it lessens his strength and multiplies his wounds.

31 Rebuke not your neighbor when wine is served,   G
nor put him to shame while he is merry;
Use no harsh words with him
and distress him not in the presence of others.

32 1 If you are chosen to preside at dinner, be not puffed
up,
but with the guests be as one of them;   B
Take care of them first before you sit down—
2   see to their needs, then take your place,
To share in their joy   G
and win praise for your hospitality.

3 You who are older, it is your right to talk,   B
but temper your wisdom, not to interrupt the
singing.

4 Where listening is in order, do not pour out discourse,   G
and flaunt not your wisdom at the wrong time.

5 Like a seal of carnelian in a setting of gold
is a company singing when wine is served.

6 In a gold mounting, an emerald seal
   is string music with delicious wine.
7 Young man, speak only when necessary,
   when they have asked you more than once;
8 Be brief, but say much in those few words,
   be like the wise, taciturn.
9 When with officials, be not forward,
   and among your elders be not too insistent.
10 Like the lightning that flashes before a hailstorm
   is the esteem that shines on modesty.
11 When it is time to leave, tarry not;
   be off for home without delay,
12 And there enjoy doing as you wish,
   but without sin or words of pride.
13 Above all, give praise to your Maker,
   who showers his favors upon you.

Notes

31   12a. This omits (with G) the *bĕnî 'im* of MS B and Syr; keeping the *'im,* one would read: "When you are seated . . ."

13. G has only 13a,c,e; the Heb and Syr call for two bicola (13b–e) after 13a. MS B has also an alternative form for 13b, and a contraction of 13de into one colon different from G's 13e—"That is why its juice flees (!) before anything."

15, 14. This order of the verses provides the (otherwise missing) subject for the verbs of v 14.

14b. *dish:* so G and Syr, evoking associations with Mark 14:20 and parallels; MS B has "basket."

16. In 16a, MS B here appears corrupt, see Segal; after *loathed* of 16b, MS B has three more cola. Of these latter, the first duplicates 15a; the others repeat 16ab in a form, tied to Syr, that can scarcely be anything other than retroversion from that source.

20. The two bicola of v 20 are in the reverse order in G. *the glutton* of G, Syr, is, in the Heb, *'îš kĕsîl;* does this use of *kĕsîl* carry an allusion to fat covering the loins, cf. Job 15:27?

20cd, 21. There were doublets for both verses in MS B; much of the text for these is eaten away in the MS.

22–27. In this section, MS B has doublets, partially garbled or expanded, for vv

22cd, 26, 27cd. That for 27cd, which in the MS follows v 28, has an end rhyme (*tîrôš, mērô'š*) that looks suspiciously like a medieval development.

26b. *hearts of the insolent:* reading *libbôt lēṣîm,* with G; so Segal. In G, *en machē/ en methē* (Ziegler, cf. Clem. Alex., Lat, and v 32) is an expansion parallel to *en baphē,* also an expansion, in the preceding colon.

28a. *and delight:* a third noun seems needed in the colon; compare the contrasting v 29a. Since MS B's *ʿdwy,* and the *ʿdwn* suggested (Segal) on the basis of Syr, are hardly to be credited, *ʿēden* as a common noun (plural in Ps 36:9) appears most likely.

28b. *wine enough:* reading at the end of the line, for MS B's *wry,* rather *(bĕʿittô) dāy,* compare G (*autarkēs*) here and in 11:24. This seems to fit also Syr *bĕwālîtāʾ,* used already for a related notion at the end of v 27b.

29a. *wormwood:* G's *pikria* three times (in Deuteronomy, Amos, and Lamentations)=*laʿănâ;* also (vs. Segal), Syr's "poverty" supposes the *ʿayin-nun* of *ʿŏnî,* which again are traces of *laʿănâ; laʿănâ* is present in MS B.

31. These two bicola are damaged in MS B.

31d. *in the presence of others:* G's *en apaitēsei* is a manifest corruption from *en apantēsei anthrōpōn* (or, a̅n̅o̅n̅, abbreviated), as seen by Smend; compare Syr and Heb.

32 1. Two cola of this verse are missing (with the bottom of a page) in MS B; v 1b as found on the same line with a crowded v 2 at the top of the following page in the MS has beside it a note in Persian (in Heb letters) saying: "This half-verse and this verse are from another copy." The Syr, with "and take no prominent place among the rich" between 1a and 1b, probably shows what sort of reading stood in the second colon of the missing line. For the Persian note, besides the facsimile of MS B, cf. Smend, *Die Weisheit . . . hebräisch und deutsch* (1906), p. 27.

2bc. With Smend, G's *di' autōn*=*baʿăbûrām.* For this, MS B's *bikĕbôdām* is a garbled copy. The *šēkel* with which MS B ends the verse is then a substitute by a confused copyist for *kābôd* turning up again at the end of the verse, where G seems to have rendered that term by *stephanon,* "crown"—cf. again Smend, who points 25:6 for a parallel rendering in G.

4. The copyist of MS B draws from two sources again for this verse, as is shown by his writing of 4a normally, then of a variant on 4a plus 4b in a smaller, crowded hand in the space intended for the second colon in the line. Neither his "in the place of wine/in place of the wine" nor his "and without music" matches G's *Where listening is in order.* That supposes *bimĕqôm haʾăzîn,* which if written without the *aleph* would make easy the distortion to *bimĕqôm hayyayin* as it appears in MS B (1° *loco*) and Syr.

5–6. These two comparisons become four for MS B, with a number of confusions and enlargements.

7–8. Here G and MS B run closer together, though v 7 in MS B is still padded; Syr lacks these verses.

9. MS B transposes *officials* and *elders* in this verse, cf. G, Syr. The verb *ṭrd* in Sirach occurs only here (in MS B) and in 11QPsᵃ for 51:19c, beginning the *ṭeth* line of the alphabet acrostic (*ṭrty* for *ṭrdty,* with the *daleth* assimilated). The usages are compatible and mutually illustrative.

10. *hailstorm:* so the Lat and MS B; Ziegler shows no variant to "thunder" in this place for the Gr tradition. The wordplay *bārād, bārāq* confirms that "hail" is original

here. MS B gives the verse in two forms, plus a rewritten 10a in the margin; Syr lacks the verse.

11–12. G here has four cola; Syr diverges widely, with about the same amount of text. MS B has six cola, two of which are an identical conflation of elements from 11a, 12a. Only G has recognizable continuity.

Comment

This section has three related poems: moderation in eating (31:12–21); the blessing of wine and its abuse (31:22–31); and proper conduct at a banquet (32:1–13). The advice given here is, in general, what is dictated by good manners and courtesy.

When invited to a banquet, one should not be greedy or make ill-advised comments (31:12; cf. NOTE), for gluttony (Heb ʿayin rāʿâ, Gr ophthalmos ponēros, lit., evil eye) "is a bad thing" (31:13a). For the text of 31:13, cf. NOTE. It could be considered a sign of envy or cupidity to make comments about the large quantity of food placed on the table; cf. Prov 23:1–3. Edersheim writes: "The praising of the food in Oriental countries is done by the host; the mere act of admiration by any one else would be regarded as dangerous" (cited by Box-Oesterley, p. 419). The eye, whose greed "God hates" (31:13b), is considered the greediest of all creatures (31:13c) and, accordingly, a source of sin; cf. Num 15:39; Job 31:1. The greedy and envious eye "shifts with everything it sees, and sends tears streaming down the face" (31:13de), because it cannot have all its desires, and begrudges others the good they receive; cf. 14:10; Matt 20:15. On the order of the verses in 31:15, 14, cf. NOTE. One should be sensitive to others at a banquet; they have feelings, too (31:15a). Hence, that which one dislikes should not be done to others (31:15b); cf. Tob 4:15. If your neighbor eyes a particular dish and reaches for it, do not reach for it at the same time (31:14; cf. NOTE). In sum, at a dinner one should be responsive to others and their tastes. The literal translation of 31:16a is "Eat like a human being what lies before you," i.e., do not bolt your food (31:16b), as animals do, or chew so loudly that you annoy your neighbors (so Spicq, p. 720). Otherwise, you will be "loathed" (31:16b; cf. NOTE). It is "good manners" to stop eating first (31:17a) and not to appear to "gorge" yourself, for otherwise you will "be despised" (31:17b). Cf. 37:29–31. The point of 31:16–17 is that you should eat in moderation and with courtesy, not too slowly lest you prolong the meal and hold up those who serve, and not too fast lest you be considered a ravenous parasite whose appetite was sharpened by the invitation to dinner. If there are many other guests you should not be the first to reach for the food (31:18). *Derek ereṣ rabba* vii states: "When two are sitting at table, the elder begins to eat first, and the younger after him; and if the younger begins first he is a glutton." Moderation not only is a mark of "a well-bred person" (lit., a person of understanding) but also enables one to sleep comfortably (31:19). On the contrary, gluttony brings on indigestion and "restless tossing" when one attempts to sleep (31:20cd; cf. NOTE). Moderation enables one to sleep soundly and to awake refreshed and with "a clear mind" (31:20ab); cf. 37:29–31. If, however, one has "eaten too much" (as can happen on a festive occasion even when one intends to eat moderately), vomiting will bring "relief" (31:21; cf. NOTE). Ben Sira's advice sounds earthy, but it is practical nonetheless. There is no point in getting sick after unintended overindulgence in food and drink. And even if one was a glutton, it is still better to avoid illness by vomiting. Ben Sira, however, is not urging the disgusting custom, practiced by wealthy Romans, of a person using an emetic to induce vomiting after he has over-eaten, so that he may continue to eat some more. The modern version of this practice, which is called bulimia, often has disastrous results for health.

In the next poem (31:22–31), Ben Sira continues his observations and ex-hortations about the use of food and especially of wine. For the text of 31:22–27 in MS B, cf. NOTE. The text of 31:22cd translated here is found before 31:21 in MS B. As regards the opening phrase, "listen to me," cf. COMMENT on 6:23. Ben Sira urges his student, whom he calls "my son" in accordance with the usage of other Wisdom authors, to "be moderate" in everything he does (31:22c), so that no "addiction" (Heb *'āsôn,* lit., harm, evil, mischief) may "afflict" him (31:22cd). In other words, moderation is a form of enlight-ened self-interest. One should be "generous with food" and so receive "bless-ings" from others (31:23a) and a good reputation that is "lasting" (31:23b). Cf. Prov 22:9. Conversely, one should not be "miserly with food" for fear of being "denounced in public" (31:24a) and receiving a bad reputation that also lasts (31:24b). The reading "testimony" (Heb *'ēdût*) in 31:24b is from MS B^mg; MS B^txt reads "knowledge" (*da'at;* note that these are the same consonants of *'ēdût* but in a different order). Cf. 14:10; Prov 23:6–8. V 25a is an allusion to Isa 5:22.

There was a Hellenistic institution called in Gr *symposion* (the basis of our English word "symposium"), at which food and drink were served as at a banquet; large quantities of wine were usually consumed at these events. In 31:25, Ben Sira warns of the perils of excessive wine-drinking at such ban-quets; cf. 1 Macc 16:15–16. In Scripture, there are many other exhortations about the risks of drinking too much; cf. Prov 20:1; 23:29–35; 31:45; Amos 6:6; Hos 7:5; Isa 5:11–12; 28:1. The case of Holofernes (Jdt 13:2–8) is dra-matic proof of the statement in 31:25b. The "forge" and "wine" are parallel in 31:26; as the former tests the quality of metal, the latter shows that the hearts (cf. NOTE) of the foolish are "insolent." Cf. the Lat proverb *In vino veritas,* "In wine, the truth." Another parallel can be seen in Theognis, 499–500 (Sanders, p. 34). The first word of 31:27a should be read as *lĕmô;* MS B has *lmy* instead of *lmw*—another case of confusion of *waw* and *yod;* cf. COMMENT on 4:2. The word *lĕmô* is a poetic form of the particle *lĕ-;* cf. Job 27:14; 29:21; 38:40; 40:4. Smend (p. 283) and Box-Oesterley (p. 423) point the word as *lĕmê,* "waters of (life)." Syr reads: "like the waters of life." The comments Ben Sira makes in 31:27–28 should gladden the hearts of readers who enjoy a glass of wine. "Wine is very life to humans" but only when taken in moderation (31:27ab); cf. 1 Tim 5:23. He does not "really live who lacks the wine which was created from the first for his joy" (31:27cd)—a clear and unambiguous affirmation of the goodness of wine as a creation by the Lord "from the first" (Heb *mērē'šît,* lit., from the beginning; cf. *bĕrē'šît* in Gen 1:1). Cf. Judg 9:13; Ps 104:15. A goodly supply of wine, "drunk at the proper time" (31:28b; cf. NOTE) is "joy of heart, good cheer, and delight" (31:28a; cf. NOTE); cf. 40:20a. The sentiments expressed in 31:25–28 have echoes in many other literatures and cultures. "Bronze is the mirror of the form [in antiquity mirrors were made from polished bronze]; wine, of the heart" (Aeschylus [525–456 B.C.], *Fragments,* 384). "Where there is plenty of wine, sorrow and worry take wing" (Ovid, *The Art of Love* [ca. A.D. 8], 1). "Good wine is a good familiar creature, if it be well used" (Shakespeare, *Othello* [1604–5], II iii 313). "Wine is like rain: when it falls on the mire it but makes it the fouler, / But when it strikes the good soil wakes it to beauty and bloom" (John Hay, "Distichs" [1871?], 7). Cf. J. Bauer, " 'Kein Leben ohne Wein' (Jesus Sirach 31,27): Das Urteil der Hl. Schrift," *Bibel und Liturgie* 23 (1955–56): 55–59; and A. A. Wieder, "Ben Sira and the Praises of Wine," *JQR* 61 (1970–71): 155–66.

In contrast to wine "drunk at the proper time" (31:28b) is "wine drunk amid anger and strife" (31:29b). In the latter case wine is not "joy of heart . . ." (31:28a) but rather "headache, wormwood [cf. NOTE], and disgrace" (31:29a). "What the sober man has in his heart, the drunken man has on his lips" (Danish proverb). "To dispute with a drunkard is to debate with an empty house" (Publilius Syrus, *Moral Sayings* [first century B.C.], 4). Too much wine becomes "a snare for the fool" because "it lessens his strength and multiplies his wounds" (31:30). Cf. Prov 23:29–35. "Drunkenness does not create vices, but it brings them to the fore" (Seneca, *Letters to Lucilius* [first century of our era], 83, 20). "Bacchus [the god of wine] hath drowned more men than Neptune" (Thomas Fuller, *Gnomologia* [1732], 830). The drunkard often causes violence or becomes its victim because of his intemperate words or actions. The four cola of 31:31 provide a transition to the following poem on proper conduct to be observed at banquets. Since wine tends to loosen the tongue and the inhibitions, Ben Sira's advice here is sound. Cf. 20:1. It is discourteous and foolish to become rowdy at a banquet and to abuse your neighbor "in the presence of others" (31:31d; cf. NOTE), for wine was created to promote good cheer among people (31:27–28) and not to provoke discord. Cf. 18:18; 20:15ab; 22:22. For other parallels to 31:24–31, see Theognis, 467–510 (Sanders, pp. 34–35).

The final poem of this section (32:1–13) offers many bits of advice and warnings about behavior at a banquet. Doubtless the mind-set and attitudes expressed here were commonly shared by the cultivated Jews of that time. Ben Sira includes in his exhortations the different kinds of people present at the sumptuous banquets of the day: the banquet master (32:1–2), the older guests (32:3–6), and the younger guests (32:7–10). The poem concludes with general aphorisms applicable to all (32:11–13). "If you are chosen to preside at dinner" (32:1a, Gr *hēgoumenon,* lit., to be leader, chief) is a reference to the custom of selecting a banquet master, called in Gr literature *symposiarchos* or *architriklinos* (this word is used to describe the official of the wedding feast at Cana in John 2:8–10). From John 2:8–10 and what Ben Sira says here, it must have been the responsibility of the banquet master to arrange the seating, prepare the menu, select the wines, and ensure good service for all the guests; cf. Esth 1:8; 2 Macc 2:27. Since it was a great honor for a person to be chosen banquet master, Ben Sira urges him to be modest in the performance of his assigned tasks and to act like one of the guests (32:1ab; cf. NOTE). As befits courtesy and consideration, he should take care of their needs first and then take his place (32:1c, 2a) "to share in their joy and win praise for [his] hospitality" (32:2bc; cf. NOTE).

Next comes advice to the elder guests. They have, of course, the "right to talk" (32:3a), but they should "temper [their] wisdom, not to interrupt the singing" (32:3b). The wise guest knows when to speak and to keep silent when there is singing. The reference here is to the singers who performed (cf. 32:5b) at these sumptuous banquets; cf. 2 Sam 19:26; Isa 5:12; 24:7–9; Qoh 2:8. The elder who is wise knows when "listening is in order" (32:4a; cf. NOTE), and he does not "pour out discourse" like a bore, or "flaunt . . . [his] wisdom at the wrong time" (32:4b). In 32:5–6 (cf. NOTE), the images of jewelry are used to evoke the pleasures one experiences when listening to a good "company singing" along with "string music" and enjoying "delicious wine." Cf. Prov 25:11; Exod 28:17–20. Ben Sira's advice to the young guest is typical, and expected. If he is wise, he will "speak only when necessary" and when the other guests "have asked [him] more than once" (32:7; cf. NOTE); cf. the words of Elihu in Job 32:6–7. The young should "be brief, but say much" and then be quiet "like the wise" (32:8). The two cola of 32:9 (cf. NOTE) are in synonymous parallelism: "when with officials" or "elders," "be not forward" or "too insistent"; cf. Job 29:7–10. For the possible dangers of being overfamiliar with "officials," cf. 13:9–13 with COMMENT. "The esteem [Heb *ḥēn,* Gr *charis,* lit., grace] that shines on modesty" may be compared to the brilliance and swiftness of "the lightning that flashes before a hailstorm"

(32:10; cf. NOTE), i.e., the modest youth receives immediate and dazzling recognition.

The final three verses (32:11–13) of this poem are applicable to all guests at a banquet. "When it is time to leave, . . . be off . . . without delay" (32:11). Overstaying your welcome is a gross violation of good manners. Home is the place to do or talk "as you wish, but without sin or words of pride" (32:12; cf. NOTE). Consideration for others at a banquet demands that you be discreet and circumspect in the way you eat, drink, and speak. "Above all, give praise to [Heb *bārēk,* Gr *eulogēson,* lit., bless] your Maker" (32:13a) —a reference to the ancient practice of saying grace, or giving thanks, at meals; cf. Deut 8:10. The faithful and grateful believer acknowledges that it is the Lord alone who is the Source of the "favors" (lit., the good things) he receives not only at table but also elsewhere in his life. Even the pagan Greeks had the custom after meals of offering praise to their gods; cf. Plato (ca. 428– 348 B.C.), *Symposium,* 176.

39. The Providence of God
(32:14–33:18)

32   14 Whoever seeks to learn from God will obtain guidance;   B
      whoever seeks God out will receive his answer.
  15 Whoever studies the Law masters it,
      but the reckless is caught in its snare.
  16 Whoever fears the LORD will know what is right
                                conduct;
      out of obscurity he draws forth a course of action.
  17 The sinner turns aside warnings
      and distorts the Law to suit his purpose.
  18 Whoever is well advised will not neglect what he learns;   G
      the proud and insolent person is deterred by nothing.
  19 Do nothing without counsel;   B
      then, having acted, have no qualms.
  20 Go not on a way that is set with snares,
      and let not the same thing trip you twice.
  21 Trust not the road, for bandits;
  22   be careful on all your paths.
  23 Whatever you do, be on your guard,
      for in this way you will keep the commandments.
  24 Whoever keeps the Law preserves himself;
      and whoever trusts in the LORD shall not be put to
                            shame.

33   1 No evil can harm the one who fears the LORD;
      through trials, again and again he is safe.   E
  2 Whoever hates the Law is without wisdom,   B
      and is tossed about like a boat in a storm.   G
  3 The prudent trusts in the word of the Lord,
      and the Law is dependable for him as a divine oracle.
  4 Prepare your words and you will be listened to;
      bind your training to your person, and then give your
                            answer.

5 Like the wheel of a cart is the mind of a fool;   E
  his thoughts revolve in circles.
6 An unscrupulous friend is like the distracted stallion
  that neighs, no matter who the rider.

7 Why is one day more important than another,
  when the same sun lights up every day of the year?
8 By the Lord's knowledge they are kept distinct;   G
  among them he designates seasons and feasts.   S
9 Some he exalts and sanctifies,   G
  and others he lists as ordinary days.   E
10 So, too, all people are of clay,
  for from earth humankind was formed;
11 Yet in the fullness of his understanding the Lord makes   G
                                              people unlike:
  in different paths he has them walk.
12 Some he blesses and makes great,   E
  some he sanctifies and draws to himself.
  Others he curses and brings low,
  and expels them from their place.
13 Like clay in the hands of a potter,
  to be molded according to his pleasure,   GII
  So are people in the hands of their Maker,   E
  to be requited according as he judges them.   G
14 As evil contrasts with good, and death with life,   E
  so are sinners in contrast with the just;
15 See now all the works of the Most High:
  they come in pairs, the one the opposite of the other.

16 Now I am the last to keep vigil,
  as one gleaning after the vintagers;
17 Since by God's blessing I too have made progress
  till like a vintager I have filled my winepress,
18 Take notice that not for myself only have I toiled,
  but for every seeker after guidance.

Notes

32 14–15. Of the four bicola in MS B here, the two that provide the basic text are the second and the fourth. The first is a combination of 14a with 15b. The third is a weak reworking of v 14. Syr has v 14 only. G reflects the earlier, related verses 2:16 and 4:12.

16. Here MS E runs parallel with MS B, doublets and all; its single folio is defective at one side, so that, on the recto, 32:16–33:14 lack the first word or two of each bicolon. V 16 in MSS B, E is correct in the first of its two forms; the second, and the Syr, are debased.

17. In 17a, MS B's margin supplies the correct *ḥāmās* for a mistaken *ḥākām;* in 17b, MS B's text is correct, though its margin and MS E combine to present a distorted form of it.

18. With two forms of this verse in the text of MSS B, E, and another in B's margin, plus Syr, only G relates adequately to the context.

21. *for bandits: mēḥetep.* So with MS B (1° *loco*), compare 50:4a and Prov 23:28. Though *byd ḥwtpw* in 15:14 (MS A) is a gloss borrowed from Syr of 4:19, the other occurrences are unexceptionable, and "of the wicked" of MS B's doublet and margin, plus Syr, is here a vague substitute (influenced by Ps 1:1?). As for G's *(en hodǭ) aproskopǭ,* it is presumably a corruption from *apo proskopōn = mēḥetep.*

22. *all your paths: ûbĕʾōrḥōtêkā* with MS B 2° *loco.* MSS B (1° *loco*), E, and G lose the parallelism by reading *wbʾḥrytk;* the reverse confusion occurs in Prov 1:19. *all* is an expansion.

23. MS B again has a doublet; 1° *loco* = Syr, 2° *loco* = G. The latter is followed here. MS E lacks the verse.

33 1–3. The second (left-hand) colon in each verse is damaged in MS B, which is then lacking for 33:4–35:10 inclusive. MS E lacks v 3 and Syr lacks vv 2, 3.

2b. Apparently G translated *ûmitmōṭēṭ = tossed about* (MSS B, E) in the same manner as it had *ûmitlaḥlēah* in 32:15b. *ship* will have been *ʾŏnîyâ,* for which MS E has *ʾznw* (Marcus) or perhaps *ʾwny* (Margolis, cited by Marcus); the difficult reading cannot be verified from the facsimile.

3a. *trusts in:* would suppose *yaʾămîn,* and the parallel favors this. MS B *yābîn.*

33:4–34:1. MS E is here the only Heb witness; it no longer (after 32:18) has the doublets characteristic of MS B. Its direct witness is limited throughout by the word or two missing on its right margin (to 33:14a) or its left edge (on the verso, 33:14c–34:1); there are a few letters illegible elsewhere, but usually comparison with G and Syr leaves little doubt as to what must be supplied.

4. MS E's "Prepare your words and afterward you will do / and a place of rest, and afterward *tgyh* (!)" hardly fits the context; Segal sees it as possibly related to 32:19 and belonging at that point. MS E's *wĕʾaḥar . . . wĕʾaḥar* can hardly be correct; in 4a, G's *kai houtōs* suggests *ûbĕkēn,* compare 32:1c where MS B's margin offers *ûbĕkē(y)n;* the

same expression occurs in 13:7 (MS A), and cf. already Qoh 8:10; Esth 4:16. For G's 14b, Segal rightly refers to Prov 3:3; 6:21; and 7:3. The verb used here by G (*syndēson*) is that ascribed (for *qšr*) to Theodotion in Prov 6:21, and to Aquila in all three places named; the occurrence in Sirach is unique.

6. *unscrupulous:* supposes *lēṣ*, with G, Syr; MS E's *śônē'* is surely secondary. *distracted:* this conveys the effect implied. The missing second word in the verse in MS E will have been a participle, either *mĕyuzzān*, "rutting," cf. Jer 5:8, as supposed by G, or, less likely, *mûkān*, "caparisoned (for battle)" as supposed by Syr, cf. Prov 21:31 and Job 39:19–25.

7. The form in MS E is debased; to judge by G, the original may have read *lāmmâ yôm miyyôm yākōl / wĕkol 'ôr haššānâ mē'im šámeš*.

8. G and Syr again prove MS E defective.

9. *exalts:* MS E and Syr read "blesses," cf. v 12, where that verb belongs.

11. MS E has a garbled alternative before the second colon.

12. MS E can be rebuilt from G with the appropriate text; but in 12a read *wehĕrîmām* with suffix, and in 12d *mimma'ămaddêhem* (besides G, cf. the frequency of *ma'ămād* at Qumran and the easy confusion of *beth* and *mem* for both auditory and visual reasons).

13b. Ziegler has repaired the Gr reading on the basis of GII (*plasai auto*) and Lat; as to the Heb, this calls for *lîṣōr kirĕṣônô* rather than MS E's *le'ĕḥōz kĕrāṣôn*.

13d. *to be requited according as he judges them:* this reference to retribution in G does not go beyond the expectations in the context, cf. 12cd. Syr has "to raise him up among all his works," and MS E has "to be stationed before him, a share." In this last, an approximation to G can be supposed if the *ḥēleq*, "share," conceals *ḥōq*, "decree, limit," which (41:3, 4) G of Sirach renders by *krima* (though not *krisin*), and for which (41:4) MS B reads *ḥlq* (but M, *qēṣ*). But no assurance as to an original text seems obtainable, and of the extant forms MS E is the least worthy of credit. Segal reads *ḥālāq* here, and makes it mean "creature," referring also to 31:13; but in that place *ḥālaq*="create" is in a doublet, and the normal text has *bārā'*. *ḥlq* in the meaning "create" is no part of the authentic language of Ben Sira, even in those passages where G uses *ktizein* to translate the verb.

14b. MS E adds, "and darkness with the light," a reading that it shares with Syr. But since Syr does not have *sinners in contrast with the just*, MS E is suspect of having derived its pair of readings from two sources, one related to G and the other to Syr. An added possibility is that the "darkness . . . light" theme derives from a copy of Sirach that passed through Essene hands. Original it could be; but proof is not in the extant materials.

16b–33. Here again Ziegler restores the correct sequence of the text as preserved in Lat, and provides the verse numeration standard for that source. In the Gr MSS, some three chapters were shifted backward from this point, so that this portion of chap. 33 becomes 30:25–40; chaps. 34, 35 become chaps. 31, 32, and the beginning of chap. 36 becomes chap. 33, vv 1–13. For the materials transposed forward in the Gr MSS, see the NOTE at chap. 30, v (27) above and also INTRODUCTION, Part VIII, 3b.

16ab. G and Syr show MS E's *w-* at the beginning of each colon to be a weakening expansion of the text; Segal, working from the facsimile, challenges Marcus's reading *wgm* rather than *gm* in 16a. *the last:* supposes *'aḥărôn* with G, Syr. Marcus convinced himself that MS E reads *'ḥryw;* but the facsimile shows the final *nun* clearly enough, and Segal reads *'ḥrwn* from the facsimile. *after the vintagers:* so MS E is restored on the basis of Syr, and cf. Ruth 2:3, 7; G's "after the vintage" renders freely.

18. *Take notice . . . toiled:* reading, with G, *rĕ'û kî lō' lî lĕbaddî 'āmaltî.* G has been supposed to read *dĕ'û* rather than MS E's *rĕ'û,* for which see G in 24:34 (*idete*); but in 41:21 (M) *mēhabbîṭ 'el, of gazing at,* is rendered in G by *apo katanoēseōs,* and the presence of *habbēṭ* (G *emblepson*) in v 15 above will have influenced the *katanoēsate* for *rĕ'û* here. *guidance:* G's *paideian* supposes *mûsār,* here as in 32:14a, with which the present line forms an *inclusio.*

Comment

The Heb word *mûsār,* "guidance, discipline," occurs in the opening (32:14a) and closing colon (33:18b) of this section, thus forming an *inclusio.* There is little else that gives unity to the section, which contains miscellaneous aphorisms and comments about the conduct of the pious (=wise) Jew and the sinful (=foolish) one.

In 32:14–17, which may be considered a unity (so, e.g., Box-Oesterley, pp. 426–27, and Ziegler, p. 276), Ben Sira compares and contrasts the person who "seeks God" and "studies the Law" and the person who is "reckless" and "distorts the Law" for his own purposes. As regards the Heb text of 32:14–15; cf. NOTE. V 14a may be translated, lit.: "Whoever seeks God will receive discipline" (Heb *mûsār,* Gr *paideia*). Discipline/*mûsār* is a key concept in the book; cf., e.g., 6:22; 21:19, 21; 22:6; 23:7; 42:5, 8; 50:27. It is impossible to seek God without discipline, which here means "fear of the Lord" (cf. 32:16). The person "who seeks God out" sincerely and energetically "will receive his answer" (32:14b), i.e., the light and the help to conduct his life wisely (=in keeping with the Law). Cf. 18:14 with COMMENT. The pious Jew "studies the Law" and "masters it" (32:15a) so that he may live his life in accord with its precepts. Cf. 2:16; 4:12; 6:37; and Ps 119:44–48. In contrast to the righteous Jew, "the reckless" (Gr has *hypocrite;* cf. 1:29) "is caught in [the Law's] snare" (32:15b), with the result that the Law, instead of being a source of life, becomes because of his bad will a trap. The pious person (who "fears the Lord") "will know what is right conduct" (32:16a, Heb *mišpāṭ*) because he finds it in the Law; cf. Prov 28:5. In 32:16b, "obscurity" refers to the uncertainties of life for which the Law, like a beacon, provides sure guidance, "a course of action." Perhaps Ben Sira alludes here to the great lighthouse of Pharos off Alexandria, which he may have seen (so Smend, p. 292). Cf. Prov 6:23; Ps 119:105. "The sinner" (cf. NOTE), however, is not interested in guidance but "turns aside warnings" that the Law provides in abundance, and even "distorts the Law to suit his purpose" (32:17b); cf. 21:6. The sinner, in other words, uses the Law when it suits his purposes or his life-style but ignores it when it does not.

A new unit may be seen in 32:18–24 (so, e.g., Box-Oesterley, pp. 427–28, and Ziegler, pp. 276–77). It speaks primarily of the person who is "well advised," the sage who pays heed to "what he learns" (32:18a); cf. Tob 4:19. In contrast, "the proud and insolent person is deterred by nothing" (lit., does not cringe in fear), but like the arrogant of Prov 21:24, he "acts with scornful effrontery." It is a mark of wisdom to "do nothing without counsel" (32:19a), nothing on impulse, nothing on whim; cf. 37:16; Prov 12:15. Once the wise have acted with forethought and prudence, they should "have no qualms" (32:19b). For to have regrets after a carefully planned course of action is not only a foolish waste of time, but also a source of discontent and uneasiness in one's inner life. For the imagery of snares and stumbling in 32:20; cf. Isa 8:14–15. There is an *a:b::b':a'* chiastic pattern in 32:20, which may be rendered, lit.: *on the way of snares:walk not::and stumble not:on a stumbling (stone) (twice).* The meaning is: avoid paths that are treacherous; but if you err on a particular course you have chosen after careful thought, do not repeat the same mistake. In 32:21–23 (cf. NOTES), there is another *a:b::b':a'* rhetorical pattern, which gives emphasis to the thought: *trust not:in the road (for bandits)::and in your paths:be careful.* Bandits who preyed on travelers were common in that day and also later; cf. Luke 10:30–35, the parable of the Good Samaritan. Ben Sira may be using this practical advice also in a metaphorical sense: the road or course of action you have chosen may have hidden pitfalls (bandits); so do not be overconfident; rather, be careful on the path you walk. Cf. Prov 22:5. V 23a (cf. NOTE) restates the idea of 32:20–22: be on guard in "whatever you do." A new note is added by 32:23b, which may be rendered, lit.: "for whoever does this keeps the commandment." "The commandment" (Heb *miṣwâ*) is a reference to Deut 4:9, which uses the same Heb phrase found here (32:23a): *šĕmōr napšĕkā,* "be on your guard"; or "watch yourself." Keeping the Law not only is a mark of wisdom, but also enables one to preserve oneself (32:24a); cf. Prov 13:3; 16:17; 19:16. It is interesting that Ben Sira makes trusting in the Lord (32:24b) a parallel to keeping the Law. The point of 32:24 is that by doing both these activities, a person promotes his own self-interest at the deepest level, i.e., he preserves himself and is not "put to shame." This verse serves as a transition to the following unit.

In 33:1a, the expression "the one who fears the Lord" is in synonymous parallelism with the phrases "whoever keeps the Law" (32:24a) and "whoever trusts in the LORD" (32:24b). It is such a person who is truly wise; cf. COMMENT on 1:11–30; 6:32–37; 15:1; 19:20; 21:6; 23:27; 24:23–29. Just as those who are loyal to the Lord by their observance of the Law and their trust in him will be preserved and "not be put to shame" (32:24), so those who fear the Lord will not be harmed by any evil (33:1a). Cf. Job 5:19; Prov 12:21; Dan 13:1–63 (the story of faithful Susanna). Through repeated trials they will be safe (33:1b; cf. NOTE); cf. 1 Cor 10:13. Those who hate the Law, however, are not wise (33:2a); cf. COMMENT on 32:24 above. Such persons are "tossed about like a boat in a storm" (33:2b; cf. NOTE), i.e., they are in grave peril, unlike the faithful, who are "safe" (33:1b); recall the fate of the wicked elders in the story of Susanna. For an image similar to the boat here, cf. Jas 1:6. The G of 32:3a has *nomǭ*, "the Law," repeated from 32:2a, instead of *logǭ*, "the word" (here translated "the word of the Lord"). In his text, Ziegler prints *logǭ* not on any Gr evidence but on the basis of MS B's *dābār*, which is certainly original. "The prudent," unlike the one who "hates the Law" (33:2a), "trusts in" or "believes in" (cf. NOTE) "the word" (33:3a) because it was spoken by God himself. In turn, "the Law," in parallel with "the word," becomes for the loyal believer as "dependable . . . as a divine oracle" (33:3b), concerning which cf. Exod 28:30; Lev 8:8; Deut 33:8; 1 Sam 14:41. The point of this verse is that for the faithful who observe the Law perfectly the Lord will fulfill all his promises contained in the Law; cf., for example, Lev 26:1–13 and Deut 28:1–14. The advice in 33:4 (cf. NOTE on the textual problems) is sound in any age and culture. Preparing your words before speaking and putting your learning and experience into an answer are the best ways to get others to listen. Cf. 32:19a and 37:16. In addition to Prov 3:3; 6:21; and 7:3, mentioned in the NOTE, cf. Isa 8:16 for the image of binding up one's training (33:4b) in order to preserve it and keep it in mind.

In the next brief unit (33:5–6), Ben Sira speaks of the fool and the "unscrupulous friend," two characters devoid of wisdom. "The mind of a fool" is like a cartwheel, and "his thoughts revolve in circles" (33:5)—strong and distasteful images—because he lacks instruction, discipline, and firm convictions. In other words, because his folly makes him incapable of weighing his words before speaking, as the wise are urged to do in 33:4, he constantly changes his mind like a wheel that is revolving. Hence, what he says makes little or no sense. "An unscrupulous [cf. NOTE] friend is like the distracted [lit., rutting, cf. NOTE] stallion"—another forceful image—"that neighs, no matter who the rider," i.e., such a "friend" speaks up or acts impulsively, no matter who is present; considerations of time or place, of courtesy or confidence, mean nothing to him.

The next poem (33:7–15) is important for an understanding of Ben Sira's thought on the antinomies or polarities or opposites that are found in creation. The poem also provides a general orientation to his teaching on theodicy. From the beginning of this section (32:14), he has characterized, on the one hand, the pious Jew as wise, sincere, prudent, intelligent, disciplined, and conscientious about the Law, and, on the other hand, the wicked as foolish, insincere, imprudent, arrogant, stupid, undisciplined, and unconcerned about the Law. In the present poem, Ben Sira attributes the differences between these two types of people to the divine ordering of the cosmos in general and of human beings in particular. In his infinite wisdom, God has established in creation a series of opposites or contrasts or contraries. All days, in and of themselves, are identical, for "the same sun lights up every day" (33:7b). Yet, according to his unfathomable will, "he designates [certain days] seasons and feasts" (33:8b), and other days "he lists as ordinary" (33:9b). God acted in like manner with regard to human beings, all of whom are the same in terms of their origin, i.e., "of clay," "from earth" (33:10). Nonetheless, for reasons that are beyond human scrutiny, God has also made "people unlike" (33:11a), blessing some and cursing others (33:12); the Israelites, of course, belong to the former, the Gentiles to the latter. I agree with Smend (p. 279) that the poem was directed against Jewish Hellenizers who questioned Israel's divine election; cf. INTRODUCTION, Part II.

The poem opens with an engaging question (33:7): "Why is one day more important than another, when the same sun lights up every day of the year?" This question sets the tone for the rest of the poem. All days seem to be the same, except for the obvious differences in length of daylight. Yet they are not, for the Lord in his "knowledge" has designated certain days to be "seasons and feasts" (33:8), exalting and sanctifying particular days while listing others as "ordinary" (33:9). Cf., for example, Gen 2:3 ("God blessed the seventh day [the sabbath] and made it holy"); Deut 16:1–15 (the laws concerning the time and manner of celebrating the seven days of Passover, the Feast of Weeks, and the Feast of Booths). The literal translation of 33:9b is "and others he placed in the days of number," i.e., these days are distinguished only by their number in the week or month. In 33:10, there is an $a:b::b':a'$ chiastic arrangement in the order of the nouns: *people:clay::earth:human(kind)*. The point of the verse is that all human beings have a common origin, viz., from the clay of the earth; cf. Gen 2:7; 3:19; 18:27; Job 4:19; 10:9; 34:15; Pss 103:14; 104:29; 146:4; Qoh 3:20; 12:7; Tob 8:6; Wis 7:1. Despite this fact, however, the Lord "in the fullness of his understanding," i.e., for his own mysterious and impenetrable reasons, "makes people unlike" and "has them walk" "in different *paths*" (33:11), i.e., he assigns to them different *destinies*. As Smend notes (p. 298), "path" in the OT often means "destiny." Some people the Lord "blesses and makes great" (33:12a)—the reference is to the call and blessing of Abraham and his descendants in Gen 12:2; 15:5; 22:17; 24:60; 28:14; Exod 32:13; Deut 1:10; Sir 44:21–23. Some the Lord "sanctifies and draws to himself" (33:12b)—the reference is to the election and role of the priests in Israel; cf. Num 16:5–7; Ezek 40:46; 42:13; 45:4. Others the Lord "curses and brings low" (33:12c)—the reference is to the Gentiles in general, who were not chosen as Israel had been, and in particular the Canaanites, whom the Lord had expelled "from their place" (33:12d; cf. NOTE); cf. Gen 9:25–27; 12:6–7; Exod 33:1–3; Deut 34:1–4; 1 Sam 2:6–8. In

10:7–18, Ben Sira gives another reason why God brings low people and nations—pride and arrogance.

The image of the potter working the clay "according to his pleasure" (33:13ab; cf. NOTE) emphasizes how completely the destinies of human beings are "in the hands of their Maker" (33:13c), "according as he judges them" (33:13d; cf. NOTE). For this imagery, cf. Isa 29:16; 45:9; 64:7; Jer 18:3–6; Wis 15:7; Rom 9:20–23. The three great pairs of opposites in the world are evil and good, death and life, and sinners and the just (33:14), to which series MS E adds darkness and light, but cf. NOTE. The reference to darkness and light (in MS E and in Syr) is an allusion to Gen 1:2–3, in which darkness is a concomitant of chaos (noncreation) and light is the first of God's creatures. These opposites or contraries, and others in the cosmos, are "all the works of the Most High" (the reading of G; MS E, God): "they come in pairs, the one the opposite of the other" (33:15). The thought expressed here is similar to that of Qoh 7:13–14: "Consider the work of God. Who can make straight what he has made crooked? On a good day enjoy good things, and on an evil day consider: Both the one and the other God has made, so that man cannot find fault with him in anything." See INTRODUCTION, Part X, 3.

A quotation from O. S. Rankin neatly summarizes the theology of this poem: "Sirach speaks of the harmony and purpose of opposites, and of physical and moral good and evil being necessary counterparts in creation. . . . The thought which he develops upon the perfect harmony and adjustment of creation would seem to be his own contribution to theodicy" (*Israel's Wisdom Literature: Its Bearing on Theology and the History of Religion*, pp. 34–35). For a detailed study of this poem, cf. G. L. Prato, *Il problema della teodicea in Ben Sira*, pp. 13–61. Cf. also P. Winter, "Ben Sira (33[36],7–15) and the teaching of 'Two Ways,' " *VT* 5 (1955): 315–18.

As regards the numbering of 33:16b–33; cf. NOTE. In the final poem (33:16–18) of this section, Ben Sira provides a brief autobiographical note that attempts to legitimate his right to teach all who seek to become wise. He frankly confesses that he is "the last to keep vigil" (33:16a; cf. NOTE), i.e., he is last in a long line of Wisdom teachers, and that he is like "one gleaning after the vintagers" (33:16b; cf. NOTE), i.e., he writes what he gleaned from the earlier books of the Bible, esp. Proverbs; cf. INTRODUCTION, Part VI. For the image of gleaning, cf. Deut 24:21; Isa 24:13; Jer 49:9; Mic 7:1. Thanks to "God's blessing," Ben Sira "made progress till like a vintager [he] filled [his] winepress" (33:17), i.e., from his careful and diligent study of the Scriptures and of Israel's traditions he was able to become wise enough to teach what he learned to others; cf. 39:1–11. What he learned from his lifetime of study and reflection was not for himself alone (33:18a; cf. NOTE) "but for every seeker after guidance" (33:18b; cf. NOTE). For other notices about the life of Ben Sira, see the Prologue by his grandson as well as 24:30–34; cf. also 39:12–13 and 51:13–28.

PART VI   (33:19–38:23)

40. Property and Servants
(33:19–33)

33   19 Listen to me, leaders of the people;   E
            rulers of the assembly, give ear!
     20a Let neither son nor wife, neither kindred nor friend,
        b   have power over you as long as you live.
     21 While breath of life is still in you,
            let no human being take your place.   G
     20c Yield what you have to no one else,
        d   lest then you must plead for support yourself;
     22 Better that your children plead with you   E
            than that you should look to their generosity.
     23 Keep control over all your affairs;
            let nothing tarnish your glory.
     24 When your few days of life reach their limit,   G
            at the time of death distribute your inheritance.

     25 Fodder and whip and loads for an ass;
            food, correction, and work for a slave.
     26 Make a slave work and he will look for his rest;   GII
            let his hands be idle and he will seek to be free.
     27 Yoke and harness are a cure for stubbornness;   GI
            and for a refractory slave, punishment in the stocks.
     28 Force him to work that he be not idle,
     29   for idleness is the teacher of much mischief.
     30 Give him work to do such as befits him;
            but if he fails to obey you, load him with chains.
        Yet never lord it over any human being,
            and do nothing that is not just.

31a If you have but one slave, treat him like yourself;
 d   you would miss him as though it were you who was
                                                    lost.
 c If you have but one slave, deal with him as a brother;
 b   your life's blood went into his purchase.
32 If you mistreat him and he runs away,
33   in what direction will you look for him?

Notes

33 19a. *people:* MS E has *ʿam rāb,* "multitude," cf., e.g., Gen 50:20. The *rāb* is expansion, lacking in G, Syr; so Segal.

20ab. *kindred:* with G, Syr; MS E *ʾwhb (wrʿ),* "friend (or companion)." *over you:* MS E lacks this (=*bĕkā,* cf. G, Syr, and v 21b).

21ab. In G, this bicolon is preceded (as 20cd) by that which here (with MS E and Syr) follows it as 21cd.

25b. MS E seems to reflect a copyist's loss of *leḥem* = "food" after the very similar *laḥămôr,* "for an ass"; so Marcus. *correction* = G's *paideia;* this would normally suggest an underlying Hebrew *mûsār.* Here, however, MS E agrees with Syr (*mardûtāʾ*) in reading the regularly Aram *mardût.* With *mûsār* having taken on a range of meanings that allows it to be a practical equivalent for *ḥokmâ,* "wisdom" (compare 6:18, 22), it is possible Ben Sira himself chose *mardût* to convey physical chastisement more directly. In 42:8, MS B's margin gives *mardût* as alternative to the *mûsār* of its running text; and Yadin sees the longer word called for by the size of the lacuna in the Masada scroll in that place. The Syr usage throughout Sirach is inconclusive evidence for a choice. The homonym for *mardûtāʾ* that means "rebellion" is never employed in the book (compare 1 Sam 20:30, where the Heb hapax legomenon *mardût* [from *mrd*] is dealt with by the Peshitta as though it meant "discipline" instead of "rebellion"; Marcus's reference to this Samuel text is unclear). In 6:23, Syr uses *mardûtāʾ* as a synonym for *yulpānāʾ* in the other half of the same bicolon; we have no Heb for this, but G's *counsel* and *advice* suggest that neither *mûsār* nor *mardût* was in the original (cf. *HTR* 64 [1971]: 400). In 22:6, the two Syriac terms occur together again (here, *lashes and discipline*), and it is *mardûtāʾ* that corresponds to G's *mastiges,* "lashes," for corporal punishment; no Heb is extant. In 31:17, *mardûtāʾ* corresponds to *mûsār* in a derived sense, here rendered "good manners." In 51:23b, 26b, first *yulpānāʾ* and G's *paideias* combine to suggest that *mûsār,* and not MS B's *midrāšî,* was the authentic Heb reading; then G's *paideias* combines with *mardûtāʾ* of Syr in treating *maśśāʾāh,* "her burden," as implying "her message" and a practical equivalence with *mûsār* (the *maśśāʾ* term is guaranteed by the parallel *her yoke* in the matching colon 26a)—cf. again *HTR* 64 (1971): 397–98. Confronted at least a dozen times with *mûsār* in the underlying Heb, Syr used *yulpānā'* for it twice, *ḥekmĕtā'* once, *mardûtā'* once—plus three variant or confused passages and a number of places where no Syr equivalent is preserved. All in all, there remains a real likelihood that the present colon and 42:8a are witnesses to a borrowing of *mardût,* in the sense of corporal punishment, into the Heb of Sirach at the time of its composition.

26. In 26a, GI is a rewritten text—"Work at/with discipline and you will find rest." Though a few MSS have *paidi,* which could be construed to mean *slave,* rather than *paideia,* "discipline," Ziegler (BZAW 77 [1958]: 284=*Sylloge,* MSU 10 [1971]: 460) points out that the grandson uses only *oiketēs* for "slave." Codex 248 supplies *and he will look for (his rest);* similarly Lat, *et quaerit.* Syr lacks the first two words of 26a because their similarity to Syr's own ending for v 25 (*wĕpulḥānā' lĕ'abdā'*) has brought about their loss. Both Syr and MS E transform *and he will look for his rest* into "and give him no rest/that he may not seek rest." G, Syr agree on *and he will seek to be free,* but for *let his hands be idle,* Syr has "if you lift up his head." MS E confounds this further with "if he lifts up his head, he will play you false." In this, Syr and MS E carry overtones of Gen 40:13; Sir 11:13.

27a. *are a cure for stubbornness:* lit., in G, "bend the neck." Compare 7:23; 30:12, and NOTES to both places. For this, MS E has, in broken context, *wḥṭr twmkw,* "and the staff of its wielder(?)." Segal emends the second word to *wĕmakkôt,* "and blows," but concedes that it is G which retains the original reading. Syr is lacking for v 27.

28, 29. For *that he be not idle,* Syr and MS E have "that he rebel not"; for *is the teacher of,* they both have "does (much mischief)."

30. *Give him work to do such as befits him:* for this, Syr has "As may suit him, give him authority in your house," a clear allusion to Joseph in Gen 39:4; Segal, following Marcus, rebuilds the text of MS E to conform to this, but for G's *load* (=*hakbēd*) *him with chains* has to read "multiply his chains/bonds" with the *harb[ēh]* that alone survives in the MS: this he concedes to be inferior to the Gr.

31–33. These verses, the last (with 34:1) to survive in MS E, are defective in the MS; with Syr, they help to establish the order of the cola in v 31a–d, which G presents in the less cogent order a,d,c,b.

31a,c. *If you have but one:* reading *heis (estin soi)* each time for G's *ei,* with MS E and (for 31c) Syr. In 31c, *a brother* is the usual Gr reading; Codex B and two other witnesses read *yourself.*

Comment

The section contains various maxims about personal independence and the treatment of slaves—important subjects for the middle-class Palestinian Jewish householder. It may be divided into three units: 7+6+3 bicola.

The opening bicolon (v 19) has an *a:b::b':a'* chiastic pattern that attracts the reader's attention: *listen to me/šim'û 'ēlay:leaders of the people/śārê*

ʿam::rulers of the assembly/ûmôšĕlê qāhāl:give ear/haʾăzînû]. There is also a
liquid (*l* and *r*) and sibilant (*š*, *ṣ*, and *z*) alliteration. This rhetorical pattern is
employed not only in the Heb text (MS E) but also in G, Lat, and Syr. By the
imperative "listen to *me*," Ben Sira again appeals to his own authority as a
Wisdom teacher; cf. 6:23; 16:24; Prov 4:10; 7:24. The titles "leaders of the
people" and "rulers of the assembly" are figurative; cf. Wis 1:1. Ben Sira uses
these titles for the purpose of motivating his readers to model themselves on
the Jewish "leaders" and "rulers," who were considered to be learned and
wise; cf. 45:26; Matt 11:25; Luke 10:21. The command to "hear" is common
also in the NT: Matt 13:9; Rev 2:7, 11, 17, 29; 3:6, 13, 22; 13:9. The rest of the
poem, in effect, urges the reader not to imitate the sorry example of King
Lear (so Duesberg-Fransen, p. 243).

In v 20, "son," "wife," "kindred" (cf. NOTE), and "friend" are the significant others in the life of a Jewish adult male; the absence of "daughter" is
noteworthy. None of these persons should be given "power over you [cf.
NOTE] as long as you live" lest you become subject to, and dependent on,
them, to your dismay. V 21a may be translated, lit.: "While you are still alive
and breath is in you." "Alive," Heb *ḥay,* and "breath," Heb *nĕšāmâ,* are an
allusion to Gen 2:7, where the phrase *nišmat ḥayyîm,* "breath of life," occurs.
Ben Sira urges care lest others "take your place" (v 21b) and run your life.
You should not be so generous as to yield your wealth to others and thus
become indigent yourself (v 20cd). Charity begins at home. It is more in
keeping with your dignity to have "your children plead with you than that
you should look to their generosity" or be at their mercy (v 22), which would
be a reversal of roles. Cf. 40:29 and Ps 123:2. A firm hand in personal affairs
is essential (v 23a); nothing should tarnish your glory (v 23b). The Heb
expressions of v 23b are used of Abraham in 44:19b; cf. also 18:15a. Only
when your death seems imminent, "distribute your inheritance" (v 24). This
verse seems to prove that the practice of writing a last will and testament was
not common in the Palestine of Ben Sira's day (so Smend, p. 301).

Some of the maxims on how to treat a slave may appear harsh to modern
readers. But since slavery was a socially and religiously accepted and acceptable fact of life at the time, Ben Sira saw fit to include this institution in his
writing. Though he advocates firmness and even severity for lazy or refractory slaves (vv 27–30ab), he also urges that one be just in treating them (v
30cd). The two cola of v 25 are in parallel, word for word. The demeaning
comparison between "an ass" (v 25a) and "a slave" (v 25b) says much about
the institution of slavery in any period of history; cf. also v 27a. For the text
of v 25b, cf. NOTE. For the thought of v 25b, cf. Prov 29:19. The point of v 26
(cf. NOTE) is that if you make a slave work hard, he will be content just to
"look for his rest" at the end of the day (cf. Exod 5:4; 6:9); but if you allow
him to be idle, "he will seek to be free"—something that slave owners have
known in every age and culture. In v 27a, "yoke and harness," which are

things used on beasts of burden, are suggested as "a cure for [a slave's] stubbornness" (cf. NOTE); cf. v 25 and Prov 29:21. "For a refractory [lit., knavish, villainous, evildoing] slave" Ben Sira suggests "punishment in the stocks" (v 27b). As regards this humiliating form of punishment, cf. Jer 20:2; 29:26; 2 Chr 16:10. V 28 (cf. NOTE) restates v 26. The point of v 29 (cf. NOTE) is that a slave's idleness can become the occasion of "much mischief [lit., evil]," i.e., he can do evil to others because he does not have enough to keep himself busy (cf. 2 Thess 3:11–12); or he can "seek to be free" (v 26b), which would be "evil" (=a loss) to his master. In Ben Sira's view, since a slave is made for work, give him enough to do (v 30a; cf. NOTE). But if he disobeys you, "load him with chains" (v 30b; cf. NOTE); cf. Lam 3:7. *Phibis,* xiv 6–11, parallels the advice given in vv 25–30ab (Sanders, p. 95). Ben Sira tempers his maxims on slaves with a concluding exhortation: "never lord it over any human being, and do nothing that is not just" (v 30cd). The Law protected the limited rights of slaves; cf. Exod 21:1–11, 20–21, 26–27; Lev 25:44–55; Deut 15:12–18; 23:16–17.

The last poem of the section offers advice to the householder who has only one slave. For the order of the cola in v 31, cf. NOTE. If as a less affluent Jew you have "but one slave" (31a,c; cf. NOTE), you would be well advised to treat him well, "like yourself" (v 31a), or "as a brother" (v 31c). V 31d may be translated, lit.: "for you have need of him as (you need) your soul." The meaning is this: since you have purchased your only slave with "your life's blood" (v 31b), you should treat him kindly in order to ensure his faithful service to you. Only in this way can you get your money's worth out of him. In other words, your own self-interest should motivate you to be good to your slave, as you are good to yourself. Cf. 7:20–21. If, however, "you mistreat him," he may run away (v 32); then where "will you look for him?" (v 33), for he is gone forever. Indeed, according to Deut 23:16–17, it was forbidden to return a runaway slave to his master; moreover, the slave had the right to live unmolested in any community he chose. Thus, to lose a slave because you mistreated him could bring you personal and economic misfortune. The relationships between masters and slaves were complex in that day. The slave was considered part of the family household, and apparently could voice his opinion (cf. 37:11). He could also rise to power; cf. Prov 19:10; 22:29; 30:22; Qoh 10:7. A Jew could become a slave through carelessness in managing his affairs; cf. Prov 11:29. But prisoners of war constituted the largest source of slaves; cf. 1 Macc 8:10–11. On the question of slavery in second-century B.C. Palestine, cf. M. L. Vincent, *RB* 29 (1920): 161–68; F.-M. Abel, *RB* 33 (1924): 566–74; and Duesberg-Fransen, pp. 244–45.

41. Trust in the Lord and Not in Dreams
(34:1–20)

34   1 Empty and false are the hopes of the senseless,   G
      and fools are sent winging by dreams.
   2 Like one grasping at shadows or chasing the wind
      is whoever puts trust in dreams.
   3 What is seen in dreams is a reflection
      that mirrors the vision of the onlooker.
   4 Can the unclean produce the clean?
      can the liar ever speak the truth?
   5 Divination, omens, and dreams are unreal;
      what you already expect, the mind depicts.
   6 Unless it be a vision specially sent by the Most High,
      fix not your heart on it;
   7 For dreams have led many astray,
      and those who based their hopes on them have
                                    perished.
   8 The Law is fulfilled without fail,
      and well-rounded wisdom is in the discourse of the
                                    faithful.

   9 A person with training gains wide knowledge;
      a person of experience speaks sense.
   10 One never put to the proof knows little,
   11   whereas with travel a person adds to his
                                    resourcefulness.
   12 I have seen much in my travels,
      learned more than ever I could say.
   13 Often I was in danger of death,
      but by these attainments I was saved.

   14 Lively is the courage of those who fear the Lord,
   15   whose hope is in their Savior;

16 Whoever fears the Lord is never frightened,
    never discouraged; for the Lord is his hope.
17 Happy the soul that fears the Lord!
18   In whom does he trust, and who is his support?
19 The eyes of the Lord are upon those who love him;
    he is their mighty shield and strong support,
 A shelter from the heat, a shade from the noonday sun,
    a guard against stumbling, a help against falling.
20 He buoys up the spirits, brings a sparkle to the eyes,
    gives health and life and blessing.

Comment

In the first poem (vv 1–8) of this section, Ben Sira deplores the practice of relying on dreams, divination, and omens. In the second poem (vv 9–20), he extols the person who through discipline and fear of the Lord gains wide experience while trusting in God.

In v 1, Ben Sira states unequivocally his position on the futility of belief in dreams: it is the "senseless" and the "fools" who take dreams seriously, and "the hopes" they derive from their dreams are "empty and false." Belief in the significance of dreams was widespread in antiquity, even in the OT; cf. Gen 40:8–19; 41:1–32; Dan 2:1–19, 27–45. Box-Oesterley (p. 433) write: "In his strong repudiation of belief in dreams Ben-Sira is much in advance of his time. Even the later Rabbis failed to reach so discriminating a standard, belief in the efficacy of dreams being practically universal among them." Trusting in dreams, which is the mark of the fool, is the same as "grasping at shadows or chasing the wind" (v 2)—an exercise in utter futility. For the imagery, cf. Hos 12:2; Qoh 1:14; 2:11, 17, 26; 4:6, 16; 6:9. Dreams have no reality in themselves; they merely reflect "the vision of the onlooker" (v 3), i.e., what the dreamer worries about or desires becomes the subject of the dream; cf. v 5b. Another possible interpretation: dreams can be made to mean whatever the dreamer reads into them. As regards v 4a, cf. Job 14:4. The point of v 4 is that one should not be guided by dreams because in many cases they can be notoriously bad leaders (so Smend, p. 306), unclear and deceptive. "I talk of dreams; / Which are the children of an idle brain, / Begot of nothing but vain fantasy" (Shakespeare, *Romeo and Juliet* [1594–95], I iv 96–98).

It is interesting that Ben Sira lumps together "divination, omens, and dreams" (v 5a), all of which are "unreal" (Gr *mataia*, "idle, foolish, meaningless"). Divination and paying heed to omens were explicitly forbidden in Lev 19:26 and Deut 18:10–14. Such practices were pagan and unworthy of the true Israelite; cf. 1 Sam 6:2; Isa 44:25; Ezek 13:6–8; 21:26. "The mind depicts" in divination, omens, and dreams "what you already expect" (v 5). Ben Sira displays here a psychological insight that is remarkably modern. "Dreams, which, beneath the hovering shades of night, / Sport with the ever-restless minds of men, / Descend not from the gods. Each busy brain / Creates its own" (Thomas Love Peacock, "Dreams," *Petronius Arbiter* [1806]). Ben Sira makes an exception for visions "specially sent by the Most High" (v 6a), because such experiences happened in Israel's history; cf., for example, Gen 28:12–16; 31:10–13, 24; 37:5–10; 40:8–19; 41:1–32; Dan 2:1–19, 27–45. Yet one still had to be careful not to be deceived. The Law is sufficient for guidance in the living of one's personal life. Dreams, visions, and the like are unnecessary; cf. Luke 16:27–31. As regards v 7, cf. Jer 23:25–27; 29:8–9. V 8a may be translated, lit.: "Without deceit the Law can be fulfilled," i.e., no deceitful practices (such as omens, dreams, and divinations) are needed, or desirable, for one to fulfill the Law. The point of v 8b is that only the faithful person has perfect wisdom, i.e., fulfills the Law exactly, and accordingly never has recourse to dreams or omens or other exotic and often deceptive means. For the equation of wisdom = keeping the Law, cf. 1:11–30 and 24:23–29. V 8 serves as a connective between this poem and the next.

The next poem (vv 9–20) develops the implications and benefits of true wisdom and fidelity to the Law. The two cola of v 9 are in parallel. The "person with training" (reading Gr *pepaideumenos* with Codices B, A, and many cursives) is the one who is disciplined, who fears the Lord, who keeps the commandments. Such a person "gains wide knowledge" (v 9a, lit., knows much); he is "a person of experience" (Gr *polypeiros;* cf. 21:22b; 25:6a [*polypeiria*]; 36:25b), who "speaks sense" (v 9b), because he is wise. One who has never been "put to the proof knows little" (v 10, cf. v 9a), for he has little experience of the real world. "But the person who travels increases his resourcefulness, or skill" (the literal translation of v 11). The implication of vv 10–11 is that travel puts a person to the test and enables him to put his knowledge into practice. It is thus that one becomes even more wise. "He that travels much knows much" (Thomas Fuller, *Gnomologia* [1732], 2335). Ben Sira refers here to the value of travel for the wise (cf. v 9). The foolish would gain little from travel. "If an ass goes travelling, he'll not come home a horse" (Thomas Fuller, *Gnomologia,* 2668). In vv 12–13, Ben Sira gives an autobiographical note, unfortunately with no details, about his own travels, which apparently were frequent; cf. 39:4. He saw much in his travels (v 12a)—other cultures, other religions, other customs; and "learned more than ever [he] could say" (v 12b)—his experiences abroad and what he learned were too much for words. Travel, however beneficial for the wise, was nonetheless dangerous (v 13a). One had to cope with disease and discomfort, which a change in food and water can occasion, as well as bandits who preyed on travelers (cf. Jesus' Parable of the Good Samaritan, Luke 10:29–35) and shipwreck (cf. Acts 27:9–44; 2 Cor 11:25–26). Despite the "danger of death" Ben Sira often found himself in, he "was saved" "by these attainments" (v 13b, lit., by these things), i.e., by his wisdom, training (v 9a), experience (v 9b), and resourcefulness (v 11).

The rest of the poem (vv 14–20) extols the virtues and blessings of the wise, of which Ben Sira himself is a prime example. The translation of v 14 above is one possible interpretation; cf. also the NAB of Pss 22:27 and 69:33. The verse may also be translated, lit.: "The spirit of those who fear the Lord will live"—an allusion to Isa 38:16–17. The reason is given in v 15, lit.: "for their hope is in the One who saves them." The one who fears the Lord need never be "frightened" or "discouraged," "for the Lord [lit., he himself] is his hope" (v 16). With the Lord at a person's side, he can face with courage any of life's perils and difficulties. Thus Ben Sira declares: "Happy the soul that fears the Lord" (v 17); cf. Ps 23:1–4. For more on vv 16–17, cf. M. L. Margolis, "A Passage in Ecclesiasticus," *ZAW* 21 (1901): 271–72. The questions in v 18 are rhetorical, introducing the answers found in vv 19–20. A similar rhetorical question, followed immediately by an answer, is seen in Pss 24:10; 121:1. V 19a repeats Ps 33:18 and the G of 15:19a except for the verb; the latter texts have "fear" (as do two Gr MSS here) instead of "love." Cf. Ps 34:16. The images of the Lord as "shield" and "support" (v 19b) are taken from Gen 15:1; Deut 33:29; Pss 3:4; 7:11; 18:2–3, 19, 36; 61:3–4; 91:1–4; Prov 2:7; 30:5. The "heat" in v 19c is Gr *kausōn*, "burning heat; scorching wind," i.e., the sirocco or khamsin, the hot, dry wind that blows in the Mediterranean region in the changes between the dry (summer) and the rainy (winter) seasons, viz., in the spring and autumn. It is an unpleasant and distressing wind often charged with sand and dust. For the images of God as "shelter" from such heat and as "shade from the noonday sun" (v 19c), cf. Isa 4:6; 25:4–5; Ps 121:5–6. For the images of "a guard" and "a help" (v 19d), cf. Pss 22:20; 91:11–12; 121:3. The Lord is Source of all the best things in life (v 20). As regards v 20a, cf. Ps 19:9: "The precepts of Yahweh . . . *rejoice the heart;* the command of Yahweh . . . *enlightens the eye.*" For the last phrase, cf. also 1 Sam 14:29. For the thought of the Lord bestowing: *health* (v 20b), cf. 1:18; Ps 30:3; *life,* cf. Pss 21:5; 36:10; and *blessing,* cf. Ps 133:3. "Blessing," Gr *eulogia* (Syr has the word in the plural), the last word of the poem, sums up all the material and spiritual goods God has bestowed on his people from the time of Abraham onward; cf., for example, 44:21; Gen 12:2–3; 22:17–18.

42. True Worship of God and His Response
(34:21–36:22)

34 ²¹ Tainted his gift who offers in sacrifice ill-gotten goods!   G
²²   Presents from the lawless do not win God's favor.
²³ The Most High approves not the gifts of the godless,
    nor for their many sacrifices does he forgive their sins.
²⁴ Like one slaying a son in his father's presence
    is whoever offers sacrifice from the holdings of the
                      poor.
²⁵ The bread of charity is life itself for the needy;
    whoever withholds it is a person of blood.
²⁶ He slays his neighbor who deprives him of his
                    living;
²⁷   he sheds blood who denies the worker his wages.

²⁸ If one builds up and another tears down,
    what do they gain but trouble?
²⁹ If one prays and another curses,
    whose voice will God hear?
³⁰ If a person again touches a corpse after he has bathed,
    what did he gain by the purification?
³¹ So with a person who fasts for his sins,
    but then goes and commits them again:
Who will hear his prayer,
    and what has he gained by his mortification?

35   ¹ To keep the Law is a great oblation,
²   and whoever observes the commandments sacrifices a
                    peace offering.
³ In works of charity one offers fine flour,
⁴   and when he gives alms he presents his sacrifice of
                    praise.

5 To refrain from evil pleases the Lord,
and to avoid injustice is an atonement.

6 Appear not before the Lord empty-handed,
7   for all that you offer is in fulfilment of a precept.
8 The just person's offering enriches the altar
and rises as a sweet odor before the Most High.
9 The just person's sacrifice is welcomed,
and the memory of it will never be lost.
10 In generous spirit pay homage to the Lord;
be not sparing of freewill gifts.
11 With each contribution show a cheerful countenance,   B
and pay your tithes in a spirit of joy.
12 Give to the Most High as he has given to you,
generously, according to your means;
13 For he is God who always repays,
and he will give back to you seven times over.

14 But offer no bribes; these he does not accept!
15   Trust not in sacrifice of the fruits of extortion,
For he is the God of justice,
who knows no favorites.
16 He does not take sides against the weak,
but he hears the grievance of the oppressed;
17 He does not reject the cry of the orphan,
nor the widow when she pours out her complaint:
18 Do not the tears that stream down her cheek
19   cry out against the one that causes them to fall?   G
20 One bitterly distressed is given a sympathetic hearing;
his plea reaches the heavens.
21 The prayer of the lowly pierces the clouds;
it does not rest till it reaches its goal,   B
Nor will it withdraw till the Most High responds,
22   judges justly and affirms the right.

God indeed will not delay,
and like a warrior, will not be still
Till he breaks the backs of the merciless
23   and wreaks vengeance upon the nations;

Till he destroys the scepter of the proud
　　and breaks off short the staff of the wicked;
24 Till he requites humankind according to its deeds,
　　and repays people according to their thoughts;
25 Till he defends the cause of his people,
　　and gladdens them by his saving help.
26 Welcome is his mercy in time of distress　　　　　　　G
　　as rain clouds in time of drought.

36　1 Come to our aid, God of the universe,　　　　　　　B
　2　and put all the nations in dread of you!
　3 Raise your hand against the foreign folk,
　　　that they may see your mighty deeds.
　4 As you have used us to show them your holiness,
　　　so now use them to show us your glory.
　5 Thus they will know, as we know,
　　　that there is no God but you.

　6 Give new signs and work new wonders;
　7　show forth the splendor of your right hand and arm;
　8 Rouse your anger, pour out wrath,
　9　humble the enemy, scatter the foe.
10 Hasten the ending, appoint the time
　　when your mighty deeds are to be proclaimed:　　　　G
11 Let raging fire consume the fugitive,
　　and your people's oppressors meet destruction;
12 Smash the heads of the hostile rulers,
　　who say, "There is no one besides me!"

13 Gather all the tribes of Jacob,　　　　　　　　　　B
16　that they may inherit the land as in days of old.
17 Show mercy to the people called by your name:
　　Israel, whom you named your firstborn.
18 Take pity on your holy city,
　　Jerusalem, the foundation for your throne.
19 Fill Zion with your majesty,
　　your temple with your glory.

²⁰ Give evidence of your deeds of old;
   fulfil the prophecies spoken in your name,
²¹ Reward those who have hoped in you,
   and let your prophets be proved true.
²² Hear the prayers of your servants,
   for you are ever gracious to your people;
   Thus it will be known to all the ends of the earth
   that you are the eternal God.

Notes

34 22. *presents:* with GII, Lat, Syr, Ziegler reads *dorēmata;* GI and a doublet in Lat have for this *mōkēmata,* "mockeries," which in a number of codices is accommodated to the *memōmēmenē* of v 21 by a distortion into *mōmēmata.*

25. *charity:* supposes Heb *ḥesed,* as read by Syr, for G's *epideomenōn,* which supposes *ḥeser,* "want/need."

35 1. *oblation:* GI has the plural for this, but vv 2–4 show that a singular is called for (with Syr and other oriental versions; the Lat evidence is divided).

8–12. In these verses especially, Syr redirects the language centered on temple sacrifices and tithes in such a way as to make almsgiving (with prayer and observance of divine Law, vv 1–7) the avenue for offerings to God.

11. MS B is again extant from this point to 38:27b, and is the unique Heb witness (except for a few citations in the Talmud) as far as 36:26. *With each contribution* reflects G, Syr, which retain the association with sacrifices and tithes that is lost in MS B's *běkol maʿăśêkā,* "With all that you do."

12, 13. the *Most High, God.* G picks up the divine name *Most High* from v 8 (its *Lord* in v 10 may have been supplied for clarity); MS B has simply "to Him," and its margin supplies *lěʾēl. God* in MS B is *ʾělôah* where G has *Kyrios* and Syr *ʾalāhāʾ. ʾělôah* is witnessed to only three times in the Heb of Sirach—here, in the margin of v 22b below, and at 45:23b, again in MS B. In that last place it is a dubious reading; see NOTE there. In general, *ʾělôah* as a construct is rather rare (here before *taślûmôt,* a noun not found in MT)—five times in MT. This can serve to illustrate the hazards of determining the divine name chosen by Ben Sira for use in a particular place, from the versions and MSS at our disposal. Cf. *CBQ* 38 (1976): 147. Choice of an equivalent in translation is yet another problem.

13. Before this verse, MS B's margin would insert the gloss "He makes the Lord his debtor who gives to the poor; and who is the source of recompenses if not He?" Compare Prov 19:17. The gloss is already in Syr.

16. *against the weak:* so with G (*epi*=Heb *ʿal*); MS B has *ʾēl,* "toward." Syr does not have v 16.

18–20. After v 17 Syr has "The bitterness of feelings of the poor he [God] hears / and their prayer tilts downward the clouds. The prayer of the poor ascends above the clouds / and enters before the Lord of majesty." This is followed by vv 21c–22a; "tilts downward the clouds" seems to reverse the imagery of Ps 18:10.

19. *the one that causes them to fall,* with G=Heb *môrîdāh;* MS B has *mĕrûdêhā,* "her homelessness." Syr does not have vv 18–19.

20a. For this colon, MS B gives *tmrwry rṣwn hnḥh,* which as it stands is unintelligible. G's *therapeuōn,* beginning v 20, does not fit the context; it is here supposed that the term reflects *rp*', and that *mar nepeš* underlies the corresponding Syr (cf. Job 3:20; 7:11; 10:1). Perhaps, for the whole colon, read, *mar nepeš bĕrāṣôn yērāṣeh?*

21a. MS B has a garbled reading (*ḥl ʿm*) for *pierces the clouds* (=G).

22b. *God:* so MS B; G, Syr both have "the Lord," and MS B's margin has *ʾādôn;* see NOTE at vv 12, 13 above.

25b. *saving help:* with MS B's *yĕšûʿātô;* G has "his mercy," and Syr, "his recompense."

26. MS B is damaged at the beginning of this verse; and in 26b it reads *kĕʿēt* for the *kĕʿābê* underlying G, Syr. The following line, which seems to have contained a doublet of v 26, is eaten away in the MS, which also contains in Persian the marginal note "This verse is from other copies, and was here left out and not written." 36:26 is missing from the verso of the same leaf, in the corresponding position, because of the same defect.

36 1. The Gr adds "sovereign" (*despota*) before *God of the universe;* it also adds, "O Lord," at the end of v 5. The divine name *Yhwh* does not occur in the prayer, vv 1–22.

3a. *your hand:* supplied from G, Syr, and the margin of MS B.

4b. *them:* so with MS B's margin, G, and Syr; MS B's text reads *bānû,* "us." The whole verse is also repeated in the margin of B, with *them,* and with a slight change in word order that matches G and Syr.

5. Lat introduces much of this verse, along with a form of v 10b, into both v 2 and v 13.

6, 7. MS B's text of this bicolon adds a verb (*wĕʾammēṣ*) which would make v 7 read, "show forth the splendor of your hand and strengthen your arm and your (right) hand." The margin of MS B repeats the whole bicolon in a somewhat garbled form which, however, agrees with G and Syr on the shorter reading for v 7. The other occurrences of *ʾmṣ* in Sirach (42:17; 45:2) and elsewhere make it seem inappropriate to this context, and the allusion to Isaiah it might carry (e.g., Isa 28:2; 40:26) is already fully provided for with *zĕrôaʿ,* "arm," cf. Isa 51:9, 10.

10a. MS B, and with it Syr, show a break in the structure after this colon. The break is resolved in both by a borrowing from Job 9:12, "for who can say to you, 'What are you doing?' " cf. also Qoh 8:4; Wis 12:12. MS B's margin further distorts this by substituting for *taʿăśeh,* "doing," the synonym *tipʿal,* an allusion to Isa 41:4; 43:13.

10b. This colon, in the form "that they may proclaim your wondrous/mighty deeds" is introduced, along with much of v 5, into both vv 2 and 13 by Lat.

11. This bicolon is vouched for by G and Syr, the latter in the form "In anger and

in fire destroy the enemy, and all the rulers and princes of the nations." It is not present in MS B.

12. The Syr form of this verse (partly anticipated in 11b; see above) is, "Put an end to the crown of the enemy / who says, 'There is none like me!' " MS B has, "Put an end to the head of the temples of Moab [cf. Num 24:17] / who says, 'There is none like me!' " B's margin reads *'ôyēb*, "enemy," for "Moab." The Gr renders "heads," in the plural, and gives 12b accordingly as "who say, 'There is no one besides ourselves.' " Segal sees the allusion to Moab's temples (sides of the skull) as a reference to the Seleucid kingdom, arguing from the use of "Moab" as the typical enemy in Isa 25:10, 11. The "temples" (*pa'ătê*) he understands with LXX, Targ., Peshitta as metaphorical for "nobles." The Gr could have reached the same point with a reading of *běrō'š pinnōt 'ôyēb:* for *pinnōt* metaphorical for "nobles," cf. Judg 20:2; 1 Sam 14:38; Isa 19:13 (repointed from *pinnat*); Zech 10:4.

13. This marks the end of the major dislocation in the Gr MSS of Sirach. The verse numbers 1–13 come from the placement of these verses, in Gr, at the head of chap. 33. V 13 here is the first half of a bicolon, the matching part of which in the Gr tradition is numbered 36:16b, with the rest of the book following in normal sequence (see the INTRODUCTION, Part VIII, 3b). Adherence to the Gr verse numbers on either side of this join has the effect that while no text at all is missing, the verse numbers 14, 15 are not used in chap. 36.

17a, 22a,d. *Kyrios* as the divine name is added in these three cola by Gr; it is not in MS B or Syr—compare with v 1a above.

Comment

Having discussed the vanity and futility of belief and trust in dreams (34:1–8), Ben Sira now turns his attention to abuses in offering sacrifices (34:21–27) and to insincerity in performing certain religious acts (34:28–31). He then extols the keeping of the Law as the greatest form of divine worship (35:1–5). The manner in which the true believer offers sacrifice is the subject of the poem in 35:6–13. There follows an exhortation (35:14–22a) to practice social justice, esp. with regard to the *persones miserabiles*—the disadvantaged people of society. See INTRODUCTION, Part X, 5 and 6. The justice of God, who requites the evil that sinners (esp. Gentiles) are guilty of, and has mercy on those in distress (esp. Israel), is detailed in 35:22b–26. The section concludes with a moving and lengthy prayer for the deliverance and vindication of the nation Israel (36:1–22). Other prayers are found in 22:27–23:6 and 51:1–12.

In the first poem (34:21–27), Ben Sira deplores the offering of sacrifices by the ungodly. The theme is set forth in the opening verse: presenting "ill-gotten goods" for sacrifice is a "tainted" "gift" (another well-attested reading has "mocking gift"). Since the Lord hates robbery and injustice (Isa 61:8), "ill-gotten goods" are "tainted." The Law forbade the offering of an animal with any blemish or defect (Lev 22:18–25); cf. also Deut 15:21; 17:1; Mal 1:8, 14. "Presents [cf. NOTE] from the lawless" are not pleasing to the Lord (34:22); cf. Prov 15:8 and 21:27. This important idea is repeated in 34:23a; cf. Amos 5:21–24. God does not forgive the lawless, who are also called the godless (Gr *asebeis*), when they offer "many sacrifices" for their sins instead of turning away from them (34:23b); cf. 7:9; Hos 8:13; Isa 1:11–15; Jer 7:21–23; Qoh 4:17; Ps 51:18–19. Offering in sacrifice what one has stolen from "the poor" is a heinous crime comparable to "slaying a son in his father's presence" (34:24)—a powerful metaphor, derived from the horror described in 2 Kgs 25:6–7, to emphasize a central theological truth of social justice. The poor are especially dear to God, and to exploit them is to sin against the Lord of justice and compassion, "the father of orphans and the defender of widows" (Ps 68:6). "The bread of charity" [cf. NOTE] is what sustains the very life of the needy (34:25a), and to withhold such assistance is to be "a person of blood" (34:25b); cf. Ps 5:7. Thus helping the poor is not simply an optional act of virtue, but is a mandate the violation of which is the moral equivalent of murder. Depriving a neighbor "of his living" and denying "the worker his wages" are also viewed as murder (34:26–27). Cf. 4:1–6; Lev 19:13; Deut 24:14–15; Jer 22:13; Mal 3:5; Tob 4:14; Jas 5:4.

The cola in 34:28a and 29a are in parallel and develop the idea introduced in 34:21. In 34:28a, the one "who builds up" is the poor person whose goods the wicked rich person seizes, i.e., "tears down," and offers as a sacrifice. Neither gains a thing but "trouble" (34:28b), i.e., the poor is deprived of what is rightfully his, and the rich sins by his theft. In 34:29a, the one who "prays" is the godless rich; the poor is the one who "curses" the rich for the social injustice of which he is guilty. In this case, God will hear (34:29b) the voice of the poor; cf. 4:6. In 34:30, Ben Sira describes as futile the performing of ritual acts of purification when one does not intend to avoid the source of defilement. (Touching a corpse [34:30a] rendered a person ritually unclean for seven days [Num 19:11]. A person so defiled had to purify himself on the third and seventh day with the lustral water in the preparation of which the ashes of a red heifer were used [Num 19:9, 12].) Similarly, it is useless for a person to fast "for his sins" and then to commit them over again (34:31ab). Cf. 2 Pet 2:20–22. Fasting, however, when combined with sincere repentance of one's sins, is praiseworthy (cf. 2 Sam 12:16; Joel 2:12–13; Pss 69:11; 109:24). The prayer of the hypocrite who fasts without repenting will not be heard (34:31cd); cf. Isa 58:3–7; Jer 14:12; Zech 7:5–14.

The next three bicola (35:1–5) form a small unit that describes what true worship of God is all about. Here Ben Sira insists that the moral prescriptions of the Law (charity toward the poor and avoidance of evil) take first place, and that external cultic practices are efficacious only when joined to interior conversion and repentance; cf. 1:28; Hos 6:6; 14:2–3; 1 Sam 15:22–23. The opening bicolon (35:1–2) with its *a:b::b':a'* rhetorical pattern neatly summarizes Ben Sira's thought: *whoever keeps the Law:makes great (his) oblation* (cf. NOTE)*::he sacrifices a peace offering:who observes the commandments.* Regarding the peace offering (35:2), cf. Leviticus 3. Contrast what is said here with the conduct of the wicked described in 34:21–27. "Fine flour" (35:3) was the principal ingredient of the cereal offering one brought as an oblation to the altar in the Temple; cf. Leviticus 2. When one does works of charity (35:3) for others in their need, one in effect "offers fine flour" to the Lord. The "sacrifice of praise" (35:4, Heb *tôdâ*) was a type of "peace offering" one made in thanksgiving; cf. Lev 7:12–21. Ben Sira again insists on almsgiving (35:4) as an essential part of Jewish religion; cf. COMMENT on 3:14–15; 3:30–4:6; 29:8–13. The assertion that works of charity and almsgiving are like sacrificial offerings to the Lord (35:3–4) calls to mind the words of Jesus in Matt 25:40: "As often as you did it [a work of charity] for one of my least brothers or sisters, you did it for me." In addition to doing positive acts of virtue (35:1–4), one is urged "to refrain from evil," which "pleases the Lord," and "to avoid injustice," which "is an atonement" (35:5). Cf. Job 28:28b: "Avoiding evil is understanding." As regards "atonement," Gr *exilasmos,* cf. 5:5a (Heb *sĕlîḥâ*); 17:29b; 18:12b, 20b; Ps 130:4; Neh 9:17; Dan 9:9.

The next poem (35:6–13) prescribes attitudes and interior dispositions that the righteous Jew should have when he makes an offering to the Lord. "To appear before the Lord" is a technical expression for going to the Temple, which the pious Jew visited on the pilgrim festivals of Passover or Unleavened Bread, Pentecost or Weeks, and Tabernacles (cf. Tob 1:6); it was explicitly forbidden to appear before the Lord "empty-handed" (35:6); cf. Exod 23:14–17; 34:20; and Deut 16:16. Although a moral life of obedience to the Lord, works of charity, and avoidance of evil, esp. injustice (35:1–5), is the best offering one can make to God (cf. Prov 21:3), one still was bound to fulfill the cultic obligations because the Law stipulated them (35:7); cf. 7:29–31. It was obedience to God's will as manifested in the Law that gave sacrifices their essential religious value; cf. 1 Sam 15:22; Hos 6:6–7; Amos 5:21–24. That is why Ben Sira affirms that the offering of the righteous Jew "enriches [lit., makes fat] the altar" and "rises as a sweet odor [Gr *euōdia*=Heb *rêaḥ nîḥôaḥ,* as in Lev 1:9 and 3:5] before the Most High" (35:8)—only the sacrifice offered by the righteous is acceptable to God. For the Syr of 35:8–12, cf. NOTE. In 35:9a, "sacrifice" renders Gr *thysia,* which in the LXX of Lev 2:1 is used to translate Heb *minḥâ,* "the cereal, or meal, offering" (cf. 35:3 with COMMENT). In 35:9b, "the memory (of it)," Gr *mnēmosynon,* Heb *'azkārâ* (as in 38:11a and 45:16c), is the portion of the cereal offering that was burned on the altar as "a sweet-smelling oblation to Yahweh" (Lev 2:2); cf. Ps 20:4. Thus 35:8 and 9 are in parallel. "In generous spirit" (35:10a) is, lit., "with a good eye." Compare with "the evil eye" in 14:10a (=the eye of the miser) and 31:13a (=gluttony). "Pay homage to" (35:10a) is, lit., "glorify," Gr *doxason,* as in 7:31a. The point of 35:10a is that one should be generous in offering sacrifices to the Lord. As regards "freewill gifts," Gr *aparchē cheirōn sou* (35:10b), lit., "the firstfruits of your hands," cf. LXX of Deut 12:11 and Sir 7:31d with COMMENT. "God loves a cheerful giver" (2 Cor 9:7); hence one should make contributions and "pay . . . tithes in a spirit of joy" (35:11; cf. NOTE); cf. 7:31; 45:20–21; and Tob 1:6–8. For the divine titles in 35:12–13, cf. NOTE. One should give to God "generously," lit., with goodness of eye; cf. 35:10a. You should give "according to your means," Heb *běhaśśā-gat yād,* lit., "as (your) hand has attained" (cf. 14:13b for the Heb phrase); for the expression of similar ideas with regard to almsgiving, cf. 1 Sam 25:8 and Tob 4:8. Before 35:13, MS B has a marginal gloss, concerning which cf. NOTE. Generosity to God will be rewarded "seven times over" (35:13); cf. 12:2, which speaks of the Lord requiting the one who does a service for the just. Cf. also Prov 19:17 and Jer 51:56. For the expression "seven times over" or "sevenfold," cf. COMMENT on 7:3b and 20:12b.

In the next poem (35:14–22), Ben Sira urges his affluent readers to beware of exploiting the powerless—the poor and the oppressed, the orphan and the widow, the *persones miserabiles* of the Bible, for whom the Lord has a special love and concern. Because a person is rich, perhaps at the expense of the weak, he should not assume that God is like a corrupt judge, for he cannot bribe him by offering lavish sacrifices, for "these he does not accept" (35:14); cf. Deut 10:17. The only way to win divine favor is by sincere repentance of one's sins. Even worse is the case of the Jew who "trusts . . . in sacrifice of the fruits of extortion" (35:15a), as if he could atone for his crimes by offering in oblation what he has unjustly wrung from the disadvantaged; cf. 34:21–24. The lapidary statement in 35:15b is the central affirmation of the poem: "For he is the God of justice," Heb *kî 'ělōhê mišpāṭ hû',* words taken from Isa 30:18c; cf. Mal 2:17. Accordingly, God "knows no favorites" (35:15c), lit., "and with him there is no lifting up of the face"—for the idiom cf. COMMENT on 4:22a. For the thoughts expressed in 35:14–15, cf. Deut 10:17–18; 2 Chr 19:7; Job 34:17, 19; and Wis 6:7. Cf. also Acts 10:34; Rom 2:11; Gal 2:6; Col 3:25. Using the same idiom, 35:16a repeats 35:15c, but specifies the group against which (cf. NOTE) God will not take sides, viz., "the weak," lit., "the poor," Heb *dāl,* Gr *ptōchos;* cf. Prov 22:22–23. In fact, God pays special heed to "the grievance [lit. supplication] of the oppressed" (35:16b).

Two particular groups of oppressed are mentioned in 35:17, "the orphan," whose cry God "does not reject," and "the widow," whose "complaint" also receives a favorable hearing. As regards these two social groups, which receive special protection in the Law because they have no one to plead their cause, cf. Exod 22:21–23; Deut 10:18; 24:17–18; 27:19; Zech 7:10; Ps 68:6; Prov 23:10–11. The widow's tears "cry out against the one that causes them to fall" (35:18–19; cf. NOTE). In Lam 1:1–2, Jerusalem is described as a widow who weeps bitterly at night, "with not one to console her of all her dear ones." Cf. also Bar 4:12, 16. The text of 35:20a is uncertain; cf. NOTE. But the meaning of 35:20 seems clear: the cry of the distressed will be heard; their plea "reaches the heavens" (lit., the clouds); cf. Gen 18:20–21; Exod 3:7–9; Pss 68:5; 104:3. For the background of 35:21a (cf. NOTE), in synonymous parallelism with 35:20b, cf. Lam 3:44: "You wrapped yourself in a cloud which prayer could not pierce." The prayer of the lowly is so insistent and efficacious that "it does not rest till it reaches its goal" (35:21b), i.e., "till the Most High [so G; MS B, God] responds, judges justly and affirms the right" (35:21c, 22a). The Heb of 35:22a may be translated, lit.: "and the righteous Judge [lit., Judge of righteousness] executes judgment." Cf. 18:25.

In the next poem (35:22b–26), which serves as a lead into the long prayer for the deliverance of the Chosen People (36:1–22), Ben Sira turns his attention from the individual victims of oppression to the nation Israel, which in that day was under foreign domination. He affirms his staunch faith in the power and will of God to break [lit., to smite] "the backs [lit., the loins] of the merciless" and wreak "vengeance upon the nations" (35:22d, 23a). Cf. Deut 33:11 for the image of God smiting the loins of a human enemy. Nor will God delay (35:22b) in executing his judgment on the oppressors of his holy people; for a similar sentiment, cf. Luke 18:7–8 and 2 Pet 3:9. Rather, "like a warrior, he will not be still" (35:22c, Heb *lōʾ yitʿappāq*, lit., he will not restrain himself, a rare verb Ben Sira borrowed from Isa 42:14; 63:15; 64:11). The language in this poem has a prophetic ring and style. An elegant *a:b::b':a'* chiastic pattern reinforces the strong statement in 35:23bc: *he destroys:the scepter of pride::and the staff of wickedness:he cuts in two.* For the image of cutting a staff in two, cf. Zech 11:10, 14. For the phrase "staff of wickedness," cf. Ps 125:3; Isa 14:5; Ezek 7:11. As regards the evil of pride, Heb *zādôn,* cf. 10:13, 18, with COMMENT. God also "requites humankind [Heb *ʾĕnôš,* here used as a collective noun to designate the Gentiles as in Ps 56:2] according to its deeds" (35:24a); cf. Prov 24:12. And he "repays people [Heb *ʾādām,* also a collective noun, in synonymous parallelism with *ʾĕnôš*] according to their thoughts" (35:24b), presumably their evil designs against his Chosen People. God himself "defends the cause of his people" (35:25a); the wording here comes from Isa 51:22. Cf. also Mic 7:9. By this action, he "gladdens them by his saving help" (35:25b; cf. NOTE)—a thought derived from Isa 25:9; cf. also Sir 2:9. God's mercy "in time of distress" is "welcome" (Gr *hōraion,* lit., seasonable) as "rain clouds [cf. NOTE] in time of drought" (35:26). For the imagery, cf. Ps 72:6; Prov 16:15; Isa 45:8; Zech 10:1.

The prayer (36:1–22) that concludes this section may be divided into four stanzas—4 + 5 + 4 + 4 bicola. It flows naturally from Ben Sira's sure faith in the God of Israel and his prophetic hope of relief from pagan oppressors (35:22b–26). In the prayer, which is a lament, he urgently pleads with God to come to the rescue of his Chosen People. Cf. Ps 44:2–9 and 2 Macc 1:24–29.

Ben Sira appeals to the past signs and wonders God performed on Israel's behalf and asks that the prophecies of deliverance be now fulfilled, so that all peoples may come to know that the Lord is "the eternal God" (36:22d); cf. the Prayer of Azariah in Dan 3:26–45. The opening colon (36:1) summarizes the prayer; it may be translated, lit.: "Save us, O God of all" (cf. NOTE). This title of God occurs also in 45:23c and in 50:22a (in G only); cf. also Rom 9:5. It is interesting in that it does not address the Lord as God of Israel, but rather as God of *all*, i.e., Jews, Gentiles, the whole universe. Two similar expressions are found in apocryphal Ps 151:4 from Qumran (11QPs^a xxviii 7–8): Heb *'ǎdōn hakkōl*, "the Lord of all," and *'ĕlōah hakkōl*, "the God of all." This epithet has a long history, deriving from the Canaanite phrase *ba'alu 'arṣi*, "Lord of earth," which became in Heb, when applied to Yahweh, *'ǎdōn kol-hā'āreṣ*, "The Lord of all the earth" (Josh 3:11, 13; Mic 4:13; Zech 4:14; 6:5; Ps 97:5). Cf. F. M. Cross, "David, Orpheus, and Psalm 151:3–4," *BASOR* 231 (1978): 69–71. The imperative "Save us" and the mention of God form the typical abrupt beginning of a lamentation psalm; cf., for example, Psalms 43, 54, 55, 56, 57, 109, 140, 141, and 143.

The rest of this stanza (36:2–5) and all of the next (36:6–12) contain pleas to humble Israel's foes, i.e., the Seleucid overlords, who after the Battle of Panium in 198 B.C. were in charge of the Holy Land. In 36:2, the phrase "all the nations," Heb *gôyīm*, may also be translated, "all the Gentiles," i.e., the Seleucids. For the wish expressed in the verse, cf. 1 Chr 14:17. The reason why the Gentiles deserve to have the "dread" of God instilled in them is given in a gloss in the Syr, "they do not know [i.e., recognize as true] [God]." Cf. Ps 79:6 and Jer 10:25. "The foreign folk" (36:3a) are again the Seleucid rulers. Regarding the "hand" of God (36:3a; cf. NOTE) being raised against a foe, cf. Isa 19:16. For the expression "your mighty deeds," Heb *gĕbûrôtĕkā* (36:3b), cf. 15:18b and Deut 3:24; Pss 20:7; 71:16; 106:2; 145:4, 12; 150:2; Isa 63:15. A literal translation of 36:4 shows the *a:b::b:a'* chiastic structure of the Heb text: *(As) you have been sanctified:before their eyes (in us)::(so) before our eyes:glorify yourself (in them;* cf. NOTE). What is meant is that just as God has manifested his holiness (and his hatred of evil) by punishing Israel for her sins by allowing the nation to become subject to foreign domination (35:4a; cf. Deut 28:36–37; Ezek 20:41; 28:25; 38:16; 39:27), so now God is asked to show his glory by punishing the Gentiles for their crimes of oppression of the Jewish people (35:4b; cf. Deut 28:7–13; Ezek 28:22; 38:21–23). It is thus that the Gentiles "will know," as the Jews know, "that there is no God but you" (36:5; cf. NOTE). Cf. 1 Kgs 8:60; 1 Chr 17:20; Isa 45:14. The word "God," Heb *'ĕlōhîm*, occurs in 36:1 and 5b, the opening and closing cola of the stanza, thus forming a rhetorical *inclusio*.

In the next stanza (36:6–12), Ben Sira continues his plea to punish the enemies of the Jews. The opening bicolon (36:6–7; cf. NOTE) is an appeal to God to repeat the "signs" and "wonders" that long ago he had done in Egypt when he liberated his people from bondage. For the combination "signs and wonders," cf. Dan 3:32(99)–33(100); 6:28. As regards the imagery of 36:7, cf. Exod 15:6; Isa 51:9; 62:8; 63:12; Ps 98:1. For the ideas of God's anger being roused and his wrath poured out (36:8), cf. Pss 78:38; 79:6; Jer 10:25. In 36:9, "the enemy" to be humbled and "the foe" to be scattered are the Seleucids. "The ending," or "end," Heb qēṣ, Ben Sira prays God to hasten (36:10a) is the end of the Seleucid oppression of the Jews and rule of the Holy Land. "The time," Heb môʿēd (lit., appointed time), is the moment of the hoped-for deliverance from the hated Syrians, "when [God's] mighty deeds are to be proclaimed" (36:10b; cf. NOTES); cf. 36:3b with COMMENT. In Dan 11:35, qēṣ and môʿēd occur together in a similar context. The mighty deeds that Ben Sira prays for are specified in 36:11–12. For the background of 36:11 (cf. NOTE), cf. Num 24:18:22 and Obad 18. In 36:12a (cf. NOTE), "the heads of the hostile rulers" may refer to the Seleucid Antiochus III the Great (223–187 B.C.), who had crushed a large part of the Egyptian army in 198 at Panium, thus gaining control over the Holy Land and the Jews, and may also refer to his son, Seleucus IV Philopator (187–175 B.C.); but this identification is less probable, for Seleucus had none of the grandeur of his father. Antiochus III was arrogant enough to say, "There is no one besides me!" (36:12b); cf. Dan 11:18 with COMMENT in L. F. Hartman and A. A. Di Lella, *The Book of Daniel*, AB 23, pp. 292–93. The *hybris* of pagan rulers will not go unpunished; cf. Isa 47:8–10 and Zeph 2:15. In 190 B.C., Antiochus was decisively defeated in the Battle of Magnesia, between Sardis and Smyrna. The victorious Roman general Lucius Cornelius Scipio forced him to come to humiliating peace terms, including payment of a large indemnity; cf. INTRODUCTION, Part II. The stanza ends with the Heb preposition zûlat, "besides [me]," the same word that concludes the previous stanza (36:5b), "besides, or but [you]."

Ben Sira's prayer in 36:13 (cf. NOTE about the numbering of the verses here) is for God to bring back to the Holy Land all the Jews who never returned after the Exile. Cyrus had allowed the Judeans exiled in Babylon to return home, but most preferred to stay put. Moreover, many Jews lived in other parts of the world. Hence Ben Sira asks God to complete the restoration of his people to the Promised Land, "that they may inherit the land as in days of old" (36:16). As regards the gathering of "the tribes of Jacob" (36:13), cf. Isa 11:11–12; 27:13; Jer 3:18; 29:14; 30:3; 31:8, 10; 32:37; Ezek 36:8–11; 39:25–27; Amos 9:14. Like the prophets here cited, Ben Sira expresses the hope for the return to Palestine of all the tribes of Jacob (=Israel). Israel is "the people called by [Yahweh's] name" (36:17a); cf. Deut 28:10; Isa 63:19; Jer 14:9; 15:16. Israel is also named Yahweh's "firstborn" (36:17b); cf. 44:23; Exod 4:22; Jer 31:9. See also Hos 11:1 and Wis 18:13. Jerusalem is the Lord's "holy city" (36:18a); cf. 49:6; Isa 48:2; 52:1; Neh 11:1, 18; Dan 9:16. It is also "the foundation of [his] throne" (36:18b)—Heb mēkôn šibtēkā also may be

translated "the place of your dwelling." Cf. Exod 15:17; Ps 132:8; 2 Chr 6:41.
In 36:19, an *a:b::b':a'* chiastic pattern gives emphasis to the petition Ben Sira
addresses to God: *(Fill) Zion:with your majesty::and with your glory:your temple.* Cf. Hag 2:7. Since Zion/Jerusalem is the Lord's earthly dwelling, it is the
place where he manifests his majesty and glory; cf. Isa 2:2–3; Mic 4:1–2; Jer
31:6. The last four cola (36:18–19) of this stanza have an end rhyme, Heb *-kā,*
"your."

The last stanza (36:20–22) of the prayer opens with a petition that God
"give evidence of [his] deeds of old" (36:20a), i.e., his great interventions in
Israel's behalf, as, for example, the call of Abraham, the bestowal of the
Promised Land, the Exodus, the Covenant on Sinai, the Conquest of the Holy
Land. V 20b may be translated, lit.: "Make stand, or establish, the vision
spoken in your name," Heb *wĕhāqēm hāzôn dubbār bišĕmekā,* a colon similar
to one found in the "Apostrophe to Zion" (11QPs^a Zion), col. xxii, ll. 13–14:
qhy hzwn dwbr ʿlyk, "Accept the vision speaking [or spoken] about you" (i.e.,
Jerusalem). The vision Ben Sira refers to is, as G and the translation here
interpret the word, "the prophecies" spoken long ago in Yahweh's name, esp.
the prophecies of deliverance and salvation. The word "vision," *hāzôn,* often
occurs in the superscriptions of the prophetic books; cf., for example, Isa 1:1;
Obad 1; Nah 1:1. In 36:21a, "those who have hoped in [God]" are, of course,
the faithful Jews who look to the Lord for vindication. V 21b, in synonymous
parallelism with 36:20b, resembles the colon that follows after the one already
cited from the "Apostrophe to Zion" (col. xxii, ll. 13–14): *whlmt nbyʾym
ttbʿk,* "and may you [i.e., Jerusalem] seek for yourself the dreams of the
prophets." This passage from the "Apostrophe to Zion" also has a remarkable relationship with Dan 9:24; cf. Hartman–Di Lella, *The Book of Daniel,*
AB 23, p. 45. In 36:22a, Ben Sira makes his final appeal, which recapitulates
the entire prayer: "Hear the prayers of your servants [or, as in MS B^{mg},
servant,]," i.e., Israel; cf. 1 Kgs 8:30; Dan 9:17. V 22b may be translated, lit.:
"according to your good favor toward your people." Cf. Ps 106:4. For the
imagery of "all the ends of the earth" (36:22c), cf. Isa 52:10. The title "eternal
God," Heb *ʾēl ʿôlām,* derives from Gen 21:33 and Isa 40:28; cf. Tob 13:6. The
words "all," Heb *kōl,* and "God," *ʾĕlōhîm/ʾēl,* occur in the opening (36:1) and
the closing bicola (36:22cd) of the poem in an *a:b::b:a* chiastic pattern
(*ʾĕhōhê:hakkōl::kōl:ʾēl*). For a fuller study of this prayer, cf. J. Marböck, "Das
Gebet um die Rettung Zions Sir 36,1–22 . . . im Zusammenhang der Geschichtsschau Ben Siras," in *Memoria Jerusalem,* pp. 93–116.

43. Choice of Associates
(36:23–37:15)

36   ²³ The gullet can swallow any food,   B
     yet some foods are more agreeable than others;
  ²⁴ The palate is the judge of delicacies put forward as   C
     gifts:
     so it is with the discriminating mind and deceitful   B
     tidbits.
  ²⁵ A double-dealing character causes grief,
     but an experienced person can turn the tables on
     him.

  ²⁶ Though any man may be accepted as a husband,   G
     yet some women are better wives than others.
  ²⁷ A woman's beauty makes her husband's face light up,   B
     for it surpasses all else that charms the eye;
  ²⁸ And if, besides, her speech is soothing,
     his lot is beyond that of mortal men.
  ²⁹ A wife is her husband's richest treasure,
     a help like himself, a staunch support.
  ³⁰ A vineyard with no hedge will be overrun;
     a man with no wife becomes a homeless wanderer.
  ³¹ Who will trust an armed band
     that skips from city to city?
     Or a man who has no nest,
     but finds lodging where night overtakes him?

37   ¹ Every friend declares his friendship,   D
     but there are friends who are only so-called friends.
  ² Is it not a sorrow to bring death close
     when your other self becomes your enemy?
  ³ "Alas, my intimate! What are you made of,
     to blanket the earth's surface with deceit?"

4 A harmful friend will look to your table,   B
    but in time of trouble he stands aloof.
5 A good friend will fight with you against the alien foe;   D
    against your enemies he will hold up your shield.
6 Forget not your comrade during the battle,
    and neglect him not when you distribute your
                    spoils.

7 Every counselor points out a way,
    but some counsel ways of their own.
8 Be on the alert when one proffers advice,
    find out first of all what he wants;
He too may have himself in mind—
    "Why should the opportunity be his?"
9 He may tell you how good your way will be,
    and then stand by to see you impoverished.
10 Seek no advice from your father-in-law;
    from one who is envious of you, keep your
                  intentions hidden.
11 Consult not with a woman about her rival,
    nor with a coward about war,
    with a merchant about business,
    with a buyer about value,
    with a miser about generosity,
    with a cruel person about physical fitness,
    with an indifferent worker about his work,
    with this year's hired person about next year's
                  sowing,
    with an idle slave about a great task: G
    pay no attention to any advice they give.

12 Instead, associate with a religious person   D
    who you are sure keeps to God's directives,
Who is like-minded with yourself
    and will feel for you if you fall.
13 Then, too, heed your own heart's counsel:
    there is nothing that you can depend on more—
14 A person's conscience can tell him his situation
    better than seven watchers on a pinnacle of rock.

15 Then with all this, pray to God
   to steady your steps in the true path.

Notes

36   23, 26. In the damaged state of MS B for these two lines (bicola), which occur together at the bottom of a page (the reverse side of the leaf that ends on its obverse with 35:26; see NOTE there), any citations or reconstructions of the Heb are very tentative, both as to running text and as to what is said to be, or to have been, in the margins. This is complicated by the fact that on the next leaf (and page) of MS B, vv 24, 25 stand at the top, and are followed before v 27 by what can only be a parallel bicolon to v 23; it, too, has (*nbr*) one damaged word; see below. Syr does not have v 26. Vattioni's arrangement is specially confusing here and for v 27.

   23. The first colon is clear in MS B, but has a word (*grgrt*) for "gullet" that lacks agreement with the verb (*'ôkēl*); Syr (*napšā'*) can hardly mean "gullet," though it might reflect Heb *nepeš* with that meaning. G has *koilia*, "belly," and Smend judged he could read two letters of *kāreś* (Jer 51:34) with that meaning in the faded margin of MS B. In view of 31:12, perhaps *gārôn*, "gullet," was the original reading. V 23b is clear as to meaning, from G, Syr, and MS B's margin; of restorations of B's running text, with Peters, Strack, Smend, Segal, *'ak yēš 'ōkel mē'ōkel nā'îm* is the most likely and would represent the basic form. The seemingly parallel line to v 23 in MS B (see above) reads *kl nbr t'kl ḥyh / 'k yš mkh mmkh tn'm;* Segal's *nekes* for *nbr* cannot be got from the facsimile. For this doubtful word, Lévi already read *nbr,* as did Strack, the latter with a footnote offering *n-b/k-r/d* as the possible readings. Smend speaks of the line (he reads, doubtfully, *nkd*) as *"eine sinnlose Variante,"* "a meaningless variant." The solution is furnished by J. Strugnell, in "Of Cabbages and Kings—or Queans," *The Use of the Old Testament and Other Essays . . . in honor of W. F. Stinespring,* ed. James M. Efird (Durham, N.C.: Duke University, 1972): 204–9. Recognizing that *mkh* is a transposition for *kāmēh,* "truffles" (at least currently, the individuating form is *kĕmēhâ,* "truffle"/"mushroom") he can account both for the presence of the animal (*ḥyh*), presumably a hog, and the sense of *nbr,* "to scratch, to root." The *kmh* term is also Aram; in Ar, *kam'* is the cognate. Reading *kol nābūr tō'kēl ḥayyâ / 'ak yēš kāmēh mikkāmēh nā'îm* (Strugnell would read *nibbār* or *nēber*), the resultant sense is, "An animal will eat whatever has been dug up (by its snout) / but some kinds of truffles are better than others." With v 23 as given, this added bicolon can be related meaningfully to vv 24, 25, and it would seem to have survived, garbled, from Ben Sira's original discourse. Neither the accepted v 23 nor this additional bicolon can be intelligibly related to v 26 of G, though G builds its vv 23, 26 on strictly parallel lines.

   24. The correct Heb text of 24a is that furnished by MS C in an isolated colon at the bottom of a page containing 5:7c, 9–13 (!)—*ḥyk yṭ'm mṭ'my zbd.* It has (with MS

B's text) an expanded orthography for *ḥēk*. Its *yiṭʿam* (so G, Syr) is correct rather than MS B's *bwḥn*, "tests," found both in the text and (twice) in the margin. *maṭʿammê zābed* (so Segal) is the reading of MS C, vs. Smend—the *ṭeth* of *mṭʿmy* in the MS was made in two strokes that failed to join; hence Smend's *mnwʿmy*. The phrase is repeated twice in MS B's margin (cf. also 40:29, B^mɛ); B's running text has a corrupt *(mṭʿmy) dbr*. The sense of *yiṭʿam* is illustrated by the parallelism in Job 12:11; 34:3, where the palate tasting (*ṭʿm*) food is compared to the ear testing (*bḥn*) words; Job is the likely source of the *bwḥn* reading here in Sirach. G's *brōmata thēras*, "food from the hunt," conveys the gratuitous and unexpected nature of the gift (*zābed*); the grandson may have been thinking of the food as God's gift (cf. Gen 30:20), from the hunt (cf. Gen 27:20). If so, a wordplay at work in the Heb between *zābed* and *kāzāb* makes it likely that the grandson was wrong, and that Ben Sira did not have in mind the gift delicacies as a sincere benefaction, much less as a divine gift (cf. 29:22–26; Prov 23:1–8). V 24b is correct in MS B's running text, and the parallelism relates to that of Job 12:11; 34:3, mentioned above: in *maṭʿammê kāzāb*, as contrasted with *maṭʿammê zābed*, the "tidbits" are words, which is how G and Syr have rendered them. The phrase *maṭʿammê kāzāb* should be compared with the deceitful, or elusive, riches (*adikō mamōnq*) of Luke 16:11; the riches are deceitful because undependable, and so it is with the "tidbits" of gossip, only too likely to be false.

25a. *double-dealing character:* cf. Jer 17:9; *causes grief:* cf. Prov 10:10.

25b. For *an experienced person* MS B has the expression, unique in Ben Sira as we have it, *ʾîš wātîq;* the Gr is *anthrōpos polypeiros,* and Segal uses this expression to relate this passage to 21:22b; 34:9b, where the same *polypeiros* occurs (cf. also 1:7, GII). None of these passages is likely to reflect *wātîq;* the Semitic term is at home in Aram and in Ar, though the Heb Bible does not have it.

26. See NOTE for vv 23, 26 above. Only the Gr tradition offers a full text of this verse. In MS B, beneath the hole where v 26b has been eaten away, stand the words *ʾk yš ʾšh yph*. These are generally taken to show that G's *thygatēr thygatros* are a slight paraphrase for *ʾiššâ mēʾiššâ,* and do not suppose a twofold *bat*, "daughter," "girl," as might appear at first glance. Here v 26 is rendered as meant by Ben Sira to introduce vv 27–31.

27–31. MSS B and C both supply text for these verses. They are joined for vv 29b, 30, 31 by MS D, the single leaf of which includes 36:29b–38:1a.

27a. The verb in MS B, text and margin (*whlyl, yhll*), need not be rewritten to *yāʾîr,* from 7:29; read *yāhēl,* cf. Isa 13:10 (already rewritten to *yāʾîrû* in 1QIsaᵃ) or *yĕhallēl* (so Syr, but with the wrong meaning: *nĕšabbaḥ,* "praises"), *makes . . . light up.*

28b. Lit., "her husband is not [one] of the sons of men"—hyperbole.

29b. *a help like himself:* G and Syr have this correct (Syr, "like yourself"). All three Heb MSS show a breakdown of the reading into *ʿîr mibṣār,* "a fortified city." The original reading will have been *ʿēzer kĕʿaṣmô;* once *ʿzr* was corrupted into *ʿyr,* the *mbṣr* (Josh 19:29, and often) from *kʿṣmw* was inevitable. The *kĕʿaṣmô* is a play on Gen 2:23, "bone of my bones"; Ben Sira uses *ʿeṣem* as a term for identity in 43:1 (M), *ʿeṣem šāmayim, heaven itself. staunch support:* lit., "supporting column."

37. For this chapter, MS D is taken as basic because its text runs almost unbroken and without marginal glosses (it gives out after three words of 38:1). MS B has some damage, and longer than usual marginal alternatives, which frequently coincide with

the readings of MS D. Both complete editions of Segal (1953, 1958) contain by over-sight a confused identification of the sources for 37:7–15. On the right-hand page the bottom six lines, vv 7–11, are all from MS B, as are the top nine lines of the left-hand page. The continuation, vv 7–13 (plus vv 14–15 overleaf), is from MS D.

37:2. *sorrow*=G=*dāwôn;* MSS D, B, and B's margin all read *dîn,* an error common to the medieval MSS each time *dāwôn* occurs: cf. 14:1 (MS A); 30:21, 23; 38:18. See Di Lella, *The Hebrew Text of Sirach,* p. 73; Rüger, p. 98, allows for *dĕyôn* as a possible reading; but the *waw* is strong in all cognates of this term.

3a. *What are you made of?*=*mē'ayin nôṣartā.* The interrogative phrase=G's *pothen;* with G, the verb should be second person (cf. 3b). MSS D, B have *maddûa' nôṣartî,* "Why was I formed?" This is introduced in D by "Alas! an intimate; he says, [etc.]"; in B by "Alas! an intimate; that he should have said, [etc.]." Syr runs 2b–3a together, reads *ra'* for *rēa',* and obtains "the enemy and the wicked, why were they created?" G is furthest off in some respects; its *ō ponēron enthymēma* is for *hôy lĕyēṣer ra'* "Alas! evil inclination": the *yēṣer* (see 15:4; 27:6) represents the same kind of borrowing of *lĕṣār* from the end of v 2 that produced "the enemy" with "and the wicked" in Syr (*hôy lĕ-* is a standard construction, and *yṣr* for *ṣr* was read after it). *pothen enekylisthēs* is, as Ziegler has seen, a direct allusion to G of 27:27. Either the *enekylisthēs* was the translator's choice for *nôṣartā* as a conscious variant on *ektisthēs* (Smend: the Lat has *creata es*) or *enektisthēs* (Peters)—Ziegler quotes both of these— or the Lat reading reflects the primitive Gr and a later hand read *enekylisthēs* (the verb appears also in Sir 23:12) to get "how did you become involved?" or the like. At least for Sir 27:27 there is a further deliberate allusion to LXX Prov 26:27b, *ho de kyliōn lithon eph' heauton kyliei,* "He who rolls a stone rolls it (back) upon himself" (the play on the verb is not in the Heb of Proverbs). The passages in their current Gr form all carry the implication that evil done reverts back upon its perpetrator. In the Heb, the first-person form *nôṣartî* is medieval, supported by neither G (nor Lat) nor Syr; the *maddûa'* has been introduced in the spirit of Job 3:12. The *mē'ayin* seen above as underlying G appears in MS A once in 13:18b and may or may not be primitive twice in that verse (13:18a for *mē'îš,* erroneous before *šālôm*). Syr *'tbryw* here seems to have been influenced by 39:28–29.

4. *but in time of*=*ûbĕ'ēt* with MS D, G, and Syr; MS B lacks the conjunction, but otherwise (with Syr) has the better text in this bicolon. The *mērēa'* with which the verse begins represents two homonyms: one a favorable description, meaning the friend of the bridegroom (Judg 14:20; 15:2, etc.), and the other, one who is *harmful* or an evildoer. The listener to 4a would know only from 4b which was meant. In 4b, "aloof," *minneged,* is from MS B; MS D's *mnwb* is faulty; cf. v 9, where *minneged* recurs. With v 4 compare 6:8, 10.

5a. G read *yaḥmōl* for *yillāḥēm* and destroyed parallelism and sense.

5b. For *your enemies,* MS D has *'ārîm,* which Smend would accept on the basis of later Aramaizing usage in Heb. But in this colon the sibilant alliteration is unmistak-able (5a ends with *zār;* then *ṣārîm, yahăzîq, ṣinnâ*) and *ṣārîm* is called for. Compare NOTE at 47:7b.

7a. *points out a way*=*yānîp yād,* MS B; the *'ōmēr ḥāzēh,* "says, 'Look!' " of MSS D, B^ms is a clarifying variant (for the relationship of *yānîp yād* to G, see Smend).

7b. *of their own*=*'ēlāyw,* cf. G; MS D has *lyw,* MS B *'l lṣ* (!).

8c. *have himself in mind* = *lĕnapšô yaḥšōb* = MS B; MS D lacks the *lamed.*

8d. G resolves the direct discourse with "lest he take chances against your interest," which is reading *yappîl* for the *yippōl* of MSS D and B and rewriting the prepositional phrase.

9. MS B is fragmentary here, and MS D has faulty readings. G and Syr agree on 9a (= *wĕ'āmar lĕkā mah ṭôb darkekā*); 9b follows MS D, with *rēšekā* for "you impoverished."

10. GI, Syr, and Heb (MSS D, B) agree on the place of this verse; early, but not primitive, Lat evidence also agrees. GII and the oldest Lat read the verse after v 6. *with your father-in-law* is the oldest Lat reading, unmatched in the extant Gr MSS. The consonants for this reading (*ḥāmîkā*) are those of MS D—in MS B, the bicolon is missing with the bottom of a leaf. The earliest G (I) appealed to the Palestinian Aram verb *ḥmy,* "to see," to get for these same consonants a (Heb!) participial form *ḥāmēkā,* "him who looks (askance) at you," in the sense of "him who is jealous of you," thus finding a parallel to 10b *mqn',* "one who is envious of you." Syr avoided both *ḥmyk* and *mqn'* and settled for "enemy," once, in an abridged line. **ḥām,* "father-in-law," instead of the usual Heb *ḥōtēn,* is the old Semitic word, at home in Akk, Aram, South Ar–Eth, and (in suffixed forms only) the MT at Gen 38:13, 25; 1 Sam 4:19, 21. In those two contexts, however, it is used from the perspective of a daughter-in-law, which is not the case in Sirach. Still, with *'ōwēn/'ōyēn* employed for the notion "looking (with envy)" in 1 Sam 18:9, and with several verbs of seeing in Hebrew (*r'h, ḥzh, hbbyṭ*) available to convey this sense of invidious conduct, GI's solution is so far incredible that the *father-in-law* choice imposes itself. Was Ben Sira so influenced by Aram that he looked beyond his broad Heb vocabulary for a verb, in such a case as this?

11. *Consult not:* supplied for clarity. The Heb construction is "With a woman, about her rival," etc., giving a series of nine situations for which the rule to be followed, *Pay no attention to any advice,* is given only in the tenth and last colon. In fact, the ninth instance about the *idle slave,* plus the final recommendation, is a bicolon missing from the Heb MSS and needing to be supplied from G. For the detail, G is the best witness throughout; next would be the combination of MS D and the marginal readings of MS B (which agree with D); then the text of MS B, which is inferior; and finally Syr, worse still. MS D has false readings as regards *coward* (Heb *rak*); *about business* (Heb *'al teger,* with Segal; the corresponding noun for *merchant* is in the Masada MS at 42:5); *indifferent (worker),* (Heb *pô'ēl šāw',* with MS B).

12a. Reading *'ak 'im 'îš mĕpaḥēd histayyēd.* For *'im,* "with," MSS D, B have *'im,* "if"; for *'îš,* "man" (so MS D), MS B has *yēš,* "there is." Both variants result from the presence of *tāmîd* in the MSS (to be discussed below); G read *'im 'îš. religious* = G *eusebous; mĕpaḥēd* (MSS D, B) is more precisely "(god-)fearing," with a stronger emphasis on the emotion of fear than either *eusebēs* or the customary *yĕrē' 'ĕlōhîm* would convey: compare the use of *mĕpaḥedet* in 42:14b (M). Since in 12b "God" needs to be introduced explicitly in this translation as the source of *miṣwâ,* "directives," the broader term of G is rendered in 12a. Superficially, there is a strong case for seeking a verb form cognate with *tāmîd* for this context: see the data for *tāmîd* = *endelechōs,* etc., in NOTE on 9:3–4, and also NOTE on 41:6. Peters (1913) would find the verb for 12a continued from *Seek . . . advice* in 10a, and read the *tāmîd* as merely an adverb. But in view of the negative in 10a (seek *no* advice) and the *pay no attention . . . to any advice* that must be supplied from G at the end of v 11 (Segal: *ʾal tibṭaḥ [ʿal ʾēlleh] ʿal kōl ʿēṣâ;* Syr is similar), that solution is surely too contorted. Here it is supposed that even if the Gr read *tāmîd* or the like for its *endelechize,* the basic text will have had *histayyēd,* "associate." Syr uses *ʿēmar,* "dwell with, be with," here and in 41:6, which again might suggest *tāmîd;* but after *with an indifferent worker* in v 11 above it supplies the clause *lāʾ teqṭor rāzāʾ,* "do not agree/conspire," which points to the presence in the context of *histayyēd,* see again NOTE on 9:3–4. The confusion of *samek* and medial *mem* in the early second century B.C. would be quite easy; compare the *samek* open at bottom left that is still employed in 1QIsaᵃ, 125–100 B.C. Since *histayyēd* is rather special to the vocabulary of Ben Sira, a confusion of its forms at times with *tāmîd* might be expected. A similar confusion of *samek* and *mem* in the transcription of Isa 49:21 led to *gôlâ wĕsûrâ* as a doublet for the preceding *wĕgalmûdâ* (*CBQ* 22 [1960]: 50).

12cd. *ʾăšer kilĕbābô kilĕbābekā;* MSS D, B have *ʾăšer ʿim,* MS B *lĕbābô,* MS D *bilĕbābô* (error, *b-* for *k-*). *wĕʾim tikkāšēl yĕʿākēr bāk: tikkāšēl* = MS B, MS D *yikkāšēl; yĕʿākēr* = G (MS D *yaʿăbōd, -b-* for *-k-, -d* for *-r*); MS B *ygyʿ ʾlyk.*

13. *heed* = *hāben,* MS B; MSS Bᵐᵍ, D *kāk* (medieval!); G = *hāken.* 13b *kî ʾēn lĕkā* (*ʾāmûn mimmennû*); *ʾēn* = G (MSS D, B *ʾim*); *lĕkā* = MS B.

15b. *steps* = *ṣĕʿādêkā* with MS B; MS D omits *yod* as though reading singular.

Comment

The text of this section, which urges discernment in the choices one must make in daily life, is difficult, as is obvious from the lengthy NOTES to the translation. The units are related only insofar as they speak of the different types of persons one may choose to associate with.

In the first unit (36:23–25), Ben Sira draws a parallel between the trained palate, which can distinguish between foods of varying qualities, and the discriminating mind, which can discern the character of people. The opening bicolon (36:23; cf. NOTE) states a general principle: all foods can be eaten, but some are better than others. For the text and interpretation of 36:24, cf. the long NOTE. In 36:25a, "a double-dealing character" renders Heb *lēb ʿāqōb,* lit., "an insidious, or deceitful, heart," a phrase that derives from Jer 17:9. "Heart" here refers to an individual, as in 3:26a. The next two Heb words, *yittēn ʿaṣṣābet,* "causes grief, or trouble," are taken from Prov 10:10a; *ʿaṣṣābet* occurs also in 38:18a. "An experienced person" (36:25b; cf. NOTE), i.e., a wise person, can, however, "turn the tables on him" (lit., can turn it [the grief, or trouble] back on him), because he has intelligence and foresight to anticipate, and so ward off, the other's deceitful actions.

The next unit (36:26–31), on the selection of a suitable wife, opens with a chauvinistic comment, which may be translated, lit.: "A woman will accept (as husband) any male" (36:26a). But a man has to be careful, implies Ben Sira, for "some women are better wives than others" (36:26b; cf. NOTE). As regards the effect of "a woman's beauty" (36:27; cf. NOTE), cf. the story of Jacob being attracted by Rachel, who was "well formed and beautiful" (Gen 29:17). Cf. 7:19 and 26:16–18. In 36:28a, the phrase, "(her) speech (is) soothing," renders Heb *marpē᾽ lāšôn*, lit., "healing of tongue," an expression taken from Prov 15:4a. Cf. 26:14. G paraphrases: "If there is on her tongue mercy and meekness (GII adds: and healing)." For the literal translation of 36:28b, cf. NOTE; the typically Semitic hyperbole suggests that the husband of such a woman is unusually blessed and lucky. For the thought of 36:29a, cf. 26:1–4. The Heb phrase *rē᾽šît qinyān*, "richest treasure," clearly derives from the middle two words of Prov 8:22a: *yhwh qānānî rē᾽šît darkô;* note that the verb *qānānî* has the same consonants as *qinyān* (with *yod* and second *nun* reversed). Thus, by describing the wife as a man's *rē᾽šît qinyān*, Ben Sira distinctly implies that she is to be compared to Lady Wisdom, "the firstborn of [Yahweh's] ways," in the majestic poem of Prov 8:22–36—a comparison that is high praise indeed. The expression "a help like himself" (36:29b; cf. NOTE) is an allusion to Gen 2:18, the LXX of which has *boēthon kat᾽ auton*, the reading of G here; cf. also Gen 2:20. "A vineyard with no hedge will be overrun" (36:30a, Heb *yĕbô῾ar*, lit., consumed by grazing) by cattle and will thus be ruined; for the imagery of the vineyard deprived of its hedge and the use of *b῾r* in the sense "to graze," cf. Isa 5:5. See also Isa 3:14 and Prov 24:30–31. Without a wife, a man "becomes a homeless wanderer" (36:30b), Heb *nā῾ wānād*, lit., "a vagabond and a wanderer," the exact words applied to Cain in Gen 4:12, 14. For the imagery of "an armed band" (36:31a) in the sense of plunderers, cf. Jer 18:22; a form of the Heb expression *gĕdûd ṣābā᾽* occurs also in 1 Chr 7:4. The "nest" (36:31c) is the home; cf. 14:26a and Prov 27:8. Since the man has no wife, he has no "nest." The point of 36:31, which expands the thought of 36:30b, is that a man without a wife and home is unreliable and restless, wandering from place to place, unwelcome and unwanted. Cf. 29:21–28.

The third unit of this section (37:1–6) deals with the friend who turns into an enemy and then with the true friend who stands by you in adversity and so deserves to be treated generously. Longer poems on true and false friendship are found in 6:5–17 and 22:19–26.

In 37:1, there is a striking *᾽aleph* and labial alliteration: *kol ᾽ôhēb ᾽ômēr ᾽āhābtî, ᾽ak yēš ᾽ôhēb šēm ᾽ôhēb*. Note also the *ē* assonance in v 1b. The point is clear: many friends are friends only in name; hence, one needs to be cautious; cf. Prov 20:6. Otherwise, the keen observations of 37:2–4 will come true. For sentiments similar to those in 37:2, cf. 8:18–19; 22:19–26; 27:16–21. See the long NOTE on the corrupt text of 37:3a. In v 3, Ben Sira expresses the anguish of the person whose friend has become an enemy through betrayal or hypocrisy; cf. Pss 41:10; 55:13–15. Cf. NOTE on 37:4. The idea of looking "to your table" (37:4a) is developed from another perspective in 40:29ab. What is meant in 37:4 is the fair-weather friend who as a matter of fact is "harmful," and when trouble strikes "stands aloof" (cf. 2 Sam 18:13; Obad 11). For other incisive observations along the same line, cf. 6:8, 10–12. With regard to 37:5a, cf. 22:25. For the sibilant alliteration in 37:5b, cf. NOTE. The thought of holding "up your shield" (37:5b) derives from Ps 35:2. The true friend is one who will stand by your side in adversity when you are attacked by enemies (37:5). The injunction of 37:6 probably is to be taken figuratively, too; i.e., forget not your friend when he is in adversity and surrounded by enemies; and when your condition becomes prosperous again, be generous to him. Cf. 27:17. In the last two words of 37:6a, there is a clever reversal of the *b* and *r* in *ḥābēr*, "comrade," and *baqqĕrāb*, "during the battle."

The fourth poem (37:7–11) and the fifth (37:12–15) offer sound admonitions and observations about seeking counsel. One must be careful in choosing not only a wife (36:26–31) and friends (37:1–6) but also counselors, if one wishes to enjoy a serene and happy life. The first qualification of good advice is the disinterest and objectivity of the person who offers it (37:7–11). It is not easy to find a person who will counsel you with no self-interest in mind. Yet one should do nothing major without first seeking advice, as Ben Sira urges in 32:19. Nonetheless, one must beware, for "nothing is given so profusely as advice" (François, Duc de La Rochefoucauld [1613–80], *Reflections,* 110); or as Ambrose Bierce writes in *The Devil's Dictionary* (1906): *"Advice, n. the smallest current coin."* Among the worst counselors is the person who suggets a course of action that will profit not you but himself (37:7–8). Another one to avoid is the jealous person who reinforces your current determination only because it will lead to your downfall, in which he will take great pleasure (37:9). See the lengthy NOTE on the phrase "your father-in-law" (37:10a). In 37:10–11, Ben Sira lists the people to avoid when seeking advice. One's father-in-law heads the list. The reason is not stated, unless perhaps he is the "one who is envious of you" (37:10b), in the sense that you are not good enough for his daughter. The "rival" in 37:11a (cf. NOTE) is a woman a man intends to marry as a second wife, or a woman who is already a man's second wife; cf. 26:6 with COMMENT. The jealousy and conflict that could arise between a wife and her rival in a polygamous marriage is dramatized in 1 Sam 1:2–7; cf. also Gen 30:1. When writing 37:11b (cf. NOTE), Ben Sira may have had in mind Deut 20:8, which allows the cowardly soldier to return home "lest he make his fellows as fainthearted as himself." Cf. also Judg 7:3. One should not consult the merchant and the buyer (37:11cd) because of their obvious interest in the result of any possible transactions; cf. Prov 20:14. Asking a miser for advice about generosity (37:11e) would be even more senseless; cf. 14:5–10. The individuals in 37:11f–i, "a cruel person," "an indifferent worker," "this year's hired person," and "an idle slave," are all unfit counselors because of their defects of character and their unconcern or inexperience regarding "physical fitness" (lit., the good of the flesh), "his work," "next year's sowing," and "a great task," respectively. Cf. A. Vaccari, "Ecclesiastico 37,10.11: critica ed esegesi," *EstEcl* 34 (1960): 705–13.

In the final poem (37:12–15) of this section, Ben Sira describes the kind of person who would give good counsel. One should "associate with a religious person" (37:12a; cf. the long NOTE), because he "keeps to God's directives" (lit., the Commandment; cf. NOTE); cf. 10:19–20, 22, 24. The counselor, "who is like-minded with yourself" "will feel for you if you fall" (37:12cd; cf. NOTE) because like a true friend he is your other self; cf. 37:2b. You should also "heed your own heart's counsel" (37:13a; cf. NOTE), because as one who fears the Lord you will be wise and prudent; cf. 1:11–30 and 6:32–37. Your "conscience" (37:14a, lit., heart) can give better advice with regard to your "situation" "than seven watchers on a pinnacle of rock" (37:14b)—an allusion to astrologers, to whom the Jews of Ben Sira's day apparently would go for consultation (so Smend, p. 332). The number seven in a context like this means "many," as in Prov 26:16, 25; Jer 15:9. Above all, "pray to God to steady your steps [cf. NOTE] in the true path" (37:15, lit., in truth); cf. Prov 16:9. Prayer is essential if one is to be enlightened to follow the best course. On the need for prayer in other situations, cf. 38:9; Isa 38:2–3. In 37:12–15, there is an ascending order of importance in the counselors one should consult: "the religious person" (v 12), your own heart and conscience (vv 13–14), and God (v 15).

44. Wisdom and Temperance
(37:16–31)

37   ¹⁶ A word is the source of every deed;   D
         a thought, of every act.
¹⁷ The root of all conduct is the mind;
¹⁸   four branches it shoots forth:
     Good and evil, death and life,
         with the tongue as their absolute mistress.
¹⁹ A person may be wise and benefit many,
         yet appear to himself to be foolish.
²⁰ Though one may be wise, if his speech is rejected,
         he will be deprived of all enjoyment.
²² When one is wise to his own advantage,
         the fruits of his knowledge are seen in his own
                                     person;
²³ When one is wise to his people's advantage,
         the fruits of his knowledge are lasting.
²⁵ (Limited are the days of one's life,
         but the life of Israel is days without number.)
²⁴ One wise for himself has full enjoyment,
         and all who see him praise him;
²⁶ One wise for his people wins a heritage of glory,
         and his name lives on and on.

²⁷ My son, while you are well, govern your appetite: B
         see that you allow it not what is bad for you;
²⁸ Not every food is good for everyone,
         nor do all dishes appeal to every taste.
²⁹ Go not to excess with any enjoyment,
         neither become a glutton for choice foods,
³⁰ For sickness alights on overeating,
         and gluttony drives the system to revolt.

31 Through lack of self-control many have died,
but the abstemious person prolongs his life.

Notes

37　16b. Omit *hî* with MS B's margin, which otherwise=MS B for v 16.

18c. *mistress=(û)môšelet* with MS B's text and G (Syr similarly); B^mg and MS D have *ûměšalleaḥ.*

19–26. The verse numbers are those of G; the order followed here is that of MS D. V 21 appears only in G; its 21b relates to an already corrupt G form of 20 b (with *sophias* for *tryphēs*), and 21a is a gloss on 20a in the pejorative form (with *sophizomenos*) given it in G. V 23 appears in MS B only in the margin, so that its order of verses is 19, 20, 22, [23], 25, 24, [26]; from 25b on, it is defective at the bottom of a page. In MS C are present vv 19, 22, 24, 26, on a page that contains 20:7 before, and 20:13 after them; the anthological character of MS C lends itself to this juxtaposition of verses about the wise. Syr lacks v 25; Segal sees the omission as based on odium for Israel. He also regards the verse as a gloss, which he compares to 17:17, another instance of specific reference to Israel in a quite generalized context. This may be true in both cases, but the verses are firmly fixed in the Gr tradition. In the present instance (v 25), the continuity of the surrounding verses is broken whether one follows the order of G or that of MSS D and B; and in the Heb the form of the verse is unstable, with text and margins of the two witnesses showing little agreement among them. As Segal says, v 25 is really an expansion on v 31 to clarify its implications; for this reason it has been put in parentheses in the translation.

20b. With Smend and Peters, the *ma'ăkal* before *ta'ănûg* in MSS D, B is rather a corrupt dittograph of the preceding *mikkol* than a reflection of the inner-Greek corruption of *tryphēs* (cf. v 24) to *trophēs.* Segal refers to Job 33:20 (*ma'ăkal ta'ăwâ*) and keeps the doublet.

22b. *in his own person*=Heb (MSS D, B) *'al gěwîyātô;* for this, Ziegler restores *epi sōmatos* as the Gr equivalent: the MSS have *epi stomatos.*

23b. *are lasting,* for G's *pistoi,* is the approximate sense called for by the context. In fact, however, the only thing to which this reading relates directly is a Gr reading *pistin* in 26a, where the Heb is *kābôd,* "glory," and where Smend and Ziegler read for the Gr rather *timēn,* the equivalent for *kābôd* in 3:11; 45:12. The Heb of both MSS D and B in the present place is *bgwytm,* a corrupt variant on the *'l gwytw* of 22b. In Syr one cannot be sure whether its 22b or 23b holds the intended equivalent for this place, and neither points to a Heb reading that would fill the gap. If *ne'ěmān,* "dependable, constant," underlies *pistoi,* it matches poorly with the image in *pěrî,* "fruits," to convey the notion of *lasting,* unless one thinks of the *fruits* as continually growing anew.

26. For 26a, compare Prov 3:35. *lives on and on,* for G's *zēsetai eis ton aiōna.* The only Heb we have for this is MS D's *(ûšěmô) 'ōmēd běḥayyê 'ōlām,* with the first and

last words of the colon preserved also in MS C. Syr *(wašĕmeh) qayyām lĕḥayyê dalĕʿālam* appears very close to this, but is in fact speaking of eternal life. That the sense of the original was different can be gathered from 39:9–11; 41:11–13; 44:12–15.

27b. *for you:* literally, "for it," the appetite.

29. *Go not to excess with=ʾal tāzîd ʾel,* with MS D; MS B *ʾl tzrʿ l-, tzr* for *tzd* and *ʾl* for *ʾl. become a glutton=tĕšuppak,* "lose control," cf. Ps 73:2, loss of balance and footing (figurative). In 29b omit *kol* with MS D, G, and Syr.

30. *overeating=bĕrōb ʾōkel* with MS D; MS B *bĕrōb taʿănûg. alights on,* lit., "nests on"; cf. Zechariah's image of the flying scroll (Zech 5:1–4). *gluttony=G's aplēstia;* for MS B's *wĕhammarbeh* or the *wĕhammēzîaʿ* of MSS D, B^mg, perhaps with Segal read *wĕhammēzîd;* compare 29a.

Comment

This section contains two poems: on wisdom (37:16–20, 22–26), and on temperance (37:27–31) or practical wisdom applied to eating and drinking.

The first poem opens with some perceptive remarks on speech and thought (37:16–18). In 37:16, it is interesting to observe how Ben Sira places in synonymous parallelism "word" and "thought," which are the sources "of every deed" and "act," for as he explains, "the root of all conduct is the mind" (37:17). The mind produces "four branches," which are given in an *a:b::b':a'* chiastic order: *good:evil::death:life;* "their absolute mistress" [cf. NOTE] is the tongue (37:18). The tongue of the wise brings forth good, which leads to life; the tongue of the fool, evil, which leads to death. Cf. 27:6; 33:14; and Prov 18:21. For the Deuteronomic connection between doing good and achieving a long life, and between doing evil and dying prematurely, cf. Deut 30:15–20; Sir 15:15–17.

The remainder of the poem is concerned with the diverse types of wise people, not all of whom are of service to others (37:19–26; cf. NOTE regarding the order of verses). The point of 37:19 seems to be that a person may be judged wise because he benefits many, but in his own eyes he appears to be foolish because he cannot manage his own affairs. Another may be wise but not wise enough; hence, "his speech is rejected," perhaps because of his imprudent manner of speaking, and he is "deprived of all enjoyment" (37:20; cf. NOTE); cf. 20:20; 21:16–17. V 21, found only in G (cf. NOTE) and Lat, may be an attempt to interpret v 20; it reads: "For grace has not been given to him from the Lord, because he is deprived of all wisdom." One who is truly wise shows "the fruits of his knowledge . . . in his own person" (37:22); i.e., he enjoys even material benefits from his wisdom. The real sage is wise for himself first before being wise for others; cf. 37:19. Cf. also Prov 12:14; 13:12; 18:20. Such a person is also "wise to his people's advantage," with the result that "the fruits of his knowledge are lasting" (37:23; cf. NOTE); i.e., the community experiences long-term benefits from his wisdom, and because of this he achieves enduring fame; cf. v 26; 39:9–11; Prov 3:35. Regarding the fruits of wisdom, cf. Prov 8:19. V 25 seems out of place (cf. NOTE on 37:19–26); its content is rephrased, in another context, in 44:13–14. The idea that *Israel* (so MS B; MS D reads *yĕšŭrûn*, lit., upright one, a poetic name for the nation in Deut 32:15; 33:5, 26; Isa 44:2) is immortal can be seen also in 2 Macc 14:15. For the thought of 37:24, cf. Job 29:11. Note that vv 22–23 are developed further in vv 24, 26, and that these four verses prepare the reader for the lengthy poem in praise of the professional wise person or scribe in 39:1–11. The wise person who employs his wisdom in the service of the community will enjoy an immortal memory (37:26; cf. NOTE); cf. 39:9–11; 41:11–13; 44:13–15; Ps 112:6, 9. Contrast this sentiment with the perhaps more realistic assessment of Qoheleth (Qoh 2:16).

The next poem (37:27–31) offers hygienic reasons for practicing moderation, esp. in eating. Overindulgence is to be avoided, says Ben Sira, simply because it is not good for your health, whereas self-control at table prolongs life and well-being; cf. 31:19–31; Prov 25:16. The poem serves as a transition to the next section (38:1–15), which is devoted to the physician.

The point of 37:27 is clear: be moderate at table while you are still feeling well; if you overeat, it's too late. Cf. 36:23 for a variation on the theme in 37:28; cf. also 1 Cor 6:12; 10:23. Ben Sira excoriates the vice of gluttony in 37:29–30 (cf. NOTES) by alluding to the episode in Num 11:18–20 in which the greedy Israelites complain in the hearing of Yahweh that they have no meat for food. As punishment for their grumbling Yahweh says he will give them so much meat to eat that it will come out of their nostrils and become loathsome to them; i.e., they will become nauseated and vomit. Nausea, vomiting, and diarrhea (or perhaps even dysentery, so Smend, p. 338) are the results of gluttony (37:30); cf. 31:20. "Intemperance is the physician's provider" (Publilius Syrus, *Moral Sayings* [first century B.C.], 483). In 37:31a, "(through lack of) self-control" renders Heb *(bĕlōʾ) mûsār*, lit., "(through no) discipline"; cf. 31:17a. The one who lacks *mûsār* is a fool; cf. Prov 1:7; 5:12–14; 15:5. The habit of intemperance can lead to an early death (cf. Prov 5:23), whereas moderation at table, like other manifestations of wisdom, prolongs life (37:31). "The glutton digs his grave with his teeth" (English proverb). "Nothing in the world is so incontinent as a man's accursed appetite" (Homer, *Odyssey* [ninth century B.C.], 7).

45. Sickness and Death
(38:1–23)

38   ¹ Make friends with the physician, for he is essential to   B
    you;
    him also God has established in his profession.
  ² From God the doctor has his wisdom,
    and from the king he receives his sustenance.
  ³ Knowledge makes the doctor distinguished,
    and gives him access to those in authority.
  ⁴ God makes the earth yield healing herbs,
    which the prudent should not neglect.
  ⁵ Was not the water sweetened by a twig
    that people might learn his power?
  ⁶ He endows humans with the knowledge
    to glory in his mighty works,
  ⁷ Through which the doctor eases pain
  ⁸   and the druggist prepares his medicines;
  Thus God's creative work continues without cease
    in its efficacy on the surface of the earth.

  ⁹ My son, when you are ill, delay not,
    but pray to God, for it is he who heals.
  ¹⁰ Flee wickedness; purify your hands,
    cleanse your heart of every sin.
  ¹¹ Offer your sweet-smelling oblation and memorial,
    a generous offering according to your means.
  ¹² Then give the doctor his place
    lest he leave; for you need him too.
  ¹³ There are times that give him an advantage,
  ¹⁴   and he too beseeches God
  That his diagnosis may be correct
    and his treatment bring about a cure.

15 Whoever is a sinner toward his Maker
   will be defiant toward the doctor.

16 My son, shed tears for one who is dead
   with wailing and bitter lament;
   As is only proper, prepare the body,
   do not absent yourself from his burial:
17 Weeping bitterly, mourning fully,
   pay your tribute of sorrow, as he deserves,
   A day, two days, to prevent gossip;
   then compose yourself because of what grief can do—
18 For grief can bring on an extremity
   and heartache destroy one's health.
19 In affliction, grief persists;   G
   the curse that rankles makes for a wretched life.
20 Set your heart on him no longer;   B
   cease to recall him; think rather of the end.
21 Recall him not, there is no hope of his return;
   no good can it do, but it will do you harm.
22 Remember that his fate will also be yours;
   for him it was yesterday, for you today.
23 With the dead at rest, let memory cease;
   rally your courage once the soul has left.

Notes

38 1–23. After v 1a (MSS D, B) the Heb is witnessed only by MS B and by sparse reflections of vv 1, 4 in Talmud and Midrash.

1. Reading *rĕʿēh rôpēʾ lĕpî ṣorkô / kî gam ʾōtô ḥālaq ʾēl. lĕpî* is from MS D; *kî* is MS B^mg and was lost from the text after *-kw* of the preceding *ṣrkw. him also:* this phrase fits 38:1–15 within the framework of 37:16–26 and 38:24–39:11, which treat of the more traditional type of Heb wisdom; Ben Sira singles out the practice of medicine for that high place in religious and civic affairs alike which doctors came to occupy among both Jews and Christians in the Near East in the centuries that were to follow: Sergius of Reshaina, the Bokhtishos, Ḥunayn ibn Isḥaq, Maimonides, Bar-Hebraeus. . . .

6. *his mighty works:* pl. with G and Syr; MS B, "his might." In 7a, *through which*

goes back to *healing herbs* of v 4, a manifestation (5b) of God's *power.* For *gĕbûrātô, his might,* cf. 43:15 (with M).

8. *on the surface of the earth:* both G and Syr suppose an expression of this kind, while MS B has *mibbĕnê ʾādām;* B^mg reads *mibbĕnê mippĕnê* (!) and then *ʾarṣô* for *ʾādām.* Segal suggests (construed after *lĕmaʿan lōʾ yišbōt* in 8b) *mēʾal pĕnê hāʾădāmâ.* 10a, 11a, 12ab are damaged in MS B.

10. In 10a, MS B's text is much debased. Restoring the first two words as does Segal, the colon reads: *sûr mimmaʿal wĕhakkēr pānîm.* G, Syr, and MS B^mg all suppose *hāsēr* for the first word; after it G (cf. 10:7) reads *maʿal.* For the following clause, it would seem on the surface that G's *kai euthynon cheiras* should equal *wĕhākēn kappāyim;* compare 37:15, and so Segal. In fact, however, 51:20a as preserved in 11QPs^a (*kappay hăbērôtî ʾēlêhā*) shows two things: first, that Segal is right in restoring *wĕhābēr kappāyim* in the present place with MS B^mg; and second, that the Greek *euthynon* is being used here as an approximation for *hābēr.* In 51:20a, G with *kateuthyna* makes the same equivalence while substituting *psychēn* for *kappay:* see the NOTE there, and *HTR* 64 (1971): 388, 395. For related passages in MT, Segal points to Jer 4:11; Job 9:30; Ps 24:4; Gen 20:5; for further Qumran references, see with 51:20 below. In 10b, *every sin* should, with G, read *pešaʿ* in the singular, vs. MS B. The bicolon as a whole should then read: *hāsēr maʿal wĕhābēr kappāyim / ûmikkol pešaʿ ṭahēr lēb;* note the alliteration and assonance of the three imperatives, a feature of Ben Sira's style seen already in 36:6. *purify your hands* is partly figurative of the proper moral dispositions for offering sacrifice (v 11); compare Ps 26:6.

11. *memorial:* Heb *ʾazkārâ,* as in 45:16. *generous:* Heb *dešen,* the fat of animal sacrifices, also used here in a partly figurative sense. *Offer your sweet-smelling oblation* is supplied from G (MS B is defective). In 11b, MS B again has a garbled text, *bĕkanpê hônêkā* for *kĕpî hônekā;* cf, G.

16d. *his burial:* with G, Syr; MS B *bigĕwîʿātām* with faulty plural suffix (also B^mg, *bigĕwîʿām).*

17. *weeping=bĕkî,* with MS B^mg and G; MS B^txt *bĕnî,* cf. v 16. *to prevent gossip=baʿăbûr dibbat ʿām,* cf. G and 51:2; MS B *baʿăbûr dimʿâ,* a nonsense. *because of what grief can do: baʿăbûr dāwôn,* cf. v 18; MS B *baʿăbûr ʿāwôn,* another nonsense. For the incapacity of MSS A, B to deal with *dāwôn,* see NOTE at 37:2.

18. *For=*G, Syr; MS B lacks the corresponding *kî. destroy one's health:* reading, with Segal, *yaknîaʿ ʿoṣmâ,* cf. G *kampsei ischyn,* for MS B's *ybnh ṣbh.*

19. Both G and Syr suppose here a bicolon not preserved in MS B; in G its text is poorly transmitted; see Ziegler. Syr is more wordy—"For thus the sad heart, rather than death, breaks the poor with cares and brings on grief; because the life of the poor becomes the heart's curse"—but hardly more helpful. The translation given for the verse is subject to grave doubts.

20a. *Set . . . no longer: ʾal tāšēt* with MS B^mg; MS B^txt *ʾal tāšēb.*

21, 22. MS B transposes these two verses.

21a. *no hope of his return:* includes the Gr elaboration (*ou gar estin epanodos*) of the Heb *ʾēn lô tiqwâ,* "there is nothing for him to expect." The Gr reference is to a coming up from Sheol—compare Wis 2:1, 5.

23a. With MS B^mg, *kišĕbōt mēt yišbōt zikrô;* MS B^txt has *mušbat mēt, wĕšābat zikrô.* Note the play on two different connotations of *šbt.*

Comment

This section contains two poems: a two-stanza poem on the physician and his healing art (38:1–15); and one on mourning for the dead (38:16–23). It is interesting that Ben Sira places this section right after the one that deals with temperance and the evils attendant upon intemperance as if to imply that even though one observes moderation at table, one still cannot avoid all sickness. Cf. Matt 9:12.

In composing the poem on the physician and his healing ability, Ben Sira probably had in mind those who on religious grounds refused or were reluctant to consult a physician in their illness. The poem may also be directed to those who were skeptical of doctors. "God heals, and the doctor takes the fees" (Benjamin Franklin, *Poor Richard's Almanack* [1732–57]). Cf. Luke 8:43–44. "A doctor is nothing more than a mental consolation" (Petronius Arbiter, *Satyricon* [first century of our era], xlii). "Cured yesterday of my disease, / I died last night of my physician" (Matthew Prior [1664–1721], *The Remedy Worse than the Disease*). "I observe the physician with the same diligence as he the disease" (John Donne, *Devotions* [1624], vi).

You are, says Ben Sira, to make friends with the physician and to respect the practice of medicine (cf. NOTE on 38:1), for if you are sick you will need him (38:1a). After all, "God has established [him] in his profession" (38:1b). Heb *ḥālaq,* here translated "has established," was taken to mean "has created" by G (*ektisen*) here and in 7:15b; 31:27d; 39:25a; 40:1a; and 44:2a. "The physician" renders Heb *rôpē',* lit., "healer," as in 10:10a. In Exod 15:26, Yahweh is called Israel's "healer" (cf. Sir 38:9b). In the poem here, however, the emphasis is on the healing "wisdom" the physician has received from God (38:2a); cf. 1:1 with COMMENT. The physician was a member of the royal court and so received "from the king . . . his sustenance" (38:2b). It is his medical "knowledge" (a gift from God), which "makes the doctor distinguished" (38:3a, lit., lifts up his head); hence, "he can stand before princes" (cf. 11:1), the lit. translation of 38:3b—another reference to physicians in the oriental courts of that day; cf. Gen 50:2. Instead of "princes," MS B^mg has "kings," a reading that would make the colon equal Prov 22:29b. Since it is God who "makes the earth yield healing herbs" (lit., medicines), "the prudent should not neglect" (or despise, reject) them (38:4), even when they may be unappealing; 38:4 corresponds to *Phibis,* xxxii 12, xxiv 2 (Sanders, p. 75). Gilead was noted for its healing balm; cf. Jer 8:22; 46:11. In 38:5, Ben Sira

alludes to the miracle of the sweetening of the water in Exod 15:23–25; he
implies that the "twig" (lit., tree or wood) had of itself, by God's design, the
ability to make the bitter water fresh. Thus, "people might learn [God's]
power" in creating such wood. The "mighty works" of God (38:6b; cf.
NOTE), in which one should glory are the "healing herbs" (of v 4a), which the
doctor prescribes to ease pain and the pharmacist uses to prepare "his medicines" (38:7–8a). The point of 38:8bc is that "God's creative work" (lit., his
work)—i.e., the "healing herbs" whose nature comes from the Lord—never
ceases to do what God has ordained for it. Thus in sickness one should not
despise or refuse these herbs but make use of them, since God created them
precisely for healing. In vv 6–8, Ben Sira encourages further study to discover
other plants and herbs with medicinal power: the God of nature has endowed
human beings with the ability to learn the mysteries of nature in order to
alleviate sickness and pain. Ancient Egyptian papyri list over five hundred
plants that could be used for medicinal purposes (so Spicq, p. 758).

The second stanza (38:9–15), which begins with the typical "My son,"
emphasizes the need for prayer and other religious exercises when one is ill.
In 38:9, the topic sentence of the stanza, there is an elegant labial (*b* and *p*)
and liquid (*l* and *r*) alliteration that highlights the importance of the thought:
běnî běhŏlî ʾal titʿabbēr, hitpallēl ʾel ʾēl kî hûʾ yirpā. The advice Ben Sira gives
here was ignored by the impious king Asa, who in his illness "did not seek
Yahweh, but only the physicians" (2 Chr 16:12). Thus, when one is sick, one
should pray as well as seek the help of physicians. The idea of God as healer
derives from Exod 15:26; cf. Job 5:18; Hos 6:1. For the alliteration and assonance of 38:10, cf. NOTE; the verse is an allusion to the Deuteronomic theory
of retribution according to which illness is viewed as a punishment for infidelity to the Law (cf. Deut 28:21–29; Prov 3:7–8). But note that this theory also
made allowance for probationary suffering to test the faithful Israelite; cf.
COMMENT on 2:1–6. Clean or pure hands (38:10a) symbolize righteousness
and freedom from sin; cf. Job 17:9; Isa 1:15–16. The injunction to "cleanse
your heart of every sin" (38:10b) alludes to Ps 51:3–4, 12. The "sweet-smelling oblation and memorial" in 38:11 (cf. NOTE) is a reference to Lev 2:1–3.
For the value of sacrifice joined with prayer (38:9, 11), cf. Ps 20:2–6. Righteousness and innocence (38:10) together with the offering of sacrifice (38:11)
are found also in 35:1–15. By the progression of thought in 38:10–11, Ben
Sira clearly implies that sacrifice without innocence or freedom from sin is
worthless; cf. Ps 51:18–19.

In 38:12, Ben Sira returns to the theme of the first stanza (38:1–8)—con-
sulting a physician when necessary. In sickness, one should pray, avoid all
evil, and offer sacrifice (38:9–11), yes; but one should have recourse to a
physician, for illness is a time that gives him "an advantage" because of his
medical knowledge and wisdom (38:2–3, 13); cf. Qoh 3:3. The doctor, aware
of his limitations, also prays to God that he may be correct in his diagnosis

and treatment of the patient (38:14). A remarkable *ô* and *ê/ē* assonance brings this poem to a close (38:15): *'ăšer ḥôtē' lipnê 'ōśēhû, yitgabbēr lipnê rôpē'*. The noun *rôpē'*, "doctor," in the first (38:1a) and last colon (38:15b), serves as an *inclusio,* another rhetorical device that signals the end of the poem; cf. 10:19–11:6, with COMMENT on 11:6. The point of 38:15 is clear: since the sinner does not revere his Maker, he "will be defiant [or arrogant; cf. Job 15:25; 36:9] toward the doctor" whose skills derive from God (38:2). This reading of 38:15b is from MS B. MS B^mg, G, and Syr read: "he will be delivered (G [most MSS]: may he fall; Syr: he will be given) into the hands of the doctor," a reading preferred by Smend (p. 342), Peters (p. 311), Box-Oesterley (p. 450), and Duesberg-Fransen (pp. 264–65). But this reading, which puts the doctor in an unfavorable light, hardly is in keeping with the tone of the rest of the poem.

For further study of this poem, cf. A. Sović, "Enkomij liječnicima u Svetom Pismu [Sir 38, 1–15]," *Bogoslovsia Smotra* 26 (1938): 165–79; H. Duesberg, "Le médecin, un sage (Ecclésiastique 38, 1–15)," *BVC* 38 (1961): 43–48; A. Stöger, "Der Arzt nach Jesus Sirach (38, 1–15)," *Arzt und Christ* 11 (1965): 3–11; P. C. Beentjes, "Jesus Sirach 38:1–15, Problemen rondom een symbool," *BTFT* 41 (1980): 260–65; and J. T. Nelis, "Sirach 38:15," *AOAT* 211 (1982): 173–84.

The next poem (38:16–23) is related to the preceding one, for sickness often is followed by death. The emphasis here is on proper burial and mourning for the dead; but sorrow must be not excessive (the wise do nothing in excess, as the Latin proverb has it: *ne quid nimis*) but moderate, lest it "do you harm" (38:21b).

The mourning rites Ben Sira prescribes—weeping, wailing, and lamenting bitterly (38:16ab)—are traditional. The Heb noun *qînâ* in 38:16b is the technical term to designate the ritual lamentation for the dead; cf. 2 Sam 1:17; Jer 7:29; 9:9, 19; Ezek 19:1; 26:17; 27:32; 32:16; Amos 5:1; 8:10. Weeping and wailing (38:16ab) were normal in lamentation; cf. Jer 9:16–19. At funerals there often were professional mourners (cf. Amos 5:16) whose loud cries were made to the accompaniment of flutes (cf. Matt 9:23). Respect for the dead included the obligation of an honorable burial (38:16cd; cf. NOTE); cf. Tob 1:17–18; 4:3–4; 6:15; 12:12; 14:12–13. The dead person, because he or she is your relative or friend, deserves to have you participate in the weeping and mourning rites (38:17ab; cf. NOTE). "A day, two days" (38:17c) is apparently a reference to the duration of the wailing and loud laments (38:16ab, 17ab) at the time of the funeral and burial, for the customary period of mourning (even for orthodox Jews today) was seven days, as in 22:12; Gen 50:10; and Jdt 16:24. If one did not take part in the public weeping and wailing for a day or two, one risked the possibility of gossip or criticism (cf. NOTE). Presumably the mourning for the remainder of the seven-day period was more subdued. After the initial day or two of intense mourning, you should "compose yourself because of what grief can do" (38:17d; cf. NOTE).

Ben Sira spells out the problems excessive grief can cause (38:18–21). Heb *ᵓāsôn* (38:18a), here rendered "extremity" (G: "death"), can also mean sudden death occasioned by accident or misfortune; cf. Gen 42:4; 44:29; Exod 21:22–23. Death can be contagious, as Duesberg-Fransen (p. 264) remark about 38:18a. "Heartache" can also "destroy one's health" (38:18b; cf. NOTE) —a keen observation. The text of 38:19 is uncertain and the translation doubtful (cf. NOTE). If this rendering be correct, the meaning would be: with health destroyed (38:18b) one would be "in affliction" and have reason to grieve further (38:19a); "the curse that rankles" (38:19b) is the death of a person's loved one, which causes him undue grief, i.e., "a wretched life." Because of the ill effects of uncontrollable mourning (38:18–19), Ben Sira urges the bereaved not to think about the deceased (38:20); the implication is: life must go on (cf. 30:21–23). "Think rather of the end" (38:20b), i.e., your own death; in that way you will make the most of the life you have left. Thinking about the deceased will not bring him back to life again (38:21a; cf. NOTE), and will not do you any good but only harm (38:21b); cf. 2 Sam 12:23; Job 7:9. Since death comes to all sooner or later (38:22; cf. also 14:12, 17), it is pointless to keep thinking about the dead; rather, one should put an end to mourning and go on living (38:23; cf. NOTE). Ben Sira perhaps is alluding to the conduct of David after learning of the death of his son born of his adulterous union with Bathsheba (2 Sam 12:19–24).

It is ironic that Patrick W. Skehan, my colleague and coauthor, suffered his fatal heart attack right after he completed the translation and notes of this section. See the Preface.

46. Vocations of the Skilled Worker and the Scribe (38:24–39:11)

I

38   24 The scribe's profession increases wisdom;   B
        whoever is free from toil can become wise.

      25 How can one become wise who guides the plow,
         who thrills in wielding the goad like a lance,
         Who guides the ox and urges on the bullock,
            and whose concern is for cattle?
      26 His determination is to plow furrows,
            and he is careful to fatten the livestock.

      27 So with every engraver and designer
            who, laboring night and day,
         Fashions carved seals,   G
            and whose concern is to vary the pattern.
         His determination is to produce a lifelike impression,
            and he is careful to finish the work.

      28 So with the smith sitting by the anvil,
            intent on the iron he forges.
         The flame of the fire sears his flesh,
            yet he toils away in the furnace heat.
         The clang of the hammer deafens his ears,
            His eyes are on the object he is shaping.
         His determination is to finish the work,
            and he is careful to perfect it in detail.

29 So with the potter sitting at his work,
   turning the wheel with his feet.
He is always concerned for his products,
   and turns them out in quantity.
30 With his hands he molds the clay,
   and with his feet softens it.
His determination is to complete the glazing,
   and he is careful to fire his kiln.

31 All these are skilled with their hands,
   each one an expert in his own work;
32 Without them no city could be lived in,
   and wherever they stay, they do not hunger.   S
But they are not sought out for the council of the   G
                                          people,
33   nor are they prominent in the assembly.
   They do not sit on the judge's bench,
      nor can they understand law and justice.
   They cannot expound the instruction of wisdom,
      nor are they found among the rulers.
34 Yet they are expert in the works of this world,   S
      and their concern is for the exercise of their skill.   G

How different the person who devotes himself to the
                                          fear of God
   and to the study of the Law of the Most High!

II

39   1 He studies the wisdom of all the ancients
      and occupies himself with the prophecies;
   2 He treasures the discourses of the famous,
      and goes to the heart of involved sayings;
   3 He studies the hidden meaning of proverbs,
      and is busied with the enigmas found in parables.

   4 He is in attendance on the great,
      and has entrance to the ruler.

He travels among the peoples of foreign lands
    to test what is good and evil among people.
5 His care is to rise early
    to seek the Lord, his Maker,
    to petition the Most High,
To open his lips in prayer,
    to ask pardon for his sins.

6 Then, if it pleases the Lord Almighty,
    he will be filled with the spirit of understanding;
He will pour forth his words of wisdom
    and in prayer give praise to the Lord.
7 He will direct his counsel and knowledge aright,
    as he meditates upon God's mysteries.
8 He will show the wisdom of what he has learned
    and glory in the Law of the Lord's covenant.

9 Many will praise his understanding;
    his fame can never be effaced;
Unfading will be his memory,
    through all generations his name will live.
10 The congregation will speak of his wisdom,   B
    and the assembly will declare his praises.
11 While he lives he is one out of a thousand,   G
    and when he dies he leaves a good name.

Notes

38   24a. *The scribe's profession:* lit., "the scribe's wisdom." After the verb, Syr adds *leh,* "for himself."

25a. *the plow:* Heb *malmād* is usually translated "oxgoad" in Judg 3:31, the only other occurrence of the word; the translation here follows G *arotrou* = Lat *aratrum,* "plow."

25b. *wielding the goad like a lance* = Heb *baḥănît mardēaʿ,* suggested by G *en dorati kentrou* (so Smend); MS B has *baḥănît mēhāʿîr,* "in wielding the lance" (cf. 2 Sam 23:8 and 1 Chr 11:11, 20).

26. The order of the cola is from G and Syr; MS B reverses the order.

26a. The last word is not fully legible in MS B; scholars commonly restore *bitĕlāmîm,* "furrows," on the basis of G *aulakas.*

26b. *to fatten the livestock,* lit., "to complete the fattening."

27b. The last word is illegible in MS B^{txt}; B^{mg} has *yinhāg* (=G *diagei*), which is translated here.

38:27c–39:15b. This section is missing from MS B; it is translated from G.

38:28a. *the anvil:* so G; Syr has "the furnace," a less likely reading since the furnace is mentioned in v 28d.

28b. *iron he forges:* lit., "the work(s) of iron."

28c. *flame:* so Syr; G *atmis,* "breath." *sears:* so Lat interprets G *tēxei* (lit., "melts").

28d. *toils away in:* lit., "contends with."

28e. *deafens*=Heb *yaḥărîš;* G *kainiei*=*yĕḥaddēš*="renews" (G misread the third consonant of the verb as *daleth* instead of *resh*—not an uncommon scribal error).

28f. *object he is shaping:* G may also be rendered "pattern (or model) of the object."

30d. *to fire*=Heb *lĕbā'ēr,* which means "to fire" and "to clean"; G *katharisai* mistakenly took the latter sense.

32b. Syr=Heb *ûba'ăšer yāgûrû lō' yir'ābû.* G, which makes no sense, reads, "and they neither sojourn nor walk around"; G *peripatēsousin* misread *yir'ābû* ("they hunger") as *ya'ăbōrû* ("they walk around")—an error that then led to the present corrupt text.

32c. This colon is found only in G MSS S^c L-672 and Syr. Cf. 21:17a.

33c. *law and justice*=Heb *ḥōq ûmišpāṭ,* the same phrase as in 45:17b, where both G and Syr have expressions similar to the ones here.

33d. *instruction of wisdom:* so Syr; G has "instruction and justice (or judgment)"— the final word is taken from v 33c, its proper place.

33e. *the rulers*=Heb *bĕmōšĕlîm,* which was misread by G as *bimĕšālîm*=*en parabolais,* "in parables." Cf. P. W. Skehan, *CBQ* 23 (1961): 40.

34b. *concern*=G *diēgēsis* (as in v 25d), suggested by Syr *rnyhwn,* "their thought"; the G MSS have *deēsis,* "prayer," which hardly suits the context. Perhaps, as Smend suggests, Syr and G (*deēsis*) are based on an original Heb *hāgût,* which means "meditation" as well as "thought, musing."

34c. *to the fear of God:* so Syr; G omits the phrase.

39 2b. *involved sayings:* G *parabolōn* (also in v 3b)=Heb *mĕšālîm; see* INTRODUCTION, PART IV, "LITERARY GENRES."

7b. *God's:* G *autou*="his," with the antecedent being God (cf. v 6d).

9b. *his fame:* lit., "his name," so Syr; G omits.

10ab. =44:15 (except for the change of number) from the Heb, from which the verse here is translated; v 10b also=31:11b.

11a. =Heb *'im ya'ămōd* [=G *ean emmeinē*] *'ĕḥād mē'elep* (cf. Qoh 7:28). Both G and Syr are corrupt.

11b. =*kai ean anapausētai* [from G] *onoma kataleipsei* [from G v 11a]. *a good name:* lit., "a name" (cf. v 9b).

Comment

The present section contains two poems: one on the vocation of the skilled worker (38:24–34), and the other on the vocation of the scribe (39:1–11). The first poem has exactly twenty-two lines (see COMMENT on 1:11–30 and 51:13–30) in three groups: (a) 1+3+3; (b) 4+4; (c) 6+1. Though the poem is concerned with the manual laborer, it opens (38:24) and closes (38:34cd) with a couplet extolling the life of the scribe, thus forming an *inclusio*. The final bicolon of the first poem (38:34cd) also serves as a lead into the second poem on the scribe, a poem with fifteeen lines: 3+4+4+4.

What we have in the present section is roughly analogous to an Egyptian work entitled "The Satire on the Trades" (*ANET*, pp. 432–34), written at the beginning of the Twelfth Dynasty (ca. 1991–1786 B.C.). The text is often called "The Instruction [or Maxims] of Duauf," but the author was apparently a person by the name of Khety, as A. H. Gardiner has pointed out in *Hieratic Papyri in the British Museum, Third Series, Chester Beatty Gift*, 1, 40, n. 1 (cited in *ANET*, p. 432). Though it was entitled an "instruction" or "teaching," this composition introduced into the Wisdom literature of antiquity the literary genre of satire.

Khety describes, with obvious relish and graphic detail, the wretchedness, tedium, and foul odors of the various Egyptian artisans. To extol the vocation and life of the scribe, he ridicules the sculptor and smith, the carpenter, the gem worker, the barber, the itinerant merchant, the mud-brick maker, the wall builder, the gardener, the tenant farmer, the weaver, the arrow maker, the courier, the embalmer, the cobbler, the laundryman, the bird catcher, and the fish catcher. The author concludes, "There is no profession free of a boss —except for the scribe: he is the boss." The scribe has the greatest office in the land; he loves writing more than his own mother. Khety concludes the work, which he addresses to his son, with these words: "Behold, I have set thee on the way of god. . . . [The scribe] reaches the halls of magistrates. . . . Behold, there is no scribe who lacks food, from the property of the House of the King—life, prosperity, health! . . . His father and mother praise god, he being set upon the way of the living."

The satire achieved such great notoriety that many copies were written during the New Kingdom (ca. 1552–1100 B.C.), especially during the Nineteenth Dynasty (1350–1200 B.C.). There are some parallels between this work and the present poems (see COMMENT below on 38:28). If Ben Sira was familiar with the satire, he not only removed from his own composition all traces of ridicule, but showed a positive appreciation for manual workers and their essential contributions to society (see 38:31–32ab, 34ab). Nonetheless, the vocation of the skilled worker is definitely inferior to that of the scribe (38:24, 34cd, and 39:1–11). One should not conclude that Ben Sira disdained all manual labor; his teaching in 7:15, 22 clearly indicates that the wise should also work with their hands. In fact, the later rabbis did just that. Saul of Tarsus, who had been a Pharisee and later became known as Paul, was a tentmaker (Acts 18:3); and he supported himself by practicing his trade even though he had the right to compensation from the Christian communities he served (1 Cor 9:3–15).

The first poem is divided into seven stanzas: introduction (38:24); the farmer (38:25–26); the seal maker (38:27); the smith (38:28); the potter (38:29–30); the products of skilled workers (38:31–34ab); concluding couplet (38:34cd). The end of four stanzas of the poem is clearly indicated by the use of the same phrases in the last bicolon of each stanza (38:26, 27ef, 28gh, 30cd): "His determination is to . . . , and he is careful to . . . ."

The introductory bicolon sets the tone of the whole section: the scribe can increase wisdom because, free from a life devoted primarily to physical labor, he himself has first become wise (38:24). For v 24a, G has "The wisdom of the scribe [is acquired] in the opportunity of leisure," thus emphasizing the necessity of free time in which one can study and reflect. In contrast, the farmer who wearies himself with the heavy work of plowing and caring for his livestock, and is content to do so, can hardly have the energy or disposition to study so as to become wise (38:25–26). In the Judaism of Ben Sira's time, the scribe (in Heb *sôpēr*) was a well-traveled, cultured, and pious Jew who was highly trained in the Sacred Scriptures, especially the Law; his principal responsibility was to instruct others in the glories of Israel's religious heritage and wisdom. In order to fulfill the demands of his vocation properly, the scribe needed adequate leisure, free from physical fatigue; hence the point of the present stanza.

The designer and engraver of seals, though his work is less strenuous than the farmer's, also lacks the leisure and talent to become wise (38:27). Yet the products his skilled hands manufactured were important for society; cf. 45:11 and Exod 28:11.

The work of the smith (38:28) seems to be the most difficult, since he must work in intense heat that "sears his flesh" and clanging noise that "deafens his ears" (see NOTE on v 28e). Obviously, at the end of a day at the anvil and furnace the smith would not be disposed to acquire the training necessary to become wise. Yet his work is necessary in everyday life. Compare this dignified description of the smith's labor with the unflattering words of "The Satire on the Trades": "I have seen the metalworker at his work at the mouth of his furnace. His fingers were somewhat like crocodiles [note: they were tough and wrinkled]; he stank more than fish-roe" (*ANET,* pp. 432–33). For some of the imagery in our poem, cf. Ezek 22:18–22.

The work of the potter (38:29–30) is perhaps the most obviously significant, for his products—drinking cups, dinner plates, storage vessels, cooking pots, and the like—were used in daily life. As often even today, the potter turns "the wheel with his feet" (v 30b); cf. Jer 18:3. The reason the potter turns out his products "in quantity" (v 29d) is clear: being fragile, they break easily; and so they must be replaced. It is thanks to this fragility that pottery fragments are found so plentifully in archaeological excavations and surface explorations. As regards the potter's feet softening the clay (v 30b), cf. Isa 41:25.

In the sixth stanza on skilled workers (38:31–34ab), Ben Sira speaks of their abilities and the essential contributions they make to the community: "Without them no city could be lived in" (v 32a). Nevertheless, he emphasizes the inability of these people to serve in positions of responsibility in the public domain (vv 32c–33). The reason why artisans "do not hunger" "wherever they stay" (v 32b) is that they readily find work to support themselves and their families. But they are not in demand "for the council of the people, nor are they prominent in the assembly" (vv 32c–33a). The reason is simple: they are not trained for civic or religious leadership in general. In particular, they are not to be found "on the judge's bench," for they cannot "understand law and justice" (v 33bc). And since they are not trained in wisdom, they are not "found among the rulers" (v 33de; see NOTE). "Yet they are expert in the works [=Syr *'ăbîdātā',* which can also mean "business" or "occupations"] of this world" [lit., of the world] (v 34ab). Hence they perform an important function in society. It is noteworthy that Ben Sira accords a place of honor to the artisan that he denies to the merchant, who "can hardly remain without fault" (26:29), for, as he explains, "between buying and selling sin is wedged in" (27:2).

The ideal scribe, who was introduced in the opening bicolon (38:24) of the poem on skilled workers, is now described in this final stanza: he is "the person who devotes himself to the fear of God [see NOTE] and to the study of the Law of the Most High" (38:34cd). The ideal scribe Ezra is depicted in similar fashion: "He was a scribe, well-versed in the law of Moses which was given by the LORD, the God of Israel. . . . Ezra had set his heart on the study and practice of the law of the LORD and on teaching statutes and ordinances in Israel" (Ezra 7:6, 10). Fear of the Lord and devotion to the Law are indispensable; without them the scribe can in no way be considered wise. The second poem (39:1–11) now describes in detail the noble life of the scribe. A major responsibility of the scribe is the study of the rest of the OT— the Wisdom books and the Prophets (39:1). Only then will the scribe pursue other learning and public service and travel in order to gain experience (39:2–4).

The contrasts between the artisans of 38:25–34ab and the ideal scribe of 38:34cd–39:11 are now seen as dramatic. Instead of the artisan's narrow determination on a single product or activity (38:26, 27ef, 28gh, 30cd), the scribe studies and occupies himself with a wide range of subjects (39:1–3). Artisans are not to be found in "the council of the people, nor are they prominent in the assembly" (38:32c–33a) or "found among the rulers" (38:33e; see NOTE); the scribe, because he has traveled widely (39:4cd) and devoted himself to the pursuit of wisdom (39:1–3, 6–8) "is in attendance on the great, and has entrance to the ruler" (39:4ab). Artisans cannot "understand law and justice" or "expound the instruction of wisdom" (38:33cd); the scribe, thanks to his diligent studies (39:1–3) and the Lord's gift of understanding (39:6ab), "will pour forth his words of wisdom and . . . direct his counsel and knowledge aright" (39:6c, 7a).

Ben Sira alludes to the threefold division of the OT in a manner similar to that of his grandson's Prologue: "the Law of the Most High" (38:34d), "the wisdom of the ancients" (39:1a), and "the prophecies" (39:1b). It is interesting that the order of the material here—Law, Wisdom books, Prophets—is the same as in the LXX and Latin Bibles; the order found in the grandson's Prologue—Law, Prophets, rest of the books (=chiefly Wisdom books)—is the same as that in the MT MSS.

In addition to his study of the OT, the scribe becomes particularly adept in the Wisdom lore not only of his own tradition, but also of other cultures (39:2–3); cf. Prov. 1:2, 6 and Wis 8:8. See INTRODUCTION, Part VII. Because of his vast learning and wide experience he is called to serve at the court of the ruler (39:4ab); cf. Dan 1:3–4, 17–21; 2:49; 3:30 (97); 5:29–30. The scribe also travels to "foreign lands" to see how other peoples live (39:4cd); the subject of his own travels Ben Sira discusses in 34:9–13.

But personal diligence and perseverance in study are not sufficient to make the scribe truly wise; prayer must be the first priority of his daily routine (39:5). The scribe at prayer will also "ask pardon for his sins" (39:5e) because these are the principal obstacles to wisdom (cf. Wis 1:4–6; Ps 51:8–9). See INTRODUCTION, Part X, 1. Ben Sira acknowledges once again that all wisdom comes from God alone, who created her (39:6ab); cf. 1:1, 6, 8–10; 33:17; 1 Kgs 3:9. With the divine gift of understanding in his purified mind (cf. Isa 11:2), the scribe is now able to engage in a threefold activity: (1) he will compose his own literary works of wisdom (39:6c), which include prayers of praise (39:6d), just as Ben Sira himself has done (cf. 39:12–35 and 50:27); (2) he will have some clear perception of God's mysteries upon which he meditates (39:7; cf. 1:2–4, 6, 8–10); and (3) he will teach others how to acquire wisdom and to glory in the Law as he does (39:8; cf. 42:2a).

Because of what in his wisdom the scribe has done for the community, many will praise him, and he will enjoy a blessed and unfading memory and lasting fame (39:9). To be remembered after death and to have an enduring name or reputation was crucial in the OT period; cf., for example, 37:26; 41:11–13; 44:14; 45:1; 46:11d; 49:1. As in 41:11–13, Ben Sira uses the word "name" three times in the final verses of the poem, in order to emphasize its significance: 39:9b (see NOTE), 9d, and 11b (see NOTE). Prov 10:7: "The memory of the just will be blessed, but the name of the wicked will rot." "The congregation" (39:10a; see NOTE: G has "the nations") acknowledges his wisdom, and "the assembly" of the elders of the people (cf. 1 Macc 12:35) declares his praises. Thus the scribe receives public recognition for his contribution to the community. The scribe is indeed "one out of a thousand" (39:11a; see NOTE), and after death his reputation is assured (39:11b; see NOTE).

For further study of this poem, cf. J. Marböck, "Sir. 38, 24–39, 11: Der schriftgelehrte Weise. Ein Beitrag zu Gestalt und Werk Ben Siras," in *La Sagesse de l'Ancien Testament,* ed. M. Gilbert (BETL 51): 293–316.

47. Praise of God the Creator
(39:12–35)

39   12 Once more I will set forth my theme   G
         to shine like the moon in its fullness!
      13 Listen, my faithful children: open up your petals
         like roses planted near running waters;
      14 Send up the sweet odor of incense,
         break forth in blossoms like the lily.
       Raise your voices in a chorus of praise;
         bless the Lord for all his works!
      15 Proclaim the greatness of his name,
         give thanks and sing his praises,
       With music on the lyre and all stringed instruments;   B
         sing out with joy as you proclaim:

      16 The works of God are all of them good;
         for every need in its own time he provides.
      17 With a word he makes the waters stand forth as though
                                              in a waterskin;
         his merest utterance makes his storehouse ready.
      18 He has but to command and his will is in effect;
         nothing can limit his achievement.
      19 The works of all humankind are present to him;
         nothing is hidden from his eyes.
      20 His gaze spans all the ages:
         is there any counting what he achieves?
       To him, nothing is small or insignificant,
         and nothing resists or surprises him.
      21 No cause then to say: What is the purpose of this?
         Everything is chosen to satisfy a need.

      22 His blessing overflows like the Nile;
         like the Euphrates it enriches the surface of the earth.

23 Again, his wrath expels the nations,
    and turns fertile land into a salt marsh.
24 For the virtuous his paths are level,
    to the haughty they are clogged with stones;
25 Good things for the good he provided from the
                                    beginning,
    but for the wicked, good things and bad.
26 Chief of all needs for human life
    are water and fire, iron and salt,
  The heart of the wheat, milk and honey,
    the blood of the grape, and oil, and cloth;
27 For the good all these are good,
    but for the wicked they turn out evil.

28 There are storm winds designed to punish,   G
    which in their fury can dislodge mountains;
  When destruction must be, they hurl their force
    and appease the anger of their Maker.
29 Fire and hail, famine, disease: B
    these too were created for punishment;
30 Ravenous beasts, scorpions, vipers,
    and the avenging sword to exterminate the wicked: G
  All these were created to meet a need   B
    and are kept in his storehouse for the proper time;
31 When he commands them, they rejoice,
    and in their assignments they do not disobey his
                                    bidding.

32 This is why from the first I took my stand,
    and wrote down as my theme:
33 The works of God are all of them good;
    for every need in its own time he provides.
34 No cause then to say: This is not as good as that—
    each shows its worth at the proper time.
35 Now with full heart and voice proclaim
    and bless his holy name!

Notes

39   12–15b. This is the last portion of the book for which the relevant page of MS B is not extant.

13a. *my faithful children:* G has *huioi hosioi,* but this form of address is more than the Heb line would carry. Lat, with *divini fructus* for this (the *fructus* is because of the floral imagery in vv 13–14) understands G to mean God's *children.* But the obvious equivalent for *hosioi* in such a phrasing, Heb *ḥăsîdîm,* is nowhere used by Ben Sira: it occurs only in the borrowing from Ps 148:14 that ends the liturgical litany appended to Sir 51:12 in MS B. Syr has *zaddîqē* to match *hosioi;* and in v 24, both versions use these same terms to render *tammîm* (so MS B), "the virtuous," on its only attested occurrence in the book. It is to be supposed *faithful* implies a relationship to God. Lat, before *Listen,* contrives to introduce *In voce dicit,* which makes God the speaker for at least 13a–14b. This, however, is very contorted, and influenced by a misunderstanding of v 12b, where G for "mid-month" has become Lat *in furore,* suggesting a mantic state and God speaking through Ben Sira. Since *tammîm* is quite unlikely as a form of direct address, the sense of G is here retained, as what remains from an unknown original.

14a. *incense:* in G, *libanos,* which occurs again in 50:8c, 9a, 12d: the first and the third times = *lĕbānôn,* the mountain, but in 9a = *lĕbônâ,* frankincense. A similar collocation in 24:13a, 15d (*Lebanon, incense*) makes the choice difficult; but the reference here to the *odor* would seem to decide the matter. Syr, which has "like the odor of Lebanon with its cedars" is then the version that is in error (cf. 24:16a, where Syr is spectacularly wrong, introducing *rhodadaphnē,* the oleander, in a typical description of a wide-branching tree identified by G as the *terebinth*).

16b. *for: l(kl)* with MS B^mg, as in v 33b.

17. Before this bicolon, G has another that is a variant form of v 21. In the same place, Syr introduces variant forms of vv 21, 34; MS B has that combination at v 21, where Syr lacks it. The earlier insert belongs only at v 21, with G and MS B; the later one only at v 34, with G, Syr, and MS B. For the Heb of v 17, read *bidĕbārô yaʿămîd kannōʾd māyim / ûmôṣāʾ pîw ʾōṣārô.* In 17a, MS B's damaged text preserves only *(y)ʿryk,* corrupt for *yaʿămîd k-;* compare G, though it read *qal* ("the waters stood") and not *hiphʿil.* Syr misread *môṣāʾ* to mean "sunrise" and emerged with "At his word the sun rises, and at his word it sets." V 17b in MS B is as given above; *ʾōṣārôt* (Strack, Vattioni) is a false reading, and *ûbĕmôṣāʾ* (Smend's reconstruction) begins with too many labial sounds, and the ellipsis was to be expected. The verb needed for 17b is the *yaʿămîd* that carries over from 17a. Ben Sira uses such forms of *ʿmd,* cf. 12:12 and 40:19, and the basic sense for the *qal,* "to stand forth, assume/maintain a station/ function," is frequent with him. The real crux is with *waterskin* in 17a, for which the reminiscence of the Exodus implicit in a reading *nēd,* "mound, heap" (Exod 15:8), goes back to G of this passage. The alternative *nōʾd* has, however, a life of its own; and

along with the present place, *kannō'd* (or *kannôd* with loss of the unspoken *aleph*) belongs also in Ben Sira's source, Ps 33:7, where it is attested by G (*askon*), Syr, Targ. Literally, of course, a skin container for water is meant; *waterskin* is as close as modern Western experience will permit for a rendering.

18a. *He has but to command* = G *en prostagmati autou;* compare perhaps *běṣawwôtô* of MS B, v 31a. Syr of 18a looks to v 31 for its borrowed paraphrase; its *lěpuqdāneh,* "his command," comes at the end of the verse, and not at the beginning as in 18a. MS B's *taḥ[tāyw],* partly restored, is unintelligible here (cf. Segal to the same effect). Prato (p. 74) makes it mean "beneath him," but the ancient translators saw nothing of the kind.

20. Of the four cola here, following MS B, G has only the first and the last. Syr has only the second and third. V 20b, *is there any counting what he achieves?,* is often set aside as a faulty duplication of 18b; but in view of the way v 29b is taken up in 30c, there is no structural argument against a similar linkage here, and v 20c, which is left hanging if 20b is removed, would be hard to account for as simply an intrusive gloss.

21. MS B follows this verse with the bicolon that is properly v 34, where it recurs in its normal place.

22a. *His blessing* = *birkātô,* with MS B^mg; MS B^txt has *brkwt.*

23b. *salt marsh* = *mělēḥâ* as in Ps 107:34; MS B has *melaḥ,* "salt," a faulty reading.

24–28. The first cola of five successive lines, vv 24–27, are damaged in MS B; as it happens, restoration with the help of G is easy. The two bicola of v 28 are missing with the bottom of the page in MS B—28ab almost completely, 28cd entirely.

24a. *For the virtuous* = *ltmym;* MS B has *tmym,* and its marginal reading is *lyšrym,* which provides the *lamed,* read also by G, *his paths* = *'orḥôtāyw* with MS B^mg and G; B^txt = *['rhw]t.*

24b. *the haughty* = *lazzēdîm,* which G and Syr render freely; MS B *lzrym,* the fault of reading *resh* for *daleth.*

25b. *and bad* = *wāra^;* MS B *wry^,* a flawed reading.

26ab. MS B puts the caesura after *mayim,* "water"; it belongs after *lěḥayyê 'ādām, for human life.*

26c. *heart of the wheat:* lit, "fat of the wheat," figurative, as in Deut 32:14; Pss 81:17; 147:14.

27–32. Extant line-ends in the Masada MS support the order of verses in MS B.

28a. Traces show MS B read *nôṣārû* here (= designed); there is a marginal reading that Strack says is illegible; the *nibrā'û* of Segal and Vattioni is rather wishful than real. Smend offers three doubtful letters, *n'ṣ[* .

28b. The verb *ya^tîqû,* "dislodge," is extant in MS B and the rest of the colon is in no doubt, from G (*kai en thymǭ autōn* = *ûbě'appām*) and Syr (*ṭûrē'* = *hārîm,* mountains).

29a. *famine* = *rā^āb* with G and Syr; MS B has *ra^.*

29b. *created* = *nibrā'û* (M preserves the ending, *[nb]r'w*).

30b. *to exterminate the wicked:* G and Syr both read "to destroy." From the facsimile, MS B clearly has *lhḥryb* in its text, and the term for *the wicked* is eaten away; there is no way of determining to which word the *-ym* (with final *mem*) in B^mg belongs. The choice of *exterminate* for "destroy" agrees with those who expect to find (rather than those who think they see) *lĕhahărîm* in this place. For the *qal* of *ḥrb,* "be desolate," cf. 16:4; for the noun *ḥērem,* "doom," cf. 16:9; 46:6.

30cd. See NOTE on vv 27–32, above. *in his storehouse . . . time:* with MS B^mg *bĕʾōṣārô ûlāʿēt;* G, in v 31, has "on the earth, for needs," which represents the corrupt reading *bāʾāreṣ* and the noun *ṣōrek* instead of *ʿēt.*

32. *took my stand=hityaṣṣabtî,* which is the reading required from the facsimile, despite Segal and others; and so G.

33a. *works=maʿăśê,* with *yod;* MS B *maʿăśeh,* for which reason B^mg reads *hkl* for *kullām.*

33b. *provides=yaspîq,* compare v 16b, and G (*chorēgēsei*) in the present place. MS B here has *[yis]pōq,* so Smend and Strack; Segal, Vattioni read *yspyq,* against the facsimile.

34a. *not as good as that=raʿ mizzeh* (as MS B has it in the doublet following v 21) with G; MS B here has *raʿ māh zeh.*

34b. *shows its worth:* MS B in the doublet following v 21, *yigbar;* here, *yagbîr.* For the last centuries B.C. there would be little to choose between these forms; the *qal* is attested at 36:7.

35a. *and voice=ûpeh* with MS B^mg and G.

35b. *his holy name=šem qodšô,* with MS B^mg. MS B^txt makes this *šem haqqādôš,* but the nearest to such a reading that occurs elsewhere in the Heb of Sirach is *qĕdôš yiśrāʾēl* in 50:17; and neither G nor Syr supposes "the Holy One" in the present text. See NOTE at 48:20c.

Comment

This long poem may be divided into five stanzas: $6+7+7+6+4$ bicola. Its theme is the goodness and purposefulness of creation and divine providence, which are manifest to the wise, who are invited to sing the praises of the Creator: hence its position here after the panegyric on the ideal scribe.

The first stanza (39:12–15), which serves as an introduction, is in the form of an invitatory, calling the faithful to proclaim with joy the greatness of the Lord. Ben Sira begins by setting forth his theme "to shine like the moon in its fullness" (39:12); for the image, cf. 50:6. He then invites his "faithful children" (39:13a; cf. NOTE), i.e., the young men he instructed, to "open up [their] petals like roses planted near running waters." In 24:14b, Ben Sira compares himself to a rosebush in Jericho. "Running waters" (39:13b) ensure abundant growth and vigor; cf. Ps 1:3; Num 24:6; Ezek 31:3–9. "The sweet odor of incense" (39:14a; cf. NOTE) in the cult was something pleasing to God; cf. 24:15; 50:9; Ezek 20:41; 2 Cor 2:15. "The lily" (39:14b) is another metaphor of luxuriant growth; cf. 50:8; Hos 14:6. The verbs of praise in

39:14cd and 15ab are all in synonymous parallelism. Praise of God "is man's most characteristic mode of existence: praising and not praising stand over against one another like life and death" (G. von Rad, *Old Testament Theology*, vol. 1, pp. 369–70). The verb "bless" occurs in 39:14d and 35b (the final colon of the poem), and the noun "name" in 39:15a and 35b, thus forming a double *inclusio*. The lyre and other stringed instruments (39:15c) were customarily used in such songs of praise; cf., for example, Ps 33:2–3; 43:4; 57:8; 150:3–4; 1 Chr 13:8; 2 Chr 5:12–13.

Now comes the content of the song of praise (39:16–31), in three stanzas. The theme of the song is this: All God's works are good (39:16a; cf. Gen 1:4, 10, 12, 18, 21, 25, 31); this colon is repeated in 39:33a. God is provident: he takes care of "every need in its own time" (39:16b; cf. NOTE); this colon is also repeated in 39:33b. Everything in creation has its appropriate time; cf. 39:34 and Qoh 3:11. The imagery of 37:17a (cf. NOTE) derives from Ps 33:7. The reference in 37:17b is to God's creation, through a word, of the basin that contained the waters under the firmament; God called this basin of water "the sea" (Gen 1:9–10). Here Ben Sira calls the basin "[God's] storehouse." The theology of creation through word has a broader application in 39:18a (but cf. NOTE); cf. 16:26–27; 43:26. "Nothing can limit [God's] achievement [lit., salvation]" (39:18b). Here Ben Sira alludes to creation as being an act of salvation; cf. Isa 40:12–31. No one can stand in the way of God's saving activity; cf. 1 Sam 14:6; Wis 11:22–26. The Creator-Savior also knows all the works of human beings and sees all things (39:19); cf. 15:19; 17:15, 19; 42:20. "His gaze spans all the ages" (39:20a)—past, present, and future. The works of the Lord are strange and hidden from men and women (11:4cd; 43:31–32), but the works of men and women of all times and places are known completely by the Lord of history. In 39:20b (cf. NOTE), "what he achieves" translates Heb *těšûʿātô*, lit., "his salvation," as in v 18b above. For the thought of 39:20, cf. Ps 147:5; Sir 42:18–25. God's creative and saving activity includes the smallest details of human history (39:20bc). Since God is all-powerful, "nothing resists" him; and since he is omniscient, nothing "surprises him" (39:20d). The all-wise Lord created everything for a purpose (39:21); cf. Qoh 3:11. We, however, may not always be able to discover the purpose or function of certain created things; cf. 42:17.

The next stanza (39:22–27) opens with God's blessing being compared to the two great rivers of the Bible—the Nile and the Euphrates (39:22). Both rivers were noted for their benefits to agriculture: the Nile, thanks to its annual flooding (cf. 47:14), fertilized the land with its silt laden with nutrients; the Euphrates, extensively tapped for irrigation, watered the fertile valley through which it flowed. Cf. 24:25–27. Presumably, God's blessing falls on the righteous, for "his wrath expels the nations" (39:23a)—a reference to the expulsion of the Canaanites; cf. COMMENT on 16:9. The "fertile land" that God turns "into a salt marsh" (39:23b; cf. NOTE) is Sodom and Gomorrah, located at the southern end of the Dead Sea; cf. Gen 13:10; 19:24–28; Deut 29:22; Ps 107:34. Sowing a field with salt, which rendered the soil barren and useless, was a severe punishment a conqueror would inflict on a defeated adversary; cf. Judg 9:45; Jer 17:6; Zeph 2:9.

In 39:24–31, Ben Sira spells out the doctrine of equilibrium in creation, i.e., how persons, things, and events ultimately fulfill God's will and design in creation. Cf. Prov 16:4. For the axiomatic thought of 39:24 (see NOTE), cf. Hos 14:10; Ps 18:26–27. In 39:16 above (cf. COMMENT), Ben Sira refers to the goodness of creation as described in Genesis 1. Now, in v 25, he states that these "good things" are "for the good" according to God's plan "from the beginning" (cf. 16:26); "but for the wicked, good things and bad" (cf. NOTE) —an allusion perhaps to the leather garments ("good things") God made for the man and woman after they sinned and to their subsequent expulsion ("bad [things]") from the Garden of Eden (Gen 3:21–24). The verse also means that while the wicked share in the good things of v 26, they will also partake of the bad things of vv 28–30. Cf. also Gen 4:13–15. In 39:26 are listed ten indispensable items for human life in ancient Palestine; the list in 29:21 includes only water, bread, clothing, and a house. Several of the items in the longer list are traditional: for grain ("the heart of the wheat," 39:26c; cf. NOTE), wine ("the blood of the grape," 39:26d; cf. Gen 49:11), and oil, cf. Hos 2:10; Jer 31:12; Neh 10:38; 2 Chr 32:28; for "milk and honey," the formulaic pair of words used to describe the Promised Land, cf., for example, Exod 3:8; 13:5; 33:3; Lev 20:24; Num 13:27; 14:8; 16:13–14; Deut 6:3; 11:9; 26:9; Jer 11:5; 32:22; for water and cloth, cf. Hos 2:7. The pairing of iron with salt (39:26b) in this list is noteworthy: manufactured iron goods were apparently considered essential for daily life in Ben Sira's day. All these items are good for the good (39:27a) because the good use them for the purpose God intended; "but for the wicked they turn out evil" (39:27b), because the wicked use them to perpetrate evil.

The next stanza (39:28–31) is devoted to a description of the forces of nature, wild beasts, and other instruments of destruction that God created in order to punish the wicked. These nine destructive creatures counterbalance the ten good things listed in 39:26. The Creator can remove mountains directly (as in Job 9:5) or indirectly through the fury of storm winds (39:28ab; cf. NOTES). These winds cause destruction, when called for, and so "appease the anger of their Maker" (39:28cd); cf. 5:6d. "Fire and hail" (39:29a) are found in a different context in Ps 148:8. Yahweh rained down sulfurous fire to destroy Sodom and Gomorrah (Gen 19:24). Hail was the seventh plague to afflict the Egyptians prior to the Exodus (Exod 9:13–26). Famine and disease (39:29a) are mentioned as possible punishments for David's census of the people (2 Sam 24:13); since he was given the choice, David chose pestilence (2 Sam 24:15). In Jer 29:17–18, sword, famine, and pestilence are mentioned together as punishments for infidelity to Yahweh. Famine and pestilence were the usual accompaniments of a prolonged siege; cf. Lev 26:25–26; Jer 21:2–9; Ezek 5:12; 7:15. "Ravenous beasts" (lit., beasts of tooth) and reptiles (39:30a) are agents of destruction also in Deut 32:24. "Scorpions" (39:29a) are an image of chastisement in 1 Kgs 12:11, 14 (=2 Chr 10:11, 14). "The avenging sword" (39:30b) is an allusion to Lev 26:25. All these instruments of destruction God created "to meet a need" (39:30c), i.e., to requite the evil of the wicked, for the Deuteronomic theology insisted that the wicked would not go unpunished in their lifetimes. See INTRODUCTION, Part X, 4. The image of God's "storehouse" (39:30d; cf. NOTE) occurs again in 43:14; cf. Job 38:22–23. "The proper time" (39:30d; cf. NOTE) is the moment of retribution, which will come sooner or later; cf. 11:26 with COMMENT. The natural forces are personified in 39:31: when God commands them to perform a mission of destruction, "they rejoice," and they do precisely what they are commanded, obeying without question the divine will. Unlike human beings, who are prone to disobedience (cf., for example, Gen 3:1–6; 1 Sam 13:12, 13; 15:1–11, 22; Lev 26:14–41; Deut 28:15–68; and the history of infidelity in Israel), nature does God's bidding unfailingly.

The final stanza (39:32–35) serves as epilogue to the poem. Ben Sira repeats his "theme" (39:32b) in 39:33, a repetition, by way of *inclusio,* of v 16, the first bicolon of the second stanza. Since all of God's works are good (39:16a, 32a), even those that are destructive (39:28–31), serving as each does to address a particular need in the divine plan of creation (39:16b, 32b), we have no reason to say, "This is not as good as that" (39:34a; cf. NOTE); cf. 39:21a. For "each shows its worth [cf. NOTE] at the proper time" (39:34b); cf. 39:21b, 30cd. As regards the double *inclusio* in 39:14d and 35b, and in 39:15a and 35b, cf. COMMENT on vv 14–15 above. In the final verse of this splendid poem, Ben Sira again invites his students to "proclaim and bless [God's] holy name" (cf. NOTE) "with full heart and voice" (cf. NOTE).

This long poem has as its deep intent to provide a theodicy, and so can be compared to the books of Job and Qoheleth. For a detailed study, cf. the excellent chapter on the functional duality of creation in G. L. Prato, *Il problema della teodicea in Ben Sira,* pp. 62–115.

48. Joys and Miseries of Life
(40:1–41:13)

40   1 A great anxiety has God allotted,   B
     and a heavy yoke, to the children of Adam:
   From the day a person leaves his mother's womb
     to the day he returns to the mother of all the living,
  2 His thoughts, the fear in his heart,   G
     and his troubled forebodings till the day he dies—
  3 Whether he sits on a throne in exultation   B
     or grovels in dust and ashes,
  4 Whether he wears a splendid crown
     or is clothed in the coarsest of garments—
  5 Are of anger and envy, trouble and dread,
     terror of death, strife, and contention.
   Even when he lies on his bed to rest,
     his cares disturb his sleep at night.
  6 So short is his rest it seems like none,
     till in his dreams he struggles as he did by day,
   Troubled by the visions in his mind,
     like a fugitive fleeing from the pursuer.
  7 As he reaches safety, he wakes up,   G
     astonished that there was nothing to fear.
  8 To all flesh, both human and beast,
     but for sinners seven times more,
  9 Come plague and bloodshed, fiery heat and drought,   B
     plunder and ruin, famine and death.
10 For the wicked evil was created,
     and because of him destruction hastens.

11 All that is of earth returns to earth,
     and what is from above returns above.

¹² All that comes from bribes or injustice will be wiped
out,   G (M)

but loyalty remains forever.
¹³ Wealth from injustice is like a flooding wadi,   B (M)
like a mighty stream with lightning and thunder,
¹⁴ Which in its rising rolls along the stones,
but suddenly, once and for all, comes to an end.
¹⁵ The offshoot of violence will not flourish,
for the root of the godless is on sheer rock;
¹⁶ They are like reeds on riverbanks,   M (B)
withered before all other plants;
¹⁷ But goodness, like eternity, will never be cut off,
and righteousness endures forever.

¹⁸ A life of abundance and remuneration can be sweet,
but better than either is finding a treasure.
¹⁹ A child and a city will preserve one's name,
but better than either is finding wisdom.
Cattle and orchards make a person flourish,
but better than either, a devoted wife.
²⁰ Wine and strong drink delight the heart,   B (G)
but better than either, the affection of friends.
²¹ Flute and harp offer sweet melody,
but better than either, a pure tongue.
²² Grace and beauty delight the eye,
but better than either, the produce of the field.
²³ A friend and a neighbor are timely guides,
but better than either, a sensible wife.
²⁴ Kindred and helper for times of stress;
but better than either, charity that rescues.
²⁵ Gold and silver make one's way secure,   G
but better than either, sound judgment.
²⁶ Wealth and vigor make the heart exult,   B (M)
but better than either, fear of God.
In the fear of the LORD there is no want;
whoever has it need seek no other support.
²⁷ The fear of God is a paradise of blessings;
its canopy is over all that is glorious.

28 My son, live not the life of a beggar;
  better to die than to beg.
29 When one has to look to a stranger's table,
  one's life is not to be considered a life.
  The delicacies offered bring revulsion to one's spirit,
  and to the intelligent inward torture.
30 In the mouth of the shameless begging is sweet,
  but within him it burns like fire.

41 1 O death! how bitter the remembrance of you
  for the person at peace in his home,
  For the one who is serene and always successful,
  who still can enjoy life's pleasures.
2 O death! how welcome your decree   M (B)
  to the weak person of failing strength,
  Stumbling and tripping on everything,
  with sight gone and hope lost.
3 Fear not death, the decree for you;
  remember it embraces those before you and those
                                              after.
4 From God this is the decree for all flesh;
  why then should you reject the Law of the Most
                                              High?
  Whether one has lived ten years, a hundred, or a
                                              thousand,
  in the netherworld there are no arguments about
                                              life.

5 A reprobate line are the children of sinners,
  and witless offspring are in the homes of the
                                              wicked.
6 Dominion is lost to the son of the unrighteous,
  and reproach remains with his seed forever.
7 Children curse their wicked father,
  for they are in disgrace because of him.
8 Woe to you, O wicked people,   M
  who forsake the Law of the Most High.
9 If you have children, mischief will be theirs;   M (B)
  and if you become a father, it will only be for
                                              groaning.

When you stumble, there is lasting joy;
and when you die, you become a curse.
10 All that is of naught returns to naught,
so too the godless—from void to void.
11 The human body is a fleeting thing,
but a virtuous name will never be annihilated.
12 Have respect for your name, for it will stand by you
more than thousands of precious treasures;
13 The good things of life last a number of days,
but a good name, for days without number.

Notes

40 2b. *till the day*=*heōs hēmeran* (so Syr); G *hēmera*. MS B lacks v 2.

3b. Read *wĕʿad lĕšaḥ bĕʿāpār wāʾēper* (cf. G); MS B: *ʿad lāšûb* [B^ms *lôbēš, lābaš*] *ʿāpār wāʾēper*.

4a. *a splendid crown:* hendiadys, lit., "a crown and head ornament." See COMMENT. G has "purple and a crown," probably to correspond to the garment mentioned in v 4b; Syr has only "crown."

4b. *is clothed:* read *ʿôṭēp*, the verb that occurs in 11:4a of MS B, which also gives an alternate form of the colon using the verb *ʿôṭeh;* here MS B wrongly repeats *ʿôṭeh* from v 4a. *ʿṭp*=Gr *periballein* in Job 23:9 and Ps 73:6; and in Sir 11:4a, where *ʿṭp* occurs in one form of MS B, G gives the noun *peribolē. the coarsest of garments:* reading *śimlat śēʿār,* lit., "garment of hair" (cf. Gen. 25:25; Zech 13:4); in the last word, only part of the *śin* and the *yod* can be read in MS B.

5a. *anger and envy*=*ʾap wĕqinʾâ*=G *thymos kai zēlos* (Syr also begins the series with "wrath"); MS B has *ʾak qinʾâ.*

5b. *strife:* reading *taḥărâ* (also found in 31:29b), the reading of MS B^mg (abbreviated *tḥ;* the scribe of MS B often abbreviates in the margin); B^txt has *taḥărâ,* which gives no sense. Here and in 31:29b *taḥărâ* is rendered by Syr *ḥeryānâ,* "strife, controversy, dispute, contention."

5c. =46:19a, but the meaning is different; see below.

5d. =*šĕnôt laylâ tĕšanneh daʾăgātô;* for a similar thought cf. 42:9, in which the noun *dĕʾāgâ* also occurs. MS B^txt has *šĕnat laylâ [t]ĕšanneh rāʿātô* (B^mg *daʿtô*); G *gnosin autou* read the last word as *daʿtô* (*resh* and *daleth* are often confused).

6b. =*ûmikkēn baḥălômôt kĕbayyôm yîgaʿ:* so G, reading with Smend, however, *kopiq* (=Arm [II]) for *skopias* found in most MSS; MS B is defective, containing only one complete word.

6c. *Troubled*=G. MS B *mṭ ṭʿ* yields no sense.

6d. =*kĕsārîd b[ôrēaḥ mippĕnê] rôdēp* of MS B as reconstructed from Syr.

7–8. These verses are fragmentary in MS B.

9a. *fiery heat and drought*=*ḥarḥûr wāḥōreb* (so point MS B); the two words occur also in Deut 28:22, but the second is pointed *ḥereb,* "sword." G has "sword" here. Vv 9–10 are missing in Syr.

9b. *famine*=*rā'āb*=G *limos;* MS B has *rā'â,* "evil."

10b. =*ûba'ăbûrô* [so MS B^mg] *tāḥûš kālâ;* MS B^txt has *ûba'ăbûr tāmûš kālâ,* which gives no sense.

11–17. Fragments of these verses are extant in the Masada MS, but only vv 16–17 are relatively intact; more letters are extant in the first colon of each respective verse than in the second.

11b. =MS B *wa'ăšer mimmārôm 'el mārôm*=Syr; G *kai apo hydatōn eis thalas-san*=*wa'ăšer mimmayim 'el yām,* "and what is from the waters (returns) to the sea."

12. This verse was omitted by MS B. Only the first four letters are extant in M: *kōl miššō[ḥad . . .];* the rest of the verse is from G (note that G omits the translation of the preposition *min* near the beginning of v 12a).

13a. *Wealth from injustice*=Masada *ḥayil mē'āwel;* neither MS B^txt *mēḥôl 'el ḥôl* nor B^mg *ḥayil mēḥôl* makes sense in the context. *is like a flooding wadi*=*kĕnaḥal* [from MS B] *šōtēp* [MS B has *'êtān,* "perennial, ever-flowing," cf. Amos 5:24]; Syr *netgarĕpûn* (with its "deceitful riches flooding" like a wadi) provides the clue to *šōtēp;* cf. Isa 30:28; 66:12; Jer 47:2 (so P. W. Skehan, *CBQ* 30 [1968]: 570–71).

13b. *like a . . . stream*=MS B^mg *wakĕ'āpîq;* B^txt *ûmē'āpîq.*

14a. =*'im šĕ'tô kēpîm* [so M and MS B^mg] *yāgōl;* MS B^txt *'im 'im š'tw kpym yāgîlû.*

15a. =*nēṣer ḥāmās lō'* [so M and MS B^mg] *yirbeh* [cf. G]; as the first two letters of the broken last word, M has either *yk-* or *yn-.* MS B^txt: *nwṣr mēḥāmās lō' yinnāqeh* [B^mg *yakkeh bô*].

15b. As the last word, read *ṣûr* with M and MS B^mg. B^txt has *sela',* "crag, cliff," which is, however, a synonym of *ṣûr;* the phrase *šēn sela'* of B^txt is taken from 1 Sam 14:4 and Job 39:28.

16a. =M *kaqĕrāmît 'al gāpôt naḥal;* "we may regard the word [*qĕrāmît*] as presumably Greek *kalamē* accommodated to Aramaic, then Hebrew, usage, by a typical Aramaic permutation of the liquid -*l*- to -*r*-, and an accommodation to the usual morphology of feminines in -*î,* thought of as an abridged absolute from -*ît*" (so P. W. Skehan, *CBQ* 30 [1968]: 571). "It is unnecessary to emend [*gpwt*] to: *špt,* as most editors; for: *gp,* in the sense of 'bank of a stream' (cf. Aramaic: *gyp,* and Syriac: *gp*), see *Makshirin* 1, 4: *'1 gp hnhr. . . .*" (so Yadin).

16b. =*lipnê kol* [so MS B^mg] *ḥāṣîr* [M *ḥṣr*] *nid'ak* [so M]; only the last two words are extant in M. "The verb *nd'k* has as its subject *nṣr* in v 15, and is masculine for that reason" (so P. W. Skehan, *CBQ* 30 [1968]: 572).

17a. =*wĕḥesed* [so MS B; M omits *wĕ-*] *kā'ad lō' yikkārēt* [M *tikkārēt*]; MS B *wĕḥesed lĕ'ôlām lō' yimmôṭ.*

18a. =*ḥayyê yôter wĕšākār* [M omits *wĕ-*] *yimtāqû.* MS B^txt misread the third word as *wĕšēkār,* "strong drink," and then read the second word as *yayin,* "wine" (cf. 40:20a); B^mg has *yôter šēkel,* "an abundance of understanding."

19bc. These two cola, attested in MS B, M, and Syr, are missing in G probably because of homoioarchton (*mišnêhem*).

19c. *a person*=šĕʾēr (so M; MS B šēm), lit., "flesh, blood relation, self" (parallel to *nepeš;* cf. Prov 11:17).

20a. *Wine and strong drink*=MS B *yayin wĕšēkār* (cf. NOTE on v 18a); Syr has "old wine," G "wine and music" (reading šîr, as in v 21a, for šēkār).

20b. *friends*=MS B *dôdîm,* which can also mean "lovers."

21b. *a pure tongue*=MS B *lāšôn bārâ*=Syr; G has "a sweet (or pleasant) tongue."

22a. *Grace and beauty*=G; MS B has a lacuna.

23a. *A friend and a neighbor*=G and Syr; MS B has a lacuna.

24a. *kindred* [lit., brother] *and helper*=Syr; G has "brothers and help." MS B has a lacuna.

27b. *over all that is glorious*=M *wĕʿal kōl kā[bôd]*=G=Syr; MS B has *wĕkēn kōl kābôd.*

28a. *My son*=bĕnî=MS Bᵐᵍ=G=Syr; Bᵗˣᵗ has *minnî,* "from me." *the life of a beggar,* lit., "a life of gifts."

28b. *than to beg*=M *mimmĕḥaṣṣēp* (or *mimmaḥăṣîp*), the reading of J. Strugnell, ErIsr 9 (1969): 112; Yadin reads *mippĕnê ḥsp.* MS B has *mimmistôlēl.* In Jewish Aram and Syr the verb *ḥṣp* is used in the *paʿel* and *aphʿel* with the meaning "to act with impudence, brazenness, insistency; to be imprudent, brazen, persistent; to beg importunately." The noun *ḥûṣpāʾ* ("brazenness, gall, boldness, impudence, daring, insolence") became a Yiddish word, popularly spelled "chutzpah," and is used today as a slang word in English.

29c. Read *migʿal* [MS B *mʿgl* reversed the consonants] *napšô maṭʿammê zebed:* so Bᵐᵍ.

29d. Read *lĕʾîš yôdēaʿ yissûr mēʿîm:* so MS Bᵐᵍ; M supports the reading of the last two words. MS Bᵗˣᵗ has *sôd mēʿîm.*

30a. *In the mouth of the shameless*=M *bĕpî ʿaz nepeš*=G=Syr; MS B is corrupt: *lĕʾîš ʿôz nepeš.*

30b. *it burns like fire*=M *kĕʾēš tibʿar*=Ps 83:15a; MS Bᵗˣᵗ *tibʿar kĕmô ʾēš*=Pss 79:5b and 89:47b; Bᵐᵍ *kĕʾēš bôʿeret*=Jer 20:9c.

41 1a. *O death*=hôy lammāwet=MS Bᵐᵍ=G=Syr; the first two consonants are also in the fragmentary Masada scroll. Bᵗˣᵗ *ḥayyîm* is corrupt.

1b. *in his home*=M and MS B *ʿal mĕkônātô; mĕkônâ* means "home, residence" also in 44:6b. G "among his possessions"=Syr.

1d. Lit., "and who still has strength to enjoy pleasures," in M and MS B; M has *kôaḥ,* "strength," whereas MS B reads the synonym *ḥayil.* Instead of "life's pleasures, or luxury," Heb *taʿănûg,* G has *trophēn,* "food," an inner Gr corruption for *tryphēn* (=taʿănûg in Prov 19:10; Qoh 2:8; Cant 7:7; Mic 2:9).

2a. *O*=MS B *heʾaḥ*=G=Syr; M is corrupt: *hʿ. how*=M *mâ*=Gᴹˢˢ; MS B *kî. your decree*=ḥoqĕkā=G; MS Bᵗˣᵗ has the plural *ḥuqqêkā* (M has only the first letter, ḥ-); Bᵐᵍ gives three variants: *ḥôq, ḥzq* (which makes no sense), and *hu(w)qqô.*

2b. *to the weak person*=lĕʾēn ʾônîm, lit., "to the one without might" (ʾôn, pl. ʾônîm). M has *[lĕ]ʾēn ʾwynym;* MS B, *lĕʾîš ʾônĕnîm,* "to the man of sorrow" (Smend's reading and translation). Lévi, Peters, Box-Oesterley, and Segal read *lĕʾîš ʾônîm;* Peters and Box-Oesterley translate, "to the man of bad luck" (ʾāwen, pl. ʾônîm). *of failing strength,* lit., "and who lacks strength." It is certain Ben Sira based his text on Isa 40:29: *ûlĕʾēn ʾônîm ʿoṣmâ yarbeh,* "and to him without might he increases strength."

2c. *stumbling and tripping* = M and MS B^mg *ʾîš kôšēl wĕnôqēš;* B^txt, *ʾîš kôšēl yinnāqēš.*

2d. *with sight gone* = M and MS B^mg *ʾepes hammarʾeh* (= M *hmrh,* so Yadin; J. Strugnell suggests the reading *ḥmdh* and renders "bereft of (sexual) delight" [ErIsr 9 (1969) 113]); B^txt, *srb.*

3a. *the decree for you* = M *ḥoqĕkā,* lit., "your decree," as in v 2a (see NOTE); MS B has *ḥu(w)qqêkā* as in v 2a. Syr has "for it is your portion, lot."

3b. *those before you and those after* = MS B *rīʾšōnîm wĕʾaḥărōnîm* = Syr; M *qadmôn wĕʾaḥărôn* in the singular. The adjective *qadmôn* is a synonym of *rīʾšôn;* cf. Isa 43:18.

4a. *decree* = *ḥōq* = G *krima,* as in vv 2a and 3a; *ḥōq* also is the right parallel to *tôrâ* in v 4b (cf. Amos 2:4). M has *qēṣ* ("end"), a reading found also in Syr; MS B reads *ḥēleq,* "portion, lot," the reading of Syr in v 3a (see NOTE).

4c. *ten years, a hundred, or a thousand* = the order in M and G; MS B reverses "ten" and "thousand."

4d. = MS B^mg *ʾên tôkĕḥôt ḥayyîm bišeʾôl* = G; B^txt, *ʾîš tôkāḥôt bišĕʾôl].* M has a hole where the colon should be.

5a. *the children of sinners* = M *tô[lĕd]ôt rāʿîm;* MS B has *dĕbar* [read *dôr,* so Smend] *rāʿîm.*

5b. = MS B (restored from G) *wĕneked ʾĕwîl [bimĕdôr rāšāʾ;* M has extant only the last two consonants of *rāšāʿ.*

6a. = *[mibbēn ʿaww]āl tôʾbad memš[āl]â,* so M reconstructed at the beginning from MS B, the last two words of which are *mimšelet rāʿ,* a corrupt reading. Syr supports M *memš[āl]â;* G has *klēronomia,* which in the rest of the LXX never renders *memšālâ.*

6b. = *[wĕʾim zarʿô] tāmî[d] ḥerpâ,* so M restored from G^MSS; cf. Syr. MS B has only the first two letters, *wr-,* which are to be restored *wĕr[îš]* (so Segal) = Syr *ḥusrānâ,* "want."

7b. = *[kî bi]glālô hāyû bûz,* so M, restored from MS B, which is missing the end of the colon. The reading *bûz* = *bĕbûz,* the preposition *bĕ-* being omitted because the first consonant of the noun is *b,* as often elsewhere in the OT and the inscriptions, esp. in the expression *byt* = *bbyt.*

8a. = *[ʾôy lākem] ʾanšê ʿaw[lâ],* so M, restored from G; MS B is missing most of v 8ab.

9a. = MS B^mg *ʾim tiprû ʿal yad ʾāsôn;* B^txt is fragmentary, and M has only the *l* of *ʿal.* Only the Lucianic MSS (*L*) have this colon; the rest of the G^MSS omit it.

9b. MS B = M.

9c. This colon is omitted by G, but that it belonged to Ben Sira's original text is proved by its presence in M and MS B.

10ab. M lacks only the first three letters of this bicolon; otherwise M = MS B. *all that is of naught . . . to naught* = *kōl mĕʾepes ʾel ʾepes* = M and MS B. G *panta hosa ek gēs eis gēn* = *kōl mĕʾāpār ʾel ʾāpār;* see Gen 3:19, where LXX translates MT *ʾāpār* by *gē.* In 40:11a, Ben Sira expresses a similar thought. *void to void* = *mittôhû ʾel tôhû;* *tôhû* is the classical expression of void or nothingness in Gen 1:2.

12b. *precious treasures* = MS B^mg *sîmôt ḥemdâ,* lit., "treasures of desire"; B^txt has *ʾôṣĕrôt ḥokmâ,* "treasures of wisdom." M is too fragmentary to decide which is the better reading. G has "great treasures of gold," and Syr, "treasures of deceit." Interestingly, Lat reads *thesauri magni pretiosi* (some MSS: *magni et pretiosi;* others: *pretiosi et magni*); one MS (Z*) has *thesauri pretiosi,* which supports MS B^ms.

13a. =*[t]ôbat ḥay mispar yāmîm,* so M and MS B^mg; B^txt, *yĕmê mispār.*

Comment

This section contains five poems: (1) 40:1–10 (thirteen bicola); (2) 40:11–17 (seven bicola); (3) 40:18–27 (twelve bicola); (4) 40:28–41:4 (eleven bicola); and (5) 41:5–13 (ten bicola). The first two poems (twenty bicola) have a pronounced pessimistic tone that contrasts sharply with the optimistic outlook Ben Sira articulates in the previous poem (39:12–35). The third poem (twelve bicola) relieves the heaviness and melancholy by a series of "better than" proverbs about the good things of life that are available in full measure only to those who fear the Lord (39:26–27). The fourth and fifth poems (twenty-one bicola) then return to the somber strains of the first two. The arrangements of these poems should be seen as deliberate: the third poem with its upbeat mood is at the center; the first two poems and the last two with their gloomy reminders provide the top and bottom parts of the sandwich construction. The literature of pessimism has a long history in antiquity; see, for example, "A Dialogue about Human Misery," sometimes called "The Babylonian Ecclesiastes," the extant tablets of which date to the seventh century B.C. (*ANET,* pp. 438–40).

Though "the works of God are all of them good" (39:16a, 33a) and God's providence in creation is marvelous and praiseworthy (39:16–35), human beings still experience anguish, anxiety, and dread. That is the point of the first poem (40:1–10). God, who is in control of the universe and of human destiny, "has allotted" to men and women "a great anxiety" and "a heavy yoke" from the time of birth to the day of burial (40:1). Ben Sira attributes to God himself the hard life human beings experience. Interestingly, the grandson in his Greek translation omits the mention of God, thus altering v 1a to read, "Much labor [or hard work] was created for every person." The expression "the mother of all the living" (40:1d) is a reference to the "dust" of the ground from which humankind was created in the Yahwistic account (Gen 2:7) and to which all must return (Gen 3:19); cf. Sir 16:29–30; 17:1–2; and esp. 51:5a, with COMMENT. For the thought of 40:1, see Job 7:1–2; 14:1–2; Ps 90:10; Qoh 2:22–23; Matt 6:34. The Fathers of the Church attributed the "heavy yoke" of human "anxiety" and other afflictions, which are detailed in this poem, to original sin with which all human beings are conceived; cf. 25:24.

No one is spared the pain of human existence; all classes of people from the highest (40:3a, 4a) to the lowest (40:3b, 4b) are subject to fears and "troubled forebodings" till death (40:2). Note the interlinear synonymous parallelism between "he sits on a throne in exultation" (40:3a) and "he wears a splendid crown" (40:4a), and between "[he] grovels in dust and ashes" (40:3b) and "[he] is clothed in the coarsest of garments" (40:4b). The "thoughts" we experience (40:2a) "are of anger and envy, trouble and dread, terror of death, strife, and contention" (40:5ab); note that the expressions used here add up to seven to suggest total or complete misery. The number seven is used again in 40:8b to connote the completeness of the sinner's destruction. In 40:3a, the reference is to the supreme civil authority; and in v 4a, to the high priest, the supreme religious authority, who wore "a splendid crown," lit., "a crown [Heb ṣānîp] and head ornament" [Heb wāṣîṣ] (cf. Exod 28:36–37). "The coarsest of garments," lit., "a garment of hair" (40:4b; see NOTE), was the clothing of the poor, or as Syr translates the phrase, "the garment of poverty." Such a garment was also worn as a protest against luxury or as a sign of simplicity or prophetic vocation (cf. 2 Kgs 1:8; Zech 13:4; Matt 3:4; and Mark 1:6). As regards the expression "terror of death" (40:5b), cf. Ps 55:5.

The thought of 40:5cd (see NOTES) echoes the sentiment expressed in Qoh 2:23: "Even at night [a person's] mind is not at rest." The graphic and realistic imagery of 40:5cd–7 is something every adult can relate to: prolonged anguish or unusual anxiety results in restless sleep and nightmares; cf. Job 7:4. One nightmare that commonly afflicts men, women, and children is described in 40:6d (see NOTE): the chase by a terrifying person. The text of G in 40:7a, translated here "as he reaches safety" (lit., "in the time of his deliverance"), is probably corrupt, since it does not correspond to what usually happens in these nightmares. Smend, whom Ziegler follows in his edition, suggests that *chreias* should be read instead of *sōterias* in all Gr MSS. This reading gives better sense: *"in the time of his [greatest] need* he wakes up"— the common experience of people who have such dreams.

The preceding troubles and terrors that afflict human beings are primarily psychological and emotional, hence internal. Now Ben Sira turns to external woes that befall "all flesh, both human and beast, but for sinners seven times more" (40:8ab). "Plague and bloodshed . . . plunder and ruin" (40:9) are the usual results of war (cf. Isa 51:19; 60:18). "Fiery heat and drought," occurring often in the Holy Land, result in "famine and death" (40:9; cf. Ezek 5:16–17; Deut 28:22). The victims of war and drought are the innocent as well as the wicked. The idea in 40:10 (see also 39:29–31) that evil was created for the wicked is related to the Deuteronomic doctrine of retribution; see COMMENT on 2:1–6. For 40:10b (see NOTE), G reads, "and because of him the flood came" (cf. Gen 6:5–7, 11–13).

In the next poem (40:11–17) Ben Sira speaks of the ill effects that come from the practice of evil and of the calamity that lies in store for the wicked.

The saying in 40:11a derives from Gen 3:19 and finds parallels in Qoh 3:20; 12:7a; Job 34:15; see also Sir 41:10a. "What is from above" is the breath of life or human spirit that "returns above" (40:11b), i.e., to God who breathed it into humans (Gen 2:7); Qoh 12:7b conveys the same idea: "the life breath returns to God who gave it." In these verses, Ben Sira and Qoheleth do not teach the doctrine of personal immortality or of eternal reward with God; that doctrine will come later (see COMMENT on 7:17; 11:26; 14:16; 17:28; and INTRODUCTION, Part X, 4). See also Ps 146:4. For 40:11b, G reads, "and what is from the waters returns to the sea"—the reference is to Qoh 1:7; see also Enoch 17:5–8. The point of 40:11, which serves as introduction to the poem, is that the impious who are prosperous will perish as do all other living beings (cf. Ps 49:6–21).

Bribery (40:12a) was severely and repeatedly condemned in the OT: 35:14 (cf. 20:29); Exod 23:8; Deut 10:17; 16:19; 27:25; 1 Sam 8:3; 2 Chr 19:7; Ps 15:5; Prov 17:23. Ben Sira affirms that what results from bribery or injustice "will be wiped out," hence will do the sinner no good. But "loyalty" or fidelity "remains forever" (40:12b); see v 17 (with COMMENT) for an expansion of the idea here. For the imagery of 40:13–14 (see NOTES), which continue the thought of v 12a, see Job 6:15–17 and Jer 15:18. What is said in 40:15 is analogous to 23:25, which speaks of the fate of the children of the adulteress. The images of 40:15–16 are similar to those in Job 8:11–12. For other descriptions of the punishment of the wicked, see 10:7–17; 41:5–10. Regarding "the root of the godless . . . on sheer rock" (40:15b), compare Matt 13:5, 21. In contrast to the godless and the impermanence of their prosperity, "goodness [Heb ḥesed], like eternity, will never be cut off" (40:17a; see NOTE), "and righteousness [Heb ṣĕdāqâ] endures forever" (40:17b)—ideas that were introduced earlier in v 12b; cf. 41:11b, 13b; Prov 10:25. The nouns ḥesed and ṣĕdāqâ occur in a similar context in 17:22. The final verse of this poem (40:17) serves as a lead into the following one.

In this poem (40:18–27), Ben Sira offers a series of ten "better than" proverbs, which culminate in the highest of human attainments, fear of the Lord. This is not the usual type of "better" proverb (ṭôb-Spruch in Hebrew-German), for it does not use the adjective ṭôb, "good," in the first colon + min, the comparative particle, in the second colon, as, for example, in 10:27 and 20:31 = 41:15. Rather, it employs a series of two nouns in a verbal or nominal sentence in the first colon and then in the second colon uses the preposition min + šĕnêhem, "better than either [lit., both]," to make the comparison. For a study of the normal "better" proverb, see G. S. Ogden, "The 'Better'-Proverb (Tôb-Spruch), Rhetorical Criticism, and Qoheleth," *JBL* 96 (1977): 489–505. The "better" proverb is found also in the ancient Egyptian Wisdom literature. Ogden (p. 489) cites some examples from "The Teaching of Amenophis the Son of Kanakht": "Better is poverty at the hand of God than riches in the storehouse. Better is bread with a happy heart than riches with vexation."

The "finding a treasure" of 40:18b is to be understood as a parallel to "finding wisdom" in 40:19b. "Wisdom" and "treasure" are paired also in 41:14b. Thus the first two parts of the series refer to wisdom, and the tenth and final part to fear of the Lord, which is "the beginning of wisdom" (1:14; Ps 111:10; Prov 1:7; 9:10). Children perpetuated one's name (40:19a), a common conviction to this day; cf. 16:1–3; Deut 25:5–6. In writing that "a city preserve[s] one's name" (40:19a), Ben Sira must have had in mind the many ancient cities that were called after their founders, such as Alexandria, Rome, and Antioch; cf. 2 Sam 5:9. A "devoted wife" is more valuable than "cattle and orchards" (40:19cd); the good wife is described as "sensible" in v 23b (see also 7:19; 25:8a; 26:1–4, 13–18). Ben Sira had a wholesome appreciation for "wine and strong drink" (40:20a; see NOTE), as is clear also from 31:27–28 and 32:5–6; but wine is not to be abused (cf. 31:25–26, 29–30). "The affection of friends" (or "lovers"; see NOTE on 40:20b) is, however, far more significant; for Ben Sira's other maxims on friends and friendship, see 6:14–17; 7:18; 9:10 ("a new friend is like new wine"); 37:5. Ben Sira places a premium on "a pure tongue" (40:21b; see NOTE); on the use and abuse of the tongue see 5:13–6:1, 5; 7:13; 19:6–17; 20:5–8, 13, 18–27; 22:6, 27; 23:1, 8–15; 27:4–7; 28:12–26.

Regarding the image of "the produce of [lit., the plants of] the field" delighting the eye more than "grace and beauty" (40:22), compare the words of Jesus in Matt 6:28–30. The Heb noun ṣimḥê, pl. construct (with śādeh, "the produce of the field") is found in the plural absolute in 43:21b; elsewhere in the Heb Bible the noun appears only in the singular. The expression ṣemaḥ haśśādeh, "the plant of the field," appears in Ezek 16:7 to describe faithless Jerusalem. The good wife, now called (40:23b) "a sensible wife" (Heb ʾiššâ maśkālet, the expression found also in 7:19a and 25:8a), is featured a second time in this ten-part series (see v 19d with COMMENT). Here Ben Sira doubtless had in mind Prov 19:14: "Home and possessions are an inheritance from parents, but a prudent wife [ʾiššâ maśkālet] is from the LORD." Almsgiving, which is a religious as well as a social obligation, is a central teaching of the Judaism of Ben Sira's day; here it is called "charity [or alms(giving)] that rescues," Heb ṣedeq maṣṣālet (40:24b); see COMMENT on 3:14–15; 3:30–4:6; 29:8–13; 35:3–4. For the thought of "kindred and helper for times of stress" (40:24a), see Prov 17:17. The value of "gold and silver," the proverbial metals to designate wealth, is obvious for the good life; but "sound judgment" is better (40:25) if one wants to live a full and happy life. Without sound judgment one could scarcely be considered wise.

Now Ben Sira turns his attention to the best or highest in the series of personal possessions—the fear of the Lord, a central theme of the book (see INTRODUCTION, Part X, 1). "Wealth and vigor" (or physical strength, well-being) are needed in order to "make the heart exult, but better than either, fear of God" (40:26ab). "Fear of God/the LORD" occurs three times, once in each of the three bicola that conclude the poem, thus emphasizing by this number (it connotes the superlative) the importance of the concept. See also 1:11–30; 15:1; 19:20; 21:6; 23:27. The one who has fear of the Lord is the only one who can be considered wise as well as virtuous (see 1:11–20, 25–27). According to the Deuteronomic doctrine of retribution, only the virtuous will prosper; hence the point of 40:26cd–27 (see also v 17). The one who possesses fear of the Lord shall have all else besides; for similar ideas, cf. Psalms 27 and 34. The phrase "a paradise [or Eden, cf. Gen 2:8–17; 3:23–24; Ezek 28:13] of blessings" (40:27a) echoes Isa 51:3. The source of 40:27b, "its canopy . . . glorious," is Isa 4:6.

The next poem has two stanzas, one on begging (40:28–30) and one on death (41:1–4). Though Ben Sira affirms elsewhere that "poverty and riches, are from the LORD" (11:14b), here he urges his disciples against any lack of industry or independence that may force them to "the life of a beggar" (40:28a; see NOTE). The maxim "Better to die than to beg" (40:28b) sums up his conviction, which he develops in 40:29; see also 29:24–28; 30:17; 37:4a. The beggar's "life is not to be considered a life" (40:29b); compare this maxim with 4:12; 17:11; 21:13. If a person is "intelligent," what is offered him brings "revulsion to [his] spirit and . . . inward torture" (40:29cd). However, "the shameless" is another story; in his mouth "begging is sweet" (40:30a; see NOTE). "But within him it burns like fire" (40:30b; see NOTE for the biblical allusions). The point of the stanza is that the wise may be poor (cf. 31:8–11) but should not be reduced to begging (cf. 31:19), a form of activity not in keeping with their personal dignity.

The second stanza of this poem (41:1–4) makes three comments about death: it is bitter for the one who is happy, healthy, and successful; it is welcome to the weak, disheartened, and disabled; it is inevitable for all. See Job 21:23–26 for three somewhat different comments. On the idea of death being "bitter" (41:1a), see 1 Kgs 15:32. In his terrible misfortunes, a form of death, Job says: "I was in peace, but [God] dislodged me" (Job 16:12a)—perhaps the background of 41:1bcd about the person "at peace" (cf. 44:6), "serene and always successful," still able to "enjoy life's pleasures." These expressions suggest the quality of the life of the wise, who do not deserve premature death. Compare Luke 12:16–20. As regards death's "decree" (41:2a), compare 14:12b, "the grave's appointed time," lit., "the decree of Sheol." For more graphic and colorful images of the physically impaired person who welcomes death (41:2; see NOTES), cf. Qoh 12:1–6. "Nobody dies prematurely who dies in misery" (Publilius Syrus, *Maxims*). Because "death, the decree for you" (41:3a; see NOTE) is inevitable, embracing everybody sooner or later (41:3b; see also 38:22), Ben Sira urges one not to fear it—something of a non sequitur. Death as "the decree for all flesh" (41:4a; see

NOTE) comes from God and is "the Law of the Most High" (41:4b); for that reason, one should accept it without question. "In the netherworld there are no arguments about life" (41:4d; see NOTE) simply because nothing takes place there except dark, dismal, shadowy existence devoid of any real life or joy (see 14:16 and 17:28, with COMMENT). See INTRODUCTION, Part X, 4. Hence it makes little difference there "whether one has lived ten years, a hundred, or a thousand" (41:4c; see NOTE); cf. Qoh 6:3–6.

The final poem has two stanzas, one dealing with the fate of the wicked and their reprobate children (41:5–10), and the other with the lasting value of the good name of the wise (41:11–13). The Heb nouns *nîn,* "line, posterity," and *neked,* "offspring, progeny," are always used in parallel with each other, not only here in 41:5 but also in 47:22cd; Gen 21:23; Job 18:19; and Isa 14:22, the only other occurrences of the words in the Heb Bible. The "reprobate line" and "witless offspring" are the Hellenizing Jews who compromised their faith by adopting pagan Greek practices and customs, or who actually formally apostatized (see v 8b). These ungodly Jews can be compared to the faithless kings of Judah (49:4–5). Especially despicable were the members of the high-priestly family who did not follow the pious example of their illustrious father Simeon II, who receives lyrical praise in 50:1–21. See INTRODUCTION, Part II, "Ben Sira and His Times." Ben Sira calls these Jews "reprobate," "sinners," "witless," "wicked" (41:5), and "unrighteous" (41:6a; see NOTE); cf. 1 Macc 3:5–8 for similar descriptions of the Hellenizers of a later day. The Greek-loving high priests, who are severely condemned in 41:6, would have been well advised to consider the doom that befell the priestly house of Eli because of the unprincipled behavior of his sons Hophni and Phinehas (1 Sam 2:12–36). Because of family solidarity and responsibility, children "are in disgrace because of" their wicked father whom they "curse" (41:7) rather than bless.

In 41:8–10, Ben Sira issues a stern warning to all Jews who give up their faith for the Greek way of life; he calls them "wicked people, who forsake the Law of the Most High" (41:8; see NOTE). Children are normally a blessing and source of joy (see 25:7c); but the children of the godless will have only "mischief" (41:9a; see NOTE). Instead of rejoicing, the father of such children will experience only "groaning" (41:9b). When he stumbles, "there is lasting joy" (41:9c; see NOTE) instead of grief; cf. Ps 35:15. And when he dies, he becomes "a curse" (41:9d) on the lips of his reprobate children (cf. v 7a) because he did not leave behind a good name (cf. vv 11–13). The Heb term *ḥānēp,* here translated "godless" (41:10b), also means "apostate" (see Job 8:15; 13:16; 20:5; 37:8; Isa 10:6; 33:14). The nouns *'epes,* "naught," and *tōhû,* "void" (41:10), occur as a parallel pair also in Isa 40:17; the word *tōhû* (41:10b; see NOTE), which designates the antithesis of creation in Gen 1:2, can also refer to moral emptiness or worthlessness (cf. Isa 24:10; 59:4), apparently the meaning here.

In dramatic contrast to the ungodly, the virtuous, i.e., the wise in the viewpoint of the biblical Wisdom writers, have a proper perspective on life and authentic human prosperity, realizing that "the human body is a fleeting thing" (41:11a) and should not count for much. But their "virtuous name will never be annihilated" (41:11b), and that is what really matters; cf. 40:12b, 17. In this stanza, the word "name" (Heb šēm) occurs once in each of its three bicola, thus emphasizing the superlative value of one's reputation; see 40:26–27, with COMMENT, where the threefold mention of "fear of God/the LORD" performs a similar function. An evil name will be blotted out or remembered as a curse (41:9–10; cf. Prov 10:7b), but the good name of the wise "will stand by" them "more than thousands of precious treasures" (41:12; see NOTE); cf. Qoh 7:1a; Prov 10:7a. Ben Sira concludes this poem by comparing social and economic prosperity, which lasts only "a number of days," with the possession of "a good name," which lasts "for days without number" (41:13; see NOTE); cf. also 37:26; 40:12b. For a parallel to 41:12–13, see *Phibis*, xx 1 (Sanders, pp. 84–85).

49. True and False Shame;
a Father's Care for His Daughter
(41:14–42:14)

41   ^{14b} Hidden wisdom and concealed treasure—

     ^c   of what value is either?
     ¹⁵ Better the person who hides his folly
        than the one who hides his wisdom.

^{14a} My children, listen to instruction about shame;
   ¹⁶   judge of abashment according to my rules,
    For not every kind of shame is shameful,
       nor is every kind of abashment to be approved.
¹⁷ Before father and mother be ashamed of immorality,
       before prince and ruler, of falsehood;
¹⁸ Before master and mistress, of deceit,
       before the public assembly, of crime;
Before associate and friend, of disloyalty,
   ¹⁹   and in the place where you settle, of theft.
    Be ashamed of breaking an oath or agreement,
       and of stretching your elbow at dinner;
    Of refusing to give when asked,
^{21a}   and of rebuffing your own kin;
   ^b Of defrauding another of his appointed share,
^{20a}   and of failing to return a greeting;
^{21c} Of gazing at a man's wife,
^{20b}   and of entertaining thoughts about another woman;
²² Of trifling with a servant girl of yours,
       and of violating her bed;
    Of using harsh words with friends,
       and of following up your gift with an insult;

42   ¹ Of repeating what you hear,
       and of betraying any secret.

Be ashamed of the right things,
and you will find favor in the sight of all.

But of these things be not ashamed,
lest you sin to save face:
2 Of the Law of the Most High and his precepts,
and of justice to acquit the ungodly.
3 Of sharing the expenses of a business or a journey,
and of dividing an inheritance or property;
4 Of accuracy of scales and balances,
and of tested measures and weights;
Of acquiring much or little
5 and of bargaining in dealing with a merchant;
Of constant training of children,
and of beating the back of a disloyal servant;
6 Of a seal to keep a foolish wife at home,
and of a key where there are many hands;
7 Of numbering every deposit,
and of recording all that is taken in or given out;
8 Of chastisement for the silly and the foolish,
and for the tottering old person occupied with
immorality.
Thus you will be truly refined.
and recognized by all as discreet.   B (M)

9 A daughter is a treasure that keeps her father   M (B)
wakeful,
and worry over her drives away sleep:
Lest in her youth she remain unmarried,
or when she is married, lest she be childless;
10a While unmarried, lest she be defiled,
c   or lest she prove unfaithful to her husband;
b Lest she become pregnant in her father's house,
d   or be sterile in that of her husband.
11 My son, keep a close watch on your daughter,
lest she make you the sport of your enemies,   G
A byword in the city and the assembly of the people,   M (B)
an object of derision in public gatherings.

See that there is no lattice in her room,
no spot that overlooks the approaches to the
house.
12 Let her not reveal her beauty to any male,
or spend her time among married women;
13 For just as moths come from garments,
so a woman's wickedness comes from a woman.
14 Better a man's wickedness than a woman's
goodness,
but better a religious daughter than a shameless
son.

Notes

41:13–42:8. These verses, except for parts of 41:19–20, are missing from Syr.

41:14bc–15. These two bicola, which are found in M, MS B, G, and Lat, are given also in 20:30–31, where the Heb text is not extant. The order of the text—vv 14bc, 15, 14a–16a, 16bc as given in our translation—comes from M and MS B; the verse numbers are from G, which has jumbled the correct order of the verses.

14b. *and concealed treasure*=M *wĕśîmâ mĕsuttāret*=MS B^mg *wĕśîmâ mĕsu(w)t-tāret;* B^txt *wĕʾôṣār mu(w)stār.* Here, as often elsewhere, M agrees with B^mg against B^txt; see, e.g., NOTES on 40:14a, 15a, b, 29d; 41:2c, d, 13a, 17a, b, 18c, 19a, 22c; 42:8b.

15a. *who hides* (his folly)=M *maṭm[în];* MS B *maspîn,* as in v 15b (M and MS B).

16a. *judge of abashment,* lit., "be put to shame, be abashed."

16bc. This verse also occurs in the florilegium MS C (=MS B).

16b. *is shameful*=M *nāʾweh lĕbôš,* lit., "is it proper to be ashamed of." MS B *nāʾeh lišmōr,* "is it proper to observe." G *diaphylaxai* supports MS B *lišmōr;* the variant *lĕbôš* points to a second ancient form of this text.

17a. *of immorality*=M and MS B^mg *ʿal paḥaz;* B^txt *ʾel* [a mistake for *ʿal*] *zĕnût,* a synonym of *paḥaz,* which is a rare word occurring only once in the MT, Gen 49:4. Here again these readings point to two ancient recensions of the Heb text.

17b. *and ruler, of* (falsehood)=M and MS B^mg *wāśar ʿal; nāśîʾ* and *śar* are in parallelism also in Prov 8:16. B^txt *yôšêb ʾel.*

18b. *the public assembly,* hendiadys; lit., "the assembly and the people."

18c. *Before associate*=M and MS B^mg *miśśôtāp;* B^txt *mēḥ[ôbēr].*

19–22. The order of the cola given in the translation comes from M; the numbering, from G, which has jumbled the order.

19a. *of theft*=M and MS B^mg *ʿa[l] yad,* lit., "of [your] hand"; cf. 42:6b with COMMENT. B^txt *ʿal zār.*

19b. *of breaking*=M *mēhāpēr;* MS B is broken at this point.

21a. *your own kin*=M šĕʾ ĕrĕkā; MS Bᵗˣᵗ rēʿekā; Bᵐᵍ rēʿĕkā.

21b. =M mēḥăšôt maḥlĕqôt mānâ; MS Bᵗˣᵗ mĕḥaš[bît]; Bᵐᵍ maḥăšābôt.

20a. As the last word of the colon, M haḥărîš is preferable to MS Bᵗˣᵗ mēhaḥărîš or Bᵐᵍ mʾḥryšw (Smend) or mēhaḥărîšû (Segal).

21c. =mēḥabbîṭ ʾe[l ʾēšet ʾîš], so M restored from G (cf. 9:9); the last two words of MS B are damaged.

20b. *another woman*=M zārâ. In Prov 2:16; 5:3, 20; 7:5; 22:14; 23:33, zārâ= "strange woman, loose woman, prostitute," which may also be the meaning here; cf. 9:3.

22a. =mitʿaśśēq ʿi[m šip]ḥâ lĕkā, so M restored from G; MS B is damaged here and in v 22b.

22c. *harsh words*=M and MS Bᵐᵍ dibrê (Bᵐᵍ dĕbar) ḥesed, lit., "words of reproach"; Bᵗˣᵗ ḥerpâ is the more common MT word for "reproach." The noun ḥesed (=reproach, shame) is an Aramaism used in the MT only twice (Lev 20:17 and Prov 14:34) and in Ben Sira only here; ḥesed is the preferred reading because in v 22d the parallel is the infinitive ḥārēp.

22d. =M ûmēʾaḥar mattāt ḥārēp; MS B ʾûmēʾaḥărê mattāt ʾal tinʾaṣ (Smend)=G.

42 1b. =M ûmēḥăšôp kol dĕbar ʿeṣâ (cf. G); MS B ûmēḥăšôp kol sôd ʿeṣâ.

5b. =[wĕʿal mûsar bānîm harb]eh, so M restored from G; MS B lacks the colon.

5c. =M wĕʿebed raʿ wĕṣēlaʿ mĕhullemet (so J. Strugnell, ErIsr 9 [1969]: 114–15); cf. Prov 18:6. As the last word, Yadin reads mhlkt. MS B lacks the colon.

6a. =[ʿal ʾiššâ mĕṭuppe]šet ḥôtām, so M restored by Strugnell on the basis of MS Bᵐᵍ ṭpšh: lit., "upon a woman who plays the fool [set] a seal."

6b. *key* and *many*=M maptēaḥ and rabbôt; MS B tptḥ and rāpôt.

7a. =M ʿal mĕ[qôm] tapqîd mispār; MS B ʿal mĕqôm tapqîd [Bᵐᵍ mpqd] yād tispôr (Bᵐᵍ taḥšôb).

7b. =M š[ĕʾēt û]mattāt hakkōl bikĕtāb; MS B ûmattāt wĕleqaḥ (Bᵐᵍ wśwʾh wtth).

8a. =ʿal m[ardût p]ôteh ûkĕsîl, so M restored from MS Bᵐᵍ; Bᵗˣᵗ has mûsar for mardût.

8b. =M and MS Bᵐᵍ [wĕś]āb kôšēl ʿôneh [Bᵐᵍ wĕʿôneh] bizĕnût; Bᵗˣᵗ wĕśāb wĕyāšîš wĕnôṭēl ʿeṣâ bizĕnût.

8d. =[wĕʾîš šānûa]ʿ lipnê kol ḥay, so M restored from MS B. Since G has a different reading—"*and you will be approved* before all"—M may have had in the lacuna a different reading from that of MS B.

9a. =[bat] lĕʾāb maṭmôn šāq[ed], so M restored from G; MS B bat lĕʾāb maṭmônet [Bᵐᵍ maṭmôn] šāqer.

9b. =[wĕdāʾăgātāh (so MS Bᵐᵍ; B dĕʾāgâ) tapr]îd nûmâ, so M restored from MS B, G, and Syr.

9c. *she remain unmarried*=M timmāʾēs, lit., "she be rejected"; cf. G. MS B tāgûr="she commit adultery."

9d. =ûbĕʿûlêhā pen t[ĕʾaṣēr], so M as read and restored (and translated) by Strugnell (ErIsr 9 [1969]: 115).

10acbd. This is the order found in M and MS B.

10a. *she be defiled*=M=tĕḥāl=G; MS B tĕpu(w)tteh.

10c. =M wĕʿal ʾîsāh [pen] tišṭeh; MS B is partially damaged but read at the beginning ûbĕbêt [baʿ]lā[h].

10b. =M *bêt ʾābîhā pen tazrîaʿ;* MS B *běbêt ʾābîhā pen* [   ]. Note in M the absence of the preposition before *bêt;* as often when a word begins with *b,* the preposition *bĕ-* is omitted.

10d. =M *ûbaʿlā[h pen tēʿā]ṣ[ēr]* as restored from G. Note that *bêt* in the first colon (v 10b) does double duty for *baʿlāh.*

11a. =M *[běnî] ʿal bat ḥazzēq mišmar;* MS B is fragmentary but has traces of *běnî* (=Syr).

11b. Translated from G; both M and MS B are too fragmentary to restore. Syr reads: "lest you make for yourself a bad name."

11d. =MS B^{mg} *wĕhôbîšatĕkā* [=G, Syr; B^{txt} *wĕhôšîbatĕkā*] *[baʿā]dat šāʿar;* M has a lacuna.

11ef. This bicolon is missing in G.

11e. =MS B *[m]ěqôm tāgûr ʾal yěhî ʾešnāb;* M omits the last word, presumably by mistake. Strugnell suggests, however, that M makes sense without *ʾešnāb,* the translation being "let there not be an opportunity for her to have illegitimate intercourse"; cf. *gwr* II in MH and Syr (ErIsr 9 [1969]: 116).

11f. =MS B; M has a lacuna.

12a. *reveal=tapen,* Strugnell's correction of M *tbn;* MS B *titten.*

12b. *among=ûbēn*=G *kai en mesō*=Syr; MS B *ûbêt.* M has a lacuna.

13a. *moths=*M *sas=*Syr=*sāsâ=*MS B *ʿāš=*G *sēs.*

14a. M and MS B^{mg} *ṭôb rôaʿ ʾîš miṭṭôb* [so Strugnell; Yadin *miṭṭîb*] *ʾiššâ;* B^{txt} is corrupt: *miṭṭôb rôaʿ ʾîš miṭṭîb ʾiššâ.*

14b. =*ûbat mĕpuḥedet mibbēn lěḥerpâ,* so M corrected (and translated) by F. M. Cross in J. Strugnell, ErIsr 9 (1969): 116. According to Strugnell, the last two words in M are *mbwl* [Yadin *mikkôl*] *ḥerpâ;* Cross corrected the third consonant to read *nun* and then placed the *lamed* before *ḥerpâ.* Cross offers an alternative translation: "but better a daughter of a religious wife than a son of the shameless one." MS B^{txt} *ûbên* (B^{mg} *ûbat*) *mĕḥārepet tabbîaʿ ʾiššâ* (B^{mg} *ḥerpâ*).

Comment

In this section there are two distinct poems: the first on true and false shame (41:14a, 16–42:8), and the second on a father's care for his daughter (42:9–14). There is a two-bicolon introduction (41:14bc–15; see NOTE); for an explanation, see COMMENT on 20:30–31. Cf. also 18:28–29 and Matt 10:27; 25:24–30.

In MS B before 41:14a, there is the title *mûsar bōšet,* "Instruction about Shame," which is also the opening phrase of the poem (41:14a); this title is not found in G, Lat, or Syr. Since shame, a natural human emotion, can be good or bad, like most other things in life, Ben Sira gives the general principle in the opening couplet (14a, 16abc): we should follow his rules about shame, for not all shame is to be approved. See also 4:20–31 and 20:22–23. The poem may be divided into two stanzas: (1) on true or correct shame (41:14a, 16–42:1d); and (2) on false shame (42:1e–8).

As regards those before whom one should feel shame, Ben Sira refers to the persons who were significant in the society of his day: parents, prince and ruler (41:17), master and mistress, the public assembly, associate and friend (41:18), relatives (41:21a), wife (41:21c), other women (41:20b), and servant girls (41:22ab). We should be ashamed of immorality (41:17a; see NOTE), a subject on which Ben Sira has written several other maxims (9:6; 18:30–32; 19:2–4; 23:16–21), and of falsehood and deceit (41:17b, 18a); see also 7:13 and 20:24–26. "Crime," Heb *pešaʿ*, is to be deplored because of the disgrace one would bear "before the public assembly" (41:18b; see NOTE). "Disloyalty" (Heb *maʿal*, which can also mean "treachery, infidelity") brings a swift end to a friendly relationship (41:18c); see also Job 21:34. "Theft" (41:19a; see NOTE) is a shameful deed condemned also in 5:14c and 20:25. The "oath," Heb *ʾālâ*, and "agreement," *bĕrît*, which also means "covenant" (41:19b; see NOTE), were sacred and inviolable; breaking either was a serious moral lapse deserving severe punishment; see Ezek 17:13–18.

Bad manners by "stretching your elbow" at table to reach for something not close to you are deplorable; see also 31:12–20. "Refusing to give when asked" (41:19d) is another serious fault, for the duty of almsgiving was incumbent on all, rich and poor alike; see 3:30–4:6; 7:32–33; 29:8–13; and esp. Tob 4:7–11, 16. "Rebuffing your own kin" (41:21a; see NOTE), i.e., turning away from your own people so as to ingratiate yourself with the Seleucid overlords, was particularly shameful; cf. 41:5–10; 1 Macc 1:11–15; 2 Macc 4:7–17. The "appointed share" (41:21b; see NOTE) refers to the sacrificial portions reserved for the priests (cf. 7:31; Exod 29:26–28; Lev 7:31–36; 2 Chr 31:19). There was an obligation "to return a greeting" (41:20a; see NOTE); cf. also 4:8b and Tob 5:10; 7:1. "Gazing at a man's wife" (41:21c; see NOTE) was morally dangerous, for it could lead to adultery; cf. 9:7–8; Prov 6:25–29; Matt 5:28. "Entertaining thoughts about another woman" (or, a prostitute, 41:20b; see NOTE) was also perilous; cf. 9:5–6; 19:2–4. "Trifling with a servant girl of yours" and "violating her bed" (41:22ab; see NOTE) were not only sexual sins but also sins of exploitation and abuse of power; cf. 2 Sam 11:1–4. "Harsh words with friends" (41:22c; see NOTE) are to be avoided, or else the friendship may cease (cf. 37:2). To follow up "your gift with an insult" (41:22d; see NOTE) was despicable, for it was contrary to the spirit of kindness and generosity that were the hallmarks of the God-fearing Jew; see also 18:15–18. Gossip is condemned in 42:1a; see also 19:7. Betraying a secret (42:1b; see NOTE) destroyed friendship; cf. 22:22 and 27:16–21. In conclusion, Ben Sira urges us to "be ashamed of the right things," and thus will we "find favor in the sight of all" (41:1cd); cf. 42:8cd, the concluding bicolon of the next stanza. "The man that blushes is not quite a brute" (Edward Young, *Night*

Thoughts [1742–45], 7. 496). "Man is the only animal that blushes. Or needs to" (Mark Twain, "Pudd'nhead Wilson's New Calendar," *Following the Equator* [1897], 1, 27).

In the following stanza (42:1ef–8) Ben Sira presents a list of things of which you should not be ashamed, lest you "sin to save face" (42:1f). Heading the list is "the Law of the Most High and his precepts" (42:2a), lit., "the statute," i.e., each individual application of the Law; the colon serves as a reminder to the Jews who are tempted to compromise their faith for the blandishments of the Greek way of life. One should not be afraid to practice "justice to acquit the ungodly" (42:2b) when they are not guilty of the charge made against them; cf. Deut 1:17 and 16:18–20. In fairness, one should share "the expenses of a business or a journey" (42:3a), and should not be ashamed of settling accounts. Nor should one be ashamed of the complicated details and attention to the rights of all involved when "dividing an inheritance or property" (42:3b). The "accuracy [lit., the dust, cf. Isa 40:15] of scales and balances, and of tested measures and weights [lit., ephah and stone]" (42:4ab, G omits v 4b) is a matter of justice about which other biblical writers also speak: Lev 19:35–36; Prov 11:1; 16:11; 20:10, 23; Amos 8:5; Hos 12:8; Mic 6:11. One need not be ashamed "of acquiring much or little" (42:4c) as long as one does so fairly and honestly; cf. 26:29–27:2. Haggling over the price to be paid to a merchant has apparently been the custom for centuries (42:5a); one needs to have patience and to be a good actor, without shame, in order to get the best price (cf. 37:11). The "constant training of children" (42:5b; see NOTE) is a duty incumbent on every parent; cf. 30:1–13, with COMMENT. Ben Sira urges the householders of his day not to be ashamed "of beating the back of a disloyal servant [or slave]" (42:5c; see NOTE). Slavery was an unfortunate reality of that society and age (cf. also 33:25–30ab and Prov 29:19); but justice and kindness were enjoined in treating slaves (cf. 7:20–21 and 33:30cd–33).

A husband should not be ashamed "of a seal [cf. 22:27b and Dan 14:11, 17] to keep a foolish wife at home" (42:6a; see NOTE); cf. also 7:26; 23:22–26; 25:13–20). "A key," metonymy for a lock, is necessary "where there are many hands" (42:6b; see NOTE) to prevent theft and the temptation thereof (cf. 41:19a, above). Keeping accurate records of every financial transaction (42:7; see NOTES) is a prudent measure that helps one avoid future injustice or embarrassment. The wise will never be ashamed to chastise "the silly and the foolish" (42:8a; see NOTE) in order to improve their lot (cf. 20:7b, 13b), and old people "occupied with immorality" (42:8b; see NOTE), as were the two lecherous elders in the Susanna story (Dan 13:5, 8–21); see also 25:2d. When one is not ashamed to do the things Ben Sira mentions, one "will be truly refined and recognized by all as discreet" (42:8cd; see NOTE); see the concluding bicolon (42:1cd) of the previous stanza.

The next poem (42:9–14) deals with a father's concern and worry over his daughter, a subject on which Ben Sira offers advice also in 7:24–25. A daughter is compared to "a treasure that keeps her father wakeful" and sleepless (42:9ab; see NOTES). Although the image of treasure is somewhat flattering, the rest of the poem manifests the author's misogynistic male chauvinism, which reaches its climax in 42:14a: "Better a man's wickedness than a woman's goodness." Ben Sira no doubt affirmed the sentiments of the Jewish morning prayer: "Blessed are you, O Lord . . . who have not made me a Gentile . . . a slave . . . a woman." For a daughter to "remain unmarried" (42:9c; see NOTE) "in her youth" was a father's worry because women usually did not marry later in life. In 42:9d (see NOTE) and 10d (see NOTE) is reflected the common ancient notion that childlessness was always attributable to the wife's sterility, never to the husband's; cf., e.g., Luke 1:25. For a girl to "be defiled" (42:10a; see NOTE) "while unmarried," lit., "in her virginity," or to "become pregnant in her father's house" (42:10b; see NOTE) was a disaster, for virginity was demanded in a bride: see Deut 22:20–22. After marriage, a daughter's adultery is also a disgrace to her father (42:10c; see NOTE); cf. Deut 22:22; Ezek 16:38–41; John 8:4–5.

In view of all these concerns, Ben Sira urges "a close watch on your daughter" (42:11a; see NOTE), as he urges the same with regard to "an unruly wife" (26:10a). Otherwise your daughter may "make you the sport of your enemies" (42:11b; see NOTE) and bring public disgrace on you (42:11cd) because of the penalties the community was enjoined to impose on the woman guilty of fornication or adultery (cf. Lev 18:20; 20:10; Deut 22:20–22). Since the "lattice" of a room provides the opportunity for looking out at passersby (cf. Prov 7:6: Lady Wisdom looks through her lattice), the father is urged to put his daughter in a room without one and in a "spot" that does not overlook "the approaches to the house" (42:11ef; see NOTES). These precautions were apparently deemed necessary to help the girl avoid temptations to immorality. For her to reveal her beauty to a male is also to be avoided (42:12a; see NOTE), presumably because one or both may be tempted to commit sin. She should not be allowed the company of married women (42:12b) because "just as moths come from garments" (42:13a; see NOTE, and compare Job 13:28 and Isa 50:9), "so a woman's wickedness comes from a woman" (42:13b)—a cynical comment that conveniently and unjustly disallows the male element in the sins of women. In 25:24, Ben Sira gives a decidedly chauvinistic interpretation of Gen 3:1–6, 19 when he states: "In woman was sin's beginning; on her account we all die." Perhaps Ben Sira tempers his meanest and grossest comment of all, "Better a man's wickedness than a woman's goodness" (42:14a; see NOTE), by observing "better a religious daughter than a shameless son" (42:14b; but see NOTE on the difficulty of the text). Cf. 16:1–3. See INTRODUCTION, Part X, 7.

50. The Works of God in Creation
(42:15–43:33)

15 Now will I recall God's works;
    what I have seen, I will repeat.
  Through the LORD's word came his works;
    he accepts the one who does his will.
16 As the shining sun is clear to all,
    so the glory of the LORD fills his works;
17 Yet even God's holy ones must fail
    in recounting all his wonders,
  Though the LORD has given his hosts the strength
    to stand firm before his glory.
18 He searches out the abyss and the human heart;
    their secrets he understands.
  For the Most High possesses all knowledge,
    and sees the things that are to come forever.
19 He makes known the past and the future,
    and reveals the deepest secrets.
20 No understanding does he lack;
    no single thing escapes him.
21 He regulates the mighty deeds of his wisdom;
    he is from eternity one and the same.
  With nothing added, nothing taken away;
    no need of a counselor for him!
22 How beautiful are all his works,
    delightful to gaze upon and a joy to behold!
23 Everything lives and abides forever,
    and to meet each need all things are preserved.
24 All of them come in twos, one corresponding to the
                            other;
    yet none of them has he made in vain.
25 One exchanges its specific good with the other;
    can one ever see enough of their splendor?

43 1 The beauty of the celestial heights and the pure
firmament,
heaven itself manifests its glory.
2 The sun at its rising shines at its fullest,
a wonderful instrument, the work of the Most
High!
3 At noon it scorches the surface of the earth,
and who can bear its fiery heat?
4 Like a blazing furnace of solid metal,
the sun's rays set the mountains aflame;
Its fiery tongue consumes the world;
the eyes are burned by its fire.
5 Great indeed is the LORD who made it,
at whose orders it urges on its steeds.
6 It is the moon that marks the changing seasons,
governing the times, their lasting sign.
7 By it we know the sacred seasons and pilgrimage
feasts,
a light which wanes in its course.
8 The new moon like its name renews itself;
how wondrous it is when it changes!
An army signal for the cloud vessels on high,
it paves the firmament with its brilliance.
9 The beauty of the heavens and the glory of the stars,
a shining ornament in the heights of God,
10 By the LORD's command it keeps its prescribed
place,
and does not fade as the stars keep watch.
11 Behold the rainbow! Then bless its Maker,
for majestic indeed is its splendor;
12 It encompasses the heavenly vault with its glory;
the hand of God has stretched it out in power.

13 His rebuke marks out the path for the hail,
and makes brilliant the flashes of his judgment.
14 For his own purposes he has let loose his storehouse,
and he makes the rain clouds fly like vultures.
15 His might gives the clouds their strength,
and lops off the hailstones.

17a The thunder of his voice makes the earth writhe;
16a   by his power he shakes the mountains.
16b A word from him drives on the south wind,
17b   whirlwind, hurricane, and storm wind.
    He makes his snow fly like birds;
        it comes to settle like swarms of locusts.
18 Its shining whiteness dazzles the eyes;
        the mind marvels at its steady fall.
19 He pours out frost like salt;
        it shines like blossoms on the thornbush.
20 Cold northern blasts he sends
        that harden the ponds like solid ground.
    He spreads a crust over every body of water,
        and clothes each pool with a coat of mail.
21 When the mountain growth is scorched with heat,
        and the flowering meadows as though by flames,   B
22 The dripping clouds restore them all,
        and the scattered dew enriches the parched land.
23 His is the plan that calms Rahab
        and plants the islands in the deep.
24 Those who go down to the sea tell of its extent,
        and when we hear them we are thunderstruck;   B (M)
25 In it are his creatures, stupendous, amazing,
        all kinds of life, and the monsters of Rahab.
26 For him each messenger succeeds   B
        and at his bidding accomplishes his will.

27 More than this we will not add;
        let the last word be "He is the all."
28 Let us praise him the more, since we cannot fathom
                                                        him,
        for greater is he than all his works.
29 Awesome indeed is the LORD,
        and wonderful is his power.
30 Lift up your voices to glorify the LORD
        as much as you can, for there is still more.
    Extol him with renewed strength,
        and weary not, though you cannot fathom him.

31 For who has seen him and can describe him?   G
   or who can praise him as he is?
32 Beyond these, many things lie hid;
   only a few of his works have I seen.   B (G)
33 It is the LORD who has made all things,
   and to those who fear him he gives wisdom.

Notes

42   15b. *I will repeat* = M *wĕʾešnennâ* = Syr *ʾenâ mĕtannē;* MS B *waʾăsapperâ.*

15c. *the* LORD'*s* = M *ʾădōnay* = G; MS B *ʾĕlōhîm. his works* = M and MS Bᵐᵍ *maʿăśāy;* Bᵗˣᵗ *rĕṣônô* (cf. the second colon).

15d. = M and MS Bᵗˣᵗ *wĕpōʿēl rĕṣônô lĕqāḥô* (Bᵐᵍ *lāqaḥ*). But the text may also be pointed thus: *wĕpōʿal rĕṣônô liqḥô* (Bᵐᵍ *leqaḥ*) = "and his [Bᵐᵍ omits "his"] teaching is a work of his will (or grace)" (so similarly Peters and Yadin). If the last word is pointed *lāqāḥû* (so NAB), then the colon = "and they [the works of v 15c] accept the doing of his will," which is close to Syr, "and all his creatures do his will." This colon is missing in most Gr MSS, being present with variants in only three MSS (Sᶜ 339, 679) and two of G's daughter versions (the Sahidic and Armenian).

16a. *shining* = M *zōheret* = G; MS B *zor[eh]et* = Syr.

16b. LORD = MS B *yyy* = M *ʾădōnay. fills his works* = M *milleʾ maʿăśāyw* (cf. G); MS B *ʿal kol maʿăśāyw* = Syr.

17b. *all his wonders* = M *kol niplāʾōtāyw* = G; MS Bᵗˣᵗ *niplĕʾôt yyy.* Bᵐᵍ *niplĕʾôt gĕbûrōtāyw* = "the wonders of his mighty deeds"; Syr reverses the words, "the mighty deeds of his wonders."

17c. *the* LORD = M *ʾădōnāy;* MS B *ʾĕlōhîm.*

18a. *the human heart,* lit., "the heart."

18b. *their secrets* = M *ûbĕmaʿărummêhem* = G; MS B *ûbĕkol maʿăru(w)mmêhem.*

18c. = M *kî yādaʿ ʿelyôn kol [dāʿat]* = G; MS B is missing v 18cd.

18d. = M *wayyabbîṭ ʾōtîyôt ʿôlām;* cf. 39:19–20. G misread the consonants *ʾtywt* (= *ʾōtîyôt*) as *ʾōtôt* = *sēmeia* found only in MSS 248–672 (the rest of the MSS made the word a singular, *sēmeion*); cf. A. A. Di Lella, *CBQ* 28 (1966): 540. The word *ʾōtîyôt* occurs also in Isa 41:23; 44:7; 45:11.

19a. = M *mĕḥawweh ḥălîpôt [wĕnihyôt],* restored from MS Bᵐᵍ and G; Bᵗˣᵗ *nihyôt.*

20a. = M *lōʾ neʿdar mippānāyw* [so Strugnell with whom Yadin agreed (ErIsr 9 [1969]: 116)] *śākel;* MS B *[lōʾ neʾ]dar mimmenû kōl śākel.*

20b. = M *wĕl[ōʾ] ʿabā[r]ô* [MS B *ḥălāpô] kol dābār;* in Isa 24:5, *ʿbr* and *ḥlp* are in parallelism.

21a. = M *gĕbûrôt ḥokma[tô tikkēn],* restored from MS B. Since Bᵐᵍ has *gĕbûrōt* (= G) (as I am reading M *gbwrt*), presumably Bᵗˣᵗ, which is broken here, had *gĕbûrat.*

21c. *With nothing added*=M *lōʾ nôʾsāp;* here the form=*nôsāp. nothing taken away*=MS B *wĕlōʾ neʾĕṣēl;* M is partly illegible.

21d. =M *wĕl[ōʾ ṣarîk] lĕkōl mēbîn,* restored from MS B.

22. This bicolon is missing in MS B.

22a. =M *hălōʾ kōl maʿăśāyw nehĕmād[îm].*

22b. =M *ʿd nyṣwṣ wḥzwt marʾeh,* as corrected (and translated) by Strugnell (ErIsr 9 [1969]: 116–17) to read *ʿdny ṣyṣ wḥzwt* (=*wĕḥădût*) *marʾeh.*

23a. =M *hakkōl ḥay wĕʿōmēd lāʿad*=G (so similarly Syr). MS B has as the first word *hûʾ,* which="God," a deliberate scribal correction to avoid giving offense (so Peters).

23b. =M *[ûlĕ]kol ṣōrek hakkōl niśmār;* MS B has as the last word *yiśmaʿ,* "obey," with which G *hypakouei* is in agreement.

24a. =M *kullām [šnayim šnayim zeh] lĕʿummat zeh,* restored from Syr; MS B shortens and alters the colon: *kullam šônîm zeh mizzeh,* "all things are different, one from the other."

24b. =M *wĕlōʾ ʿāśâ mēhem [šāwʾ],* restored from Syr; the last word of MS B is fragmentary.

25a. *its specific good*=M *ṭôbām,* lit., "their good."

25b. =M *[û]mî yiśbaʿ lĕhabbîṭ hôdām*=Syr. MS B^{txt} has as the first word *ûmê,* which is clearly corrupt (B^{mg} corrects to *ûmî*); the end of the colon is damaged.

43 1a. =M *tōʾar mārôm wĕrāqîaʿ lĕtōhar;* MS B is corrupt.

1b. =M *ʿeṣem šāmayim [marʾeh hădā]rô;* MS B^{txt} *wĕʿeṣem šāmayim marbîṭ hădārô* (B^{mg} *nĕhārâ*).

2a. =M *šemeš môpîaʿ bĕṣēʾtô nksh;* Yadin relates *nksh* to *keseh,* "full moon," in Ps 81:4. MS B^{txt} *šemeš mabbîaʿ bĕṣārāto* [B^{mg} *môpîaʿ bĕṣēʾtô*] *ḥammâ.*

2b. =M *kĕlî nôrāʾ mʿśy* [read *maʿăśeh,* as in v 4a] *[ʿe]lyôn*=G=Syr; MS B *mah nôrāʾ maʿăśê yyy.*

3c. =M *wĕlipnê ḥōreb mî yitkal[kāʾ]l* (or *yitkôlēl,* so P. W. Skehan, *JBL* 75 [1966]: 262); MS B *lipnê ḥorbô mî yitkalkāl.* The reading *ḥorbô* of MS B may be better, since it is reflected in G, Lat, and Syr.

4a. =M *kûr nāpûaḥ mʿśy* [read *maʿăśeh,* as in v 2b] *mûṣāq,* lit., "a blazing furnace, the work of casting." MS B is corrupt.

4b. =*šāl[ûaḥ še]meš* [so M restored from MS B^{mg}] *yassîq* [so B^{mg}, B^{txt} *yadlîq*] *hārîm.*

4c. =M and MS B^{mg} *lĕšôn* [B^{txt} *lśʾwn*] *mārʾôr ti[q]môr nôšābet.*

4d. From MS B; M has a lacuna.

5a. *the* LORD=M *ʾădōnay*=MS B^{txt} *yyy*=G=Syr; B^{mg} has *ʿelyôn.*

5b. =*ûbidĕbārāyw* [so G; cf. Syr] *yĕnaṣṣaḥ ʾabbîrāyw* (so MS B^{txt}; B^{mg} *ynṣḥ*). M has only part of the first word. For *ʾabbîrîm* as "steeds, horses," cf. Jer 8:16; 47:3; and 50:11. The colon is difficult and subject to various translations; cf. G and Syr. Smend reads *ûdĕbārô yĕnaṣṣaḥ ʾabbîrô,* "and his [God's] word assures victory to his mighty servant" [=the sun]. Commentators (and translators) are not in agreement on the meaning of the colon.

6a. =M *wĕgam [yā]rēaḥ yaʾărîaḥ ʿittôt,* lit., "and the moon indeed makes the times (or seasons) travel."

6b. From MS B; M has a lacuna.

7a. =M *lô môʿēd ûmimmennû ḥāg,* lit., "By it [comes] the sacred season and from it the pilgrimage feast." MS Bᵗˣᵗ *bām* [Bᵐᵍ *bô*] *môʿēd ûzĕmannê* [Bᵐᵍ *ûmimmennû*] *ḥôq,* "By them [i.e., sun and moon] [comes] the sacred season and prescribed times." G reads: "From the moon (comes) the sign of the feast day"; Syr, "For from the moon (come) the signs of the feast days." The reading of Bᵗˣᵗ (*bām,* the plural referring to sun and moon) is important in religious history, for, as Yadin observes, "we may assume that B*text* here is perhaps influenced by the *Ben Sira* recension originating with the Dead Sea Sect, where a deliberate attempt was made to introduce the sun as a factor in determining the seasons. . . ."

7b. =G and Syr; MS B, which is not fully legible, is difficult to restore.

8a. =M *ḥōdeš kišĕmô hû'* *mit[ḥaddēš],* restored from MS B. MS Bᵗˣᵗ *ḥōdeš bĕhodšô* [Bᵐᵍ *kišĕmô*] *hû'* [Bᵐᵍ *wĕhû'*] *mithaddēš.* The reading of M and Bᵐᵍ receives support from G and Syr, though these versions apparently had difficulty in rendering the Heb play on words. For the reading of Bᵗˣᵗ, cf. Num 28:14 and Isa 66:23.

8b. From MS Bᵗˣᵗ; M has a lacuna. G = "it increases marvelously in its changing" = Syr.

8c. *An army signal* = M and MS B *kĕlî ṣābā';* the reference is to the fire signals used to control and direct the movements of an army or camp (so Smend and Box-Oesterley). *cloud vessels on high* = M and MS B *niblê mārôm,* lit., "the waterskins of the heights"; in Job 38:37, the phrase is *niblê šāmayim,* which is parallel to *šĕḥāqîm,* "clouds."

8d. From MS Bᵗˣᵗ; M has only the first word intact, *mĕraṣṣēp* = Bᵗˣᵗ; Bᵐᵍ *m'rṣ.*

9a. =M *tôr* [=*tô'ar* of MS B, as also in v 18a] *šāmayim wĕhôd* [MS B *wahădar*] *kôkēb.* G makes the stars the subject of vv 9–10.

9b. =M *ʿădî maśrîq bimĕrô[mê 'ēl],* restored from MS B; as the first two words, Yadin reads *'d wĕmaśrîq;* Bᵐᵍ *waʿădî maśrîq* supports my reading of M. For *ʿădî maśrîq,* Bᵗˣᵗ has *wĕʿôrô mazhîr.*

10a. *by the* LORD*'s command* = M *bidĕbar 'ădōnay* (MS B *'ēl*). G and Syr have "by the commands of the Holy One."

10b. =M and MS Bᵗˣᵗ *wĕlō' yāšôaḥ bĕ'ašmūrôtām;* Bᵐᵍ has *yšwn* for *yāšôaḥ. as the stars keep watch,* lit., "in their watches," the reference being to the stars mentioned in v 9a; cf. Bar 3:34.

11–33. Syr omits these verses.

11b. =M *kî mĕ'ôd nehdār[â bĕkābôd],* restored from MS Bᵐᵍ; Bᵗˣᵗ *ne'dārâ.*

12a. =M *ḥûg [hiqqîpāh] bikĕbôdāh,* restored from MS B; as the first word, Bᵗˣᵗ has *ḥôq,* Bᵐᵍ *ḥôd,* both of which are corrupt.

12b. =M *[wĕ]yad 'el nāṭattāh bigĕb[ûrâ]. the hand of God:* G has "the hands of the Most High." *in power:* omitted by G.

13a. =M *gaʿărātô* [so also MS Bᵐᵍ] *[tatwe]h bārād;* Bᵗˣᵗ *gĕbûrātô tatweh bārāq* (Bᵐᵍ *bāqār,* corrupt), "His power marks out the path of the lightning." G, "By his command he sends the driving snow."

13b. =M *ûtĕnaṣṣaḥ zîqôt mišpāṭ;* the last word of MS B is damaged.

14a. =M *lĕmaʿănô* [so also MS Bᵐᵍ] *pāraʿ 'ôṣār;* Bᵗˣᵗ *lĕmaʿan bārā' 'ôṣā[r].*

14b. =M *wayyāʿap ʿābîm kĕʿāyiṭ;* MS B is damaged after the first word.

15ab. =M; MS B is damaged throughout. For the second word of the first colon, *ḥzq,* read *tĕhazzēq,* a feminine verb like the verb *watĕgaddeaʿ* in the second colon.

17a, 16ab, 17bcd, 18. The order of these bicola is from M, MS B^mg, and a significant number of G MSS *(O*-V *L'*-157") as well as the Sahidic.

17a. *makes . . . writhe*=M and MS B^mg *yāḥîl* (cf. Ps 29:8)=G *ōdinēsen* (so MSS A 248–315 *a*-534 *b* 336 542 543 679 Sa); B^txt *yāḥûl.*

16a. *he shakes*=M *yānîp;* MS B^mg *yaz'îm,* "he makes indignant."

16b. =M *'imrātô taḥărîp têmān;* MS B *'ēmātô tĕhārēp têmān.*

17b. =M and MS B^mg *'il'ôl sûpâ ûsĕ'ārâ;* B^txt *zal'ăpôt ṣāpôn sûpâ ûsĕ'ārâ.*

17c. =M *kĕresep* [also MS B^mg; B^txt *(bĕ)resep] yĕpārēaḥ šilgô.* For *yĕpārēaḥ,* an Aramaism, MS B^txt has *yānîp* (cf. NOTE on v 16a); B^mg has a variant but is not legible.

17d. =M and MS B^mg; B^txt *drtw* reverses the first two consonants of *ridtô.*

18a. *dazzles*=*yiqqâ,* lit., "pierces, stings"; M has *yhq,* MS B^txt *yagheh,* B^mg *yehgeh.*

18b. *marvels at*=*yitmah;* M *ytmyh,* MS B *yehĕmeh.*

19a. *pours out*=M and MS B^mg *yišpōk*=G; B^txt *yiškôn.*

19b. =M *wayyiṣmaḥ kisĕneh ṣiṣṣîm;* MS B *wĕyāṣîṣ kassappîr ṣi(y)ṣṣîm.*

20b. =M *ûkĕregeb yaqpî' māqôr;* MS B^txt *ûkĕrāqāb . . . mĕqôrô* (B^mg *miqweh). like solid ground,* lit., "like clods."

20d. From MS B; M is completely damaged.

21a. =M *[yĕbûl hārî]m ḥōreb yaśś[îq],* so P. W. Skehan's reading, restored from MS B (*JBL* 85 [1966]: 262); MS B has *ḥorbô.*

21b–23a. From MS B^txt; M is completely damaged.

22b. Read *wĕṭāl* (MS B *ṭāl*) as the first word of the second colon. *enriches*=*yĕdaš-šēn*=G; MS B *lĕdaššēn.*

23a. *calms Rahab*=*mašqîṭ rahab* (cf. G); MS B *maššîq rabbâ.*

23b. *and plants*=*wayyiṭṭa'*=G; MS B *wayyēṭ.* Only the last word, *'yîm,* "the islands," survives in M.

24a. *its extent*=MS B *qāṣēhû,* lit., "its end, boundary."

24b. *we are thunderstruck*=MS B *ništômām;* M, which has the complete colon, jumbled the consonants of the word: *nšmtm.*

25b. *and the monsters of Rahab*=M *[û]gĕbûrōt rahab*=G; MS B *rbh* (=*rabbâ*) reversed the second and third consonants.

26–33. M lacks these verses.

29b. *and wonderful*=*wĕniplē't;* MS B *wĕniplā'ôt. his power*=B^mg *gĕbûrātô*=G; B^txt *dĕbārāyw.*

30c. =MS B^mg *mĕrômĕmāyw* [B^txt *mĕrômîm] hahālîpû kōaḥ.*

31. This verse was omitted by MS B. *For*=MSS S 336 542 753; the other Gr witnesses omit *gar.*

32a. =G; MS B has only the first word and part of the last word.

32b. *have I seen*=MS B *rā'îtî;* G="have we seen," thus disrupting the *inclusio* with 42:15b at the beginning of this lengthy poem.

Comment

This lengthy poem may be divided into four substantial stanzas: 15+14+16+8 bicola. In form and content, it is similar to Job 38–41, Prov 30:15–16, 18–20, 24–31, and Wis 7:17–22a, all of which bear a striking resemblance to the "onomasticon" from Egypt. See also Job 28; 36:27–37:18; and Sir 38:24–39:11. The onomasticon was a type of literature devised as an aid to the scribes. It contained a list of names of places, occupations, titles, flora and fauna, natural phenomena, and the like. See INTRODUCTION, Part IV, "Literary Genres," and R. J. Williams, "Wisdom in the Ancient Near East," *IDB-Sup*, p. 950. Our present poem has one overriding theme: the praise of God, who is the omnipotent and omniscient Lord of all creation.

The first stanza (42:15–25) opens with an allusion to Ps 77:12, the recalling of God's mighty works in creation (42:15ab; cf. NOTE); v 15b=Job 15:17. The world exists thanks to "the LORD's word" (42:15c; cf. NOTE), a reference to creation by word in Genesis 1; Ps 33:6; Wis 9:1; Jdt 16:14; cf. also John 1:1–3. The meaning of 42:15d is uncertain (cf. NOTE); if my translation is correct, then the meaning is that God is favorable to "the one who does his will" (see 43:33b, the last colon of the poem), as he is to the created works that obeyed his will by coming into existence. As clear as the shining sun (42:16a; cf. NOTE) is "the glory of the LORD" that "fills his works" (42:16b; cf. NOTE). One would have to be physically and spiritually blind not to see God's glory in creation; cf. Ps 19:2–5 and Rom 1:19–22. "God's holy ones," Heb *qĕdôšê 'ēl* (42:17a), are the angels, as in Job 5:1, 15:15; Ps 89:8; Zech 14:15; Dan 8:13. The point of 42:17 is that, even though the LORD gives the angels, called "his hosts" in v 17c (cf. also Pss 103:20–21; 148:2), "the strength to stand firm before his glory," they are incapable of recounting adequately the splendors of creation; how much less capable are human beings! Cf. also 18:4–7; 43:27–31.

God's omniscience is the subject of 42:18–21. The Lord knows all about "the abyss" (Heb *tĕhôm*) and "the human heart" (42:81a; cf. NOTE), two realities that are inscrutable to ordinary mortals. The *tĕhôm*, a word used in the myths of the Ancient Near East, recalls not only "the abyss" or "the deep" (as in Gen 1:2) but also the monster Tiamat in the Babylonian creation story *Enuma eliš* (*ANET*, pp. 60–72). God has not only complete knowledge (42:18c) but also sovereign control over all the mysterious and chaotic forces of the *tĕhôm;* cf. Pss 33:7; 36:7; 89:10–11; Isa 51:9–10; Job 9:13; 26:12–13;

38:16. As regards the secrets of "the human heart" or mind, cf. Jdt 8:14; Prov 15:11. Divine omniscience extends not only to the past but also to the future (42:18d, 19a; cf. NOTES, and cf. Isa 41:21–23) as well as to "the deepest secrets" (42:19b). God's understanding knows no limits (42:20; cf. NOTES); cf. 39:19–20; Ps 139:1–6; Wis 1:6–10. "The mighty deeds of [God's] wisdom" are all in order (42:21a; cf. NOTE); nothing in creation is out of place (cf. also 16:26–28). Since God is immutable, "from eternity one and the same" (42:21b), nothing can be added or taken away from him or his marvelous creation (42:21c; cf. NOTE); cf. also 18:6 and Qoh 3:14. Nor does he have "need of a counselor" (42:21d); for the thought, cf. Isa 40:13–14; Rom 11:34.

The concluding verses (42:22–25) of this stanza praise the beauty, harmony, and splendor of creation. All God's works are beautiful, a delight and joy to the eye (42:22; cf. NOTES) and an inspiration to the poet. "Beauty being the best of all we know / Sums up the unsearchable and secret aims / Of nature" (Robert Bridges, *The Growth of Love* [1876], 8). "Everything" created "lives and abides forever" (42:23a), not in the sense of being eternal (cf. NOTE for the change of subject from "everything" to "God," which is more dogmatically acceptable), but in the sense of being stable in its nature. Everything also has a specific purpose in creation (42:23b; cf. NOTE), an idea mentioned also in 39:33–34. The words of 42:24a (cf. NOTE) are found also in 33:15b: all things "come in twos, one corresponding to the other"—e.g., night and day, light and darkness, hot and cold, dry and wet, good and evil, high and low. Nothing was created "in vain" (42:24b); one thing "exchanges its specific good with the other" (42:25a) in harmonious equilibrium (cf. Qoh 7:14). The stanza ends with "their splendor," Heb *hôdām,* an expression that characterizes all created things.

The second stanza (43:1–12) depicts specific creatures and the beauty and usefulness with which God in his wisdom and might has endowed them: the heavens, the sun, the moon, the stars, the rainbow. The heavens with their "celestial heights" and "pure firmament" (cf. Gen 1:6–8; Exod 24:10) are not only beautiful but manifest their own glory (43:1; cf. NOTES), which is a reflection of God's glory; cf. Ps 19:2. The sun, one of the greatest works of creation, is described as "a wonderful instrument, the work of the Most High" (43:2b; cf. NOTE for MS B's different reading). The "fiery heat" of the sun at noon is a common image (43:3); cf. 14:27. "O dark, dark, dark, amid the blaze of noon, / Irrecoverably dark, total eclipse" (John Milton, *Samson Agonistes* [1671], l. 80). "The sun's rays" are so strong that they "set the mountains aflame," and "its fiery tongue consumes the world" (43:4bc)— hyperbolic images to give one a feeling of the sun's awesome power, which was derived from "the LORD [who] made it" (43:5a; cf. NOTE). It is at God's orders that the sun "urges on its steeds" (43:5b; cf. NOTE for the problems of the text and its various translations); if my translation is correct, the sun is pictured as having steeds to pull it across the firmament (cf. Ps 19:7).

The moon receives even more space in the poem than the sun. The reason is that the moon marks the religious festivals (43:7a), which were of great significance for Ben Sira. Since the Jews of antiquity followed a lunar calendar, the moon is said to mark "the changing seasons, governing the times" (43:6; cf. NOTES); cf. Ps 104:19 and *Phibis,* xxxii 2 (Sanders, p. 79). By the moon people knew "the sacred seasons and pilgrimage feasts" (43:7a); cf., e.g., Num 28:11; Hos 2:13; Amos 8:5; Isa 1:13. See the NOTE on 43:7a for the reading of MS B, which suggests that the sun was also used to mark the festivals; cf. also S. Iwry, "A New Designation for the Luminaries in Ben Sira [43:5] and in the Manual of Discipline (IQS)," *BASOR* 200 (1970): 41–47. For the pilgrimage feast, Heb *ḥag,* see Exod 10:9; 23:14, 17; Judg 21:19; 1 Kgs 12:32–33; Isa 30:29; Amos 8:10; Nah 2:1; Tob 1:6. For the wordplay on the Heb words for "new moon" and "renews itself," see NOTE on 43:8a. The moon is described as "an army signal" for the clouds (43:8c; see NOTE for an explanation of the image). At night, the moon "paves the firmament with its brilliance" (43:8d), a striking image; cf. Gen 1:16. Ben Sira now uses a series of lyrical metaphors to depict the splendor of the moon: "the beauty of the heavens and the glory of the stars, a shining ornament in the heights of God" (43:9; cf. NOTES). The moon does exactly what God wills (43:10a) and "does not fade" even when "the stars keep watch" (43:10b; cf. NOTE); indeed, the moon outshines even the brightest stars.

The stanza concludes with a couplet on the rainbow. When we look at the rainbow, we should be prompted to "bless its Maker, for majestic indeed is its splendor" (43:11). The rainbow was often used as an image of spectacular beauty; cf. 50:7b and Ezek 1:28. The rainbow was also the sign of the covenant that God made with Noah after the Flood (Gen 9:12–17). The "glory" of the rainbow in "the heavenly vault" is remarkable because "the hand of God has stretched it out in power (43:12; cf. NOTES).

The next stanza (43:13–26) speaks of the various elements in nature doing the will of their almighty Creator: hail, lightning, rain clouds, hailstones, thunder, earthquakes, storm winds, snow, frost, ice, rain, dew, and the sea with all its marvelous creatures. Like other biblical authors, Ben Sira, who probably had in mind Psalm 29 with its graphic description of God's majesty and might in the storm, attributes meteorological phenomena and the other forces of nature directly to God himself. The image of God's "rebuke" marking out "the path of the hail" (43:13a; cf. NOTE on the textual variants) is derived from Ps 18:16 (= 2 Sam 22:16): "The bed of the sea appeared, and the foundations of the world were laid bare, at the rebuke of the LORD, at the blast of the wind of his wrath," and Ps 104:7; cf. also Job 26:11; Isa 50:2; 51:20. Lightning is described as "the flashes of [God's] judgment" (43:13b); the thunderstorm with its awesome displays of lightning, winds, and hail may be viewed as a foretaste of God's judgment of the world; cf. Ps 18:8–20 (= 2 Sam 22: 8–20); Isa 29:6. Thus God lets "loose his *storehouse*" (Heb *'ôṣār*) of the forces of the storm "for his own purposes" (43:14a; cf. NOTE), one of which is for judgment. Job 38:22 also speaks of "the storehouses [ʾōṣĕrôt] of the snow" and "the storehouses of the hail"; cf. also Sir 39:30d; Deut 28:12; Jer 51:16. The "rain clouds," Heb ʿābîm, are compared to "vultures," Heb ʿāyiṭ (43:14b; cf. NOTE), which means "bird(s) of prey" in general; cf. Isa 60:8. God's "might gives the clouds [Heb ʿānān] their strength" to produce rain and "lops off the hailstones" (43:15) as if from a block of ice in the sky.

"The thunder of his voice [or, more lit., the sound (or voice) of his thunder] makes the earth writhe [or, shakes the earth]" (43:17a; cf. NOTE), a clear reference to Ps 29:8. "By his power he shakes the mountains" (43:16a; cf. NOTE) through earthquakes; see Ps 18:8, 16=2 Sam 22:8, 16. God's mighty word (43:16b; cf. NOTE) makes "the south wind" blow as well as the "whirl-wind, hurricane, and storm wind" (43:17b; cf. NOTE); these winds are often cited in contexts dealing with the divine wrath and judgment (cf., e.g., Isa 29:6; 40:24; 41:16; Jer 23:19; 30:23; Ezek 13:11, 13). In contrast to the earth-quake (43:17a, 16a) and destructive winds (43:16b, 17b), which are symbols of God's anger, "[God's] snow" is depicted serenely as flying "like birds" (43:17c; cf. NOTE) and settling "like swarms of locusts" (43:17d), i.e., in an orderly fashion (the locust swarm was considered well organized; cf. Prov 30:27); cf. Ps 147:16a. "Its shining whiteness [lit., the beauty of its whiteness] dazzles the eyes" (43:18a; cf. NOTE); children of all ages take delight in snow. The snowfall itself is marvelous to behold (43:18b; cf. NOTE). People who live in places where snow is plentiful and often unpleasant may react more sympa-thetically to Hal Borland's comment, "A snowdrift is a beautiful thing—if it doesn't lie across the path you have to shovel or block the road that leads to your destination" ("Snowdrifts—January 26," *Sundial of the Seasons* [1964]).

The frost is also lovely, shining "like blossoms on the thornbush" (43:19b; cf. NOTE); God pours it out "like salt" (43:19a; in Ps 147:16b, God "strews" frost "like ashes"). The cold north wind, which God sends, freezes the ponds solid (43:20b; cf. NOTE); cf. Ps 147:17. God "spreads a crust over every body of water, and clothes each pool with a coat of mail"—colorful images that suggest Ben Sira enjoyed the sight of a frozen pond. When "the mountain growth" (cf. Job 40:20) and "flowering meadows" are burned up and dried out (43:21), "the dripping clouds" and "scattered dew" bring them back to life (43:22; cf. NOTE). For a parallel, see *Phibis,* xxxii 6 (Sanders, p. 79). An important source of moisture in Palestine, dew (like rain) was considered a blessing (cf. Gen 27:28; Deut 33:28; Job 29:19; Ps 133:3; Prov 19:12; Hos 14:6); and the lack of dew, a curse (cf. Gen 27:39; 1 Sam 17:1).

The most convincing evidence of God's great wisdom and almighty power is 43:23a: his "plan that calms Rahab" (the mythical sea monster in Isa 30:7; 51:9; Job 9:13; 26:12; Pss 87:4; 89:11; cf. NOTE). Rahab is parallel to "the deep," Heb tĕhôm (43:23b). In Job 26:12 and Ps 89:11, Rahab is parallel to "the sea," Heb yām (43:24a), which in turn is parallel to tĕhôm in Job 28:14;

38:16, 30. Regarding this section on the majesty and splendor of the sea (43:23–26), cf. Ps 104:24–26. The imagery in 43:23 is employed to give poetic expression to creation theology. "Rahab" is the personification of "the deep," *těhôm*, which, as in Gen 1:2, represents the antithesis of creation. For the phrase "that calms Rahab" (43:23a; cf. NOTE), cf. Mark 4:39; 6:50–51. When God conquers the deep, it sinks, and then the islands appear. Cf. also v 25f and 42:18, with COMMENT above. The phrase "those who go down to the sea" (43:24a) is found also in Ps 107:23a. Sea voyagers tell us of the grandeur and "extent" of the sea (43:24a; cf. NOTE), and we marvel at what we hear (43:24b). In the sea are God's "creatures, stupendous, amazing, all kinds of life, and the monsters of Rahab" (43:25); cf. Pss 104:25–26; 107:23–24 for the background of this verse. "The monsters of Rahab" (43:25b; cf. NOTE) are Leviathan, "the fleeing . . . coiled serpent," and "the dragon that is in the sea" (Isa 27:1; cf. also Job 3:8); "the helpers of Rahab" (Job 9:13); the "monster in the sea" (Ezek 32:2); and the "large fish, that swallowed Jonah" (Jonah 2:1). But all sea creatures, including "the monsters of Rahab," are under God's sovereign control; nothing in the sea can get out of hand to threaten creation or reduce it to primeval chaos (Gen 1:2); cf. Wis 14:1–7. Each one of the sea creatures, as well as all the other works of God mentioned earlier in the poem, is now called a "messenger," Heb *mal'āk*, Gr *angelos*, which "succeeds" because at God's bidding it "accomplishes his will" (43:26), thus fulfilling the purpose for which it was created. Cf. Ps 104:4.

The final stanza (43:27–33) of this masterful poem, which corresponds to the opening stanza (42:15–25), begins with Ben Sira's humble comment that he has said enough about the wonders of creation: "More than this we will not add" (43:27a). "The last word" (cf. Qoh 12:13) is "He [God] is the all" (43:27b), i.e., all of creation as a whole and in each of its parts cannot be explained except through God, who is the source and abiding sustainer of everything (so Spicq). Cf. Col 1:17; Heb 1:3. Although the clause "He is the all" (Heb *hû' hakkōl*) could be taken at face value in a pantheistic sense, such a meaning would be contrary to all of Ben Sira's thought, esp. in the present poem, which celebrates the uniqueness of God and his creative activity. The Latin renders the sense well: *ipse est in omnibus,* "He is in all," i.e., God is revealed in the splendid creatures he has made. The idea that God is beyond human comprehension and so is to be praised (43:28a), is found also in Ps 145:3. Since God is "greater . . . than all his works" (43:28b), which are themselves magnificent, Ben Sira describes the LORD as "awesome" and "his power" as "wonderful" (43:29), ideas found also in Ps 96:4–6, 10; cf. Dan 9:4. He then invites you to "lift up your voices to glorify the LORD as much as you can, for there is still more" (43:30ab). The contemplation of the beauties of creation should inspire not only awe and reverence but also songs of praise for the all-wise and all-powerful Creator; cf. also Psalm 104. We should never weary of extolling God even though we "cannot fathom him" (43:30cd); see v 28a above, where the verb "fathom" occurs again. "For who has seen [God] and can describe him? or who can praise him as he is?" (43:31; cf. NOTE). In 42:17ab, in the opening stanza of the poem, Ben Sira put this idea in a different way: "Even God's holy ones," who presumably see God, "must fail in recounting all his wonders." Cf. also Ps 106:2.

In the final couplet of the poem, Ben Sira makes four statements that are typical in Wisdom literature: (1) Beyond the marvels he has described, "many things lie hid" (43:32a); for a similar thought, cf. Job 26:14. (2) Ben Sira says: "Only a few of [God's] works have I seen" (43:32b; cf. NOTE), Heb *rāʾîtî,* which forms an *inclusio* with the parallel verb *ḥāzîtî* in 42:15b, in the opening bicolon of the poem. Our author admits that the universe is vast, and that he has seen only a small part of it. (3) He confesses his faith in Yahweh, "who has made all these things" (43:33a); cf. Gen 1:1–2:4a. The universe and all that is in it are not self-explanatory; only the creative work of God can explain the existence and presence of all things. (4) God "gives wisdom" only "to those who fear him," Gr *tois eusebesin* (43:33b; MS B has only part of the expression, *ûlĕʾa[nšê ḥesed],* lit., "to the pious, or the godly")—a sentiment Ben Sira affirms emphatically in the opening poem of the book, 1:1–10; cf. also 1:11–30 and 50:28–29. Cf. 42:15d, with COMMENT.

This stanza, which concludes the poem on creation and its splendors, also prepares us for the next section, entitled in MS B "Praise of the Ancestors of Old." In fact, the phrase *ʾanšê ḥesed,* "the pious, godly," in the final colon of the stanza (43:33b; cf. above) also occurs in the opening colon of the next section (44:1a) to designate the noble ancestors of Israel. For further study of this stanza see H. Duesberg, "Il est le Tout: Siracide 43, 27–33," *BVC* 54 (1963): 29–32.

For a detailed study of the entire poem see G. L. Prato, *Il problema della teodicea in Ben Sira,* pp. 116–208.

PART VIII (44:1–50:24)

51. Praise of Israel's Great Ancestors
(44:1–16)

44 ¹ I will now praise those godly people,
 our ancestors, each in his own time—
² The Most High's portion, great in glory,
 reserved to himself from ancient days:
³ Rulers of the earth, of royal rank,
 persons renowned for their valor,
 Or counselors with their shrewd advice,
 or seers of all things in prophecy;
⁴ Resolute governors of the folk,
 or lawgivers with their rules;
 Sages with their literary discourse,
 or framers of proverbs and pointed maxims;
⁵ Composers of melodious psalms,
 or authors with lyric themes;
⁶ Stalwart, self-reliant persons,
 at peace in their own estates—
⁷ All these were glorious in their time,
 each illustrious in his day.
⁸ Some of them have left behind a name
 so that people recount their praises;
⁹ But of others no memory remains,
 for when they perished, they perished completely,
 And are as though they had never lived,
 they and their children after them.
¹⁰ Yet these also were godly people
 whose virtues will not be forgotten;
¹¹ Their wealth remains in their families,
 their heritage with their descendants.

12 Through God's covenant with them their family
                                    endures,
    and their offspring for their sakes;
13 For all time their progeny will last,
    their glory will never be blotted out.
14 Their bodies are buried in peace,
    but their name lives on and on;
15 At gatherings their wisdom is retold,
    and the assembly declares their praises.ᵃ

---

16 ᵃ ENOCH walked with the LORD and was taken up,   B
    a sign for the knowledge of future generations.

Notes

44   1–17. The Masada MS in this, its last extant column, has usually only the first colon preserved in each line; it is eked out here with the aid of MS B, except as noted below.

1. For the opening *'ăhallĕlâ-nā'*, with MS B (M is defective), compare 42:15a *'ezkĕrâ-nā'* in M, both text and margin.

2. Reading *rāb kābôd ḥēleq 'elyôn / wĕgōrālô mîmôt ôlām*, for which the translation is rather a paraphrase. The language comes in part from Deut 32:7–9, from which the understanding of *ḥēleq 'elyôn* here derives: the phrase stands for the collectivity of Israel, which is equated with the heroes of the past (vv 9–13 make this possible). The phrase *rāb kābôd* anticipates *ḥēleq* and modifies it grammatically—compare the way in which the individual figures of Moses (45:1), Aaron (45:6), Joshua (46:1), Samuel (46:13), David (47:2), and Simeon the high priest (50:1) are characterized before being named. In the second colon, the expression *wĕgōrālô* is understood as parallel to *ḥēleq:* the Lord's possession for the future (cf. Ps 125:3; Sir 11:22), with no reference to an acquisition by lot. M already has *wgdlh* for this, and G's *tēn megalosynēn autou* supposes *(w)gdlw;* the parallel would then be with *kābôd*. In vv 7 and 13, however, the "glory" in this context is that of the forefathers, not of the Most High directly; and coherent sense and syntax are not obtainable with the *gdl* reading. For this and other details in 44:1–15, cf. P. W. Skehan, "Staves, Nails and Scribal Slips (Ben Sira 44:2–5)," *BASOR* 200 (1970): 66–71.

4b. *rules = (bi)mĕḥōqĕqōtām*, lit., "staves," cf. Num 21:18 and *BASOR* 200, pp. 67–68.

4d. G omits this colon, and Syr merged it with 5a. *pointed maxims=maśměrōtām,* lit., "nails," or "spikes"; cf. Qoh 12:11 and *BASOR* 200, p. 69.

5a,b. *melodious=ʿal ḥōq* (MS B); M and B^ms have (*ʿal) qāw. lyric=(bě)miktām,* a term confined to Psalm titles, and conjectured for Isa 38:9, the song of Hezekiah. Nobody knows the actual meaning of the word, but its presence here (against MS B, G, and Syr: *bikětāb,* "in writing," which conflicts with *authors=nōśěʾê,* referring to a vocal activity) is guaranteed by an elaborate end-rhyme pattern in *-tām,* vv 1–8; see *BASOR* 200, pp. 69–70.

10. *not . . . forgotten:* by God, that is; see the following verses. MS B is flawed; *forgotten* follows G (=*tiššakēaḥ;* cf. 3:14, MS C).

11b. *with their descendants:* MS B is flawed; read *libnê bānîm.* Cf. Ps 103:17; Prov 13:22.

12b. for their sakes=*baʿăbûrām;* cf. G.

16a. MS B includes the words *nimṣāʾ tāmîm,* which belong in v 17. This reference to Enoch, who is spoken of again in 49:14, is not present in the Masada fragments or Syr, though G and MS B do have it. His popularity in the last centuries B.C. as the custodian of ancient lore would seem to have prompted this expansion on Ben Sira's text, putting Enoch at the head of the list of ancient ancestors. Cf. Gen 5:24.

Comment

Chaps. 44–49 form a distinct and unified division of the book, having as subject matter "Praise of the Ancestors of Old," the title that appears before 44:1 in MS B. In most of the MSS of G as well as Lat and Syr, the title reads: "Praise of the Ancestors." Cf. 24:1. In some MSS of G and Syr, the title is not present. Ben Sira himself may have inserted the title (so Smend, p. 415). Peters (p. 375) thinks the original title is preserved in G, suggesting that Heb *ʿôlām,* "of old," in MS B repeats the last word of 44:2b. The present section (44:1–15) serves as introduction to the historical panorama of Israel's heroes who are worthy of praise. If MS B and G are correct, Enoch is the first individual named (44:16), and the list of ancestors comes to an end with another mention of Enoch in 49:14a, thus forming an *inclusio,* which signals the conclusion of this division. But cf. NOTE on 44:16 above.

The present chapters flow quite naturally from the preceding section (42:15–43:33), which extols the power and glory of God displayed in the splendor and might of the natural world. An appendix (50:1–24) sings the praises of the high priest Simeon II, who as a contemporary of Ben Sira can hardly be reckoned as one of the Ancestors of Old. Similar historical surveys are found also in Ezek 20:4–44; Neh 9:6–37; Psalms 78; 105; 106; 135; 136; Jdt 5:5–21; Wis 10:1–12:27; 1 Macc 2:51–64; Acts 7:2–53; Jas 5:10–11; and

Heb 11:2–39. In these chapters, Ben Sira emphasizes God's gracious call and election of Israel and the divine covenant with Abraham and his descendants. What the God of the universe and of all peoples had done in his loving-kindness toward Israel is gloriously proclaimed by the long line of patriarchs, matriarchs, kings, prophets, teachers, and other heroes of the faith. It is primarily for this reason that these individuals are admirable and praisewor-thy. This portrait gallery drawn from Israel's sacred history is meant to reinforce the conviction and courage of Ben Sira's contemporaries.

Throughout these chapters, Ben Sira manifests an easy and thorough famil-iarity with the earlier Scriptures—the Pentateuch (the Law), Deuteronomy, Joshua, Judges, Samuel and Kings, Chronicles, Nehemiah, Psalms, Proverbs, and Job. Following the basic narrative contained in these sources, he attempts to show how Israel's ancestors have something significant to say to believers of his day.

In this introductory section, Ben Sira lists in general terms the twelve categories of heroes (44:3–6) about whom he will write in some detail. He has in mind only the stalwarts of Israel. The pagan worthies who could also fit into these categories are simply not part of his purview. Cf. J. L. Duhaime, "El elogio de los Padres de Ben Sira y el Cántico de Moisés (Sir 44:50 y Dt 32)," *EstBib* 35 (1976): 223–29. All of Israel's ancestors (44:1b) were "godly people," Heb *'anšê ḥesed*, lit., "people of piety" (44:1a; cf. also 44:10a)—the essential quality that makes them worthy of note and praise and imitation. In 40:17, *ḥesed* is in synonymous parallelism with *ṣĕdāqâ*, "righteousness." Cf. 41:11b; 46:7a; 49:3b; Isa 57:1; Hos 6:6; Neh 13:14; 2 Chr 35:26; 1 Macc 2:42. It is from such godly people that Ben Sira's contemporaries are descended. In 44:1b, the expression "each in his own time" (lit., in their generations), indi-cates that Ben Sira will speak of the ancestors in chronological order.

For the text and meaning of 44:2, cf. NOTE. In the twelve cola of 44:3–6, Ben Sira lists the twelve classes of individuals to be praised. Cf. 24:13–17, where Gr *hōs*, "like," is used twelve times. The number twelve was consid-ered sacred in the Bible: twelve tribes of Israel (cf. 44:23e), twelve months in the year, twelve Apostles, twelve courses of foundation stones and twelve gates in the heavenly Jerusalem (Rev 21:12–14). In 44:7, all these categories of people are said to be "glorious in their time," lit., in their generation (44:7a). It is to be observed that 44:1–7 form a single periodic sentence, with the expressions "in their generations" (44:1b) and "in their generation" (44:7a) forming an *inclusio.* The "rulers" in 44:3a include people such as David (cf. 47:1–11) and Solomon (cf. 47:12–22). The "persons renowned for their valor" (44:3b) are Joshua (cf. 46:1–8), Caleb (cf. 46:9–10), and the Judges (cf. 46:11–12). The "counselors" (44:3c) are Nathan (cf. 47:1); Isaiah, who served at the royal court (cf. 48:20, 22); and Jeremiah (cf. 49:6). The "seers" (44:3d) are prophets such as Samuel (cf. 46:13–20), Elijah (cf. 48:1–11), Elisha (cf. 48:12–16), Isaiah, Jeremiah, Ezekiel (cf. 49:8), and the Twelve

Minor Prophets (cf. 49:10). The "resolute governors" (44:4a) are people such as Joseph (cf. 49:15); and the "lawgivers" (44:4b), those such as Moses (cf. 44:23f–45:5). The "sages" (44:4c) include Solomon and Job (cf. 49:9). The "framers of proverbs and pointed maxims" (44:4d) are those such as Solomon, the supposed author of Proverbs and Qoheleth, and presumably scribes such as Ben Sira himself. The expression "composers of melodious psalms" (44:5a) is a reference to David (cf. 2 Chr 7:6) and the guilds of temple singers. The phrase "authors with lyric themes" (44:5b; cf. NOTES), refers to people such as Solomon, the reputed author of the Song of Songs, and to Hezekiah (cf. Isa 38:9). "Stalwart, self-reliant persons" (44:6a) are the patriarchs Abraham (cf. 44:19:21), Isaac (cf. 44:22), and Jacob (cf. 44:23a–e). "[Persons] at peace in their own estates" (44:6b) probably refers to those such as Job. The twelve categories of ancestors are summed up in the phrase "all these" (44:7a). Israel's ancestors were not only "glorious in their time [and] illustrious" (44:7), but are also a source of pride for the contemporary believer. There is a pleasing rhyme in -ām at the end of each of the seven bicola in 44:1–7—a further indication that these verses form a single period.

Some of those alluded to in a general way in 44:1–7 "have left behind a *name*" (44:8), i.e., an honorable reputation. For a good parallel, see *Phibis,* ii 12 (Sanders, p. 94). These are the "godly people" who are spoken of in detail in 44:16–49:16. The "others" of whom "no memory remains," for they perished completely (44:9)—they and their children—may be the impious and disloyal Israelites of the past, esp. the godless kings of both southern and northern kingdoms whom Ben Sira passes over in silence (so Smend, p. 419, and Box-Oesterley, p. 481). But, more probably, as Spicq (pp. 801–2) argues, the "others" in 44:9 belong to a class of the pious who are simply not remembered by future generations; cf. Isa 57:1–2. The phrase "these also" in 44:10a naturally refers to the forgotten ones of the preceding verse. The point of 44:10, therefore, is that the faithful who for whatever reason are no longer remembered by later generations of Israelites were themselves "godly people whose virtues will not be forgotten" (cf. NOTE) by God; cf. Wis 3:1–3. Ben Sira then devotes the rest of this section (44:11–15) to singing the praises of these "forgotten " heroes of the faith. The remembered heroes will be extolled at length in 44:16–49:16.

For the thought of 44:11, cf. 45:25cd. In 44:11–15, Ben Sira recounts the blessings that come upon those who remain loyal to the Lord; cf. Deut 28:1–14; Lev 26:3–13. These blessings are part of the Deuteronomic theory of retribution to which Ben Sira subscribes; see COMMENT on 2:1–6 and INTRODUCTION, Part X, 4. Fidelity to the Sinaitic Covenant is what ensures the safety of one's family, offspring, and reputation (44:12–13). Cf. P. A. H. de Boer, "*bbrytm 'md zr'm* Sirach xliv 12a," VTSup 16 (1967): 25–29. In 44:13a, the reading of the Masada MS, "their progeny," Heb *zar'ām* (so also G), is to be preferred to that of MS B, "their memory," Heb *zikrām* (so also Syr), a reading influenced by 39:9c. "Their glory" (44:13b) is the reading of M, G, and Syr; MS B has "their righteousness." It is to be noted in 44:13 that "their progeny" is in synonymous parallelism with "their glory," the reason being that children made secure a person's "glory" or "name" (cf. 44:14b), i.e., good reputation (cf. 44:8a). The faithful also receive a decent and honorable burial (44:14a); cf. 38:16c; Tob 14:1, 12–13. For the thought of 44:14b, cf. 41:11b. See COMMENT on 39:10, a verse that is repeated here as 44:15.

52. The Early Patriarchs
(44:17–23e)

44 17 NOAH, the just man found without reproach,   B
     in the time of destruction kept the race alive:
  Because of his worth there were survivors,
     and with a pledge to him the deluge ended.
18 A lasting sign sealed the assurance to him
     that never should all flesh be destroyed.
19 ABRAHAM, father of many peoples,
     kept his glory without stain:
20 He obeyed the Most High's command,
     and entered into a covenant with him;
  In his own flesh the ordinance was incised,
     and when tested, he was found steadfast.
21 For this reason, God promised him with an oath
     to bless the nations through his descendants,
  To make him numerous as the grains of dust,   G
     and exalt his posterity like the stars,
  Giving them an inheritance from sea to sea,   B
     and from the River to the ends of the earth.
22 For ISAAC, too, he renewed that promise
     because of Abraham, his father:
  The covenant with all his forebears God fulfilled for
                                       him,
23   and the blessing rested upon the head of ISRAEL.
  God acknowleged him as the firstborn.
     and gave him his inheritance;
  He fixed the boundaries for his tribes
     and their division into twelve.

Notes

44:17–51:30. For this portion of Ben Sira, the only available Heb witness is MS B; except that 44:17a survives in the Masada MS, and 51:13–20a (from the alphabet acrostic poem) is extant in 11QPsª. Of the eighteen lines on each page of MS B, as far as 49:11, the bottom six are partly eaten away.

44 21a. In the translation here, in v 23b, and in 45:2–4, God is introduced as subject, as the context demands, but the subject is not expressed in Heb.

21b–d. The bicolon 21cd is lacking from MS B, and G and Syr differ. For 21b–d, Syr has "that through his descendants all the nations of the earth would be blessed; that he would make his descendants numerous as the sands of the seashore, and that he would set his descendants above all other nations."

22. *that (promise)* = *kēn*, with MS B^{mg} and G; MS B^{txt} has "(he raised up) a son" = *bēn*.

23b. *as the firstborn* = *bibĕkōrâ;* cf. Deut 21:17; so MS B^{mg}. Syr sees this as an allusion to Exod 4:22 and Sir 36:17. MS B^{txt} and G read *bibĕrākâ/bĕbirkōtāyw,* "with a blessing/his blessings."

23d. *fixed the boundaries:* an allusion to Deut 32:8–9.

Comment

Ben Sira now begins his historical survey of Israel's glorious ancestors. Enoch (44:16, the text of which is found at the end of the previous section) may be the first person in the long list of names; and if so, this division of the book (44:16–49:16) begins and ends by way of *inclusio* with the name of Enoch (44:16a and 49:14a), as I noted above. But cf. NOTE on 44:16.

If, however, Noah (44:17) is the first name, then Ben Sira has bracketed his list with the second founder of the human race, after the Deluge, and Adam, the father of the human race, who appears as the last name and last word of 49:16. Noah is called "the just [or righteous] man," Heb *ṣaddîq,* who was found "without reproach," or blameless, Heb *tāmîm* (44:17a). These two Heb words were taken from the description of Noah in Gen 6:9 and 7:1. Job is also described as *tām* (Job 1:1, 8; 2:3), "blameless." Because of his righteousness in the midst of a depraved and lawless human race (Gen 6:5, 11), Noah was spared by an act of divine graciousness so that he could keep "the race alive"

(44:17b) after the devastation of the Flood (cf. Gen 7:1, 9:1). The "pledge to him" (44:17d), Heb *bĕrîtô* (lit., "covenant with him"), is God's commitment to Noah that he would never again destroy bodily creatures or devastate the earth by the waters of a flood (Gen 9:11–15). The "lasting sign" (44:18a; cf. also 43:6b) is the rainbow which would remind God and Noah and his descendants that the covenant of divine commitment had been made (cf. Gen 9:12–17).

Ben Sira now turns his attention to the other persons with whom God had made a covenant: Abraham, Isaac, Jacob/Israel, Moses, Aaron, Phinehas, and David (44:19–47:11).

Abraham is called in 44:19a the "father of many peoples," Heb *'ab hămôn gôyīm*, lit., "the father of a multitude of peoples," words taken directly from Gen 17:4–5; cf. also Gen 12:2–3; 15:5; Isa 51:2; Matt 3:9; Rom 4:1, 16; Gal 3:7. Abraham "kept his glory without stain" (44:19b), i.e., neither Pharaoh nor Abimelech touched Sarai even though to protect himself Abraham had said she was his sister; cf. Gen 12:10–20; 20:1–18. Compare what is said of Solomon in 47:20. The reference in 44:20a is to Abraham's unquestioning obedience to God's commands; cf. Gen 12:1–4; 15:1–6; Neh 9:8. The covenant with Abraham (44:20b) is described in Gen 17:9–14. This covenant had as its sign circumcision (44:20c). The moving account of Abraham's test by God (44:20d) is found in Gen 22:1–14; cf. 1 Macc 2:52; Jas 2:21. The expressions in 44:21a–d are echoes of Gen 22:16–18. The thoughts and phrases of 44:21ef are derived from Exod 23:31; Deut 11:24; Josh 1:4; Ps 72:8; and Zech 9:10. "The River" (44:21f), as in Gen 31:21; Exod 23:31; Num 22:5; Josh 24:2, 3, 14, 15, is the Euphrates.

As regards Isaac (44:22ab) and the renewal of the great promise (cf. NOTE) originally made to Abraham (Gen 12:2–3, 7; 15:18; 17:1–8; 22:17–18), cf. Gen 17:19; 26:3–5, 24. The reference to "the covenant with all his forebears" (44:22c) is to the covenant with Noah (Gen 9:11–17) and the covenant with Abraham (Gen 17:9–14). For the story of the blessing of the firstborn son (44:23a–c), which Jacob (=Israel) conspired with his mother Rebekah to steal from his brother Esau, see Gen 27:1–29; cf. also Gen 28:3–4. In 44:23b, Ben Sira alludes to the recognition God gives to Jacob/Israel as the firstborn (cf. NOTE) in Gen 28:13–15; cf. also Exod 4:22: "Thus says the LORD: 'Israel is my son, my first-born.'" Cf. Hos 11:1. For the twelve tribes of Israel (44:23de; cf. NOTE), cf. Gen 49:1–28.

53. Praise of Moses, Aaron, and Phinehas
(44:23f–45:26)

44   ^{23f} From him he had spring the man   B
       who should win the favor of all the living:

45   ¹ Dear to God and humans,
       MOSES, whose memory is a boon.
  ² God made him like the angels in honor,
       and strengthened him with fearful powers,
  ³ Wrought swift miracles at his words
       and sustained him in the king's presence.
He gave him the Commandments for his people,   G
       and revealed to him his glory.
  ⁴ For his trustworthiness and meekness   B
       God selected him from all humankind;
  ⁵ He permitted him to hear his voice,
       and led him into the cloud,
Where he gave into his hand the Commandments,
       the law of life and understanding,
That he might teach his precepts to Jacob,
       his covenant decrees to Israel.

  ⁶ He raised up also, like Moses in holiness,
       AARON his brother, of the tribe of Levi.
  ⁷ He made his office perpetual
       when he endowed him with its dignity;
He brought him to the fore in splendor
       and enveloped him in an aura of majesty.
  ⁸ He clothed him with sublime magnificence
       and adorned him with the glorious vestments:
Breeches and tunic and robe
  ⁹   with pomegranates around the hem,
And a rustle of bells round about,
       through whose pleasing sound at each step

He would be heard within the sanctuary,
    and the families of his people would be remembered;
10 The sacred vestments of gold, of violet,
    and of crimson, wrought with embroidery;
The breastpiece for decision, the ephod and cincture
11   with scarlet yarn, the work of the weaver;
Precious stones with seal engravings
    in golden settings, the work of the jeweler,
To commemorate in incised letters
    each of the tribes of Israel;
12 On his turban the diadem of gold—
    a frontlet engraved with the sacred inscription,
Majestic, glorious, renowned for splendor,
    a delight to the eyes, beauty supreme.
13 Before him no one was adorned with these,
    nor may they ever be worn by any
Except his sons and them alone,
    generation after generation, for all time.
14 His cereal offering is wholly burned
    as an established offering twice each day;
15 For Moses ordained him
    and anointed him with the holy oil,
In a lasting covenant with him
    and with his family, as permanent as the heavens,
That he should serve God in his priesthood
    and bless his people in his name.
16 He chose him from all humankind
    to offer holocausts and choice offerings,
To burn sacrifices of sweet odor for a memorial,
    and to atone for the people of Israel.
17 He gave to him his laws,
    and authority to prescribe and to judge:
To teach the precepts to his people,
    and the norms to the descendants of Israel.
18 Strangers were inflamed against him,
    were jealous of him in the desert,
The followers of Dathan and Abiram,
    and the band of Korah in their defiance.

¹⁹ But the LORD saw this and became angry;
   he destroyed them in his burning wrath.
  He brought against them a miracle,
   and consumed them with his flaming fire.
²⁰ Then he increased the glory of Aaron
   and bestowed upon him his inheritance:
  The sacred offerings he allotted to him,   G
   with the showbread as his portion;
²¹ The oblations of the LORD are his food,
   a gift to him and his descendants.
²² But he holds none of the people's land,
   nor shares with them their heritage;
  Rather, the LORD is his portion and inheritance
   in the midst of the Israelites.

²³ PHINEHAS, too, the son of Eleazar,   B
   was the courageous third of his line
  When, zealous for the God of all,
   he met the crisis of his people
  And, at the prompting of his noble heart,
   atoned for the people of Israel.
²⁴ Therefore on him again God conferred the right,
   in a covenant of friendship, to provide for the
                                    sanctuary,
  So that he and his descendants
   should possess the high priesthood forever.
²⁵ For even his covenant with David,
   the son of Jesse of the tribe of Judah,
  Was an individual heritage through one son alone,
   but the heritage of Aaron is for all his descendants.

  So now bless the LORD
   who has crowned you with glory!
²⁶ May he grant you wisdom of heart
   to govern his people in justice   G
  Lest the benefits you confer should be forgotten, B
   or the virtue of your rule, in future generations.

Notes

44 23fg. Lat, Syr, and Eth, following a faulty ("Lucianic") Gr text, read these two cola as referring to more than one person (Moses and Aaron?), and as belonging with the preceding lines; that chap. 45 begins in the middle of a sentence in the standard numbering of the Gr verses (followed here as elsewhere) is a consequence of this.

45 1–3d. The first cola of each of these four lines, and nearly all of v 3cd, are largely eaten away in MS B.

1a. *Dear=ʾāhûb,* lacking in MS B, supplied from G and Syr, which are in agreement; cf. 46:13a.

2a. *God made him like the angels in honor=[wayĕkabbĕdēhû kēʾ]lōhîm,* following Peters, Segal, and the sense of G; cf. Exod 4:16; 7:1; Ps 8:6.

2b. *fearful powers:* with MS B's margin, *bĕmôrāʾîm*=G, Syr; MS B's text has an erroneous *bmrwmym*="in the heights."

3a. Restored from G; MS B is defective, and Syr lacks this colon.

3cd. Following G and Syr, which agree; MS B is defective.

6ab. MS B compresses two cola into one and lacks *kāmôhû* and *ʾāḥîw,* supposed by G. It is possible that the name of Aaron was first mentioned only in v 20, and that its addition here in G, Syr, and MS B has unbalanced the cola and the lines.

7c. *brought him to the fore in splendor=wayĕʾaššĕrēhû bĕkābôd*=G; MS B *wayĕšārĕtēhû bikĕbôdô,* in which the subject is erroneously changed from God to Aaron, "and he ministered to him in his glory."

7d. *in an aura of majesty=bĕtôʿăpôt tôʾar*=G; *tôʾar* is also in MS B^ms. B^txt is *bĕtôʿăpôt reʾēm,* an uncalled-for harmonization with Num 23:22; 24:8, the flaring horns of the wild ox. *tôʿăpôt* finds its most natural etymology in a transposed form from *ypʿ* < older *wpʿ,* with the idea of looming, hence prominence and loftiness. Following v 7d, MS B has an added colon, patched together out of vv 8a, 9a.

8b. *with the glorious vestments: bigdê ʿōz;* both G and Syr suppose *biklê ʿōz,* but MS B's *bĕkābôd wāʾôz* is more easily understood as a corruption from a text containing *bigdê.*

9–14. Syr omits this description of the habiliments of the high priest.

9a. A Persian note in the margin of MS B says: "This copy reaches to here," indicating a fragmentary source.

9a,b. *pomegranates* followed by *bells,* as in G; MS B has the reverse order, but *hāmôn* belongs with *paʿămônîm* both for alliteration and for sense.

11bc. MS B unbalances these lines by adding "on the breastpiece" and "every precious stone," cf. Ezek 27:22; 28:13, omitting from 11c *maʿăśēh ḥārāš* or the like, and reading only *bĕmillûʾîm* or the like (reconstructed from a flawed text) for *in golden setttings, the work of the jeweler,* as in G; compare Sir 35:6a *millûʾôt pāz.*

11d–13a. In these five lines, the second colon in MS B is largely eaten away at 11e,

12b,d; at 13a,b, the whole line is lacking; 14a is also damaged. The missing text is supplied from G.

12a. *On his turban the diadem of gold* = ʿăṭeret pāz mēʿal miṣnaptô = G; MS B erroneously read mēʿîl ûmiṣnāpet (with wěṣîṣ for ṣîṣ in 12b).

20c–21b. The order of the cola follows G; the sequence in MS B is 20c, 21a, 20d, 21b, and of these the first two are damaged in the MS.

22a–d. Only the second of the four cola is preserved in MS B; and 22d is lacking in G and abridged in Syr. In MS B, a *lamed* where 22d should end lends credit to the *Israel* reading of Syr.

23b. Here again, MS B is damaged. With Segal, read bigěbûrâ [nāḥal šělîšî], though Segal notes the reading is quite doubtful.

23c. MS B has leʾělôah kōl, "corrected" (with a *yod* and a ṣērê!) to lēʾlôhê kōl; the presumption is that the error was rather one of passing from one *hē* to another, and that the basic reading should be lʾlwhy hkl; compare 36:1 (so Smend; and see *CBQ* 38 [1976]: 147).

25c. MS B has nḥlt ʾš lpny kbwdw: in the light of G and the parallelism, this should read naḥălat ʾîš libnô lěbaddô, whence the translation given.

25e,f. Both cola, present in MS B, are lacking in G; Syr lacks 25f. After yyy = *the Lord,* MS B adds haṭṭôb, an expansion that destroys the balance of the poetic line.

26b. This colon, lacking in MS B, is supplied from G.

26d. *in future generations* = lědôrôtām, with G; MS B's lědôrôt ʿôlām overweights the line, as also does Syr.

Comment

In this section, Aaron receives the lion's share of attention, thirty-two bicola. Obviously the levitical priesthood was of special interest to Ben Sira. There are only nine bicola devoted to Moses, and ten to Phinehas. For the reason why chap. 45 begins in the middle of a sentence, cf. NOTE on 44:23fg.

The phrase "from him" (44:23f) refers to Jacob. Curiously, Ben Sira skips from Jacob to Moses. Jacob's sons, except for a passing notice of Joseph in 49:15, receive no further mention. Moses did indeed "win the favor of all the living" (44:23g)—of his own people, obviously; of Pharaoh's daughter (Exod 2:5–10); of Reuel the priest of Midian and his daughters (Exod 2:16–22); and of the Egyptians, in particular Pharaoh's servants (Exod 11:3). Since Moses was loved by God and chosen to save the people from bondage in Egypt and was regarded highly by others, Ben Sira describes him as "dear [cf. NOTE] to God and humans" (45:1a); cf. Exod 33:11; Num 12:7–8; Deut 34:11. The Heb phrase zikrô lěṭôbâ, "his memory (is) *a boon*" (45:1b) (G and Syr have *a blessing*), is a variant of the fuller expression yěhî zikrām liběrākâ, "may their memory be for a blessing" (46:11d), a pious prayer used also by later Jews when they recalled their dead. For the text of 45:2a, cf. NOTE; here *'ĕhōhîm*, which usually means "God" or "gods," is translated "angels," as is Ps 8:6; cf. Gr *hagiōn*, "(honor of) the holy ones." The "fearful powers" (45:2b; cf. NOTE) and "swift miracles" (45:3a) refer to the signs Moses performed to help the people believe in him (Exod 4:1–9) and the wonders performed in Egypt prior to the Exodus (Exod 7:8–11:10; Deut 4:34; 26:8; 34:11–12). The reference in 45:3b is to Moses standing in the presence of the Pharaoh (Exod 7:1–7). "The Commandments" (45:3c), if the Decalogue is meant, are found in Exod 20:2–17 and Deut 5:6–21. But cf. also Exod 6:13. Moses has prominence among the ancestors because God "revealed to him his glory" (Exod 33:18–23; 34:5–8). The "trustworthiness and meekness" of Moses (45:4a) are mentioned in Num 12:3, 7; cf. Heb 3:2, 5. As Smend (p. 427) correctly notes, the phrase "all humankind" (lit., "all flesh") in 45:4b means all Israel (as in 50:17a), and not all human beings. Cf. 45:16a. Moses was privileged to hear God's voice (45:5a); cf. Exod 33:11; Num 12:8; Deut 34:10. God also led Moses "into the cloud" (45:5b); cf. Exod 20:21; 24:18. In 45:5c, "the Commandments" are certainly the decalogue (cf. COMMENT on 45:3c above). "Into his hand" is a reference to Exod 32:15 and Deut 9:15. Ben Sira describes the Decalogue as "the law of life and understanding" (45:5d); cf. 17:11; Lev 18:5; Deut 30:15–16; 32:46–47; Ezek 20:11. The thought of 45:5ef echoes Ps 147:19.

Ben Sira now turns his attention to his favorite subject, the levitical priesthood, esp. as embodied in the high priest, whose vestments and liturgical functions are described here in great detail (45:6–22). The only other section that is comparable in length is the appendix to this part of the book, which praises the High Priest Simeon II (50:1–24). For the text of 45:6ab, cf. NOTE. Aaron is called a holy one (45:6a) also in Ps 106:16b; cf. Num 16:1–7. In Exod 4:14 (the J tradition), Aaron is described as Moses' brother (45:6b). The parents of Moses and Aaron, according to Exod 6:20 (the P tradition) are Amram and Jochebed; but cf. Exod 2:1–2 (the E tradition), where the parents of Moses are described simply as "a certain man of the house of Levi" and "a Levite woman." Exod 29:9 and 40:15 describe the priesthood of Aaron and his sons as "perpetual" (45:7a). Aaron's "dignity" (45:7b) derives from the fact that God consecrated him and his sons to be priests (Exod 29:44; 40:13–15). Now comes a lengthy description (45:8–13) of the "splendor" and "majesty" (45:7cd; cf. NOTES) of Aaron's "glorious vestments" (45:8b; cf. NOTE).

The stipulations for making the "breeches" (45:8c) are given in Exod 28:42; the "tunic" of fine linen (i.e., the ordinary outer garment), in Exod 28:39; and the special violet "robe" (45:8c–9; cf. NOTE), in Exod 28:31–35; 39:20–26. "The breastpiece for decision" (45:10c) was a pocketlike square receptacle for holding the Urim and Thummim, used to ascertain God's will in doubtful matters (Exod 28:30), and formed part of "the ephod," to which it was attached by chains and rings of gold; cf. Exod 28:6–30. "The ephod" (45:10c) is a priestly vestment the nature of which is uncertain; it probably was a kind of apron that hung from the priest's shoulders by means of straps and was secured around his waist by means of an attached belt (cf. Exod 28:6–14). The "cincture" (45:10c) and its manufacture are described in Exod 28:4–5, 39–40. "Scarlet yarn" and "precious stones with seal engravings in golden settings" (45:11a–c; cf. NOTE) were employed in making the breastplate and ephod; cf. Exod 28:6–21. The breastplate had on it twelve precious stones, arranged in four rows, each with three stones. On each stone was inscribed the name of one of the tribes of Israel (45:11b–e); cf. Exod 28:17–21. On the ephod there were two onyx stones, on each of which were inscribed six of the names of the sons of Israel (Exod 28:9–12). The "turban" (or miter) to which was attached "the diadem of gold—a frontlet engraved with the sacred inscription" (45:12ab) is mentioned in Exod 28:36–38; the inscription read: "Sacred to Yahweh" (Exod 28:36; 39:30). Apparently, this diadem was a spectacular sight to behold (45:12cd). Ben Sira prays in 45:13 that the sacred and splendid high priestly vestments may not be worn by "a stranger," Heb zār, here translated "any (except . . .)." Aaron's sons alone had the right to be high priests. Unfortunately, only a few years after Ben Sira wrote these lines, the high priesthood became not a matter of legitimate succession but of paying a suitably large bribe to the pagan Antiochus IV Epiphanes; cf. INTRODUCTION, Part II.

Now Ben Sira describes the liturgical functions and the grandeur of Aaron as high priest (45:14–22). The "cereal offering," Heb minḥâ, offered "each day" (45:14), half in the morning and half in the evening, was "wholly burned" according to the prescriptions of the Law (Lev 6:12–16). This was "an established [or continual] offering," Heb tāmîd (45:14b), the name it was called in Ben Sira's day and later. The ordination of Aaron and his sons by Moses (45:15) is described in Lev 8:1–13; cf. Exod 28:41. The anointing "with the holy oil" (45:15b) became a sign of "a lasting covenant with [Aaron] and with his family" (45:15cd) that the priesthood would remain forever in his family; cf. Num 25:13 and Mal 2:4–5, 8. The colorful phrase "as permanent as the heavens" (45:15d), lit., "as the days of heaven," occurs also in 50:24d and derives from Deut 11:21 and Ps 89:30b. As priest, Aaron had the responsibility of serving God (cf. Exod 28:3, 41, 43) and blessing the people in God's name (45:15ef); cf. Lev 8:22; Deut 10:8; Num 6:23–27. God "chose" Aaron "from all humankind" (45:16a), lit., "from all the living," a phrase which, like the one in 45:4b (cf. above), refers to all Israel; cf. Num 16:5, 7; 17:16–23. "Holocausts," as the term signifies, were completely burned on the altar; so also were the "choice offerings," lit., "the portions of fat, or fat pieces," which the ancients considered to be the best part of the animal (cf. Deut 32:14; Ps 63:6a; Ezek 39:19). The wording of 45:16c comes from Lev 2:2, 9. As regards the priest's atoning "for the people of Israel" (45:16d), cf. Lev 16:32–34. The references in 45:17ab are to texts such as Deut 17:8–12; 33:8–10. The priests had the duty of teaching the precepts and norms to the people (45:17cd); cf. Lev 10:11; Hos 4:4–6; Mal 2:6–7. The episode mentioned in 45:18–19 is recorded in Num 16:1–17:15. In 45:18a, Heb zārîm, "strangers," were not permitted in the priesthood. According to Num 17:5, an 'îš zār, "a strange man," in the context of priesthood, is one who is not of Aaron's seed. The "miracle" (Heb 'ôt, "sign") in 45:19c is the opening of the earth's mouth and the swallowing of Dathan and Abiram as well as the fire that came forth from Yahweh to consume "the band of Korah" (Num 16:30–35; cf. Ps 106:16–18). After the rebellion of Dathan and Abiram against Aaron ended in disaster, God increased "the glory of Aaron" (45:20a); cf. Num 18:1–7. In Num 18:20, Yahweh says to Aaron: "You shall not have any heritage [or inheritance] in the land of the Israelites nor hold any portion among them; I will be your portion and your heritage among them." The first bicolon of 45:20 and the last bicolon of 45:22 refer to Aaron's "inheritance" (or heritage), thus forming an *inclusio.* Since Yahweh alone is Aaron's "portion and inheritance" (45:22c), Aaron and the other priests are given a share in "the sacred offerings" of the other Israelites (Num 18:8–19). For the text of 45:20c–22d, cf. NOTES. As regards "the showbread" (45:20d), cf. Lev 24:5–9 and also Matt 12:3–4. Aaron and "his descendants" are to eat "the oblations of the LORD" (45:21a) as "a gift" (45:21b); cf. Deut 18:1 and Num 18:9–19. But Aaron was to hold "none of the people's land" (45:22a), i.e., as hereditary land such as the other Israelites were entitled to; certain cities, however, were assigned for the priests and Levites to live in (cf. Num 35:1–8).

It is interesting to observe that Ben Sira passes over Aaron's son Eleazar and eulogizes next Aaron's grandson Phinehas (45:23–26), i.e., "the courageous third of his [Aaron's] line" (45:23b; cf. NOTE). Eleazar was the third son of Aaron (cf. Exod 6:23; Num 3:2–4); he became chief prince of the Levites and supervisor "over those who had charge of the sanctuary" (Num 3:32). Ben Sira seems intent on proving that Phinehas was the legitimate successor to the high priesthood (45:24–25); according to 4 Macc 18:12, there had been disputes about the authentic succession of high priests. As regards the phrase "the God of all" (45:23c; cf. NOTE), see COMMENT on 36:1. "The crisis of his people" that Phinehas met (45:23d) is described in Num 25:1–15. In his zeal for "the God of all" (45:23c), Phinehas slew a certain Israelite man and a Midianite woman who had participated with other Israelites in the idolatrous worship of the god Baal of Peor, and who had tried to escape punishment for their sin (Num 25:6–8). It was by this act that Phinehas "atoned for the people of Israel" (45:23f); cf. Num 25:10–13; Ps 106:28–31. The expression "covenant of friendship," Heb běrît šālôm, lit., "covenant of peace" (45:24b), is taken from Num 25:12. It was through this covenant that God promised that the priesthood would remain forever in the family of Phinehas (Num 25:12–13); cf. 1 Macc 2:54. After "the sanctuary" in 45:24b,

G has a noteworthy addition: "and of his people." Thus G suggests clearly that Phinehas is leader not only in religious affairs but also in the political realm. "When the grandson of Ben-Sira wrote, the political power of the High Priest had been strongly asserted. The High Priest had become ethnarch. One consequence was that the office became the sport of constant political intrigues" (so Box-Oesterley, p. 489). Cf. INTRODUCTION, Part II. The parallel between the heritage of David and the heritage of Aaron (45:25a–d) was first drawn by Jer 33:14–22. The "covenant with David" (45:25a) is mentioned in 2 Sam 7:11–16; 23:5; Isa 55:3; Jer 33:21, 26; 2 Chr 13:5; 21:7; Ps 89:3–5, 29–30. The meaning of 45:25a–d is not certain. What Ben Sira probably means when he writes that the "covenant with David" "was an individual heritage through one son alone" (45:25c; cf. NOTE) is that the kingship was transmissible to "one son alone" by direct succession, whereas "the heritage of Aaron is for all his descendants" (45:25d), i.e., the priestly power is granted to every male in Aaron's line in the sense that every one of these descendants could exercise the priestly office and claim their rewards as priests.

In the little hymn (45:25ef–26) at the end of this section, Ben Sira prays for other high priests, esp. the contemporary Simeon II and his sons, who are the legitimate representatives of Phinehas. The opening colon (45:25e) is rephrased in 50:22a, the opening of the prayer (50:22–24) for Simeon II. The reference to being "crowned . . . with glory" (45:25f) comes from Ps 8:6b. The sentiment expressed in 45:26a is repeated in 50:23a. For the vocabulary of 45:26b (cf. NOTE), cf. Ps 72:2a, the LXX of which is quoted by G. Psalm 72, however, is a prayer for the king. Instead of "should be forgotten," Heb *yiššākaḥ* (45:26c), G reads: "should cease" = Heb *yišbōt*, a reading preferred by Smend (p. 438) and Box-Oesterley (p. 490). In the final bicolon (45:26cd) of this prayer, Ben Sira expresses his appreciation and concern for "the benefits" the high priests confer on the community, and for "the virtue of [their] rule," lit., "[their] power," "in future generations" (45:26d; cf. NOTE). Ben Sira probably alludes here to the intrigues of the Tobiads against Simeon II and his son Onias III, the legitimate high priests because they were descended from Phinehas. Cf. INTRODUCTION, Part II. For further study of 44:17–45:26, cf. F. V. Reiterer, *"Urtext" und Übersetzungen: Sprachstudie über Sir 44,16–45,26 als Beitrag zur Siraforschung*. Arbeiten zu Text und Sprache im Alten Testament, 12, 1980.

54. Joshua, Caleb, the Judges, and Samuel
(46:1–20)

¹ Valiant conquerer was JOSHUA, son of Nun, B
    aide to Moses in the prophetic office,
Formed to be, as his name implies,
    the great savior of God's chosen ones,
Wreaking vengeance on the enemy
    and giving to Israel their inheritance.
² What glory was his when he raised his hand
    to brandish his sword against the city!
³ Who could withstand him
    when he fought the battles of the LORD?
⁴ Was it not at his same hand the sun stopped,
    so that one day became like two?
⁵ He called upon the Most High God
    when he was hard pressed, with enemies on every
                  side;
And God Most High gave answer to him
    with the driving force of glistening hail
⁶ Which he rained down upon the hostile army
    till on the slope he destroyed the foe;
That all the doomed nations might know
    the LORD was watching over his people's battles.
And because he was a devoted follower of God
⁷   and in Moses' time showed himself loyal,
He and CALEB, son of Jephunneh,
    when they opposed the rebel assembly,
Averted God's anger from the people
    and suppressed the wicked complaint—
⁸ Because of this, those two alone were spared
    of the six hundred thousand infantry,
to lead the people into their inheritance,
    the land flowing with milk and honey.

9 The strength God gave to Caleb
　　remained with him even in his old age
　Till he won his way onto the summits of the land,
　　so that his family, too, received an inheritance,
10 That all the people of Jacob might know
　　how good it is to be a devoted follower of the LORD.

11 The JUDGES, too, each one of them,
　　whose hearts were not deceived,
　Who did not abandon God:
　　may their memory be ever blessed,
12 Their bones flourish with new life where they lie,　　G
　　and their names receive fresh luster in their　　B
　　　　　　　　　　　　　　　　　children!
13 Honored among people, dear to his Maker,　　G
　　pledged in a vow, from his mother's womb,　　B
　As one consecrated to the LORD in the prophetic office
　　was SAMUEL, the judge who offered sacrifice.
　At God's word he established the kingdom
　　and he anointed princes to rule the people.
14 By the law of the LORD he judged the assembled folk,　　G
　　and he made the rounds of the settlements of　　B
　　　　　　　　　　　　　　　　　Jacob.
15 As a trustworthy seer he was sought out
　　and his message proved him a true prophet.　　G
16 He, too, called upon God　　B
　　when he was hard pressed, with enemies on every
　　　　　　　　　　　　　　　　　side,
　　and offered up a suckling lamb;
17 Then the LORD thundered from heaven,
　　and the tremendous blast of his voice resounded;
18 He brought low the rulers of the enemy
　　and destroyed all the lords of the Philistines.
19 When Samuel approached the end of his life,
　　he testified before the LORD and his anointed
　　　　　　　　　　　　　　　　　prince,
　"No bribe or secret gift have I taken from any one!"
　　and no one could gainsay him.

20 Even after his death his guidance was sought;
   he made known to the king his fate
And from the grave he raised his voice
   as a prophet, to put an end to wickedness.

Notes

46 1c. *as his name implies*=G=*kišĕmô,* cf. 6:22; MS B *bymyw,* "in his time"; cf. 44:7b.

1d. *God's:* lit., "his," with the reference only implied, cf. NOTES at 44:10, 21a.

2b. *sword: kîdôn,* anciently a hacking implement, the Egyptian *harpē,* loosely translated "scimitar" (AB, NAB) in the Goliath narrative, 1 Sam 17:6. In the texts from Qumran, the term means a short, thrusting sword, and so presumably here.

4–6. These lines are damaged in MS B.

4a. *his same hand:* cf. 2a; Ben Sira is presumably thinking of a parallel with the stance of Moses at the battle with Amalek (Exod 17:8–16) in which Joshua was the field commander (see also Exod 14:16, 21, 26). In Joshua 10, it is the voice of Joshua that commands the sun; cf. here vv 5, 6.

5d. *with . . . glistening hail:* follows G, which is already a paraphrase. The Heb has "with hailstones and *'elgābîš.*" The last word is a synonym for hail(stones) that occurs also in Ezekiel. Since it has a cognate in Akk taken to mean "rock crystal," the presumption is that it conveys the luminosity of the hail and implies hailstones of exceptional size.

9a. *God:* see the NOTE at 1d above.

12a. *Their bones . . . where they lie:* this language, present here in G and Syr, but not in MS B, is used of the twelve Minor Prophets in 49:10. It would seem to allude to the story of the bones of Elisha in 2 Kgs 13:20–21. Since the Book of Judges shows an interest in the burial places of the individual Judges (cf. Judg 10:1–5; 12:8–15), and the Book of Joshua (24:30) in that of Joshua, it would seem Ben Sira developed this expression for the present context and applied it again in 49:10.

12b(c)–13a. As in 44:23–45:1, here again G confuses the transition between two sections of the discourse. The wording it presupposes yields for 13a *nikbad 'ănāšîm wa'ăhûb . . .* (for the last word, "of his Lord," as G has it, goes against Heb idiom). MS B has *'ôhēb 'ammô ûrĕṣûy 'ōśēhû,* "friend of his people and favored by his Maker," Syr is garbled like G, but it does vouch for the *'ōśēhû* reading of MS B (cf. 33:13c); for the participles, it supposes those underlying G. The translation follows the text underlying G, with *'ōśēhû* as the final word.

13bc. G identifies Samuel as "prophet of the Lord," but otherwise omits these cola. *pledged in a vow* is an attempt at specifying the means by which Samuel was "obtained by request" (Heb *hammĕšô'āl*) by his mother in prayer to the Lord. The Heb word is a play on the name Samuel, parallel to the *Joshua . . . savior* (=*tĕšû'â*) wordplay in

46:1. That Samuel was a *nāzîr,* one *consecrated to the Lord* according to the terms of Num 6:1–21, in his case perpetually, derives from 1 Sam 1:11, 22. In 1:22, it is made explicit in 1QSamª: see the discussion in P. K. McCarter, Jr., *I Samuel* (AB 8, 1980): 49–50, 53–56, 61. *in the prophetic office:* the Heb expression is that used of Moses (and, by association, Joshua) in 46:1; it occurs again in 46:20d, and cf. 44:3d. Samuel's dedication as a *nāzîr* at the shrine of the Ark of the Covenant at Shiloh was the preparation for the gift of prophecy that the Lord there bestowed on him.

13d. *who offered sacrifice:* Heb *ûmĕkahēn.* Ben Sira, who is presumed to have been of a priestly family himself, does not say of Samuel that he was a priest, but that he did perform priestly functions: cf. Ps 99:6.

13e–18. These lines in MS B are damaged; 14c perhaps reflects 1 Sam 10:17–25.

14b. *settlements=*Heb *'ohŏlê;* MS B, G, and Syr all agree in reading the divine name *'ĕlôhê (ya'ăqōb).* The allusion to 1 Sam 7:16–17 seems certain; the transposition of letters in the text then antedates the Gr translation.

15b. The translation supposes that what the grandson saw in his Heb text was *ûbidĕbārāyw nôda' ne'ĕmān,* and that his *horaseōs* reflects the *hōzeh* of 15a, which he there overtranslated as "prophet." Compare 1 Sam 3:20; 9:9, 19. MS B's *wĕgam* is clearly out of place (cf. 16a), and its *rô'eh* could as well be corrupt from *nôda'=*G as from *rô'eh* as is usually supposed.

19a. *When Samuel approached the end of his life:* the Heb has "and when it was time for him to rest on his (death)bed"; cf. Isa 57:2. The context of 1 Samuel 12 is the choice of Saul as king and the laying down by Samuel of his civic function as chief magistrate of the people; the poetry of Ben Sira looks to the event which Samuel, concerned for his sons, had in mind.

19d. *gainsay him:* this is followed in MS B by the sentence "and even to the time of his decease he was found prudent in the sight of the Lord and of all the living," which is a gloss that weakens Ben Sira's text.

20d. *wickedness:* G has "the wickedness of the people"; Syr has "sins," simply. The Heb for this is lacking, but from G it can be reconstructed as *(lĕhašbît) 'āwôn 'ām.* The guilt in question is Saul's, and the likelihood is that *'ām,* "people," was no more than a faulty dittography of *'āwôn,* "guilt," in the prototype of G. In 7:6, Ben Sira uses the parallel phrase *lĕhašbît zādôn* absolutely, to end a line.

Comment

This section is divided into two parts: the first on the leaders Joshua and Caleb (46:1–10); the second on the Judges in general and on Samuel, the last of the Judges.

Joshua, Heb *yĕhôšûa',* which means "Yahweh is salvation," was the worthy successor of Moses to lead the Chosen People (cf. Num 27:18–23). According to Num 27:18, he was "a person in whom there is spirit," i.e., he had the wisdom, courage, and strength of character to be a great leader; cf. Deut 34:9. He was "aide to [Heb mĕšārēt, lit., a minister of, the same word used to describe him in Exod 33:11] Moses," and like Elisha, who assisted and later succeeded Elijah (1 Kgs 19:21; 2 Kgs 2:9–15), he followed Moses "in the prophetic office" (46:1b). Joshua is called "valiant conqueror" (46:1a), for it was he, and not Moses, who was to cross the Jordan and conquer the Promised Land (cf. Deut 34:4; Josh 1:1–11). "As his name implies" (cf. NOTE and COMMENT above), Joshua was "formed to be . . . the great savior [Heb tĕšû'â (gĕdôlâ), lit., (a great) salvation] of God's [cf. NOTE] chosen ones" (46:1cd); cf. 47:22. "Wreaking vengeance on the enemy" (46:1e) is a reference to Josh 10:13: "And the sun stood still, and the moon stayed, while the nation took vengeance on its foes," i.e., the Amorites. V 46:1f refers to Deut 1:38, which says Joshua "is to give Israel its inheritance" (cf. also Deut 3:28). The raising of Joshua's hand "to brandish his sword" (46:2a; cf. NOTE) was a signal for his troops to attack the city of Ai (Josh 8:18–19, 26). Because Yahweh was with Joshua, no one "could withstand him" (46:3a)—a clear reference to Josh 1:5. "The battles [or wars] of the LORD [lit., of Yahweh]" is an allusion to Josh 8:14. The phrase "wars of Yahweh" occurs also in 1 Sam 18:17; 25:28; and Num 21:14 ("The Book of the Wars of Yahweh"). As regards Joshua's "hand" (46:4a) stopping the sun (cf. Josh 10:12–13), cf. NOTE. Interestingly, the expression "the Most High God" (46:5a and c), Heb 'ēl 'elyôn, occurs here for the first times in the book; elsewhere in the extant Heb fragments, it occurs only in 47:5a, 8b; 48:20a. The name "the Most High" (Heb 'elyôn) is found alone a total of fifteen times in the Geniza and Masada MSS of our book. Curiously, 46:5 clearly is based on Josh 10:7–14, in which the name of God is always "Yahweh," and not "the Most High God." Apparently, the phrasing of 46:5ab was traditional; cf. 46:16ab. In Josh 10:11–12, Yahweh killed more of the Amorites with giant hailstones "than the Israelites slew with the sword"—the point Ben Sira suggests in 46:5d (cf. NOTE) and 6ab. "The slope" in 46:6b is the descent from Beth-horon down which the Amorites were fleeing when they were struck by the hailstones (Josh 10:10–11). As regards the phrase "the doomed nations," cf. Josh 6:17 and Sir 16:9 with COMMENT. The allusion in 46:6d is to Josh 10:14; 23:3–10. Ben Sira describes Joshua as "a devoted follower of God" (46:6e), a phrase borrowed from Num 14:24; Josh 14:8, 9, 14; in Josh 24:29, Joshua is called "servant of Yahweh."

Joshua (and Caleb, mentioned in 46:7b) "in Moses' time showed himself loyal" (46:7a) by supporting Moses and Aaron while all the rest of the community grumbled against them (Num 14:1–10), a scene alluded to in 46:7c. Ben Sira seems to attribute the averting of "God's anger from the people" (46:7d) to Joshua and Caleb; according to Num 14:11–20, it was Moses' pleading with Yahweh that resulted in the sparing of the people. "The wicked complaint" (46:7e) is the grumbling of the Israelites in Num 14:1–3. Because of their loyalty to Yahweh and to Moses, Joshua and Caleb were the only ones "spared of the six hundred thousand infantry" (46:8ab): cf. 16:10; Num 11:21; 14:29, 30, 38; 26:65; Deut 1:35–38. It was they who led "the people into their inheritance" (46:8c; cf. Deut 1:38; Josh 11:23). The Holy Land was traditionally described as "the land flowing with milk and honey" (48:8d); cf., for example, Exod 3:8, 17; 13:5; 33:3; Lev 20:24; Deut 6:3; 11:9; Josh 5:6; Jer 11:5; 32:22; Ezek 20:6.

According to Josh 14:7, 10–11, Caleb at the age of eighty-five was as strong as he was the day Moses sent him forth to reconnoiter the land, when he was forty—the reference in 46:9ab. "The summits of the land" (46:9c) are the mountain region inhabited by the Anakim whom Caleb conquered in his old age; cf. Josh 11:21; 14:10–12. The inheritance of Caleb and his family (46:9d) is mentioned in Num 14:24 and Josh 14:9, 13–15. Caleb's devotion to Yahweh (46:10b) is noted several times in biblical tradition: Num 14:24; Josh 14:8, 14.

In the next unit, Ben Sira has a brief introduction on the Judges in general (46:11–12) and then a long panegyric on Samuel, the last and greatest of the Judges (46:13–20). The praise of the Judges as a group is somewhat hyperbolic. Contrary to what is said in 46:11bc, Samson was deceived by Delilah (Judg 16:16–20), and Yahweh did abandon him (Judg 16:20). But since the Judges were persons raised up by God to save the people from their enemies, Ben Sira prays that they may enjoy a blessed memory (46:11d; cf. COMMENT on 45:1b). The allusion in 46:12a to the Judges' bones flourishing is to the story in 2 Kgs 13:20–21, which describes how a dead man thrown into Elisha's grave came back to life; for more on this colon, cf. NOTE. The sentiment that the Judges' names may "receive fresh luster in their children" (46:12b), viz., the Israelites, has a parallel in Tob 4:12, in which Tobit commands his son not to marry outside his father's tribe because "we are children of the prophets." For more on the name or reputation of a person surviving in his children, cf. COMMENT on 44:13–15.

There is a definite change of subject in 46:13a (cf. NOTE), which begins the praise of Samuel. Indeed, Samuel was "honored among people" and "dear to his maker" (46:13a; cf. NOTE), for he led God's people at a critical point in their history. Because Hannah, Elkanah's wife, had been barren, she prayed to Yahweh to grant her a son, whom she promised to give back to the service of Yahweh for his whole life (1 Sam 1:2, 10–11). When her prayer was heard, she named the boy Samuel, "since she had asked the LORD for him" (1 Sam 1:20); it is to this episode that Ben Sira refers in 46:13b (cf. NOTE for the wordplay on the name Samuel and "obtained by request"). Samuel was "consecrated to the LORD" (46:13c; cf. NOTE) as a perpetual Nazirite; cf. 1 Sam 1:11, 22, 27–28. As regards "the prophetic office" (46:13c) Samuel enjoyed, cf. NOTE. Samuel was a judge "who offered sacrifice," or "who performed priestly functions" (46:13d; cf. NOTE); cf. 1 Sam 7:7–9. He was the one who, by Yahweh's permission, established the monarchy by anointing Saul as King

(46:13e); cf. 1 Sam 9:15–17; 10:1. In addition to anointing Saul, Samuel anointed David (1 Sam 16:13)—the allusion in 46:13f. Samuel judged the people "by the law of the LORD"—a reference to 1 Sam 7:2–6. According to 1 Sam 7:16–17, Samuel in fulfilling his duty as judge "made a yearly journey, passing through Bethel, Gilgal and Mizpah" and would then "return to Ramah, for that was his home. There, too, he judged Israel. . . ." Ben Sira refers to this activity in 46:14b (cf. NOTE). Samuel's trustworthiness as a seer (46:15a) is attested in 1 Sam 9:6. The reference in 46:15 (cf. NOTE) is to 1 Sam 3:20; 9:9. According to Jer 28:9, the fulfillment of a prophet's word proves him true; conversely, according to Deut 18:22, if the prophet's oracle is not fulfilled or verified, he is a false prophet.

Samuel "called upon God" (46:16a) when "he was hard pressed, with enemies on every side" (46:16b)—a reference to the Philistines going up against the Israelites gathered in Mizpah (1 Sam 7:7–8). Samuel "took an unweaned lamb [46:16c] and offered it entire as a holocaust to the LORD. He implored the LORD for Israel, and the LORD heard him" (1 Sam 7:9). With thundering and a tremendous blast of his voice (46:17), the LORD routed the Philistines (46:18); this episode is recorded in 1 Sam 7:10–13. Ben Sira uses the noun *sĕrānîm* (= Gr *tyrannoi*) to designate "the lords [of the Philistines]" (46:18b); this word applies only to leaders of the Philistine pentapolis (cf. Josh 13:3; Judg 3:3; 16:5, 8, 18, 23, 27; 1 Sam 6:16, 18). For the literal translation of 46:19a, cf. NOTE; the same words occur in 40:5c. In 46:19, Ben Sira refers to the story of Samuel's unimpeachable integrity in 1 Sam 12:1–5 (for the gloss after 46:19d in MS B, cf. NOTE). Cf. P. C. Beentjes, "Inverted Quotations in the Bible: A Neglected Stylistic Pattern [Sir 46:19]," *Bib* 63 (1982): 506–23. Though 1 Sam 12:2 says only that Samuel is "old and gray," Ben Sira seems to think the episode took place at the end of Samuel's life (46:19a). But Samuel does not die till 1 Sam 25:1. After his death, Samuel was consulted by Saul (46:20) via the witch of Endor; cf. 1 Sam 28:8–19. What Samuel's voice told Saul in prophecy (46:20cd) was that the king was doomed. Because Saul had disobeyed Yahweh's command to destroy Agag, king of Amalek, together with the best of the fat sheep and oxen, and the lambs and all that was worthwhile (1 Sam 15:8–9), Samuel told Saul he had been rejected as king (1 Sam 15:10–23). Later, Samuel's ghost predicted that Saul and his sons would be killed by the Philistines (1 Sam 28:19). Saul and his sons died in the battle on Mount Gilboa (1 Sam 31:1–6).

55. Nathan, David, and Solomon
(47:1–22)

47 ¹ After him came NATHAN   B
    who served in the presence of David.
² Like the choice fat of the sacred offerings,
    so was DAVID in Israel.
³ He made sport of lions as though they were kids,
    and of bears, like lambs of the flock.
⁴ As a youth he slew the giant
    and did away with the people's disgrace
When his hand let fly the slingstone
    that shattered the pride of Goliath.
⁵ He called upon the Most High God,
    who gave strength to his right arm
To flatten the skilled warrior
    and restore the eminence of his own people;
⁶ Therefore the women sang his praises
    and ascribed to him tens of thousands overcome.
When he assumed the royal crown, he fought
⁷   and subdued the enemy on every side.
He campaigned against the hostile Philistines
    and broke their power till our own day.
⁸ With his every deed he offered thanks;
    of God Most High he proclaimed the glory.
With his whole heart he loved his Maker
⁹ᶜ   and daily had his praises sung;   GII
¹⁰ᵃ He added beauty to the feasts   G
  ᵇ   and solemnized the seasons of each year
⁹ᵃ With string music before the altar,
  ᵇ   providing sweet melody for the psalms
¹⁰ᶜ So that when the Holy Name was praised,
  ᵈ   before daybreak the sanctuary would respond.

11 The LORD forgave him his sins   B
    and exalted his strength forever;
He conferred on him the rights of royalty
    and established his throne in Israel.

12 Because of his merits he had as his successor
    a wise son, who lived in security:
13 SOLOMON reigned during an era of peace,
    for God made tranquil all his borders.
He built a house to the name of God,
    and established a lasting sanctuary.
14 How wise you were when you were young,
    overflowing with instruction, like the Nile in flood!
15 Your breadth of understanding covered the earth,   G
    which you filled with sayings of hidden meaning.
16 Your fame reached distant coasts,
    and you were loved for your happy estate;
17 With song and proverb and riddle,   B
    and with your answers, you astounded the nations.
18 You were called by that glorious name
    which was conferred upon Israel.
You heaped up gold like so much iron,
    amassing silver as though it were lead;
19 But you surrendered yourself to women
    and gave them dominion over your body.
20 You brought a stain upon your glory,
    shame upon your marriage bed,
Wrath upon your descendants,
    and groaning upon your deathbed.
21 Thus two governments came into being,
    when in Ephraim power was usurped.
22 But God does not withdraw his commitment,
    nor permit even one of his promises to fail—
He does not uproot the posterity of his chosen ones,
    nor destroy the offspring of his friends;
So he gave to Jacob a remnant,   G
    to David a root from his own family.

Notes

47 3. *lambs of the flock* = G = *běnê ṣōʾn*. MS B's *běnê bāšān*, "bulls of Bashan," is as incredible here as the three lines out of four in the same MS beginning with *wěgam* (46:19ef, 20ab; 47:1—and cf. 46:15b, 16a).

4b. *the people's:* with G, Syr; MS B's *ʿôlām* is corrupted from *ʿām*.

5d. *restore the eminence:* literally, "raise up the horn." The reverse image, of breaking the horn, is *broke their power* in 7c.

7b. *he campaigned against the hostile Philistines* = *wayyiḥan bipělištîm ʿārîm*. The verb in MS B is regularly read *wytn,* but the *taw* is more likely *ḥeth.* The verb *ḥnh,* "encamp," is used by Ben Sira elsewhere (MS A 4:13, 15; 14:24), though not in a hostile sense. With *b-* following, it takes on the meaning "campaign against" (Judg 9:50), which is called for in the present context. *ʿārîm,* Aramaizing for *ṣārîm,* occurs in later Heb and Jewish Aram in the meaning "enemies" (here, *hostile*). If correct here (compare 37:5 where it is intrusive), it could be a play on *ʿărēlîm,* "uncircumcised," the usual epithet for the Philistines. But it is more likely an error in transmission.

8–10. The second colon of each of four lines in MS B is damaged; of 10ab almost the whole line is eaten away. The translation of vv 8c–10 is based on taking G 8cd as an expansion of one colon (Heb 8c, here followed); this is succeeded by 9c of Ziegler's Gr (= the broken 8d of the Heb; in Ziegler, it is a supplement from GII), then by 10ab, 9ab, 10cd in that order. Syr severely abridges this, and in MS B only 10cd is verifiable in place. G 9ab have been related to the remnants of these cola in MS B and its margin (partly not shown in the facsimile; see Smend and Segal); thus G's "musicians" has been read as *string music* and the word for *psalms* supplied explicitly.

11b. *exalted his strength:* literally, "raised his horn"; compare the NOTE on 5d above. The recurrence of this imagery in the present passage depends on its traditional association with David (Pss 89:19, 25; 132:17); see later Luke 1:69.

11d. *in Israel:* with G and Syr; MS B, "over Jerusalem."

15. The verse is damaged in MS B and scarcely represented by three words in Syr. The *psychē* of G in 15a can hardly stand for Heb *nepeš* in this place; it is here supposed that the *lēb* of *rōḥab lēb* in 1 Kgs 5:9 underlies it as the basis for an allusion. V 15b in MS B, *wtql[s b]mrwm šyrh,* is highly suspicious, both as to *qls* in a favorable sense ("praise"? "celebrate in song"? Peters) being Heb of the age of Ben Sira, and as to what "the heavens" and "song" have to do with the context. To import the Song of Songs into this does not clarify the sentence structure.

16. Lacking in MS B, this verse is present in G and Syr, which agree on 16a. V 16b in G would seem to refer to the visit of the Queen of Sheba, 1 Kings 10, especially vv 4–9. Syr 16b is "and they waited to hear you," which alludes to 1 Kgs 10:24 in the language of Job 29:21–23.

20c–22d. In MS B, the lines are damaged at the beginning, with 22cd almost completely gone.

Comment

In this section, Ben Sira gives brief notice to Nathan the prophet who serves as a link between Samuel-Saul and David and Solomon, who receive the lion's share of praise (sixteen bicola each).

By mentioning Nathan at the head of this part, Ben Sira calls attention to the succession of prophets in Israel from the time of Moses—an important conviction in the OT. Cf. 46:1, 13, 20; 48:1–4, 12, 22; 49:6, 8, 10; Amos 2:11; 3:7–8; Hos 12:14; Jer 7:25. Nathan (47:1) was the outstanding prophet in David's time; cf. 2 Sam 7:2–17; 12:1–15. In 1 Kgs 1:26, Nathan refers to himself as David's servant (47:1b).

The literal translation of 47:2 makes the point more clearly: "Indeed as the (choice) fat is *lifted up* [Heb *mûrām, hophʿal* participle of *rûm*] from the holy offering, so was David (lifted up) from Israel." The Heb verb *rûm*, in the *hiphʿil* or *hophʿal*, is a technical term for separating the fat from sacrificial animals; cf., for example, Lev 4:8, 10, 19. In Ps 89:20, which refers to David, the same verb, in the *hiphʿil*, is used: "I *have lifted up* a youth over my people." Ben Sira seems to have had both the Leviticus and Psalm 89 texts in mind when writing 47:2. The point of 47:2 is dramatic and bold. David is compared to the choicest part of the sacrificial animal, the fat on the inner organs (intestines, liver, and kidneys), which the Israelites were forbidden to eat, for it had to be burned on the altar; cf. Exod 29:13, 22; Lev 3:3–5, 9–11, 14–16. When David tended his father's flocks, if a lion or bear carried off a sheep, he would go after it and rescue the prey from its mouth (1 Sam 17:34–36): the background of 47:3 (cf. NOTE). David's slaying of the Philistine giant, Goliath (47:4), is told in colorful detail in 1 Sam 17:32–51. "The people's disgrace" (47:4b; cf. NOTE) alludes to David's comment before his encounter with Goliath (1 Sam 17:26). With regard to "the pride of Goliath" (47:4d), cf. Prov 16:18. Like Joshua (46:5a) and Samuel (46:16a), David "called upon the Most High God" (47:5a; cf. also 48:20a), an allusion to David's words in 1 Sam 17:37, 45–47. The expression "the skilled warrior" (47:5c) derives from 1 Sam 17:33. The Philistines had attempted to humiliate God's people by the proud challenge of Goliath, who said: "I defy the ranks of Israel today. Give me a man and let us fight together" (1 Sam 17:10). With God's help, David flattened the skilled Goliath (47:5c); thus did he "raise up the horn of his people," the literal translation of 47:5d (cf. NOTE). The raised horn, symbol of power (cf. 1 Sam 2:1; Pss 18:3; 89:18) and glory (cf. Ps 112:9), stands in stark contrast with the shattered "pride of Goliath" (47:4d).

David's defeat of Goliath was the beginning of the end of Philistine power in the Holy Land. Hence the women of Israel sang of his exploits: "Saul has slain his thousands, and David his ten thousands" (1 Sam 18:7; 21:12; 29:5)— the reference in 47:6ab. As king, David defeated his enemies "on every side" (47:6c, 7a), viz., the Moabites (2 Sam 8:2), the Arameans (2 Sam 8:5–12; 10:15–19), the Edomites (2 Sam 8:14), the Ammonites (2 Sam 10:1–14; 11:1), and the dreaded Philistines (2 Sam 5:17–25; 8:1; 21:15–22). It was David who put an end to the Philistine power (lit., horn; cf. NOTE on 47:5d) for good (47:7bc; cf. NOTE). "Till our own day" (47:7c, lit., till today) is a stereotyped phrase in the Bible; cf., for example, Gen 19:37–38; 26:33; 32:33; Matt 27:8; 28:25. In 47:8–10 (for the order of the verses, cf. NOTE), Ben Sira extols David as composer of psalms, esp. of praise. In biblical tradition, the Law (or Torah) was attributed to Moses, Psalms to David, and Wisdom (e.g., Proverbs, Qoheleth) to Solomon. David is presented as a person who prayed constantly (47:8a)—an exaggeration, to say the least, of the real historical David. He is said to have fulfilled the great Deuteronomic commandment (Deut 6:5) to love Yahweh "with his whole heart" (47:8c). According to 1 Chr 15:16; 16:4–6; and 23:5, David was responsible for giving music an important function in the cult (47:9c,ab, 10cd). By so doing, "he added beauty to the feasts" (47:10a), something that was needed, for as Smend (p. 451) suggests, the Zadokites of David's time had become lax in their duties, with the result that public worship was flat and colorless. Following the tradition in 1 Chr 23:31–32, Ben Sira attributes to David the solemnizing of the religious festivals, "the seasons of the year" (47:10b). According to 1 Chr 23:5, David had also devised musical instruments to be used in chanting of the psalms (47:9ab). The chanting of psalms "before daybreak" (47:10d) is mentioned also in Ps 57:9; cf. Ps 119:62. David's "sins" (so G; Heb "sin") are finally mentioned in 47:11a, though only in general. He committed adultery with Bathsheba, who then conceived a child (2 Sam 11:1–5), and to cover up his crime he brought her warrior husband, Uriah the Hittite, back to Jerusalem from the front in Rabbah with the hope that he would sleep with his wife. Uriah, however, refused to go home and to sleep with his wife, for in holy war soldiers were required to abstain from women (cf. 1 Sam 21:5–6). Finally David dismissed Uriah with a letter for his general Joab: "Place Uriah up front, where the fighting is fierce. Then pull back and leave him to be struck down dead" (2 Sam 11:15). Yahweh, however, *forgave* (47:11a, Heb *he῾ĕbîr*) David his sins (2 Sam 12:13 with the same Heb verb) and "exalted his strength forever" (47:11b; cf. NOTE for the literal translation and references). The Davidic royal house and throne (47:11cd; cf. NOTE) are to last forever (2 Sam 7:12–16)—the expression of Messianic hope; cf. also 47:22.

The next poem (47:12–22) is devoted to David's son and successor, Solomon. Because Solomon, despite a good beginning to his reign, turned out to be unfaithful to the Covenant (47:18cd–20; cf. 1 Kgs 3:3; 11:1–11), Ben Sira attributes Solomon's prosperous and peaceful reign (47:12b–13ab) to David's "merits" (47:12a); cf. 1 Kgs 11:11–13, 32–33. Solomon is described as "a wise son" (47:12b), a reference to 1 Kgs 5:21 (cf. also 1 Kgs 3:9–12, 16–28; 5:21). Thanks to David's victories (47:7), Solomon "lived in security . . . during an era of peace" (47:12b–13a); cf. 1 Kgs 5:5. The very name Solomon (Heb šĕlōmōh) suggests peace (Heb šālôm). It was Yahweh who had given Solomon "peace on all sides" (1 Kgs 5:18)—the point of 47:13b. Solomon built the temple (47:13c; cf. 1 Kgs 6:1–38), a privilege denied to David (2 Sam 7:5–7, 13; cf. 1 Kgs 5:17). Ben Sira calls the temple "a house to the name of God" [lit., to his name], a phrase he borrowed from 2 Sam 7:13 and 1 Kgs 5:19. The temple was also called the "sanctuary" (47:13d), a term used in 1 Chr 22:19. The idea of the sanctuary being "lasting" (47:13d) derives from Ps 78:69. In 47:14–20, Ben Sira uses direct address, as he does of Elijah in 48:4–11. Solomon was wise when he was young (47:14a)—a reference to 1 Kgs 3:9–12, 16–28; 5:9–11; 10:1–8. The Nile is again used as a symbol of abundance in a comparison in 47:14b; cf. 24:27; 39:22.

Solomon's "breadth of understanding" (47:15a; cf. NOTE) is mentioned in 1 Kgs 5:9–11, 14. His "sayings of hidden meaning" (47:15b) is a reference to 1 Kgs 5:12. Solomon's fame reached "distant coasts" (47:16a), an allusion to 1 Kgs 5:14 as well as to 1 Kgs 10:1–13, the story of the visit of the queen of Sheba (the leading principality in what is now the Yemen). The queen of Sheba was amazed not only at Solomon's wisdom but also at his palace, food, attendants, temple sacrifices, and prosperity (1 Kgs 10:4–9)—the allusion in 47:16b (cf. NOTE). According to 1 Kgs 5:12, Solomon uttered three thousand proverbs (Heb māšāl) and composed a thousand and five songs (Heb šîr); both words occur at the beginning of 47:17a, but in reverse order. "The Song of Songs by Solomon," as Cant 1:1 puts it, is the masterwork. The "riddle," Heb ḥîdâ (47:17a), is a word found also in Prov 1:6b, a book attributed to Solomon. For the meaning of ḥîdâ as "riddle," cf. Judg 14:12–14. Heb mĕlîṣâ (47:17b), here translated "with your answers," is a rare word, which is found only here and in Hab 2:6; Prov 1:6. In Hab 2:6, the word means "satire" (the verb lyṣ, from which the noun is derived, has, in the hiphʿil, the meaning "to deride" or "to scorn" [Prov 14:9; 19:28; Ps 119:51]). In Prov 1:6, mĕlîṣâ, being in parallel with māšāl, "proverb," means "parable" or "allusive saying" (lyṣ, in the hiphʿil, also means "to interpret" [Gen 42:23]). The reference in 47:17 is to 1 Kgs 5:9–14. The "glorious name which was conferred upon Israel" and also given to Solomon (47:18ab) by Nathan the prophet is yĕdîdyāh, which means "beloved of Yahweh" (2 Sam 12:25). In Jer 11:15, Yahweh calls Israel "my beloved," Heb yĕdîdî; cf. Deut 28:10, Isa 63:19; Jer 14:9; 15:16.

After eight bicola in praise of Solomon, Ben Sira devotes eight bicola

(47:18cd–22) to describe Solomon's sins and the results thereof. For the connection between 47:18cd and 19, cf. Deut 17:17. Solomon's amassing of gold (47:18c) is mentioned in 1 Kgs 10:14–17, 21–23, 25 (=2 Chr 9:13–16, 20–22, 24); of silver (47:18c), in 1 Kgs 10:27 (=2 Chr 9:29), though the comparison in the latter text is with stones, and not lead. Foreign women, however, were the real cause of Solomon's downfall (47:19–20); cf. 1 Kgs 11:1–10. The literal translation of 49:19a is "And you gave to women your loins"—forceful language. The whole verse is a rephrasing and application of the injunction in Prov 31:3: "Give not your vigor to women, nor your strength to those who ruin kings." Unlike Abraham, who "kept his glory without stain" (44:19b; cf. COMMENT), Solomon "brought a stain upon [his] glory" and "shame upon [his] marriage bed" (44:20ab; cf. Gen 49:4) by having intercourse with foreign women, whom Yahweh had forbidden the Israelites to marry (1 Kgs 11:2; cf. Exod 34:16). Solomon brought "wrath upon [his] descendants" (47:20c) because, being born of foreign mothers, they shared not in God's blessing but in his anger; cf. Ezra 9:2; Mal 2:15; Wis 3:16–19. The worst disaster would come after Solomon's death. The "groaning upon [Solomon's] deathbed" (47:20d) is probably an allusion to the reaction of the people at the answer they received when they asked the new king Rehoboam to lighten the heavy load his father Solomon had placed on them; Rehoboam said, "My father beat you with whips, but I will beat you with scorpions" (1 Kgs 12:14). As a result of Rehoboam's arrogant disregard for the people's request, the kingdom was split in two (47:21a). Rehoboam ruled in Judah; Jeroboam usurped power in Ephraim (47:21b), i.e., Israel. Cf. 1 Kgs 12:16–25. According to 1 Kgs 11:11–13, 33, the division of the kingdom was punishment for Solomon's idolatrous practices, about which Ben Sira, curiously, says not a word. The "commitment" that "God does not withdraw" (47:22a) is a reference to 2 Sam 7:14–16; 1 Kgs 11:13, 39; Ps 89:29–38. The literal translation of 47:22b is "nor does he let fall to the ground any of his words" (cf. Josh 23:14; 1 Sam 3:19; 1 Kgs 8:56; 2 Kgs 10:10). Because God is faithful to his promises (47:22ab), the Davidic kingship will endure forever (47:22cd). The "remnant" (47:22e) is the group of people that remained faithful in Jacob; cf. 48:15e. For the idea of the "root" from David's own family (47:22f), cf. Isa 11:1, 10. The three bicola of 47:22 express the Messianic hope of Ben Sira's day; cf. also 47:11 and 48:10.

For further study of 47:12–22, see P. C. Beentjes, " 'The Countries Marvelled at You': King Solomon in Ben Sira 47:12–22," *BTFT* 45 (1984): 6–14.

56. The Northern Kingdom: Elijah and Elisha
(47:23–48:15d)

47 23 When Solomon slept with his ancestors,   B(G)
    he left behind him one of his sons,
  Broad in folly, lacking in sense,
    who by his policy made rebels of the people;
  Until one arose who should not be mentioned by name,
    the sinner who led Israel into sin,
  Who brought ruin to Ephraim
24   and caused them to be exiled from their land.

25 Their sinfulness grew more and more,   B
    and they lent themselves to every evil

48   1 Till like a fire there appeared the prophet
    whose words were as a flaming furnace.
2 Their staff of bread he shattered,
    in his zeal he reduced them to straits;
3 By God's word he shut up the heavens
    and three times brought down fire.
4 How awesome are you, ELIJAH!
    Whose glory is equal to yours?
5 You brought a dead child back to life
    from the netherworld, by the will of the LORD.
6 You sent kings down to destruction,
    and nobles, from their beds of sickness.
7 You heard threats at Sinai;
    at Horeb, avenging judgments.
8 You anointed the bearer of these punishments,
    the prophet to succeed to your place.
9 You were taken aloft in a whirlwind,
    by fiery captors, heavenward.

10 You are destined, it is written, in time to come
    to put an end to wrath before the day of the LORD,
To turn back the hearts of parents toward their
                  children,
    and to reestablish the tribes of Israel.
11 Blessed is he who shall have seen you before he dies!
    ^a . . . .
12 When Elijah was enveloped in the whirlwind,
    ELISHA was filled with his spirit;
Twice as many signs he wrought,
    and marvels with every utterance of his mouth.
His life long he feared no one,
    nor was any able to intimidate his will.
13 Nothing was beyond his power;
    from where he lay buried, his dead body prophesied.
14 In life he performed wonders,
    and after death, marvelous deeds.
15 Despite all this the people did not repent,
    nor did they cease their sinning
Until they were rooted out of their land
    and scattered all over the earth.

---

^a 11b for we too shall certainly live.   GI

Notes

47   23ab. The line is damaged in MS B, which for the conventional *with his ances-tors* of G (lacking altogether in Syr) has a participle read by some as *mĕyō'āš*, "in despair" (cf. Qoh 2:20); there is no certainty as to the reading. V 23b is missing in MS B after the verb.

23cd. The line was structured by Ben Sira so that it began with *rĕḥōb*, "broad" (in form a stative adjective such as MT tends to level out of the language), and ended with *ʿām*, "people." This provided the name of Rohoboam, *rĕḥabʿām*, without actually using it, though MS B, G, and Syr all read it back in explicitly, and disturb the line in so doing.

23ef. Here, too, though MS B's *'al yĕḥî lô zēker*, "who should not be mentioned by name" (vouched for by Syr, though not in G), shows Ben Sira avoided it, the name Jeroboam ben Nabat appears in all extant forms of the text.

23g, 24a. These are transposed in G; the line 23g, 24a in MS B (vouched for by Syr) has a consistent metaphor in *mikšōl*, "stumbling block" (=*ruin*), and *lĕhaddîḥēm*, "to jolt them loose" (=*and caused them to be exiled*), that confirms its authenticity.

25ab. This transition to the Elijah narrative has again (cf. Notes to 44:23; 46:12b) been botched by G (as Smend and Segal have seen), because the *ʿad ʾăšer qām nābîʾ* of 48:1 was read as *ʿad ʾăšer nāqām yābōʾ*, or the like. Thus G, now at least, includes a partial doublet (and not really a gloss) in 47:25b–48:1a.

48 4b. *whose*=G, Syr=*ûmî* for MS B's *ʾăšer*.

7a. *you heard*=G=*haššômēaʿ* for MS B's *wḥšmyʿ* (similarly Syr).

8a. MS B inverts the order of vv 7 and 8; cf. G and Syr. Segal argues for the order of MS B and, with most, follows G and Syr in reading *malkê (tašlûmôt)* for B's *mĕlēʾ*. But the designation of Hazael (2 Kgs 8:13) and the anointing of Jehu (2 Kgs 9:1–6) were the work of Elisha, who is both the *mĕlēʾ tašlûmôt* of 8a and the *nābîʾ* of 8b. G *basileis*=*malkê* (also Syr) was influenced by v 6a, and the Gr translator shows his confusion by reading "prophets" and "successors" in 8b, where the singular reference is directly to Elisha, as in 1 Kgs 19:16 (and so Syr).

9a–12b. It is regrettable that these lines have been subject in MS B to the damage (to the second colon of each) spoken of in the Note at 44:17 above; 11b and 12ab are almost completely gone, a specially severe loss.

9b. *heavenward*=Syr; the Heb word is missing, and G gives no equivalent.

10b. *the day of the* Lord=Syr; the Heb is missing, and G has *thymou*, "(the time of God's) anger."

10d. *tribes of Israel:* G and Syr have "tribes of Jacob," but the last (missing) word in the line in MS B ended in a *lamed,* which survives.

11. There was undoubtedly a second colon in the original text, but what it contained is no longer evident. For 11a, MS B has *ʾšr rʾk wm[t]*. Enough of the final *taw* is preserved so that there can be no reasonable doubt this is to be read *ʾašrê* [with G and Syr] *rāʾăkā wāmēt* (and so Segal). The missing 11b should have contained a reason of sorts for this paradoxical statement, understood as in the translation given here. G of 11a (*makarioi hoi idontes se kai hoi en agapēsei kekoimēmenoi;* see Ziegler) puts this into the plural and softens it by expansion: "Blest are they who shall have seen you, and they who [shall] have fallen asleep in [the] love [of God]." Whether the more usual Gr reading *kekosmēmenoi,* "who are adorned [with love]," was a deliberate or an accidental modification cannot be said. The *agapēsei* itself, in the sense of the love of God for humans and of humans for God, presents a favorite theme and term of the GII glossator (see the Note on 11:15–16), which, however, already had its roots in GI (see 1:10 and the Note there; 2:15–16). Yet in the present place Smend is almost certainly correct in seeing *agapēsei* as a later reading based on an earlier *kai en anapausei kekoimēmenoi* (the omitted *hoi* will have been part of the reinterpretation): "(who shall have seen you) and then lain at rest." This relates to the grandson's usage in the similar verse, 38:23. To 11b of G, given above as a modified form of the text, the corresponding Syr has "(Blest is he who shall have seen you and died;) but he shall not die, but shall certainly live." Out of these data, plus the tail of a long letter surviving early in the space for the eaten-away 11b in MS B, and a *hē* that survives at the end of

the colon, Segal reconstructs for the Heb 11b *kî 'ap hû' hāyōh tihyeh*. Who it is that may have been said to certainly live, in this final colon, is settled differently by different students of the text. For Smend, it is Elijah—he reads *wĕ'ašrêkā kî hāyōh tihyeh*. Segal follows the indication in Syr, and understands his reconstruction of MS B to speak of the individual who shall have seen Elijah before dying: he, too, shall certainly live. In view of the strong evidence that Ben Sira did not believe in the resurrection of the dead, Segal is hard put to conjure up the possibility of a few meritorious individuals (he does not say, like Elijah himself) for whom the author might have allowed an exception. But if the Syr is already a modified text (in v 10 of Syr, Segal sees a Christian influence), perhaps already its source, and that of G, and even MS B, were modified in this place. Could the original Heb 11b, not represented in MS B, have read *kî 'ap 'ănahnû nōah nānûah*, "for we too shall certainly come to rest" in the sense of the *nûhat 'ōlām* of Sir 30:17b? Then *hāyōh nihyeh* would have been a tempting amelioration by the grandson's day. Lat strangely managed to minimize G's wording with "For we live our lives only, but after death our fame will not be such [as his]."

12cd. This bicolon is not in G; Syr does have it, though it puts its "twofold" with the *spirit* "of prophecy" in 12b.

13b. *prophesied* = G = *nibbā'*; MS B has the false reading *nibrā'*.

Comment

This section opens with a unit that describes the folly of Rehoboam, Solomon's successor, who ruled in Judah, and the evil of Jeroboam, who became king of Israel after the division of the realm (47:23–24). There follow longer units on the prophets Elijah and Elisha, who exercised their ministries in the Northern Kingdom (47:25–48:15).

At the death of Solomon (47:23a; cf. NOTE) after a forty-year reign, his son Rehoboam became king (47:23b; cf. NOTE), as 1 Kgs 11:43 records. Ben Sira deliberately avoids the mention of Rehoboam's name, but clearly and cleverly plays on the name, as explained in the NOTE on 47:23cd. Rehoboam's colossal folly, which made "rebels of the people" (47:23cd), is described in 1 Kgs 12:1–19. The one whose name "should not be mentioned" (47:23e) is Jeroboam (cf. NOTE). He "led Israel into sin" (47:23f; cf. 1 Kgs 14:16) by making two calves of gold, placing one in Bethel, the other in Dan, i.e., on the southern and northern boundaries of the kingdom of Israel. He also built temples on the high places and made priests from men who were not Levites. Though these measures were religious in nature, they were politically motivated: he wanted to prevent his people from journeying to the temple in Jerusalem for fear they would give their allegiance to the house of David, i.e., to Rehoboam (cf. 1 Kgs 12:26–32). Because of this apostasy, Jeroboam ruined

Ephraim (Israel), which was eventually (in 722 B.C.) taken into exile in Assyria (47:23g–24a; cf. NOTE); cf. 2 Kgs 17:20–23.

The sinfulness of the kings and people of the Northern Kingdom (47:25ab; cf. NOTE and 2 Kgs 17:21–22) provides the transition to the poem on Elijah, a name that means "Yah[weh] is my God." The wording of 47:25b derives from 1 Kgs 21:20, 25; 2 Kgs 17:17. The word "fire" (Heb *'ēš*) forms an *inclusio* in 48:1a and 3b. The mention of Elijah's appearing "like a fire" (48:1a) is an allusion to the wordplay in 2 Kgs 1:10, 12, in which the prophet is called *'îš 'ĕlōhîm*, "man of God," who could call down from heaven *'ēš 'ĕlōhîm*, "the fire of God," to consume his adversaries. Elijah's words are said to be "as a flaming furnace" (48:1b), an expression borrowed from Mal 3:19 (cf. Mal 3:23). These images of fire and flaming furnaces aptly portray the zeal (48:2b) Elijah brought to his service of the Lord. The wording of 48:2a derives from Lev 26:26; Ezek 4:16; 5:16; 14:13 (cf. Isa 3:1); these texts are the basis of the common maxim "Bread is the staff of life" (Jonathan Swift, *Tale of a Tub* [1704]). In 48:2a, G and Syr interpret rather than translate: "who [Syr: and he] brought down on them a famine," a reading based on Ps 105:6a. The reference is to the famine in 1 Kgs 18:3 (cf. 1 Kgs 17:1); see also Luke 4:25 and Jas 5:17. Elijah's zeal (48:2b) was legendary (cf. 1 Kgs 19:10, 14); he brought upon the people the punishments predicted in the Law (cf. Lev 26:1–26; Deut 28:38–42, 62). Elijah's shutting up "the heavens" (48:3a) is recorded in 1 Kgs 17:1; cf. Deut 11:17. The three times he "brought down fire" (48:3b) are found in 1 Kgs 18:38 (to consume the holocaust, wood, stones, dust, and water in the trench around the altar), and 2 Kgs 1:10 and 12 (to consume King Ahaziah's captain and his fifty men and a second captain and his fifty). After this four-bicolon introduction (47:25–48:3), Ben Sira finally mentions the name Elijah, addressing him in the second person (48:4a); similar direct address was used also of Solomon in 47:14–20.

Elijah is characterized as "awesome," with a "glory" that none can equal (48:4; cf. NOTE). Then Ben Sira lists the prophet's exploits that earned him his reputation. The "dead child" Elijah restored to life (48:5) was the son of the widow of Zarephath (1 Kgs 17:17–22). The kings he destroyed (48:6a) were the descendants of wicked King Ahab (cf. 1 Kgs 21:19–24); the "nobles" (48:6b, lit., the honored ones) is a reference to King Ahaziah, who had been injured in a fall and was confined to bed, where he then died, as Elijah had predicted (2 Kgs 1:2–4, 6, 16–17). Interestingly, Ben Sira regards the mountain of God, Horeb, as identical with Sinai (48:7); the reference is to the episode in 1 Kgs 19:8–18. Sinai in the J and P sources of the Pentateuch is the name of the mountain on which Yahweh appeared to Moses; in the E and D sources, the name is Horeb. Elisha is "the bearer of these punishments" (cf. 1 Kgs 19:15–17; 2 Kgs 8:12–15; 9:1–10) and "the prophet to succeed" Elijah (48:8; cf. NOTE); Elijah anointed Elisha as prophet in 1 Kgs 19:16. For the colorful account of Elijah's being taken "heavenward" (48:9; cf. NOTE), cf. 2

Kgs 2:1, 11. In 48:10, Ben Sira uses the expression "it is written," thus indicating that he is quoting, or referring to, a Scripture text for his belief in the return of Elijah, viz., Mal 3:23–24; cf. Luke 1:17; Matt 11:10, 14; 17:10–13. For a study of 48:10c and Luke 1:17, cf. P. Winter, *ZNW* 49 (1958): 65–66. The phrase "to reestablish the tribes of Israel" (48:10d; cf. NOTE) derives from Isa 49:6. Here we have another expression of Ben Sira's messianic hope; cf. COMMENT on 47:22. The reference in 48:11a is to those who will be around to see Elijah when he returns. The second colon of 48:11 is now impossible to reconstruct with any certainty; cf. the lengthy NOTE. What GI has for 48:11b, "for we too shall certainly live," could not reflect Ben Sira's original thought, for G (and Syr as well) expresses belief in a blessed afterlife —an idea that was totally foreign to Ben Sira; cf. 7:17b with COMMENT and INTRODUCTION, Part X, 4.

After Elijah was taken up "in the whirlwind" (48:12a; cf. also v 9), the prophet Elisha (the name means "God has saved") "was filled with his spirit" (48:12b)—a reference to the story in 2 Kgs 2:9–10, 15. In biblical tradition, Elisha was noted for the "signs he wrought" and "marvels," "twice as many" as Elijah (48:12cd); the reason Ben Sira says "twice as many" is that Elisha received a double portion of Elijah's spirit (2 Kgs 2:9–10), the portion of the eldest son who received twice as much as any of the other heirs but obviously not twice the inheritance. For the stories about Elisha's "signs" and "marvels," cf. 2 Kgs 2:13–14, 19–22, 23–24; 3:11–19; 4:1–7, 8–17, 18–37, 38–41, 42–44; 5:1–27; 6:1–7, 13–17, 18, 19–23; 6:24–7:20; 8:1–15; 13:14–19. G may have omitted 48:12cd (cf. NOTE) because this bicolon seems to make Elisha a greater person than Elijah. Elisha's fearlessness and courage, which are praised in 48:12ef, are recorded in 2 Kgs 3:9–15; 6:13–16; 6:31–7:2; cf. Matt 14:3–4. In 48:13a, Ben Sira adapts the language of Gen 18:14, which speaks of Yahweh's limitless power, and applies it to Elisha—hyperbole, to say the least. Elisha's "dead body *prophesied*" (48:13b; cf. NOTE), an interesting use of the verb, when a dead man, cast into Elisha's grave, "came back to life and rose to his feet" (2 Kgs 13:21). V 14a repeats v 12cd, and v 14b refers back to v 13b. In the six Heb words of v 14, there is remarkable balance and structure: the first words of each colon (*life* and *death*) are in antithetic parallelism; and the other words are in an *a:b::b':a* chiastic pattern: *ʿāsâ* (he did):*niplāʾôt* (wonders)::*timhê* (marvels of):*maʿăśeh* (deed). Despite the splendor of Elijah's and Elisha's lives and prodigies, "the people did not repent" (48:15a), nor did they put an end to their sins (48:15b). The repentance of the people as a result of Elijah's showdown with the prophets of Baal (1 Kgs 18:39) did not endure. Accordingly, as Yahweh had repeatedly threatened through the Law and the prophets, the people of Israel were exiled from their land and "scattered all over the earth" (48:15cd); cf. Lev 26:33–35; Deut 4:25–27; 28:36, 63–68; Jer 9:12–15; Zech 7:9–14. The reference is to the destruction of the Northern Kingdom by Assyria and the captivity and exile of the people in 722 B.C.

57. Judah: Hezekiah and Isaiah
(48:15e–25)

48   ^{15e} But Judah remained, a tiny people,   B
     with its ruler from the house of David.
  ¹⁶ Some of them did what was right,
     but others were extremely wicked.

  ¹⁷ HEZEKIAH fortified his city
     and had water brought within it;
     With bronze tools he cut through the rocks
     and dammed up a mountain site for a reservoir.
  ¹⁸ During his reign Sennacherib led an invasion,
     and sent his adjutant;
     He shook his fist at Zion
     and blasphemed God in his pride.
  ¹⁹ The people's hearts melted within them;
     they were in anguish like that of childbirth.
  ²⁰ But they called upon the Most High God
     and lifted up their hands to him;
     He heard the prayer they uttered,
     and saved them through ISAIAH.
  ²¹ God struck the camp of the Assyrians
     and routed them with a plague.
  ²² For Hezekiah did what was right
     and held fast to the paths of David,
     As ordered by the illustrious prophet   G
     Isaiah, who saw the truth in visions.
  ²³ In his lifetime he turned back the sun
     and prolonged the life of the king.
  ²⁴ By his dauntless spirit he looked into the future   B
     and consoled the mourners of Zion;
  ²⁵ He foretold what should be till the end of time,
     hidden things that were yet to be fulfilled.

Notes

48   17c. In G, the tools are of iron; MS B has *knḥšt,* with the *k-* an easy error for *b-*. *Bronze* picks are a possibility for the period in question, and *bbrzl* for "iron" would be hard to confuse with *bnḥšt;* Syr lacks the line 17cd. Neither Ben Sira nor his grandson was an archaeologist.

20a. Since *called upon the Most High God* is a recurrent theme in this section of Sirach (46:5, 16; 47:5), G's "(called upon) the Lord, the Merciful" is clearly an interpretive variant, based on the context here and in 2 Kings/Isaiah; cf. 2:11 and 50:19, the latter the only place in Sirach where "the Merciful" (*raḥûm*) is employed as a divine name in the Heb.

20c. *the prayer they uttered*=MS B's *běqôl těpillātām;* G and Syr with "swiftly" seem to have taken *bql* as being from *qll.* G also supplies "the Holy One" as subject (nowhere in Sirach is the corresponding Heb *haqqādôš* a name for God) while Syr supplies "God"; in the Heb, as in the translation here, the subject is implied (from 20a). G *ex ouranou* in this colon is simply an allusion to the *ʿelyôn* of 20a, which will have been in the grandson's source.

21b. For *and routed them with a plague* G has "and his angel (did away with them)," borrowing from 2 Kgs 19:35 || Isa 37:36. The term "plague" for this kind of divine visitation is used in the Pentateuch and 1–2 Samuel but is only implied in the Sennacherib narrative.

22cd–23. These two bicola are lacking in the Heb, with the loss of the two bottom lines of a column in MS B.

Comment

In this section, Ben Sira turns his attention from the Northern Kingdom of Israel to the Southern Kingdom of Judah, and to one of its great kings, Hezekiah, and the outstanding prophet of his reign, Isaiah.

After the Assyrians destroyed Samaria in 722 B.C., thus putting an end to the kingdom of Israel, only the kingdom of "Judah remained, a tiny people" (48:15e); cf. Isa 24:6. But a successor of David sat on its throne (48:15f), in contrast with Israel, which had usurpers as kings. Ben Sira condenses the history of Judah into one bicolon: some of the kings and people did "what was right, but others were extremely wicked" (48:16). The Deuteronomic history expresses approval of a king by using the phrase "he did what was right," or the equivalent; cf. 1 Kgs 15:11, Asa; 22:43, Jehoshaphat; 2 Kgs 12:3, Joash; 15:3, Azariah; 18:3, Hezekiah (see Sir 48:22a below); 22:2, Josiah.

Hezekiah was one of the truly great kings of Judah, at least from the religious viewpoint of the Deuteronomic historian. Ben Sira shares that view. He begins his praise of Hezekiah, whose name means "Yahweh will make strong," by noting the improvement he effected in Jerusalem (48:17). "Hezekiah fortified [Heb yĕḥizqîyāhû ḥizzēq; note the wordplay] his city" (48:17a), i.e., the capital, Jerusalem; cf. 2 Chr 32:5. He also bored a tunnel, 1,749 feet in length, from the Spring of Gihon to the Pool of Shiloh/Siloam (cf. 2 Kgs 20:20; 2 Chr 32:30), thus assuring Jerusalem a good supply of water (48:17bc). "With bronze tools [cf. NOTE] he cut through [the Heb verb is ḥṣr] the rocks [Heb ṣûrîm]" (48:17c). The verb ḥṣr and the noun ṣûr both occur twice in the so-called Inscription of Siloam found inside the tunnel; it describes how Hezekiah's engineers made the boring—quite an unusual technical accomplishment for the eighth century B.C. For the text of the Inscription, cf. ANET, p. 321. For the damming up of a mountain in 48:17, cf. Isa 22:9–11. The account of the invasion of Sennacherib (48:18) is told in 2 Kgs 18:13–37; 2 Chr 32:1–20; Isa 36:1–22. Sennacherib's "adjutant" (48:18b) is the commander, mentioned in 2 Kgs 18:17, 19–35, who addressed the delegation sent by Hezekiah. The expression "to shake his fist at Zion" (48:18c) is found also in Isa 10:32. The Assyrian commander is said to blaspheme God (48:18d) because of his arrogant words to Hezekiah's delegation recorded in 2 Kgs 18:22, 32–35; Isa 36:7, 14–20; cf. also Isa 37:6, 23–24. As regards the fear and anguish of Hezekiah's people (48:19), cf. 2 Kgs 19:3; Isa 37:3. Curiously, Ben Sira says the people "called upon the Most High God" (48:20a; cf. NOTE) and prayed with hands outstretched (48:20b), the usual manner of praying; but according to 2 Kgs 19:14–19 and Isa 37:15–20, it was Hezekiah alone who prayed. God answered their prayer (48:20c; cf. NOTE) and "saved them through ISAIAH" (48:20d), who delivered to Hezekiah God's word that Sennacherib would not succeed in capturing Jerusalem but instead would be punished (2 Kgs 19:20–34; Isa 37:21–35). "The angel of the LORD . . . struck down one hundred and eighty-five thousand men in the Assyrian camp" (2 Kgs 19:35; cf. Isa 37:36); Ben Sira says that "God struck the camp" himself (48:21a). It is interesting that Ben Sira speaks of "a plague" routing the Assyrians (48:21b), whereas 2 Kgs 19:35 and Isa 37:36 say nothing of the kind; cf. NOTE.

There is another wordplay, in 48:22ab, on the name of Hezekiah, who "did what was right [cf. COMMENT on v 16a above] and held fast to [Heb wayyaḥăzēq, lit., was strong in] the paths of David" (cf. COMMENT on v 17a above); cf. 2 Kgs 18:3, 5–6; 20:3. By Ben Sira's time, thanks especially to the Chronicler, David had a reputation for piety and fidelity. Hezekiah had a close relationship with Isaiah and followed the instructions he received from the prophet (48:22c); cf. 2 Kgs 19:1–7; 20:1–11. Isaiah was noted for his prophetic "visions" (48:22d); cf., for example, Isa 1:1; 2:1; 6:1–13. Through Isaiah's intercession, Hezekiah received a sign that he would be cured of his illness—the shadow cast by the sun on the stairway to the terrace of Ahaz went back the ten steps it had advanced (2 Kgs 20:8–11; Isa 38:7–8): 48:23a; cf. 46:4. Thus was Hezekiah's life "prolonged" (48:23b)—by fifteen years (2 Kgs 20:6; Isa 38:5). With "his dauntless spirit" (the phrase is adapted from Isa 11:2) Isaiah "looked into the future" (48:24a)—a reference to the prediction that there would be a return from the Exile; cf. Isa 40:3–11. Thus did the prophet console "the mourners of Zion" (48:24b); cf. Isa 40:1–2; 49:8–13; 61:1–3. The mention of Isaiah's predictions "till the end of time" of "hidden things" (48:25) is an allusion to Isa 42:9. From vv 24–25, which allude clearly to Second and Third Isaiah, it is obvious that Ben Sira attributed the whole Book of Isaiah to the eighth-century B.C. prophet.

58. Josiah and the Prophets; Heroes Early and Late
(49:1–16)

49   1 The name of JOSIAH is like blended incense   B
   made lasting by a skilled perfumer.
 Precious is his memory, like honey to the taste,
   like music at a banquet.
2 For he grieved over our betrayals
   and destroyed the abominable idols;
3 He kept his heart fixed on God
   and in times of lawlessness he practiced virtue.
4 Except for David, Hezekiah, and Josiah,
   they all were wicked;
 They abandoned the Law of the Most High,
   these kings of Judah, right to the very end.
5 So he gave over their power to others,
   their glory to a foreign nation
6 Who burned the holy city
   and left its streets desolate,
7 As JEREMIAH had foretold; for they had mistreated him
   who even in the womb had been made a prophet,
 To root out, pull down, and destroy,
   and then to build and to plant.
8 EZEKIEL beheld the vision
   and described the different creatures of the chariot
                                              throne;
9 He also referred to JOB,
   who always held fast to the ways of righteousness.
10 Then, too, the TWELVE PROPHETS—
   may their bones flourish with new life where they
                                              lie!—
 Gave renewed strength to Jacob
   and saved him with steadfast hope.

11 How can we extol ZERUBBABEL,   G
    who was like a signet ring on God's right hand,
12 And JESHUA, son of Jozadak?
    In their time they rebuilt the altar
    And erected the holy temple,   B
    destined for everlasting glory.
13 Exalted be the memory of NEHEMIAH!
    He rebuilt our ruined walls,
    Restored our shattered defenses,
    and set up gates and bars.

14 Few on earth have been such as ENOCH;
    he too was taken up within.
15 Was another like JOSEPH ever born?
    Even his dead body was provided for.
16 Glorious, too, were SHEM and SETH and ENOSH;
    but beyond that of any living being was the splendor
                      of ADAM.

Notes

49 1b. *made lasting:* lit., "salted"; cf. Exod 30:35.

2a. *grieved:* lit., "sickened"—in MS B *nḥl,* a by-form of *neḥĕlâ,* cf. Amos 6:6; G and Syr appear to have been confused by it in their rendering of the colon.

5. *power:* another occurrence of "horn"; see NOTE at 47:11. *others:* MS B reads *lĕʾāḥôr,* "[he left their power] in the lurch"; but the *lĕʾaḥēr* read by G and Syr is demanded by the parallel, *foreign nation.* In MS B, *foreign* is preceded by "foolish," a gloss based on Deut 32:21.

6. *holy city:* G prefixes "chosen," a gloss based on Ps 132:13.

7. *As Jeremiah had foretold:* this is a paraphrase for "by the hand(s) of Jeremiah," which equates the events in vv 5–6 with the mission of Jeremiah as described in his own words in 7cd. *they:* the *kings of Judah,* from v 4.

7cd. With Peters (1913), the last word in the overcrowded line in MS B must be *ûlĕhāʿēz;* no longer reading is credible. This form always has an unfavorable meaning in Sirach and in MT, however; and with G, the line should end without it and in agreement with Jer 1:10. The *lĕhārōs* (from Jer 1:10) is an insert by the regular scribe of MS B into the original caesura in the line. Ben Sira adapted the $2+2+2$ disposition of the infinitives in Jeremiah to his own line structuring by an arrangement of 3+(wĕkēn+2). Syr does not have 7cd.

8ab. *vision:* G adds "of the Glory." For 8b it has "which he [i.e., God] showed him upon the chariot with the cherubim."

9. There is no doubt the bicolon reflects what Ezekiel had to say about Job (Ezek 14:14, 20), and that this is all Ben Sira says about him. Extra traces after *Job* at the caesura in MS B may be a transfer of ink, adventitious in this place, to be associated with the stain in the paper in this area. They do not yield a word. G read *Job* as "enemy" (*'iyyôb* as *'ôyēb*) and so confused the sense of the verse.

10b. See NOTE at 46:12.

10d. The last two words need to be supplied from G, as MS B is defective; *be'ĕmûnat tiqwâ* would correspond (so Segal). *and saved him=*G=*wyšʿwhw* as the original reading in MS B (against Cowley-Neubauer, *wyšybwhw*). So also Strack, Segal, Smend, all following Peters. Smend saw a "correction" of this in the MS to *wyšʿnwhw*, which as an active form from *šʿn* would be hard to account for; it cannot be justified as ancient, since Syr also contains *dĕmitparĕqîn* in its paraphrase of the colon.

11-12ab. These two bicola are missing from MS B with its loss of the two bottom lines of the page. 12b. *the altar:* so with Syr; G's *oikon,* "house," can be taken to mean the *bêt-'ĕlōhîm,* i.e., the open-air sanctuary precincts; cf. 50:1cd.

12cd. From this point to the end of the book, the pages of MS B show only minimal damage and the text is nearly intact.

13cd. G transposes these two cola.

14b. *he too:* as was Elijah, cf. 48:9. *within:* beyond the firmament of the heavens, Gen 1:6–8; but implied is, into the divine Presence, for which the same word is used (cf. 45:20, *the showbread;* Isa 63:9).

15a. After this colon G introduces 50:1a; see the NOTE there.

16a. *Glorious:* with G=*nikbādû;* MS B's *npqdw* wrongly employs here the same verb *provided for* as in 15b.

Comment

This final section in praise of Israel's great ancestors has exactly twenty-two bicola, thus signaling the conclusion of this portion (44:1–49:16) of the book; see COMMENT on 1:11–30 and 51:13–30. In his praise of the heroes of faith, Ben Sira skips from King Hezekiah (715–687/6 B.C.) and the prophet Isaiah (whose ministry began in ca. 742 and lasted more than fifty years) to King Josiah (640–609 B.C.). The reason is obvious: the two intervening kings, Manasseh (687/6–642) and Amon (642–640) were scoundrels, according to the Deuteronomic historian who evaluated the nation's history exclusively from the religious point of view (cf. 2 Kgs 21:2–22). Josiah, whose birth had been predicted by a man of God (1 Kgs 13:2) during the reign of Jeroboam I

(922–901 B.C.), "pleased the LORD and conducted himself unswervingly just as his ancestor David had done" (2 Kgs 22:2). Hence, for Ben Sira, the very "name [G and Lat: memory, cf. v 1c] of Josiah is like blended incense [lit., incense of spices] made lasting [cf. NOTE] by a skilled perfumer" (49:1ab). Josiah's "memory" is "precious" (lit., sweet), "like honey to the taste" (49:1c; for the expression, cf. Prov 24:13b), and "like music at a banquet" (49:1d; for the thought, cf. 32:5–6). Josiah deserves a blessed memory, "for he grieved [cf. NOTE] over our betrayals"—a reference to his tearing of his garments when he heard the contents of the book of the Law that had been discovered during the repair of the Temple (2 Kgs 22:10–13, 19). Josiah also "destroyed [lit., put an end to; cf. 2 Kgs 23:5, 11] the abominable idols" (lit., the vain abominations); for the account of his activities, cf. 2 Kgs 23:4–15, 19–20, 24. The Deuteronomic historian lavishes the highest praise on Josiah, for in terms of religious observance there was no king before or after him who could compare with him (2 Kgs 23:3, 25); it is this sentiment that Ben Sira expresses in 49:3: "He kept his heart fixed on God," lit., he gave his heart perfectly (Heb wayyattēm libbô) to God. The noun tōm, which occurs in the phrase tom-lēbāb, "integrity of heart" (Gen 20:5–6; 1 Kgs 9:4; and Ps 101:2), derives from the root tmm; hence Ben Sira's use of that verb here. In 49:3b, the phrase "times of lawlessness" (Heb yěmê ḥāmās; cf. COMMENT on 10:23b), refers to the days when people practiced idolatry publicly before Josiah's religious reforms (2 Kgs 22:17). But Josiah himself always "practiced virtue" (Heb ʿāśâ ḥesed); cf. COMMENT on 44:1b.

In Ben Sira's judgment, the kings of Judah, "except for David, Hezekiah, and Josiah," "were wicked," for "they abandoned the Law of the Most High" (49:4). According to 1 Kgs 15:11–14 and 22:43, Asa and Jehoshaphat were also good, reforming kings who are praised even in 2 Chr 14:1–4 and 17:3–6. But Ben Sira includes these two monarchs among the wicked because of the faults 2 Chr 16:7–12; 19:2; and 20:35–37 attribute to them. Moreover, during the reigns of both kings the high places did not completely disappear (1 Kgs 15:14; 22:44; 2 Chr 15:17; 20:33). Because of the infidelity of most of Judah's kings, the Most High "gave over their power to others" (49:5a; cf. NOTE), "their glory to a foreign nation" (49:5b; cf. NOTE), i.e., the Babylonians, "who burned the holy city," leaving it utterly desolate (49:6; cf. NOTE); cf. 2 Kgs 25:1–15. The designation of Jerusalem as "the holy city" occurs also in Isa 48:2a; 52:1d; Neh 11:1, 18; cf. Dan 9:24b. Jeremiah prophesied the destruction of Jerusalem and the nation (49:7a; cf. NOTE); cf. Jer 36:2–4, 29–32; 37:8–10; 38:3. Not only the kings (49:7a; cf. NOTE) but also the nobles and people mistreated and persecuted Jeremiah (49:7a); cf. Jer 20:7–8, 10; 37:13–16; 38:4–6. In 49:7b, Ben Sira refers to Jeremiah's being made a prophet "even in the womb" (Jer 1:5). The description of Jeremiah's vocation "to root out, pull down, and destroy, and then to build and to plant" (49:7cd; cf. NOTE) derives from Jer 1:10.

In Ezek 1:4–28, the prophet describes at great length his exotic inaugural vision, to which Ben Sira simply alludes when he mentions "the different creatures of the *chariot throne*" (49:8b; cf. NOTE), Heb *zĕnê merkābâ*, lit., "the kinds of chariot." In Ezekiel's vision, however, the word *merkābâ* does not occur; but as early as 1 Chr 28:18, the word was used in the sense of "chariot throne." Here and in 44:16 and 49:16, Ben Sira refers to sapiential, priestly, and apocalyptic traditions. For a study of the expression *zĕnê merkābâ* in light of the pseudepigrapha and Qumran literature, see J. Marböck, "Henoch—Adam—der Thronwagen: Zu frühjüdischen pseudepigraphischen Traditionen bei Ben Sira," *BZ* N.F. 25 (1981): 103–11. Ezekiel "referred to JOB" (Sir 49:9a; cf. NOTE) as well as Noah and Daniel (Ezek 14:14, 20); all three were proverbially upright believers. Job is listed between the so-called major prophets (Isaiah, Jeremiah, and Ezekiel) and the so-called minor prophets, "the TWELVE PROPHETS" (49:10a), probably because, according to some rabbis, Job was considered a prophet to the Gentiles; apparently, Josephus also placed Job among the prophets (*Against Apion,* i, 8). Ben Sira speaks of Noah in 44:17–18 and Job here; but he says nothing of Daniel, probably because the Book of Daniel was not yet completed (cf. L. F. Hartman and A. A. Di Lella, *The Book of Daniel,* AB 23, pp. 9–18). It should be observed that Ben Sira lists "the TWELVE PROPHETS" (49:10a) as a single book and places them after Ezekiel, as in the Hebrew canon. For the meaning of 49:10b, see NOTE and COMMENT on 46:12a, which is identical with the present colon; in neither place is there any reference to resurrection of the dead (cf. COMMENT on 7:17; 11:26; 14:16; 17:28). It is curious that Ben Sira speaks of the Twelve Prophets giving "strength to Jacob" and saving "him with steadfast hope" (49:10cd; cf. NOTE); he thus reflects a tradition that the message of these prophets was one of consolation and hope. A similar tradition prompted the rabbis to direct that the gloomy last verse of Malachi, "Lest I come and strike the land with doom" (3:24), which closes the Book of the Twelve, be followed in reading by a repetition of the penultimate verse (3:23), which conveys a more hopeful sentiment.

In the next section (49:11–13), Ben Sira extols the leaders who returned from the Babylonian Exile to reconstruct the temple and walls of the city of Jerusalem. Zerubbabel and Jeshua, son of Jozadak, were the ones responsible for rebuilding the altar and "the holy temple" (49:11–12; cf. NOTE); the account of their activities is told in Ezra 3:1–6:22. Ben Sira derived the image of Zerubbabel as "a signet ring on God's right hand" (49:11b) from Hag 2:23, in which a promise is made to Zerubbabel that reverses the punishment of his grandfather Jehoiachin (Jeconiah, Coniah) in Jer 22:24 (cf. Zech 6:11–13 in the NAB, with its note). The newly constructed temple was "destined for everlasting glory" (49:12d)—a reference to the Messianic hope of Judaism (Hag 2:6–9). It is noteworthy that Ben Sira says nothing of Ezra the scribe (Ezra 7:6–10) but speaks with affection of Nehemiah (49:13; cf. NOTE), who despite opposition rebuilt the walls and defenses of Jerusalem in fifty-two days (Neh 2:17–7:3). Cf. P. Höffken, "Warum schwieg Jesus Sirach über Esra?," *ZAW* 87 (1975): 184–201. Thus, with temple and city walls restored, the religious worship and civil authority prescribed in the Law could be enforced.

As a transition from the Praise of the Ancestors of Old to the praise of Simeon (50:1–24), Ben Sira inserts here a minipoem on the most famous of Israel's forebears (49:14–16). Like Elijah, who was "taken aloft in a whirlwind" (48:9), Enoch "too was taken up" alive to heaven by God (49:14b; cf. NOTE and 44:16a), a reference to Gen 5:24; cf. 2 Enoch 18:2. Thus Elijah and Enoch shared a special privilege. But Joseph alone had the distinction of having his mummy, "his dead body," "provided for" (49:15b); his body was transported from Egypt to the Holy Land and then was buried in Shechem (Gen 50:25–26; Exod 13:19; Josh 24:32). As regards 49:16a, Seth, son of Adam (Gen 4:25; 5:3), represents the righteous in the antediluvian world; and Shem, son of Noah (Gen 6:10), is the father of the Semites, of whom Abraham was born (Gen 11:10–26). Enosh, the first-born son of Seth, was an upright person, for during his day "people began to call upon the name of Yahweh" (Gen 4:26). In 1 Chr 1:1, the names Adam, Seth, and Enosh also appear; in Luke 3:38, the same names appear in reverse order. "Shem and Seth and Enosh" were indeed "glorious" (49:16a; cf. NOTE). But "the splendor of Adam" (Heb *tip'eret 'ādām*) is "beyond that of any living being" (49:16b), for Adam, who was created directly by God (Gen 2:7) and made in God's image and likeness (Gen 1:26–27), could be considered "the son of God," as Luke 3:38 puts it. Cf. Wis 10:1. This idealization of Adam occurs here for the first time in Jewish literature; later it played an important part in the development of the Messianic doctrine of the Second Adam (so Box-Oesterley, p. 507). Regarding *tip'eret 'ādām,* cf. J. Marböck, *BZ* N.F. 25 (1981): 103–11, who discusses this phrase in light of 1QS 4,23; 1QH 17,15; CD III,20. The noun *tip'eret,* "splendor, glory" (49:16b), occurs again in the very next colon, 50:1a, in the phrase *tip'eret 'ammô,* "the glory of his people," referring to the High Priest Simeon; thus *tip'eret* is a *mot crochet* connecting this poem and the next one (50:1–24).

59. Simeon, Son of Jochanan
(50:1–24)

50   ¹ Greatest among his kindred, the glory of his people,   B
      was SIMEON the priest, son of Jochanan,
  In whose time the house of God was renovated,
     in whose days the temple was reinforced.
  ² In his time also the retaining wall was built
     for the residence precinct with its temple of the
                 King.
  ³ In his day the reservoir was dug,
     the pool with a vastness like the sea's.
  ⁴ He took care for his people against brigands
     and strengthened his city against the enemy.
  ⁵ How splendid he was as he looked forth from the Tent,
     as he came from the house of the veil!
  ⁶ Like a star shining among the clouds,
     like the full moon at the holy-day season;
  ⁷ Like the sun shining on the temple of the King,
     like the rainbow appearing in the cloudy sky;
  ⁸ Like the blossoms on the branches in springtime,
     like a lily by running waters;
  Like the verdure of Lebanon in summer,
  ⁹   like the blaze of incense at the sacrifice;
  Like a vessel of beaten gold   G
     studded with an assortment of precious stones;
  ¹⁰ Like a luxuriant olive tree thick with fruit,   B
     a plant whose branches run with oil;
  ¹¹ Wearing his splendid robes,
     and vested in sublime magnificence,
  As he ascended the glorious altar
     and lent majesty to the court of the sanctuary.

12 When he received the sundered victims from his
                                          brother priests
   while he stood before the sacrificial hearth,
His sons ringed him about like a garland,
   like young cedars on Lebanon;
And like poplars by the brook they clustered around
                                                   him,
13   all the sons of Aaron in their dignity,
With the offerings to the LORD in their hands,
   in the presence of the whole assembly of Israel.
14 Once he had completed the service at the altar
   and arranged the sacrificial hearth for the Most
                                                   High,
15 And had stretched forth his hand for the cup,   G
   to offer blood of the grape,
And poured it out at the foot of the altar,
   a sweet-smelling odor to God the Most High,
16 The sons of Aaron would sound a blast,   B
   the priests, on their trumpets of beaten metal;
A blast to resound mightily
   as a reminder before the Most High.
17 Then all the people with one accord
   would quickly fall prostrate to the ground
In adoration before the Most High,
   before the Holy One of Israel.

18 Then hymns would reecho,
   and over the throng sweet strains of praise resound.
19 All the people of the land would shout for joy,
   praying to the Merciful One,
As the high priest completed the service at the altar
   by presenting to God the sacrifice due;
20 Then coming down he would raise his hands
   over all the congregation of Israel;
The blessing of the LORD would be upon his lips,
   the name of the LORD would be his glory.
21 Then again the people would lie prostrate,
   receiving the blessing from the Most High.   G

²² And now, bless the God of all,
    who has done stupendous things on earth;   B
Who makes humans grow from their mother's womb,
    and does with them according to his will!
*²³ May he grant you wisdom of heart,
    and may he abide among you as peace;
*²⁴ May his kindness toward Simeon be lasting;
    may he fulfill for him the covenant with Phinehas
So that it may be not abrogated for him
    or for his descendants, while the heavens last.

---

*²³ May he grant us joy of heart   G
    and may there be peace in our days
    in Israel, as in the days of old.

*²⁴ May his kindness remain constantly with us
    and may he save us in our days.

Notes

50 1a. This colon is correctly placed here by MS B and Syr. G, once more confused when its source presents a character sketch of the hero being praised before it actually names him (see NOTES on 44:23ef; 46:12b–13), transfers the colon to follow 49:15a and makes it refer to Joseph; cf. Gen 49:26b=Deut 33:16b.

1cd. *house of God . . . temple:* compare NOTE on 49:12b above; the *temple* was the building comprising the Holy Place and the Holy of Holies. *renovated*=Heb *nibdaq,* agreeing with G; cf. the same verb in a somewhat different sense in 34:10. MS B has *npqd,* a verb that occurs correctly in 49:15b, but again by error in 49:16a; see NOTE there.

2–3. Following the order of G and Syr. MS B transposes these two verses, which have identical beginnings (with *ʾăšer*); but *bĕdôrô* belongs in v 2 and *bĕyāmāyw* in v 3; compare the order of these terms in 1cd.

2ab. Difficult text. The Gr paraphrase is "And under him [=*in his time*] was constructed [cf. 1 Pet 5:10 for *themelioō*] the elevation for the courtyard, the lofty eminence for the sacred precincts." As given here, "the retaining wall"=*qîr;* "residence"=*māʿôn,* normally used of God's heavenly dwelling, Deut 26:15; Ps 68:6. In a context in which God is repeatedly El Elyôn, *the Most High God* (cf. vv 14–17 below), the temple as the emplacement of his throne represents by its lofty site this heavenly counterpart. *precinct=pinnôt;* i.e., the angles of the elevated enclosure are mentioned to convey its reinforced, its enclosed, and its lofty character. The *temple=hēkāl* has here also the secondary meaning of (God's) "palace," for God is the *King* within it, as in the applied usage of Ps 29:9–11, and cf. v 7 below.

3b. *like the sea's=G=kayyām;* in MS B, this is corrupted into *bām.*

6b. MS B wrongly repeats *mibbēn* (=*among*) from 6a, to overload the colon.

8a. *blossoms:* in G, "roses"; cf. 24:14, in Jericho, and 39:13 where, to judge by Syr, the rose is introduced into the context by G—as also here.

9bc. In all forms of the text, this is the only comparison within vv 6–9 that extends over two cola. The words for *vessel, gold,* and *precious stones* are clear in MS B; for the rest, G has been followed because the Heb in MS B is both damaged and obscure.

10. Segal notes that the imagery drawn from vegetation is otherwise concentrated in v 8, and would accordingly transpose this verse before 9bc. G, Syr, and MS B all agree on the present place, however; and in fact both parts of v 10 in MS B have to do with the olive tree, which is an especially appropriate image for the high priest in the temple, since (1) Jeshua, or Joshua, son of Jozadak, is one of Ben Sira's heroes (49:12a) and (2) Zech 4:1–3, 11–14 provides the same image for that high priest Jeshua. It would seem that MS B and Syr have the correct text for 10b, and that G's "like a cypress standing against the clouds" is borrowed from the imagery for wisdom in 24:13.

11b. MS B repeats *bigdê,* "robes," from 11a; but with G and 45:8, the parallelism calls for *kĕlîl,* "the perfection of," here rendered *sublime.*

15. G and Syr both have this verse; MS B does not. It was lost to the Heb because in it the divine name *ʿelyôn,* which had ended v 14 and would again end v 16, stood once more at the end of the line, making it possible for the two bicola of v 15 to be skipped by homoioteleuton. See COMMENT on 15d.

18b. *sweet strains . . . resound:* with G=*heʿĕrîbû rinnâ* (or, *rannēn,* or as at Qumran, *ronnâ*) in place of MS B's *heʿĕrîkû nērô,* a confused reading. *of praise* is an interpretive expansion.

21b. In MS B, two words of this colon are eaten away; most likely, in the limited space, is Schechter's reconstruction [*hāʿām kullô*] *mippānāyw,* which Strack accepts and Segal mentions after excluding other attempts. For Peters, the Gr *para hypsistou* is a false interpretation of *mippānāyw,* which Peters understands to mean "before Simeon." The only other occurrence of *mippānāyw* in the extant Heb of Sirach is in MS E, in the troubled colon 33:13d, where "God" is the only antecedent possible.

22a. *And now=G=wĕʿattâ* is the standard opening for a conclusion (cf. Prov 8:32); MS B *ʿattâ. the God of all=G=ʾĕlôhê hakkōl,* cf. 36:1a; 45:23c; and the NOTE in the latter place. MS B has "the Lord, the God of Israel," which visibly overloads the line. Syr has *laʾlāhāʾ,* simply.

23a. *wisdom of heart:* G has "joy of heart," cf. 30:22; Cant 3:11—likely a term related to *wisdom* (*sōphrosynēn/phronēsin*) has been altered in G to *euphrosynēn,* "joy," cf. Ziegler.

23b. *and may he abide among you as peace:* this is normally translated "and may peace abide among you." It is here supposed that the preposition in *bĕšālôm* is not an error induced by the following *bĕnêkem* (Smend), that it is meaningful as the so-called *beth essentiae* (GKC §119*i;* Joüon §133*c*), and that the subject of *yĕhî* is still *'ĕlôhê hakkōl* from 22a. G is one source of the usual translation; Syr can be taken either way. Segal, in discussing the name of Solomon in 47:18a, argues from Judg 6:24, *Yhwh-šālôm,* and a passage in Sifrê to Numbers (vi, 24) for *šālôm* as a divine appellation.

23–24. The shorter Gr ending given above as an alternative form was a deliberate adaptation of Ben Sira's text in view of the changed conditions of a later day. V 23c *as in the days of old*=G=*kîmôt 'ôlām;* cf. Deut 32:7; Ps 90:14–15. V 24b *save us:* G *lytrousthai*=Heb *hôšîa'* in 48:20; 49:10; 51:3 (cf. the end of the verse). In 51:2, it serves for *pādîtā/ḥāśaktā/hiṣṣaltā;* see further the NOTE there.

Comment

Almost as a conclusion to his "Praise of the Ancestors of Old," but quite distinct from it, Ben Sira adds the present lengthy panegyric on the High Priest Simeon. The *mot crochet, tip'eret* ("splendor, glory"), in 49:16b and 50:1a, clearly links the two sections together. From the graphic and effusive description of the high priest's liturgical activities and vestments (50:5–21) we can conclude that Ben Sira frequently witnessed Simeon's officiating at the Temple services. Most likely, Ben Sira knew Simeon personally. The person in question is Simeon II, son of Jochanan (Gr Onias; see also Josephus, *Antiquities,* xii, 4, 10); he served as high priest from 219 to 196 B.C. Simeon II was given the title "the Righteous," or "the Just," because he was the last of the priestly house of Zadok to observe the Law faithfully; see INTRODUCTION, Part II. That is why Ben Sira calls him "greatest among his kindred, the glory of his people" (50:1a; cf. NOTE). The phrase "in whose time" (50:1c) indicates that Simeon is no longer living; G, "in whose life," makes the point even clearer. Simeon renovated the Temple and fortified its precincts (50:1cd–4; cf. NOTES); cf. Josephus, *Antiquities,* xii, 3, 3, and INTRODUCTION, Part II. Simeon dug "the reservoir," "the pool with a vastness like the sea's" (50:3; cf. NOTE), in order to provide the city and Temple with water in the event of a siege—the same reason that Hezekiah bored a tunnel from the Spring of Gihon to the Pool of Shiloah (cf. 48:17, with COMMENT). Although Simeon "strengthened his city against the enemy" (50:4b), Jerusalem was later to be assaulted repeatedly (cf., e.g., 1 Macc 1:20–24, 29–32; 6:62).

The next section (50:5–21) describes Ben Sira's emotionally charged reaction to the sight of Simeon ministering as high priest in the Temple. Almost all commentators understand the ceremonies described here as being those of the Day of Atonement, or the Yom Kippur. But F. Ó Fearghail, "Sir 50,5–21:

Yom Kippur or The Daily Whole-Offering?," *Bib* 59 (1978): 301–16, has argued convincingly from a comparison of our passage with the tractate Tamid vi,3–vii,3 that the ceremonies involved correspond more closely to those of the Daily Whole-Offering. I summarize his arguments below. The parallels between the two texts may be seen in this chart:

Tam vi,3–vii,3	*Sir 50:5–21*
a. High priest's incense offering, prostration	(missing)
b. High priest's exit from Holy Place	b'. Simeon's exit from house of the veil (v 5)
c. Priestly blessing	(see below)
d. Burnt offering	d'. Burnt offering (vv 11–14)
e. Drink offering, trumpet blasts	e'. Drink offering (v 15)
f. Singing, trumpets, prostration	f'. Trumpets, prostration, singing (vv 16–19)
	c'. Priestly blessing, prostration (vv 20–21)

There are two discrepancies: (1) Ben Sira makes no mention of the incense offering; (2) he places the priestly blessing at the end. The reason why the incense offering is not spoken of is that v 5 probably refers to Simeon's exit from the Holy Place after the morning incense offering. There are several possible reasons for the blessing at the end: (1) Ben Sira followed the scheme of 45:15, in which the blessing occurs last; (2) since Ben Sira is writing poetry, he feels no need to give the exact sequence of ceremonies; (3) he organized the ceremonies in order to end his praise of Israel's worthies on the impressive note of the priestly blessing. If Ben Sira had in mind the Day of Atonement, he would have chosen at least some elements proper to the ceremonies of that day; but the order of events in vv 5–21 does not correspond to the description of that liturgy in either the Mishnaic tractate Yoma or the somewhat confused account of Leviticus 16.

Simeon looked "splendid" as he "came from the house of the veil," Heb *mibbêt happārōket* (50:5b). Commentators who interpret this section as referring to the Day of Atonement understand "the house of the veil" as the Holy of Holies, for the high priest was allowed to enter there only on that one day in the year. In Exodus and Leviticus, *pārōket,* they argue, is the inner curtain that divided the Holy of Holies from the Holy Place; the outer curtain at the entrance to the Holy Place was called *māsāk* (Exod 36:37). But as Ó Fearghail points out, in Num 18:7 *pārōket* may well refer to the outer curtain; in the Peshitta, *pĕrāsā'* denotes the inner and outer curtains and also those within the Temple court (cf., e.g., Exod 26:7, 14, 33, 36, 37; 27:16, 21; 30:6), and the LXX Pentateuch uses *katapetasma* for both *pārōket* and *māsāk.*

Thus, in 50:5b, *pārōket* (=G *katapetasma*) may refer to the outer curtain. Ó Fearghail then argues that "the house of the veil" is best understood as the Temple building itself, which is designated by one of its principal characteristics, viz., the curtain dividing the Holy of Holies from the Holy Place. This interpretation receives support: (1) from the parallelism in 50:5: "the house of the veil" is a synonym for "the Tent" (v 5a), i.e., the Temple; and (2) from the Syr, which reads: "How glorious he was when he came from the Temple, when he appeared from beneath the veil." When Antiochus IV sacked the Temple in 169 B.C., "the curtain" or "veil" (Gr *katapetasma*) was part of his plunder (1 Macc 1:21–24); cf. Matt 27:51; Mark 15:38; Luke 23:45; Heb 10:20.

Ben Sira now waxes eloquent in describing the splendid sight of Simeon emerging from the Temple, using ten exuberant metaphors (50:6–10). The image of "a star shining" (50:6a) derives from Ps 148:3b. The "full moon at the holy-day season" (50:6b; cf. NOTE) is a reference to the feasts of Passover and Tabernacles, both of which began at the full moon. "The King" in 50:7a is God, for in the OT God often receives that title (cf., e.g., 1 Sam 12:12; Pss 44:4; 74:12; 98:6; 145:1; Isa 6:5; 41:21; 43:15; 44:6; Jer 46:18; 51:57). The wording of 50:7b, "like the rainbow appearing in the cloudy sky" (lit., clouds), is adapted from Ezek 1:28, in which the prophet uses the metaphor to describe the splendor that surrounded the vision of Yahweh. The images of "blossoms on the branches" (50:8a; cf. NOTE), "lily by running waters" (50:8b), and "verdure of Lebanon" (50:8c) were especially meaningful to the agricultural people of Palestine; cf. 24:13–17, 30–31; 39:13–14; Isa 30:25; 44:3–4. The Heb phrase *peraḥ lĕbānôn* ("the verdure of Lebanon") comes from Nah 1:4 and refers to the magnificent sight and fragrance of the lofty cedars that grow there (Isa 10:34; 14:8; Hos 14:6–7; Cant 4:11). "Incense" (50:9a) is a figure also used to describe Josiah (49:1ab); "the sacrifice," Heb *minḥâ*, is the cereal offering on which frankincense and oil were placed; part of this combination was then burned on the altar (Lev 2:1–2; 6:7–8). Simeon is now said to have the splendor of "a vessel of beaten gold studded with . . . precious stones" (50:9bc; cf. NOTE); cf. 45:11. For the background of the metaphor of the "olive tree" (50:10), see the extensive NOTE and cf. Pss 52:10; 128:3; Isa 61:19; Neh 8:15.

The high priestly robes Simeon and his predecessors wore during Temple services were indeed magnificent (50:11ab; cf. NOTE); for a full description, see 45:8–12; Exod 28:2–43 (cf. Exod 29:29–30); and Josephus, *Jewish War,* v, 5, 7, and *Antiquities,* iii, 7, 1–7. "The glorious altar," which Simeon "ascended" (50:11c), is a reference to the bronze altar (cf. Exod 27:1–2) located in the court facing the Temple (2 Chr 4:1; cf. 1 Kgs 8:64; 2 Kgs 16:14); this altar had steps (cf. Ezek 43:13–17). "The court of the sanctuary" (50:11d) is "the great courtyard" mentioned in 2 Chr 4:9. During the Daily Whole-Offering when Simeon officiated, he "received the sundered victims [Heb

něṭāḥîm, lit., pieces of carcass] from his brother priests [lit., brothers]"
(50:12a). The word něṭāḥîm is most often used in reference to the pieces of an
animal offered as a holocaust (cf. Exod 29:17; Lev 1:6, 8, 12; 8:20; 9:13). "The
sacrificial hearth," Heb ma'ărākôt, which occurs in 50:12b, 14b, means, lit.,
"rows" or "layers" (of wood for burning the holocaust); cf. Gen 22:9; Judg
6:26; 1 Kgs 18:23. The Heb phrase kišěṭîlê 'ărāzîm, "like young cedars"
(50:12d), occurs nowhere else in the Heb Bible; the first word, however,
occurs one other time in a similar expression kišěṭîlê zêtîm, "like young olive
trees," in Ps 128:3. "The sons of Aaron" (50:13a), i.e., the priests, "clustered
around" Simeon "like poplars by the brook," Heb 'arbê naḥal (50:12e), a
phrase found also in Lev 23:40; Job 40:22; and Isa 44:4; the poplar tree
appears also in Ps 137:2. The priests carried "the offerings to the LORD," Heb
'iššê yyy, lit., fire offerings of Yahweh (50:13b); cf. Lev 1:9, 13, 17; 2:2, 9; 3:5;
23:18. The wording of 50:13c comes from 1 Kgs 8:22. In 50:14a, 19c, the
expression "the service at the altar," Heb lěšārēt mizbēaḥ (lit., to serve the
altar) is similar to one in Joel 1:13b, měšārětê mizbēaḥ, "ministers of the
altar." See COMMENT on 50:12b regarding "the sacrificial hearth" (50:14b).

According to Num 28:7, a fourth of a hin of wine—a hin=ca. 1.65 gallons
—was poured out in the sanctuary as the drink offering for the lamb immo-
lated during the Daily Whole-Offering. Here (50:15c; cf. NOTE) the drink
offering is poured out "at the foot [lit., foundations] of the altar." Josephus
(Antiquities, iii, 9, 4) agrees with Ben Sira: "they pour the wine as a libation
around the altar," Gr peri ton bōmon. The phrase "blood of the grape"
(50:15b) occurs also in 39:26d; Gen 49:11; Deut 32:14. "A sweet-smelling
odor" (50:15d) is what the drink offering is called in Num 15:7, 10. "God the
Most High" (50:15d)=Heb 'ēl 'elyôn; G has "the Most High, the All-King,"
hypsistǫ pambasilei, a word order that is not likely because the colon needs to
end in 'elyôn (cf. NOTE). Now "the sons of Aaron" (50:16a), i.e., "the priests"
(50:16b), would "sound a blast . . . on their trumpets of beaten metal," i.e.,
silver, as stipulated in Num 10:2. Josephus describes this trumpet: "In length
a little short of a cubit, it is a narrow tube, slightly thicker than a flute, with a
mouthpiece wide enough to admit the breath and a bell-shaped extremity
such as trumpets have" (Antiquities, iii, 12, 6). The trumpet blast serves "as a
reminder before the Most High" (50:16d); in Num 10:10, a similar expression
occurs. Then "all the people," as G correctly renders Heb kol bāśār (lit., all
flesh), "would quickly fall prostrate to the ground" (cf. 2 Chr 29:28) to adore
"the Most High," "the Holy One of Israel" (50:17), a title commonly used in
Isaiah (e.g., Isa 1:4; 5:19, 24; 10:20; 12:6; 17:7; 31:1; 37:23; 41:14, 16, 20;
45:11; 60:9, 14); cf. also 2 Kgs 19:22; Jer 50:29; Pss 71:22; 78:41; 89:19.

While "the throng" lay prostrate, choirs of singers made "sweet strains of
praise resound" (50:18b; cf. NOTE); cf. 47:9c; 2 Chr 29:28. It is interesting
that the phrase "all the people of the land," Heb kol 'am hā'āreṣ (50:19a), is
in synonymous parallelism with "the throng," Heb hāmôn (50:18b), in atten-

dance at the Temple ritual. In the earlier OT literature, ʿam hāʾāreṣ meant citizens who had full legal and political rights; cf. 2 Kgs 21:24; 23:30; Ezek 7:27; 12:19. The congregation prayed to "the Merciful One," Heb rāḥûm (50:19b); God is often spoken of as "merciful" (Deut 4:31; Exod 34:6; 2 Chr 30:9, Neh 9:17, 31; Pss 78:38; 86:15; 103:8; 111:4; 145:8; Joel 2:13; Jonah 4:2). Only once, in Ps 112:4, is "merciful" used to describe a human being. When the high priest presented "to God the sacrifice due," Heb mišpāṭāyw ʾēlāyw, lit., to him that which is due him [God], he "completed the service at the altar" (50:19cd). He would then come down the steps of the altar (cf. 50:11c) and "raise his hands over all the congregation of Israel" in order to bless them (50:20abc). In Lev 9:22, Aaron raises his hands over the people and blesses them *before* descending from the altar; but in Lev 9:23, Aaron blesses the people a second time after coming down from the altar. In that blessing (cf. Num 6:22–27) the high priest would pronounce "the name of Yahweh" (50:20d). This colon provides one of the key arguments (for the other argument, see COMMENT on 50:5b) for those who understand vv 5–21 as describing the Day of Atonement, for it is often assumed that the ineffable name "Yahweh" was to be pronounced by the high priest only during that liturgy and at no other time in the year. But, as Ó Fearghail (*Bib* 59 [1978]: 306–7) points out, the evidence is conflicting as to when "Yahweh" was no longer pronounced in the daily priestly blessing; in Ben Sira's time, however, there is solid evidence that the name was still pronounced daily. The people again "would lie prostrate" (cf. 50:17), this time to receive "the blessing from the Most High" (50:21; cf. NOTE); cf. Num 6:27.

The expression "And now" clearly marks the conclusion of this section (50:22a; cf. NOTE). Ben Sira invites his readers/listeners to "bless the God of all" (50:22a; cf. NOTE). Martin Rinckart composed his hymn "Nun danket alle Gott" ("Now Thank We All Our God") on the basis of this text (so Box-Oesterley, p. 511). Indeed, God "has done stupendous things [cf. Ps 136:4a] on earth" (50:22b), especially in Israel, as Ben Sira takes great pains to demonstrate (44:1–50:21). It is God who controls the destinies of human beings "according to his will" (50:22cd); cf. 36:22b with COMMENT and 48:5. The text of 50:23a (cf. NOTE) is virtually identical with 45:26a. God alone, by abiding "among you," can be "peace" (50:23b; cf. NOTE). Note the differences in the texts of 50:23–24 in MSS B and G (cf. NOTE). In 50:24a, "Simeon" stands for his priestly descendants, for by this time Simeon was already dead (cf. COMMENT on 50:1c). "The covenant with Phinehas" (50:24b) is mentioned also in 45:24–25; see COMMENT there. Ben Sira prayed that this covenant "be not abrogated for [Simeon] or for his descendants, while the heavens last" (50:24cd). As a matter of unfortunate fact, Simeon's priestly line came to end with the assassination of his son Onias III (cf. 2 Macc 4:34), before Ben Sira's grandson made his Greek translation; hence the deliberate differences in the G of 50:24.

For further study of chaps. 44–50 in praise of Israel's ancestors, see T. Maertens, *L'Éloge des Pères (Ecclésiastique XLIV–L (LumVie* 5, 1956); R. T. Siebeneck, "May Their Bones Return to Life!—Sirach's Praise of the Fathers," *CBQ* 21 (1959): 411–28; J. L. Duhaime, "El elogio de los Padres de Ben Sira y el Cántico de Moisés (Sir 44–50 y Dt 32)," *EstBib* 35 (1976): 223–29; T. R. Lee, *Studies in the Form of Sirach 44–50* (SBLDS 75, 1986); B. L. Mack, *Wisdom and the Hebrew Epic: Ben Sira's Hymn in Praise of the Fathers.*

CONCLUSION (50:25–51:30)

60. Judah's Neighbors; Postscript to the Book (50:25–29)

50 25 My whole being loathes two nations, B
    the third is not even a people:
26 Those who live in Seir and Philistia,
    and the foolish folk who dwell in Shechem.

27 Training in wise conduct, and smooth-running
                proverbs,
    have been written in this book G
Of Yeshua ben Eleazar ben Sira, B
    who poured them out from his understanding heart.
28 Happy the one who reflects on these,
    wise will he be who takes them to heart!
29 If he carries them out, he will be equal to any G(B)
                challenge,
    for the fear of the LORD will provide him with
                depth.

Notes

50 25b. MS B has *whšlyšyt* (and *the third*); the *tau* is an error.

27–29. MSS B, G, and Syr are all in need of patching in these verses, and the reconstruction here is a mosaic of what they contain.

27a. *Training in wise conduct*=Prov 1:3a; so MS B. *smooth-running proverbs*= *mišlê 'opnayim*, for MS B's *ûmôšēl 'opnayim* (note that a dual is being supposed; cf. Prov 25:11); i.e., proverbs that run freely as though equipped with (matching) chariot wheels (cf. Duesberg-Fransen, p. 327). The reference would be to the balanced cola, with similar quantity and stresses, before and after the caesura in most of Ben Sira's bicolon lines. For 27a, Syr loosely quotes Prov 1:6b as "all the proverbs of the wise and their riddles."

27b. Present in G and Syr, but not in MS B. In G, Ben Sira (from 27c) is made the subject, and most Gr and Lat MSS make the verb first person, so that Ben Sira speaks for himself.

27c. MS B introduces (from v 24a) "Simeon," as though that, rather than *Yeshua*, were the author's personal name. Syr (compare v 27 above) omits the colon completely; G adds to the name as given "the Jerusalemite."

27d. MS B both doubles and garbles this colon: *'šr nybʿ bptwr lbw / w'šr hbyʿ btbwnwt*. There is no excuse for introducing *nbʾ*, "to prophesy," in this place. Forms related to G's *anōmbrēsen* occur in Sir 18:29; 39:6, but in neither place do we have the Heb. See, however, Prov 18:4b, *naḥal nōbēaʿ mĕqôr ḥokmâ*, where both Theodotion and Quinta employ *anombreō* for *nbʿ*. With this, compare Sir 10:13b, G *exombrēsei=* MS A *yabbîaʿ*, where *mĕqôr(ōh)* is the subject, as in Proverbs. Only the *hiphʿil* is normal; to it the *qal* participle (in Proverbs) attaches itself. The colon reconstructs as *'ăšer hibbîaʿ bitĕbûnôt libbô;* compare Ps 78:72; Prov 11:12; 28:16.

28. All the sources nearly agree, for once. G *anastrephēsetai* is unusual for *yehgeh*, "reflects"; but the latter is supported by Syr *nernē'*. Syr adds at the end "and does them," all it retains of v 29a.

29ab. For this bicolon, MS B has only "For the fear of the LORD is life," beginning the line that also contains 51:1ab. Syr has "The height of the fear of the Lord is exalted above everything; hold on to it, my son, and do not let it go." This is from the Syr of 25:11–12, the whole repeated in 40:26, with the likelihood that the last part derives in some way from the Heb of 6:27b. There remains G. In 11:10, GII has *ean gar* and a finite verb to render a participle (though the *gar* is really for a preceding copula). Here the *ean gar tauta poiēsēs* is probably for *'ōšeh 'ēlleh;* cf. 32:23b,d in MS B. *pros panta=lakkōl.* For *ischysei*, Smend proposes *yigbar*, referring to MS B's margin at 39:24; Segal supplies *yeḥĕzaq; yûkal* is also possible. V 29b has been variously rewritten, but G should be taken absolutely at face value=*kî yirʾat Yhwh ḥeqrô* with the sense given here in translation. *the fear of the* LORD is in all three sources (it is the subject of Syr's substitute lines); and G's *ichnos* is seen to be for *ḥēqer* from 42:19 (both M and MS B), where *ichnē apokryphōn=ḥēqer nistārôt*. See also Job 8:8; 11:7, for *ḥēqer* as the depth of knowledge acquired by probing, penetration. After 29b, GII reproduces 43:33b (see the NOTE there) indicating an alternate place at which to end the book; the same witnesses add a doxology, similar to that in MS B and Syr after 51:30.

Comment

The couplet (50:25–26) on the three peoples that Ben Sira detests is in no way related to the preceding section or to the Postscript (50:27–29). This minipoem opens with a numerical proverb: "two nations" (50:25a), "the third" (50:25b; cf. NOTE); other examples of this type of proverb are found in 23:16–18; 25:7–11; 26:5–6, 28 (cf. INTRODUCTION, Part IV, 1). The language is deliberately intemperate. Jewish hatred for the inhabitants of Seir, i.e., the Edomites or Idumaeans, had a long history. For the Edomites had assisted the Babylonians in devastating the land and conquering the people and had then occupied southern Judah after the destruction of Jerusalem in 586 B.C.; they also became the bitter enemies of the Jews who had returned from Babylon after 537 (cf. Ps 137:7; Ezek 25:12–14; 35:1–15; Obadiah 10–14; Mal 1:2–5; Lam 4:21; Jdt 7:8–18). The Philistines, the proverbial enemies of Israel who were finally subdued by David (2 Sam 5:18–25; 8:1), stand here for those who have accepted paganism and Hellenization (cf. INTRODUCTION, Part II) in Palestine, a word that derives ultimately from Heb *pĕlešet*, "Philistia" (50:26a). Ben Sira expresses his deepest contempt for the Samaritans, "the foolish folk [Heb *gôy nābāl*, an expression taken from Deut 32:21d] who dwell in Shechem" (50:26b), who are "not even a people" (50:25b). The Jews despised the Samaritans because they were heretical descendants of the mixed population in the North: Israelites who had survived the Assyrian destruction of the Northern Kingdom in 722 B.C. and intermarried with the pagan peoples from Mesopotamia who had settled there (cf. 2 Kgs 17:24–41). The Jews, who considered the Samaritans spurious worshippers of Yahweh, detested them even more than pagans. Because the Samaritans were not allowed to help in rebuilding the Temple after Cyrus allowed the return from Babylon, they harassed and intimidated the people of Judah and halted construction for a while (Ezra 4:1–24). Later, during the Maccabean wars, the Samaritans allied themselves with the Seleucids (1 Macc 3:10; Josephus, *Antiquities*, xii, 5, 5). Cf. J. D. Purvis, "Ben Sira and the Foolish People of Shechem," *JNES* 24 (1965): 88–94.

In the Postscript, or Subscription (50:27–29), our author gives us his full name and a minihomily on carrying out the advice contained in the book. "Training in wise conduct," Heb *mûsar śēkel* (lit., training of prudence), and "smooth-running proverbs" (50:27a; cf. NOTE) are what "have been written in this book" (50:27b; cf. NOTE) "of Yeshua ben Eleazar ben Sira" (50:27c; cf.

NOTE), "who poured them out from his understanding heart" (50:27d; cf. NOTE). If, as seems to be the case, Ben Sira added these words himself, he was following the model of Prov 1:1–3 and Qoh 1:1, 12; 12:9–10; accordingly, he cannot be faulted for immodesty. "Happy the one [Heb *'ašrê 'îš*, which derives from Ps 1:1a] who reflects [or meditates] on these [proverbs and training in wise conduct; cf. 50:27a]" (50:28a; cf. NOTE). He will be wise "who takes them to heart," Heb *nôtēn 'al libbô*, an expression found also in Qoh 7:2; 9:1. But it is not enough only to meditate on Ben Sira's wise sayings; one must also "[carry] them out," Gr *poiēsē̦*, lit., do them. By so doing, "he will be equal to any challenge," Gr *pros panta ischysei*, lit., he will be strong for all things (50:29a; cf. NOTE). That is to say, he will have the strength and courage to overcome the blandishments and pervasive temptations of Hellenization and so remain faithful to the religion and values of Israel; cf. INTRODUCTION, Part II. The reason is that "the fear of the LORD will provide him with depth" of knowledge (50:29b; cf. NOTE); cf. Matt 7:24–25; Luke 6:47–48. Thus at the end of his book Ben Sira emphasizes once again the importance of "the fear of the Lord," which is "the beginning of wisdom" (1:14a). The one who possesses such wisdom not only fears the Lord but also keeps the Law of Moses; cf. 1:11–30; 6:32–37; 15:1; 19:20; 21:6; 23:27; 24:23–29.

61. Ben Sira's Prayer
(51:1–12)

I

51 1 I give you thanks, LORD and King;   G
        I praise you, my savior God!
        I proclaim your name, my life's refuge,   B
     2 because you have redeemed me from death,
        Held back my body from the pit
            and freed my foot from the clutches of the
                                                    netherworld.

II

You have delivered me from the slanderous tongue,
    and from the lips of lying miscreants:
You have been with me in the face of my attackers,
 3 have helped me in your abundant mercy
Out of the snare of those looking for my downfall,
    the clutches of those seeking my life.

III

From multiple dangers you have saved me:
 4 from flames that beset me on every side,
From the midst of the fire, without a whiff of it
                                        remaining;
 5 from the depths of the belly of the netherworld—   G
From malicious lips, slimy deceivers,   B
 6 arrows sped by treacherous tongues.

IV

Close as I was to death—
    my life, to the depths of the netherworld—
7 Wherever I turned, there was no one to help me;
    though I looked for support, there was none.
8 Then I remembered the LORD's mercies,
    his solicitude from times long past;
How he delivers those who take refuge in him
    and defends them against evil of every kind.

V

9 I raised my voice from the dust,
    my plea from the gates of the netherworld;
10 I extolled the LORD, "You are my Father!
    my mighty savior, only you!
Do not leave me in this time of crisis,
    on a day of ruin and desolation!
11 I will praise your name constantly,
    singing to you with my prayer!"

VI

Then the LORD heard my voice;
    he listened to my plea!
12 He redeemed me from evil of every kind
    and kept me safe in time of crisis;
For this I give thanks and offer praise,
    and I bless the name of the LORD!

Notes

51   1ab. G and Syr agree on the first colon; G's second colon is MS B's first. The second colon in MS B reads: "I give you thanks, God of my father [or: my God, my Father—cf. Exod 15:2, but also v 10a]"; in Syr, it is "and I praise your name each day" (influenced by 11a?). For the order of G and Syr, compare v 12cd.

1c–2a. G here has been influenced by Exod 15:2 LXX, as Peters saw. Its *exomologoumai* for MS B's *'ăsappĕrâ* (=Syr) is drawn from v 1a; the *mā'ôz* of 2a suggested *boēthos*, cf. Ps 52:9, *mā'uzzô*, LXX *ton boēthon autou*, and this in turn suggested Exodus (*boēthos kai skepastēs egeneto moi eis sōtērian*='*ozzî wĕzimrāt Yāh wayĕhî lî lîšû'â*). Nothing might have happened if the Gr translator had read *ḥayyay* after *mā'ôz*, but he apparently read *ḥyy* with *hē;* and Exodus' *eis sōtērian* must have recalled the *'elōhê yiš'î,* which had just led to *(theon) ton sōtēra mou* in 1b above. Needing help, he looked forward to the end of v 2 and the beginning of v 3 to find *hāyîtā lî* and *'zrtny.* *'zr* equates with *boēthos* in LXX more easily than *'wz/m'wz,* and so the *'zrtny* became *boēthos,* the *hāyîtā* became *egenou,* and the combination (with *moi* for *lî* added out of Exodus and the end of v 2) traveled to the beginning of v 2 with *hoti skepastēs kai* from Exodus as extra baggage. (Note that the use of *exomologoumai tǭ onomati sou* instead of, e.g., *diēgēsomai to onoma sou,* Ps 21[22]:23 in 1c, as mentioned above, would seem to have been to prepare for the *hoti* clause; cf. Pss LXX 53:8; 117:21, 28cd; 137:2.)

2b–3a. G of these cola further exemplifies the technique just described. V 2 of Heb calls for four verbs of deliverance: *pādîtā, ḥāśaktā, hiṣṣaltā, pĕṣîtanî.* G's *elytrōsō* matches none of these: it has been borrowed from v 3. In v 3 the equation *'zrtny*= *boēthos* has been noted above. The verb thus eliminated is followed in the Heb by a string of three *min*-phrases; to govern them, the *hôša'tanî* from the end of the verse was seized upon and given (see the NOTES at 49:10; 50:23–24) its normal equivalent from this translator, *elytrōsō,* which then traveled also to v 2, as said. At the end of v 3, the *ṣārōt*=*thlipseōn* lacks a dependent pronoun, and with the following verb transferred elsewhere, the Gr translator had a lame colon, which he eked out with *hōn eschon.* Small wonder that in v 2a *mimmāwet napšî,* plus all of 2c, have vanished along with the assortment of governing verbs. In 2b, *body* is the Gr (and modern) equivalent for the Heb *bāśār* "(living) flesh."

2de. MS B contains doublets and G has (in its 2cd) one expansion. Since *dibbat 'ām* is a biblical phrase (Ezek 36:3) and is not reflected in the Gr of Sirach, *(mid)dibbat lāšôn* is guaranteed primitive by G's *diaboles glōssēs.* The *(ek) pagidos* is an expansion in G to fill out the colon from which the verb *(pĕṣîtanî)* has been suppressed. The *šôṭ* is a doublet of *śāṭê,* so that the full primitive line in Heb=*pĕṣîtanî middibbat lāšôn ûmiśśĕpat śāṭê kāzāb.*

3a. G *kai onomatos (sou)* after *mercy* is an inappropriate expansion in the context, an ancient error of some kind.

3b. Peters, followed by Smend and Ziegler, is the source of *brochōn=snare*(s); the reading in the codices is *brygmōn*=Lat *rugientibus*. Peters saw *brōma* as=*belaᶜ* for *selaᶜ* of the Heb; perhaps the assonance with *brochōn* induced its use without that much textual support.

4b. *From the midst*=G=*mittôk* for MS B's garbled *mkbwt. without a whiff of it remaining*=*lĕʾên pōḥāh,* "till there was not a whiff of it [the fire]." The vocalization of *pôḥ (*pwḥ*) is doubtful, but the expression (paraphrased by G as "by which I was not consumed") includes a term for "scent, odor" with the Syr and Ar cognates *pawḥāʾ* and *fawḥ*. The reference is to escape from the flames without even the smell of smoke from it, as in Dan 3:27(94). The term *lĕʾên* need not, though it usually does, introduce a phrase that describes loss and foreboding: cf. 1 Chr 22:4; 2 Chr 20:25. Vv 4b–6a are simply lacking in Syr.

5a. Following G completely (*ek bathous koilias hạdou*); MS B has *mrḥm [. . .] wm lʾm[. . .],* but *reḥem* is not *koilia* and *tĕhôm* is not Hades, nothing corresponds to *bathous,* and the broken-off *lʾm-* is an unsolved puzzle. G may have been borrowing from 6c to deal with whatever it saw here, but (cf. 2ab; 6bc) another reference to Sheol would certainly have been in place.

5b. *slimy deceivers:* Heb, *ṭôpĕlê šeqer,* "daubers of something worthless, deceptive" —but the verb implies that what they daub is slimy, and that they also are.

10b. G, not using direct discourse, omits this title; cf. v 1b.

11b. *singing to you*=G=*ʾzmrk* for MS B's *ʾzkrk,* "I will mention your name."

11c. G, employing direct discourse for vv 11–12, omits this colon.

Comment

The material in chap. 51 comprises two appendices to the book; cf. post-script in 50:27–29. Curiously, the Gr MSS and most of the Lat MSS give this chapter the title "Prayer of Jesus, Son of Sirach." Actually, however, only vv 1–12, the first appendix, contain Ben Sira's prayer or psalm; vv 13–30, the second appendix, contain his autobiographical poem on wisdom. Between vv 12 and 13, MS B presents a litany of praise, sixteen bicola in length, of doubtful authenticity since it is not contained in G or Syr or any of their daughter translations (cf. COMMENT on 51:12 i–xvi). The authenticity of the prayer and of the autobiographical poem has also been questioned by some scholars because of the postscript in 50:27–29, which seems to exclude any further material from the book. But this reason is hardly convincing. I agree with Smend (p. 495) that the language, form, and contents bear witness to their authenticity. Moreover, the two compositions are found not only in MS B but also in G, Lat, and Syr, and, as already noted, have in the Gr and Lat MSS a title that implicitly attributes the pieces to Ben Sira.

The prayer or psalm in vv 1–12 may be divided into six stanzas, arranged in two groups, each of three stanzas; (a) 3+3+3 bicola; and (b) 4+4+3 bicola. The prayer may be classified as a declarative psalm of praise by an individual who has survived a major peril. The psalm does not indicate which specific slanders or dangers Ben Sira experienced and survived, thanks to God's deliverance. As a result, an individual praying this psalm could readily see in it his own experiences that call for praise after the Lord has heard his lament/petition. Smend (p. 495) considers the psalm "rather colorless in content and form." I disagree, for the psalm displays an artistically balanced form and structure that corresponds to its content. In the following diagram of the psalm, "1st pers.," "2d pers.," or "3d pers." refers to the verb and/or pronoun (or noun) object of the verb; the only two clearly identifiable persons are the poet (1st pers.) and Yahweh (2d and 3d pers.). Note how the content of the first three stanzas (I–III) corresponds to the content of the second three stanzas (IV–VI), but in reverse order:

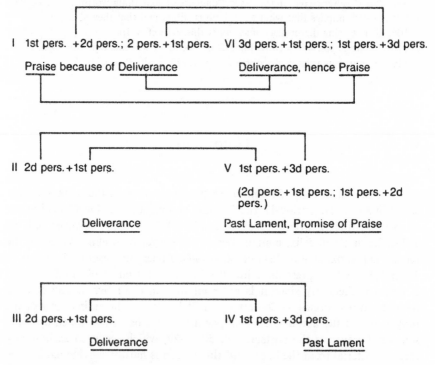

I 1st pers. +2d pers.; 2 pers.+1st pers.   VI 3d pers.+1st pers.; 1st pers.+3d pers.

Praise because of Deliverance   Deliverance, hence Praise

II 2d pers.+1st pers.   V 1st pers.+3d pers.

(2d pers.+1st pers.; 1st pers.+2d pers.)

Deliverance   Past Lament, Promise of Praise

III 2d pers.+1st pers.   IV 1st pers.+3d pers.

Deliverance   Past Lament

Observe the following: (1) The first three stanzas have 1st pers. and 2d pers., and the second three have 1st pers. and 3d pers. (with stanza V having a quotation in the 2d pers. + 1st pers. and 1st pers. + 2d pers.). (2) There is an *a:b::b:a* chiastic *inclusio* in the key ideas and phrases of stanzas I and VI:

praise (Heb *ʾ ôdĕkā, ʾăhallelkā,* v 1ab; cf. NOTE):*deliverance (pādîtā napšî,* v 2a)::*deliverance (wayyipdēnî,* v 12a):*praise (hôdêtî wā'ăhalĕlâ,* v 12c). (3) The name "Yahweh" occurs in the first (v 1a; cf. NOTE) and last cola (v 12d), thus forming a second *inclusio,* which marks out the limits of the psalm. (4) The first three stanzas are essentially a song of praise (v 1) for the deliverance Yahweh has granted in the past (vv 2a–6a); the second three record: a past lament over former adversities (vv 6b–7b), which includes Ben Sira's remembrance of Yahweh's past mercies (v 8); his plea for help (vv 9–10); his promise of future praise (v 11ab); and his description of Yahweh's deliverance (vv 11cd–12ab); and a couplet of praise (v 12cd).

The first stanza has splendid balance, rhythm, and structure among the elements comprising the declarative psalm of praise by the individual: (a) declaration of Ben Sira's intention to extol God; (b) his reasons for praising God, viz., God has come to the rescue. Cf. Ps 138:1–2, where this typical pattern is also found. In 51:1–2c, the three bicola, or poetic lines, contain three verbs extolling God (*I give you thanks,* v 1a; *I praise you,* v 1b; *I proclaim your name,* v 1c); three titles of God (LORD *and King,* lit., *O Yahweh, King,* v 1a; *my savior God,* v 1b; *my life's refuge,* v 1c); three saving activities, the reasons for praising God (*you have redeemed me,* v 2a; *[you have] held back my body,* v 2b; *[you have] freed my foot,* v 2c); three objects from which God saved the poet (*from death,* v 2a; *from the pit,* v 2b; *from the clutches of the netherworld,* v 2c). Moreover, each bicolon ends in *-î:* Heb *yiš'î, napšî, raglî,* which create a pleasing rhyme. The three verbs, *I give thanks, I praise,* and *I proclaim,* and the three nouns, *death, pit,* and *netherworld,* are often found in synonymous parallelism in the OT, esp. in the Psalms: e.g., Pss 6:6; 22:23; 49:15; Isa 28:15, 18; Hos 13:14. The title "Yahweh, King" (51:1a) is analogous to "God, King" in Ps 145:1; cf. 2 Macc 1:24. The title "my savior God" (51:1b, lit., the God of my salvation) occurs also in Pss 18:47; 25:5; 27:9; Mic 7:7; Hab 3:18. The title "my life's refuge" (51:1c) comes from Ps 27:1c. God is often said to "redeem [one] (from death)" (51:2a); cf., e.g., Pss 26:11; 49:16; 55:19; 69:19; 71:23; 116:8; 1QH 3:19. As regards 51:2b, cf. Job 33:18 and Isa 38:17. The expression "freed my foot" (51:2c) derives from Pss 25:15; 116:8.

In the second stanza (51:2d–3c), Ben Sira continues the theme of divine deliverance, the reason for his praise (51:1). In 51:2de (cf. NOTE), "the slanderous tongue" and "the lips of lying miscreants" are in synonymous parallelism; cf. Ps 40:5. Good Israelite that he was, Ben Sira firmly believed that Yahweh was with him in the face of attackers (51:2f); cf. Pss 3:2; 56:10; 124:2; Deut 32:10. He received help because of God's "abundant mercy" (51:3a; cf. NOTE), a phrase that occurs also in Pss 5:8; 69:14; 106:7, 45. Praying for deliverance "out of the snare" (51:3b; cf. NOTE) derives from Ps 141:9; cf. Ps 140:6; Prov 18:7; 22:25. For the expressions "those looking for my downfall"

(51:3b), cf. Jer 20:10; "those seeking my life" (51:3c), cf. Pss 35:4; 40:15; 63:10; 70:3.

The third stanza is more of the same. Like the Psalmist, Ben Sira acknowledges that God has saved him "from multiple dangers," Heb *ṣārôt* (51:3d); cf. Pss 31:8; 71:20; and 120:1. The *ṣārôt* are then spelled out in detail: "flames" (51:4a), cf. Isa 43:2; 47:14; "fire, without a whiff of it remaining" (51:4b; cf. NOTE), cf. Ps 66:12 and Dan 3:23–27(94); "depths of the belly of the netherworld" (51:5a; cf. NOTE), cf. Jonah 2:3 and Pss 71:20; 86:13; "malicious lips, slimy deceivers" (51:5b; cf. NOTE), cf. Job 13:4, 7; Ps 119:69; "arrows sped by treacherous tongues" (51:6a), cf. 28:13–15, 17–22; Pss 52:3–6; 64:4; Jer 9:2, 7.

A striking *a:b::b':a'* chiastic pattern opens the fourth stanza: *lammāwet:napšî::ḥayyātî:lišĕʾôl,* "(Close) *to death:*(was) *my soul::my life:to the netherworld* (the lowest parts)" (the literal translation of 51:6bc). The use of Heb *taḥtîyôt,* a f. pl. adjective used as a noun, "the lowest parts," after the noun *šĕʾôl* is not unique; in Ps 88:7 and Lam 3:55, *taḥtîyôt* is used after *bôr,* "pit," and in Ezek 26:20 and 32:18, 24, after *ʾereṣ,* "earth." For the thought of 51:6bc, cf. Pss 86:13; 88:4, 7. Heb *māwet,* "death," and *šĕʾôl,* "netherworld," are in synonymous parallelism, as often in the OT (e.g., 2 Sam 22:6 [=Ps 18:6]; Isa 28:15, 18; 38:18; Hos 13:14; Pss 6:6; 49:15; 89:49; Prov 5:5; 7:27). Ben Sira does not specify in which way he was "close . . . to death, . . . to the netherworld"; this expression could be used to describe either a serious illness or a mortal danger from outside. For the clauses "there was no one to help me" and "though I looked for support, there was none" (51:7ab), cf. Ps 107:12; Isa 59:16; 63:5. The vocabulary of remembering "the LORD's mercies [Heb *raḥămê yyy*], his solicitude [Heb *ḥăsādāyw,* lit., his kindnesses] from times long past" (51:8ab) comes from Ps 25:6. For the clause "who take refuge in him" (51:8c), cf. Ps 16:1. God "defends [his faithful] against evil of every kind" (51:8cd)—words taken from Gen 48:16a; cf. also v 12 and Ps 121:7.

The fifth stanza records Ben Sira's poignant and urgent plea to Yahweh for help. The phrases "from the dust" (Heb *ʾereṣ,* lit., earth, 51:9a) and "from the gates of the netherworld" (*šĕʾôl,* 51:9b, cf. Isa 38:10; Matt 16:18) are in synonymous parallelism; elsewhere in the OT, *ʾereṣ* can mean "netherworld" (e.g., Pss 147:6 and 148:7 [cf. F. M. Cross, Jr., and D. N. Freedman, *JNES* 14 (1955): 247–48]). Both phrases are poetic images to suggest that the poet is at the point of death (cf. 51:6bc, with COMMENT); cf. Pss 18:5–7; 120:1. As introduction to his petition, Ben Sira "extolled the LORD [Heb *wāʾărômēm yyy*], 'You are my Father!' " (51:10a); the vocabulary of this colon comes from Exod 15:2. Accordingly, *contra* Smend (p. 500) and Box-Oesterley (p. 513), *wāʾărômēm* need not be emended to *wāʾeqrāʾ,* "and I cried: ('O LORD, you are my Father')." There is an *a:b::b:a'* chiastic pattern in the rest of the bicolon: lit., *"My Father* (are):*you::*(indeed) *you:*(are) *the hero of my salvation"* (51:10ab; cf. NOTE). In the OT, Yahweh is often called "Father" (cf., e.g.,

23:1a, 4a; Deut 32:6; Isa 63:16; 64:7; Jer 31:9; Mal 1:6; Ps 68:6). The expression "my mighty savior," lit., the hero of my salvation, is modeled on such phrases as "the rock of my salvation" (Ps 89:27; cf. Ps 95:1) and "the strength of my salvation" (Ps 140:8). The words "this time of crisis" (lit., the day of danger, cf. 51:3d) and "a day of ruin and desolation" (51:10cd) are quoted from Zeph 1:15; cf. also Job 30:3; 38:27; 1QH 5:30; 9:6. After his fervent appeal for help, Ben Sira promises God constant praise and prayerful song (51:11ab; cf. NOTE); cf. Ps 145:1–2. The verbs "to praise" and "to sing" used here are found together also in Ps 135:3.

The sixth and final stanza has the word "the LORD," i.e., Yahweh, Heb *yyy* (as always in MS B) in its opening colon (51:11c; cf. NOTE) and closing colon (51:12d), forming an *inclusio,* which marks off its limits. The verbs "heard" (Heb *šāmaʿ*) and "listened" (*wayyaʾăzîn*) in 51:11cd are found in parallel also in 4:15 and 33:19 and often elsewhere, e.g., Gen 4:23; Num 23:18; Judg 5:3; Isa 1:2, 10; Pss 17:1; 84:9; 143:1. The words "my voice" (Heb *qôlî*) and "my plea" (*taḥănûnay*) are likewise in parallel; in Pss 28:2, 6; 31:23; 116:1; 130:2; 140:7, the noun *qôl,* which in these cases means "sound," is used in conjunction with *taḥănûnay:* "the sound of my plea." By using *qôlî* in 51:11c and *taḥănûnay* in 51:11d as objects of the verbs "hear" and "listen," respectively, Ben Sira employs the literary device known as "breakup of a stereotyped phrase;" i.e., the words *qôl taḥănûnay,* instead of being used in a single phrase (as in the psalms cited above), are each used separately but in parallel (as here). For examples from the Psalter of the breakup of stereotyped phrases, cf. M. Dahood, *Psalms III,* AB 17A, pp. 413–14. The next bicolon (51:12ab) also has double parallelism: "[Yahweh] redeemed me [Heb *wayyipdēnî*] from evil of every kind [*mikkol raʿ,* the same phrase as in v 8d] and kept me safe [or, delivered me, *wayĕmallĕṭēnî*] in time of crisis [*bĕyôm ṣārâ,* lit., in the day of danger, as in v 10c]"; the second colon is modeled after Ps 41:2: "In the day of evil Yahweh will deliver him." Ben Sira concludes his hymn by using the verbs of the opening bicolon (51:1ab), "I give thanks" and "I praise," together in 51:12c, thus forming an *inclusio* (see COMMENT above); to these he adds (51:12d) the verb "I bless" (Heb *wāʾăbārĕkâ*), which, as elsewhere in the OT, is also parallel to the verbs "to give thanks" and "to praise" (cf., e.g., Ps 145:2). The idea of blessing the name of Yahweh (51:12d) occurs frequently in the OT; cf., e.g., Pss 96:2; 100:4; 145:2.

For a fuller study of the text and poetic features of this prayer, see A. A. Di Lella, "Sirach 51:1–12: Poetic Structure and Analysis of Ben Sira's Psalm," *CBQ* 48 (1986): 395–407.

62. Hymn of Praise from the Time of Ben Sira
(51:12 i–xvi)

51 12 i Give thanks to the LORD, for he is good,   B
   for his mercy endures forever;
   Give thanks to the God of [our] praises,
   for his mercy endures forever;
   Give thanks to the Guardian of Israel,
   for his mercy endures forever;
   Give thanks to him who formed all things,
   for his mercy endures forever;
v Give thanks to the Redeemer of Israel,
   for his mercy endures forever;
   Give thanks to him who has gathered Israel's
                              dispersed,
   for his mercy endures forever;
   Give thanks to him who rebuilt his city and his
                              sanctuary,
   for his mercy endures forever;
   Give thanks to him who makes a horn to sprout
   for the house of David, for his mercy endures
                              forever;
   Give thanks to him who has chosen the sons of Zadok
                              as his priests,
   for his mercy endures forever;
x Give thanks to the Shield of Abraham,
   for his mercy endures forever;
   Give thanks to the Rock of Isaac,
   for his mercy endures forever;
   Give thanks to the Mighty One of Jacob,
   for his mercy endures forever;
   Give thanks to him who has chosen Zion,
   for his mercy endures forever;

Give thanks to the King of the kings of kings,
   for his mercy endures forever;
xv He has raised up a horn for his people,
   be this his praise from all his dutiful ones,
For the children of Israel, the people close to him.
   Praise the Lord!

Comment

This litany or hymn of praise, located between 51:12 and 13, is found in
MS B but in none of the ancient versions (G, Syr, and their daughter translations). Its authenticity, therefore, is open to serious question; cf. A. A. Di
Lella, *The Hebrew Text of Sirach*, pp. 101–5, for a survey of scholarly opinions and bibliography. Arguments for or against authenticity are not conclu-
sive. But since the psalm is contained only in MS B and in its present location
does not seem to suit the context, I favor the view that it was not composed
by Ben Sira. Apparently, however, the psalm dates at least from the time
when the Zadokites were still high priests (as is clear from 51:12 ix), i.e.,
before 152 B.C., when the Hasmonean Jonathan, brother of Judas Maccabeus,
was awarded the high priesthood for his support of Alexander Balas, the
Syrian king (1 Macc 10:15–21), thus bringing the Zadokite high priestly line
to an end. If the psalm is genuine Ben Sira material, the grandson may have
omitted it from his translation in order to avoid embarrassing the reigning
Hasmonean high priestly line; Syr probably followed G in omitting the psalm.
It is possible that a member of the Essene Community at Qumran composed
the psalm and inserted it into the copy of The Wisdom of Ben Sira that
eventually found its way into the cave near Jericho, which in about A.D. 800
was found to contain ancient MSS, including copies of our book. The
Qaraites who recovered the MS(S) of Sirach from this cave made the copies
that were eventually discovered in the Cairo Geniza between 1896 and 1900.
Cf. INTRODUCTION, Part VIII, 4, and A. A. Di Lella, *The Hebrew Text of
Sirach*, pp. 78–105, 150–51. Evidence for a Qumran origin of the psalm can
be seen in the use of the phrase *lĕ'ēl hattešbŏḥôt*, "to the God of [our] praises"
(51:12 ii); the reverse of that expression, *tešbŏḥôt 'ēl*, "the praises of God," is
found on one of the standards in the War Scroll (1QM iv 8). Ben Sira never
uses the word *tešbŏḥôt* himself, nor even its root. Moreover, the Essenes of
Qumran, who hated the Hasmonean high priests, considered the Zadokite

priests as the only ones that still kept the Covenant; cf. Di Lella, *The Hebrew Text of Sirach,* pp. 104–5.

The psalm is patterned after Psalm 136 insofar as the refrain, "for his mercy endures forever," occurs in fourteen of the sixteen verses. Its opening verse reproduces Ps 136:1 verbatim; the same words, however, occur also in Pss 106:1; 107:1; and 118:1, 29; cf. Jer 33:11. The expression "the God of [our] praises" (51:12 ii) does not occur elsewhere in our book, as noted above, nor in the rest of the Heb OT. The meaning is clear, however: "the God who is the recipient of our praises" (cf., e.g., 51:1b, 12c, 17b, 29b; Pss 48:1; 66:2; 69:31, 35; 74:21; 104:33, 35). The phrase "the Guardian of Israel," Heb *šômēr yiśrā'ēl* (51:12 iii), comes from Ps 121:4; cf. Ps 121:5–8 for the implications of the text. God is the one "who formed all things," Heb *yôṣēr hakkōl* (51:12 iv), an expression borrowed from Jer 10:16b and 51:19b (cf. Sir 24:8a). "The Redeemer [Heb *gō'ēl*] of Israel" (51:12 v) derives from Isa 49:7b (cf. also Isa 44:6ab). The wording "who has gathered Israel's dispersed," Heb *mĕqabbēš nidḥê yiśrā'ēl* (51:12 vi), is right out of Isa 56:8b (cf. also Isa 11:12b; 27:13; Ps 147:2b). For the sentiment that God "rebuilt his city [i.e., Jerusalem] and his sanctuary [Heb *miqdāš,* i.e., the temple, cf. Isa 60:13c]" (51:12 vii), cf. Ps 147:2a; Isa 44:28; Dan 9:26; Tob 13:10, 12, 16–18. The vocabulary of "who makes a horn to sprout for the house of David" (51:12 viii) comes from Ps 132:17a, which, however, omits the expression "the house of," but cf. Ezek 29:21: "I will make a horn sprout for the house of Israel." The text is messianic, promising that an offspring of David will rule the people (cf. Jer 23:5; 33:15–17; Isa 11:1–5); see J. L. McKenzie, "Royal Messianism," *CBQ* 19 (1957): 25–52. This verse deals with the political authority of the nation. God himself is the one "who has chosen [Heb *bôḥēr*] the sons of Zadok as his priests" (51:12 ix), a conviction Ben Sira certainly would have shared, though he probably did not write the psalm, as pointed out above; cf. 45:23–25 and 50:24, with COMMENT. This verse deals with the religious authority of the priests. In the restored Temple that Ezekiel describes in chaps. 40–48, only "the sons of Zadok" are allowed to serve as priests, for they alone remained faithful while the Levites and the other Israelites strayed from Yahweh (Ezek 40:46; 43:19; 44:15–16; 48:11–12).

For the divine titles "the Shield of Abraham" (51:12 x), cf. Gen 15:1 and Pss 18:3; 115:9–11; "the Rock of Isaac" (51:12 xi), cf. Gen 49:24d; Deut 32:4, 15, 18, 30, 31; 2 Sam 23:3; Pss 18:3; 43:10; 71:3; Isa 30:29; and "the Mighty One of Jacob" (51:12 xii), cf. Gen 49:24c; Ps 132:2b, 5b; Isa 1:24; 49:26; 60:16. The names Abraham, Isaac, and Jacob often appear together in the Bible; cf., e.g., Exod 2:24; 3:6, 15–16; 4:5; 6:3, 8; Num 32:11; Deut 1:8; Jer 33:26; Tob 4:12; Matt 8:11; Luke 13:28; Acts 3:13. Curiously, in Lev 26:42 the names occur in reverse order. The belief that it is God "who has chosen [Heb *bôḥēr*] Zion [i.e., Jerusalem]" (51:12 xiii) is a given of OT theology; cf., e.g., 1 Kgs 8:44, 48; 11:13, 32; 14:21; 2 Kgs 21:7; 23:27; 2 Chr 6:6; Ps 132:13a;

Zech 1:17; 2:16; 3:2. The participle *bôḥēr* occurs here and in 51:12 ix. The two passages are clearly related, for just as "the sons of Zadok" alone are the legitimate priests, so also Jerusalem is the only city where the full Temple ritual may take place (cf. 51:12 vii). The centralization of cult in Jerusalem was a fundamental doctrine of Deuteronomic theology (Deut 12:1–14; 16:6; cf. also Tob 1:4; 14:5, 7); cf. G. von Rad, *Old Testament Theology*, vol. 1, pp. 226–31; and A. A. Di Lella, "The Deuteronomic Background of the Farewell Discourse in Tob 14:3–11," *CBQ* 41 (1979): 385. Thus the rival temple, which the Samaritans had constructed on Mount Gerizim near Shechem and which was still standing in Ben Sira's day (50:26b records his caustic remark about Samaritans: "the foolish folk who dwell in Shechem"), was considered by Jews to be an utter abomination; the Jews destroyed this temple in 128 B.C. In the OT, Yahweh is often called "King" (e.g., Sir 50:7a; Isa 6:5; Jer 46:18; 48:15; 51:57; Pss 98:6; 145:1) or "King of glory" (Ps 24:7–10) or "great King" (Mal 1:14; Pss 47:3; 95:3), but never "the King of the kings of kings" (51:12 xiv), a title analogous to "God of gods, and Lord of lords" in Deut 10:17. *Pirqe Aboth*, iv 32, has, however, the expression: "The King of the kings of kings, the Holy One, blessed be He" (cited by Box-Oesterley, p. 515). The last two verses of the psalm (51:12 xv–xvi) are an exact quotation from Ps 148:14. The word "horn" in 51:12 xv means power, as in 47:5d, 11b, on which cola see NOTES and COMMENT.

As should be clear from the above analysis, the psalm is completely biblical in its phrasing, orientation, and theology; for similar prayers, cf. Dan 3:(52)–(90); Tob 3:2–6; 13:1–18; 2 Macc 1:24–28; 3 Macc 2:2–20; 6:2–15. The psalm also has some similarities with the Jewish work called "The Eighteen Benedictions," or the *Shemoneh 'Esreh;* but the precise relationship of these two pieces is uncertain. For a translation of the texts of the *Shemoneh 'Esreh* that correspond to verses of our psalm, cf. Box-Oesterley, pp. 514–15. See also A. Marmorstein, "Jesus Sirach 51,12ff.," *ZAW* 29 (1909): 287–93; and T. Vargha, "De Psalmo hebraico Ecclesiastici c. 51," *Anton* 10 (1935): 3–10.

63. Autobiographical Poem on Wisdom
(51:13–30)

51   13 *aleph*   When I was young and innocent,   11QPs^a
                      I kept seeking wisdom.

14 *beth*   She came to me in her beauty,
                  and until the end I will cultivate her.

15 *gimel*   As the blossoms yielded to ripening
                            grapes,
                  the heart's joy,

daleth   So my feet kept to the level path,
                  for from earliest youth I was familiar
                            with her.

16 *hē*   In the short time I paid heed
                  I met with great instruction.

17 *waw*   Since in this way I have profited,
                  to my Teacher I will give grateful
                            praise.

18 *zayin*   I resolved to tread her paths;
                  I have been jealous for the good and
                            will not turn back.

19 *ḥeth*   I burned with desire for her,
                  never relenting.

ṭeth   I became preoccupied with her,
                  never weary of extolling her.

yod   I spread out my hands on high,
                  and I came to know her secrets.

20 *kaph*   For her I purified my hands;
                  in cleanliness I attained to her.   G (B)

lamed	At first acquaintance with her, I gained understanding such that I will never forsake her.	
21 *mēm*	My whole being was stirred to seek her; therefore I have made her my prize possession.	B
22 *nūn*	The Lord has granted me my tongue as a reward, and with my lips I will praise him.	G (Syr)
23 *samekh*	Come aside with me, you untutored, and take up lodging in the house of instruction;	
24 *ʿayin*	How long will you be deprived of wisdom's food, how long will you endure such bitter thirst?	Syr (B) B (Syr)
25 *pē*	I open my mouth and speak of her: gain wisdom for yourselves, without money.	
26 *ṣadhe*	Submit your neck to her yoke, and let your mind weigh her message.	
qoph	She is close to those who seek her, and the one who is in earnest finds her.	
27 *resh*	See for yourselves! I have labored only a little, but have found much.	Syr (B)
28 *shin*	Hear but a little instruction; you will win silver and gold through her.	
29 *taw*	Let your being rejoice in the mercy of God, and be not ashamed to give him praise.	G

30 *pē*   Work at your tasks in due season,
   and in his own time God will give   G (11QPsᵃ)
      you your reward.

Notes

51   13–20a. These verses are translated from 11QPsᵃ, published by J. A. Sanders, *The Psalms Scroll of Qumrân Cave 11 (11QPsᵃ)*, pp. 70–85, and plates xiii and xiv; they form the *aleph* to *kaph* lines of the alphabetic acrostic. For further study of the text of these verses and a restoration of the *lamed* to *taw* plus *pē* lines, see P. W. Skehan, "The Acrostic Poem in Sirach 51:13–30," *HTR* 64 (1971): 387–400. Skehan's translation is the basis of the translation here, though I have made some revisions; I also quote in the notes below and COMMENT several of Skehan's observations. Cf. also M. Delcor, "Le Texte hébreu du cantique de Siracide LI,13 et ss. et les anciennes versions," *Textus* 6 (1968): 27–47, and I. Rabinowitz, "The Qumran Hebrew Original of Ben Sira's Concluding Acrostic on Wisdom," *HUCA* 42 (1971): 173–84. See COMMENT regarding the form of this poem in MS B.

13a. *and innocent=běṭerem těʿôtî*, lit., "before I erred." Sanders and Skehan read *tʿyty=tāʿîtî* (a perfect tense); but since *waw* and *yod* are written so much alike in 11QPsᵃ, the *tʿwty=těʿôtî* (infinitive construct with suffix) reading is not only possible but preferable because *běṭerem* is never followed by a perfect tense in biblical Hebrew. G *prin ē planēthēnai me* also supports the reading of an infinitive construct with suffix.

13b. *I kept seeking=ûbiqqaštîhā*, a *waw*-consecutive perfect which equals an imperfect that contextually implies continuous action in past time. *wisdom*, lit., "her." "Wisdom is the obvious theme; yet, by an artifice no doubt intended, the word *ḥokmâ* occurs nowhere in the poem" (so Skehan); G has "wisdom" and then adds: "openly in my prayer. (v 14a) Before the temple I asked for her."

14a. *in her beauty=btrh*: "the orthography lacking *aleph* for this noun is to be found in 1Q Isaᵇ 52:14 (*wtrw*); Masada Sir. 43:9,18 (*twr*); and (*htwr*) a second time in 11Q Psᵃ, col. 28, line 9, Ps. 151. This last suggests the copyist of 11Q Psᵃ may not have had *tʾr* in mind for Sir. 51:14, since he fails to use *waw* (compare *ʾwzny*, v. 16); but his source may have been in the sparser orthography, and no other word presents itself as plausible" (so Skehan).

14b. *the end=swph*: "This is to be read with terminative *he* rather than with a suffix, compare *wʿd—gzrh* 1 Chr. 14:16; so the Greek" (so Skehan). *I will cultivate her=ʾdwršnh* (lit., "I will seek her out"): "The shift in place in the stem vowel in this form (MT would be *ʾedršennāh*) is the less surprising because of the *resh* in the unstressed syllable" (so Skehan).

16a. *I paid heed=hiṭṭîtî ʾo(w)znî*, lit., "I inclined my ear."

17a. The *waw* line of the poem has the word *wʿlh*, which is to be vocalized *"waʿālā(h)* from the root *yʿl*, in a meaning of 'advantage, profit.' Given the Aramaic influences on late Hebrew, this is not unreasonable (compare *wᶜd*, noun and verb)" (so Skehan). Sanders reads the word as *wĕᶜālā(h)*, "and a nurse." MS B has *ᶜullāh*, "her yoke,"=Syr.

17b. *grateful praise=hôdô*, lit., "his praise." The masculine suffix refers to God, "my Teacher," for which phrase G has: "to him who gives me wisdom." Sanders reads the consonants *hwdy* and translates "my ardor, my manhood."

18a. =11QPsᵃ *zammôtî wā'ešḥāqehā*, lit., "I resolved and wore her down (by treading)." The verb *šḥq* occurs in a similar context in 6:36b. Sanders reads the second verb *w'šḥqh*, "and I made sport." Skehan corrects 11QPsᵃ to read *wā'eḥšĕqâ bāh*, translating the whole colon "I became resolutely devoted to her."

18b. *and [I] will not turn back*=11QPsᵃ *wĕlô' 'āšûb*; G *kai ou mē aischynthō*=*wĕlô' 'ēḇôš*.

19c. *I became preoccupied*=11QPsᵃ *ṭrty npšy* read as *ṭrdty:* "the orthography represents an assimilation of the *daleth* into the following *tau*" (so Skehan, and similarly Sanders); in 32:9b the infinitive construct of *ṭrd* occurs.

19d. *of extolling her*=*wbrwmmh* for "the meaningless *wbrwmyh* of 11Q" (so Skehan).

19e. =11QPsᵃ *ydy prś[ty lmrwm]*, restored from G; for arguments favoring this reading, cf. *CBQ* 28 (1966): 93–94. Skehan reads the line *ydy ptḥ[h šᶜrh]*, "My hand opened her gate."

19f. =11QPsᵃ *[wb]mᶜrmyh 'tbwnn;* the same phrase occurs in 42:18b in M. Sanders reads *[w]mᶜrmyh* (=*maᶜărummēhā*) and translates, "and [I] perceive her unseen parts, her nakedness" (cf. 2 Chr 28:15).

20a. =11QPsᵃ *kpy hbrwty 'l[yh]*. This is the last full colon of 11QPsᵃ.

20b. From here to the end, MS B is in part retroversion from Syr.

20c. *understanding*, lit., "heart"=G, MS B, and Syr.

20d. *I will never forsake her*=Syr (though in vv 20–21 Syr has the 3d s.m. pronoun instead of the f.).

21a. *My whole being*=MS B *mēᶜay*, lit., "my internal organs (intestines, belly)"=Syr=G (most MSS); some G MSS (*L* 547 603) have "my heart." *to seek her*=G=*lĕdoršāh;* MS B *lĕhabbiṭ bāh*=Syr="to look upon her."

21b. Lit., "therefore I have possessed her (as) a good possession"=MS B=Syr; G omits "her."

22. =G=Syr. MS B has altered this verse somewhat: "The LORD has given me a reward, my lips, and with my tongue I will praise him."

23b. *in the house of instruction*=*bĕbêt mûsār*=G *en oikō paideias*=Syr *bêt yulpānā'*. MS B has *bĕbêt midrāšî*, "in my house of instruction." For the reading of *mûsār*, cf. 6:22 and NOTE on 33:25b.

24a. *How long*=Syr=MS B. *of wisdom's food*=*mēᵒoklāh* (Skehan's conjecture), lit., "of her food." G and Syr have "these things"=Heb *'elleh;* MS B *min 'ellû wā'ellû* is secondary.

24b. =MS B *wĕnapšĕkem ṣāmē'â mēᵒôd*=G; omit *tihyeh* at the end of the colon in MS B.

25a. *I open my mouth*=*pātaḥtî pî*=Syr=G; MS B transposes the two words. *of her*=MS B and Syr; G omits the phrase.

25b. =MS B=Syr; G omits "wisdom."

26. =MS B but without initial *waw* on *ṣawwěʾrêkem;* the *waw* disrupts the acrostic pattern. *Your mind=napšěkem,* lit., "your soul, yourself." *and the one who is in earnest=wěnôtēn napšô,* lit., "and the one who gives himself"—the idiom is found also in 7:20b; 30:21a; 38:34c; and 1 Chr 22:19 (so Skehan). G omits v 26d.

27–28. MS B is a retroversion, with corruptions, of Syr.

27b. *much:* G adds "rest" (cf. 6:28a).

28b. *through her=bāh=*G; Syr *bî=*MS B, "through me."

29a. *in the mercy of God:* lit., "in his mercy."

30. This is the *pē*-line (*paʿǎlû=*G *ergazesthe*) of the twenty-three-line acrostic.

30b. *God:* lit., "he." The last two words of the colon are found also in 11QPsᵃ: *šěkarkem běʿittô=*MS B.

Comment

The concluding poem of our book is autobiographical (see also 33:16–18). Part of the poem (see NOTE on 51:13–20a) is found in 11QPsᵃ, which dates to the first half of the first century of our era; this Dead Sea Scroll, containing one of the oldest fragments of our book, was discovered in early February 1956 by Arab Bedouin but was not unrolled till November 1961. Over a century ago, before the recovery of the MSS of Sirach from the Cairo Geniza in 1896–1900, G. Bickell ("Ein alphabetisches Lied Jesus Sirach's," *ZKT* 6 [1882] 319–33) argued that the Syr form of the poem was made from a Heb text that was an alphabetic acrostic, like the concluding poem in the Book of Proverbs (31:10–31). He then proceeded to retranslate the poem into Heb, primarily from the G.

The text of the poem in 11QPsᵃ proves that Bickell was right. The poem is an elegant twenty-three-line alphabetic acrostic. The Heb alphabet has twenty-two letters, *śin* and *šin* counting as one, and other acrostics have twenty-two parts (like Prov 31:10–31, the concluding poem of that Wisdom book, and Psalms 37, 119, and 145). Though the poems in 1:11–30 and 6:18–37 are not acrostic, they do have exactly twenty-two lines, like many other poems in the book (see INTRODUCTION, Part IX). In some acrostics, the reason for the twenty-third (or last) line, the *pē* line (as in Psalms 25 and 34), is this: the *aleph* line is the beginning of the poem, the *lamed* line is the exact middle, and the *pē* line is the end, these three letters thus forming the word *ʾalep,* which is the name of the first letter of the alphabet, and which as a verb in the *piʿel* means "to teach" (cf. P. W. Skehan, *CBQ* 23 [1961]: 127). It is generally acknowledged that the acrostic pattern served as an aid to memory. The text of our poem in MS B does not preserve the full acrostic, because it was for the most part retroverted into Heb from Syr, as I. Lévi demonstrated many years ago (*L'Ecclésiastique,* Part I, pp. xxi–xxvii), and as M. Delcor has reconfirmed more recently (*Textus* 6 [1968]: 45–47). For other examples of retroversion in the Geniza MSS of our book, cf. A. A. Di Lella, *The Hebrew Text of Sirach,* pp. 106–47.

The twenty-three bicola of the poem are divided into ten short stanzas, each of two or three bicola, combined into three larger units of six, eight, and nine bicola, respectively: 2+2+2 bicola, 3+2+3, and 3+2+2+2. ". . . The threefold division is marked mainly by the employment of 3 s.m. pronoun suffixes (with the Lord referred to) toward the close of each unit: a slender, but distinctive feature when seen in the context" (so Skehan); see NOTE on 51:17b, and the translation of 51:22b, 30b. It may also be observed that at or near the end of each larger unit the praise of God is mentioned (51:17b, 22b, and 29b); in this way Ben Sira emphasizes that the wise have the joyful responsibility to praise the Lord; cf. 15:9–10.

Ben Sira begins by informing us that from the time he was "young [Heb *na'ar,* as in Jer 1:6] and innocent" (51:13a; cf. NOTE) he "kept seeking wisdom" (51:13b; cf. NOTE). Thus he followed his own advice to the young men he instructed in 6:18a; cf. Wis 8:2, a reference to 1 Kgs 3:7–9. Though wisdom is a gift from the Lord (1:26), one must nonetheless strive for it (Prov 8:17). Wisdom, which is personified in this poem, came to Ben Sira "in her beauty" (51:14a; cf. NOTE) presumably while he was still relatively young (cf. 51:15d), and he determined to "cultivate her" "until the end" of his life (51:14b; cf. NOTE). The pursuit of wisdom was a lifelong affair for our author, as it is for everyone else (6:18).

For the imagery of "the blossoms yielded to ripening grapes, the heart's joy" (51:15ab), cf. Hos 9:10a–d and Isa 18:5. "The ripening grapes are a figure of the youth's own adolescence" (so Skehan). Ben Sira's "feet kept to the level path" (Heb *mîšôr,* which can also mean "uprightness, fairness," as in Ps 67:5; Isa 11:4; Mal 2:6; cf. Ps 27:11), i.e., he kept the Law faithfully, and accordingly "from earliest youth [he] was familiar with her [wisdom]" (51:15cd). In the theological perspective of our book, one cannot attain wisdom without keeping the Law or fearing the Lord; cf. 1:11–30; 6:32–37; 15:1; 19:20; 21:6; 23:27; 24:23–29. Though Ben Sira "paid heed" to wisdom for only a "short time" (51:16a; cf. NOTE), he nevertheless "met with great instruction" (51:16b); a similar thought occurs in 6:19cd. Because he profited from wisdom, he gives "grateful praise" (51:17b; cf. NOTE) to his "Teacher," i.e., God, who is the author and bestower of wisdom; cf. 51:22b, 29b; 1:1–10, 26.

Ben Sira begins the second larger unit (51:18–22) by using the image of walking (51:18a; cf. NOTE), as in 51:15c. Firm resolution kept him on wisdom's paths. The theme of 51:18–19d "is desire and pursuit of wisdom, not possession" (so Skehan). The "good" for which the poet is jealous (51:18b) is wisdom. He never relented in his burning desire for wisdom (51:19ab); cf. 6:26, 32–37; Wis 8:2. He "became preoccupied with her" (51:19c; cf. NOTE) and was "never weary of extolling her" (51:19d; cf. NOTE); striving for wisdom cannot be a half-hearted affair (cf. 14:20–27). Ben Sira "spread out [his] hands on high" (51:19e; cf. NOTE); cf. 1 Kgs 8:22 and 2 Chr 6:13, where Solomon is said to "spread out his hands toward heaven." It was the custom to spread out the hands when one prayed: cf., e.g., Exod 9:29, 33; Isa 1:15; 2 Chr 6:12, 29; Ezra 9:5; Tob 3:11. When Solomon, the proverbial wise man, also prayed for wisdom, his prayer was answered by God (1 Kgs 3:6–12; Wis 7:7). God answered Ben Sira's prayer, too: "I came to know [wisdom's] secrets" (51:19f; cf. NOTE); cf. 1:1, 26. In addition to prayer, pure hands (51:20a; cf. NOTE) and "cleanliness" are also needed before one can attain to wisdom (51:20b; cf. NOTE). Skehan calls attention to a useful parallel to 51:20a in 1QH xvi 10: "and I have chosen to purify my hands according to your will." Cf. also Pss 26:6a and 73:13b. From the moment Ben Sira became acquainted with wisdom, he "gained understanding" (51:20c; cf. NOTE); the latter expression occurs also in Prov 15:32b and 19:8a. Therefore he "will never forsake her" (51:20d; cf. NOTE), heeding the injunction of Prov 4:6. His pursuit of wisdom being wholehearted (51:21a; cf. NOTE), he "made her [his] prize possession" (51:21b; cf. NOTE), Heb qinyān ṭôb; cf. 36:39a with COMMENT and Prov 4:7. Therefore Yahweh granted him his "tongue as a reward" (51:22a; cf. NOTE), a statement that "is unmistakably based on Isa. 50:4" (so Skehan); that is to say, he became an effective teacher. Cf. 2:8. Ben Sira's response to God's gift is praise (51:22b), as in 51:17b; cf. 51:29b.

In the final larger unit (51:23–30), Ben Sira invites the unlearned to come to him for instruction so that they may themselves acquire wisdom. This invitation is modeled on Prov 9:1–6, 11, 16; cf. also Sir 14:20–27 and 24:7–8, 19. In 51:23a, the imperative "come aside" = Heb sûrû = Syr sĕṭaw, is exactly what the acrostic requires: the same verb "is used in the invitations by wisdom and folly in Prov 9:4" (so Skehan). Commentators have noted that MS B's bĕbêt midrāšî, "in my house of instruction" (51:23b; cf. NOTE), marks "the earliest known use of the expression. But both the Greek and the Syriac (paideias, yulpānā') call rather for bĕbêt mûsār, with no suffix. And indeed, this appears to provide us with a play on words elsewhere employed, in a similar context, by the author of Sirach. Sir. 6:22 . . . conveys that mûsār is not directly accessible to man, because its very name can be understood as 'withdrawn.' This is playing with the root sûr, and our v. 23 does the same: 'Come aside . . . and take up lodging in the house of (withdrawn, remote) instruction' " (so Skehan); cf. 6:22 with COMMENT. As regards "wisdom's food" and "bitter thirst" (51:24; cf. NOTES), cf. Prov 9:5; Isa 55:1; Amos 8:11; John 4:13–14. When Ben Sira opens his "mouth," he speaks of wisdom (51:24a; cf. NOTE); this is apparently a reference to his lectures to the young men who came to him for instruction; cf. INTRODUCTION, Part II. The colon, "gain wisdom . . . without money" (51:25b; cf. NOTE), derives from Isa 55:1–3; compare Prov 4:5–7.

Wisdom's "yoke," to which the young are urged to submit their neck (51:26a; cf. NOTE), features also in the exhortation of 6:23–31, on which cf. COMMENT. For the expression, cf. Jer 27:8, 11–12. Like the command of God, which is very near to the people (Deut 30:11–14), wisdom "is close to those who seek her" (51:26c), but one must earnestly seek her (for the phrase, cf. 1 Chr 22:19) in order to find her (51:26d; cf. NOTE); cf. 6:26. As proof, Ben Sira now appeals to his own experience: he "labored only a little, but . . . found much" (51:27; cf. NOTE); the antithetic parallelism between "a little" and "much" highlights the thought; cf. 6:19cd. Even if one "hear but a little instruction," one "will win silver and gold through her" (51:28; cf. NOTE); this bicolon is in synonymous parallelism with the previous one. The point of both bicola is that wisdom pays off even in the practical realm, and not only in the religious; cf. Prov 8:14–21. In the final stanza of the poem (and the book), Ben Sira appeals to his audience to "rejoice in the mercy of God" (51:29a; cf. NOTE and 35:25–26), and to "be not ashamed to give him praise" (51:29b), for praise of God is the most appropriate response for mercies received, including the gift of wisdom; cf. 51:17, 22; Wis 8:21–9:18. His final exhortation to his students is: "Work at your tasks" of seeking wisdom "in due season," i.e., whenever you get the opportunity (51:30a; cf. NOTE); cf. 6:31–37. If you do so, then "in his own time," parallel to "in due season," "God will give you your reward" (51:30b; cf. NOTE), i.e., the gift of wisdom; cf. 1:1–10, 26.

In *The Psalms Scroll of Qumrân Cave 11 (11QPsᵃ)*, pp. 79–85, and *The Dead Sea Psalms Scroll*, pp. 112–17, J. A. Sanders gives an erotic interpretation of our poem; for his translation of certain expressions in keeping with his viewpoint, see NOTES on 51:17a, 17b, 18a, 19f. For a critique of this interpretation, cf. my review of the former book in *CBQ* 28 (1966): 92–95. See also T. Muraoka, "Sir. 51:13–20: An Erotic Hymn to Wisdom?," *JSJ* 10 (1979): 166–78. For a more balanced study, see C. Deutsch, "The Sirach 51 Acrostic: Confession and Exhortation," *ZAW* 94 (1982): 400–9.

After 51:30, MS B has this subscription: "Blessed be Yahweh forever [=Ps 89:53a], and praised be his name from generation to generation. Thus far the words of Simeon, the son of Yeshua, who is called Ben Sira. The Wisdom of Simeon, the son of Yeshua, the son of Eleazar, the son of Sira. May the name of Yahweh be blessed from now to eternity [=Ps 113:2]." The majority of MSS of G have "Wisdom of Jesus, son of Sirach." The oldest Syr MS (B.L. 12142, sixth century) has: "Blessed be God forever, and praised be his name from generation to generation. Thus far the words of Joshua, the son of Simeon, who is called Bar [=Heb Ben] 'Asira. The end of the writing of the Wisdom of Bar Sira." Codex Ambrosianus of the Peshitta (from the sixth or seventh century) has "Blessed be God forever, and praised be his name from generation to generation. The writing of Bar 'Asira is finished." The subscription in the Mosul edition of the Peshitta is similar to B.L. 12142, but it adds the curious note: ". . . in the time of the Maccabees." Our author's real name is Yeshua (or Jesus), the son of Eleazar, the son of Sira; cf. 50:27c with NOTE.

INDEXES

INDEX OF AUTHORS

Citations providing complete bibliographical information are indicated with an asterisk (*).

INDEX OF SUBJECTS

O

Oath   323, 357, 481
  See also Speech; Swearing
Obedience   152, 154, 155
  See also Docility; Parents
Old Age   212, 348
  aged parents   156
  Ben Sira as old man   341
  dignity of aged   405
  disrespect to old   156, 212
  distribution of estate   405
  foolish old men   341
    aged adulterer   341
  right of elders to speak   391
  Wisdom of the old   192, 195, 212–
    13, 341. *See also* Parents
Omens   408–9
  See also Dreams; Divination
Onias (variant in Gr MSS for [Simeon
    ben] Jochanan)   9, 550
Onias III   9, 200, 514, 554
  pro-Ptolemaic policy   200
Onomasticon. *See* List
On Women (Semonides)   91
Oppression. *See* Social Justice
Order, ascending or descending
    (rhetorical device)   201, 214,
    433
Origenistic recension of Greek II   56
  witnessed in Syrohexaplar   62
  See also Wisdom of Ben Sira, textual
    witnesses
Orphan   167, 207, 419
  See also Social Justice

P

Pagans. *See* Gentiles; Hellenism;
    Ptolemies; Seleucids
Pairs (stereotyped, formulaic,
    fixed)   66, 67, 68, 69, 70, 71,
    72, 142, 177, 212, 229, 232,
    263, 265, 422, 460, 474, 565,
    566, 567, 570
  breakup of stereotyped pair   567
Panegyric   458, 520, 550
Pantheism   80, 495
Papyrus Insinger. See Phibis
Parallelism   67–73

antithetic   67, 70, 156, 229, 231, 232,
    233, 234, 534, 579
synonymous   65, 66, 67–73, 152,
    155, 164, 166, 171, 176, 195,
    211, 212, 224, 234, 240, 247,
    254, 256, 259, 263, 265, 271,
    272, 301, 302, 326, 377, 389,
    391, 398, 399, 403n., 405, 409,
    417, 420, 436, 458–59, 470,
    472, 494, 500, 502, 553, 565,
    566, 567, 579
synthetic   67, 69, 195
Parasite   375–76. *See also* Begging;
    Poor
Parents   41–42, 154–57, 206
  distribution of estate   405
  duties of children toward
    parents   154–57
  impiety toward parents as impiety
    toward God   157
  parents' blessing   155–56
  parents' disgrace   156
  parents in old age   156
  See also Children; Old Age
Passion. *See* Sensual desire
Patience   151
Patriarchal societies   90, 91
  See also Women
Perseverance   152, 195
  See also Resolution
Persian Empire   13
Personification   357, 461, 495
  Wisdom as woman   78, 139, 171,
    264–65, 332, 577
Pessimism, literature of   469
Pharaoh   302, 505, 511
  God's hardening Pharaoh's
    heart   81, 275
  Pharaoh's daughter   510
  Pharaoh's servants   510
Pharos   397
Phibis   48–49, 50, 184, 189, 218, 253,
    286, 292, 406, 441, 475, 493,
    494, 501
  use by Sirach   48–49
  See also Egyptian Wisdom literature
Philistines   521
  code word for Hellenized Jews   558
  power in Holy Land   525–26
Phinehas   505, 510, 513–14
  action against Baal of Peor   513